I0084001

Crosscurrents

Crosscurrents

US Relations with Nationalist China, 1943–1960

Martin B. Gold

LEXINGTON BOOKS

Lanham • Boulder • New York • London

Published by Lexington Books
An imprint of The Rowman & Littlefield Publishing Group, Inc.
4501 Forbes Boulevard, Suite 200, Lanham, Maryland 20706
www.rowman.com

86-90 Paul Street, London EC2A 4NE

Copyright © 2023 by The Rowman & Littlefield Publishing Group, Inc.

All rights reserved. No part of this book may be reproduced in any form or by any electronic or mechanical means, including information storage and retrieval systems, without written permission from the publisher, except by a reviewer who may quote passages in a review.

British Library Cataloguing in Publication Information Available

Library of Congress Cataloging-in-Publication Data

Names: Gold, Martin, 1947- author.
Title: Crosscurrents : US relations with Nationalist China, 1943–1960 / Martin B. Gold.
Other titles: US relations with Nationalist China, 1943–1960
Description: Lanham : Lexington Books, 2023. | Includes bibliographical references and index.
Identifiers: LCCN 2022046776 (print) | LCCN 2022046777 (ebook) | ISBN 9781793631145 (cloth) | ISBN 9781793631169 (paperback) | ISBN 9781793631152 (epub)
Subjects: LCSH: United States—Relations—China. | China—Relations—United States. | United States—Relations—Taiwan. | Taiwan—Relations—United States.
Classification: LCC E183.8.C5 G628 2023 (print) | LCC E183.8.C5 (ebook) | DDC 327.0973051—dc23/eng/20220928
LC record available at https://lccn.loc.gov/2022046776
LC ebook record available at https://lccn.loc.gov/2022046777

♾ ™ The paper used in this publication meets the minimum requirements of American National Standard for Information Sciences—Permanence of Paper for Printed Library Materials, ANSI/NISO Z39.48-1992.

Dedicated to Dwight David Eisenhower
A Hero in War and a Hero in Peace

Contents

Acknowledgments

I have been privileged to have exceptional help in preparing this book for publication. I begin by thanking Joseph Parry, executive acquisitions editor at Rowman & Littlefield Publishing Group. This is the seventh book I will have worked on with this publisher. In 2017, it published *A Legislative History of the Taiwan Relations Act: Bridging the Strait.* That book focused on President Jimmy Carter's 1979 recognition of the People's Republic of China, his withdrawal from a long-standing Mutual Defense Treaty between the United States and the Republic of China on Taiwan, and the passage of the Taiwan Relations Act. Many months ago, I approached Joseph about looking at the beginning of this story, how the Mutual Defense Treaty developed in the first place, along with the Formosa Resolution, each concerning rising and persistent tensions in the Taiwan Strait. He concurred with me that the story, and its historical antecedents, needed to be completed. I am grateful for his confidence, and so much appreciate his patience as this book has come together.

I also wish to thank Yan He, the China Documentation Center librarian at the Gelman Library, George Washington University. She was an indispensable guide in assisting me to locate some of the primary source materials I have used throughout the chapters.

Heather Moore is the photo historian at the US Senate. She helped greatly in finding and making available many of the photos that accompany the text. Heather's archives are vital to researchers on the Senate, so I know from experience it is important to visit her as a book takes shape. Her enthusiasm for and dedication to her work also make it a joy. Heather is an outstanding public servant.

My longtime colleague and friend, Allegra Han, has given substantial and dependable help as this book came together. We have worked jointly for many years, during which I have happily engaged her positive attitude and dedicated professionalism. I appreciate her, always.

I acknowledge and thank Sonia Robinson and Andrea Melendez at my firm, Capitol Counsel, for their able technical assistance on this book. They have been helpful in moments when help was needed most. I further acknowledge the cooperative and helpful guidance of Emilia Rivera at Rowman & Littlefield.

Celeste Gold, my wife, has made the largest contribution of all, combing through the text with meticulous care and making numerous, well-founded suggestions for how it might be improved. To do that, she took time from her exceedingly busy schedule as a US Senate staffer. As always, the reader is the leading beneficiary of her thoughtful work. She has also shared, without complaint, the many hours over many months necessary to research and write this book. Celeste has made these sacrifices for all my books, none of which could have come together without her. Hers are labors of love. I could not be more grateful.

Martin B. Gold
Washington, DC
Paris
August 2022

Introduction

Diplomatic relations between the United States and the People's Republic of China began more than 40 years ago, following two decades of mostly abject hostility. What started in the 1970s primarily as a quasi-alliance against a common Soviet enemy, turned into a vibrant partnership of complementary economies, but has since evolved into a competition between distrustful and strategic rivals. Though points of agreement and division have changed through the years, the subject of Taiwan has remained the principal irritant.

Prior to 1895, Taiwan belonged to China. However, China relinquished control to Japan that year in the Treaty of Shimonoseki, which ended the Sino-Japanese war. For the next five decades, Japan exercised sovereignty. In November 1943, President Franklin Roosevelt, Prime Minister Winston Churchill, and Generalissimo Chiang Kai-shek convened in Egypt at a summit to plan a strategy for the China-Burma-India Theater in World War II. From that meeting came the Cairo Declaration, which provided that Chinese territories occupied by Japan would be returned to China after the war. However, the declaration was a statement of intent, not a transfer of title. The Pacific war formally ended with the Treaty of San Francisco in 1951. In that treaty, Japan renounced "all right, title, and claim to Formosa and the Pescadores." However, the treaty itself did not pass sovereignty to anyone.

Thus, for many years after the war, Washington openly asserted that the legal status of Taiwan remained to be determined.[1] One reason America maintained this position was the inconvenient fact that, by 1951, there was a Communist government in mainland China. To acknowledge that Taiwan was Chinese would be tantamount to legitimizing Communist claims to an island that the United States deemed essential to its own defense.

After losing the mainland, the Chinese Nationalists occupied Taiwan, treated it as if it were Chinese territory, and declared that their government, the Republic of China, was the legitimate government of the entire country. The United States continued to recognize the ROC and supported it with a treaty that obliged it to come to its defense. America's allies were consistently less enthusiastic about this policy than Washington. First Britain, and then other US partners, cut ties with the Republic of China in Taipei and established relations with the People's Republic of China in Beijing.

Seeking to counter the Soviet Union and to extricate the United States from Vietnam, President Richard Nixon explored an opening to the People's Republic. And, for its part, the PRC saw benefits in using the United States to balance against the Soviets.[2] In February 1972, a breakthrough came as Nixon made his historic journey to the mainland. To ease a path to normalized relations between Washington and Beijing, both countries addressed the Taiwan issue carefully. In the Shanghai Communiqué, issued at the end of Nixon's trip, the United States acknowledged that Chinese on both sides of the Taiwan Strait believed there was one China and that Taiwan was part of it. While the United States did not accept that position, it also did not challenge it. Normalization was not achieved at that moment, but the door to that objective had been opened.[3] In 1973, both China and the United States opened liaison offices in each other's capital.

In 1979, America took the next step. In a communiqué establishing diplomatic relations with the People's Republic of China, the United States stated that the PRC is the legitimate government of the entire country. In that context, and consistent with the PRC's demands, the United States has not supported separating Taiwan from the mainland, either to create two Chinas or one China and an independent Taiwan.

As part of normalization, the United States also agreed to end a quarter-century-old mutual defense treaty with the Republic of China. Although the PRC had denounced the pact as illegal from the time it was signed in 1954, and insisted that the United States abrogate it immediately, President Jimmy Carter withdrew from the treaty under its express terms, which allowed either party to cancel on a year's notice. Thus, it remained in force until the end of 1979.

Although the United States would no longer recognize the ROC, it had a significant web of governmental and nongovernmental relationships there that it wished to continue. As well, Taiwan enjoyed substantial political support among US politicians and voters. While there was general acknowledgment across party lines that modernizing America's China policy was overdue, there was concern about abandoning an old ally, who was without fault in the rupture. The difficult and often violent history of Communist/Nationalist relations offered an important basis for US concerns and the United States was unwilling to simply leave Taiwan to its fate.

After normalization, the United States maintained only unofficial relations with the people of Taiwan. That meant no embassy and no liaison office but involved establishing the American Institute in Taiwan and continuing access to many US programs that did not require diplomatic relations. It also meant supporting robust commercial and other private activity.

To structure these mostly cultural and economic arrangements, President Carter proposed the Taiwan Relations Act in January 1979. The measure passed by large majorities in Congress, after a vigorous debate in both the Senate and House. To China's special and ongoing chagrin, Congress added a military dimension. The act provided for the continued sale of defensive arms to Taiwan,[4] claimed that the use of coercion against Taiwan would be a matter of "grave concern" to the United States, and committed America "to maintain the capacity of the United States to resist any resort to force or other forms of coercion that would jeopardize the security, or the social and economic system, of the people on Taiwan."[5]

This legislation reinforced the US position that the Taiwan question should be peacefully resolved, as expressed in the Shanghai Communiqué and elsewhere. China agreed not to explicitly contest that language in the communiqué, since it was a unilateral expression of US policy.

However, elsewhere in the communiqué, the PRC restated its long-standing insistence on the one-China policy and that resolving differences with Taiwan is an internal matter, not subject to outside interference.[6] In the years thereafter, Beijing offered periodic olive branches to the Chinese across the strait, but at no time has it renounced the use of force if peaceful unification proved unavailing.[7]

With this framework set out through adroit diplomacy, the United States and China were able to move forward toward normalized relations. The resolution of the Taiwan question was deferred. It has been managed in an ambiguous fashion that has allowed bilateral relations to proceed and sometimes prosper but has never been concluded to the satisfaction of either Beijing or Washington, much less of Taipei.

This book traces a period before the PRC and the United States came to terms. It begins in 1943, before there was a PRC at all. At the time, China and the United States were in a necessary but uneasy alliance against Japan, in which the presence of a mutual foe barely concealed the misgivings each partner had for the other. President Franklin Roosevelt and Generalissimo Chiang Kai-shek had a common enemy, but they also had conflicting priorities, and neither could fully deliver what the other truly needed.

Sino-American wartime relations were marred by disappointment and disillusionment. Roosevelt wanted a China fully committed to the war effort but found a counterpart hedging against the fear of civil war in its aftermath. Chiang wanted a major US commitment of supplies and forces to the China Theater but found an ally that prioritized defeating Germany first. Roosevelt wanted a China that could act as a major power to maintain order in Asia after the Japanese were vanquished, but found instead a government exhausted by war, riven by cronyism and corruption, and unable to consolidate political stability within its own borders.[8] Chiang hoped for American backing to maintain power against the rising threat of Communist insurrection, and got some, but never to the measure he wanted.

Near the end of the war, and its immediate aftermath, discord in the relationship was palpable. America sought to mediate between the Nationalists and Communists to avert the instability of a civil war. But neither Chinese side truly believed a coalition government was desirable or even workable. Led first by US ambassador Patrick J. Hurley and then by Special Envoy General George C. Marshall, these negotiations were fruitless. The civil war proved unavoidable and was decisively resolved in the Communists' favor once it occurred. The conflict left both Chinese factions angry with the United States—Chiang because he felt American support was inadequate, and Mao Zedong because he felt that the most economic help the United States continued to give the Nationalists prolonged the war.

As the Communists were winning the civil war and the Nationalists were regrouping, President Harry Truman provided modest economic assistance to the Nationalists and did not immediately recognize Mao's government. Nevertheless, the administration made it clear it had no designs on Taiwan and no intent to prop up the Nationalist regime. Mao readied an amphibious invasion to finish the war, and an absolute Communist victory appeared inevitable.

Before it could occur, war broke out on the Korean Peninsula in June 1950. Seeking to confine the conflict to Korea, Truman reversed himself and, in effect, intervened in the Chinese civil war. He interposed the US Seventh Fleet in the Taiwan Strait with express orders to prevent either side from assaulting the other. With the fleet in place, the Communists could not attack Taiwan, nor could the Nationalists attack the mainland. Again, both the Communists and Nationalists were frustrated with the United States for impeding their ambitions, whether realistic or not.

In Korea, Communist China and the United States became actual enemies. Threatened by the presence of United Nations forces near its border, China entered the war in late November 1950 to substantial initial effect. Already sour relations between the PRC and the United States became embittered. Meanwhile, Chiang Kai-shek had been thrown a lifeline. The erstwhile ally the United States had been prepared to abandon before Korea became a cornerstone of US policy to contain the spread of Communism in Asia. And even more important to the United States than retaining Chiang in power was keeping the strategically situated island of Formosa out of Communist hands. On the surface, the interests of the Nationalists and those of the Americans appeared to coincide.

Things seemed to align even better when Dwight D. Eisenhower became president in 1953. Within three weeks of taking office, Eisenhower revised the fleet's mission. While it would continue to protect Chiang from the Communists, it would no longer protect the Communists from Chiang. For the Nationalists, an opportunity to recover the mainland seemed not as farfetched.

And yet Washington had major reservations. Knowing that Chiang had no prospect of recovering the mainland without American logistical help, the United States was wary that he would maneuver it into a war against the PRC. Given the fact that, in 1950, Beijing and Moscow had formalized an alliance, it was imaginable that such a conflict could expand to include Soviet Russia. Thus, while America built an architecture of bilateral and multilateral alliances in Asia, Nationalist China was initially left outside of it.

The Korean armistice was signed on July 27, 1953. In its aftermath, Beijing once more turned attention to securing control over Formosa. Communist attacks in 1954 against Nationalist-held islands close to the mainland caused the United States to reconsider its qualms about an alliance with Chiang. In late 1954, Washington and Taipei concluded a mutual defense treaty that finally gave Chiang the protective umbrella he was seeking. However, it came at the price of an agreement that gave the United States veto power over its ability to launch offensive military action against Communist China.

In January 1955, before the Senate had time to advise and consent to the treaty, Eisenhower pushed through Congress a resolution authorizing him to deploy the US military in defense of Formosa. The president insisted on going to Capitol Hill even though Truman had not sought congressional authorization before committing US troops in Korea. Key Democrats argued that Eisenhower's constitutional powers as commander-in-chief were sufficient to address problems in the strait. However, Eisenhower believed that lining Congress up alongside the Executive would send a strong domestic and international message about US policy, so he successfully persisted.

The authority the president sought would include not just the defense of Formosa but also related possessions then in Nationalist hands, if the United States deemed an attack on them to presage an attack on Formosa. These possessions included the island groups of Quemoy and Matsu, near the Chinese coast.

The Formosa Resolution, as it was called, was the first time in the Twentieth Century Congress passed Authorization for the Use of Military Force (AUMF) in lieu of a Declaration of War. Soon after, in early February 1955, the Senate consented to the treaty. Although the resolution and the treaty were considered in a Congress controlled by Democrats, and notwithstanding misgivings, both passed by strong majorities. Debate on these measures was spirited, especially regarding the defense of Quemoy and Matsu, and framed issues that would again arise during deliberations on subsequent

AUMFs. The administration's policy, which included the potential use of nuclear weapons, was controversial. It met substantial resistance from US allies, who believed Washington's priorities were misplaced and risked war for little gain.

Although the threat of conflict receded in 1955, when the Communist Chinese reduced tensions, it returned with a vengeance three years later. In September 1958, the Communists began shelling Nationalist positions on Quemoy. Once more the possibility of war was real, fissures in US alliances were exposed, and this time with elevated partisan divisions in a US midterm election year. America gave logistical assistance to the ROC. However, in bellicose speeches and private meetings, Chiang urged a more vigorous posture, including bombing the mainland. In response, the United States exercised its veto to keep matters from spiraling out of control. After a period of tension, the crisis abated, and the situation in the strait, although not peaceful, was at least stabilized.

The dual crises in the Taiwan Strait in the 1950s could readily have spilled over into kinetic conflict for the United States, not just with the PRC but also with the USSR. Not only Chiang, but senior American military leaders and some members of Congress were spoiling for a fight. At the same time, allied nations were prepared to conciliate the Communists by weakening Chiang. In his memoirs, President Eisenhower describes these pressures as crosscurrents, which buffeted his administration and through which he had to navigate. Eisenhower's patient, courageous, and temperate leadership was key to averting war while avoiding appeasement. One can doubt whether overwhelming support would have existed in Congress if the president had been someone other than Eisenhower, who enjoyed broad affection and trust among the American people. This book is dedicated to the memory of an outstanding American, first known to his country as a leader of warriors but whose stature became all the greater for how he kept the peace.

———————————————————

Editorial Note: Throughout this book, the term "Formosa" is almost always used in lieu of the term "Taiwan." The word Formosa was a European term, distinct from Taiwan, which is Chinese. During the period covered in this book, 1943–1958, "Formosa" was in common usage in the United States. Thus, the 1943 Cairo Declaration spoke of the return of "Formosa" to China, not "Taiwan." And in 1955, Congress passed the "Formosa Resolution," not the "Taiwan Resolution." Similarly, islands near Taiwan were known years ago as the "Pescadores," not as the "Penghu."

On the same basis, I use spellings elsewhere in this book that were in use at the time. These will sometimes involve the Wade-Giles system of transliterating Chinese names, rather than Pinyin, which came into common usage in the United States after relations were normalized with the PRC. Thus, Nationalist China's leader will be Chiang Kai-shek, not Jiang Jieshi. I have endeavored to show the alternate version in brackets the first time any name appeared in the text.

NOTES

1. China has consistently and vigorously asserted this position, not just with the United States, but in many international forums. For a discussion of how the policy is used to exclude Taiwan from such forums, see Jessica Dunn and Bonnie Glaser, "The Distortion of UN Resolution 2758 and Limits on Taiwan's Access to the United Nations," *German Marshall Fund*, March 24, 2022.

2. At the time of Nixon's trip, Chairman Mao Zedong [Mao Tse-tung] was still alive. Mao died in 1976. After a two-year power struggle, Deng Xiaoping [Teng Hsiao-ping] rose to be China's principal leader. Deng was the leader of Reform and Opening Up, a governing philosophy to modernize China's economy. For that purpose, Deng needed access to Western markets, technology, and capital. Thus, by 1979, there were major incentives to reach normalized relations with the United States in addition to maneuvering against the Soviet Union.

3. In his memoirs, President Nixon wrote,

"Taiwan was the touchstone for both sides. We felt that we should not and could not abandon the Taiwanese; we were committed to Taiwan's right to exist as an independent nation. The Chinese were equally determined to use this communique to assert their unequivocal claim to the island. We knew that no agreement concerning Taiwan could be reached at this time. While both sides could agree that Taiwan was a part of China—a position supported by both the Peking and Taiwan governments—we would have to oppose the use of military force by Peking to bring Taiwan under Communist rule."

Richard Nixon, *RN: The Memoirs of Richard Nixon* (New York: Grosset & Dunlap, 1978), pp. 570–571.

4. In a meeting with Chinese vice premier Deng Xiaoping just before the December 15, 1978, joint announcement of normalized relations, Leonard Woodcock, chief of the US Liaison Office to the People's Republic of China, informed Deng that President Carter intended to sell arms to Taiwan even after the Mutual Defense Treaty expired. Deng took vigorous exception to this policy but chose not to let China's objection derail normalization. In January 1979, Deng visited Washington and urged Carter to withhold arms sales because they would make negotiations on reunification more difficult. For his part, Carter urged Deng to renounce the use of force against Taiwan. Neither leader did what the other wanted.

5. See Taiwan Relations Act, PL 96-8, 22 USC 3301, et seq.

6. In the Shanghai Communiqué, the Chinese side stated,

"The Chinese side reaffirmed its position: the Taiwan question is the crucial question obstructing the normalization of relations between China and the United States; the Government of the People's Republic of China is the sole legal government of China; Taiwan is a province of China which has long been returned to the motherland; the liberation of Taiwan is China's internal affair in which no other country has the right to interfere; and all US forces and military installations must be withdrawn from Taiwan. The Chinese Government firmly opposes any activities which aim at the creation of 'one China, one Taiwan,' 'one China, two governments,' 'two Chinas,' an 'independent Taiwan' or advocate that 'the status of Taiwan remains to be determined.'"

7. On January 1, 1979, the day that diplomatic relations between Beijing and Washington officially commenced, the PRC issued its "Message to Compatriots in Taiwan." It presented a soft line toward the resolution of cross-strait differences, quite distinct in tone from the military exercises directed at Taiwan from the mainland in the present day or periodic bellicose overtures in the intervening years. In part, the January 1 message stated,

"It is our fervent hope that Taiwan returns to the embrace of the motherland at an early date so that we can work together with a great cause of national development. Our state leaders have firmly declared that they will take present realities into account in accomplishing the great cause of reunifying the motherland and respect the *status quo* on Taiwan and the opinions of people in all walks of life there and adopt reasonable policies and measures in settling the question of reunification so as not to cause the people of Taiwan any losses. On the other hand, people in all walks of life in Taiwan have expressed their yearning for their homeland and old friends, stating their desire to identify themselves with and rejoin their kinsmen and raised diverse proposals which or expressions of their earnest hope for an early return to the embrace of the motherland."

"Message to Compatriots in Taiwan," January 1, 1979. www.china.org.cn.
8. Sinologist John King Fairbank has written about the deterioration of Chiang's regime between the time it established its capital at Chungking and the end of war.

"The Nationalist government, which in 1938 was forced into exile beyond the Yangtze gorges, among the mountains and paddy fields of Szechwan, had become a rallying point for the best talent in modern China, the first fruit of the new patriotism and technical training. Eight years later, the leadership which returned down the river to Nanking and Shanghai in late 1945, was worn and demoralized. During exile in the mists of Szechwan, the top personnel of the government had changed very little. Cabinet reshuffling only brought the same faces to different windows. But by retaining personal power, the Kuomintang leaders had devitalized their organization. Politically, they marked time while waiting for the war to end. The best men among them knew how to modernize China technologically, but they were unable to mobilize the back country and a continuing social revolution. The revolution consequently passed them by." (Fairbank, *The United States and China*, p. 255)

Chapter 1

A Fraught Partnership

America strongly believed in building alliances to contain Communism, more urgently so after Communist Party chairman Mao Zedong [Mao Tse-tung] announced the establishment of the People's Republic of China on October 1, 1949. Mao's victory over Generalissimo Chiang Kai-shek [Jiang Jieshi] in the Chinese civil war ended two decades of bitter recriminations and often violent conflict. Mao's success was an immense setback and policy failure, not just for the Chinese Nationalists, but also for the United States.

Washington had hoped for something very different in China. During World War II, President Franklin D. Roosevelt planned that it would assume significant responsibility for winning the war and maintaining order in Asia. Sinologist Nancy Bernkopf Tucker captures the president's motives. "Anxious about the power vacuum that would exist in Asia once Japan's forces had been disarmed and sent home, he wanted to build a Chinese state capable of controlling the East and keeping the Russians out."[1]

Thus, the elevation of China into major power status was one of Roosevelt's key initiatives until late in the war, a guardian of peace. As FDR wrote to Generalissimo Chiang Kai-shek on October 27, 1943, "I am pressing for the full-blown partnership of China, Great Britain, Russia, and the United States."[2]

Chiang had led China since the mid-1920s and had, in the early stages of the war, enjoyed a reputation in the United States as a stalwart and courageous leader of resistance against Japanese invaders. Thus, in 1938, six months after the general war between China and Japan began in earnest, *Time* magazine declared, "But while Japan launched her great adventure without outstanding leadership, China, the victim of the adventure, has had the ablest of leadership. Throughout 1937, the Chinese have been led—not without glory—by one supreme leader and his remarkable wife. Under this man and wife, the traditionally disunited Chinese people—millions of whom seldom used the word 'China' in the past—have slowly been given national consciousness."[3]

In his memoirs, Secretary of State Cordell Hull explained why China was so central to Roosevelt's postwar planning. It would usurp defeated Japan as the leading power in Asia and would not be distracted elsewhere. "The only major strictly Oriental power would be China," Hull wrote. "The United States, Britain, and Russia were also Pacific powers, but the great interests of each were elsewhere. Consequently, if there was ever to be stability in the Far East, it had to be assured with China at the center of any arrangement that was made."[4]

For this plan to work, China needed a stable government. However, Roosevelt worried that, after the war ended, a civil conflict between the Nationalist and Communist factions would erupt. That could not only dash Roosevelt's hopes for Asia but could also sidetrack his efforts to preserve the USSR as an ally.[5] Continuing amicable and cooperative relations with the Soviets was indispensable to the president's vision for the postwar world.

Although the United States and Britain had emphasized the European theater ahead of Asia, China remained significant to the allied war effort until Japan surrendered.[6] Tokyo was unable to extricate itself from its protracted misadventure in China. As a result, approximately 1 million Japanese soldiers remained mired in China rather than being redeployed to fight US and allied forces.[7]

In addition, until quite late in the war, America embraced the idea of attacking Japan from air bases it could construct on Chinese territory.[8] Roosevelt wrote to Prime Minister Churchill on November 10, 1943, about the importance he placed on this possibility. "We have under development a project whereby we can strike a heavy blow at our enemy in the Pacific early next year with our new heavy bombers. . . . I am sending a similar message to the Generalissimo asking him to expedite construction of five advanced bases in the Chengdu area financed by Lend-Lease funds."[9]

Thus, Roosevelt understood the importance of having China as an ally and keeping her in the war. However, because of demands in other theaters, he could not supply all the logistical support Chiang needed. In lieu of materiel, the president initially offered symbolic gestures to demonstrate goodwill.[10] In 1943, the United States removed two irritants that had long complicated US-China relations. In January, it entered the Sino-American Treaty for the Relinquishment of Extraterritorial Rights, renouncing special legal rights that had existed for a century.[11] The Senate approved the treaty unanimously. The European allies, who also enjoyed such rights, similarly abandoned them.[12] Later in the year, the president asked Congress to repeal the Chinese exclusion laws, a body of discriminatory legislation, originating in 1882, that sharply restricted Chinese immigration to the United States and barred

American citizenship for persons of Chinese descent born anywhere outside the United States itself.[13] Roosevelt signed the repeal legislation, known as the Magnuson Act, on December 17, 1943. These were war measures, intended to buttress the Western position in China against Japanese propaganda and diplomacy.[14] The high-profile conference in Cairo was an additional overture to Chiang, an apparent course correction for sidelining him earlier in the war.

By then, China had been at war for six years, far longer than any of its allies. Through 1943, the United States and Britain had not been of much help. Quite to the contrary, Chiang felt they were marginalizing the China-Burma-India Theater, in favor of prosecuting the war in Europe.[15] He wanted them to take on a much greater role in fighting the Japanese and considered symbolic political gestures insufficient. It was possible that a disgruntled generalissimo might explore peace terms with Japan.

Chiang had a potentially compelling incentive to quit the war. Doing so would allow him to prioritize confronting the Communists, who he always considered his more dangerous enemy. Governor Thomas E. Dewey,[16] who traveled to Formosa during an extensive Asia trip in 1951, wrote many of Chiang's closest advisers urged him to conclude a separate peace. "They knew the strength of the Communist armies in the north, and from long experience, they mistrusted all assurances of cooperation from Stalin. They felt that the ultimate danger would come from the Communists, arguing powerfully that they should settle with Japan and get busy eliminating the Communist armies."[17] According to Chiang's close ally, Representative Walter H. Judd, the Japanese made 11 offers to Chiang to negotiate peace after Pearl Harbor so they could turn full attention to war against the United States.[18] Ultimately, Chiang disregarded that advice.

For well over a year after American entry into the war, China was excluded from United Nations' war planning. A case in point was the January 1943 Anglo-American Casablanca Conference in which China was not invited to participate. T. V. Soong, Chiang's brother-in-law and China's foreign minister, wrote to Harry Hopkins, FDR's special assistant, complaining, "At the Casablanca Conference, when Far Eastern matters were discussed, China was not consulted as there were no representatives present. Only after decisions were made, were they communicated to the Chinese Government."[19]

A February 11, 1943, memorandum from Maxwell Hamilton, chief of the US State Department's Far Eastern Division, warned that US political messaging on China's importance did not correlate with reality in the war effort, and that the inconsistency was becoming a problem. "There has been much publicity to the effect that China is one of the 'Big Four' of the United Nations. Some Chinese believe that China is not actually so considered or treated and, as a result thereof, are disappointed and resentful."[20]

The following week, Stanley Hornbeck, adviser on political relations to the secretary of state, cautioned that the United States would have to give better evidence of its commitment to support its Chinese ally. If that were not forthcoming, he said, China might withdraw from the war.[21]

A TRIPARTITE MEETING IN CAIRO

Roosevelt attempted to address this problem by staging a November 1943 conference in Cairo between himself, Chiang, and Prime Minister Winston Churchill. FDR had initially broached the possibility of such a gathering in a June 30, 1943, note to Chiang. His gesture followed reports from US intelligence sources that Chinese leaders were miffed that the president had not conferred with Chiang earlier in the war. The omission was taken as a sign that China was of secondary, even inconsequential, importance in allied war planning. Feeling disrespected and determined not to lose face, the Chinese did not take the initiative to seek such a consultation. But on July 9, invitation received, Chiang responded to FDR's proposal enthusiastically embracing the idea of a meeting any time after September 1943. With this agreement to meet in hand, planning for the conference proceeded.[22]

British historian Robert Bickers notes, "Roosevelt put a great deal of personal effort into making sure that Chiang felt the conference was a success."[23] Notwithstanding substantial British qualms about what Churchill thought was disproportional US perceptions of China, and the risk of elevating and empowering it, London went along.[24]

Roosevelt's efforts succeeded and Chiang's ego was assuaged. In his diary, Chiang characterized the summit in Cairo as "the greatest triumph in the history of China's foreign affairs."[25]

The conference between Roosevelt, Churchill, and Chiang began on November 22 and ended on November 26. Madame Mayling Soong Chiang, the generalissimo's American-educated wife, participated as a translator.[26]

The president and Chiang met several times, both with Churchill and without him. At a dinner on November 23, attended by the Chiangs; Roosevelt; and FDR's adviser, Harry Hopkins, the generalissimo gave assurances that the Nationalists were not hoarding supplies to use against the Communists and were putting maximum effort into the war. Chiang also tended to dismiss claims that the Communists were meaningfully engaged in fighting the Japanese, said the Communists must be kept under constant surveillance, and expressed grave suspicions about the Soviet Union.[27] He suspected that they would aid his domestic enemies, if given the opportunity to do so.

In addition,there was mistrust based on Stalin's relationship with Tokyo. To ensure that Japan might get bogged down in China and be unable to attack the USSR, the Soviets in the mid-1930s rendered substantial arms assistance to the ROC. But Chiang wanted more. He fruitlessly explored a mutual defense treaty with Moscow. Unable to secure Stalin's agreement, Chiang settled for a 1937 nonaggression pact.[28] As the fighting in China turned grim in late 1937 and early 1938, Chiang tried to coax the Soviets to enter the conflict. But Stalin was primarily concerned about potential conflict with Germany. He rebuffed Chiang.

The generalissimo's last major attempt came when the Japanese assaulted the Yangtze transport center of Wuhan, where Chiang had moved his capital after the fall on Nanjing [Nanjing] at the end of 1937. The fight for Wuhan began in June 1938 and ended in October. Again, Stalin refused. After, Wuhan fell, Chiang retreated west to Chungking, which remained the Nationalist capital until the end of the war.[29]

Instead, on April 13, 1941, Stalin concluded a five-year neutrality pact with Japan.[30] The accord meant Stalin was free to deal with Germany, and Japan was free to deal with the United States and Britain. Neither had to worry about rearguard attacks in Asia. Meanwhile, Chiang was left to fend for himself.

As historians Brendan Simms and Charlie Laderman have chronicled, the day after the Japanese attack on Pearl Harbor, Chiang summoned a Soviet representative in Chungking to demand that the Soviets declare war on Japan.[31] But the Soviets remained faithful to the neutrality pact, which remained in force until Stalin abrogated it a few days before the war ended in 1945.[32]

At dinner, Roosevelt heard the generalissimo out. But given reports he had been getting from official sources and journalists, FDR was skeptical of Chiang's representations about China's war effort.[33] Before retiring for the evening, the president spoke with his son, Elliott. Professor Ronald Ian Heiferman writes, "Roosevelt also told his son that despite the disclaimers of the Generalissimo and his wife, he believed that many of Chiang's best forces were not being committed to the war against Japan but were being deployed instead against Communists in the northwest of China."[34] Nevertheless, the president said, Chiang was a useful ally, because he engaged Japanese troops that would otherwise be deployed against the United States.[35]

This consideration would remain key even when US aerial strategy later shifted to attacking Japan from positions in the Pacific rather than from mainland China. As Heiferman summarizes it, "Although there was little chance that the Chinese could achieve a definitive victory over Japan in China, this was not necessary. . . . Keeping China in the war by providing minimal amounts of supplies and puffing up the egos of China's leaders was a cheap strategy requiring few American combat troops and equally few casualties."[36]

The conference in Egypt culminated in the Cairo Declaration, a statement which remains important in US-China relations to this day because of what it said about Formosa [Taiwan]. The declaration noted, "The three great allies are fighting this war to restrain and punish the aggression of Japan. They covet no gain for themselves and have no thought of territorial expansion. It is their purpose that Japan shall be stripped of all the islands in the Pacific which she has seized or occupied since the beginning of the First World War in 1914, and that all the territories Japan has stolen from the Chinese, such as Manchuria, Formosa, and the Pescadores [Penghu], shall be restored to the Republic of China."

This formulation mirrored a Chinese policy memorandum given to Roosevelt in Cairo.[37] The paper covered a broad range of military and political topics, mostly related to the Pacific. It stated that "Japan shall restore to China all the territories she has taken from China since September 18, 1931. Japan shall also return Dairen [Dalian] and Port Arthur, and Formosa and the Pescadores Islands to China."[38]

John Paton Davies argued that Roosevelt was too hasty in accepting Chiang's proposal but did so on the basis that accepting allied territorial demands was necessary to keep wartime coalitions operating. FDR's thinking applied not only to Chiang's claims at Cairo but, later, Stalin's at Yalta. It generated complex political and security problems for FDR's successors. "FDR believed that a display of generosity, gratuitous offerings of enemy territory to the Chinese and the Russians, would persuade Chiang to stay in the war against Japan and Stalin to enter it—when each had every intention of doing what Roosevelt thought he had to pay them to do." Davies added, "Subsequent presidents have had reason to regret that in the case of Formosa a decision on the disposition of the island had not been withheld until a peace conference and determined by a plebiscite."[39]

Ever since, Chinese governments have regarded the Cairo Declaration as a definitive international acknowledgment of China's sovereignty claims over Formosa. But it bears repeating that the declaration was a statement of intent and did not resolve the legal question of how Japan, then indisputably sovereign on Formosa, was to convey sovereignty to China. That proved to be a complicated proposition. Originally, the United States and Britain thought the legal transfer would occur whenever a peace treaty was reached with Japan. But by the time that happened, in 1951, the Communists ruled mainland China, and the Americans decided the treaty should not convey sovereignty after all. Given the security complications arising from changed circumstances, they decided it was preferable to say the status of Formosa's sovereignty remained undetermined.[40]

For the time being, however, FDR's Cairo meetings with Chiang had gone well. As the president cabled Secretary of State Hull on December 3, "My conferences with the Generalissimo were very satisfactory and I liked him."[41]

The reaction in Chungking was parallel. The American ambassador to China, Clarence Gauss, captured the mood there in a December 4 dispatch to Secretary of State Cordell Hull. "The resulting tripartite declaration was considered by Chinese a great diplomatic victory for China as (1) constituting a promised by the United States of America and Britain to effect return to China of territories taken from her by Japan; (2) ensuring Manchuria against feared future encroachment by Soviet Russia; and (3) entailing no additional commitments of service on China's part other than that related to the unconditional surrender of Japan." Gauss also reported a highly favorable reaction in the Chinese press.[42]

However, Chiang's moment of triumph was exceptionally brief. As Roosevelt's speechwriter, Robert Sherwood, pointed out, "When the Generalissimo and Madame departed for Chungking on November 28th, their hopes were high that at last China's demands were to be met with measures that were more than mere words. These hopes, however, were short lived. The agreement at Cairo did not stick for more than 10 days."[43]

As would promptly become clear, there were overriding priorities in other theaters.[44] From Egypt, Roosevelt and Churchill flew to Tehran, where they met with Soviet leader Joseph Stalin in the first "Big Three" conference of the war. Commitments had been made to Chiang in Cairo about seaborne attacks in Burma against Japanese positions. This was code-named Operation Buccaneer. It was to be coordinated with Operation Tarzan, which was to involve Chinese army assaults further north.[45] Taken together, these attacks were intended to relieve Tokyo's grip on Burma, which had severely impeded the flow of supplies into southwestern China.

However, these promises had been made notwithstanding grave British misgivings. London's interests lay in the Mediterranean and Europe, not in a diversion of resources to the China-Burma-India Theater. But Chiang disagreed, wanting an amphibious operation on Burma. Only if there was a commitment to such an assault would Chiang agree to a coordinated land attack. Tensions between China and Britain were barely concealed. British scuttling of such plans occurred almost immediately, when Roosevelt, Churchill, and Stalin met in Tehran.[46]

A CHANGE OF PLANS

Responding to Stalin's insistence that the Americans and British open a second front against Hitler, the Big Three decided on November 30, 1943, to commit to a cross-channel invasion. Code-named Operation Overlord, it was tentatively set to occur in May 1944. Churchill had doubts about the Overlord strategy but gave way under Soviet and American pressure. The

US minutes of that day's plenary session note that "the Prime Minister stated that having taken this important decision, the main question now was to find enough landing craft for all our needs." The effect was that such equipment and personnel could not be diverted for operations in Burma.[47]

As FDR told his advisers, he decided to yield to Churchill on Buccaneer because Churchill had relented on Overlord.[48] Thus, the Big Three were harmonized and the Germany-first priority was reaffirmed.

On December 5, Roosevelt's special assistant Harry Hopkins cabled British foreign secretary Anthony Eden with the message, "It looks like Buccaneer is out."[49] The decision was particularly damaging to Chiang. British scholar Hans van de Ven remarked, "Now, finally, a clear strategy for the defeat of both Germany and Japan was in place—one that reduced yet further the strategic significance of China."[50]

After Tehran, Roosevelt and Churchill returned to Cairo. On December 6, they jointly cabled Stalin to affirm the idea that Overlord would have proper logistical support. "To provide for the reinforcement of cross channel operations, we have directed the greatest effort be made to increase the production of landing craft in the United States and the United Kingdom, and for the same purpose, the diversion of certain landing craft from the Pacific has also been ordered."[51]

That same day, the president let Chiang know about the altered plans. He wired, "Conference with Stalin involves us in combined grand operations on European continent in late spring giving fair prospect of terminating war with Germany by end of summer of 1944. These operations impose so large a requirement of heavy landing craft as to make it impracticable to devote a sufficient number to the amphibious operation in the Bay of Bengal simultaneously with launching of Tarzan to ensure success of operation." The president argued that this outcome, although doubtlessly disappointing to Chiang, was in China's best interest. "I am influenced in this matter by the tremendous advantage to be received by China and the Pacific through the early termination of the war with Germany."[52] As van de Ven put it, "Coming so soon after promises of significant support for China, this was a slap in the face for Chiang."[53]

The Sino-American relationship again turned south. The generalissimo was feeling betrayed and let the president know so.[54] On December 9, Chiang responded to Roosevelt's message. He noted that, before Cairo, there had been many questions in China about allied commitment to the CBI Theater. However, he said, that such doubt had been dispelled in Egypt. "Prior to the Cairo Conference there had been disturbing elements voicing their discontent and uncertainty of America and Great Britain's attitude in waging a global war and, at the same time, leaving China to shift as best as she could against our common enemy. At one stroke the

Cairo Communiqué decisively swept away this suspicion in that we three had jointly and publicly pledged to launch a joint all-out offensive in the Pacific."

However, he said, the changes could dissipate all those gains and precipitate a devastating collapse of morale in China. "If it should now be known to the Chinese army and people that a radical change of policy and strategy is being contemplated, the repercussions would be so disheartening that I fear of the consequences of China's ability to hold out much longer."

The generalissimo bitterly acknowledged the priority being given to beating the Germans first but pointed out important downsides if the CBI were starved to do it. "I am aware and appreciate your being influenced by the probable tremendous advantages to be reaped by China as well as the United Nations as a whole in speedily defeating Germany first. For the victory in one theater of war necessarily affects all other theaters; on the other hand, the collapse of the China theater would have equally grave consequences on the global war."

Having little choice but to acquiesce, Chiang told Roosevelt, "I have therefore come to this conclusion that in order to save this grave situation, I am inclined to accept your recommendation. You will doubtless realize but in so doing my task and rallying the nation to continue resistance is being made infinitely more difficult."

Chiang grimly predicted, "From the Declaration of the Tehran conference, Japan will rightly deduce that practically the entire weight of the United Nations forces will be applied to the European front thus abandoning the China theater to the mercy of Japan's mechanized air and land forces."[55]

As he forecasted, within four months, the Japanese launched a major offensive that wrought terrible damage in southern and eastern China. In its aftermath, Chiang assigned blame for the disaster to demands imposed on him by America.

In an October 9, 1944, letter to Patrick Hurley, Chiang bitterly set out his grievances. Hurley forwarded the letter to FDR. Chiang wrote, "At the Cairo conference, commitments were finally made by representatives of the United States and Great Britain which appeared to ensure the kind of Burma campaign which I could approve. Unhappily those commitments were abandoned shortly after I left Cairo."

The backtracking presented political complications for Chiang and exacerbated his already tense relations with his military adviser and Chief of Staff US General Joseph Stilwell. Chiang reported, "Stilwell then came to me and announced that he proposed to proceed with a limited offensive in north Burma. I again warned him of the consequences, stating specifically that I feared the project would be difficult and costly and would engage all of China's limited resources at a time when this would be dangerous."

Already skeptical of Chiang's commitment to the war effort and disdainful of him personally, Stilwell reacted contemptuously. Chiang wrote, "He treated my warning lightly, and insisted that if I maintained my attitude, China would be suspected of wishing to withhold any real contribution to the allied cause. . . . It was not long before my warning was substantiated."[56]

Writing again to Roosevelt on December 23, Chiang complained about vital decisions from which he had been excluded. China's relationship with its allies was again painful for everyone. Feeling like his views and China's vital interests were being disregarded, Chiang was generally fed up. He told the president, "As regards the general strategy decided by the British-American Council of Chiefs of Staff to use all available resources to defeat Germany first, I was not present during the deliberations and was therefore not in any position to express my views." The consequences of putting China on the backburner were becoming evident. Chiang wrote, "Judging by the latest military dispositions in activities, the allied strategy of relegating the China War Theater to the background has given rise to serious misgivings on all sides. The success of the Burma campaign is a matter of life and death for China."[57]

FDR decided to put the best face on an obviously problematic situation. Having returned to the White House from Cairo and Tehran, he replied on December 30, "Your acceptance of the strategy of concentrating all necessary means to defeat Germany first unites all of us completely."[58]

DISILLUSIONMENT WORKS IN TWO DIRECTIONS

It was not only Chiang who was disenchanted with his ally. Roosevelt drew conclusions from the Cairo conference that reinforced what he had been hearing about China's commitment to the war and Chiang's openness to a coalition that could avert a destabilizing civil war with the Communists. The president concluded that the United States should explore whether direct contact with the Communists could be fruitful. According to Heiferman, "In light of the fact that the Generalissimo was unwilling to engage the Japanese in Burma in any substantial campaign without the simultaneous launching of Operation Buccaneer, Roosevelt was ready to act more forcefully on establishing contacts with Mao's Yan'an government despite Chiang's wishes."[59] The United States Army Observation Group, informally known as the Dixie Mission, began operating in Yan'an in July 1944, with Chiang's very grudging acquiescence.

Roosevelt's faith in Nationalist China diminished as the war progressed, goaded by a steady stream of negative commentary from Stilwell.[60] On the advice of Army Chief of Staff George Marshall, FDR had assigned Stilwell to

Chiang in January 1942. Thus, Roosevelt was an audience for the General's caustic and critical reports. Critical US embassy dispatches, and negative press commentary, augmented Stilwell's views and took their toll.[61] For example, a cable to Secretary Hull from George Atcheson, the chargè d'affaires in China, noted, "Recent allied victories have had a noticeably good effect on the morale of the Chinese oligarchy of officials, bankers, et al. The scenes of victory are however too distant to inspire Chinese government and people to bestir themselves to increase China's war effort. . . . The Chinese continue to wait for the allies (chiefly the United States) to defeat Japan."[62]

Daniel Kurtz-Phelan of the Council on Foreign Relations wrote that China was often on the short end of allied assistance. "Their share of global Lend-Lease assistance to American allies was one percent of the total in some years, never more than four percent. Why, they asked, should they do more of what the Americans wanted? Chiang threatened collapse, demanded billion-dollar payments, hinted at capitulation."[63] Tired of the shakedown, and receiving a stream of reports from the War Department, State Department, and journalists, Roosevelt grew impatient.

Japan's massive 1944 Ichigo Offensive further weakened American reliance on Chiang. Ichigo's dual purposes were to destroy American-controlled airfields in eastern China from which attacks could be launched on the Japanese home islands and to connect Japanese positions and supply lines in Indochina with those in Manchuria.[64] The offensive was broadly successful and established Tokyo's control in much of southern China for the first time in the war. The repositioning of Japanese troops for the offensive also eased pressure on Communist-held areas in the north.[65]

While Chiang's regime did not collapse under the weight of the offensive, it was seriously damaged. Ichigo took a significant toll on his armed forces and undermined Nationalist prestige and political support, both domestically and abroad.[66] Richard Bernstein, former Beijing bureau chief for *Time*, noted such perceptions were distorted but devastating. "The government resisted far more than the Communists, who resisted very little, and whose losses were a small fraction of those suffered by the KMT's forces. And yet, both at home and abroad, Chiang came to be perceived less and less as a heroic fighter. More and more it came to be the Communists who were deemed to be waging the good fight, the main force of Chinese resistance."[67]

At the same time, US victories in the South Pacific opened a potentially more rapid path to victory over Japan. By the autumn of 1944, the American military leaders would forswear the idea of landing on the east coast of China and attacking Japan from there.[68] This change not only diminished the importance of the China Theater, but it also upended Communist plans. While the main body of Nationalist forces was concentrated in the interior of China, Mao's forces were closer to the coast and better positioned to help with allied landings. The Communists reasoned that cooperation could weaken US ties with the Nationalists and open the door to direct American military assistance.[69]

Even though plans had changed, Washington still had to keep China in the war. The United States was preparing to launch an invasion of the Japanese home islands beginning in December 1945. Expecting bitter resistance and substantial American casualties, US planners needed to keep Japanese forces distracted.[70] Davies recounted that if Tokyo concluded that Washington had given up on the CBI, Japan would then feel it could transfer forces from there to resist America in the central and western Pacific.[71]

Thus, the United States had to ensure that Japanese armies would not be repositioned to contest the invasion.[72] Appearing before a Senate committee after the war, former US ambassador to China Patrick J. Hurley summarized the strategy he had been executing during the final year of the conflict. "My directive was to prevent the collapse of China during the war, and we did; my directive was to sustain the leadership of Chiang Kai-shek—we did; my directive was to harmonize the relations between the military establishment of the United States and of China—we did; my directive was to keep the Chinese Army in the field and contain as many Japanese as possible to protect our men on the beaches and in the jungles—and we did."[73]

COAXING THE SOVIETS

However necessary these measures were to mitigate American casualties, the president's military advisers, including Army Chief of Staff General George Marshall and General Douglas MacArthur, considered them insufficient. Senior military urged Roosevelt to secure Soviet agreement to enter the war.[74]

Reporting on a 1945 conversation in Manila with MacArthur, then-secretary of the navy James Forrestal outlined the general's thinking. "He felt that we should secure the commitment of the Russians to active and vigorous prosecution of a campaign against the Japanese in Manchukuo[75] of such proportions as to pin down a very large part of the Japanese army; that once this campaign was engaged, we should then launch an attack on the home islands."[76]

Years later, in testimony before the Senate Committee on Foreign Relations, John Stewart Service argued that, in retrospect, the price paid for Soviet support proved excessive. "I think there was another way in which military advice was very important, and I think quite wrong. That was the insistence that we needed the Soviet Union's help in a land war against the Japanese. Marshall apparently held to this view past Yalta right into the late spring of

1945, that we needed Russian assistance, and, therefore, the President was led to pay a very heavy price at Yalta."[77]

Bernstein also contends that the Yalta bargaining was unnecessary, both because the United States did not need Stalin's help to defeat Japan and the Soviets would have entered the war anyway to ensure account was taken of its interests in the Far East.[78]

However, that was not obvious in 1945 and the United States made it a great priority to see that the Soviet-Japanese Neutrality Pact was canceled.[79] At Yalta, Stalin made clear he might do so, provided his interests in the Far East were addressed.

The topic came up during the first Big Three meeting, 14 months earlier in Tehran. With his struggle with Germany then being fought on Soviet soil, Stalin sidestepped making tangible pledges.[80] However, an August 1943 State Department analysis anticipated the Soviets would be much more forward-leaning in Asia once Hitler was vanquished. "The Soviet government will take full advantage of every possible opportunity to prepare for a more positive action in the future. . . . It is reasonable to expect that Soviet Russia will at some time in the future depart from its present policy of not offering material assistance to the Chinese Communists and not openly opposing the Japanese."[81]

In preparation for Tehran, Stalin let the Americans know that the subject was open, even if he needed to defer making formal commitments.[82] Following a meeting of foreign ministers in Moscow, Secretary of State Hull dispatched two secret and urgent cables to Roosevelt, both sent on November 2, 1943. The first read, "Most secret for the President from Hull. A message has been given me from the person highest in authority to be given to you personally in extreme secrecy. The message promises to get in and help defeat the enemy." The second stated, "In the Far East after German defeat."[83]

MEETING IN THE CRIMEA

By the time FDR arrived in Crimea in February 1945 for the Yalta Conference with Stalin and Churchill, he had concluded that the predominant power in Asia would be the Soviet Union, not China.[84] At Yalta, Roosevelt negotiated with that in mind, making secret agreements with Stalin and Churchill that affected China, while keeping the US Foreign Service and the Chinese Government in the dark.[85] However, at the time, the president reasoned that Soviets embracing Chiang's government would stabilize China, marginalize the Chinese Communists, and advance America's vision of continued big-power cooperation after the war.[86]

There had been no thought of inviting Chiang to the conference. He was no longer the imaginary great power. British scholar Diana Preston writes that, in the aftermath of Ichigo, the United States was disillusioned over Chiang's lackluster military performance and his hollowed-out authority.[87] Thus, she says, "In these circumstances, in Roosevelt's mind, there was no question of Chiang being invited to Yalta or to any pre-summit."[88]

By early 1945, the Soviets' military position had dramatically improved. Stalin was prepared to declare war on Japan once Germany surrendered. However, he insisted his people would never support doing so unless they had tangible interests at stake.[89] In a December 1944 meeting in Moscow, Stalin had outlined those interests for US ambassador Averell Harriman.[90] They came up again in Crimea, first at a brief meeting between Stalin and Roosevelt on February 8, 1945, and again on February 10, following further discussions on that day between Stalin and Harriman.

Soviet demands involved regaining rights in China and adjacent regions that Tsarist Russia enjoyed, but that were stripped away after Russia's defeat in its 1905 war with Japan. These included recognition of "preeminent" Soviet interests in the port of Dairen [Dalian],[91] the right to lease a naval base at Port Arthur, joint Soviet-Chinese operation of the China-Eastern Railroad and the South Manchurian Railroad, the maintenance of Outer Mongolia as an independent country (rather than it reverting to Chinese territory),[92] and restoration of Russian claims in South Sakhalin Island and adjacent territories. When Stalin formally raised these issues on February 10, Roosevelt and Prime Minister Churchill acquiesced.[93]

The conditions were stipulated as the last section in the "Protocol of Proceedings of Crimea Conference," which they signed with Stalin on February 11, 1945.[94] The Big Three expressly stipulated that "the heads of the three great powers have agreed that these claims of the Soviet Union shall be unquestionably fulfilled after Japan has been defeated."[95]

As historian S. M. Plokhy noted in his history of the Yalta Conference, "It was one thing to compensate Stalin with territories taken from a common enemy, as was the case with Japan, and quite another to hand over the lands of a friend and an ally, as he had done with China. But his concern was with the overriding national interest as he understood it at the time: to shorten the war and save American lives." Given that priority, the president did not feel he had a choice but to go along. Plokhy continued, "the Soviet refusal during the first days of the conference to discuss joint operations against Japan convinced Roosevelt that there would be no effective cooperation with the Red Army, and perhaps even no Soviet participation in the war in the Far East, unless Stalin's conditions were met."[96]

To secure Soviet Far Eastern rights that Stalin negotiated at Yalta, it was necessary for the USSR to conclude a treaty with China, whose government had not been represented there. How was that negotiation to be arranged?

In a Memorandum of Conversation that Harriman dictated on February 10, this passage appears:

> THE PRESIDENT asked Marshal Stalin whether he (Stalin) wished to take these matters up with T.V. Soong when he came to Moscow or whether Stalin wished the President to take them up with the Generalissimo.
> MARSHAL STALIN replied that as he was an interested party, he would prefer to have the President do it.
> THE PRESIDENT then asked when the subject should be discussed with the Generalissimo, having in mind the question of secrecy.
> MARSHAL STALIN said he would let the President know when he was prepared to have this done.[97]

Thus, it became America's responsibility to inform the Chinese, which would occur once Stalin advised the United States that he was ready to redeploy sufficient forces to enter the Pacific war. The Conference Protocol recited, "It is understood that the agreement concerning Outer Mongolia and the ports and railroads referred to above will require concurrence of Generalissimo Chiang Kai-shek. The President will take measures in order to maintain this concurrence on advice from Marshal Stalin."[98] The Soviet leader essentially regarded this as a mere formality.[99] Preston comments that "privately he considered the Chinese Nationalist leader a nonentity and did not intend to allow squeamishness about consulting him to pose an obstacle."[100] In any event, by the time the moment for consultation arrived, Roosevelt had died, and the responsibility fell to President Harry Truman.

As Michigan Republican senator Homer Ferguson was later to observe, "We were making an agreement with Russia which concerned the integrity and the sovereignty of one of our allies in the Far East, namely, China, to give away, in violation of the very principles we were for which we were fighting in the Pacific, certain territory and rights, provided that Russia came into the war."[101] Roosevelt's speechwriter, Robert E. Sherwood, judges that FDR's concurrence in these conditions represented "the most assailable point in the entire Yalta record."[102]

Walter Robertson, who served in the Eisenhower administration as assistant secretary of state for Far Eastern Affairs, considered Yalta a betrayal of Chiang, because it sold out China's strongest economic assets. Robertson noted that much of the Japanese-built industrial capacity in Manchuria remained intact and could have fueled China's postwar recovery. "At Yalta, secretly, without the knowledge of the Republic of China or of Mr. Churchill at that time, Mr. Roosevelt and his advisers, in order to get the Russians to come in the war against the Japanese—a war which was already won—offered them these rich provinces of Manchuria—provinces which at Cairo in December 1943 had been pledged to be returned to the Republic of China."[103]

As part of its agreement to enter the Pacific war, the Soviets promised to take steps to reach agreements with China, theoretically bringing Chiang an important new ally, and closing off support for the Chinese Communists in their struggle with the Nationalists. "For its part, the Soviet Union expresses it readiness to conclude with the National Government of China a pact of friendship and alliance between the USSR and China in order to render assistance to China with its armed forces for the purpose of liberating China from the Japanese yoke."[104]

A CONFERENCE AT POTSDAM

Following Roosevelt's death on April 12, 1945, Harry S. Truman became president. Germany surrendered on May 8. From July 17 to August 2, 1945, there was another Big Three meeting, this time held at the Berlin suburb of Potsdam, to discuss terms for concluding the war and constructing a durable peace. Truman and Stalin were at Potsdam throughout the conference. Clement Attlee replaced Churchill midstream, following the success of the Labor Party in British elections.[105] Before Churchill departed on July 26, he and Truman jointly issued a declaration regarding Japan. Paragraph eight of the declaration reaffirmed the agreement at Cairo with respect to Formosa. It read, "The terms of the Cairo Declaration shall be carried out and Japanese sovereignty shall be limited to the islands of Honshu, Hokkaido, Kyushu, Shikoku, and such minor islands as we determine."[106]

As was the case in Crimea, Chiang was not present in Potsdam for negotiation or consultation. The text of the declaration notes, "Approval of President Chiang Kai-shek obtained by radio." Professor van de Ven writes that by that stage of the war effort, the generalissimo was inconsequential. "If Chiang's domestic reputation suffered serious damage, internationally he had become an irrelevance."[107]

THE SOVIETS ENTER THE WAR AND
MAKE A TREATY WITH CHINA

Stalin joined the Pacific war on August 9, 1945, a week following the Potsdam Conference. It was three days after the United States dropped an atomic bomb on Hiroshima and the day of the attack on Nagasaki.[108] Soviet armies quickly swept across sections of Manchuria in well-prepared actions against depleted Japanese forces.[109]

Highly reluctant to negotiate with Stalin, and resentful about behind-the-back dealings affecting Chinese sovereignty, the Nationalists felt compelled by the United States to go along with an accord the Soviets mostly precooked and dictated. Ravaged by eight years of war, and confronting internal tensions with the Chinese Communists, the Nationalists would need ongoing American support. As Robertson told Congress, "They first said they would not send emissaries. We were putting tremendous pressure on China to send these emissaries there, and when they got there all of the details of this agreement had been spelled out for them."[110]

From Roosevelt's perspective, the arrangement served the dual objective of hastening the end of the war, potentially removing a source of instability for China, and cushioning against a potential future conflict between Washington and Moscow.

For months after Yalta, the deal-making remained secret from Chiang. It was not until June 1945 that he received official notice of the agreement that affected his country.[111] During the war, Chiang had been nervous about Soviet's intentions toward his government, and thought that Stalin would, if possible, help the Chinese Communists depose him.[112] After he learned about Stalin's requirements, his apprehension grew.

While the Chinese Government was not easy to persuade, it could not withstand the American pressure.[113] Of this moment, Chiang Kai-shek has written, "On February 11, 1945, the United States Britain and Soviet Russia had concluded a secret agreement at Yalta. The Republic of China was not represented at the discussions. We were, therefore, not bound legally by said agreement. But it would be unrealistic to deny the influence which American policies towards Soviet Russia and China had exerted on Sino-Soviet negotiations in the spring of 1945."[114]

In his memoirs, Wellington Koo, China's ambassador to the United States from 1946 to 1956, states, "Our Legislative Yuan was strongly opposed to ratification at the beginning and there were popular demonstrations against the Sino-Soviet Agreement. But China had been under strong 'persuasion' from the United States to send a mission to Moscow to conclude the treaty."

A further consideration motivating an agreement was the presence of major Soviet forces in Manchuria. Chinese diplomat James Shen has written, "After the Soviet army moved into Northeast China in force, Chiang Kai-shek had little choice but to conclude the August 1945 Sino-Soviet Treaty of Friendship and Alliance."[115]

China had suffered a lasting wound and felt greatly aggrieved. Koo reflects the attitude of the Nationalist government. "It was surprising that the American foreign policy, supposedly based on the principles of democracy, self-determination and peace, should have taken for its guidelines the now discredited policy of spheres of influence and interest in the world, divided among the great powers at the expense of, and with disregard for, the rights and aspirations of oppressed peoples."[116]

Of crucial importance to concluding this pact was the support that the Americans and British gave to Soviet demands. Several years after the accord took effect, Sinologist George W. Atkinson remarked, "It is unthinkable that any strong independent Chinese Government would have granted such advantageous terms to any other power, had that power stood alone. The crux of the matter lay in American and British support for Soviet claims. By secret agreement at Yalta, the 'Big Three' pledged their support of free China, but, at the same time, had taken other pivotal decisions concerning Soviet 'rights' in China."[117]

Instigated in the Crimea, treaty negotiations between the Soviet Union and the Republic of China concluded on August 14, 1945. The provisions reflected Yalta's understandings, and therefore were exceedingly favorable to Moscow, but would have stabilized an important relationship for China if the Soviets had scrupulously observed them.[118] However, Stalin had compelling reasons not to do so, given an opportunity to replace a generally pro-American Chinese regime with one beholden to the USSR. John Paton Davies foresaw this in 1943, predicting in a policy memo that "following the defeat of Japan, Russia would no longer be threatened on its eastern borders, because the Kremlin's present need of Chiang Kai-shek's cooperation would have passed, because Stalin would then presumably prefer to have a friendly if not satellite Chinese government on his flank."[119] Initially after the war, however, the Soviets recognized Chiang as China's legitimate leader and counseled the Chinese Communists to work with his government.[120]

NOTES

1. Nancy Bernkopf Tucker, *Patterns in the Dust: Chinese-American Relations and the Recognition Controversy: 1949–1950* (New York: Columbia University Press, 1983), p. 7.

2. *Foreign Relations of the United States 1943: The Conferences at* Cairo *and* Tehran (Washington, DC: US Government Printing Office, 1961), p. 47. As China specialist John Paton Davies wrote in his autobiography, "Roosevelt went to Cairo in large part to achieve a meeting of minds with Chiang, on whom he relied so much in war and in the fashioning of the conditions for world peace. . . . Yet he took with him no one with knowledge of the Chinese and their language. . . . Without the inhibiting presence of a knowledgeable American at his side, Roosevelt plunged into cultivation of Chiang and soliciting the Generalissimo's collaboration in building a Rooseveltian world order." John Paton Davies, Jr., *China Hand* (Philadelphia, PA: University of Pennsylvania Press, 2012), p. 149.

3. "Man and Wife of the Year," *Time Magazine*, January 3, 1938, p. 12.

4. Cordell Hull, *The Memoirs of Cordell Hull* (New York: Macmillan Company, 1948), p. 1587.

5. See Sumner Welles, *Seven Decisions that Shaped History* (New York: Harper and Bros., 1950), p. 152. Steven I. Levine, "On the Brink of Disaster: China and the United States in 1945," in Harry Harding and Yuan Ming, Eds., *Sino-American Relations 1945–1955: A Joint Assessment of a Critical Decade* (Wilmington, DE: Scholarly Resources, 1989), p. 11.

6. Soon after Japan attacked Pearl Harbor, Prime Minister Churchill traveled to visit President Roosevelt and frame a joint approach to the war. Notwithstanding the fact that it was Japan that attacked the United States, Churchill and Roosevelt agreed that, although the war would be fought in Asia as well as Europe, Germany was the principal enemy and must be defeated first. David Bercuson and Holger Herwing, *One Christmas in Washington* (Woodstock, NY: The Overlook Press, 2005), p. 127. Journalist Daniel Kurtz-Phelan writes, "The United States had good reason to focus its resources on the war in Europe. Without Japan, Germany could still fight and maybe win. Without Germany, Japan was finished. So, the United States would start with Europe, condemning China to a low priority in its war effort." Daniel Kurtz-Phelan, *The China Mission: George Marshall's Unfinished War* (New York: W.W. Norton & Company, 2018), p. 27.

7. Tang Tsou, *America's Failure in China, vol. 1* (Chicago, IL: University of Chicago Press, 1962), p. 43

8. Roosevelt's adviser, Stanley Hornbeck, observes that unless the United States and its allies invested sufficient resources into the China-Burma-India Theater so that China could remain in the war, the airfields might not be available by the time the allies got around to needing them. "It is by no means certain that at a time when, say, nine months or twelve months or eighteen months from now, we might wish to use Chinese airfields for direct offensives against Japan, we will find those airfields available." *Foreign Relations of the United States, China 1943* (Washington, DC: US Government Printing Office), p. 44.

9. *FRUS Cairo and Tehran 1943*, p. 172.

10. Daniel Kurtz-Phelan addresses the contradiction between US words, which appeared to elevate the importance of China, with the insufficient flow to Chiang of materiel and other support. Not only did Chiang notice it, but so did Army Chief of Staff General George Marshall. "US resources were already over committed, in the sprawling multi-front war Marshall had to manage. So, we took other measures, more symbolic to elevate and ally. The United States scrapped the exclusion laws. It gave up quasi-imperial privileges in China and leaned on the British to do the same—aside from control of Hong Kong, which would be relinquished, Churchill said over his dead body" (Kurtz-Phelan, p. 24).

11. The Senate approved the treaty unanimously. Historian Herbert Feis writes that "the American government hoped that this act would be convincing proof so we were ready not only to accord China full sovereignty but help her to maintain it; And that it would remove the last vestige of the accusation that the United States was pursuing in China selfish or imperialist ends." Herbert Feis, *The China Tangle* (Princeton, NJ: Princeton University Press, 1953), p. 62.

12. Chiang's adviser, Hollington Tong, states that "the idea that Western powers should have enclaves of political control within Chinese territory, in the

form of the foreign settlements, had tortured the pride of the Chinese people. They were holdovers from the days of the declining Manchu empire. Chiang, before the Japanese attack, was negotiating for their abrogation, but he had encountered a great reluctance, particularly on the part of the British. Now, at the initiative of the United States, China's war allies had decided to make this gesture to show their appreciation of China's wartime contributions." Hollington K. Tong, *Chiang Kai-shek's Teacher and Ambassador; An Inside View of the Republic of China from 1911–1958* (Bloomington, IN: AuthorHouse, 2005), p. 123.

13. People of Chinese descent born inside the United States were considered American citizens by virtue of the birthright citizenship provisions of the Fourteenth Amendment to the US Constitution.

14. Hans van de Ven, *China at War* (Cambridge, MA: Harvard University Press, 2018), pp. 174–175.

15. The Germany-first strategy was first agreed upon months before the United States became an actual belligerent in the war. According to historians Brendan Simms and Charlie Laderman, near the end of March 1941, "British and American military leaders agreed during secret staff talks that in the event of a world war involving Japan they would nonetheless pursue a 'Germany first' strategy." Brendan Simms and Charlie Laderman, *Hitler's American Gamble: Pearl Harbor and Germany's March to War* (New York: Basic Books, 2021), p. 30.

16. Thomas E. Dewey was governor of New York from 1941 to 1955 and was the Republican nominee for president in 1944 and 1948.

17. Thomas E. Dewey, *Journey to the Pacific* (Garden City, NY: Doubleday, 1952), pp. 130–131.

18. Walter H. Judd Oral History, Eisenhower Administration Project Number 117, Columbia University, p. 33.

19. Ibid., p. 53. Soong's remonstrance did not result in prompt improvement. On August 18, he told Secretary Hull that "the Chinese government can no longer hide from its people, whose will determined the decision to oppose Japan in 1937, and from the army, the fact that China is not a party to either the consultations or decisions for the conduct of allied war operations and allied peace plans." Soong beseeched the secretary that China be made a part of all allied decision-making (Ibid., p. 96).

20. Ibid., p. 7.

21. Ibid., pp. 9–10.

22. FRUS, *China: 1943*, pp. 54, 58, 69, 73.

23. Robert Bickers, *Out of China: How the Chinese Ended the Era of Western Domination* (London: Penguin Books, 2018), p. 232.

24. Churchill did not share Roosevelt's enthusiasm for China. Bickers writes, "The British were perplexed and irritated that so much time was taken up with China. . . . Churchill still thought it was an 'affectation' to pretend China was a 'great power'" (Ibid.). Roosevelt's adviser, Robert Sherwood, said of Churchill, "He always went along with the proposition that the supply route to China must be reopened in order to sustain Chinese morale and to keep this gigantic mass of humanity in the war, but it is apparent that he did this out of deference to Roosevelt's sentiments—or perhaps he thought of them as 'whims'—and not from any profound convictions of

his own." Robert E. Sherwood, *Roosevelt and Hopkins: An Intimate History* (New York: Harper & Brothers, 1948), pp. 772–773. In his history of the war, Churchill relates one of his concerns about binding China to the established powers. "There were five hundred million people in China. What would happen if this enormous population developed in the same way as Japan had done in the last century and got hold of modern weapons?" Winston Churchill, *The Second World War, Vol. IV: The Hinge of Fate* (London: Cassel, 1951), p. 139.

25. Bickers, p. 232. Herbert Feis notes wistfully that the newly constructed image of China as a great power did not comport with facts on the ground in the country. "The Chinese armies were in poor condition, not in shape or in state of mind for hard, effective action. The Chinese people were tired and suffering. . . . Those who knew the state of China in December 1943 had much reason to wonder whether the Chinese government and people could manage their affairs well enough to justify that concept of greatness with which the Cairo Declaration is imbued" (Feis, p. 110).

26. Born Soong Meiling in 1898, she attended secondary school in Georgia and was a 1917 graduate of Wellesley College. After graduation, she returned to China. Meiling married Chiang Kai-shek in 1927. After his death in 1975, she emigrated to the United States. Madame Chiang lived in New York until her death in 2003.

27. Heiferman, p. 79.

28. Historian John Garver analyzes the 1937 pact. "First, it provided the political basis for large-scale Soviet military sales and assistance to the ROC. Second, it ensured that neither side would strike a deal with Japan while the war was still underway. If either signatory was attacked by Japan, the other signatory was to render Japan no assistance of any kind., direct or indirect, at any time during the entire conflict, and would refrain from taking any action or entering into any agreement which might be used to advantage by Japan." John W. Garver, "Chiang Kai-shek's Quest for Soviet Entry into the Sino-Japanese War," *Political Science Quarterly*, Vol. 102, No. 2 (Summer 1987), p. 302.

29. The fall of Wuhan was a turning point in Chiang's relations with Moscow. Garver explains, "once it became clear to trying that the Soviet Union would not enter the Sino Japanese war, his policies began to change. After the fall of Wuhan, Soviet Chinese relations entered a new stage. The Soviet Union continued to support China's war effort until June 1941, but the scale of aid declined" (Ibid., p. 315). In June 1941, Hitler attacked the Soviet Union. Beset by Operation Barbarossa, the USSR could no longer manage to assist China.

30. At the time he signed the 1937 nonaggression pact, Chiang expressed concern that the Soviets would double-cross him and sign a similar agreement with Japan, which the Soviets did (Ibid., p. 302).

31. Brendan Simms and Charlie Laderman, *Hitler's American Gamble: Pearl Harbor and Germany's March to Global War* (New York: Basic Books, 2021), p. 192.

32. The German invasion of the USSR, Operation Barbarossa, began on June 22, 1941.

33. For example, when Madame Chiang joined the president on February 19 for his weekly news conference, she was asked, "Madame Chiang, I am going to ask this

question . . . my impression is that there is more unanimity of opinion in support of the Chinese than almost any other, and the one criticism, or the one question that I have heard was that the Chinese people government, or whatever it is, are not supporting their own war with manpower as well as they might. . . . The one tremor of criticism, or question, that I heard around the capitol yesterday come after your two magnificent speeches, was that the Chinese are not utilizing their manpower to their full extent." Madame chalked up any shortfall of effort to munitions supply and answered, "We are using as much manpower as there are munitions to be used. We can't fight with bare hands. We have fought with no overhead protection throughout 5 1/2 years. But we can't go there and fight with our bare hands, although we have fought with nothing but swords in hand-to-hand combat. But it is not true when it is said that China is not supporting the front with her manpower, because we are." Press Conferences of President Franklin D. Roosevelt 1933–1945, Franklin D. Roosevelt Presidential Library and Museum, Number 891, February 19, 1943.

34. Ronald Ian Heiferman, *The Cairo Conference of 1943* (Jefferson, NC: McFarland & Company, Inc., 2011), p. 80.

35. Ibid., pp. 80–82.

36. Ibid., p. 104. John Garver astutely notes that Stalin, early in the Pacific War, and Roosevelt later, used China for much the same purpose. "Roosevelt was doing the same thing Stalin had done—paying for Chinese soldiers to tie down Japan." And Garver adds, "Chiang's subsequent dealings with the Americans were shaped by his earlier experiences with the Soviets. Nor was Chiang Kai-shek the last of China's leaders to fear great power manipulation of what political analysts of later generations would call 'the China card'" (Garver, p. 316).

37. Herbert Feis states that Roosevelt and Churchill agreed without reservation and demanded nothing from Chiang in return (Feis, p. 106).

38. *FRUS Cairo and Tehran 1943*, p. 389. The American draft communiqué read, "We are determined that the islands in the Pacific which have been occupied by the Japanese, many of them made powerful bases contrary to Japan's specific and definite pledge not to militarize them, will be taken from Japan forever, and the territory they have so treacherously stolen from the Chinese such as Manchuria and Formosa will of course be returned to the Republic of China" (Ibid., p. 401). Taiwan and the Pescadores had been ceded to Japan by the 1895 Treaty of Shimonoseki, concluding a war between China and Japan. After war between China and Japan broke out in 1937, the Chinese Government declared the Treaty of Shimonoseki abrogated. See "White Paper: The Taiwan Question and Reunification of China," Embassy of the People's Republic of China, May 17, 2004.

39. Davies, *China Hand*, p. 150.

40. Alan D. Romberg, *Rein in at the Brink of the Precipice* (Washington, DC: The Stimson Center, 2003), pp. 2–3.

41. *FRUS, Cairo and Tehran 1943*, p. 784.

42. *FRUS China 1943*, pp. 177–178.

43. Sherwood, p. 774.

44. *FRUS Cairo and Tehran 1943*, p. 577. British scholar Rana Mitter writes, "During this contentious meeting, although China was treated as an ally of the

Western powers, it was sidelined because the European theater and the opening of a second front in Europe were given top priority." Rana Mitter, *China's Good War* (Cambridge, MA: The Belknap Press of Harvard University Press, 2020), p. 216.

45. According to Robert Sherwood, "It was quite clear, however, that Chiang Kai-shek was not interested in the ground operations in the north, in which his own Chinese divisions would provide the bulk of the manpower, unless the British would agree to synchronize with them the major moves by land, sea, and air in the South to cut off the Japanese lines of supply and reinforcement, including the railroad that they had constructed from Bangkok to Rangoon" (Sherwood, p. 772).

46. Ibid., p. 80.

47. "The original plan of opening the Burma Road, the strategic idea of making a landing on the Chinese coast, and the program of reforming and retraining the Chinese army, if effectively implemented, would have increased the possibility of China's being both strong and friendly at the end of the war, but the global shortage of men and resources prevented the early execution of this strategy" (Tsou, p. 46).

48. Heiferman, p. 152.

49. *FRUS Cairo and Tehran 1943*, p. 803.

50. van de Ven, p. 172.

51. Franklin D. Roosevelt, Papers as President: Map Room Papers, 1941–1945, Franklin D. Roosevelt Presidential Library & Museum, FDR and Stalin 1943, December 6, 1943.

52. *FRUS China 1943*, p. 178.

53. van de Ven, p. 172. Daniel Kurtz-Phelan adds, "When Chiang got his own war summit and sat side-by-side with Churchill and Roosevelt in Cairo, commitments to China collapsed almost immediately afterward, when the European front turned out to need more help—a stab of humiliation in what was to be a moment of glory" (Kurtz-Phelan, p. 28).

54. Heiferman, p. 155.

55. Franklin D. Roosevelt, Papers as President: Map Room Papers, 1941–1945, Franklin D. Roosevelt Presidential Library & Museum, FDR and Chiang Kai-shek 1943, December 9, 1943.

56. Compounding this problem, Chiang wrote, was as Ichigo rolled along, "Stilwell exhibited complete indifference to the outcome in east China." Franklin D. Roosevelt, Papers as President: Map Room Papers, 1941–1945, Franklin D. Roosevelt Presidential Library & Museum, FDR and General Hurley 1944–1945, October 9, 1944. On October 18, FDR wrote to Chiang, absolving Stilwell and taking responsibility along with Churchill for the strategy in Burma. "General Stilwell was not responsible for the decisions with respect to attacking in North instead of South Burma. This decision was made by the Combined British and American staff and was fully approved by the Prime Minister and myself." Franklin D. Roosevelt, Papers as President: Map Room Papers, 1941–1945, Franklin D. Roosevelt Presidential Library & Museum, FDR and General Hurley 1944–1945, October 18, 1944.

57. *FRUS Cairo and Tehran 1943*, pp. 855–856. Chiang had advocated the opposite strategy: defeating Japan first and thereafter mobilizing full resources against Germany. By the end of December 1941, the Soviets, as well as the Americans and

British, had rejected that approach (van de Ven, pp. 159–160). Apart from military considerations, the cancellation of Buccaneer generated political problems for Chiang. On October 20, John Stewart Service wrote a memo for General Stilwell about how invested China was in the Burma campaign. "The public has been led by allied propaganda to believe that such a campaign will be conducted with the coming of the dry season and feels that success of the campaign will enable China to receive sufficient war supplies for its armed forces and to solve some of its economic problems through the import of needed materials. There will be widespread disappointment among the Chinese people if the campaign does not take place." *FRUS China 1943*, pp. 154–155.

58. Franklin D. Roosevelt, Papers as President: Map Room Papers, 1941–1945, Franklin D. Roosevelt Presidential Library & Museum, FDR and Chiang Kai-shek 1943, December 30, 1943.

59. Heiferman, p. 163.

60. Tucker writes, "The President assumed that the Chinese would continue to tie down the Japanese armies while Americans fought to free Europe from Fascist control. While Roosevelt chided Chiang for hoarding his arms and ammunition and urged him to keep the fight against Japan alive, the Generalissimo worried instead about the struggle with Communist armies which would erupt as soon as the Japanese scourge lifted. American disenchantment with Chiang proceeded apace, accelerated by the Kuomintang's refusal to liberalize its regime" (Tucker, p. 7). Roosevelt's commitment to Chiang peaked at the Cairo Conference of the end of the year. "In early 1944, the two leaders clashed over the question of whether or not American-trained and -equipped Chinese forces would fight in northern Burma, and much of the confidence that remained between Chungking and Washington was broken" (Reardon-Anderson, p. 31).

61. "Most of the correspondents, taking their cues from the American officers, who were Stilwell's men, believed that Generalissimo Chiang had mishandled the war. The correspondents failed to perceive the larger issues in this controversy" (Tong, p. 142).

62. *FRUS China: 1943*, p. 111. Ambassador Gauss reinforced this view in an October 18 cable to Secretary Hull. "The Chinese have persuaded themselves that the war in Europe will shortly end and the United States, possibly with help from Great Britain, will defeat Japan; that the Chinese are too tired and too worn and too ill-equipped to make greater effort, especially when such effort may not be necessary; and that the Chinese can sit back, holding what they have against the Japanese, and concentrate their planning upon China's post war political and economic problems" (Ibid., p. 142). Davies writes, "He preferred passively to depend on the Americans to supply him by air until such time as, in routing the Japanese in the Pacific, they opened East China coastal ports for him" (Davies, *China Hand*, p. 147). Feis speaks of conflicting purposes between China and the United States that were difficult to reconcile. "American intent was centered on the wish to win the war as quickly as possible. To this end, the American government sought to apply all the human effort and resources of the United States and expected China to do the same. . . . But while it was being won the Chiang Kai-shek regime wanted to be sure that it would survive

in power. It was convinced that the maintenance of its position was essential for an orderly and unified China after the war. Hence, it was afraid to take military chances" (Feis, p. 74).

63. Kurtz-Phelan, p. 28. For example, at the Casablanca conference in January 1943, at which China was not present, allied war planners had developed concepts for an assault on Japanese-occupied Burma. Chiang was heartened by this development, but disappointed at lax execution. Thus, at a conference of the Combined Chiefs of Staff on May 17, 1943, T. V. Soong, Chiang's brother-in-law and senior representative, said that China would make a separate peace if the promises emanating from Casablanca were not carried out (Feis, p. 67).

64. Richard Bernstein, *China 1945: Mao's Revolution and America's Fateful Choice* (New York: Alfred A. Knopf, 2014), pp. 84–85. John Paton Davies notes that Ichigo compromised airfields that had been "a major factor in the war." Davies, *Dragon by the Tail*, p. 290.

65. van de Ven, p. 198. Ichigo caused a massive repositioning of Japanese forces, which took pressure off the Communists. M. Taylor Fravel writes, "Japan left a largely garrison force in north China to protect existing Japanese positions, allowing the CCP and the Red Army to rebuild and grow." M. Taylor Fravel, *Active Defense* (Princeton, NJ: Princeton University Press, 2019), p. 53. Professor John King Fairbank notes, "The Japanese had to relax their pressure on the North China Liberated Areas and Border Region. For the Communists, the war began to wind down when the long-planned Japanese Ichigo Offensive in 1944 rolled down from Honan south of the Yangtze, destroying much of the Nationalists' best armies." John King Fairbank, *The Great Chinese Revolution: 1800–1985* (New York: Harper & Row, 1986), p. 258.

66. van de Ven, p. 177. "Besides greatly reducing the sphere of Chungking's authority, the East China Crisis dealt a shattering blow to the stability and morale of the Kuomintang regime. While the government had always been viewed with some misgivings, both in China and among the allies, the collapse of the Nationalist army in 1944 drove its critics to seek for other alternatives. The most obvious alternative was some new political arrangement which would give a greater role to the Communists." James Reardon-Anderson, *Yenan and the Great Powers* (New York: Columbia University Press, 1980), pp. 29–30.

67. Bernstein, p. 86.

68. Tsou, p. 70.

69. Carter, p. 141.

70. Charles Stephenson, *Stalin's War on Japan: The Red Army's Manchurian Strategic Offensive Operation, 1945* (Yorkshire: Pen & Sword Books, 2021), p. 4.

71. Davies, *China Hand*, p. 146.

72. Stephenson, p. 8.

73. Statement of Ambassador Patrick J. Hurley on December 5, 1945 (Ibid., p. 65).

74. Testimony of John Stewart Service, p. 37. See also Stephenson, p. 8.

75. Manchukuo was the name the Japanese gave to the puppet state they had set up in Manchuria.

76. Walter Millis and E. S. Duffield, *The Forrestal Diaries* (New York: Viking Press, 1951), p. 31. Robert Sherwood states that Roosevelt's overriding concern about the Far East was what steps were necessary to defeat Japan while minimizing American losses. Other policy considerations were subordinated to that one.

> "The immensely costly operations at Iwo Jima and then at Okinawa were about to be launched, and the plans had been made for the major invasion of the Japanese home islands in the fall of 1945. MacArthur's calculations were based on the assumption that the Russians would contain the great bulk of the Japanese forces on the Asiatic mainland as they had contained the Germans in Eastern Europe. Obviously, the entry of the Soviet Union forcibly into the Japanese war by midsummer—before the major invasion—could mean the saving of countless American lives and might even make the final invasion unnecessary." (Sherwood, p. 867)

77. Testimony of John Stewart Service, p. 37. Charles Stephenson takes a contrary view, arguing FDR did the best he could, given that the USSR could act in far eastern Asia without American permission and before the United States could intercede to stop it. He says, "Russia could do more or less what it liked and the United States was in a very weak position to prevent it. Should the US try to frustrate them, the Soviets could wait for Japan to be defeated and then walk in with less resistance than they would face in August 1945. Meanwhile, America would have taken on Japan without Soviet help" (Stephenson, p. 10).

78. Bernstein, p. 196.

79. The pact dated from April 1941. Historian S. M. Plokhy notes that Japan did not attack the Soviet Union after the German invasion in June 1941, which allowed Stalin to move troops from the Far East to defend Moscow. S. M. Plokhy, *Yalta: The Price of Peace* (New York: Penguin Group, 2010), p. 217. Professor Tsuyoshi Hasegawa, who studied the influence of Soviet entry into the war on Japan's decision to surrender, writes, "The more the military situation deteriorated the more the Japanese policymakers focused on the Soviet Union. For the army, determined to wage a last-ditch battle to defend the homeland, it became essential to keep the Soviet Union out of the war. For the peace party, the termination of the war through Moscow's mediation seemed to offer the only alternative to unconditional surrender." Tsuyoshi Hasegawa, *Racing the Enemy: Truman, Stalin, and the Surrender of Japan* (Cambridge: Belknap Press, 2006), p. 4.

80. *FRUS China 1943*, p. 318.

81. Ibid.

82. Tsou, p. 242. Sherwood writes that at the initial Big Three meeting on November 28, 1943, Stalin told his allies that "when Germany was finally defeated the necessary Russian reinforcements could be sent to Eastern Siberia." Then, Stalin continued, "We shall be able by our common front to beat Japan." Sherwood adds, "This was the first assurance given to Roosevelt or Churchill to that important effect" (Sherwood, p. 779).

83. The information was so sensitive that Hull broke it into two cables, the first sent via navy communications and the second via army communications (*FRUS Cairo and Tehran 1943*, p. 147). See also Feis, who wrote, "Just before the Secretary of State left Moscow for home, Stalin made a short statement of dramatic consequence.

Stalin asked him to tell the President the Soviet Union would enter the Pacific war and help defeat the enemy in the Far East as soon as soon as the Germans were beaten. This promise was unasked and unqualified. . . . Stalin's statement was not repeated to the Chinese government. . . . But the prospect of Soviet entry into the Pacific war gave further impetus to the wish to settle the future of China and straighten out Sino-Soviet relations" (Feis, pp. 100–102).

84. Testimony of John Stewart Service, p. 33.

85. Ibid.

86. Robert L. Messer, "Roosevelt, Truman, and China: An Overview," in Harry Harding and Yuan Ming, Eds., *Sino-American Relations 1945–1955: A Joint Assessment of a Critical Decade* (Wilmington, DE: Scholarly Resources, 1989), p. 67.

87. "Japan's Operation Ichigo Offensive in the summer of 1944 conquered further large swathes of southeast China including all the air bases from with the US air force had hoped to bomb Japan in the lead-up to any invasion." Diana Preston, *Eight Days at Yalta: How Churchill, Roosevelt, and Stalin Shaped the Post-War World* (London: Picador, 2019), p. 39.

88. Ibid.

89. Sherwood, p. 867.

90. Harriman was under instructions to ascertain the Soviets' political demands in the Far East. Plokhy, p. 219.

91. In 1948, Hollington Tong, director of the Chinese Government Information Office, spoke of the disparity between what Chiang and Roosevelt discussed in Cairo on the subject of Dairen and the outcome of Yalta. In Cairo, FDR had raised the possibility of making Dairen a free port at the end of the war. Chiang stated he might consider it, provided Chinese sovereignty was not infringed. However, the Big Three at Yalta recognized the preeminent rights of the Soviet Union in the port and did not bother to inform Chiang. Tong stated, "The nature of the commitment later made by President Roosevelt at Yalta differed from what President Roosevelt himself had suggested to President Chiang at Cairo. The Yalta commitment was not known to the government of China at the time it was made" (*FRUS Cairo and Tehran 1943*, p. 891).

92. Mongolia was under the control of China during the Qing Dynasty, which was overthrown in 1911. Mongolia declared independence at that time, which the Chinese contested. Independence was resolved by the formation in 1924 of the Mongolian People's Republic, which had a long border and close relations with the USSR. At Yalta, Stalin made one of his preconditions for entering the Pacific war that Mongolian independence be preserved.

93. Soviet diplomat Andrei Gromyko, who was present at Yalta, gave to and translated for Stalin a letter from Roosevelt that acquiesced in Soviet claims to South Sakhalin and the Kuriles. In his memoirs, Gromyko quotes Stalin's reaction. "This is an important letter. The Americans recognize the justice of our position on Sakhalin and the Kuriles. Now in return they will try to insist on our participation in the war against Japan. But that's another question altogether." Gromyko continued,

"as I left him, I had the feeling that his positive response to Roosevelt letter would have an influence on the session that was to start in about an hour's time. Certain significant events had led up to the letter. Already, back in Tehran, Roosevelt had asked Stalin about

Soviet help in the war against Japan. It became apparent then that the opening of a second front by the Allies was being linked to the USSR's willingness to help the USA in the East. The USA and USSR reached an understanding in principle on that occasion, but it was not regarded as a firm agreement, and the final word on the question was not given until after Roosevelt's letter about Sakhalin and the Kuriles."

Andrei Gromyko, *Memoirs* (New York: Doubleday, 1989), p. 90.

94. The understanding on the Far East was negotiated between Roosevelt and Stalin, with Churchill not present, although the prime minister joined them in signing the final agreement (Sherwood, p. 866). Ambassador Leighton Stuart says of these concessions, "This permitted Russian troops to enter, just as the war was ending, Manchuria, where they brutally slaughtered Chinese, publicly raped their women, looted their possessions, and plundered this allied nation of two billion dollars' worth of industrial machinery." John Leighton Stuart, *Fifty Years in China: The Memoirs of John Leighton Stuart Missionary and Ambassador* (New York: Random House, 1954), p. 180.

95. "Yalta Conference Agreement, Declaration of a Liberated Europe," February 11, 1945, History and Public Policy Program Digital Archive, National Archives. http://digitalarchive.wilsoncenter.org/document/11617

96. Plokhy, p. 228.

97. Franklin D. Roosevelt Papers as President (Map Room Papers 1941–1945), Franklin D. Roosevelt Presidential Library & Museum, The Crimean Conference, Memorandum of Conversation (Harriman), February 10, 1945.

98. According to Chiang's biographer, Jonathan Fenby, the deal gave the Soviets major advantages in the Far East. "This handed Stalin inducements in Manchuria on the shape of joint operations of the main railway, Soviet use of Port Arthur, and the neighboring city of Dairen becoming a free port. The independence of Mongolia was recognized, meaning that Moscow would be able to make its influence felt there." Jonathan Fenby, *Chiang Kai-shek: China's Generalissimo and the Nation He Lost* (New York: Carroll & Graf Publishers, 2004), p. 451.

99. In a February 8 Memorandum of Conversation, Harriman recounts a discussion with Soviet foreign minister Vyacheslav Molotov in which he notes Soviet skepticism on the need to consult the Chinese at all. "It took me some time to explain to Molotov the reasons" for it. Franklin D. Roosevelt Papers as President (Map Room Papers 1941–1945), Franklin D. Roosevelt Presidential Library & Museum, The Crimean Conference, Memorandum of Conversation (Harriman), February 8, 1945.

100. Preston, p. 193.

101. *Congressional Record*, March 27, 1953, p. 2381.

102. Sherwood, p. 867. The agreement on the Soviet position in Manchuria was one of the final acts of the Yalta Conference, which had lasted nine days and covered much other consequential ground. Sherwood contends, "It is my belief that Roosevelt would not have agreed to that final firm commitment had it not been that the Yalta Conference was almost at an end and he was tired and anxious to avoid further argument" (Ibid.).

103. Oral History Walter S. Robertson, Princeton University Library, p. 8, http://arks.princeton.edu/ark:/88435/3n204436h (accessed February 4, 2022).

104. Stephenson, p. 6. Tsou comments that this language framed a military alliance against Japan but did not extend to supporting the political authority of the Nationalist government (Tsou, p. 252).

105. Office of the Historian, US Department of State, "The Potsdam Conference, 1945" www.history.state.gov (accessed March 17, 2022).

106. Log of President Harry S. Truman's Trip to the Berlin Conference, President Truman's Travel Logs, 1945, Rose A. Conway Papers, p. 118. www.trumanlibrary .gov (accessed March 17, 2022).

107. van de Ven, p. 180.

108. Tsuyoshi Hasegawa argues that it was the Soviet entry into the war and not the atomic bombs that hastened the Japanese surrender. "Even after the Potsdam Proclamation was issued, the Japanese clung to the hope that Moscow mediation would bring about more favorable surrender terms. Thus, Soviet entry into the war shocked the Japanese even more than the atomic bombs because it meant the end of any hope of achieving a settlement short of unconditional surrender. Eventually, the fear of Soviet political influence in Japan's occupation drove the Emperor to accept unconditionally the Potsdam surrender terms" (Hasegawa, p. 4).

109. Bernstein, p. 279. Alarmed by Soviet actions in Europe and buoyed by the successful testing of the atomic bomb, the United States had reason to regret coaxing Stalin into the war. As well, Stalin was determined to move quickly. Van de Ven states, "Increasingly concerned about Soviet behaviour in eastern Europe, even before the end of the war with Japan, the Americans had tried to keep them out of east Asia. President Truman approved the dropping of atomic bombs on two Japanese cities to shorten the war, and so save American lives, but also in the hope that Japan's surrender would take place before Soviet armed forces entered Korea and Manchuria. However, the Soviets had their own fears, including a revival of Japanese militarism and concern about the Americans' ultimate objectives" (van de Ven, p. 230).

110. *Congressional Record*, March 27, 1963, p. 2382.

111. "China, though, was to learn nothing of these matters at the time. Fearing security leaks, Roosevelt kept the agreement from Chiang and his regime. . . . The reason behind this veil of secrecy was obvious. If the Japanese authorities got word of what was afoot then they would reinforce their already heavily fortified border regions with the Soviet Union. Moreover, they might launch an offensive with a view to blocking or damaging the vital Trans-Siberian Railway. Any such operation could have disastrous effects on the build-up for the planned offensive" (Stephenson, p. 6). Not only was Chiang not informed, neither were the Communists. "Stalin, who did not believe in the ability of the Communists to take power, had kept them in the dark about Yalta, and did not consult them before reaching the agreement with the Nationalists" (Fenby, p. 451).

112. In October 1943, US ambassador Clarence Gauss predicted that, following the defeat of Germany, the Soviets would provide a lifeline to the Chinese Communists. "The end of the war in Europe will find a militarily strong Soviet Russia which may be expected to take an active interest in the Far Eastern situation. That interest is likely to include the Chinese Communists, and every day that passes brings nearer

the possibility of Russian interference in the Communist situation in China" (*FRUS China 1943*, p. 357).

113. As Hollington Tong writes, "The idea of a post-war partnership between Russia and the United States was accepted in the United States after the Tehran conference. It was politically dangerous to reject the gratuitous advice, which was coming to us from Americans" (Tong, pp. 142–143).

114. Chiang Kai-shek, *Soviet Russia in China: A Summing Up at Seventy* (New York: Farrar, Strauss, and Cudahy, 1957), p. 135.

115. Shen Zhihua, *Mao, Stalin, and the Korean War* (London: Routledge, 2012), p. 44. US ambassador to the Soviet Union Averell Harriman was confident that the Soviets would, in fact, intervene because their territorial claims were satisfied, and thus they would be able to dominate China. *Forrestal Diaries*, p. 55.

116. The Wellington Koo Memoir, New York Times Oral History Program, Chinese Oral History Project of the East Asian Institute of Columbia University, Part II, pp. F-319–320.

117. George W. Atkinson, "The Sino-Soviet Treaty of Friendship and Alliance," *International Affairs* (Royal Institute of International Affairs), Vol. 23, No. 3 (Jul. 1947), pp. 357–366. https://www.jstor.org/stable/3017226. Stuart Schram writes that the Soviets had strong leverage to coerce the final measure of Nationalist cooperation in signing the treaty. It involved control over Manchuria. "In the course of the negotiations in Moscow, Stalin had cynically underscored the point at issue, warning Chiang's Foreign Minister T.V. Soong on 10 August that if the treaty was not signed immediately, the Chinese Communists would get into Manchuria first." Schram, *Political Leaders of the Twentieth Century: Mao Tse-Tung* (Westport, CT: Praeger Publishers, 1966), p. 235.

118. John Paton Davies writes, "I commented by radiogram to the Department on September 4 that Moscow did not require the treaty for the achievement of any of the immediate objectives now being attained by the Red Army advance. The pact's advantage to the Soviet government was that it lent legality to situations which might otherwise lead to disputes and complaints" (Davies, *China Hand*, p. 264).

119. Davies, *Dragon by the Tail*, p. 272. Chinese scholar Shen Zhihua emphasizes that Stalin always put Soviet national security ahead of ideological interests. As to the Far East, Soviet interests were served by stability in China, rather than a civil war. Moscow's attitude changed when Stalin concluded Chiang was too dependent on the Americans to be allowed to assert control in Manchuria, a region from which the Nationalists had been absent during a 15–year Japanese occupation. "To resist American pressure and put the brakes on the Nationalists, the Soviet Union not only prevented Nationalist forces from landing in Northeast China ports, but also indicated its support for a Chinese Communist takeover of the Northeast" (Shen, p. 53).

120. Ibid., p. 45. Tensions had existed between the Soviets and Mao for more than a decade, with Moscow believing that the Chinese Communist leadership had been insufficiently subject to its dictation (Ibid., p. 47).

Chapter 2

An Impossible Coalition

UNITED AND DISUNITED FRONTS

Notwithstanding Stalin's urging, and American hopes, the simmering conflict between adverse Chinese factions was on the verge of reigniting. Chiang Kai-shek and Mao Zedong had been rivals for nearly two decades. Before 1927, they had briefly worked together under the banner of the Nationalist Party, known in Chinese as the Kuomintang (KMT), in a fragile United Front coalition. The KMT had roots in anti-dynastic movements dating back to 1894 and had formally organized itself as the Nationalist Party in 1912. Its leader was Sun Yat-sen. The Communist Party was newer, having set up with Soviet help in Shanghai in 1921. Intellectuals Chen Duxiu and Li Dazhao were its founders, along with a small cadre of other revolutionaries including Mao.

Sun was not himself a Communist, but he accepted assistance from the USSR after being turned aside by Western governments. Moscow helped him organize his party and governmental structures along Soviet lines. Believing the nascent Chinese Communist Party was too small to be consequential, the Soviets counseled its members to join the KMT as well and encouraged Sun to accept them. Both the Chinese Communists and Sun agreed.

Time magazine wrote about their cooperation. "When the Chinese Communist party allied itself with Dr. Sun Yat-sen's nationalist revolutionary movement, Mao worked in the combined executive committees of the Communist Party and the Kuomintang. In this capacity, he met a young, Kuomintang leader who, like himself, was a country boy with an urge to take a hand in China's destiny. He was Chiang Kai-shek."[1]

Sun succumbed to cancer in 1925, at age 58. His death deprived the United Front of its unifying figure. Shortly after that, tensions exploded between the KMT's leftist and rightist factions, the latter under Chiang's leadership.

As the generalissimo consolidated his position within the KMT, an armed struggle erupted. In 1927, Chiang decimated the Communists in Shanghai, destroyed the United Front, and drove his enemies into the countryside where they established base areas.[2]

Leading a military campaign known as the Northern Expedition, Chiang sought to bring the country together under KMT leadership. It was largely successful, either through conquest or by coopting local warlords. Victorious, Chiang established his government in Nanjing [Nanking] in 1927.

Meanwhile, Chiang continued to seek eradication of the Communists, conducting a series of campaigns to against their positions in rural base areas. After the initial failure in the early 1930s, Chiang neared success against a main Communist bastion in Jiangxi [Kiangsi] Province in south-central China.

Facing annihilation, the Communists under Mao and Zhou Enlai [Chou En-lai] initiated a major and circuitous retreat of more than 5,000 miles, which began in October 1934 and ended a year later far to the north in Shaanxi Province. Known as the Long March, it left Mao's forces decimated, losing 90% of their personnel. Regrouping, the Communists made their headquarters at the provincial city of Yan'an [Yenan].

While the Communists were still reeling from the rigors and privations of the Long March, Chiang planned to finish them off. He may well have succeeded, but for complications posed by Japan's aggression on the mainland of Asia. Since the Treaty of Portsmouth in 1905, which ended the Russo-Japanese War, Tokyo had enjoyed rights in resource-rich Manchuria. Located in northeastern China, it was mainly controlled by Chinese warlords. The Chinese population of the area was increasing rapidly.[3]

In 1931, concerned that incipient Chinese nationalism might undercut its interests, the Japanese conducted a full-scale invasion and occupation of Manchuria.[4] Establishing the puppet state of Manchukuo there the following year, Japan entrenched itself in the region and presented a looming menace to the remainder of the country.[5] Believing that his forces were too weak to repel the Japanese, and that China needed to eradicate its own insurgencies before confronting foreigners, Chiang traded space for time.[6] He did not disturb the Japanese in Manchukuo and prioritized moving against his domestic opposition.

In December 1936, Chiang traveled to Xi'an [Sian] in central China to plan a campaign against the Communist base in Yan'an, some 185 miles to the north. The Communists, who the Nationalists had pursued relentlessly, countered with an appeal for unity against the Japanese. Their strategy was both self-preservative and patriotic, and it had some appeal within the Nationalist army. To exhort his forces to finish off the Communists, Chiang made his journey.[7]

Marshal Zhang Xueliang [Chang Hsueh-liang] was the principal Nationalist commander in Xi'an. He was also the son of Zhang Zuolin, a Manchurian
warlord who the Japanese had assassinated in 1928. Known as the Young
Marshal, Zhang Xueliang replaced his father as the power in Manchuria
until ousted by the Japanese in 1931. Frustrated that China had not been able
to dislodge the Japanese, Zhang thought that Chiang's priorities were misplaced.[8] He also believed he would be a suitable replacement for Chiang as
leader of Nationalist China.[9] He planned a coup against Chiang, conspiring
with Mao's agents in Xi'an.[10]

On December 12, Zhang's soldiers kidnapped Chiang. They held the
generalissimo for two weeks until he agreed to form a United Front with the
Communists to oppose Japan. Having characterized the Japanese as a disease
of the skin and the Communists as a disease of the heart, Chiang was reluctant
to agree.[11] For their part, the Communists would have been pleased to see
Chiang killed.[12]

However, the Soviets intervened to support Chiang's leadership, because
they feared that a fractured China would leave the USSR exposed to potential
Japanese aggression, and that no one but the generalissimo could hold China
together.[13] Mao was outraged but had to comply.[14] He sent Zhou Enlai to
Xi'an to negotiate for Chiang's release.[15]

According to Mao's biographers, Jung Chang and Jon Halliday, "Stalin's
goal was to use China to steer Tokyo away from the Soviet Union by
dragging the Japanese into the vast interior of China and bogging them down
there. Moscow worked hard to fan sentiment in China for such an all-out war
with Japan, while keeping its own agenda under wraps."[16]

In the ensuing negotiations, the Nationalists insisted that the Communists
acknowledge Chiang as China's leader and suspend actions against the
central government. For their part, the Communists demanded that their party
and army could continue to operate, and that they would retain autonomy in
Yan'an.[17]

Rebuffing Nationalist commanders who wanted to bomb the city, the
generalissimo's irrepressible wife flew to Xi'an to help parley for his
freedom.[18] A member of a highly prominent family, Madame Chiang was a
formidable political force in her own right.

Born Soong Mayling [Song Mei-ling] in 1898, she was the youngest of three
daughters of Charlie Soong, a prominent Shanghai businessman who had been
a strong supporter of Sun's movement to free China from dynastic feudalism.
Her eldest sister, Ai-Ling, married H. H. Kung, reputed to be China's wealthi-
est man and a descendant of Confucius. Another sister, Qing-Ling, succeeded
Ai-Ling as Sun's secretary and then married him in 1915. The girls also had
a brother, T. V. Soong, born four years before Mayling. At different times,
he served as China's finance minister and the country's foreign minister. Like

her siblings, Mayling was educated in the United States. She married Chiang in 1927 and remained wed to him for nearly 50 years.

On Christmas Day 1936, upon conclusion of the negotiations, Chiang was released, to enormous public relief and jubilation.[19] Along with his wife, he returned to Nanjing, accompanied by the Young Marshall, who was under arrest.[20] A second United Front was formed, providing the Communists with room to survive and prosper.[21]

As the Soviets had understood, at that moment no one could match Chiang's stature. *Time Magazine* recounted, when it named Chiang and Madame "Man and Wife of the Year" for 1937, the reaction across Chinese officialdom and the army to the kidnapping "proved that Chiang had remade China. . . . Instead of rushing to seize Chiang's power, Chinese soldiers, and officials from all parts of the country began a bombardment of telegrams demanding the release, rescue, or ransoming of Chiang Kai-shek at any cost. It was the ultimate testimony that after centuries the Chinese people had at last found a leader."[22]

However, the new coalition worried Tokyo. A Nationalist China stronger and more cohesive could only imperil Japan's interests in Asia. Japanese militarists considered that a war with China should be fought before the balance of power altered. Their army acted with increased impunity not just in Manchuria but below the Great Wall, increasing the likelihood of a preemptive general war.[23]

The spark was an incident on July 7, 1937, at the Marco Polo Bridge near Beijing [Peking, Peiping]. Full-scale war between China and Japan soon erupted. In his 1943 book, *China's Destiny*, Chiang described China's reaction. "We were, of course, a weak nation but we could not refuse to fight to preserve our nation, nor could we refuse to assume the responsibility passed down to us by our forefathers. We therefore decided upon a policy of total resistance, and once the War of Resistance was launched, we were determined to see it through."[24]

By August, fighting had spread to Shanghai. Chinese forces were finally overcome near the end of November. The conflict proceeded west along the Yangtze River and reached Nanjing at the beginning of December.

Unable to defend the city, Chiang evacuated Nanjing after two weeks of fighting.[25] He retreated first to Wuhan and ultimately to Chungking [Chongqing], which served as China's capital from late 1937 until 1946. Substantial portions of China fell under Japanese occupation. Under Japanese pressure, Chiang was in no position to threaten the Communists again. As Representative Walter Judd, one of the KMT's foremost congressional stalwarts, explained, "The Japanese attack saved the Communists. . . . Naturally, he had to turn from the Communists in order to fight the external enemy, the Japanese."[26]

The new United Front suspended the Chinese civil war, but the truce was not sturdy.[27] This problem was on vivid display in the New Fourth Army Incident of January 1941. The New Fourth Army was a Communist force of some 9,000 personnel under nominal Nationalist control. Based south of the Yangtze River it disregarded Chiang's orders to reposition itself north of the river by the end of December 1940. In retribution, a substantially larger Nationalist concentration attacked the New Fourth Army in a battle that raged from January 6 to 17. Seven thousand Communist troops were killed. Subsequently, the Communists reorganized the New Fourth Army, this time wholly outside the Nationalist command. Historian James Carter assesses, "In the decades that followed, the New Fourth Army Incident became a touchstone, illustrating either Communist disobedience or Nationalist treachery, in both cases proving that the other side was too selfish to commit to cooperation against the Japanese. Although the Nationalists and Communists—led by Chiang Kai-shek and Mao Zedong respectively, continued their alliance through the defeat of Japan, from January 1941 onward, it may have been a foregone conclusion that they would wind up fighting one another for control of China."[28]

As Communist leader Liu Shaoqi [Liu Shaochi] later told Stalin, Chiang's breakup of the first United Front left no illusion on either side that the marriage of convenience would last. "Even as the cooperation began, we were preparing to overthrow Jiang Jieshi. At the time of the anti-Japanese war of resistance, we prepared steadily for eight years since this time Jiang Jieshi was also planning to destroy the Communist Party. So, when the anti-Japanese war of resistance ended, Jiang Jieshi turned to face us, but we were ready."[29]

Duplicity was the hallmark of the second United Front. Sinologist John King Fairbank remarked, "Far from combining with the KMT, Mao planned to carry on the social revolution in Soviet areas as a basis for fighting Japan on the nation's behalf. If this strategy worked, the separate armed forces of the CCP would develop their own bases and popular support while also riding the wave of national resistance to the invader. The basis for Mao's national Communism was already laid."[30]

By 1941, the second United Front was in disarray, marked by perpetual tensions and sporadic confrontations between Nationalist and Communist forces.[31] During the war, the Communists substantially expanded the dimensions of their territory in northern China, the numbers of people living under their control, and the strength of their armies.[32] Historian M. Taylor Fravel noted that by the time of the Japanese surrender in 1945, "the Red Army had grown from the remnants of the Long March to approximately 910,000 soldiers along with two million militia."[33] Chiang, whose geographic and political power base was elsewhere, was unable to restrain these Communist gains.[34]

In an effort to confine the Communists, the Nationalists blockaded Red base areas.[35] Between 200,000 and 400,000 Nationalist troops were assigned to this objective, which diverted them from fighting the Japanese. Some estimates of these Nationalist troops devoted to this purpose are even higher.[36]

Anticipating a deadly fight with the Communists for control of the country, Chiang hoarded military resources. In a memo dated March 9, 1943, diplomat John Paton Davies described Chiang's reasoning, "Acutely aware of their relative military exhaustion, of the fact that they can be no stronger politically than they are militarily, of the importance of appearing as powerful as possible at the peace table, and of the likelihood of civil war with the Chinese Communists after the peace, the Chinese Government is, not surprisingly, pursuing a policy of conservation of military strength."[37]

In a message to Roosevelt immediately prior to the Cairo Conference, Patrick Hurley, then FDR's personal representative in China, recounted a discussion with Chiang on military strategy. Hurley warned the president that the Nationalists would exaggerate their contribution to the war but were focused on other priorities. He counseled, "In evaluating the Generalissimo's conversation, it is advisable to consider with some skepticism the Chinese capacity, or readiness, to contribute materially to offensive warfare. It is advisable likewise to give consideration to the relative importance placed by the Chinese Central Government upon conserving its strength for maintenance of its post war internal supremacy as against the more immediate objective of defeating Japan."[38]

Writing to Secretary Hull during this same period, Ambassador Gauss noted, "It is generally believed that the Central Government is committed to a policy of liquidation of the Chinese Communist Party by one means or the other, and that this policy will be carried out if and when the Kuomintang decides that it can be achieved without great danger to its internal position and to China's international position."[39]

NATIONALIST STRENGTH ERODES

All Chinese armed forces fought against Japan, but the burden of the eight-year war truly fell more heavily on the Nationalists. Theodore White and Annalee Jacoby attempted to quantify it. "At peak periods of Japanese activity, perhaps 40% of all the Japanese in China were battling Communists or garrisoning Communist-held land. But during the significant campaigns it was the weary soldiers of the central government who took the shock, gnawed at the enemy, and died." They added, "During the campaigns of 1937–38 or the eastern China campaign of 1944, more than 70% of the Japanese effort was concentrated against the troops of Chiang Kai-shek and his warlord allies."[40] As to the Communist effort, Mao admitted, "Our policy is to devote seventy percent of our effort to our own expansion, twenty percent to coping with the government, and ten percent to fighting the Japanese."[41]

The conflict ended with the Nationalists badly debilitated and with the Communists broadly revitalized.[42] Needing to balance competing power centers within the KMT to maintain power himself and separated by war from his power base in southern and eastern China, Chiang was a shadow of the dynamic leader of the Northern Expedition, incapable of making reforms necessary to secure popular support. Historian Tang Tsou summarized the effects of the war on the KMT.

> In the first place, it decimated the Nationalist army and drove the Nationalist government from its home base. . . . Secondly, it gave the Communists opportunity to expand their control over the most important regions of China. Third, it greatly weakened the upper classes, which had been the strong and capable supporters of the Nationalist government and created conditions which alienated the middle classes from the government. Finally, the stresses of war caused a demoralization of the bureaucracy and the army.[43]

ROOSEVELT'S PERSONAL REPRESENTATIVE ARRIVES

The United States had been increasingly concerned that the long-standing grievances between Nationalists and Communists would degenerate into civil war, triggering massive destabilization and potential Soviet intervention.[44] The Americans were determined to avoid that outcome, if possible, and would make a major effort to prevent it.[45] Thus, American Brigadier General Patrick J. Hurley arrived in China in August 1944 with the mission of strengthening Chiang's military and engineering the formation of a coalition government between the Nationalists and Communists.[46]

Hurley went as FDR's personal representative. His appointment was from a June conversation between Chiang and US vice president Henry Wallace. The vice president was in China during Japan's Ichigo Offensive and expressed alarm to Chiang about the deterioration of conditions in the CBI.[47] Wallace said that Chinese factionalism and discord between the generalissimo and General Stilwell were hampering the war effort.[48] Chiang recommended that Roosevelt appoint someone who could act as a direct liaison between himself and the president. In response, Roosevelt named Hurley, a former US secretary of war under President Herbert Hoover.[49]

Hurley was given a difficult assignment. His first objective was to press Chiang to launch a ground offensive in Burma, then under Japanese control. He was also charged with getting Chiang to grant General Stilwell command authority over Chinese ground and air forces.[50] The Joint Chiefs of Staff

(JCS) had recommended such reforms to the president in light of Ichigo and the failure of Nationalist troops to counter it.[51] But Chiang wanted no part of these ideas and procrastinated.

Frustrated, Roosevelt prepared a tough letter to Chiang, imploring him to act.[52] Fed up with what he considered the generalissimo's dithering, Stilwell personally delivered the letter, ignoring Hurley's counsel to communicate more diplomatically.[53]

Dated September 19, 1944, Roosevelt's message stated,

> I have urged time and again in recent months that you take drastic action to resist the disaster which has been moving closer to China and to you. Now, when you have not yet placed General Stilwell in command of all forces in China, we are faced with the loss of a critical area in east China with possible catastrophic consequences. . . . Only drastic and immediate action on your part alone can be in time to preserve the fruits of your long years of struggle and the efforts we have been able to make to support you. Otherwise, political and military considerations alike are going to be swallowed in military disaster.[54]

Chiang felt dishonored and humiliated. Historians Theodore White and Annalee Jacoby describe the scene. "Chiang read the message in stony silence, with his knee trembling nervously. . . . Stilwell left shortly in an atmosphere of frigid formality while Chiang privately indulged in one of his famous rages. He declared to his intimates that he did not need America; if need be, he could go along on his own without American aid. The Generalissimo's wrath was incandescent."[55]

Often at odds with Stilwell,[56] and concerned about abdicating leadership in China to the Americans,[57] Chiang flatly rejected the demands. Instead, he insisted that the general be recalled. Blaming Stilwell for disasters in eastern China during Ichigo, Chiang wrote to Roosevelt, on October 6, 1944,

> Let me repeat that we are in entire agreement on all points of policy, and that I am grateful to you for the splendid and unvarying friendship and great aid that you have always given to China. But in good conscience, considering my tremendous responsibility to the nation, I cannot knowingly confide the execution of policies of such profound importance to an officer who in my opinion does not possess the qualifications essential for success.[58]

Assessing this impasse, Hurley stood up for Chiang. In an October 13, 1944, report to FDR, Hurley declared, "The two men are fundamentally incompatible, and they are mutually suspicious of each other. The Generalissimo reacts favorably to logical persuasion and leadership. You can do business with the Generalissimo. He reacts violently against any form of coercion squeeze play or ultimatum. Stilwell is incapable of understanding or cooperating with Chiang Kai-shek politically."

Hurley recommended to the president that he concede to the recall. "There is no issue between you and Chiang Kai-shek except Stilwell," said Hurley. "My opinion is that if you sustain Stilwell in this controversy, you will lose Chiang Kai-shek and probably you will lose China with him." He described severe potential consequences of rebuffing Chiang. These involved "a prolongation of the war and increased cost to America in materiel and blood." Hurley continued, "If we permit China to collapse, if we fail to keep the Chinese army in the war, all the angels in heaven swearing we were right in sustaining Stilwell will not change the verdict of history. America will have failed in China."[59]

Stilwell resisted being dismissed, appealing to his patron in Washington, General Marshall. If the United States bowed to Chiang, Stilwell wrote, the Chinese war effort would essentially shut down and the American investment in training and equipment plus combat support would have been wasted.[60] "Two and a half years of struggling have proved to me that if China is to make any effort in this war which will contribute to overall plan to defeat Japan, CKS must be pushed into doing it. . . . It is not a choice between throwing me out or losing CKS and possibly China. It is case of losing China's potential effort if CKS is allowed to make rules now."[61]

However, to keep China in the war and prevent further degradation of its relations with the United States, Roosevelt gave in. John Paton Davies summarizes the upside-down power relationship that had evolved between the KMT and the Americans. "Stilwell and others of us had miscalculated the power of the United States to impel the wasted regime of Chiang Kai-shek to perform as ordered by Washington. Here, the president had berated and threatened the Generalissimo, attempting to goad him to action. And if Chiang did not wish to act, as he did not, all he had to do was to stall and go limp, which he did."[62]

Stilwell left China on October 19, 1944.[63] However, his dismissal came at a heavy price for bilateral relations. Dismayed, the president wrote to Chiang, "A full and open explanation for General Stilwell's recall will have to be made. The American people will be shocked and confused by this action. I regret the inevitable harm it will do to the sympathetic attitude of the American people toward China."[64]

The tension over Stilwell exposed a major conflict of interest between Chiang's position and Roosevelt's at that stage of the war. Determined to safeguard assets for a fight against the Communists, the generalissimo wanted to husband resources.[65] While that served Chiang's interests, it contradicted Roosevelt's. To minimize American casualties, the president sought maximum Chinese engagement. As Richard Bernstein summarizes,

"This was the fundamental incompatibility of the priorities of Chiang and Roosevelt, the one striving to preserve himself, the other to save the lives of his nation's soldiers."[66]

John Paton Davies argues that persistent illusions blinded American policymakers to the reality of trying to work their will in China:

> The American public and government after Pearl Harbor looked upon the Chinese as needing only American assistance to launch a spirited counteroffensive. Americans attributed to the Chinese, the impatient, pugnacity, then animating themselves. In reality, the war against "the common enemy" was a side issue for China and his regime. His main concern was to conserve such strength as he had, add to it from American bounty, and prepare for a civil war against the Communists.[67]

A US public relations disaster for Chiang followed Stilwell's dismissal. On October 31, a front-page column appeared in the *New York Times* under the byline of Brooks Atkinson, who had just returned from an assignment in Chungking. It bluntly discounted China's value as an ally, telling readers that "the decision to relieve General Stilwell has the most profound implications for China as well as American policy toward China and the allied war effort in the Far East." It speculated that "the United States has decided from now on to discount China's part in a counteroffensive."

Atkinson painted a devasting picture of the generalissimo as a mandarin concerned with little else besides navigating treacherous domestic politics and preserving personal authority at the cost of the war effort. He wrote that "inside China it represents the political triumph of a moribund anti-democratic regime that is more concerned with maintaining its political supremacy than in driving the Japanese out of China." And Atkinson criticized the administration for continuing to support Chiang. "America is now committed at least passively to supporting a regime that has become increasingly unpopular and distrusted in China, that maintains three secret police services and concentration camps for political prisoners, and that stifles free speech and resists democratic forces."[68]

Compounding Chiang's image problems in America, an adjacent story in the paper indicated that Ambassador Clarence Gauss was resigning in connection with Stilwell's dismissal. Attributed to the United Press International, the story stated, "Mr. Gauss, long an advocate of a 'strong' policy in China, was said to feel that withdrawal of the general had cut the ground from the American position."[69] The Atkinson story quickly led to numerous additional negative articles in other media outlets.[70] These helped transform Chiang's image from a valiant resister against aggression to a corrupt and diffident warlord.[71]

According to Professor Hans van de Ven, "Stilwell's recall marked the moment when China changed from being the USA's favourite ally to a constant source of problems, worry, and disappointment."[72] A top Chiang adviser, Hollington Tong, adds that Stilwell's negative commentaries and open disdain severely colored how American leaders thought about Nationalist China. "Stilwell had a strong influence on General George Marshall and Presidents Roosevelt and Truman. He played a key role in the intriguing policy change to 'no significant support' for China after World War II, which most likely led to the Communist victory on mainland China."[73]

The controversy over Stilwell convinced American leaders that the United States would be best served by extricating itself from China. But Chiang concluded that the United States had no alternative and would continue to support him. According to Tang Tsou, "the Generalissimo was confirmed in his belief that the United States was so dependent on him to protect her Far Eastern interests, and so lacking in firmness of purpose in the pursuit of her policy, that she would finally yield to his insistent demands and accept his views no matter what he did or refused to do."[74]

Upon the resignation of Clarence Gauss in November 1944, Roosevelt named Hurley ambassador. The brief time that Hurley had served as Roosevelt's personal representative was the sum of the general's experience in China.

SEARCHING FOR AN ELUSIVE COALITION

Freshly appointed, Hurley traveled in November to the Red stronghold at Yan'an to explore whether Chinese factions could be unified in some form of coalition.[75] He was the highest ranking American to have conferred with the Communist leadership, but not the first.

US diplomats John Stewart Service, John Paton Davies, John Carter Vincent, and George Atcheson were all experienced "China hands" and had a deep and realistic understanding of conditions in the country. As early as January 23, 1943, Service had promoted the idea of a US mission to Yan'an to assess how the Communists might assist in the war against Japan. In a memorandum to State, he wrote, "I suggest the American representatives best suited to visit the Communist area are Foreign Service Officers of the China language service." Essentially, Service was describing himself.[76]

Endorsed on June 24, 1943, by Service's superior, Davies, the proposal found its way to the FDR's adviser, Harry Hopkins, who recommended it to the president. Roosevelt cabled Chiang on February 9, 1944, seeking his agreement to move forward.[77] Chiang was not pleased.

It took time for the mission idea to reach fruition because of the generalissimo's resistance and attempts to deflect it.[78] Chiang initially responded on February 22 that US observers could go to any place then under Nationalist control, which would of course exclude Communist areas.[79] More correspondence followed, without a breakthrough.

Then, in June 1944, Vice President Wallace finally won Chiang's grudging agreement to permit access to Communist-held territory.[80] In so doing, Chiang relented from conditions that would have required the Communists first pledge fealty to the National Government and bring their base areas and military under government control.[81]

Led by Col. David D. Barrett, the observers, known officially as the US Army Observer Group and colloquially as the Dixie Mission (because it was assessing the situation in rebel-held areas), began operating in Yan'an in July 1944.[82] It would continue until March 1947.[83] The US embassy assigned Service to accompany the mission as a political reporter. Apart from assessing the Communist leadership and situation, the US observers also explored how it might be possible to coordinate Communist support for anticipated American landings in China. By virtue of their power center in north China, they could be the indigenous forces most useful to American forces. The Communists warmly received the Dixie Mission, hoping, in part, that their friendly relations with the United States might yield direct provision of arms and deter Chiang from pursuing civil war.[84] Having observed both the Nationalist and the Communists firsthand, Service and his colleagues were impressed with Communist organization and esprit de corps, in contrast to what they considered the advanced decay of the KMT. The Dixie observers doubted Chiang's government could survive, whether in coalition with the Communists or not. Service and other diplomats believed that the Chinese Communists were well positioned to assume a leading role in postwar China.[85]

Professor James Reardon-Anderson comments that:

> The arrival of the Dixie Mission demonstrated for the first time publicly that Washington could and would impose its will on the Nationalist government, which had tried to prevent contact with the Communist areas. It constituted a quasi-official recognition of Yenan by the United States government. It gave the Communists a chance to make their case for foreign assistance directly and with evidence of their military and political successes in hand. Finally, it opened a direct line to Washington and offered hope that this connection would pay dividends in the months to come.[86]

In lengthy meetings with the observers, Mao argued for the kind of coalition in which Communist autonomy over their base areas and continued control over its armed forces would be recognized, pending a political settlement.[87] By contrast, Chiang was insisting that the Communist forces be subordinated to the national army before any political reforms would occur, in effect making it a precondition that the Communists disarm and submit to his authority.[88] The sides were far apart and would remain so, notwithstanding periodic negotiations.

Hurley's subordinates did not trust the generalissimo's stewardship of the war effort, especially when it came to hoarding weapons. Thus, they advocated arming the Communists directly. They argued that doing so would strengthen the fight against Japan, promote relations between Mao and the United States, and foster Chinese Communist independence from the Soviet Union.[89] However, the ambassador disagreed. Considering it his mission to reinforce the National Government in all feasible ways, he insisted it be the conduit for any assistance the United States might offer to the Communists. Service and his colleagues could never convince the ambassador to the contrary.

Hurley tried to break the political impasse that was impeding the formation of a coalition.

In Yan'an, he negotiated with Mao a five-point draft that purported to be a basis for a coalition arrangement.[90] It would have placed Communist forces under Nationalist rule while guaranteeing the Communists recognition as a political party and a role in the government.[91] The third point of five was a recitation of American values put into a Chinese framework and was entirely Hurley's workmanship. On November 10, 1944, Hurley and Mao signed the draft.[92] The text read:

BASIS FOR AGREEMENT

1. The Government of China, the Kuomintang of China, and the Chinese Communist Party will work together for the unification of all military forces in China for the immediate defeat of Japan and the reconstruction of China.

2. The present National Government is to be reorganized into a coalition national government embracing representation of all anti-Japanese parties and nonpartisan political bodies. A new democratic policy providing for reform in military, political, economic, and cultural affairs shall be promulgated and made effective. At the same time, the National Military Council is to be reorganized into the United National Military Council consisting of representatives of all anti-Japanese armies.

3. The coalition National Government will support the principles of Sun Yat-sen for the establishment in China of a government of the people, for the people and by the people. Both parties will pursue policies designed

to promote the progress and development of democratic processes in government. The coalition National Government will pursue policies designed to promote progress and democracy and to establish justice, freedom of conscience, freedom of press, freedom of speech, freedom of assembly and association, the right to petition the government for a redress of grievances, the right of writ of habeas corpus, and the right of residence. The coalition National Government will also pursue policies intended to make effective the two rights defined as freedom from fear and freedom from want.

4. All anti-Japanese forces will observe and carry out the orders of the coalition National Government and its United National Military Council and will be recognized by the Government and the Military Council. The supplies acquired from foreign powers will be equitably distributed.

5. The Coalition National Government of China recognizes the legality of the Kuomintang of China, the Chinese Communist Party, and all anti-Japanese parties. The Government of China recognizes and will legalize the Chinese Communist Party as a political party. All political parties in China will be given equal, free, and legal status. There will be but one national government and one army in China.

Upon concluding the negotiations, Mao cabled Roosevelt to express gratitude for American "good offices."[93] Agreement in hand, Hurley returned to Chungking and presented this proposal to the Nationalists. He thought if he could secure Chiang's acquiescence, the Communists would have no choice but to abide by the terms. Hurley anticipated the USSR would reach an accord with the Nationalist government, leaving Mao without an external patron on whom he could rely.[94]

However, Hurley's subordinates understood Mao's situation differently. They observed that the Communists enjoyed broad and sustainable indigenous popularity and that loyalty to the Nationalists was thin and eroding across many sectors.[95] In October 1944, Service commented: "Unless the Kuomintang goes as far as the Communists in political and economic reform and otherwise proves itself able to contest this leadership of the people (none of which it shows signs of being willing or able to do), the Communists will be the dominant force in China within a comparatively few years."[96]

The following month, John Paton Davies wrote that Chiang faced political demise even if he nominally headed a coalition government. "Should the Generalissimo accept this compromise proposal and a coalition government be formed with Chiang at the head, the Communists may be expected to continue effective control over the areas which they now hold. They will also probably extend their political influence throughout the rest of the country, for they are the only group in China possessing a program with positive appeal to the people." The KMT's defeat was inevitable, Davies continued.

"Chiang's feudal China cannot long exist alongside a modern, dynamic popular government in North China. The Communists are in China to stay. And China's destiny is not Chiang's, but theirs."[97]

A REJECTED PROPOSAL

Not without reason, Chiang had little confidence that a stable coalition government could be established on terms acceptable to him. He believed that Hurley was naïve about the nature of the threat posed by the Chinese Communists and, potentially, the Soviet Union.[98] On November 16, he refused Hurley's negotiated terms.[99] As Service later recounted, "Quite understandably, Chiang Kai-shek thought he could not afford to be reasonable, because if he let the Communists in, that would, he believed, be the end of him."[100]

Spurned by the Nationalists, Hurley backed away from the proposal and stood firmly with Chiang, undermining the goodwill he had built with the Communists, who questioned whether a mediator who had obviously picked a side could be trusted.[101] When the Nationalists made a three-point counterproposal, the Communists rebuffed it. Then, the Communists published the original five-point plan that Chiang had rejected.[102] The publication was a blow to Hurley who had told FDR he had an agreement with both sides to keep the papers confidential until there was an agreement or final disagreement.[103]

Zhou angrily wrote to Hurley:

> The refusal of the Generalissimo and the National Government of our minimum five-point proposal, clearly showing disagreement with our suggestions for a coalition government and united military council, and the submission of the three-point counterproposal, preclude the possibility of my returning to Chungking for further negotiations. We find it impossible to see any fundamental common basis in these new proposals. We feel that publication of our five-point proposal is now called for in order to inform the public and to bring out the changing attitude of the Government.[104]

Having lost confidence in the ambassador, the Communists tried to work around him. To evade Hurley's insistence that all US aid be channeled through Chiang, they attempted to communicate directly with Roosevelt.[105]

In January 1945, Mao Zedong and Zhou Enlai proposed to travel to Washington to meet with the president.[106] They sent their message via US military observers in Yan'an, with express instructions that Hurley not be informed.[107] Learning of the Communists' attempted circumvention, the ambassador strongly advised the administration against agreeing to the visit. Given Roosevelt's trust in Hurley, and without benefit of a contrary view, the White House brushed aside the Communist overture.[108]

On January 15, 1945, Hurley sent the president an extremely detailed message of over 2,500 words, summarizing the ebbs and flows of failed negotiations to that time. It was this message in which Hurley spotlighted Mao and Zhou's effort to work around him and recommended they not be received.[109]

Hurley reported that after the government's rejection of the five-point plan, and the Communists' refusal of the three-point counteroffer, Zhou had come back to Chungking for a month of additional negotiations, including a discussion with Chiang himself outside of Hurley's presence. Thereafter, Zhou returned to Yan'an for consultations.

After these additional talks, Chiang told Hurley he was prepared to make further concessions to the Communists. While opposing a formation of a coalition and insisting that the Communists be subordinate to the National Government, Chiang offered them representation in key structures such as the War Cabinet and in the Military Council. He also proposed to recognize the Communists as a legal political party. As Hurley wrote, "The Gissimo's position is that while he would be willing to give representation and recognition as a political party to the Communists, he would be adverse to a coalition government. He explained to me that he would not like a situation similar to that existing in Yugoslavia and Poland." Hurley told Roosevelt he believed Zhou would have accepted those terms had the offer been made during the Chungking negotiations, but that the Communists' position had hardened.

Notwithstanding Hurley's multiple overtures in December, Zhou refused to reopen talks, claiming that the government lacked sincerity and asking for various remonstrances of Nationalist good faith. Initially, Hurley had found the hard line from Yan'an difficult to explain. He wrote, "At the time, I was unable to account for the drastic change of position of the Communists." He reported that the Communists continued to propound new conditions, which had to be met before negotiations could even commence.

Summarizing for Roosevelt the situation in mid-January 1945, Hurley stated,

> I have heretofore recited to you the elements which constitute the opposition to the unification of China. Briefly again they are:
>
> 1.   The stand-pat element in the KMT party
> 2.   Serious opposition in the Communist Party
> 3.   The opposition of the representatives of all the imperialist governments[110]
> 4.   Doctor Soong was not favorably inclined in the beginning but is now wholeheartedly in favor of the agreement with the Communists. He would like to have credit for having avoided civil war in unified China.[111]
> 5.   In addition to these we have had constant opposition from some of our own diplomatic and military officials who sincerely believe that the Chiang Kai-shek government must fall.

However, Hurley claimed to have discovered the reason behind the Communist recalcitrance, involving circumvention of the ambassador by his own subordinates.

It has taken from the first of January until now to find the fundamental cause of the break. Here it is: during the absence of General Wedemeyer from headquarters, certain officers of his command formulated a plan for the use of American paratroops in the Communist-held area. The plan provided for the use of Communist troops led by Americans in guerrilla warfare. the plan was predicated on the reaching of an agreement between the United States and the Communist Party, bypassing completely the National Government of China and furnishing American supplies directly to the Communist troops and placing the Communist troops under command of an American officer.

Hurley reminded the president of the instructions he was given when sent to Chungking. They were to promote China's political and military unity under the leadership of Chiang Kai-shek. However, he complained, his mission was complicated by back-channel discussions with the Communists about recognition and lend-lease supplies. Such talk removed any incentive for them to negotiate. He continued, "If the Communists, who are an armed political party, should succeed in making such arrangements with the United States Army, it would be futile for us to try to save the National Government of China."

Hurley told FDR that he had uncovered the machinations when he learned through Wedemeyer that Mao and Zhou were seeking to visit Washington for direct discussions at the White House. "The Communists are not yet aware that I know of their effort to bypass me and go directly to you."

He concluded, "Having discovered the real reason for the change of attitude of the Communist toward negotiations with the National Government and toward me, I will use every effort to continue negotiations until we have convinced the Communists again that they cannot use the United States in their effort to supplant the National Government of China." Once arrangements satisfactory to both sides were made for political and military unification, Hurley said, then Chiang and Mao should jointly be granted a meeting at the White House.[112]

A TORTURED AND FUTILE ROUND
OF NEGOTIATIONS

On August 28, 1945, high-level negotiations resumed. Hurley flew with Mao and Zhou to the Chungking, where they commenced seven weeks of talks with Chiang. The atmosphere seemed hopeful at first and opening of the talks was front-page news in the *New York Times*.[113] Upon arrival at the airport, Mao stated, "I have come to Chungking, in response to an invitation from Chiang Kai-shek, President of the National Government, to discuss important issues of unity and national reconstruction." He continued, "The present time is of extreme importance. At the present time the guarantee of peace, the realization of democracy, and the consolidation of internal unity is of the utmost urgency."[114]

The *Times* story also revealed that Communist troops were engaged in mop-up operations against holdout Japanese troops and Chinese collaborators. These were occurring across a wide swath of geographic areas, from near Hong Kong in the south to Qingdao [Tsingtao] in the east, in the vicinity of Nanjing in south-central China.

The article also carried assurances the Soviet government gave to the Associated Press that the spirit and letter of its new treaty with Chiang would be observed, notwithstanding Communist efforts to gain Stalin's assistance.

> Moscow dispatches to the Associated Press said the Soviet Union, sticking closely to the terms of the new treaty, would not support the demand of Chinese Communists for recognition in areas they have taken from the Japanese. The Soviet Union was said to favor a liberal, democratic Chinese government that would be representative of all people and democratic parties, but at the same time recognizes the sovereignty of the Chiang government.[115]

However, the negotiations again proved inconclusive. Mao had been reluctant to make the trip, but Stalin had pressed him to go.[116] His presence in Chungking conveyed the impression of someone open to peace and wanting to avert a civil war. Richard Bernstein argues that it was a conflict for which the Communists were not yet ready, and that Mao's tactics were an effort to defer the fighting until a more propitious moment. "The purpose of negotiations in his eyes was not to reach a compromise agreement, but to buy time, to deter aggressive action by your enemy even as you exploit opportunities to enhance your power as well as your reputation as a peacemaker. Then, when conditions are ripe, you abandon negotiations, blaming your adversary for their breakdown, and go all out for military victory."[117]

THE WAR ENDS AND SO DOES HURLEY'S TENURE, WHILE MARSHALL'S BEGINS

In early August, three major events occurred that rapidly accelerated an end to the war. On August 6, the Americans dropped an atomic bomb on Hiroshima.

On August 9, they dropped another on Nagasaki. And on August 9, the Soviet Union entered the war against Japan. Emperor Hirohito announced on August 15, 1945, that Japan would surrender.[118] Formal ceremonies took place on September 2 on the USS *Missouri*. Neither the Nationalists nor the Communists expected the war to end so quickly, and the circumstances set off maneuvering for territory and political advantage, such as that mentioned in the *Times* article.

Years later, John Stewart Service testified to senators that a coalition could not be arranged because neither the Nationalists nor the Communists were interested in compromise, and each ultimately aimed to annihilate the other. "They were jockeying for position in the struggle for mastery in China, which would immediately break out, we were sure, as soon as the Japanese were defeated."[119]

Unable to construct a political settlement, confronting renewed fighting, and facing substantial dissension within his own embassy, Hurley resigned on November 27, 1945. For months, he had been complaining about his staff, telling senior administration officials that the China-based diplomats were too sympathetic to the Communists and were hindering his work.[120] These were ideas embraced in Hurley's lengthy cable to Roosevelt at the beginning of 1945.

In an incendiary press conference on his resignation day, the ambassador alleged that "professional foreign service men sided with the Chinese Communist armed party and the imperialist bloc of nations whose policy it was to keep China divided against herself." Hurley continued, "Our professional diplomats continuously advised the Communists that my efforts in preventing the collapse of the National Government did not represent the policy of the United States."[121]

As historian Carolle Carter wrote, "Patrick Hurley's assignment in China had been to bring the Kuomintang and Communists together. He started his task in an evenhanded manner, but when negotiations collapsed, he revealed himself as a partisan of the national government."[122]

Truman was surprised and taken aback by Hurley's resignation.[123] Wanting to pursue the chance for peace in China, the president on recommendation of his cabinet promptly appointed retired General George C. Marshall as US special envoy.[124]

In a December 18, 1945, letter to Marshall, Truman made clear his mission was to renew the effort to pursue a coalition government. "I desire that you endeavor to persuade the Chinese Government to call a national conference of representatives of the major political elements to bring about the unification of China and, concurrently, to effect a secession of hostilities particularly in north China. . . . The fact that I have asked you to go to China is the clearest evidence of my very real concern with regard to the situation there."

Hollington Tong comments scathingly on America's insistence that China have a coalition government:

> The nemesis of China during all the years from 1944 to 1949 was this obsessed determination of official Washington to impose a coalition government upon it. The coalition idea bedeviled and soured all the relationships between Chiang Kai-shek and Washington. All too many Americans use this coalition proposal with the communists as a yardstick by which to test the good faith of Chiang and his American relationships. The test was cruelly unfair because Chiang never believed in the coalition and only went along with the idea to keep peace with General Marshall and other insistent American advisers.[125]

To force the issue, Truman was willing to press the Nationalists very hard, while having little to no leverage to push the Communists at all.[126] Marshall's appointment was a hinge moment in US relations with Chiang. It represented the decisive eclipse of those advisers who believed that a KMT government without Communist participation was viable.

In his instructions to Marshall, Truman made clear he could threaten to withhold various forms of aid if the generalissimo proved uncompromising:

> In your conversations with Chiang Kai-shek and other Chinese leaders you are authorized to speak with utmost frankness. Particularly, you may state in connection with the Chinese desire for credits technical assistance in the economic field and military assistance (I have in mind the proposed US military advisory group which I have approved in principle) that a China disunited and torn by civil strife could not be considered realistically as a proper place for American assistance along the lines enumerated.[127]

Truman included with his letter a memorandum from Secretary of State James Byrnes. It referenced a statement that the secretary had given on December 7 to the Senate Foreign Relations Committee. Byrnes told the senators that a goal equally important to the wartime objective of defeating Japan was that postwar China should stand strong and united. That involves securing for the Communists and other outliers the chance for political engagement, while recognizing and standing by the National Government. As Byrnes testified, "We believe, as we have long believed and consistently demonstrated, that the government of Generalissimo Chiang Kai-shek affords the most satisfactory basis for a developing democracy. But we also believe that it must be broadened to include the representatives of those large and well-organized groups who are now without any voice in the government of China."

For the administration, this formula was not wishful thinking. It was prepared to strongarm Chiang into a coalition. James Forrestal recounts a cabinet meeting of November 27, 1945, in which Byrnes had spoken about influencing Chiang by threatening to withhold US assistance. "Mr. Byrnes said that, taking everything into account, perhaps the wise course would be to try to force the Chinese government and the Chinese Communists to get together on a compromise basis, perhaps telling Generalissimo Chiang Kai-shek that he will stop aid to his government unless he goes along with this."[128]

Left to their own devices, the Chinese could not achieve such a coalition, the secretary said. They would be too fractious to iron out their differences without foreign intervention. "It will not be solved by the Chinese leaders themselves. To the extent our influence is a factor, success will depend upon our capacity to exercise that influence in such a way as to encourage concessions by the central government, by the so-called Communists, and by the other factions."[129]

But what would happen if the attempt at leveraging failed? Should Chiang refuse to go along, would the United States truly withdraw all support? Before leaving for his mission, Marshall got clarification from Truman, who allowed that if Chiang could not be persuaded to act as the United States wished him to act, America would not actually abandon him. Chiang believed that too. As Daniel Kurtz-Phelan observes, "Withdrawing all support from Chiang was out of the question, even if he resisted Marshall's efforts." Thus, he continues, "Even if Chiang did little of what Marshall demanded, then United States would have to do most of what he wanted."[130]

Assuming his role in China on December 20, 1945, Marshall wound up passing a frustrating year there, failing to achieve the kind of successful coalition that had also eluded Hurley.[131] But success was beyond the capacity of even someone with Marshall's prodigious ability. Neither Chinese side could imagine surviving in a durable government with the other.[132] The abiding mistrust that colored their own troubled history persisted. Mao's and Chiang's core objectives were mutually exclusive. Hans van de Ven wrote, "While Chiang Kai-shek was prepared to make many concessions, his bottom line was a single army and a unified government under his leadership. He had battled for this his whole adult life, and now, after the defeat of Japan, he was trying to make it a reality. The Communists for their part were unwilling to give up their own armed forces."[133] Similarly, Nancy Bernkopf Tucker observed that neither side truly believed in the necessity of power sharing and each thought it could win a decisive victory. "Neither the CCP nor the KMT desired an end to China's struggle which would require significant concessions, each anticipating a day when it could hurl overwhelming might at the other and emerge as the single ruling party in the nation."[134]

Still, they negotiated, or at least went through the motions. According to Professor Lucien Bianco, both sides were aware that the Chinese people were war-weary and would condemn whoever appeared to disdain talks in favor of renewed fighting. In addition, the Nationalists were concerned with offending the Americans, who pushed hard for a bargained settlement.[135]

Marshall's intercession began in January 1946 and showed early promise.[136] To shore up political support in Washington, he returned to the United States in March for a hiatus of two months. During his absence, prospects for an accord dimmed, Stuart lamented. Such fragile trust as may have been built broke down, with charges flying in both directions about truce violations and other allegations.[137] Fighting renewed in Manchuria concurrent with the withdrawal of Soviet forces in early spring and escalated in the months thereafter, periodically interrupted by desultory negotiations.

By early 1947, there was a full-scale civil war. Symbolically, Chiang ordered the Communists to close the liaison offices they had operated in KMT territory since the Second United Front started a decade earlier. A brief story in the *New York Times*, datelines Nanjing February 28, 1947, notes, "The last formality connected with moves for all-out warfare with the Communists was taken here tonight when the government ordered Communist delegations to leave Kuomintang China. The step amounted to the final breach of relations between two warring parts of China and locked the door against any prospects for peace in the predictable future. . . . Today's Government move brings about most complete break between the Communists and the Kuomintang since the two parties came together to fight the Japanese in 1937."[138]

Sinologist Frank Dikötter writes that the burden of negotiating did not fall on both sides evenly and how the Communists used the talks to their advantage:

> Chiang was dependent on continuing American economic and military assistance and had little choice but to acquiesce, even though the prospect of any lasting agreement between both camps seemed more remote than ever. The Communists, on the other hand, had nothing to lose: they used the truce to regroup and expand ever further in Manchuria, entrenching themselves in the countryside away from major cities and the railways. The suave and unassuming Zhou Enlai, Mao's envoy to the peace talks, was a master of deception, cultivating a close relationship with Marshall to present the Communists as agrarian reformers keen to learn from democracy. . . . Mao would agree to almost anything on paper, as long as nobody was checking on what he was doing on the ground.[139]

Chiang was sure the Soviets worked to undermine the talks because, if Marshall had succeeded, it would have weakened their efforts to dominate postwar China. Thus, Moscow had an incentive to sidetrack negotiations and aggravate fissures between the Nationalists and the United States. He wrote, "What Soviet Russia did during this period was to incite the Chinese Communists to ignore their own pledges by starting a rebellion on the one hand,

and to carry out a smear campaign against the United States on the other. . . . It was her hope that after the failure of American effort and after General Marshall had gone home, she herself could play the role of mediator so that she could manipulate the political situation in China."[140]

In January 1947, General Marshall resigned from his position in China to become secretary of state.[141] His departure ended the American project to facilitate conciliation there. The United States would not send another mediator. And, in any case, the conflict had mushroomed beyond mediation.[142]

On August 18, 1949, in an essay titled "Farewell, Leighton Stuart!" Mao wrote a caustic critique of the failed negotiations. The essay reflected the anger and deep mistrust Mao felt for the United States. "At the outset of its help to Chiang Kai-shek in fighting the civil war, a crude farce was staged in which the United States appeared as mediator in the conflict between the Kuomintang and the Communist Party; this was an attempt to soften up the Communist Party of China, deceive the Chinese people and thus gain control of all China without fighting. The peace negotiations failed, the deception fell through, and the curtain rose on the war."[143]

Americans were predisposed to take the Nationalists' side because they were well acquainted with the Chiangs, through a diet of largely favorable news coverage as well as Madame Chiang's Christian upbringing, American education, and extensive goodwill efforts during the war.[144] Davies wrote of "a sentimental, condescending, proprietary love of fictional Chinese, who Americans fancied reciprocated with due gratitude admiration and loyalty. Americans identified these mythic Chinese with the idealized Chiangs."[145]

By contrast, they had little connection with the Communists, who seemed more mysterious and remote, if not menacing. White and Jacoby offered a compelling portrait of the Communists of Yan'an who Americans had little basis to understand.

> The leaders of the Communist Party were a highly interesting group. They could be studied only from the outside, for what went on in their inner councils was a tight secret. Their primary characteristic was their sense of unity. They had been fighting together for 20 years, against the Kuomintang and then against the Japanese; their families had been tortured, murdered, lost. They had been subjected to every form of police espionage and suppression. The weak had fallen; the faint of heart had surrendered. Those who were left were tough as leather, hard as iron; they trusted one another and hung together in a unity that showed no fissure or factionalism.[146]

Notwithstanding sympathetic literature such as Edgar Snow's 1937 *Red Star over China*, the Communists were comparatively unknown in the United States. And if they were susceptible to foreign influence, it was not American but Soviet.

NOTES

1. "Man of Feeling," *Time*, February 7, 1949, p. 20. Lucien Bianco, a chronicler of the Chinese revolution, profiles Chiang,

"In turn, wily and cruel, he defeated or disarmed his enemies one after another. Dividing his opponents within the Kuomintang as well as without had long been his chief occupation; and his talents in this sphere were indisputable. Small wonder, then, that military struggle and political intrigue took precedence over the sufferings of the peasantry or the problems of economic development. The man the Chinese press called 'the Super Warlord' had all the characteristics, and all the strength, of the founder of a dynasty. With rare determination, he pursued a single end, or rather, two ends that, in his eyes, merged into one—the establishment of his own authority and that of the state."

Lucien Bianco, *Origins of the Chinese Revolution, 1915–1949* (Palo Alto, CA: Stanford University Press, 1971), p. 121.

2. Memorandum prepared by John Paton Davies, *FRUS 1943 China*, p. 259.

3. In his memoirs, former secretary of war Henry Stimson outlined the Sino-Japanese frictions that existed in 1931 Manchuria, "Shortly stated, the issue in Manchuria was between the Chinese aspiration toward complete national independence and the Japanese conviction that security of basic Japanese interests required the maintenance of extensive economic and political rights in Manchuria. . . . During the first three decades of the 20th century, some 30 millions of Chinese poured northward into Manchuria, where they continued to think of themselves as Chinese in Chinese territory. The few hundred thousand Japanese in the area were a mere handful, sufficient only to act as a continual goad to rising Chinese pride." Henry L. Stimson, *On Active Services in Peace and War* (New York: Harper Brothers, 1947), pp. 221–222.

4. Details about the 1931 Japanese attack are set out in the Lytton Commission report, an official inquiry by the League of Nations in response to an appeal by the Chinese government. League of Nations, "Appeal by the Chinese Government, Report by the Commission of Inquiry," October 1, 1932.

5. Japan had coveted this position on the mainland of Asia at least since the Russo-Japanese War of 1905 (Stephenson, pp. 16–17).

6. "While Chinese territory was thus systematically nibbled away, Chiang Kai-shek temporized. By an ironic quirk of fate, this intransigent Nationalist was compelled to fall back before the enemy and negotiate. Instead of fight, his uncharacteristic response was an ineluctable necessity; knowing that China was not ready to meet Japan, head on, he pulled back, avoided open conflict, and patiently set about putting together a modern army" (Bianco, p. 144).

7. Theodore F. White and Annalee Jacoby, *Thunder Out of China* (New York: William Morrow & Company, 1946), p. 46.

8. "'First unity, then resistance' was the phrase Chiang Kai-shek used in November 1931 to explain his approach to resisting Japanese aggression. In speeches and articles, he insisted that China would be able to fight back against Japan only if the country was unified, its leadership had broad support, and it was governed by a strong and effective administration" (van de Ven, p. 32).

9. Jung Chang and Jon Halliday, *Mao: The Untold Story* (New York: Alfred A. Knopf, 2011), p. 176.

10. Ibid., p. 182.

11. "Modern Chinese History III: The Nanjing Decade 1927–1937," chinafolio.c om (accessed October 29, 2021). See also van de Ven, pp. 62–63, "During the coup, Chiang gave all the signs of being willing to die a martyr's death."

12. Chang and Halliday, pp. 184–185.

13. See memorandum of John Paton Davies, *FRUS 1943 China*, p. 261. Professor Hans van de Ven writes of the Communists, "They were astounded, no doubt, when Moscow told them that their call for Chiang s dismissal and trial was 'inappropriate' as it undermined 'a united front to resist Japan.' Moscow ordered them to firmly advocate a peaceful settlement" (van de Ven, p. 62).

14. Chang and Halliday, p. 186. Fairbank, *The United States and China*, p. 268.

15. Bianco, p. 147.

16. Chang and Halliday, p. 177.

17. van de Ven, p. 143. Feis, p. 84.

18. "China's Near Tragedy," *New York Times*, April 18, 1937, p. 68. A September 14, 1941, story in the *Times* recounts, "More than her husband's life, the fate of China itself hung trembling in the balance as she stepped from her plane into the dangerous center of rebel violence and intrigue. For days there was no news of her. Then on Christmas afternoon she brought back the injured Generalissimo without the payment of a ransom or the signing of a promise." F. Tillman Durdin, "Worth Twenty Divisions," *New York Times*, September 14, 1941, p. 145.

19. Van de Ven, p. 57. Lucien Bianco observes that the outcome for Chiang was a Pyrrhic victory. Building a coalition for the express purpose of confronting and frustrating Japanese ambitions signaled to Japan that its prospects in China could dim and that it should press its advantage while it could. "The war that thus began, and in beginning made him a national hero, was to be the direct cause of his downfall" (Bianco, p. 148).

20. Zhang Xueliang remained under house arrest in Taiwan until after Chiang's death in 1975. He emigrated to the United States in 1995 and died in Honolulu in 2001 at the age of 100.

21. "Open fighting between the Kuomintang and the Communists stopped, as did Chiang s Communist extermination campaigns. During the spring of 1937, negotiations between Chou Enlai and a representative from the KMT resulted in restoration of communications between the KMT and the CCP, lifting of the economic bill a blockade of the Red-controlled areas, the release of some political prisoners, and an end to the kidnapping and torture of Chinese Communists by the Blue Shirts who now turned their attention to Japanese spies." Hannah Pakula, *The Last Empress: Madame Chiang Kai-shek and the Birth of Modern China* (New York: Simon & Schuster, 2009), p. 272. The Blue Shirts were a Fascist faction within the KMT. See W. F. Elkins, "Fascism in China: The Blue Shirts Society 1932–37," *Science and Society*, Vol. 33, No. 4 (Fall-Winter 1969), p. 426. "In his choice of authoritarian methods., Chiang came much closer to Germany and Italy, whose achievements he greatly admired, then to Soviet Russia. By way of example, the men

who controlled the party machinery made use of a fascist-style secret police, The Blue Shirts, to suppress their internal enemies—whether they were simply liberals or men suspected of Communist sympathies" (Bianco, p. 117).

22. "Man and Wife of the Year," *Time Magazine*, January 3, 1938, p. 14.

23. "The major result of the Sian (Xi'an) Incident however was the decision of Japan to get on with its plans to conquer China, since the ongoing unification of the Chinese who would only make them harder to subdue. What the Japanese now needed was an incident that they could escalate into open hostilities. . . . And on July 7, 1937, Japan manufactured an incident that it could blow up into a casus belli" (Pakula, p. 273).

24. Chiang Kai-shek, *China's Destiny* (New York: Roy Publishers, 1947), p. 136.

25. In the undefended city, Japanese forces went on a two-month spree of killing, rapes, and torture, beginning in mid-December 1937. Estimates of Chinese dead in this massacre exceeded 300,000. USC Shoah Foundation, "Nanjing Massacre," www .sfi.usc.edu (accessed September 1, 2022). "When the city fell on December 13, 1937, Japanese soldiers began an orgy of cruelty seldom if ever matched in world history. Tens of thousands of young men were rounded up and herded to the outer areas of the city, where they were mowed down by machine guns, used for bayonet practice, or soaked with gasoline and burned alive." Iris Chang, *The Rape of Nanking* (New York: Penguin Books, 1998), p. 4.

26. Judd, p. 17.

27. Herbert Feis recounts, "By 1943, each side had its own black book of suppression and betrayal by the other. Many of the leaders on both sides of the great break within the Kuomintang Party in 1927 had remained alive and were in comparable positions sixteen years later. Their memory of past dealings with one another expressed itself in distrust" (Feis, p. 85). Zhang Baijia of the Institute of Modern Chinese History recounts that pressures within the KMT to dissolve the second United Front emerged within a year and a half after its formation. "The rightists in the KMT complained loudly that the Communist Party 'has become the greatest hidden peril.' They advocated a policy of 'restricting and fighting against the CCP.' . . . By the end of 1939, the diehards in the KMT launched the first campaign of anti-Communist actions since the Anti-Japanese War had started." Zhang Baijia, "Chinese Policies Toward the United States, 1937–1945," in Harry Harding and Yuan Ming, Eds., *Sino-American Relations 1945–1955: A Joint Assessment of a Critical Decade* (Wilmington, DE: Scholarly Resources, 1989), p. 16.

28. James Carter, "The New Fourth Army Incident: The Nationalist Massacre that Sealed with Winning Side's Fate," January 6, 2021. www.supchina.com (accessed July 1, 2022). Lucien Bianco notes that the incident "did much to confer on the Reds the halo of martyrs" (Bianco, p. 154).

29. Digitalarchive.wilsoncenter.org, "Discussing the Overthrow of Jiang Jieshi with Stalin, 27 July 1949."

30. Fairbank, *The Great Chinese Revolution*, p. 239.

31. On January 20, 1943, John Stewart Service reported, "The United Front is now definitely a thing of the past and it is impossible to find any optimism regarding the possibility of its resurrection as long as present tendencies continue and the

present leadership of the Kuomintang, both civil and military, remains in power." He added, "It is now no longer wondered whether a civil war can be avoided, but rather whether it can be delayed until at least after a victory over Japan" (*FRUS 1943 China*, p. 194).

32. Hearing, Senate Committee on Foreign Relations, "United States-China Relations," July 21, 1971, Testimony of John Stewart Service, p. 10. "For the next few years, the Red Army focused largely on expanding areas under its control as well as those beyond it. . . . The CCP increased the size of its regular and militia forces while avoiding large scale engagements with Japanese forces that might place those forces at risk."

33. Fravel, p. 54. Tang Tsou recounts that in 1937, a year after the Long March, the Communists controlled 35,000 square miles of territory and a population of 1.5 million. By the end of the war, they controlled 225,000 square miles of territory and a population of 65 million. Their army increased in size from 100,000 in 1937, to over 900,000 by 1945, augmented by militias of approximately 2 million (Tsou, p. 51). Historian Hans van de Ven notes that "Communist power expanded in two distinct timeframes." Those were 1937–1939 and again 1944–1945. With the latter expansion, states van de Ven, they controlled approximately one-fourth of China's population and were able to "move into Manchuria, train their armies in waging large-scale warfare and, finally, to surround the cities from the countryside and so defeat the Nationalists" (van de Ven, *China at War*, pp. 6–7).

34. Fairbank, *The United States and China*, p. 270.

35. Ibid., pp. 5–6. On November 30, 1943, Ambassador Gauss reported to Secretary Hull about "definite apprehensions for the future which gnaw on the official Chinese mind as justification for conservation of military resources and for diverting more than a half a million soldiers (including some of the best Chinese divisions) from the Japanese front to blockade the Chinese Communist forces. The Chinese are apprehensive lest in time the Russians sweep down through Manchuria and with the aid of the Chinese Communists occupy north China as well as Manchuria" (*FRUS 1943: China*, p. 172). The Nationalists were not the only ones worried about that. In June 1943, John Paton Davis anticipated that, if Chiang attempted to annihilate the Communists, Mao would seek support from the Soviets, who would provide it. Davies argued, "Following the defeat of Japan, Russia would no longer be threatened on its eastern borders, because the Kremlin s present need of Chiang Kai-shek s cooperation would have passed, because Stalin would then presumably prefer to have a friendly if not satellite Chinese government on his flank." Under such circumstances, Davies reasoned, the Communists would prevail. He added, "It may be assumed that a Russo-Chinese bloc, with China as a subservient member of the partnership, would not be welcomed by us" (Ibid., p. 263).

36. Fairbank, *The United States and China*, p. 307. US ambassador Clarence Gauss put it somewhere around 500,000 (Carter, p. 19).

37. *FRUS 1943: China*, p. 26. Fairbank writes, "by the wars end in 1945, The CCP had created a dynamic, centrally controlled movement in its own areas and exerted great attraction upon intellectuals in free China. Having done less of the fighting against Japan than the Nationalist government and having avoided the burdens of

city government and modern services, it was prepared to bid for power in the countryside" (Fairbank, *The United States and China*, p. 282).

38. *FRUS: Cairo and Tehran*, p. 265. *FRUS 1943: China*, p. 26.

39. Ibid., p. 352.

40. White and Jacoby, p. 210. Apart from adverse military circumstances,
wartime conditions generated overwhelming inflationary pressures, leading to the
alienation and disintegration of civil society. Due to the Japanese occupation, the
Nationalists had been unable to sell war bonds or raise sufficient taxes, so they
covered war costs by printing money. Frank Dikötter notes that "by 1947, the cost of
living was approximately 30,000 times what it had been in 1936, a year before Japan
attacked China." Frank Dikötter, *The Tragedy of Liberation: A History of the Chinese
Revolution 1945–1957* (New York: Bloomsbury Press, 2013), p. 18.

41. Tang Tsou, Vol. I, 1963, p. 39.

42. Ibid., p. 49.

43. "Deeply suffering from a demoralizing effects of a protracted foreign war and
intermittent civil strife, the Chinese people were restless and discontented, and deeply
stirred by the nationalistic impulses affecting all Asia. The dictatorial Kuomintang
regime under Chiang Kai-shek's authoritarian leadership failed to recognize the
urgent need for internal reforms that alone could have enabled it to maintain popular
support" (Foster Rhea Dulles, p. 24).

44. "In the first two and a half years after Pearl Harbor the United States
discouraged the Nationalist government from suppressing the Chinese Communists
by force and endeavored to prevent the outbreak of a civil war" (Tsou, p. 141). Even
before Pearl Harbor, the United States worried that a disunited China would not
be able to stem Japanese aggression in the Far East. Zhang Baijia recounts, "The
Americans were deeply worried over the danger of a renewed full-fledged Chinese
civil war. In February 1941, Roosevelt sent Lauchlin Currie as his special envoy
to China with a letter to Chiang. In the letter, the President expressed his hope that
'the KMT and the CCP eliminate their differences and closely unite to achieve
their common purpose of fighting the Japanese" (Zhang, p. 17). During the Cairo
conference FDR twice mentioned to Chiang the importance of preserving Chinese
cohesion during the fight against Japan (Ibid., p. 21).

45. Historian Barbara Tuchman writes that unity was crucial to strategies to
defeat Japan and avoiding Soviet interference that might destabilize China after
the war.

> "Coalition was the central factor in American plans because only in this way would it
> be possible, while still supporting the legal government, to utilize Communist forces on
> territory against the Japanese entrenched in the north. A patched-up unity was more the
> imperative from our point of view because of the need to avert civil war between the
> Chinese parties. This above all was the thing we most feared because it could defeat our
> major objective, a stable, united China after the war and because civil chaos would tempt
> outsiders if the conflict erupted before the Japanese had been defeated and repatriated.
> And then there was the looming shadow of the Soviet Union. In the absence of coalition,
> we feared the Russians might use their influence when they entered the war to stir up the
> Communists and increase the possibility of a disunited China afterwards."

Barbara W. Tuchman, "If Mao Had Come to Washington: An Essay in Alternatives," *Foreign Affairs*, October 1972.

46. Before Congress, Service testified that in a civil war the Communists would necessarily turn to the Soviet Union for whatever support they could get. America would wind up on the losing side, and alienate the winner, who would become a Soviet client government. However, if the war did not occur, American interests in China would be enhanced or at least preserved (Service, p. 19).

47. FDR asked Wallace to make clear to Chiang American dissatisfaction on several major points. "Chiang's whining for $1 billion, his forebodings of conflict with the Russians and the Chinese Communists, and the incompetence of his armies and dealing with Ichigo aroused the president's anxiety" (Davies, *Dragon by the Tail*, p. 305).

48. Reardon-Anderson, p. 31. Wallace told Chiang that he assumed that the KMT and the Communists, both being Chinese, were basically friends, who might need help from a mediator in bridging their differences. Davies reports, "If these Chinese friends could not get together, Wallace went on, they might 'call in a friend' and that friend, Roosevelt had indicated, might be none other than himself," Davies adds. "This was Washington first dabbling mediation in the whirlpool of enmity between Chang and the Communists" (Ibid., p. 306). Chiang was unimpressed by this proposal. "Beneath the show of courteous compliance, Chiang opposed Roosevelt acting as a friend between friends" (Ibid., p. 308).

49. Feis, pp. 155–156.

50. John Paton Davies noted the patchwork authority, loose command structure, and divided loyalties that weakened the Chinese military, notwithstanding its substantial size. "The Chinese army it is not an army in the sense that we use the word army. Rather it is an agglomerate of feudalistic military forces held more or less together by personal loyalties, endowments, grants in aid, threats of superior weight and indifferent toleration. The Generalissimo s relation to this armed mass is variable. A few divisions he can count upon to obey his orders fairly faithfully, within the limits of their ability. Others, no. . . . Many orders are issued only after negotiation with the commander or his Chungking representative" (*FRUS 1943 China*, p. 27).

51. Tao Wenzhao, "Hurley's Mission to China and the Formation of US Policy to Support Chiang Kai-shek Against the Chinese Communist Party," in Harry Harding and Yuan Ming, Eds., *Sino-American Relations 1945–1955: A Joint Assessment of a Critical Decade* (Wilmington, DE: Scholarly Resources, 1989), p. 81. Theodore F. White and Annalee Jacoby write of the efforts of US ambassador Clarence Gauss to promote reforms necessary to counter the Japanese. "Through the summer of 1944 the American embassy kept pressing matters that seemed undebatable—a clean and vigorous administration, unity, and thoroughgoing reform. . . . It urged Chiang to create a representative government for China to express the will of all groups and all parties, to let fresh air into the closed atmosphere its one-party dictatorship" (White and Jacoby, p. 218).

52. Historian Barbara Tuchman observes that the problem with the letter is that Chiang could not or would make necessary reforms, and that the United States, having called him out, was unwilling to withdraw its support. "It made no sense to

send a message of implied unfitness to rule to a chief of state unless it was backed by a readiness to cease investing support in him. In the absence of such readiness the message was a crippled ultimatum from which the senders must inevitably retreat." Barbara Tuchman, *Stilwell and the American Experience in China: 1911–1945* (New York: The Macmillan Company, 1970), p. 493.

53. Tuchman describes the scene as Stilwell presented Roosevelt's message.

"Before entering the conference room, he sent for Hurley and showed him the text. Hurley's diplomatic instinct counseled softening and he offered to paraphrase the terms verbally for the Generalissimo. . . . Stilwell refused, took it in himself, and as he wrote afterwards with rather horrid satisfaction, "handed this bundle of paprika to the Peanut and then sank back with a sigh. The harpoon hit the little bugger right in the solar plexus and went right through him." Chiang read the Chinese version with no show of emotion, looked at Stillwell and said, "I understand," and after sitting for a moment in silence, jiggling one foot, closed the meeting." (Ibid., pp. 493–494)

54. Quoted in Kurtz-Phelan, p. 27.

55. White and Jacoby, pp. 220–221. Tuchman writes, "To Chiang Kai-shek the message was unquestionably a shock. His wrath after the meeting was reported to have been tremendous and it did not take him long to recognize the implications. He knew he could not accept the American demand made in such terms without opening the way to his own discard. If the Americans succeeded in imposing Stilwell on him against his will, they might do this likewise in the manner of the Communists" (Tuchman, *Stilwell*, p. 494).

56. On March 9, 1943, midstream in Stilwell's tenure, Davies wrote to Ambassador Gauss, "Chinese and Americans have criticized General Stilwell for getting on badly with the Chinese. General Stilwell is not a man who willingly compromises. He has not concealed from the Chinese what he thinks of their incompetence and corruption. Naturally many of them have thereby been offended" (Ibid., p. 29). Herbert Feis writes of the tension between Stilwell and the Chinese. "The Chinese around Chiang Kai-shek were hurt by his blunt way of dismissing their ideas, of treating as trivial matters that meant much to them. They felt reduced in standing and in face by his directness and wounded by his epithets. Moreover, they regarded his opposition as the dam which was holding back American aid" (Feis, p. 74).

57. Chiang cast the issue as resistance to imperialism. Tuchman says, "Although he was grateful for the abolition of extraterritoriality and the Exclusion Act, the Americans were now trying to infringe on China's sovereignty in another way" (Tuchman, *Stilwell*, p. 498). The same kind of issue would arise later in the context of the Yalta agreement, which obligated the United States to coerce Chiang to accept Soviet claims in Manchuria.

58. Franklin D. Roosevelt, Papers as President: Map Room Papers, 1941–1945, Franklin D. Roosevelt Presidential Library & Museum, FDR and General Hurley 1944–1945, October 6, 1944.

59. Franklin D. Roosevelt, Papers as President: Map Room Papers, 1941–1945, Franklin D. Roosevelt Presidential Library & Museum, FDR and General Hurley 1944–1945, October 13, 1944.

60. Tuchman, *Stilwell*, p. 499.

61. Franklin D. Roosevelt, Papers as President: Map Room Papers, 1941–1945, Franklin D. Roosevelt Presidential Library & Museum, FDR and General Hurley 1944–1945, letter from General Stilwell to General Marshall, October 10, 1944.

62. Davies, *Dragon by the Tail*, p. 332.

63. Testifying in the 1971 Senate hearings, former diplomat John Paton Davies noted, "He was removed because Chiang could not accept a foreigner taking command of all Chinese forces. It was inevitable" (Testimony of John Paton Davies, p. 29).

64. Van de Ven, p. 193.

65. Bernstein asks, "Was it wrong for him to believe that saving China meant not fighting Japan, which was nearly defeated anyway, but making sure that a Communist dictatorship didn't position itself to take power once Japan had been disposed of by the valiant Americans?" (Bernstein, p. 151).

66. Ibid.

67. John Paton Davies, Jr., *Dragon by the Tail* (New York: W.W. Norton, 1972), pp. 338–339.

68. Brooks Atkinson, "Long Schism Seen," *New York Times*, October 31, 1944, p. 1. The leading police services were the Military Bureau of Investigation and Statistics, whose focus was military, and the Central Bureau of Investigation and Statistics, whose focus was civilian. Historian Suzanne Pepper comments,

"Both organizations operated extensive and competing intelligence-gathering networks throughout the country but were ultimately responsible to Chiang Kai-shek. Their respective spheres of operations were not precisely defined and sometimes overlapped. In theory at least, the former concentrated on military matters while the latter focused on civilian administration, both within the KMT and without, and on economic, labor, educational, and cultural matters. . . . As with most such organizations, the Bureaus did not confine themselves to the passive task of intelligence gathering. Both engaged in underground cloak and dagger work in the Japanese-occupied territories during World War Two. Foreign observers in KMT China regularly referred to entire secret service operation as Chiang s Gestapo. This reflected the tasks for which both bureaus were best known and most feared, namely, their efforts to ferret out, spy upon, intimidate, and, if possible, silence Communist suspects and domestic critics of the KMT regime."

Suzanne Pepper, *Civil War in China: The Political Struggle 1945–1949* (Lanham, MD: Rowman & Littlefield Publishers, 1999), p. 47.

69. "Envoy's Resignation Seen," *New York Times*, October 31, 1944, p. 4. Davies comments on the disconnect between the reality of Chiang and the myth FDR and Secretary of State Hull had erected of China as a member of the Big Four. "Perpetuation of the Chiang myth had become essential to the Roosevelt-Hull prospectus for a world of international-interracial peace and harmony. The United States, near the peak of its wartime might, was close to being, in its relations with Kuomintang China a captive nation" (Davies, *Dragon by the Tail*, p. 322).

70. "Every correspondent or former correspondent in CBI [China, Burma, India Theater] wrote all the things that he had not been permitted to publish for years. News stories, editorials, columnist and radio commentators contributed to what Joseph C.

Harsch of CBS called the 'bursting of a great illusion the long-delayed wash day for China s dirty linen'" (Tuchman, *Stilwell*, p. 506).

71. Tuchman includes a profound thought attributed to S. I. Hsuing, one of Chiang's biographers. In 1948, he "obliquely suggested that many great men would be considered greater if they had had the sense to die earlier, for example, Napoleon before Waterloo, Wilson before Versailles and 'Chiang Kai-shek before the recall of General Stilwell'" (Tuchman, *Stilwell*, p. 509). Professor Lucien Bianco concludes, "In China, the war hastened the collapse of a weak regime. It stripped bare the Kuomintang's ineffectuality and rendered its contradictions more acute; chaos and negligence are the two words that constantly recur in the descriptions of neutral and even sympathetic observers." Thus, Bianco states, "It was during the Second World War that the Communists won the civil war; this is true, but it is not the whole truth. We must add a further point: it was during the Second World War that the Kuomintang lost the Civil war. War puts every belligerent power to the test and shows up outmoded regimes for what they are" (Bianco, p. 159).

72. van de Ven, p. 190.

73. Tong, pp. 142–143.

74. Tsou, p. 122.

75. "In two telegrams sent to the Chinese Communist leadership in mid-August 1945, Stalin insisted that China had to avoid civil war, which, he asserted, would lead to national catastrophe, and urged Mao to attend the Chongqing talks promoted by Hurley and Chiang" (Shen, p. 49). Several years later, Stalin would express contrition to the Chinese Communists for this and other arm twisting. In a June 1949 meeting in Moscow with Liu Shaochi, one of the CCP's top leaders, Stalin said, "Since we did not understand the situation, we gave the Chinese revolution bad advice, causing problems in your work and interfering with you" (Ibid., p. 80). "There had been significant examples where the Soviet and Chinese Communists were at odds, such as the 1945 Treaty, which Mao opposed, Stalin's ongoing advice through 1948 that the Communists should join a coalition government, which Mao ignored, and Stalin's advice in 1949 that the Communists should refrain from crossing the Yangtze, which Mao also ignored." Michael Lynch, *The Chinese Civil War 1945–49* (Oxford: Osprey Publishing, Ltd.), pp. 76–77.

76. *FRUS 1943 China*, p. 198. On June 24, John Paton Davies endorsed the proposal to establish US representation in Communist territory. "In view of the risks to the United States implicit in the present trend towards civil war in China and in view of our complete lack of official information, both political and military, from the Chinese Communist area, it is recommended that a Consulate General be established in Chinese Communist territory and that a military observer mission also be sent to that area" (Ibid., p. 258). Historian Carolle Carter observes. "Davies believed that a serious gap in American sources of information existed because contact was lacking. Everything learned about the activities in Communist China with secondhand information." Carolle J. Carter, *Mission to Yenan: American Liaison with the Chinese Communists, 1944–1947* (Lexington, KT: University of Kentucky Press, 2021), p. 16.

77. "In it he stated that although the principal concentration of the Japanese army was in North China, only meager news was available from the region and

from Manchuria. The President therefore found that highly advisable to dispatch an American observer mission immediately. To the north of Shensi and Shansi Provinces and to other parts of North China, as necessary to increase the flow of information and to survey the possibility of future operations" (Ibid., p. 18).

78. White and Jacoby, p. 216.

79. Carter, p. 18.

80. Reardon-Anderson, p. 31. The previous month, journalists were permitted to go to Yenan (Carter, p. 20).

81. Carter, p. 22.

82. James Reardon-Anderson describes Barrett as "a plump, vigorous professional soldier who had spent two decades in China, spoke the language fluently, and had great empathy for things and people Chinese" (Ibid., p. 38).

83. Carter, p. 197.

84. Zhang Baijia, p. 22.

85. See "Hearings Before the Committee on Foreign Relations, United States Senate, Ninety-Second Congress, First Session, on the Evolution of US Policy Toward Mainland China," US Government Printing Office, 1971, pp. 66–68.

86. Ibid., pp. 36–37.

87. "Mao's emphasis on the Communists in the Nationalists functioning separately, each in its own sector of the country, meant that the Reds alone would deal with the Americans in that section of China controlled by them" (Davies, *Dragon by the Tail*, p. 326).

88. Reardon-Anderson, p. 44.

89. Testimony of John Stewart Service, p. 20.

90. "His message was simple and to the point. The United States did not want to interfere with the internal politics of China" (Reardon-Anderson, p. 52). Hurley opened the discussion with a five-point plan, which Mao countered. This led to a negotiated plan, also five points, that Hurley would endorse and present to Chiang (Ibid., pp. 52–53).

91. "He went up to Yan'an in November 1944 with some terms he had worked out which were agreeable to the Nationalist Government. But when he got to Yan'an the Communists convinced him those terms were quite unreasonable, and that there needed to be a really broad-base, in which the Communists would have a voice, some share, and if such a government were set up then they would turn control of their armies to that government" (Service testimony, p. 20).

92. Tuchman describes Hurley as a "go-between, with optimism, enthusiasm, and a minimum of acquaintance with the causes, nature, and history of the problem." She goes on to say, "To Hurley, who thought the Communists were a kind of Chinese populist Farmer Labor Party whose aim was a democratic share in the national government, the terms seemed so workable and such a triumph of his own diplomacy that he signed the document along with Mao" (Tuchman, *Foreign Affairs*).

93. Roosevelt replied, "I look forward to vigorous cooperation with all the Chinese forces against our common enemy, the Japanese invaders of China" (Reardon-Anderson, p. 54).

94. Tsou, p. 193.

95. American diplomat John F. Melby, who served under Hurley, described this attitude in a 1989 oral history for the Association for Diplomatic Studies and Training.

"They saw the situation and said 'it's hopeless.' All the career officers without exception agreed that the Communists were going win. Didn't mean they looked on it with any great favor. On the other hand, they just thought the Nationalists were hopeless. They were corrupt beyond measure. They were going to get worse. And as John Davies put it in one memorandum the fact that the future in China belongs to the Communists. So what were we going to do about it? Are we going to live with it or are we going to fight it? And how can we fight it? And are we prepared to take on the whole Chinese community? Obviously, the answer was no. Just saying the future belongs to the Communists didn't mean that you agreed with it. 'It' being the idea or with them. It was simply that you knew that at the time, they were absolutely incorruptible. They were dedicated. They knew what they were doing. They were in touch with the masses." (John F. Melby oral history, www .adst.org (accessed July 2, 2022))

96. Joseph W. Esherick, *The World War II Dispatches of John Stewart Service* (New York: Random House, 1974), p. 249.

97. *United States Relations with China: With Special Reference to the Period 1944–1949* (The China White Paper) Department of State Publication 3573, Far Eastern Series 30, pp. 572–573. In his autobiography, Davies elaborated on this point. Writing of Hurley, he said "what he did not understand was that the concept of a loyal opposition did not exist in China and that Chiang s system of balancing off a variety of competing opportunists could not survive the introduction of western democracy with its free-for-all popular participation, particularly when one of the competing forces would be a dynamic, proliferating, disciplined organization determined to destroy that system and seize power" (Davies, *China Hand*, p. 228).

98. Hurley painted what time has established was a naïve picture of Soviet interests, based on a conversation in Moscow with Stalin, with whom Hurley met on his way to China. See Feis, pp. 180–181. Hurley's view radically diverged from the generalissimo's assessment. In a November 20, 1944, cable, Hurley told Roosevelt about a recent discussion with Chiang.

"I recalled to him Marshal Stalin s renunciation of world conquest as a fundamental policy of Communism. I told him that in my opinion Marshal Stalin is now committed to the proposition that Communism can succeed in alone without an attempt being made to force it on the rest of the world. I also said that in my opinion Russia is no longer subsidizing or directing Communist activities in other countries. . . . I said that I realized there are Communist political parties and other nations, but in my opinion such parties are neither directed nor subsidized from Russia."

(*FRUS 1943 Cairo and Tehran*, pp. 101–102) However, Hurley's views were basically consistent with those of other senior advisers. A November 23 memo that Harry Hopkins appears to have prepared states, "there are definite indications that the Soviet government . . . wants peace within China and a strong central government, and recognizes that this objective can be obtained only through the Generalissimo." Hopkins previewed US efforts to promote a coalition government. He wrote that

Moscow "desires some solution of the Chinese communist problem either by the Generalissimo's acceptance of them as an independent political party or by bringing them into the government in some manner" (Ibid., p. 376).

99. Those terms involved subservience rather than pluralism. "Basically, Chiang's whole political program was vitiated by a short-sighted determination to hold on tenaciously to his own power and a corresponding refusal to share power and control with political leaders who did not blindly obey and follow him" (Tsou, p. 291). In an oral history, US diplomat John F. Melby recounted how the five-point agreement came together and Hurley's naïve perspective and futile mediation.

"Hurley arrived all pro-Communist. He said, "they're just a bunch of Oklahoma Republicans with guns." And he went scooting to Yan'an, which was Communist headquarters at this time. And Hurley produced a draft agreement. Or rather, Mao Zedong had produced an agreement. And Hurley said "this is fine. Except it's missing something." So Hurley added the American Bill of Rights. Mao looked at it, and his eyes bugged out. He said "Chiang Kai-shek will never buy this!" And Hurley said, "yes he will if I tell him to." Mao said, "OK go ahead. If you can sell it, it's fine with us." So, they all signed it and Hurley took it back to Chungking with him and showed it to Generalissimo Chiang Kai-shek. His eyes bugged out too. He said, "you must be crazy to bring me this! I'll never sign anything like this." At this point, Hurley started getting very pro-Nationalist."

John F. Melby oral history. The Association for Diplomatic Studies and Training Foreign Affairs Oral History Project, p. 17. www.adst.org (accessed July 2, 2022).

100. Testimony of John Stewart Service, p. 20.

101. "This outcome originated from the ambassador's belief that his mission was to prevent the collapse of the National government and to help Chiang unify all military forces in China" (Zhang Baijia, p. 24). Picking sides destroyed Hurley's credibility. Tucker writes, "Obviously unreliable, Hurley became increasingly identified with Chiang and the Communists tried to avoid dealing with him, privately calling him *ta-feng* (big wind)" (Tucker, p. 45). Barbara Tuchman comments, "Concluding that negotiations through a mediator who had committed himself to the other side were useless, they broke off the talks" (Tuchman, *Foreign Affairs*). Mao let Colonel Barrett know of his displeasure. "The Chairman had never been sanguine about the chances for an agreement with Chiang; what bothered him more was Hurley's apparent reversal. After reviewing Hurley s role in drafting the Communist five points, Mao found it 'difficult to understand' how the American could ask Yenan to accept the government reply" (Reardon-Anderson, p. 55). If a power-sharing coalition was impossible, Mao told Barrett, the Communists could create an independent government in the areas it controlled and seek Soviet assistance. "The possibility of a Chinese Communist-Soviet alliance, coupled with a civil war, which would result if a basis for unity could not be found, was one scenario the Americans wanted to avoid" (Ibid.).

102. *The China White Paper*, p. 76. Professor Steven Levine speaks of the Communists' alienation from the United States after the breakdown. "Chinese Communist leaders, led on by signs of interest displayed mostly by mid-level American officials, courted Washington s assistance. However, the United States, notwithstanding its difficulties with Chungking, was unwilling to jilt Chiang in favor of a dubious would-be paramour who still seemed to bear the marks of Moscow s embrace. The bitterness

of this rejection poured into the beaker of revolutionary anti-imperialism formed the anti-Americanism that suffused Chinese Communist ideology during the civil war and afterward" (Levine, p. 10).

103. Franklin D. Roosevelt, Papers as President: Map Room Papers, 1941–1945, Franklin D. Roosevelt Presidential Library & Museum, FDR and General Hurley 1944–1945, November 16, 1944.

104. *The China White Paper*, p. 76.

105. Schram, p. 230. Hurley's deputy George Atkinson cabled State that Hurley's policy was unworkable and counterproductive to US interests.

> "Despite the fact that our actions and our refusal to aid or deal with any group other than the central government have been diplomatically correct, and our intentions have been good, the conclusion appears clear that if this situation continues, and if our analysis is correct, the probable outbreak of disastrous civil conflict will be accelerated and chaos in China will be inevitable. . . . In the event the high military authorities of the United States agree that some cooperation is desirable or necessary with the Communists and with other groups who have proved that they are willing and in a position to fight Japan, it is our belief that the paramount and immediate consideration of military necessity should be made the basis for a further step in the policy of the United States." (Ibid., p. 89)

106. Reardon-Anderson, p. 64.

107. Tuchman, *Foreign Affairs*. In her 2021 book about the Dixie Mission, Carolle Carter sets out the text of the communication that went to General Wedemeyer's headquarters. Dispatched by Major Ray Cromley, the acting chief of the Dixie Mission, it read

> "Yenan government wants to dispatch to America an unofficial rpt unofficial group to interpret and explain to American civilians and officials interested in the present situation and problems of China. Next is strictly off the record suggestion by same: Mao and Chou will be immediately available either singly or together for exploratory conference at Washington should President Roosevelt express desire to receive them at White House as leaders of a primary Chinese party. They expressly desire that it be unknown rpt not known that they are willing to go to Washington in case Roosevelt invitation is not now forthcoming. This is to protect their political [*sic*] *vis-à-vis* Chiang." (Carter, p. 146)

108. Tucker, p. 45. "The ambassador learned of the plot before it could hatch and demanded a full investigation, which convinced him that US Army officers had caused the breakdown of negotiations and that Yenan had tried to deceive the American government. He dismissed Barrett from the Dixie Mission, and thereafter his antagonism toward the Communists mounted" (Reardon-Anderson, p. 64).

109. The attempted circumvention provoked an understandable, negative reaction in Hurley, who by now trusted the Communists as little as they trusted him. Professor Carolle Carter notes, "According to some historians, Hurley s attitude toward the Communists changed when he found out that Mao and Chou were scheming to go to Washington without his knowledge." Searching for a way to break through to top US decisionmakers, and feeling stymied by Hurley's bias, Communist leaders had proposed an extraordinary step. Carter says, "Clearly. Mao and Chou believed it necessary to maneuver around Chiang and Hurley in order to put their case directly to their

American 'friends' and the 'progressives.' They apparently thought they could appeal to the president s reason, hence their interest in approaching him directly" (Carter, pp. 147–149).

110. On January 2, 1945, Hurley had written to Roosevelt about the negative attitudes that European powers held toward American policy in China. He said, "All of the British-Dutch-French diplomatic and other organizations in China are definitely opposing the American policy in China. The British ambassador has said to General Wedemeyer and also to me that the American policy to unify China is detrimental if not destructive to the position of the white man in Asia. The British-Dutch-French policy is to keep China divided against herself and prevent China from emerging from this war as a free united democratic nation. None of the imperial nations have taken any interest whatever in the war against Japan in China." Their purpose, Hurley said, was to justify restoration of European imperialism in the region. Franklin D. Roosevelt, Papers as President: Map Room Papers, 1941–1945, Franklin D. Roosevelt Presidential Library & Museum, FDR and General Hurley 1944–1945, January 2, 1945. It was a repeated warning. On November 26, 1944, Hurley had explained, "The British, French, and Dutch are bound together in a vital, common interest—namely repossession of their colonial empires and the re-establishment therein of imperial governments. This common interest is vital because without their empires Britain, France, and the Netherlands would be impoverished and weak" (Ibid., November 26, 1944).

111. T. V. Soong was Chiang's brother-in-law and held a number of high-level positions in the Chinese government before and during the war.

112. Franklin D. Roosevelt, Papers as President: Map Room Papers, 1941–1945, Franklin D. Roosevelt Presidential Library & Museum, FDR and General Hurley 1944–1945, January 15, 1945.

113. The main headline of the day was about the imminent Japanese surrender ceremonies, scheduled for September 2. It read, "M'Arthur Starts Trip to Japan as Halsey Sails into Tokyo Bay." The adjacent story on Mao's trip was headlined, "Mao in Chungking for Talks on Unity" (*New York Times*, August 29, 1945, p. 1).

114. Ibid.

115. Ibid.

116. Mao had turned down two prior invitations from Chiang but accepted the third, but with great reluctance. Bernstein writes, "According to his Russian interpreter, Shi Zhe, he was very distressed and even angry about the order to go to Chungking but he understood its source in the Soviet leaders eagerness not to provoke nuclear armed Americans into active opposition to Soviet and Chinese Communist aims in China. A year later, Mao argued an interview with left wing journalist Anna Louise Strong that, unlike Stalin, he had never been worried about an atomic bomb attack on China, confident as he was in the ability of the ideologically awakened masses to defeat even a technically superior foe" (Bernstein, p. 286). It was Mao's first flight. Nervous about flying and fearful of being killed or captured, he convinced Hurley to fly with him to Chungking (Ibid., pp. 286–290).

117. Ibid., p. 292.

118. Mao believed that it was the Soviet intervention, and not the bombs, that forced the Japanese surrender (Ibid., p. 287).

119. Testimony of John Stewart Service, pp. 18–19. During the war, the mistrust was palpable. On May 6, 1943, Service's colleague, John Carter Vincent, reported to Secretary Hull that "the determination of the Kuomintang leadership, probably stronger than a year ago, to liquidate the Communists continues to be a sure barrier to cooperation. The very objective of the negotiations, from the standpoint of the Kuomintang, is the elimination of the Communists as a force in China, and if this elimination cannot be accomplished through negotiations, an attempt will be made when what may be considered a propitious moment arrives to effect it by force" (*FRUS 1943 China*, p. 231).

120. Millis, pp. 98–99. Tang Tsou frames the fundamental disagreement between Hurley and the career Foreign Service officers working in China.

"General Hurley believed that a united and democratic China could be brought about by giving strong support to Generalissimo Chiang, advising him to reach a settlement with the Chinese Communists, but without exerting pressure on him to achieve such purpose or to undertake necessary reforms. . . . In contrast to Hurley s views, the foreign service officers thought that an American policy of unconditional support for Chiang Kai-shek would only make the Generalissimo more intransigent and prevent a compromise settlement with the Chinese Communists. They believed that a united and democratic China could be brought about only by exerting pressure on the Generalissimo to offer the Communists reasonable terms."

(Tsou, pp. 143–144) One of those foreign service officers, John Paton Davies, writes in his autobiography, "All Foreign Service Officers, of course, favored the perfectionist goal of preventing civil war and unifying China. The difference between some of us and Hurley was that we thought his objective was probably then unattainable and since 1943 came with a pressing practical issue of what policy the United States should follow in anticipation of and during a civil conflict from which the Communists would probably emerge victorious. Hurley s insistence on unqualified support of Chang was, we believed, in error" (Davies, *China Hand*, p. 269).

121. Ibid., p. 67. Barbara Tuchman notes, "Hurley accepted no guidance from his staff. Because he was over his head in the ancient and entangled circumstances which he proposed to settle, he fiercely resented and rejected the counsel of anyone more knowledgeable about China than himself. When the coalition blew up in his face and he found Chinese affairs resisting his finesse, depriving him of the diplomatic success he had counted on, he could find an explanation only in a paranoid belief that he was the victim of a plot by disloyal subordinates" (Tuchman, *Foreign Affairs*). Testifying before the Senate Foreign Relations Committee on December 10, 1945, Secretary of State James F. Byrnes affirmed that he had reviewed State Department records and found no evidence of the disloyalty that Hurley alleged in his testimony several days prior (Tsou, pp. 156–162).

122. Carter, p. 134.

123. "Attending a cabinet meeting after learning that Hurley had been venting his rage in a public statement, Truman yelled, 'see what a son-of-a-bitch did to me!' The president thought Hurley duplicitous because he had in a manner that would ensure a congressional inquiry and would increase partisan political debate over the crisis in China" (Ibid., p. 177).

124. "He was a hero unconnected to partisan politics, he was a man who could be trusted not to involve the United States in a foolish war, and he was someone who would probably not be accused of betraying China" (Ibid.). "Hurley's resignation and the dispatch of the Marshall mission signified the triumph of those who believed in the necessity of forcing Chiang to offer the Communists better terms in order to obtain a political settlement. The foreign service officers' judgment that the Nationalist regime was not viable found an echo in General Marshall s despair of achieving his objectives through cooperation with the Kuomintang and his ultimate decision to withdraw from China" (Tsou, p. 145). Gordon H. Chang notes that one of Marshall's key negotiating objectives in avoiding a civil war was to reduce Soviet influence on the CCP. "He feared that continued fighting would force the Communists to seek help from Moscow and make the country more vulnerable to Soviet penetration." Gordon H. Chang, *Friends and Enemies: The United States, China, and the Soviet Union, 1948–1972* (Stanford, CA: Stanford University Press, 1990), p. 11.

125. Tong, pp. 175–176.

126. Chiang has written about the devastating effect this disparate treatment had on Nationalist fortunes. Referencing a moment in April 1946, when a cease-fire agreement broke down, he states, "It was a matter of great regret that our ally, the United States, should stop its supply of arms to the Chinese Government at the very moment when the Chinese Communists began their anti-American activities. Earlier in April, following the Chinese Communist breach of the ceasefire agreement, the American government had stopped its US $500,000,000 loan to the Chinese Government. Now it interrupted its military aid to China. At the same time, it took no action whatever against the Chinese Communists despite their violations of the ceasefire agreement" (Chiang, *Soviet Russia*, pp. 185–186).

127. *The China White Paper*, pp. 605–606.

128. Millis, p. 122.

129. Ibid., p. 606. Byrnes's use of "so-called" reflected a benign wartime view by State Department specialists that Chinese Communism was far from doctrinaire. In a June 24, 1943, memo, John Paton Davies, second secretary at the American embassy in Chungking wrote, "Forward observers (including Americans) who have recently visited the Communist area agree that the Communist regime in present policy is far removed from orthodox Communism; that is administratively remarkably honest; that popular elections are held; that individual economic freedom is relatively uncurbed; that the regime appears to have strong popular support and that it is described less accurately as communist than as agrarian democratic" (*FRUS 1943 China*, p. 260).

130. Kurtz-Phelan, p. 44.

131. Millis, p. 113.

132. John Leighton Stuart, *Fifty Years in China: The Memoirs of John Leighton Stuart Missionary and Ambassador* (New York: Random House, 1954), p. 161. Professor Michael Lynch, who has written a history of the Chinese civil war, argues that Chiang and Mao were both products of a culture that disdained compromise necessary to build a coalition. "Both Chiang and Mao were firm in their conviction that compromise was not a solution to any of China s major problems. Complete victory over opponents was the only option, both politically and militarily. . . . They

had grown up in a China torn by crisis and upheaval, where strength was admired and weakness despised. . . . At its most basic, politics in 20th century China was a matter of one claimant for power trying to destroy all elements of opposition. Absent was any democratic notion of legitimate opposition or government by consent" (Lynch, p. 75).

133. van de Ven, p. 234. John Leighton Stuart, who succeeded Hurley as ambassador, states of the negotiations, "The government representatives were skeptical of Communist good faith and their colleagues were even more dubious or frankly opposed to any attempted cooperation with so treacherous a foe." For their part, the Communists, who Chiang nearly annihilated in 1927 and again in 1934–1935, were unwilling to trust the Nationalists. Stuart adds, "The hindrances were their fears of non-survival unless their areas were protected by their own armed forces and their suspicions in general of the government group." John Leighton Stuart, *Fifty Years in China: The Memoirs of John Leighton Stuart, Missionary and Ambassador* (New York: Random House, 1954), p. 161.

134. Tucker, p. 8.

135. Bianco, pp. 170–171.

136. "The Communists had welcomed Marshall from the outset. Come before they needed his cooperation, and they hoped he would reverse. Hurleys pernicious line" (Reardon-Anderson, p. 133).

137. According to Stuart, the worst of these problems involved Communist incursions into Manchuria with the connivance of the Soviet Union, which, notwithstanding its 1945 treaty with Chiang, turned over to the Reds large quantities of Japanese military equipment. "After this flagrant disregard of the terms," Stuart says, "the Nationalists felt naturally justified in any form of retaliation" (Stuart, p. 161).

138. Tillman Durdin, "Red Envoys Ordered Out," *New York Times*, March 1, 1947, p. A6.

139. Dikötter, pp. 15–16.

140. Chiang, *Soviet Russia*, p. 163.

141. The Senate confirmed Marshall as secretary of state on January 8, 1947, the same day that Truman sent them the nomination.

142. Foster Rhea Dulles concludes, "The Truman administration had failed to take into account Chiang's unbending resolve to maintain the one-party dictatorship of the Kuomintang, Mao's firm determination to establish a Communist dictatorship, and the absence of any effective third force in providing a possible bridge between these contending factions" (Foster Rhea Dulles, p. 28). Bianco concludes,

> "Neither side ever really considered granting China's exhausted people a respite. The movement that had been gathering for us for a good half-century was not going to come to a halt just when the decks had been cleared for the final showdown. The problem was not imperialist aggression, which for the first time in 100 years was not an immediate threat, but the absolute opposition between two national political forces with antithetical programs and irreconcilable ambitions. One intended to seize power, the other to retain it; one was determined to promote social revolution in the countryside, the other to prevent it." (Bianco, p. 172)

143. Mao Zedong, "Farewell, Leighton Stuart!" *Selected Works of Mao Zedong*, www.marxists.org (accessed February 4, 2022). Mao argued that the contemporaneous *China White Paper* exposed US perfidy and imperialist purposes, so that people inclined to friendly feelings for Western countries might reconsider and repent. "There are still some intellectuals and other people in China who have muddled ideas and illusions about the United States. Therefore, we should explain things to them, win them over, educate them and unite with them, so they will come over to the side of the people and not fall into the snares set by imperialism. But the prestige of US imperialism among the Chinese people is completely bankrupt, and the White Paper is a record of its bankruptcy. Progressives should make good use of the White Paper to educate the Chinese people." It will be noted that publication of the *China White Paper* also aggrieved the Nationalists, who felt that it reflected badly and unfairly on them. Quoted in Rankin, p. 128.

144. White and Jacoby, p. 227.

145. Davies, *China Hand*, p. 266.

146. White and Jacoby, p. 227.

Chapter 3

Estrangement and a Lifeline

At the time of the Japanese surrender, the Nationalists held a major initial edge over the Communists in manpower and weaponry. But raw numbers proved not to matter, and after the civil war ignited, these advantages dissipated rapidly. The change began with Red victories in Manchuria in 1947 that the Soviets helped to facilitate.[1] Communist successes there caused Stalin to reevaluate his short-lived alliance with Chiang.[2] As Ambassador Karl Rankin has written, "In the thirty-year Treaty of Friendship and Alliance signed in 1945, the Soviet Union agreed to 'render to China moral support and aid in military supplies and other material resources' and to give such support and aid only to the Nationalist government of China. Once the Kremlin had obtained a legal foothold in Manchuria, however, the undertaking to support only the Nationalist government was conveniently forgotten."[3]

For three major reasons, the United States avoided combat engagement in China: the rising Soviet threat in Europe, a reluctance to getting drawn into the quagmire of China's internal affairs, and frustration with the Nationalists' failure to adopt US suggestions for reforms.[4]

The commander of US forces in China was General Albert C. Wedemeyer, who replaced Stilwell in November 1944 and served in China until April 1946. His objectives were to facilitate the surrender and repatriation of Japanese forces by moving Nationalist troops by sea and air to take control of areas temporarily under US control, to forestall the possibility the Japanese would surrender to the Communists, and to ensure the Nationalists would recover Japanese weaponry.[5] As Professor Lucien Bianco recounted, "to be sure, with the sudden end of the war had caught Chiang Kai-shek with almost all his forces in southwestern China, 600 to 1500 miles away from the disputed territories in the north and northeast; but that disadvantage was soon remedied."[6] Assisted by 50,000 US forces, the movement of some half a million Nationalist troops took place in September and October 1945. But for the airlift, Communist forces would have been positioned to establish dominance in those regions.

The airlift amounted to an intervention for Chiang, and the Communists bitterly resented it. Professor Robert Messer comments, "By transporting Chiang's troops into north China by means of the most massive airlift in history, the United States escalated its involvement internal politics. As with subsequent attempts to aid Nationalists against the Communists, this intervention immediately after the war was quantitatively insufficient, but qualitatively its political and psychological importance was very real."[7]

In a December 1945 hearing, Secretary of State Byrnes tried to reassure senators that the US role in China would be limited. "In recent weeks, the necessary presence of our troops in China has been a source of understandable concern to the American people. . . . I have made it very clear that our troops are in China for the sole purpose of facilitating the surrender of large numbers of Japanese to the armies of the National Government."[8]

In his book, *Soviet Russia in China*, Chiang extended gratitude for the American intervention, while acknowledging that the Communist perspective was different:

> American forces had fought side by side with Chinese Government troops in the China Theater. When the war ended, they assisted the latter in accepting the surrender of Japanese armed forces. Both during and after the war, the help of the American forces was sincerely appreciated by the Chinese people. The Chinese Communists, however, charged that by assisting the government in accepting Japanese surrender . . . the Americans were "interfering in China's internal affairs."[9]

COLLAPSE IN MANCHURIA

The target of these efforts was the crucial prize of Manchuria, the country's industrial heartland. Occupied by the Japanese from 1931 to 1946, it suffered comparatively little war damage, and most of its infrastructure was intact at the end of the war.[10]

What was to happen to the factories and armaments the Japanese abandoned? While the Nationalists and Communists each hoped to take control of this critically important region, the Soviets also had interests.[11]

Historian William Stueck notes the breadth of Soviet activity in the region. "Upon entering Manchuria, Soviet armies set about stripping its industrial plant, facilitating the entry of Chinese Communist troops and their capture of Japanese stockpiles of light arms and ammunition, and obstructing the movement of the Nationalists, who were struggling to beat the Communists and to keep portions of that strategic region."[12]

American assistance was only marginally effective in helping Chiang to secure Manchuria because the war had ended suddenly, without time to get Chiang's troops fully in place and because the USSR shared a long border there and quickly established a dominating presence.[13]

Reneging on his promise to disengage in Manchuria after the Japanese surrender, Stalin instead enabled the arming and positioning of the Chinese Communists, affording them important advantages.[14] In addition, the Soviets seriously impeded efforts to land Nationalist troops in Manchuria on American seaborne transports, forcing their disembarkation at distant and militarily disadvantageous points.[15] However, wishing to avoid confrontation with the Soviets, the United States did not confront their tactics.[16]

Washington supported the Nationalist government through economic aid and materiel but, apart from the airlift, avoided military intervention. In addition to concerns about the costs of commitment, and whether it was sensible to engage in a land war in Asia, Truman was under considerable public pressure to demobilize US armed forces.[17] Overall American service personnel numbered 12.2 million in 1945, when the Japanese surrendered, of which more than 8.2 million were in the army. By July 1947, army strength had shrunk to 1.3 million.[18] By February 1948, the number was just under 900,000.[19] Walter Judd contended that the pressure was, to some degree, Communist inspired. "The drive was on to get our soldiers home from Europe and Asia just as fast as possible, regardless of the consequences. The Communists plugged ceaselessly the line 'get the boys home, get the boys home, stop Truman's military intervention in China, stop American military meddling in a civil war in China.'"[20] America had not appetite for further interventions. As John King Fairbank remarked, "This was a moment when the American people were least prepared, emotionally and intellectually, to face a Chinese crisis. We had no intention in the winter of 1945–46, of finding another war in East Asia."[21]

The CBI Theater was deactivated on May 1, 1946, and by June of that year, the number of Marines in north China was half of what it had been just after the Japanese surrender.[22] This paralleled the departure of Soviet troops from Manchuria, who withdrew from China in the spring of 1946. Dr. James Reardon-Anderson observed that such reductions diminished both American and Soviet influence on how events in China would unfold—the descent into civil war. He wrote, "Yenan, and Chungking as well, had heeded the foreigners because they recognized the importance of foreign power on the mainland. Now the Russians were gone,[23]and the Americans were going. Left to their own devices, Chinese on both sides agreed to fight."[24]

Thus, while the Truman administration deployed the US military for limited objectives, armed conflict on Chiang's behalf was avoided.[25] Americans would not deploy troops to defend a government they by then considered corrupt, out of touch with the Chinese people, and unwilling or unable to reform.[26]

GENERAL WEDEMEYER REPORTS

Secretary of State Marshall recommended to President Truman that Wedemeyer, whose mission had ended, be sent back to China to assess the rapidly deteriorating situation there. He was to recommend guidelines on how, if at all, the United States could constructively engage. On July 9, 1947, the president issued a directive to the general that read, in part:

> You will proceed to China without delay for the purpose of making an appraisal of the political, economic, psychological and military situations—current and projected. In the course of your survey, you will maintain liaison with American diplomatic and military officials in the area. In your discussions with Chinese officials and leaders in positions of responsibility you will make it clear that you are on a fact-finding mission and that the United States Government can consider assistance in a program of rehabilitation only if the Chinese Government presents satisfactory evidence of effective measures looking towards Chinese recovery and, provided further, that any aid which may be made available shall be subject to the supervision of representatives of the United States Government.
>
> In making your appraisal it is desired that you proceed with detachment from any feeling of prior obligation to support or to further official Chinese programs which do not conform to sound American policy with regard to China. In presenting the findings of your mission you should endeavor to state as concisely as possible your estimate of the character, extent, and probable consequences of assistance which you may recommend, and the probable consequences in the event that assistance is not given.[27]

Acting as the president's special representative, Wedemeyer was in China from July to September 1947. He was appalled by the rapid and ongoing Nationalist collapse. On July 29, 1947, he sent an alarming report to Marshall, "Confidence in the Government has been severely shaken due to its inability to cope with the Communist situation and to economic problems. Uniformly, we are impressed by all contacts, that drastic reforms and changes in key positions of the Government must be made, or the Generalissimo's position as President will become untenable, resulting unquestionably in his downfall."

Wedemeyer offered highly divergent assessments of the morale, leadership, and fighting spirit of the Communists and the Nationalists. The former was on the cusp of victory; the latter, almost without hope. "Having noted the apathy among many Chinese with whom we have come in contact, there are, on the other hand, reports which would indicate excellent spirit, almost a fanatical fervor, within Chinese Communist ranks. This of course can be partly attributed to their recent military successes and the booty and prizes attained thereby. However, their leaders and perhaps many in the ranks seem to believe in their cause."

By contrast, the Nationalists seemed doomed. "I feel that the Nationalist Chinese are spiritually insolvent," Wedemeyer continued. "They do not understand why they should die or make any sacrifices. They have lost confidence in their leaders, political and military, and they foresee complete collapse. Those in positions of responsibility are therefore corruptly striving to obtain as much as they can before the collapse. Nationalist soldiers reflecting this general attitude, simply do not want to fight and their response is increasingly apathetic and ineffective."[28]

After a series of interim updates, Wedemeyer submitted his final report on September 19, 1947. Its recommendations stated that, subject to certain stipulations, including implementation of "urgently required political and military reforms," the United States should give China "aid designed to protect China's territorial integrity and to facilitate her recovery." It also recommended that Manchuria be placed under a United Nations trusteeship or a Five-Power guardianship. One of those powers would be China.[29]

The report was not made public for nearly two years, principally because of the shocking recommendation that China could not manage its own affairs and should defer to external political authority. In any case, the proposal was not implemented. As Secretary of State Dean Acheson[30] explained in a May 12, 1949, memo to Truman, "It was the opinion of General Marshall that the assumption by the United Nations of responsibility at that time for the solution of the problem of Manchuria would probably have been fatal to that organization and that for the Chinese Government to take such action would have undermined its prestige in China, as an admission that it could not act as sovereign over one of its own most important areas."[31]

The Communists prevailed in Manchuria, inflicting heavy losses on the Nationalists. The turning point was the Liaoshen Campaign between mid-September and early November 1948. Against American advice, Chiang had overextended his forces in Manchuria, garrisoning the cities while the Communists dominated the countryside. Historian Harold M. Tanner wrote, "By the time of the Liaoshen Campaign, the Communists had taken control of most of the Northeast. Through a series of offensives, Communist commander Lin Biao (1907–1971) had forced the Nationalist armies into three mutually isolated areas, centering on the cities of Changchun, Shenyang, and Jinzhou. Lin's goal in the Liaoshen campaign was to cut off and annihilate the Nationalist armies in these areas."[32] His success destroyed the Nationalist position in Manchuria and eliminated many of Chiang's best troops.[33]

Besieged, Chiang's forces ultimately surrendered or defected in great numbers.[34] The Nationalist effort in the civil war never recovered and was quickly followed by routs in the Huai-hai Campaign (November 6, 1948, to January 10, 1949) that opened the Yangtze River region to Communist conquest, and the Pingjin Campaign for Beijing and Tianjin (November 29, 1948, to January 31, 1949).

In his memoirs, Chinese ambassador Wellington Koo recounts that Chiang ignored US advice and pursued what proved to be a problematic military strategy in Manchuria because of political considerations within the KMT Party:

> We had lost our initiative and finally lost the whole mainland because we did not withdraw our forces from Manchuria, which we should have done by all rules of military strategy. I might add that such withdrawal was recommended by General Marshall and the American military advisors, too. I think I explained previously that the Generalissimo felt unable, for fear of the loss of support of the Manchurian group to follow the recommendation because it would have been such a blow politically to the leaders of Manchuria, who were already feeling very unhappy about the probable loss of their entire province. The support of the Manchurian group, with its large armed forces, was, of course, very much needed by the Generalissimo in conserving his leadership position against the repeated attempts of other factions to dislodge him from it.[35]

By 1948, the momentum of the entire conflict had shifted decisively in the Communists' favor, while the Nationalist effort was being hollowed out by pessimism within the government and the public, rampant inflation, and student strikes and demonstrations. There was also rising anti-Americanism in China, stemming from the belief that the United States was propping up a government doomed to collapse and prolonging a conflict that a war-weary people just wanted to end.[36] Fairbank wrote, "the chaos, disorders, and dangers of 1948–49 turned city dwellers irrevocably against the Nationalist government and therefore against American aid to it. Having backed that government increasingly since 1937, we could not, in the Chinese view, divest ourselves of responsibility for its evils, even though our aid had been well intended, often critical of those selfsame evils, and consequently limited in scope and amount."[37]

As the tide turned, the Truman administration was in an awkward and untenable position. It was stuck with a leader in whom it had lost faith, but it was unwilling to jettison, especially considering sunk costs and Chiang's support on Capitol Hill.[38] At a cabinet meeting on February 12, 1948, Marshall spoke of assumptions he intended to communicate to Congress. "We regard the China problem under present conditions of disorder, of corruption, inefficiency and impotence of the central government as practically unsolvable; that we cannot afford to entirely withdraw our support of the Chiang Kai-shek government and that neither can we afford to be drawn in on an unending drain on our resources."[39]

THE CHINA LOBBY

As the Nationalist position grew dire, Chiang's advocates in the United States pressed for US intervention on his account, if not with American troops, then at least with stepped-up military and economic assistance. Some of his staunchest supporters were in Congress, especially among Republicans such as Senators William F. Knowland (R-CA), Styles Bridges (R-NH), Homer Ferguson (R-MI), H. Alexander Smith (R-NJ), William Jenner (R-IN), and Joseph R. McCarthy (R-WI). Another advocate for Chiang was Senator Pat McCarren (D-NV), a fervent anti-Communist. Among the leading boosters in the House were the spellbinding orator Walter Judd (R-MN) of Minnesota, a physician who had lived in China for 10 years as a medical missionary, and John Vorys (R-OH).[40]

Working hand in glove with them was the China Lobby, an array of steadfast private sector advocates for the Nationalists, most prominently Henry Luce, publisher of *Time*, *Fortune*, and *Life* magazines, Generals Douglas MacArthur and Claire Chennault, as well as merchant and publicist Alfred Kohlberg, who headed the American China Policy Association, and the Committee to Defend America by Aiding Anti-Communist China.[41] Nationalist China's ambassador Wellington Koo was deeply engaged with the lobby in an effort to mobilize US public opinion.[42]

According to Nancy Bernkopf Tucker, their adherents closely collaborated across public and private sectors. "The Chinese Embassy kept in touch with many prominent participants in this so-called China Lobby. . . . Members of Congress, whether Cold Warriors, anti-New Dealers, partisan Republicans, or sincere friends of China, became constant targets for Kuomintang appeals." Within that targeted audience, the Nationalists had a pervasive influence. Tucker continues, "Up-to-date 'evidence' provided by the Nationalists also appeared in Congressional speeches of many who personally knew little about Chinese affairs. On occasion, the Embassy even drafted such speeches."[43] And the information flow moved quite actively in both directions. Sympathetic Americans, in Congress and in the Executive Branch, were sources of intelligence and strategy to the Nationalists.[44]

With the advent of the so-called Truman Doctrine in 1947, the United States committed itself to resist the advance of Communism.[45] The first public manifestation of this policy came in the president's March 12, 1947, speech to Congress calling for aid to Greece and Turkey. The Marshall Plan, providing economic assistance to Western Europe, soon followed, as did the formation of NATO.

The China Lobby took heart in these developments. It was successful in getting Congress to add aid to China in the Marshall Plan funding bill in 1948, and on several other occasions,[46] Chiang's supporters argued that Communism was a worldwide problem, and that fighting it could not be confined to Europe.[47] Representative Judd expressed the philosophy:

> We could have followed in Asia the policy we followed successfully in Europe. . . . If we had treated France and Italy and Greece and Germany the way we did China, they'd have gone Communist too. They couldn't possibly have survived without our enormous help. That is why we started the Marshall Plan. Then after we got their economics going, we had to adopt NATO to give military support. . . . Now this is what was needed in China, but we didn't give it. We didn't give proper aid to the Chinese government which wanted to keep China independent. Instead, we told them that they had to take Communists into the government.[48]

However, the Truman administration did not embrace this view because Stalin seemed like a more immediate threat in Europe than he was in Asia and because the United States had become cynical about the quality of Nationalist leadership. Preoccupied with the Soviet menace, and unable to intervene everywhere, America needed to pick its fights.[49]

This disconnect was a source of profound consternation to the generalissimo and his allies. At its core was the important personal perspective of Secretary Marshall, whose views on the Nationalists had been conditioned by Stilwell's wartime reports, the Stilwell recall, and his own postwar experience as a mediator. As Chiang's biographer, Jonathan Fenby, recounts, "Nationalists reflected bitterly on the difference between Greece, where the Truman Administration committed itself fully to a government victory in the civil war with the Communists, and China, where it took a much cooler attitude. What they did not appreciate was how the playing field had tilted. George Marshall had got a close-up view of the regime and its leader and could not encourage any increase in support."[50]

While in both Europe and Asia the United States confronted Communism, the circumstances were more different than similar. The United States did not simply funnel money to the Europeans, instead insisting that the beneficiary countries present detailed and effective plans for how assistance funds would be spent. The administration could not believe that with the civil war ongoing and with a poor Nationalist record of internal reforms, the same requirements could be imposed in China. Thus, in contrast to the carefully arranged and systematic Marshall Plan program the United States structured for European recovery, American assistance to China was relatively haphazard.[51] China specialist John Paton Davies noted the disparity. "I think Europe and the Mediterranean were one problem, and the China situation another. It had so far deteriorated by the period of 1947–1948 that Acheson threw his hands up on China but was very aggressive on Europe and the Mediterranean."[52] While House Republicans would not let the Marshall Plan pass without including money for Chiang, the program retained an overwhelmingly European focus.

Chiang strongly hoped the Republican candidate, New York governor Thomas E. Dewey, would defeat President Truman in 1948. The Nationalists had counted congressional Republicans among their staunchest supporters. Bipartisanship, which was so much present in the US response to Communism in Europe, did not extend to Asia.[53] However, if Dewey won, the generalissimo could hope for a fresh start.[54]

It was not to be. In the 1948 general election, Truman prevailed in a historic upset.[55] Dewey's loss instigated much soul searching within the Republican Party, which concluded it had been too accommodating on foreign policy, and toughened its posture on China, an issue on which it thought Democrats to be vulnerable.[56]

In a postelection note to Truman, Chiang combined congratulations with an urgent call for assistance. He asked for substantial financial aid, a clear statement of support from the United States, and the dispatch of a senior American officer to assess the military situation.[57] Neither the president nor Congress in general was inclined to be receptive, to the degree Chiang wanted.[58]

If the Nationalists retained support on Capitol Hill, it was mostly with the Republicans. Fifty-one House Republicans wrote to the new secretary of state Dean Acheson on February 24, 1949, to demand answers on US-China policy. A month into his tenure, the secretary met with 30 of them a few days later, commenting that the direction of policy could not be determined "until some of the dust and smoke of the disaster clears away." Republicans were outraged at what they interpreted as the secretary's indifference to the looming catastrophe in China, but the administration stood firm.[59]

Truth be told, Chiang disliked being dependent on American aid, even though he had been adept at keeping it flowing. In a diary entry in 1948, he wrote, "If I should make a few requests or show a little dependence on other nations or foreigners, no matter how good and friendly their national character, I would necessarily become their slave, and there could not be what is called equality, freedom, and justice. Only if a nation can be independent and strengthen itself without asking for help and relying on others, can it exist in the world."[60]

MADAME CHIANG IN AMERICA

With the Communists advancing rapidly, the generalissimo's wife decided to highlight his dilemma and reinforce his message by traveling to the United States. She would cite Chiang's dismal situation and repeat his view that America bore meaningful responsibility for it, based on the Yalta agreements as well as the US insistence that Communists be included in a coalition government.[61]

To Americans, Madame Chiang had been a symbol of China.[62] Three times, she and Chiang appeared together on the cover of Henry Luce's *Time* magazine, and one time she appeared alone. Once, she was featured solo on the cover of *Life*, *Time*'s sister publication. In 1943, at Eleanor Roosevelt's invitation,[63] she made an extensive and well-received trip to the United States to increase support for China's war effort, making major speeches in New York, Boston, Los Angeles, and in Washington, DC, before the Senate as well as in a nationally broadcast address to the US House of Representatives.[64] Of her speech before the House, the *New York Herald Tribune* wrote, "The extraordinary ovation which greeted Madame Chiang in the House of Representatives—at her entrance and for sentence after sentence of her moving speech—was after all a personal tribute to a great individual. The gallantry of her long journey in wartime, her wisdom, her dignity, and her loveliness have won admiration throughout America."[65]

As we have seen, the gallant image Madame hoped to convey about China's war posture did not line up with assessments from some of Roosevelt's most senior advisers and reports from US diplomats and China-based journalists. Professor Ronald Ian Heiferman notes that "they described a government, plagued by factionalism, unable to wage a real war with the Japanese, husbanding its resources for use against the Chinese Communists, and waiting for the United States to win the war for them."[66] Although her barnstorming was a great public relations triumph, it generated less assistance than Chiang hoped because of what insiders already knew about the reality of China.

Headstrong, Madame dismissed skepticism from her husband that the new trip could be productive. She informed US ambassador Leighton Stuart of her plans, engaging him for interface with the State Department and logistical assistance, not his counsel.[67] Nor, for that matter, did she consult with her own ambassador, Wellington Koo.[68]

On November 26, 1948, Stuart cabled Secretary Marshall, "Mme. Chiang sent for me immediately after talking to you. She did not ask my advice regarding trip and as much as I should have liked to do so, I did not feel I could assume responsibility for endeavoring to dissuade her. It is obvious that she plans desperate plea for military aid, arguing United States responsibility for present situation because of Yalta[28] and because of our advocation of 'broadly based' government."[69] Marshall agreed to Madame Chiang's request, and the United States furnished her transportation.

A *New York Times* dispatch of November 28, datelined in Nanjing, described the desperate circumstances under which she made the trip and the lifeline she was seeking. "Mme. Chiang was flying to the United States to persuade Washington to underwrite the Chinese Government with unqualified moral and material support. The political situation here has reached a point where the survival of the Chinese Government seems to depend almost entirely on the possibility of such a commitment."[70]

The *Times* told readers that the US government faced a quandary. Previous aid to China had been ineffective in preventing the major advance of Communist forces. American leaders were dubious about Chiang's ability to survive and whether further investments would be worthwhile. "Thus far Washington has been cautiously lukewarm to the idea of becoming committed to an unpopular government that might not even be in Nanking by the time any new aid program could be implemented."[71]

Madame arrived in Washington on December 1, 1948. By then, angered and alienated by the Chiangs and the China Lobby, the president would not permit her to stay at the White House. As Truman described the circumstance to historian, Merle Miller, "She came to the White House for more handouts when I was President. I wouldn't let her stay at the White House like Roosevelt did.[72] I don't think she liked it very much, but I didn't care one way or the other about what she liked and what she didn't like." Of Chiang, Madame, and her relatives, Truman exclaimed, "They're all thieves. I discovered after some time that Chiang Kai-shek and the Madame and their families, the Soong family and the Kungs, were all thieves, every last one of them, the Madame and him included. And they stole seven hundred and fifty million dollars out of the thirty-five billion that we sent to Chiang," diverting it for personal use and to fund the China Lobby. Truman concluded, "I don't like that. I don't like that at all, and I don't want anything to do with people like that."[73]

Instead, Secretary Marshall and his wife, Katherine, invited her to Dodona, their home in Leesburg, Virginia.[74] At the time, Marshall was hospitalized at Walter Reed for kidney surgery, where he would remain throughout her visit. In December 1948, Madame stayed with Katherine at Dodona.

Personal courtesies were one thing, but policy direction was another. And there the Truman administration and the Nationalists sharply diverged. Madame sought to keep the United States in a situation from which Washington was determined to extricate itself. As Ambassador Stuart forecast, and as the generalissimo predicted, Madame could not succeed.[75]

Anticipating her requests, the State Department prepared a rebuttal. In a memorandum to Marshall from W. Walton Butterworth, director of Far Eastern Affairs, argued:

> The US Government is sympathetic with the difficulties of the Chinese Government and recognizes the threat to China's independence from an insidious form of foreign imperialism exerted through international communism. US interest and sympathy has been shown by its aid both during and since the war, the most recent instance being the present China aid program. However, the President made clear in his message transmitting the China aid bill in February 1948 that this Government could only provide aid to enable the Chinese Government itself to take those measures necessary to provide the framework within which peace and true economic recovery could be achieved, that the solution of China's problems was chiefly a Chinese responsibility and that US aid could not, even in a small measure, be a substitute for action that could be taken only by the Chinese themselves. The US Government is concerned over the recent serious turn of events. However, the pattern of these developments does not indicate that increased aid would in itself offer a solution.[76]

Butterworth's comments coincided with Marshall's own views, which the secretary bluntly expressed to Madame Chiang when he met with her at Walter Reed Hospital on December 3. In their meeting, Madame requested a statement of unswerving support for Chiang's beleaguered government. As well, she asked that a senior officer be dispatched to China for purpose of reinvigorating the Nationalists' military. Finally, she sought $3 billion in economic and military assistance.[77]

Marshall did not foreclose on conveying some economic aid but rejected her other pleas.[78] He observed that if the United States made a public declaration of support, it would have to acknowledge before the American people the true situation in China. Such candor might have the perverse effect of undermining Chiang, the secretary said. In a note he later prepared to memorialize the discussion, Marshall wrote:

> I explained to Madame why a statement at the present time was not advisable; that President Truman and I had discussed it and felt it was impossible to reconcile the facts of the case as we understood them and as we would desire to explain to the American public and a statement favorable to the Generalissimo's Government at this time; that the latter would have to be so watered down that it would do more harm than good. I told her that in the circumstances, despite the urgent necessity of informing the American public of the facts of the situation as we understood them, we, for the time being at least, were foregoing any statement rather than say something that would be destructive of the position of the Generalissimo.[79]

Marshall also refused to consider appointing an American to redirect the Nationalist armed forces. He told Madame that such a step would essentially require "taking over the Chinese government," and that it "would be highly inadvisable for this government to put its representative in that position."[80]

On December 9, Madame Chiang met at the White House with President Truman. It went no better than her session at Walter Reed. Like Marshall, Truman wanted to cut American losses. He rejected Madame's appeals for the assignment of an American military leader and for $3 billion in new American aid.[81]

Harry Truman was famous for plain speaking, but Madame Chiang seemed unable to understand or unwilling to accept what she heard and put a positive spin on the meeting. Her distorted characterization was soon communicated to Ambassador Stuart, who was astounded by what he learned. On December 11, Stuart cabled the State Department:

> British Ambassador told me December 10 that Vice Foreign Minister George Yeh had just told him that as a result of encouraging news received from Washington within the previous 48 hours regarding military aid, the Chinese Government was "altering its plans." What plans or in what way they were being altered was not stated. I told my colleague I knew nothing to support such a statement and considered any such report from Washington to be ill-founded.[82]

Concerned that the State Department may not have kept him fully informed, Stuart added, "I appreciate that Madame and Ambassador Koo may clutch at any straw and color their reports accordingly. I would appreciate Department informing me if there is any development which should alter the position which I have consistently expressed that any military or economic aid beyond that already authorized could not even be considered until Congress meets."[83]

Acting secretary Robert Lovett, who was serving during Marshall's hospitalization, promptly replied to Stuart, debunking the rumors. In a December 13 cable, Lovett wrote. "In conversations with Madame Chiang, both President and Secretary have expressed sympathy with Chinese difficulties but have not given any indication of any change in US position and have made no commitments beyond implementation of the present China Aid Program. For your info neither Ambassador Koo nor any other Chinese official was present during Madame's conversation with President."[84]

Rumors circulated in China that the generalissimo was ready to resign in a settlement the Soviets would broker. Madame believed that support in Congress for the Nationalists would disintegrate if that happened. She pressed Chiang to carry on. On December 21, she sent him a cable, "I spoke with leaders in the US Congress, all of whom thought that you should persist and wait for assistance. . . . Aid from America will come sooner or later. . . . I insist that you not give up. As long as you can sustain your position anywhere on the mainland, the assistance from America will finally arrive."[85]

Madame remained in Washington for the rest of the month, continuing to speak with friends on Capitol Hill.[86] On the morning of December 27, she had a final session with Marshall at the hospital.

Marshall again rejected the idea of sending a military officer and did not relent on aid. Madame brought up the prospect of Chiang's resignation.[87] As Marshall later described it, "(She) explained that she had had a message from the Generalissimo this morning (it may have been last night) stating that the members of the Government were pressing him; that if there was to be no more American aid, he should make an accord with the Soviets, and that he had to make the decision immediately, today presumably; that he would resign in that event, but he had to be advised immediately." Marshall directed her to Lovett.[88]

At 3:00 p.m., Madame saw Lovett, who made none of the commitments she sought. However, he forcefully pushed back against the resignation threat that Madame communicated to Marshall and made certain to separate the United States from it. Lovett stated, "I took occasion to explain to the Madame that under no conditions could the United States be placed in the position of deciding for the Generalissimo whether or not he would step aside, that this was a decision for the Generalissimo alone to make and was purely and simply a Chinese problem, that nothing we might say or do or not say or not do should have any bearing on the decision."

Madame Chiang's intense lobbying had failed. The lady who as recently as her 1943 American visit had been hailed as a symbol of Chinese resistance to Japanese aggression was now treated skeptically and disdainfully in the American press.[89]

In the November 28 dispatch alerting readers to her trip, the *Times* accurately speculated that the administration would not necessarily have the last word about China aid. If she failed, the *Times* said, Madame would amp up her lobbying and try to mobilize US public opinion.

Her mission to Washington having proved unproductive, Madame relocated to New York, where she spent essentially all of 1949 in residence at her sister's home in the Bronx section of Riverdale. It was her mission to invigorate the China Lobby, reinforcing Chiang's base of supporters in the United States.[90] She put prodigious energy into the task. As historian Kevin Peraino notes, "Madame Chiang did her best to organize the pro-Chiang forces in the United States. She organized regular strategy sessions at the mansion, gathering her closest allies and attempting to unify the fractured Nationalist sympathizers."[91] Madame's biographer, Laura Tyson Li, further observes, "From her base in the Bronx mansion above the Hudson, she took charge of the Nationalist lobbying forces in the US, marshaling the formidable powers of command for which she had years ago earned the epithet 'Madamissimo.'"[92] In her efforts, she worked closely with the pro-Nationalist bloc of congressional members.[93]

After abandoning Nanjing in November 1948, Chiang moved his government successively to south to Guangzhou, then west to Chongqing, and Chengdu. Unable to maintain Nationalist authority in any of these places, he departed for Formosa on December 10, 1949. From there, Chiang's Republic of China ultimately would carry on, claiming it was the lawful regime for the entire country.

The collapse of Chiang's government dismayed many Americans, especially considering rising anti-Communist sentiment then seizing the country. China scholar John King Fairbank argued that, for reasons of commission and omission, the US was terribly unprepared to accept the turn of events in China:

> The epitaph for America's China policy in the 1940s should begin by noting Americans profound ignorance of the Chinese situation. They were preoccupied with their official contacts with the Nationalists and their own logistic war effort in China. They sensed the Nationalist deterioration but had little detailed knowledge of it. The CCP side of the picture was meanwhile almost entirely blank to Americans. The few observers who got to Yan'an responded to the upbeat optimism and determination of the CCP, but there were no American observers in North China except for a very few journalists, who however had very limited observations. The result was that CCP power was completely underestimated. In 1948, the American estimate was that the Nationalists could not defeat the CCP, but neither could the CCP defeat the Nationalists. This view showed a total incomprehension of reality in China.[94]

On December 31, 1948, the generalissimo announced to KMT Party leaders that he would resign to facilitate peace negotiations. "If peace can be secured, I am not at all concerned about my own position," he stated, "I will follow only the consensus of popular feeling."[95]

Chiang stood down from the presidency on January 21, 1949, leaving the responsibility to Vice President Li Zongren.[96] However, as acting president, Li would prove to be a figurehead, with Chiang retaining power within the KMT Party. In the early months of 1949, Chiang would transfer substantial cultural, economic, and military resources to Formosa.[97] At the end of May, Chiang, and his son, Chiang Ching-Kuo, joined him there.[98]

On January 31, 1949, the Communists entered Beijing. By April, their forces crossed the physical and psychological barrier of the Yangtze River.[99] The Nationalist capital of Nanjing[100] soon fell and, within two months, so did

Shanghai. Although there were pockets of resistance in southern and western China, the end of the conflict was soon at hand.[101]

Atop the Gate of Heavenly Peace facing Tiananmen Square, Mao Zedong proclaimed the founding of the People's Republic of China on Saturday, October 1. Scattered fighting continued elsewhere in the country. As autumn turned to winter, the Communists were victorious in almost all parts of the mainland.

On January 8, 1950, and still in New York, Madame Chiang made an emotional, nationally broadcast farewell speech to America. Madame expressed gratitude to the United States, denounced Great Britain for recognizing the PRC,[102] and pledged to continue the fight against Communism. "It is either in your hearts to love us or your hearts have been turned from us. It is either in your mind and will to aid China in her struggle for liberty or you have abandoned liberty," she said.[103] Several days later, Madame flew to Taipei to join her husband.[104] Citing health reasons, Li Zongren stepped down at the start of February 1950, and Chiang resumed the presidency.

America maintained assistance to Chiang, even as he faced certain defeats from the Communists who were planning a cross-strait invasion. The principal reason for continued support was domestic US politics.[105] As John Paton Davies later explained, "I think the State Department was terrified, of the China Lobby and what could be done to anyone who would suggest there was any alternative to Chiang. He had become a monkey on our back. We had a fixation, so that we had no liberty of choice."[106]

Along with his colleagues John Stewart Service and John Carter Vincent, Davies himself fell victim to a China Lobby-inspired State Department purge of China specialists that began with Service's dismissal in 1951 over allegations concerning the transfer of classified documents to the left-wing publication *Amerasia*, and accelerated once John Foster Dulles replaced Dean Acheson at the helm of the State Department.[107] Historian Stephen Kinzer notes that Dulles, who had been present in Paris during negotiations on the Treaty of Versailles, was haunted by the memory of the treaty's failure in the Senate and was motivated to avoid similar breakdowns with Congress. "Foster never forgot the trauma of Woodrow Wilson's collapse after his failure to win Senate approval for American entry into the League of Nations period from it he drew the lesson that makers of American foreign policy must work closely with Congress and avoid alienating any of its prominent members. This made him eager, in his own words, 'to find a basis for cooperation with McCarthy.' Since McCarthy considered the State Department a nest of dissolute leftists, that meant firing people."[108]

Dulles's biographer, Richard Immerman, commented, "To most of the Republican old guard, this purge was the minimum price for their allegiance to the Administration."[109]

MAO IN MOSCOW

Two months after his triumph in the civil war, Mao made his first trip abroad, arriving by train in Moscow on December 16 for talks with Joseph Stalin on the possibility of a Sino-Soviet agreement.[110] China's objectives were to obtain significant economic assistance and to cement a tight security relationship.[111] Mao remained in the Soviet capital for two months, leaving on February 17, 1950.

The negotiations were complicated. Stalin wanted to preserve Soviet gains in the Far East, acquired in his 1945 Yalta-inspired treaty with Nationalist China. That pact guaranteed the Soviets' enhanced military, commercial, and geographical rights, essentially restoring it to a position Tsarist Russia had enjoyed in the Far East before Japan defeated it in the Russo-Japanese War of 1905 and affording open access from Vladivostok to the ocean. Again, Stalin had insisted on these concessions as a condition for entering the Pacific war, making them clear to the Americans as early as the Tehran Conference in December 1943. At Yalta, Roosevelt acquiesced, agreeing to facilitate negotiations with Chiang on Soviet demands concerning railway and port rights.[112] Inasmuch as the 1945 treaty was based on Yalta, the Americans and British did not challenge it. Stalin was cautious about disturbing these advantages.[113]

In their initial meeting, Stalin explained the problem to Mao:

> As you know, this treaty was concluded between the USSR and China as a result of the Yalta Agreement, which provided for the main points of the treaty (the question of the Kurile Islands, South Sakhalin, Port Arthur, etc.). That is, the given treaty was concluded, so to speak, with the consent of America and England. Keeping in mind this circumstance, we, within our inner circle, have decided not to modify any of the points of this treaty for now, since a change in even one point could give America and England the legal grounds to raise questions about modifying also the treaty's provisions concerning the Kurile Islands, South Sakhalin, etc.[114]

Although Mao was frustrated, he got the message.[115] Plenty of patience and further negotiations were necessary. As he cabled his senior colleague Liu Shaochi, who was awaiting word in Beijing, "With regard to the question of the treaty, Stalin said that because of the Yalta Agreement, it is improper for us to overturn the legitimacy of the old Sino-Soviet treaty. If we abolish the old treaty and sign a new one, the status of the Kurile Islands will be changed, and the United States will have an excuse to take them away."[116]

During his visit, Mao also discussed the possibility of Soviet support for taking Formosa. Believing from 1949 discussions between Stalin and Liu that the Soviets would refuse direct intervention, Mao suggested "volunteer pilots" and "secret military detachments." Concerned that such engagement, however camouflaged, could generate war with the United States, Stalin demurred.[117] If Mao wanted to attack Formosa, he would have to rely on his own resources.

Eventually, Stalin changed his mind about a treaty. Mao's biographers June Chang and Jon Halliday offered an explanation. Frustrated by the pace of negotiations and the disrespectful treatment he was receiving in Moscow, Mao had dropped the suggestion that he was willing to work with the West:

> He let it be known, not least by speaking out loud in his bugged residence, that he was "prepared to do business with Britain, Japan and America." And contrary to what he had told Stalin upon his arrival in Moscow (that he was not going to "rush to be recognized" by Britain), talks went ahead with Britain which led to London recognizing Mao's regime on 6 January 1950. The British press, meanwhile, reported that Mao had been put under house arrest by Stalin., and this "leak" could well have been planted by Mao's men. It was "possible," Mao later said, that this shift in policy towards the West helped "in Stalin's change of position," noting that real negotiations "began right after this."[118]

Another of Mao's biographers, Alexander V. Pantsov and Steven I. Levine, confirm that Britain's decision to recognize the PRC triggered Stalin's willingness to negotiate a new treaty.[119]

On January 2, 1950, Mao reported to the Central Committee of the Chinese Communist Party, "Our work here has achieved an important breakthrough in the past two days. Comrade Stalin has finally agreed to invite Comrade Zhou Enlai to Moscow and sign a new Sino-Soviet Treaty of Friendship and Alliance and other agreements on credit, trade, and civil aviation."[120]

Known as the Sino-Soviet Treaty of Friendship and Alliance, the new accord would fully replace the 1945 post-Yalta treaty that Stalin had been so reluctant to alter. Mao was effusive about its benefits to China:

> By taking this action, we will gain enormous advantages. Sino-Soviet relations will be solidified on the basis of the new treaty; in China, workers, peasants, intellectuals, and the left wing of the national bourgeoisie will be greatly inspired, while the right wing of the national bourgeoisie will be isolated; and internationally, we may acquire more political capital to deal with the imperialist countries and to examine all the treaties signed between China and each of the imperialist countries in the past.[121]

A HAVEN ON FORMOSA

As Mao consolidated power, Chiang was adrift, with no meaningful possibility of continuing the war on any major scale, much less any chance to regain the mainland. More immediately, Chiang faced the dual problems of stabilizing his government on Formosa, whose population was mainly composed of people native to the island and harbored a deep resentment against the cavalier newcomers from the mainland who had taken over and ruled imperiously over the island. Tensions erupted on February 28, 1947, over harsh police treatment of a widow selling contraband cigarettes. Violent protests shook Taipei and spread throughout Formosa, causing from 18,000 to 28,000 deaths. For many years thereafter, discussion of the 228 Incident, as it became known, was actively suppressed on the island. Troops were ferried from the mainland. Formosa was pacified after nearly three months. The 228 Incident was followed in 1949 by the imposition of martial law under an amendment to the Nationalist Constitution.[122] Titled "Temporary Provisions Effective for the Period of National Mobilization for Suppression of the Communist Rebellion," the amendment was in effect until 1991. Martial law operated from May 20, 1949, to July 14, 1987.

Apart from local resentment and discord, Chiang also faced the prospect of the PRC launching an amphibious operation to finish the civil war. The Communists have already attempted such an assault once, attacking the Nationalist-held island of Quemoy in the Battle of Guningtou. It occurred between October 25 and 27, 1949. In that instance, Communists met stout resistance from Nationalist defenders and withdrew after failing to overrun the Nationalist garrison. Having been routed off the mainland, the Nationalists got a strong boost in morale.

Undeterred, Mao planned a large-scale invasion, which was to occur late the following year.[123] US aid to help the Nationalists repel it appeared doubtful.[124]

By the end of 1949, Chiang had himself retreated to the Nationalist enclave of Formosa and had very minor pockets of resistance on the mainland. Protected mainly by the strait, he lacked the strength to survive a major assault.

NO CHANCE OF INTERVENTION

At this late hour, while Mao was negotiating with the Soviets, the United States announced it would not intervene on Chiang's behalf. Secretary of State Dean Acheson rejected Republican efforts to reexamine American policy or provide further aid to the Nationalists.[125] The failure of the Marshall Mission strongly influenced Acheson's views. Early months at the helm of State reinforced his cynicism. According to Tucker, "he became convinced of the party's financial deceit, its inability to rule, even its incapacity to unite in pursuit of a common goal." Investing further in the KMT was not productive, Acheson thought. He was open to finding a way forward with the PRC.[126]

On January 5, 1950, Truman asserted that American military intervention on Chiang's behalf would not occur.[127] He further declared the United States would not seek territorial advantage with respect to Formosa or otherwise take steps to involve itself in the civil war. "The United States has no predatory designs on Formosa, or on any other Chinese territory," stated Truman. "The United States has no desire to obtain special rights or privileges, or to establish military bases on Formosa at this time. Nor does it have any intention of utilizing its Armed Forces to interfere in the present situation. The United States Government will not pursue a course which will lead to involvement in the civil conflict in China."[128]

Truman knew that Chiang retained considerable support in Congress. Traversing the political minefield of not abandoning him entirely, but not alienating the new Chinese government, the administration offered the Nationalists limited economic aid via the Economic Cooperation Administration that was originally set up to administer the Marshall Plan.[129] Truman went on, "Similarly, the United States Government will not provide military aid or advice to Chinese forces on Formosa. In the view of the United States Government, the resources on Formosa are adequate to enable them to obtain the items which they might consider necessary for the defense of the island. The United States Government proposes to continue under existing legislative authority the present ECA program of economic assistance."[130]

Chiang's problems mushroomed the next day, when the British government recognized the People's Republic of China, notwithstanding US objections. The British had substantial commercial interests in China proper, especially in Shanghai, and possessed the Crown Colony of Hong Kong.[131] Both had their foundations in the 1843 Treaty of Nanjing, which ended the first Opium War. The treaty opened Shanghai and four other ports to British trade and granted the British perpetual rights to Hong Kong Island. Seeking to protect its position there, and particularly sensitive to attitudes in India, Britain was the first Western country to recognize Mao's government.[132] But, the British-Chinese relationship progressed tortuously. The two countries did not exchange ambassadors for several years, and the British angered the PRC by failing initially to support its admission into the United Nations.[133] British efforts to maintain a commercial foothold on the mainland also failed, because Mao was bent on "eliminating every aspect of the hold that global capitalism had everywhere in China."[134] There was also turmoil in Hong Kong. It became a haven for the Chinese escaping the revolution and its effects. Although there had been a tradition of open frontiers between China and the Crown Colony, the British closed the border in 1950 because of a massive refugee flow.[135]

Congressional Republicans were irritated, both with the British decision and Truman's announcement.[136] Adding to their dismay, Acheson reinforced the administration disengagement policy with January 12 comments before the National Press Club.[137]

In his speech, Acheson differentiated between areas the United States must defend and other places where conflicts might arise, but for which the response must come from the United Nations. "This defensive perimeter runs along the Aleutians to Japan and then goes to the Ryukyus. We hold important defense positions in the Ryukyu Islands, and those we will continue to hold. In the interest of the population of the Ryukyu Islands, we will at an appropriate time offer to hold these islands under trusteeship of the United Nations. But they are essential parts of the defensive perimeter of the Pacific, and they must and will be held."

"The defensive perimeter runs from Ryukyus to the Philippine Islands," the secretary continued. "Our relations, our defensive relations with the Philippines are contained in agreements between us. Those agreements are being loyally carried out and will be loyally carried out. Both peoples have learned by bitter experience the vital connections between our mutual defense requirements."

Acheson omitted reference to Korea, which was divided at the 38th Parallel, and to Formosa, which Truman had just said would not involve American military intervention.[138] As to those places, the secretary added, "So far as the military security of other areas in the Pacific is concerned, it must be clear that no person can guarantee these areas against military attack." If such an assault did come, said Acheson, responsibility for defense would first rest with those under attack, with potential assistance subsequently provided by the UN.[139]

Acheson's statement, combined with Truman's, left the generalissimo isolated, without an obvious strategy to survive. The president had disclaimed any intention to provide military aid. The secretary had excluded Formosa from the US defense obligations. Although Republicans in Congress protested, the administration could not be moved. As Chiang's biographer, Jay Taylor, observes, "The statements of Acheson and Truman made clear that, as in 1937, he again faced an overwhelming enemy alone, and this time he had no refuge up a great river or across another strait. For a moment, he was badly rattled."[140]

LITTLE CHANCE OF RECOGNITION

While the United States did not follow its British allies in recognizing Mao's government, it did not foreclose on doing so. Acheson assembled a working group under Ambassador Philip Jessup to review the issue of recognition. In January 1950, the Jessup team recommended having diplomatic relations with the Communist government.[141] The theory was that an American diplomatic presence in the PRC would protect American commercial and missionary interests and help promote a Sino-Soviet schism.[142] Acheson took the recommendation to President Truman, who, angered at the Communists' disregard for international obligations and the shabby treatment they had given American diplomats, refused.[143]

Senior State Department analysts hoped that Mao would mimic the example of the Yugoslav Josip Broz Tito, who, although a Communist, exerted independence from Soviet domination.[144] The basis for this theory was that both Mao and Tito had come into authority by their own wiles and, unlike other Communist regimes, had not been installed by the Soviet Union.[145] A retrospective 1973 staff study for the Senate Committee on Foreign Relations observes that, initially, the Truman administration considered recognizing the PRC as an incentive to secure Beijing's adherence to international obligations and to coax decoupling from the Soviet Union. The study speculated that "if those obligations had been met, in whole or even in part, the Administration would very likely have followed the policy consistent with its overall objective of encouraging Titoism in China by recognizing Peking."[146] But those aspirations were not realized.

Among those with hopes for a more independent China was Leighton Stuart, the US ambassador in China since July 1946. Unlike ambassadors from other countries, Stuart remained in Nanjing after the Nationalist government abandoned the city in April 1949. Stuart was born in China and had decades of experience in the country, including serving as president of Yenching University in Beijing, which he helped to found in 1919. From his years at Yenching, Stuart was acquainted with Huang Hua, a former student there and by 1949 a senior aide to Zhou Enlai. Stuart and Huang met in Nanjing on May 13, 1949, the first of several interactions, instigated by Stuart's aide, Philip Fugh. Discussions between Huang and Stuart or Fugh continued into June. The contacts were informal, taking place at the ambassador's residence and not at the embassy, as Stuart was still accredited to the Nationalist government.[147]

In an article published in China in 1992, Huang describes the circumstances of these interactions.

On 10 March 1949 Stuart telegraphed the State Department and asked to remain in Nanjing to contact our Party in order to establish new relations. In his return telegram on 6th April, Acheson authorized Stuart to have meetings with our Party leaders. Acheson instructed him not to say anything definitive, to keep the talks secret, and to avoid any leak of information which might cause reactions from the opposition party in Congress. Therefore. Stuart did not leave Nanjing, even though the Guomindang [Kuomintang] government requested all foreign embassies to move southward to Guangzhou [Canton] with it and instructed diplomats to follow it to Guangzhou.[148]

Stuart affirmed to Huang that the United States would abstain from further intervention in the civil war, and that it would consider recognizing the Communist government if it had popular support and would adhere to existing Chinese international obligations. While the Communists considered this message, they continued a propaganda barrage against the United States and their abrasive treatment of American diplomats still in China.[149]

In a subsequent discussion with Fugh soon thereafter, Huang declared that the Communists regarded agreements entered by the predecessor government as having no effect and condemned any effort to continue support for Chiang:

> I told Fugh that the Communist Party of China Central Committee and the People's Liberation Army General Headquarters had announced many times their denunciation and non-recognition of all traitorous treaties between the Guomindang and foreign governments. . . . If the United States wished to resume its courtship of the Chinese people as well as to establish diplomatic relations with China, it must first withdraw all its armed forces from China, break off its relations with the Guomindang government, and terminate the policy that infringed upon China's independent sovereignty and territorial integrity.[150]

In early June, Fugh raised with Huang the question of whether Stuart would be welcome to continue the ambassador's long-standing practice of visiting Yenching University on his birthday. It could provide an occasion to see Communist leaders and explore whether there was a basis for normal relations between them and the United States.

Huang was intrigued. Several weeks later, he advised Stuart that if the ambassador traveled to Beijing, Mao and Zhou would welcome him there.[151] Huang wrote:

> On 28 June, I informed Stuart that I had received Peiping's telegram and the trip to Yenching was approved. It was going to be possible for him to get to meet the Chinese leaders as he had wished. Stuart told me he was very glad to get the message. Congress however could be adjourned by the end of July. Stuart worried whether he would have enough time to work out something. Moreover, divided factions existed on Capitol Hill and his trip to Peiping at this moment would bring about criticism and could easily cause problems. He decided to report this to Acheson and let him make the final decision.[152]

Thus, Stuart sought guidance from State, cabling that he had received a "veiled invitation from Mao and Chou to talk with them [while] ostensibly visiting Yenching."[153] Stuart observed that such contact could open useful discussions with the Communists on the future of US-China relations, open a window into Communist thinking, and strengthen "anti-Soviet elements" within the Party. He also noted the potential for a misinterpretation by other nations of the gesture and the prospect of domestic political criticism within the United States. Senior staff at the State Department shared this trepidation.

While Stuart's note was pending, Mao delivered a June 30 speech titled, "The Dictatorship of the People's Democracy." In it he scotched any notion of Tito-like independence from Moscow. Instead, Mao credited the Soviet Union for providing China with an enlightened path to emerge from dynastic feudalism and to adapt to the modern world:

> It was through the Russians that the Chinese found Marxism. Before the October Revolution, the Chinese were not only ignorant of Lenin and Stalin, they did not even know of Marx and Engels. The salvoes of the October Revolution brought us Marxism-Leninism. The October Revolution helped progressives in China, as throughout the world, to adopt the proletarian world outlook as the instrument for studying a nation's destiny and considering anew their own problems. Follow the path of the Russians—that was their conclusion.

As a new China was emerging, Mao argued that it could not straddle between East and West. "The forty years experience of Sun Yat-sen and the twenty-eight-year experience of the Communist Party have taught us that in order to attain victory and consolidate it, we must lean to one side. According to these experiences, the Chinese people must lean either to the side of imperialism or that of socialism. There can be no exception. There can be no sitting on the fence; there is no third road."[154] For the Chinese revolution to take root, Mao continued, Soviet support would be indispensable. "In the epoch in which imperialism exists, it is impossible for a genuine people's revolution to win victory in any country without various forms of help from the international revolutionary forces, and even if victory were won, it could not be consolidated." Mao denounced the United States as "a great imperialistic power" that "wants to enslave the world."[155]

Historian Tang Tsou commented that Mao was being "deliberately provocative" in this declaration because he saw little benefit in hedging his bets. "Ideological convictions thus combined with hostility toward the United States to lead Mao to make a sharp break with the age-old Chinese policy of using barbarians to control barbarians."[156]

In the face of Mao's June 30 remarks, the administration had little reason to assume the risks Stuart outlined.[157] Truman told Acheson that the visit should not proceed. On July 1, Stuart received a cable stating, "Following highest level consideration, URTEL 1410, you are instructed under no, repeat no, circumstances to make visit Peiping. Principal reasons for negative decision are those contained URTEL."[158]

A 1973 Senate Foreign Relations Committee Staff Study observes that "there were compelling domestic political reasons for the Administration to veto this trip and in general proceed cautiously in dealing with the question of recognition." For example, several days earlier, 21 senators, including five Democrats, had written to Acheson urging that the United States not recognize the Communist government. In response, Acheson promised Chairman Tom Connally of the Senate Foreign Relations Committee that the administration would consult the committee before moving forward on recognition. The Staff Study notes that "this response was typical of the Administration's caution in handling any subject concerning China. The effort at fending off initiatives from Congress and within its own ranks to give military support to the surviving non-Communist elements in China was politically expensive and the Administration was extremely anxious to avoid the blame for the extinction it assumed would come to Chiang Kai-shek." The study adds, "In such an environment, a trip to or even through Peking by an American Ambassador would have been interpreted as the coup de grace for the Nationalist regime on Formosa."[159]

As it happened, even if such contact had occurred, it was not likely to yield much. Mao did not trust that Stuart's apparent openness accurately portrayed the US posture, and told Moscow, "We would be happy if all the capitalist embassies got out of China for good."[160]

Historian Chen Jian argued that Mao had established preconditions that doomed the Huang-Stuart negotiations. Apart from abandoning the KMT regime, Mao had insisted that the United States treat China as an equal. That meant apologizing for and rectifying a century of what Mao charged was America's imperialistic approach to China. Chen writes, "Mao's definition of inequality, meant a total negation of America's role in China's modern history and posed the crucial challenge to the existing principles of international relations, to which the United States and other Western countries adhered. In Mao's opinion, America's willingness to change its attitude toward China represented a pass-or-fail test for policymakers in Washington; and he simply did not believe they would pass the test."[161]

The path to normal relations being blocked, Stuart prepared to leave the country. In late July, he had his final meeting with Huang, who recounted:

Stuart came to see me one more time for his departure paper. Stuart asked my opinion of America's future China policy. I told him the United States could do nothing at the present stage but give up its errant policy and prove the sincerity of pursuing a true friendship with the Chinese people. The United States, however, had not stopped supporting the Chinese reactionaries in the civil war and was organizing "the Pacific treaty organization." The Chinese people would firmly oppose these imperialist policies.[162]

The ambassador was recalled on August 2 and departed from China.[163] He never returned.

As Stuart was leaving, the State Department released a compilation of documents intended to explain what had happened in China in recent years and to justify US policy during the period. Formally titled *United States Relations with China, with Special Reference to the Period 1944–1949*, it was otherwise known as the China White Paper. The publication failed to defuse domestic criticism. The Communists seized upon it to prove a pattern of US interference in China's internal affairs. In his July 30, 1949, letter of transmittal to the president, Acheson declared, "the unfortunate but inescapable fact is that the ominous result of the civil war in China was beyond the control of the government of the United States. Nothing that this country did or could have done within the reasonable limits of its capabilities could have changed that result; nothing that was left undone by this country has contributed to it. It was the product of internal Chinese forces, forces which this country tried to influence but could not. A decision was arrived at within China, if only a decision by default."

In his August 18 essay, "Farewell, Leighton Stuart!", Mao condemned the former ambassador personally and added broad attacks on US foreign policy, including on the White Paper.[164] Mao stated,

> The war to turn China into a US colony, a war in which the United States of America supplies the money and guns and Chiang Kai-shek the men to fight for the United States and slaughter the Chinese people, has been an important component of the US imperialist policy of world-wide aggression since World War II. The US policy of aggression has several targets. The three main targets are Europe, Asia, and the Americas. China, the center of gravity in Asia, is a large country with a population of 475 million; by seizing China, the United States would possess all of Asia. With its Asian front consolidated, US imperialism could concentrate its forces on attacking Europe. US imperialism considers its front in the Americas relatively secure. These are the smug over-all calculations of the US aggressors.[165]

Repelled by a US record of pro-KMT bias during the Hurley and Marshall missions and throughout the civil war, Mao could not be turned.[166] On the contrary, he was convinced he must secure early and significant Soviet backing. In his "Leighton Stuart" essay, he wrote of "the towering presence of the Soviet Union, this unprecedentedly powerful bulwark of peace bestriding Europe and Asia." Moscow could help with the recovery of an economy that had been devastated by years of warfare and rampant inflation and in addressing the potential threat that the revolution could be upended before consolidated.[167] Mao was determined that the Chinese Communists would stand with the Soviets.[168]

In a 1953 Statement of Policy, the US National Security Council assessed that the Sino-Soviet alliance, for whatever tensions might exist within it, was fundamentally beyond the Western capacity to dismantle. "It also seems improbably that the West can through accommodation create a situation in which Chinese conflicts of interest with the Russians are greater than Chinese conflicts of interest with the West," the statement observed. It mentioned Mao's positioning as the Communists were coming to power in China, noting "the initial Chinese Communist choice of partnership with the Russians in 1949, when the Western powers, including the United States, had obviously reconciled themselves to the defeat of the Nationalists and the supremacy of the Communists in China, and were making gestures of accommodation."[169]

PROBLEMS IN KOREA

For the generalissimo, early 1950 looked decidedly grim. In quick succession, there was Truman's statement of January 5, Acheson's Press Club speech of January 12, and the signing of the Sino-Soviet 25-year defense pact on February 15. Hollington Tong describes a May 1950 meeting in Washington with John Foster Dulles, then an adviser to the State Department. "He did not hold out any hope of American aid. The impression he gave me in our confidential talk was that the American government had made up its mind that it was now too late to do anything effective and that most American experts felt that Formosa could survive only three or four months longer."[170]

But Chiang was about to be saved. On June 25, 1950, North Korean armies crossed the 38th Parallel in an effort to overthrow the South Korean government and unify the Korean peninsula.[171] North Korean leader Kim II Sung acted after securing Stalin's agreement, permission the Soviet had originally been reluctant to give because of the unsettled situation in Europe, where tensions between the USSR and the West were combustible.[172] As Professor Shen Zhihua, a Chinese Cold War scholar, observed, "In 1948, when the Americans and the Soviets were in sharp conflict in Europe, Stalin could not afford to put Korea at the top of his agenda."[173]

However, given the success of the Maoist revolution, and statements from Truman and Acheson, Stalin assessed that the situation in Asia had turned in the Communists' favor.

Thus, Stalin accepted Kim Il Sung's assurances that North Korea could quickly overrun South Korean positions, that any Western response would be ineffectual, and that the risk of American engagement was small. A quick victory in Korea would further strengthen Soviet security and add to a sense of momentum for the Communist bloc.[174]

The Chinese had asked for Soviet personnel to support an invasion of Formosa, but Kim requested arms alone. The probability of direct conflict with the United States over Korea seemed low, but over Formosa, potentially higher. Needing to manage risk, Stalin greenlighted Kim's invasion, while deflecting the Formosa issue.[175] Historian Stuart Schram has written that the hostilities in Korea served Soviet purposes at the expense of Mao's interests. "To be sure, Mao was as interested as anyone in fighting 'American imperialism,' but he could well have waited to do so until the internal situation was consolidated, and he had settled accounts with Chiang Kai-shek."[176]

Stalin maneuvered Mao to backstop Kim, and the war began.[177] According to Hans van de Ven, "With the invasion of South Korea promising the definitive removal of US influence from the Korean Peninsula, and the ousting of a hostile South Korean government with links to Chiang Kai-shek on Taiwan, and little being asked of the Chinese in the way of support, Mao Zedong [Mao Tse-tung] readily gave his approval."[178]

After the North Koreans crossed the 38th Parallel, the United States promptly secured United Nations Security Council Resolution 82 to counter the aggression.[179] The Security Council averted a Soviet veto, because the USSR was boycotting the United Nations in protest over the UN's failure to replace the Nationalist Chinese government in the UN with the PRC.

INTERPOSING THE SEVENTH FLEET

Truman quickly accepted Acheson's advice, rendered at a June 25 Blair House dinner, to have the US Seventh Fleet police the Taiwan Strait, preventing attacks in either direction.[180] The objectives of his order of June 27 were to confine fighting to the Korean Peninsula,[181] protect the Nationalists, secure the support of Chiang's stalwarts in Congress, and avoid a wider war. Frustrated that he could not pursue his plans for an amphibious attack on Formosa, Mao stood down. He was outraged.[182]

Journalist Rudy Abramson, Governor Averell Harriman's biographer, observed that Truman's action "boldly risked junking the US policy against using arms to defend the Nationalists against the Communists, even though the purpose was also to make sure that Chiang Kai-shek did not attack the mainland." Reversing course, it was an enormously fateful moment, keeping the United States entwined with internal Chinese politics from which there again seemed no easy exit. Abramson went on to say, "With that decision, the United States had thrown itself back into the China conflict, a position it had profoundly hoped to escape."[183]

US diplomat Karl Rankin, who was President Eisenhower's ambassador to the ROC, described how Chiang responded to this lifeline. "In return for our willingness to assist in the defense of Taiwan—shortly afterward extended to include Penghu, or the Pescadores—the Chinese Government was quite prepared to forego any and all offensive action against the Communists for an indefinite period after the outbreak of hostilities in Korea. . . . The government on Taiwan proffered its agreement immediately in a manner intended to give the appearance of bilateral rather than unilateral action."[184]

The effects of Truman's order were to reverse the US hands-off policy in the region and cancel Mao's amphibious assault.[185] A United States National Intelligence Estimate issued on April 1, 1952, concluded, "provided that the present US policy with respect to Taiwan continues unchanged, and provided US naval and air forces are available to defend Taiwan, Chinese Communist operations against Taiwan would almost certainly fail."[186] However, all that stood between Chiang and annihilation was the Seventh Fleet. The NIE added, "If US policy with respect to Taiwan should change and the US did not participate in the defense of Taiwan, the Chinese Nationalist forces could not successfully defend Taiwan against a large-scale Communist operation."[187] To maintain control of Taiwan, American protection was indispensable.

Blocked from attacking across the strait, Mao repositioned his troops away from coastal areas and moved them to the vicinity of the North Korean border.[188] When UN forces, under the command of General Douglas MacArthur, approached the Chinese border, Beijing counterattacked. According to Professor Robert Accinelli, "A major reason why Mao chose to fight in the peninsula was his belief that the United States intended to crush the Chinese revolution, using Korea, Taiwan, and Vietnam as staging areas for an offensive against China's territory. Taiwan and Korea were inextricably meshed in the minds of Mao and his comrades."[189]

Entering the war at the end of November 1950, Chinese armies pushed the UN away from the border and drove south down the Korean peninsula before the situation stabilized in the vicinity of the 38th Parallel.[190] On February 1, 1951, by a vote of 44–7, with nine abstentions, the UN General Assembly adopted Resolution 498 (V). It declared that the General Assembly "finds that the Central People's Government of the People's Republic of China, by giving direct aid and assistance to those who were already committing aggression in Korea and by engaging in hostilities against United Nations forces there has itself engaged in aggression in Korea."[191]

Late in 1950, Beijing offered cease-fire terms that would have required US withdrawal from the strait and the seating of Communist China in lieu of Nationalist China at the UN.[192] The administration refused, a position popular with the China Lobby and its many friends in Congress.

A POISONED ATMOSPHERE

The president's Seventh Fleet order had profound political implications for US relations with the PRC. It destroyed the remaining goodwill, if any, that Mao retained for the United States, and shut down any chance that Beijing and Washington could normalize relations. Having announced that the United States would not intervene in the civil war, Truman had reversed course. The presence of the Seventh Fleet preserved a regime on Formosa that was tattered militarily, opposed by significant segments of the native Formosan population, and unlikely to have repelled the amphibious assault.

Historian Nancy Bernkopf Tucker observed, "Not only did American action frustrate a long and bitterly sought conclusion of the revolutionary struggle by preserving Chiang Kai-shek's regime, but to the CCP it proved beyond doubt the deceitfulness of the world's foremost imperialistic power. Earlier American pledges to refrain from precisely such a measure appeared to have been lies."[193]

Just as Beijing could not attack Taipei, Truman's policy also restrained Chiang from attacks against the mainland, which amounted to harassing pinpricks that did not truly threaten the Communist regime.[194]

TROOP DEPLOYMENTS IN KOREA

Although 21 nations participated in the UN force in Korea, the United States supplied 90% of the troops. Truman appointed General Douglas MacArthur as commander. Chiang offered to contribute 33,000 troops to the war effort,[195] but Truman declined, affirming the recommendation of the Departments of State and Defense not to import the Chinese civil war into the Korean conflict. In an interview with historian Merle Miller, Secretary of State Acheson explained, "We did not wish to raise the political complications which would have been raised if we had introduced the Nationalist-Red Chinese controversy into the battle in Korea. . . . It would have been a divisive and not a unifying action if we took it."[196]

In any case, Truman was personally dubious about the value of Chiang's troops. As he told Miller, "They weren't any damn good, never had been. We sent them about three billion five hundred million dollars' worth of materiel, sent that to the so-called free Chinese, and then about five million of Chiang's men between Peking and Nanking surrendered to three hundred thousand Communists, and the Communists used that materiel to run Chiang and his men out of China. I told you. He never was any damn good."[197]

Late in 1952, President-elect Eisenhower and his team reviewed the issue of Nationalist troop deployment in Korea. Fulfilling a campaign promise,

Eisenhower visited the war zone in early December. In the context of that visit, he consulted with Major General William C. Chase, who led the US Military Assistance Advisory Group (MAAG) on Formosa.[198] Chase returned to Formosa to sound out Chiang about whether the deployment, first offered in 1950, was still possible.

But now Chiang was hesitant, because the military balance vis-à-vis the PRC had become unfavorable to him. According to a cable from Karl Rankin, "Gimo observed that question whether troops shld be sent or not was matter for consideration but added with emphasis his first concern must be security of Formosa." Chiang had become concerned that deployment would pro-voke air bombardment from the PRC. Since his 1950 offer, Chiang added, the Soviets had substantially strengthened the PRC air force, without com-mensurate US support for his defenses. While the Nationalist air force had been stronger in 1950, it was now inferior. To provide effective air defense, Chiang argued, the United States would need to base a substantial force of jet fighters on Formosa. Rankin summarized, "He hoped such force wld actu-ally be based here before any invitation recd to contribute Chi Nat forces for Korea."[199]

On December 24, the *Washington Post* indicated that the Nationalist deployment was still under active consideration. Alarmed at this story, Assis-tant Secretary of State John Moore Allison expressed reservations about it to the secretary of state-designate John Foster Dulles. Allison cited seven objec-tions: the cost of equipping, transporting, and maintaining Chiang's troops; the greater efficiency of spending such funds on equipping South Korean forces; doubts about the fighting capacity of the Nationalist Chinese; the likelihood that Chiang would seek a quid pro quo of a major buildup of US air power on Formosa; making the Korean conflict part of the Chinese civil war; stirring dissension among US allies; and the likely reluctance of South Korean president Syngman Rhee to have Chinese Nationalist troops put into Korea. "I am strongly of the opinion," Allison concluded, "that the possible advantages to be gained by the introduction of Chinese Nationalist divisions to Korea is far outweighed by the adverse factors listed above."[200]

AN INFLECTION POINT

The Korean conflict was a fundamental inflection point in how the United States approached Asia, including its relations with Chiang's Republic of China. Both Korea and the ROC became frontline states in the fight against Communism.[201] Promptly, Chiang was converted from a disrespected and largely abandoned client to an indispensable American ally. And the shift was not temporary but became settled American policy. As expressed in a

March 4, 1952, memo from the JCS to Secretary of Defense Robert Lovett, "the self-interest of the United States demands that Formosa be strengthened as an anti-Communist base militarily, economically, politically, and psychologically. The denial of Formosa to Communism is of vital importance to the long-term United States position in the Far East."[202]

The issue became not whether Chiang should just be sustained and protected on Formosa, or whether the United States should go further, and use him for offensive actions against the Chinese Communists. Each strategy had its benefits and risks. On April 9, 1952, the Joint Chiefs held a planning session at the Pentagon with representatives of the Department of State and the Central Intelligence Agency. A prime topic was whether to remove restraints on Chiang. Senior diplomat Charles Bohlen, soon to serve as ambassador to the Soviet Union, pleaded for caution. Otherwise, he feared, Chiang would draw the United States into widened conflict with the PRC, "We should not foreclose the possibility of removing the shackles if that becomes desirable. I, however, would have great doubts about the wisdom of passing on to the Nationalist Government any indication that the shackles will be removed." Bohlen surmised it was likely that the Nationalists would interpret doing so as a US commitment to their defense or even enabling their return to the mainland.

Bohlen added, "The Chinese Nationalists do not disguise their objective in any way. If we changed our policy, we would give the Chinese Nationalists the ability to involve the US in war with a major power. . . . The Chinese know that the only way they can get back on the mainland is with US support. This is not the kind of risk we would take with very many governments in the world." Army Vice Chief of Staff John E. Hull responded, "I don't think it will ever be within their capabilities."

However, Allen W. Dulles, deputy director of Central Intelligence, noted that constraining Chiang indefinitely might lead to the disintegration of his forces and even a revolution. The Nationalists would not accept being confined to Formosa without a foreseeable opportunity to recover the mainland. "It is not inconceivable that a revolution might occur in Formosa. The situation is not a level one. US controls are not adequate. Over a period of time, it would be our estimate that the situation will deteriorate, that the army will not sit there idle forever. They want to go home. If they have no way of fighting their way back, they will go back as individuals."[203]

"If we do not foresee a combined Chinese Nationalist-US capability adequate to bring down the Communist Chinese," said Paul Nitze from State, "Even so, we do not want to lose Formosa and we ought to address ourselves . . . to building a healthier situation so that the island will not collapse around us."[204]

Joint Chiefs chairman Omar Bradley argued for maintaining the status quo. Igniting a wider war with China to restore Chiang seemed reckless to him. Keeping Formosa out of Communist hands was the true US national security interest, although he was skeptical about sending American troops to secure it.[205]

> The chance of overthrowing the Chinese Communist government is slim—certainly without US action. We are not prepared to begin a general war with Communist China and our discussion seems to indicate that is the only way in which that regime can be overthrown. . . . If we are not going to war with Communist China, then what do we do in Formosa? . . . We have said many times and still say that the loss of Formosa would be bad but that it would not be so bad as to justify sending US forces there to hold it.[206]

WHAT ABOUT QUEMOY AND MATSU?

Outside that discussion, there remained the momentarily peripheral question of how Truman's policy affected Nationalist-held islands near the Chinese coast, primarily Quemoy [Kinmen or Jinmen] and Matsu [Mazu]. It was an issue that would rise to great prominence in the Strait Crises of 1954–1955 and 1958, and in congressional debates on the Formosa Resolution and the Mutual Defense Treaty between the United States and the Republic of China. A March 9, 1952, cable from Secretary Acheson to the US embassy in Taipei [Taibei] affirmed the United States was not obligated to defend the islands but would not impede Chiang from doing so. "While US cannot under Presidential Directive of June 27, 1950, commit its forces def any islands now under the control of Chi Govt other than Taiwan and the Pescadores, it is US hope that the Chi Govt will defend such islands. US does not consider current directive to CINCPAC with respect to Formosa as preventing such action." Acheson cautioned the embassy to avoid discussing the issue with the Nationalists, if possible. If the Communists got wind of the fact that the United States would not defend Quemoy and Matsu, they might be tempted to attack. Acheson added a special caution, "In event considered nec again discuss matter with Natl Govt you should convey US position to highest auth only."[207]

On May 14, Howard Jones, a counselor at the embassy, responded to Acheson. The Nationalists intended to defend the islands but might need help from the Seventh Fleet. "Since Chi Govt without active support Seventh Fleet wld find it impossible maintain successful defense in face determined, well-mounted attacks."[208] Given the Truman-Acheson policy, such intervention was unlikely to be forthcoming.

THE JAPANESE PEACE TREATY

The Treaty of San Francisco, which formally ended the war with Japan and terminated the six-year American military occupation, was signed on September 8, 1951.[209] John Foster Dulles represented the United States and was its principal architect.[210] Forty-nine nations participated, but the United States took care to exclude both the Nationalist and Communist Chinese from the occasion. Chiang took the exclusion as an insult. Traveling in Formosa shortly thereafter, Governor Thomas E. Dewey experienced Chiang's anger at the humiliation.

Dewey recounts that Britain proved to be the principal obstacle to Nationalist China signing the treaty. "If the British government did not sign, then the British Dominions probably would stand aside and with them most of Europe. The British Foreign Office could not be persuaded to sign the treaty with the Nationalist government of China since they had recognized Red China, even though Red China had not recognized Britain; to persuade them to omit Red China from the signatories was a great triumph of American diplomacy."[211] The excuse of British intransigence did not satisfy Chiang, who never ceased to regard Nationalist China's exclusion as "a serious omission and failure."[212]

In addition, on September 8, Washington and Tokyo entered upon a security treaty, which permitted the continued basing of US forces in Japan, and which remained in effect until it was revised in 1960.[213] With strong American encouragement, the Japanese, who had considered some options for Cold War neutrality, announced they would conduct diplomatic relations with the Nationalist China. Taipei and Tokyo concluded a separate treaty on April 28, 1952.[214] As Chiang noted in a 1964 interview, Dulles helped to engineer a rapprochement between the former enemies. "Mr. Dulles urged both the Japanese Government and the Chinese Government in this respect, because Mr. Dulles saw that it would be to our mutual advantage and mutual interest to have an early resumption of relations."[215] Japan would continue to recognize Chiang's government until switching to the PRC in 1972 after President Nixon's trip to China.

NOTES

1. New York governor Thomas E. Dewey, who traveled to Formosa in the summer of 1951, observed,

"Precious military supplies were flown into Manchuria by their limited Air Force to pockets of Nationalist resistance at a time when it was perfectly clear that Manchuria could not be held. The practical reason for this action was not merely to try to save the priceless resources and industry of the area, but that many members of the Legislative Yuan represented districts in Manchuria and north China. They clamored for more aid to Nationalist troops in those areas. These demands mounted in intensity until it became apparent that the government and Generalissimo Chiang would lose their support if some action was not taken." (Dewey, p. 106)

2. Tsou argues that the Yalta construct failed because it did not reflect China's postwar realities. The Communists had attained such a strong position that even a treaty between Stalin and Chiang could not marginalize them. Tang Tsou observes that the Soviet reappraisal was not long in coming. "Once Moscow had reached a new estimate of the military and revolutionary potentiality of the Chinese Communists, and once the American program of seeking a settlement between the Nationalists and Communists had completely broken down, she gave open diplomatic support to the Chinese Communists" (Tsou, p. 240). Diplomat Karl Rankin wrote in his memoirs about the period after Chiang and the Soviets signed the Treaty of Friendship and Alliance. "In the succeeding years that treaty had been flagrantly violated by giving large scale support to the Chinese Communists. Without that support, the legal government of China could not have been driven from its homeland." Karl Rankin, *China Assignment* (Seattle, WA: University of Washington Press, 1964), p. 18.

3. Rankin, pp. 101–102. To this assessment, Dewey adds, "When peace came to the rest of the world that did not come to China. Mao Tse-tung's Chinese Communist armies received from the Russians a fresh supply of captured Japanese arms, so the war weary and exhausted Chiang government faced a new attack from a fresh, well-supplied enemy. Betrayed by Russia in 1945 almost as soon as the ink was dry on Stalin's 30-year treaty of friendship and alliance, Chiang also found himself deserted by his other wartime ally, the United States. Instead of support, he got abuse public repudiation" (Dewey, p. 110). Enhanced cooperation with Mao also worked against American interests in Asia. As Chinese scholar Shen Zhihua observes, "the Chinese Communists were the only factor the Soviets could use in their China policy to check the Nationalist governments policy toward the Soviet Union and American power in China" (Shen, p. 62).

4. Stuart, p. 183.

5. Tucker comments that the airlift may have been counterproductive because it alienated the Communists and somehow convinced Chiang that he need not compromise because he would be able to assume dominion over the whole of China (Tucker, p. 9). Davies notes,

"Clinging to the policy of sustaining Chiang, Washington immediately launched an airlift of Nationalist troops from the back country to take the surrender of the Japanese who had so obligingly rebuffed the Communists. Thus, at the outset of the civil war, the American government allied itself with the Nationalist side. Rather than disarming the enemy forces in north China and repatriating them, the American- borne Nationalists invited the Japanese to hold the cities and communication lines against the Communists while Chiang's detachments ventured into the countryside against the Reds. Washington assigned more than 50,000 US Marines to join the Japanese trustees in custodial duties on behalf of the Generalissimo." (Davies, *China Hand*, pp. 265–266)

6. Bianco, p. 169.

7. Messer, p. 72.

8. Statement of Secretary of State James F. Byrnes, hearings before the Senate Foreign Relations Committee, December 7, 1945, p. 147. US ambassador Patrick Hurley underscored why it was necessary, if feasible, to assist Chiang with this task. "If the US and the United Nations allowed an opposition party in China which has a military force to accept the Japanese surrender and to take over Japanese armaments, a civil war will be unavoidable" (van de Ven, p. 212).

9. Chiang, *Soviet Russia*, p. 140. Chiang goes on to comment, "The Communist propagandist insinuated that while Russian troops were being withdrawn from Manchuria, American forces were being landed in north China to help the Government carry out its 'anti-democratic' policies. One purpose of this propaganda was to arouse public opinion in the United States and to force the American Government to withdraw its troops from the China Theater. Another purpose was to prevent Government troops from going to north China to accept the Japanese surrender, especially to stop them from going to Manchuria to reestablish Chinese authority in that region" (Ibid.).

10. Fravel, p. 54.

11. Stuart Schram explains the importance to Mao of taking the surrender of Japanese forces rather than having them surrender to the Nationalists. "Mao's intention was effectively that the military forces under his command should accept the surrender of the Japanese and puppet troops everywhere possible, so as to obtain important stocks of arms while expanding and consolidating the Communist territorial basis" (Schram, p. 235). See also Herbert Feis on the logistical problems that existed at the time of the hasty Japanese surrender. "The armies of the Chinese government at the end of the war were weaker and less qualified and equipped than had been hoped; and they were scattered in the far-off interior and in the south" (Feis, p. 196). "The American government did not have the timeline on which it had counted to make up its mind as to what military support to give the Chinese government after the end of the war" (Feis, p. 298).

12. William Stueck, "The Marshall and Wedemeyer Missions: A Quadrilateral Perspective," in Harry Harding and Yuan Ming, Eds., *Sino-American Relations 1945–1955: A Joint Assessment of a Critical Decade* (Wilmington, DE: Scholarly Resources, 1989), p. 96. Professor Stueck identifies two principal Soviet objectives. The first was to exploit China, as Eastern Europe had been exploited, in order to facilitate Soviet recovery from the war. The second was to prevent the emergence from the war of a strong, unified China that would ally with the United States (Ibid., p. 99).

13. "What Americans couldn't do, though, was get Nationalist forces into Manchuria. Indeed, Chiang's armies, whether under their own steam or with US assistance, could only enter the region at all with Soviet acquiescence" (Stephenson, p. 151).

14. Tsou, p. 286. "The Soviets delayed the withdrawal of their troops from Manchuria for five months, and the last of their tanks only rumbled across the border in April 1946. They handed the countryside over to the Communists and allowed Lin Biao to deploy his forces on the outskirts of all major cities" (Dikötter, p. 15).

"By early 1946. Yenan could claim an armed force with 300,000 in Northeast. It is clear that this army could not have been moved into Manchuria, recruited, supply, or equipped without active Soviet cooperation. The Russians also assisted in the creation of new Communist political organs in the northeast. . . . Finally, while providing aid and comfort to the Communists, the Russians obstructed the Kuomintang army entry into the northeast. . . . Despite their promise to assist in the restoration of Nationalist control over the region, the Russians had kept government forces out while providing timely and valuable aid to the Communists." (Reardon-Anderson, pp. 107–108)

15. At the same time, the Soviets assured the Nationalists that they were being faithful to the treaty. For example, on November 16, 1945, Moscow instructs the Soviet ambassador to tell the Chinese Foreign Ministry that the USSR will permit Nationalist forces to land in Manchuria without hindrance. The ambassador is also instructed to say that "the Soviet government also considers it necessary to state that the Soviet Military Command, strictly observing the Soviet-Chinese agreement, has not given and is not giving any assistance to the Communists units in Manchuria." "Note to the Soviet Ambassador in China," https://digitalarchive.wilsoncenter.org/document/208926 (accessed February 21, 2022).

16. US policy "was to assist the Nationalists but not to the extent of armed involvement with the Communists" (Ibid., p. 152). Walter Robertson recounts that the Russians in Manchuria proved to be a major impediment to both the Nationalists and the Americans. "They wouldn't allow us—who had won the war there in the Pacific, almost without allied help—to send in even our consular representatives. . . . The Russians wouldn't let us take the armies of the Republic of China into Manchuria to take over the territory as they gave it up" (Robertson, p. 8).

17. Stueck, p. 97.

18. "Research Starters: U.S. Military by the Numbers," www.nationalww2museum .org (accessed July 1, 2022).

19. The number of US forces in China reached a high of 113,000 shortly after the end of the war. Their mission was to assist with the surrender and repatriation of Japanese forces. Within little more than a year, the size of the American contingent was reduced to about 12,000, consistent with accomplishment of their mission and the general demobilization of the US military. Xixiao Guo, *The Journal of American-East Asian Relations*, Vol. 7, No. 3/4 (Fall-Winter 1998), pp. 157–185 https://www .jstor.org/stable/23612918.

20. Judd, p. 27.

21. Fairbank, *The United States and China*, p. 308.

22. Reardon-Anderson, p. 158.

23. Ibid., pp. 166–167.

24. Ibid.

25. The mission of the remaining Marines was to support General Marshall's mediation efforts. Noting the cabinet meeting of August 2, 1946, Forrestal noted remarks by Undersecretary of State Dean Acheson.

"The reason for the Marines being in China now was to support policy and efforts by General Marshall to bring about order, a constitutional government, and a unified National Army. He said it was true that the existing Nationalist government of Nanking was not all that could be desired, and that Marshall was not getting any great help in his endeavors to secure peace. But he felt that we should back Marshall up to the limit until he himself has said there is no longer any hope of gaining his objective and that it is time to come out and reconsider our position in China and our general policy in the Far East."

    (Millis, pp. 190) Historian Robert Accinelli observes, "During Marshall's tenure in the State Department, the Truman administration had rejected both an all-out commitment to save the Nationalists from defeat and a complete break with them, settling on a policy, of limited economic and military assistance. The disintegration of KMT forces in late 1948 left no doubt in the minds of State Department officials that Chiang's cause was beyond recovery." Robert Accinelli, *Crisis and Commitment: United States Policy Toward Taiwan, 1950–1955* (Chapel Hill, NC: University of North Carolina Press, 1996), p. 5.

    26. Tsou, p. 89. Foster Rhea Dulles notes the Nationalist' failure to meet demands for land redistribution, to control inflation, and to address problems of nepotism and corruption. Anger over these failings, he says, was communicated from the countryside to Chiang's troops, and generated massive desertions (Foster Rhea Dulles, p. 29). Nancy Bernkopf Tucker writes that American arms sent to the Nationalists often wound up in Communist hands. Chiang intransigence in the face of US military and political advice was grounded in the idea that he was indispensable to the US Cold War structure and so the Americans would never abandon him (Tucker, pp. 9–10).

    27. *Foreign Relations of the United States, The Far East: China 1947, Vol. VII* (Washington, DC: US Government Printing Office), pp. 640–641.

    28. Ibid., pp. 683–684.

    29. *The China White Paper*, pp. 773–774.

    30. Acheson followed Marshall as Secretary of State. He took office on January 21, 1949.

    31. *Foreign Relations of the United States the Far East: China 1949, Vol. IX* (Washington, DC: US Government Printing Office), p. 1366.

    32. Harold M. Tanner, *Where Chiang Kai-shek Lost China* (Bloomington, IN: Indiana University Press, 2015), p. 5.

    33. Ibid., p. 4.

    34. Koo, pp. H-361–362. Dikötter writes of Chiang's Manchurian effort, "The loss of Manchuria, he confided in his private journal, would open all of north China to the Communists. He was staking everything he had on one huge gamble rather than retreating and holding the line along the Great Wall" (Dikötter, pp. 19–20).

    35. Koo, pp. H-361–362.

    36. Stuart, p. 188. Elsewhere in his memoirs, Stuart writes, "We incurred the animosity not only of the Communists but of a number of Chinese intellectuals who had lost respect for their government and longed for the peace which was supposedly hindered chiefly because of our aid" (Ibid., p. 209). For example, in 1948, Congress appropriated $125 million, which could be used in any way the Chinese government deemed desirable. They used the full amount to purchase military supplies, which were slow to arrive. The delays engendered what Stuart called "bitter invectives" from the Nationalists, while the Communists were also bitter because American aid was prolonging the war (Ibid., pp. 244–245). John King Fairbank also notes

the disaffection of intellectuals from the KMT. "Given the record of corruption and terrorism which overtook the comandante government in proportion as its problems multiplied, and its leadership move to the right, it is not surprising that the Chinese intelligentsia in their political thinking became steadily more estranged from it" (Fairbank, *The United States and China*, p. 257).

37. Ibid., p. 315.

38. Michael Lynch argues that America had far too much in sunk costs to abandon Chiang, from equipment, to the airlift, to military advisers. "Such an outlay made it impossible simply to write off its political and economic investment. The result was that it continued to finance and support Chiang and the Nationalists, despite deep differences of opinion within the US government." Lynch also cites political considerations that kept Truman's feet to the fire even when it was clear Chiang would lose. "In Congress the hardening of the Cold War produced a vocal China Lobby, largely made up of Republicans, which argued strongly that the Nationalists—whatever their failings—were an Asian bastion against the spread of international communism and therefore could not be deserted" (Lynch, pp. 81–82).

39. Stuart, p. 372. Cronyism was rampant within the Nationalist army and was, in fact, Chiang's method of remaining atop the political power structure (Tsou, pp. 111–112).

40. Judd served in Congress from 1943 to 1963. He gave the keynote address at the 1960 Republican National Convention. He was considered a leading possibility to join the national ticket that year with Richard M. Nixon, losing out to Ambassador Henry Cabot Lodge, Jr.

41. "Dubbed the China Lobby by the New York Communist Party in 1949, the pro-Chiang coalition never actually formed a tightly organized lobbying group. What center the Lobby had revolved around its representatives from Nationalist China who operated out of New York and Washington, DC. Contacts between the Chinese and their American supporters tended to lack any formal unity. A few individuals worked as paid lobbyists, but the majority of Americans who aided the Nationalists did so informally" (Tucker, p. 80). Professor Robert David Johnson states the China Lobby was "a combination of hardline anti-Communist supplicants of KMT leader Chiang Kai-shek, former Christian missionaries, and those influenced by the religious portrayal of China centered on the *Time/Life* empire of Henry Luce." Johnson adds that "the Lobby claimed to have one million members behind a policy of massive military and economic assistance to Chiang's beleaguered forces in the Chinese civil war." Robert David Johnson, *Congress and the Cold War* (Cambridge: Cambridge University Press, 2006), p. 33.

42. "Ambassador Koo believed that the most effective influence could be brought to bear not by the Chinese themselves, but rather by properly inspired Americans" (Ibid., p. 95).

43. Ibid., p. 76.

44. "From their American sympathizers, the Nationalists solicited and received confidential information about the inner workings of government agencies. . . . Most helpful in providing such intelligence were congressmen like Walter Judd, State Department representatives like John Foster Dulles, and the military" (Ibid.).

45. The State Department explains, "With the Truman Doctrine, President Harry S. Truman established that the United States would provide political, military and economic assistance to all democratic nations under threat from external or internal authoritarian forces. The Truman Doctrine effectively reoriented U.S. foreign policy, away from its usual stance of withdrawal from regional conflicts not directly involving the United States, to one of possible intervention in faraway conflicts." "The Truman Doctrine, 1947," www.history.state.gov (accessed April 16, 2022).

46. "China aid requests usually came up as amendments to European assistance programs which the President deemed essential for national and international stability—in 1947 in conjunction with interim aid, in 1948 with the European Recovery Program, and in 1949 as part of the military assistance program. To assure itself of the votes needed to pass these measures, the Administration had to include provisions for Chiang's Kuomintang regime and could not follow its reasoned inclination to disassociate the United States from a losing cause" (Ibid., p. 165). Daniel Kurtz-Phelan takes a somewhat different perspective on the assistance to China. "At 10 percent of what would go over the same period to Western Europe, an economy more than five times larger, the package was hardly insignificant. But it was less than the Nationalists wanted, in scale and kind, and Marshall knew it was likely to achieve little other than 'buying time'" (Kurtz-Phelan, p. 342).

47. Walter Robertson states, "We poured 14 billions of dollars into Europe to prevent the Communists from taking over Greece, Turkey, France, and Western Europe; and in China we withheld a $500 million loan to force the Communists in" (Robertson, p. 9).

48. Judd, pp. 31–32. Daniel Kurtz-Phelan notes that Marshall himself disagreed with that view. Comparatively wealthy as it was, America obviously had limited resources and had to allocate them where they would do the best. That was Europe, not China, he believed. "He had to weigh proliferating news, to distinguish the vital from the secondary, vital and achievable from vital but futile. . . . His thirteen months in China gave him ample cause for skepticism, at a time when every dollar, officer, or weapon sent to Chiang was a dollar, officer, or weapon not available elsewhere" (Kurtz-Phelan, pp. 339–340).

49. Ibid., p. 11.

50. Fenby, p. 481. Marshall had long been skeptical of Chiang, given the generalissimo's performance during the war with Japan and his hostility to General Joseph Stilwell. Tsou observes, "It is not accidental that the man who later took steps leading to the permanent withdrawal of the United States from China, thus ending an era of 100 years of friendly Sino-American relations, was none other than General Marshall, who as Stilwell's immediate superior and close friend, had intimate knowledge of Stilwell's tribulations and difficulties in dealing with Chiang" (Tsou, p. 124). China scholar John King Fairbank elaborates on the role Secretary of State Marshall played in constraining assistance to Chiang. "He knew the score, and when he returned to the United States as Secretary of State in 1947, he succeeded in preventing the Americans for going in to a super-Vietnam to quell the Chinese Revolution." John King Fairbank, *The Great Chinese Revolution 1800–1985* (New York: Harper & Row, 1986), p. 267.

51. Before the Marshall Plan was framed, 16 European nations submitted reconstruction plans to which the aid would be directed. As Marshall himself stated when he announced the program at a Harvard University commencement address,

> "It is already evident that, before the United States Government can proceed much further in its efforts to alleviate the situation and help start the European world on its way to recovery, there must be some agreement among the countries of Europe as to the requirements of the situation and the part those countries themselves will take in order to give proper effect to whatever action might be undertaken by this Government. It would be neither fitting nor efficacious for this Government to undertake to draw up unilaterally a program designed to place Europe on its feet economically. This is the business of the Europeans. The initiative, I think, must come from Europe. The role of this country should consist of friendly aid in the drafting of a European program and of later support of such a program so far as it may be practical for us to do so. The program should be a joint one, agreed to by a number, if not all European nations."

"The Marshall Plan Speech at Harvard University, 5 June 1947," oecd.org (accessed August 16, 2021).

52. Testimony of John Paton Davies, p. 35. Ambassador Stuart describes the attitude of the Department of State as one of "frustrated, unsympathetic defeatism" (Stuart, p. 273).

53. Nancy Bernkopf Tucker writes about the sharp difference between the bipartisan foreign policy on Europe and the high degree of partisanship on Asia. "China policy, however, forgotten in the shuffle of pressing European and domestic crises, never earned sufficient status to merit party cooperation. The Administration made no effort to secure Republican support for its decisions. . . . After Marshall's mission failed, and the entire Roosevelt-Truman strategy appeared doomed, Republicans happily recalled that they had nothing to do with the disaster" (Tucker, p. 163).

54. Ibid., pp. 59–60. Ambassador Stuart recounts, "The Generalissimo and his comrades had been led to believe that the election of Thomas E. Dewey was practically assured and that this would mean prompt and powerful military aid to China instead of the Truman Marshall hesitations" (Stuart, p. 219).

55. Republicans were enormously disappointed with the outcome. The bipartisan foreign policy related to Europe fractured as to Asia, and recriminations abounded concerning the expected loss of China. As Tucker reports, "Utilizing charges that the Democrats harbored Communists in the government and knowingly betrayed Chiang Kai-shek, the GOP hoped to overcome the attraction of Roosevelt's domestic legacy and scare the American public into voting Republican" (Tucker, p. 12).

56. Ibid., p. 163. "Looking back at the campaign which had culminated in Harry Truman's victory, Republican leaders identified bipartisanship as a major part of the problem" (Ibid., p. 182).

57. Jay Taylor, *The Generalissimo: Chiang Kai-shek and the Struggle for Modern China* (Cambridge, MA: The Belknap Press of Harvard University Press, 2009), p. 394.

58. "Having already spent great quantities of money on Chiang Kai-shek, the Administration as well as most of Congress opposed squandering additional funds. Repeatedly during 1947 and 1948, Congress further cut minimal appropriations for

assistance to Nationalist China" (Tucker, p. 13). Robert Messer notes, "The aid was not enough to save the Generalissimo, and most insiders agreed he was beyond saving, but for appearances sake the aid continued to flow" (Messer, p. 73).

59. "Foreign Relations: Until the Dust Settles," *Time*, March 7, 1949.

60. Quoted in Tsou, p. 105. Michael Lynch notes, "Chiang was never entirely happy with his reliance on the USA. He would have liked to continue playing off the Russians and the Americans against each other indefinitely" (Lynch, p. 81).

61. Roosevelt's maneuvering to secure concessions from Chiang in order to satisfy Stalin generated substantial dissatisfaction in China, which Madame expressed in this instance. On June 26, 1947, Forrestal noted a conversation with Marshall. "I made the observation that we could not draw entirely oblique conclusions about China today without realizing that part of the antipathy, which Marshall had quoted was now mounting in China, derived from the Yalta Agreement in which we gave away certain of the sovereign rights of China in order to get the Russians into the war. . . . Marshall agreed that this unfortunate fact was a substantial factor in the present unpopularity of the USA in China" (Millis, p. 286). Chiang never excused the Big Three for negotiating his future behind his back. On January 6, 1947, General Marshall, about to depart from China, paid a final call on Chiang and was treated to a diatribe about the Yalta betrayal. Ambassador Stuart writes, "The Generalissimo was very outspoken about the Yalta agreement concerning which China had not been consulted, and he added that although he himself was able to forgive those who were responsible, yet the Chinese nation bitterly resented this treatment, and he hoped this would be reported to President Truman" (Stuart, p. 177).

62. "A charismatic intellectual who challenged traditional ideas of silent and subservient Chinese women, she took a leading role in Nationalist politics, running Chiang's air force at one point. As icons of Western-friendly modernity and of unbending resistance to the excesses of Maoism, Madame Chiang and her husband were highly regarded in the US, and she was even featured three times on the cover of *Time* magazine. At home, however, some regarded her as arrogant and an apologist for the authoritarian ways of the KMT regime." Tony Karon, "Madame Chiang Kaishek, 1898–2003," *Time*, October 24, 2003.

63. Mrs. Roosevelt extended the official invitation. The idea for the trip was first broached in October 1942 by Wendell Willkie, the 1940 Republican nominee, who visited Chungking as part of a round-the-world wartime tour. Ronald Ian Heiferman, *The Cairo Conference of 1943* (Jefferson, NC: McFarland & Company, Inc., 2011), p. 22.

64. Grace C. Huang, "Madame Chiang's Visit to America," in Joseph W. Esherick and Matthew T. Combs, Eds., *1943: China at the Crossroads* (Ithaca: Cornell University, 2018). Madame was exceedingly well received in Congress and elsewhere on her US trip. Hollington Tong recounts, "She was invited to deliver successive addresses to the United States Senate and the House of Representatives. In both of these appearances, she proved a brilliant spokeswoman of the Chinese point of view. American goodwill toward China probably reached an all-time high during these action-filled weeks of Madame Chiang's 1942–1943 visit" (Tong, p. 125). *Time* recounted her appearance before the Senate on February 18, 1943, "Madame Chiang

stepped to the rostrum, listened as Vice President Wallace introduced her, shot a smile at the Senators, and then, after apologizing for not having a set speech, knocked their silvery blocks off extemporaneously. . . . The US Senate is not in the habit of rising to its feet to applaud. For Madame Chiang it rose and thundered." "Madame," *Time*, March 1, 1943, p. 24.

65. *New York Herald Tribune*, February 19, 1943, quoted in Heiferman, p. 24.

66. Heiferman, p. 32.

67. Hollington Tong recounts,

"During a cabinet meeting held on the residence of President Chiang on November 26, 1948, Madame Chiang came down from upstairs and called President Chiang out for an urgent consultation. Later we learned that she had had a long-distance telephone conversation with General Marshall who was then Secretary of State. She told him that she wanted to see him before he entered the hospital for medical attention and that she would be willing to leave China immediately. She would get the decision of the President before she hung up the phone. The President hastily decided to let her go to America to submit the Chinese case for American aid personally through General Marshall." (Tong, p. 159)

68. "Madame Chiang . . . neither informed the embassy of her purposes nor used its services to conduct her business. Only rarely did she confer with Koo and then imparted as little information about her intentions as possible" (Tucker, p. 69).

69. "The Ambassador in China (Stuart) to the Secretary of State, November 26, 1948," *Foreign Relations of the United States, The Far East: China 1948 Volume VIII*, www.history.state.gov. The ambassador's reference to Yalta involved President Roosevelt's agreement to press certain pro-Soviet conditions on China in exchange for Stalin's agreement to join the war against Japan. Stuart's comment about a "coalition government" concerned efforts in 1945 by then-ambassador Patrick Hurley and in 1946 by Special Envoy George Marshall to avert a Chinese civil war by promoting a unity government of Nationalists and Communists. The China Lobby considered efforts to force a coalition government on Chiang to be shameful (Judd, p. 35).

70. Henry R. Liebman, "Mme. Chiang Flying to US to Get Help," *New York Times*, November 29, 1948, p. 18.

71. Ibid.

72. From February 17 to 28, 1943, Madame Chiang was Roosevelt's guest at the White House.

73. Merle Miller, *Plain Speaking: An Oral Biography of Harry S. Truman* (New York: Berkley Publishing Corporation, 1973), pp. 279–280. Whether Truman's sense of the situation was accurate is disputed. Chiang's biographer, Jay Taylor, states, "Chiang had never stolen from the state and he did not have his own private cache of gold" (Taylor, p. 401).

74. During 1946, the year that General Marshall was in China as Truman's special envoy, he and Katherine spent substantial time with generalissimo Chiang and Madame Chiang. The couples knew each other well.

75. Pakula, p. 563.

76. "Memorandum by the Director of the Office of Far Eastern Affairs to the Secretary of State, December 2, 1948," *FRUS, The Far East 1948: China*, www.history.state.gov.

77. Pakula, p. 564.

78. Shortly thereafter, Paul G. Hoffman, head of the Economic Cooperation Authority, advised Truman against further loans to China (Ibid., p. 566). The ECA was originally established to administer Marshall Plan assistance. It was later renamed the United States Agency for International Development.

79. "Memorandum of Conversation by the Secretary of State, December 3, 1948," *FRUS The Far East 1948: China Volume VIII*, www.history.state.gov.

80. Ibid.

81. Graham Hutchings, *China 1949: Year of Revolution* (London: Bloomsbury Academic, 2021), p. 19.

82. "The Ambassador in China (Stuart) to the Secretary of State, December 11, 1948," *FRUS 1948, The Far East 1948: China, Volume VIII*, www.history.state.gov.

83. Ibid. Tucker writes, "Madame Chiang, for instance, did not see the impropriety of appealing to Secretary of State George Marshall for aid when his retirement was imminent. She misinterpreted his friendship as encouragement" (Tucker, p. 69).

84. "The Acting Secretary of State (Lovett) to the Ambassador in China (Stuart), December 13, 1948," *FRUS, 1948, The Far East Volume VIII*, www.history.state.gov.

85. Pakula, p. 568.

86. Laura Tyson Li, *Madame Chiang Kai-shek: China's Eternal First Lady* (New York: Atlantic Monthly Press, 2006), p. 301.

87. The notion of making a separate deal with the Soviets was reminiscent of Chiang's periodic wartime threats to conclude a separate peace with Japan if the United States did not provide certain levels of support. Tang Tsou writes, "The United States had to cope with Generalissimo Chiang, a master of political maneuvers, who turned his very weakness into a position of diplomatic strength. . . . He employed a threat of rupturing the alliance as a trump card to back his demands and counter American pressures" (Tsou, pp. 89–90).

88. "Memorandum of Conversation by the Secretary of State, December 27, 1948," *FRUS 1948 The Far East:1948 Volume VIII*, www.history.state.gov.

89. Kurtz-Phelan, p. 347. Her treatment in the American press was initially fawning and remained so for years. For example, in an April 1937 account in the *New York Times* of the nan Incident of the previous December, readers saw reference to her "penetrating intelligence," "extraordinary personality," and "brilliant career." "China's Near Tragedy," *New York Times*, April 8, 1937. An article in the *New York Times Magazine* of November 7, 1937, stated, "Madame Chiang is constantly proving her extraordinary abilities. She is wise in many of the ways of two worlds, for her Chinese background has been livened with a foreign perspective acquired through years of study in America. She is easily the world's most powerful woman." The *Times* speculated that she might have an even more extraordinary political role to play for her country. "It is quite within the realm of probability that this little Chinese woman will become the real leader of China in the event her husband is incapacitated." Anthony Billingham, "The Man and The Woman Whom China Obeys," *New York Times Magazine*, November 7, 1937, p. 7. Such coverage continued well into the war. An April 18, 1943, article titled "China's Leaders Speak," states, "In her speech as you can detect some of the ingredients that make Madame Chiang one of

the world's most outstanding women. She cherishes her ideals and her principles and her love of mankind. She represents the liberal thinking people of all countries. She and the Generalissimo combine to make the perfect couple who seem almost a legend." Helen Kuo, "China's Leaders Speak," *New York Times*, April 18, 1943, p. 68.

90. At that point, the China Lobby was not the potent force it would soon become (Accinelli, p. 7).

91. Kevin Peraino, *A Force So Swift: Mao, Truman, and the Birth of Modern China 1949* (New York: Crown Publishing Group, 2017), p. 81.

92. Li, p. 302.

93. Ibid. Chinese law professor Rao Geiping depicts the role, strategies, and objectives of the China Lobby.

"They took advantage of the differences between the Republican and Democratic parties over China policy and made efforts outside normal diplomatic channels. . . . Their goal was not only to encourage US aid to Chiang but also to discriminate against those who held realistic views on Chinese affairs. In so doing they relied on the KMT's broad social connections in America. . . . Madame Chiang summoned important KMT members in America to her headquarters in H. H. Kung's residence in New York every week to design strategy and organize a public relations campaign, and she bypassed the embassy to contact Chiang directly. . . . The China lobby's role in Chinese-US relations should not be neglected."

Rao Geiping, "The Kuomintang Government's Policy Toward the United States, 1945–1949," in Harry Harding and Yuan Ming, Eds., *Sino-American Relations 1945–1955: A Joint Assessment of a Critical Decade* (Wilmington, DE: Scholarly Resources, 1989), p. 56.

94. Fairbank, *The Great Chinese Revolution*, p. 268.

95. Taylor, p. 397.

96. Chiang's biographer, Jay Taylor, recounts that Mao told Stalin of his concern that the United States would rally to support acting president Li, potentially with a combination of atomic weapons and Japanese troops. Taylor writes, "Stalin was not worried. Through his British spies Kim Philby and others, he had a good sense of the likely range of Anglo-American policies in China—and such an intervention was not being mentioned in Washington, not even by the Generalissimo's most ardent supporters in the 'China Lobby'" (Taylor, p. 398).

97. "Chiang had also sent 300,000 of his best soldiers, twenty-six gunboats of the Chinese navy, and the entire Chinese air force to Taiwan. Although 900,000 soldiers remained on the mainland, only 120,000 of these belonged to Li's old partner General Pai and could thus be relied on by the Acting President. Chiang had taken away everything from General Li except the ability to make peace, honorably or dishonorably, with the Communists" (Pakula, p. 571).

98. After the generalissimo's death in 1975, Ching-kuo would succeed him in the presidency.

99. Ambassador Stuart depicts Chiang's crisis. "The government had been steadily losing popular support on even respect. As the communist forces advanced in the victorious March toward the Yangtze River, the grandiose plans for defense crumbled amid political bickering, desertions, or betrayals, [and] disorderly retreats" (Ibid., p. 242).

100. Nanjing was the capital of Nationalist China from 1927 to 1937, after which Chiang abandoned it in the face of Japanese assaults. In 1946, after the war, he reestablished the capital at Nanjing, where it remained until 1949.

101. Hutchins, pp. 131–152.

102. In her radio address, Madame declared, "Already the moral weaklings are forsaking us. It is with a heavy heart that I note former ally, Britain, which sacrificed millions of lives on the altar of freedom, has now been taken by its leaders into the wilderness of political intrigue. Britain has bartered the soul of a nation for a few pieces of silver. I say, 'for shame' to Britain." "Mme. Chiang Vows Long War on Reds in Goodbye to US," *New York Times*, January 9, 1950, p. A1.

103. Li, p. 318.

104. Jung Chang notes that her arrival in Taiwan was a huge morale booster at a time when there was widespread belief there that the Nationalists could not hold out. People who had the means to leave were attempting to do so. Instead, Mei-ling did not stay in the United States and joined her husband on the island (Chang, p. 246).

105. "China policy after Acheson took charge at the State Department was fluid, provisional, and ridden with conflicting purposes. Anticipating the impending Kuomintang defeat, the department chose not to cut all American links with Chiang, but instead to distance the United States from his doomed government, narrow the conduit of aid, and retain freedom of action in China. The American posture toward the Chinese Communists was neither actively accommodationist nor unreservedly hostile" (Accinelli, pp. 5–6).

106. Testimony of John Paton Davies, p. 36.

107. David M. Oshinsky, who has chronicled McCarthy career, writes that

"services days in government were numbered. In 1951, the Civil Service Loyalty Review Board declared him a loyalty risk, and Atchison quickly dropped the axe. The reason, ostensibly, was the *Amerasia* affair. But that was a smokescreen. In the following months, other China hands who had nothing to do with *Amerasia*, were also dismissed. What they had in common was a vision that Chiang would lose in China that America would be wise to adjust its policies accordingly. When Chiang did lose come his supporters raised the angry cries of sellout and treason. In Joe McCarthy, they found the perfect instrument of revenge."

David M. Oshinsky, *A Conspiracy So Immense: The World of Joe McCarthy* (New York: Oxford University Press, 2005), p. 129.

108. Stephen Kinzer, *The Brothers: John Foster Dulles, Allen Dulles, and Their Secret World War* (New York: Henry Holt and Company, 2013), p. 143.

109. Richard H. Immerman, *John Foster Dulles: Piety, Pragmatism, and Power in US Foreign Policy* (Wilmington, DE: Scholarly Resources, Inc., 1999), p. 118.

110. Mao had hoped to visit sooner, making several overtures to do so in 1948, as he drew closer to winning the civil war. However, Stalin deflected him, finally sending Soviet Politburo member, Anastas Mikoyan, to China at the end of 1948 for consultations (Shen, p. 69). These consultations reinforced Mao's view that close ties to the Soviet Union would be essential to survival of a Chinese Communist government. "We cannot imagine being without the Soviet Union," Mao told his party in March 1949 (Ibid., p. 76). "The Secretary had no desire to share the fate of his

Democratic predecessor, whom the Republican right had pilloried. . . . Scrupulously attentive to the political and public relations facets of his job, je constantly kept an ear cocked for the thunder on the right" (Accinelli, p. 113).

111. Immerman, p. 91.

112. Plokhy, pp. 216–220.

113. "From Finland through the three Baltic states to Eastern Europe, and then from the Near East to Mongolia, onto Northeastern China and the northern part of the Korean Peninsula, and to the islands north of Japan, Stalin had achieved Russia's longstanding strategic goal of building broad national security buffer zones all around it" (Shen, p. 19).

114. "Record of Conversation between I.V. Stalin and Chairman of the Central People's Government of the People's Republic of China Mao Zedong on 16 December 1949," www.digitalarchive.wilsoncenter.org.

115. "Mao found particularly insulting Stalin's refusal to conclude an official intergovernmental treaty with him because Stalin felt that his existing treaty with the Guomindang regime was adequate. This latter treaty, it will be recalled, was an unequal treaty that disfavored the Chinese side and was very advantageous for the USSR." Alexander V. Pantsov and Steven I. Levine, *Mao: The Real Story* (New York: Simon & Schuster, 2012), p. 371.

116. "Cable, Mao Zedong to Liu Shaochi on the First Meeting with Stalin, December 18, 1949," www.digitalarchives.wilsoncenter.org.

117. Shen, p. 93.

118. June Chang and Jon Halliday, *Mao: The Unknown Story* (New York: Alfred A. Knopf, 2005), p. 352.

119. "Mao was now satisfied, but still he could not restrain himself from registering his 'surprise' at Stalin's decision. 'But changing this agreement goes against the decisions of the Yalta Conference?!' he noted, not without malice, reminding Stalin of the very argument Stalin himself had used to object to signing the treaty with the PRC. 'True it does' Stalin replied, 'and to hell with it'" (Pantsov and Levine, pp. 371–372).

120. "Cable, Mao Zedong to the Central Committee of the CCP, January 2, 1950," www.digitalarchives.wilsoncenter.org. Zhou was then Premier as well as Foreign Minister.

121. Ibid.

122. On February 28, 1947, protests and rioting broke out in Taipei against Nationalist rule and soon spread elsewhere on the island. Recounting the circumstances, Thomas J. Shattuck of the Foreign Policy Research Institute wrote in 2017,

"Though a vibrant and thriving democracy today, the Republic of China (Taiwan) was once a nation plagued with corruption, mass violence, and totalitarian rule. In Taiwan, the period immediately following the 228 Incident is known as the "White Terror" for the massive suppression, murder, and imprisonment of political dissidents, or anyone who the Kuomintang (KMT), known as Nationalists in English, perceived as a threat to its one-party rule. The Martial Law that was implemented in the aftermath of the incident was not lifted until 1987.The story of the 228 Incident—named after the day on which the terror began, February 28—can be traced back to 1945 and the rampant dissatisfaction that local

Taiwanese had for the governing officials of the Republic of China after the end of World War II. The Kuomintang controlled the island while the party engaged in a war against the communists and Mao Zedong."

Thomas J. Shattuck, "Taiwan's White Terror: Remembering the 228 Incident," www.fpri.org (accessed April 21, 2022). See also Nicholas D. Kristof, "The Horror of 2–28: Taiwan Rips Open the Past," *New York Times*, April 3, 1992, p. A4. Bianco explains that the turmoil in Taiwan caused disaffection among the intelligentsia on the mainland, where Chiang was still in control but under severe Communist pressure (Bianco, p. 192).

123. Edward F. Chen, "Battle of Guningtou: The Republic of China Fights for Survival," www.warfarehistorynetwork.com (accessed June 30, 2022).

124. By then, there had been vast sunk costs. John King Fairbank cites, "United States A to China between VJ Day and early 1948 cost over $2 billion, in addition to some billion and a half committed during World War Two" (Fairbank, p. 311).

125. Tucker, pp. 184–185.

126. Ibid., p. 188.

127. The origin of Truman's statement was a January 3 meeting with Acheson and other senior advisers. State drafted Truman's statement, which the president modified after taking into account the views of JCS chairman Omar Bradley. "To satisfy Bradley, who wanted to retain enough elbow room to sever Taiwan from the mainland under wartime conditions, the president had consented to insert the qualifying words 'at his time' as well as to excise language in the State Department's original version that disavowed any desire to detach Formosa from China" (Accinelli, pp. 13–14).

128. Tucker remarks, "Not only had the President of the United States asserted that American troops would not be sent to preserve the Nationalist's hold on Taiwan, but Truman had also acknowledged in his remarks that Taiwan belonged under Chinese control" (Tucker, p. 55). A Senate Staff Study notes that the Joint Chiefs, the China Lobby, and pro-Chiang members of Congress disliked this policy and wanted to do something more active for the Nationalists. "The United States and Communist China in 1949 and 1950: The Question of Rapprochement and Recognition: A Staff Study, Committee on Foreign Relations United States Senate" (Washington, DC: US Government Printing Office, 1973), p. 6.

129. Truman would permit release of $9 million in unexpended military aid but offer no new military aid (Ibid., p. 186). Of Dean Acheson, Foster Rhea Dulles writes, "No one could have been more fully convinced in 1949 that any further military assistance to the Nationalists would only prolong the war already lost and arouse among the people desirous for peace a deep resentment against the United States" (Foster Rhea Dulles, p. 33).

130. Harry S. Truman, "Statement on Formosa," 1950, china.usc.edu. The ECA was the Economic Cooperation Administration, originally established in 1948 to administer assistance under the Marshall Plan.

131. Walter Robertson notes that "In January 1950, the British recognized the Communist regime. They had $1,200,000,000 property values in China. . . . They hoped to save their property and establish a working position with the Chinese" (Robertson, pp. 48–49).

132. Former ambassador Karl Rankin said in his memoirs, "British action in 1950 to recognize Red China was taken, not to save the world, but in response to British and Commonwealth political and economic interests" (Rankin, p. 237).

133. Tucker, p. 24.

134. See Hutchings, pp. 65–68. The PRC did not disturb the Crown Colony, which reverted to Chinese control only in 1997. Britain's perpetual rights to Hong Kong Island had proved impractical to maintain in the absence of other parts of the Crown Colony that were subject to an expiring time-limited lease.

135. "The British had closed the border in 1950 after some 3 million people from China headed for Hong Kong, seeking sanctuary from war and revolution. More than 100,000 had crossed the small bridge at Lo Wu every day at the peak of the exodus in 1949." Michael Sheridan, *The Gate to China: A New History of the People's Republic and Hong Kong* (New York: Oxford University Press: 2021), pp. 40–41.

136. "China bloc Senators received their 'forewarning' on the day of Truman's statement. Even if unintentional, such an oversight aggravated worsening relations by reminding Congress of its powerlessness in the realm of foreign affairs" (Tucker, p. 164). Professor Robert Accinelli writes that Truman's January 5 statement failed to resolve national policy or to quiet partisan disagreement. Although the dissent was bitter and vocal, Truman's action was consistent with public opinion. "A poll taken in late January showed that 50 percent of a national sample approved of the President's decision not to send military assistance of Chiang Kai-shek while only 20 percent objected" (Accinelli, p. 15). This division of opinion would not hold up throughout the remainder of 1950. The Korean War began in June. China entered the war in October, and public opinion hardened against the Communists (Accinelli, p. 5).

137. "Corroborating these official declarations, and possibly of even more importance to the Chinese Communist analysis, a secret State Department guidance paper on Taiwan became public during January. The document indicated that the American government expected Taiwan's imminent fall and proposed to take no action to prevent it. Rather, authorities in Washington urged their foreign service representatives abroad to minimize Taiwan significance whenever opportunities for such propaganda statements allowed" (Tucker, p. 56).

138. According to Professor Shen Zhihua, relying upon high-level Soviet sources, Acheson's speech affected Stalin's attitude about North Korea's invasion plans. Reluctant to approve the attack because he feared American intervention, Stalin changed his mind (Shen, p. 122).

139. "Remarks by Dean Acheson before the National Press Club, January 12, 1950," www.trumanlibrary.gov.

140. Taylor, p. 425.

141. Jessup's attitude was reflected in a letter he wrote on December 8, 1949, to Senator H. Alexander Smith, in which he stated, "Whether or not one believes that we should return to a policy of using withholding of recognition as an indication of disapproval, the history of the matter seems to me to make it clear that such a policy is not effective unless there is a very high degree of cooperation with other governments interested" (Senate Staff Study, p. 1).

142. Ibid., p. 7.

143. Robertson, pp. 74–75. Sentiment in Congress was also strongly opposed. Foster Rhea Dulles comments that "against the desire wholly to disengage from the civil war by accepting the legitimacy of the People's Republic stood all the forces not only of anti-Communism but of tradition, sentiment, and loyalty to a wartime ally" (Foster Rhea Dulles, p. 60). In a 1966 oral history for Princeton University, former Indian ambassador to the United States Gaganvihari Mehta surmised that if China had not intervened in the Korean War, it was probable that the United States would have recognized the Beijing government and that the PRC would have been admitted to the United Nations. Oral History of Gaganvihari Lallubhai Mehta, Princeton University Library, p. 10. http:/arks.princeton.edu/ark:/88435/02871214 (accessed December 27, 2020).

144. These hopes were not realized, at least in the early years of the alliance. A US National Intelligence Estimate of September 10, 1952, noted that "Communist China and the USSR present a united front to the world. Since the establishment of the Chinese Communist regime in 1949 there has been no reliable indication that either country has adopted any important course of action without the consent of the other." Looking ahead in a two-year window, the NIE concluded that neither Western concessions nor pressure would "disrupt Sino-Soviet solidarity" during the period. *Foreign Relations of the United States, 1952–1954, Vol. XIV, China and Japan, Part 1*, pp. 97–101. The Korean War foreclosed this thinking. "Although he had hoped to extend diplomatic recognition to Peking, circumstances no longer permitted advances toward a Communist power" (Tucker, p. 204).

145. David Allan Mayers, *Cracking the Monolith: US Policy Against the Sino-Soviet Alliance, 1949–1955* (Baton Rouge, LA: Louisiana State University Press, 1986), p. 16. Serving as consul general in Hong Kong, Karl Rankin cabled the State Department on November 16, 1949, to disabuse it of such hopes. "The only expectations upon which the United States is warranted in basing its Far Eastern policy are that the Communists will control China for a long time to come, that they will follow Russian direction at least in foreign relations, and that they will constitute a highly dangerous influence in the affairs of their neighbors to the east and south" (Rankin, p. 36).

146. Senate Staff Study, p. 3. The study quotes NSC 48/2, issued December 30, 1949, which states, "The United States should exploit, through appropriate political, psychological, and economic means, any rifts between the Chinese Communists and the USSR, and between the Stalinists and other elements in China, while scrupulously avoiding the appearance of intervention" (Senate Staff Study, p. 5).

147. Senate Staff Study, p. 7. See also the 1974 oral history of former US diplomat John Wesley Jones, who served in Nanjing under Ambassador Stuart. Oral History Interview with John Wesley Jones, June 8, 1974, LBJ Library, www.discoverlbj.org (accessed July 1, 2022).

148. Huang Hua and Li Xicabing (Translator), "My Contacts with John Leighton Stuart After Nanjing's Liberation," *Chinese Historians*, 5:1, 47–56, DOI: 10.1080/1043643x, 1992,11876866.

149. Robert Blum, *Drawing the Line: The Origin of American Containment Policy in East Asia* (New York: W.W. Norton, 1982), p. 55. In November 1948, the

Communists overran Mukden (Shenyang) in Manchuria and proceeded to hold the American Consul General Angus Ward and his staff incommunicado for over a year, before deporting them at the end of 1949. This was the most egregious action within a general atmosphere of hostility. They also refused to honor the diplomatic credentials of diplomats, like Ward, who had been accredited to the KMT government. However, they did not accord the same treatment to Soviet diplomats. Professor Chen Jian comments that the CCP's treatment of Ward and his staff "reflected the party leadership's determination to 'make a fresh start' in China's external relations, which required the party to 'clean the house before entertaining guests.' As well as to 'lean to one side' (the side of the Soviet Union)." Chen Jian, *Mao's China and the Cold War* (Chapel Hill, NC: University of North Carolina Press, 2001), p. 40. Referencing the Ward case, Foster Rhea Dulles observes, "In this incident and such later actions as the seizure of our consular properties in Peking, the Chinese Communists appeared to be doing everything possible to humiliate the United States." Of Mao, Dulles adds, "Instead of smoothing the way toward foreign recognition, he was far more interested in these symbolic acts of retribution for all the indignities China had suffered in the past at the hands of foreigners" (Foster Rhea Dulles, p. 52).

150. Huang, p. 52. Chen Jian observes, "In retrospect, these two conditions were impossible for the Americans to meet. . . . Indeed, reflected in Mao's perception of 'equality' was a profound Chinese 'victim mentality.' When Mao pointed out that Sino-American relations had been dominated by a series of unequal treaties since China's defeat in the Opium War of 1839–42, he revealed a deep-rooted belief that in a moral sense the United States and other Western powers owed the Chinese a heavy historical debt" (Chen, p. 42).

151. Tucker, p. 47.

152. Huang, p. 55.

153. Ibid., pp. 61–62. "Not just any price for recognition was acceptable to the Communists, especially if payment jeopardized recent achievements won by prolonged, arduous struggle. To emphasize the point, CCP representative Huang Hua told the ambassador that it would be up to Washington when the appropriate time arrived to make the first move in establishing relations with the People's Democratic Government; at the same time, however, Huang displayed a lively interest in American recognition of Communist China on terms of equality and mutual benefit" (Mayers, p. 44). While eager to pull away from the Nationalists, Truman was not yet ready to embrace the Communists and to face criticism on Capitol Hill for moving too quickly (Tucker, p. 174). Nevertheless, before the Korean War, Secretary of State Acheson kept the door to recognition open.

154. Quoted in Tang Tsou, *America's Failure in China, Vol. 2* (Chicago, IL: University of Chicago Press, 1963), p. 505.

155. From *Sources of Chinese Tradition: From 1600 Through the Twentieth Century*, compiled by Wm. Theodore de Bary and Richard Lufrano, 2nd ed., vol. 2 (New York: Columbia University Press, 2000), pp. 452–453.

156. Tsou, p. 505.

157. Tucker notes that "deep-seated hostility against the imperialists stood as a barrier to relations. The capitalists, many party leaders believed, would never treat

them equally and simply wanted Chinese riches to prevent the impending collapse of Western civilization. . . . Ideological imperatives also persuaded some Chinese Communist leaders that cooperation with the West, and most especially the United States, could not be countenanced" (Tucker, p. 42). Among problems the United States identified were the refusal of the Communists to adhere to all international agreements the Nationalists had concluded and the Communists' refusal to recognize continuing diplomatic status of foreign representatives then in China.

    158. Blum, p. 64.

    159. Senate Staff Study, p. 11.

    160. Blum, p. 68. Peking University professor Wang Jisi discusses Communist China's deliberate attempt to decouple itself from Western influence. "The CCP's rise to power in 1949 wiped out US political, economic, and cultural ties to the Chinese mainland. In response to Washington's effort to contain and isolate China, Beijing forged an alliance with Moscow and soon found itself directly fighting the United States during the Korean War. At around that time, the CCP waged an ideological campaign to rid educated Chinese of the mindset of 'being pro-America, fearing America, and worshipping America.'" Wang Jisi, "The Plot Against China? How Beijing Sees the New Washington Consensus," *Foreign Affairs*, July/August 2021.

    161. Chen Jian, p. 43.

    162. Huang, p. 56. In 1970, before the thaw in China-US relations, historian Foster Rhea Dulles explained a deeply rooted truth that underpinned China's deep skepticism of the West. "Wholly apart from today's conflict between communism and democracy, the clash of two antithetical economic and political systems, is the traditional Chinese resentment of the West and anti-imperialism that has always been directed against this country as well as the European powers. This has been a stronger force than the surface ties of friendship. A great deal in the past helps to explain why the Communists were so successful in 1949 in arousing in the Chinese people and almost fanatic hostility toward the United States" (Foster Rhea Dulles, p. 7).

    163. Stuart died in the United States in 1962. In his will, he said he wished to be buried in China, where he was born. That was not possible at the time. His ashes were interred in Hangzhou, China, in 2008.

    164. In his essay, Mao says of Stuart, "John Leighton Stuart, who was born in China in 1876, was always a loyal agent of US cultural aggression in China." As well, he writes, "Leighton Stuart is a symbol of the complete defeat of the US policy of aggression. Leighton Stuart is an American born in China; he has fairly wide social connections and spent many years running missionary schools in China, he once sat in a Japanese jail during the War of Resistance; he used to pretend to love both the United States and China and was able to deceive quite a number of Chinese." Mao Zedong, "Farewell, Leighton Stuart!" *Selected Works of Mao Zedong*, www.marxists .org (accessed March 9, 2022).

    165. Ibid. Stuart left China quietly and returned to the United States. He died in Washington in 1962, expressing in his will a desire to be buried in China, where his wife and parents were also buried. For 46 years his wish went unheeded. Finally, in 2008, after negotiations between General John Fugh, the son of Philip Fugh, and Zhejiang Province Communist Party leader Xi Jinping, permission was granted

for burial in China. Stuart was buried in Hangzhou on November 17, 2008. David Barboza, "John Leighton Stuart, China Expert, Is Buried There At Last," *New York Times*, November 19, 2008, www.nytimes.com (accessed July 1, 2022).

166. See He Di, "The Evolution of the Chinese Communist Party's Policy Toward the United States, 1944–1949," in Harry Harding and Yuan Ming, Eds., *Sino-American Relations 1945–1955: A Joint Assessment of a Critical Decade* (Wilmington, DE: Scholarly Resources, 1989), pp. 31–50.

167. Chen Jian writes, "Mao and his comrades never regarded the Communist seizure of power in China in 1949 as the revolution's conclusion. Rather Mao was very much concerned about how to maintain and enhance the revolution's momentum after its nationwide victory. . . . While defining the American threat, Mao and his fellow CCP leaders never limited their vision merely to the possibility of direct American military intervention in China; they emphasized long range American hostility toward the victorious Chinese revolution especially the US imperialist attempt to isolate the revolution from without and to sabotage it from within" (Chen, pp. 47–48).

168. Mao's concern about conspiracies by counterrevolutionaries was hardly unique. Similar rationales drove formation of the Cheka secret police after the 1917 Bolsheviks seizure of power in the Soviet Union in 1917, and later haunted Stalin. Fear of foreign intervention proved realistic, with invasion by anti-Bolshevik European and American forces following the revolution. Other revolutionaries, from those in France at the end of the eighteenth century to Cuba in the 1960s, faced similar concerns and pursued strategies ranging from preemptive war to superpower protection schemes to ward off opposition.

169. *FRUS 1952–1953, Vol. XIV China and Japan, Part 1*, p. 297.

170. Tong, p. 179.

171. With the defeat of Japan, which had occupied Korea since 1910, the United States and the Soviet Union took responsibility of securing the Korean Peninsula. Soviet forces occupied the northern half, while American troops occupied the southern half. Over the next few years, each of the major powers installed local regimes friendly to their interests. Kim Il Sung headed North Korea and Syngman Rhee led South Korea. Each hoped to unify the peninsula under his own leadership. The Republic of Korea, headed by Rhee, was established on August 15, 1948. The Democratic People's Republic of Korea, headed by Kim, was founded on September 10, 1948.

172. Peraino, p. 264. In 1949 discussions, Mao encouraged Kim to proceed with an invasion in early 1950, but then asked him to defer so as not to distract attention and resources from the invasion of Taiwan, set to occur at about the same time. Stalin clarified for Kim that the Soviets would provide logistical support, but not combat intervention. Troops, he said, would have to come from Mao (Taylor, p. 427, Peraino, p. 264). Once the North Korean invasion was launched, Mao deferred the proposed assault against Taiwan until 1951 (Li, p. 328). By that time, the issue was moot, because Truman had ordered the Seventh Fleet into the Taiwan Strait.

173. Shen, p. 41.

174. Peraino, p. 264.

175. Ibid., p. 124.

176. Schram, p. 264.

177. Ibid., p. 159. However, Stalin influenced the war. As a 1952 US National Intelligence Estimate noted, "the Korean War appears to be directed from joint Sino-Soviet military headquarters. The Chinese Communists are undoubtedly strongly influenced by Soviet military advisors, and it is probable that no major decisions are made in the Korean War without Soviet approval." *FRUS, 1952–1954, Vol. XIV, China and Japan, Part 1*, p. 100.

178. van de Ven, p. 257.

179. On July 9, 1971, during his first trip to China, Dr. Henry Kissinger spoke to Premier Zhou Enlai about the effect of this portentous moment. "There's no question that if the Korean War hadn't occurred, a war which we did not seek and you did not seek, Taiwan would probably be today a part of the PRC. For reasons that are now worthless to recapitulate, a previous Administration linked the future of Korea to the future of Taiwan, partly because of US domestic opinion at the time." *Foreign Relations of the United States, 1969–1976, Vol. XVII, China 1969–1972*, p. 368.

180. *Foreign Relations of the United States, 1950, Korea, Vol. VII*, p. 161. Foster Rhea Dulles, p. 94. Chen Jian notes that, at approximately the same time, the Nationalists broke up a CCP spy network on Formosa, weakening the chance that an amphibious invasion force could join up with a CCP-inspired local insurrection (Chen, p. 166). At an August 31, 1950, press conference, Truman implied that if the Korean War was settled, there would be no further reason for the Seventh Fleet to protect Taiwan. This fostered alarm in Taipei, which was already uncertain about its future (Rankin, pp. 54–55). Truman made the decision to use the Seventh Fleet for this purpose at a Blair House meeting on the evening of June 25. Accinelli notes, "this recommendation for neutralization of the Strait—the idea that John Foster Dulles and Dean Atchison had first put forward to previous month—emerged from the deliberations of State, Defense, and intelligence officials who had been working on the crisis. Acheson's endorsement was critical because of the weight his views carried with the president" (Accinelli, p. 30). Accinelli further notes, "In deciding to seal off Taiwan by military means, Truman and Acheson did not intend to take Chaing Kai-shek again under the American wing. The salvation of the Generalissimo and the Kuomintang was a byproduct of the intervention, not one of its purposes" (Accinelli, p. 32).

181. "Once US air and naval forces were bound for Korea, it became urgent to protect the southern flank of the military operation and to prevent hostilities from spreading beyond the peninsula" (Accinelli, p. 31).

182. "In the face of this new development, Mao declared angrily that the American president had proved his own previous statements about not intervening in Taiwan to be fraudulent and the United States had thus 'openly exposed its own imperialist face'" (Schram, p. 264). "The Chinese Communists remained convinced we had no purpose other than to thwart their rightful goal of liberating the one part of Chinese territory still remaining in Nationalist hands" (Foster Rhea Dulles, p. 97). Alan D. Romberg of the Stimson Center writes that the PRC never reconciled itself to Truman's order, much less to the US-ROC Mutual Defense Treaty that followed it a half-decade later. "The PRC believes that President Truman's 1950 intervention order to the Seventh Fleet, and the later creation of a US military alliance with Taipei, were

solely responsible for blocking reunification, and that the United States thus owes China a debt" (Romberg, p. 8).

183. Rudy Abramson, *Spanning the Century: The Life of W. Averell Harriman* (New York: William Morrow and Company, Inc., 1992), p. 449.

184. Rankin, p. 155.

185. Rankin believed that the public had a misimpression about the role the Seventh Fleet played during the Korean conflict. "Not infrequently during the Korean War no American naval vessel was seen within several hundred miles of Taiwan" (Ibid., pp. 83–84). See also Foster Rhea Dulles, p. 94.

186. Ibid., p. 24.

187. Ibid. In his memoirs, Rankin described a message to State of August 18, 1950. "I suggested that a policy of avoiding long term commitments could be interpreted by the Chinese Government as indicating our intention to continue to support only until the Korean War was over and a treaty concluded with Japan. Then we might be expected to recognize the Chinese Communists, who would be free to cut the throats of the political and military leaders who had collaborated with us on Taiwan" (Ibid., p. 49).

188. Two years later, the JCS assessed and reaffirmed Truman's decision. In a memo to Secretary of Defense Robert Lovett, they asserted that the United States should "continue that part of the mission presently assigned to the 7th Fleet relative to the protection of Formosa until such time as conditions in the Far East permit the Chinese Nationalists on Formosa to assume the burden of the defense of that island." Office of the Historian, US Department of State, *FRUS, 1952–1954, Vol. XIV, China and Japan, Part 1*, p. 16.

189. Accinelli, p. 53.

190. US officials reacted angrily to the Chinese intervention. "They faced a formidable new foe who, in their judgment, had contemptuously challenged American power and UN authority. They could find no extenuating circumstances for what they looked upon as a blatant act of aggression by a compliant Soviet proxy" (Ibid., p. 55).

191. United Nations, *Yearbook of the United Nations*, 1951, pp. 225–226. Senator Knowland later pointed out that Congress had prodded the UN action by passing resolutions in the House on January 19 and the Senate on January 21. The resolutions are nearly identical. The Senate resolution stated, "It is the sense of the Senate that the United Nations should immediately declare Communist China an aggressor in Korea" (*Congressional Record*, March 6, 1953, p. 1973).

192. Accinelli, p. 68.

193. Tucker, pp. 195–196. Two decades later, this reversal and its effect on the status of Formosa remained an open wound in US-China relations, barring a path to normalization until it was closed. On July 9, 1971, at Dr. Henry Kissinger's first meeting with Premier Zhou Enlai, the premier referenced it within minutes after the session convened. Speaking of the early days after the People's Republic was founded, Zhou said,

"At the time, the US government considered this an internal affair of China. This was during the period of 1949 to the beginning of 1950. By then, Taiwan was already restored to the motherland, and China was that motherland. The US stated that it had no territorial ambitions regarding Taiwan or any other Chinese territories. And, therefore, the U S declared that it wouldn't interfere in China's internal affairs and would leave the Chinese people to settle internal questions. This attitude was proclaimed in all your documents of that time, although some documents adopted an attitude hostile to us—you wouldn't agree that the Chinese Communist party was leading a new China, but you couldn't do anything about it. Therefore, you made a statement that you would not interfere in China's internal affairs. Within a short period afterwards, the Korean War broke out and you surrounded Taiwan and declared the status of Taiwan was still unsettled. Even up to the present day the spokesman of your State Department says that this is your position. That is the crux. If this crucial question is not solved, then the whole question will be difficult to resolve." (*FRUS 1969–1976, Vol. XVII, China 1969–1972,* pp. 366–367)

194. Some of the Nationalist "pinpricks" were done with CIA collaboration through a front known as Western Enterprises, Inc., which was officially headquartered in Pittsburgh. Nationalist aviators flew on "Black Bat" missions to gather intelligence and sow dissension in mainland China. The program was particularly active during the Korean conflict. See "Black Bats-CIA Connection Emerges," April 4, 2008, www .npr.org (accessed July 4, 2022). "One form of harassment that the United States already practiced was the covert program of coastal raids by the Nationalists carried out under the auspices of the COA's front organization, Western Enterprises. This program, had, however become stagnant by the spring of 1954 because the raids had proven unproductive" (Accinelli, p. 138).

195. Karl Rankin, then Chargè in the Republic of China, spoke to Chiang on October 25, 1952, about the generalissimo's proposal to send ROC troops to Korea. Rankin reported to State, "answering query re: utility of sending ChiNat troops to Korea, Generalissimo said it wld provide valuable training for them and encourage surrenders of ChiCom troops. He did not believe it cld contribute decisively to the course of events in Korea" (Office of the Historian, US Department of State, Ibid., p. 113). "The troops being tendered were of uncertain quality and inadequately equipped, and the Joint Chiefs felt that they were better employed defending Taiwan" (Accinelli, p. 39).

196. Miller, p. 274. The matter was quite actively discussed between the Department of State and the Department of Defense. One such interchange took place on August 19, 1952, at the Pentagon. Secretary of Defense Robert Lovett stated that "we have been working to see what means we could find to relieve the demands on US troops in Korea. There is a proposal . . . that we have under consideration which calls for the equipment of two Chinese Nationalist divisions to be used in one of several areas." Under Secretary of State David Bruce was highly negative. "We feel our allies would oppose the use of Chinese Nationalists in Korea, and the Asians generally would be strongly opposed to their use." Bruce continued, "We would anticipate no difficulty in getting Chiang's consent to use them in Korea or elsewhere. We would have difficulty with our allies. We have a very strong view that it would be injudicious to approach Chiang" (*FRUS, 1952–1954, Vol. XIV, China and Japan, Part 1,* pp. 88–89).

197. Miller, pp. 273–274.

198. The first members of the Military Advisory Group arrived in May 1951. It was a tenuous beginning. "An undercurrent of mistrust, even outright anti-Americanism,

was reportedly present at senior levels of the government and armed forces" (Accinelli, p. 91).

199. *FRUS, 1952–1954, Vol. XIV, China and Japan, Part 1*, pp. 117–118. On January 2, 1953, secretary of state-designate Dulles spoke with Nationalist Chinese foreign minister George Yeh, who "said that his government did take a favorable view of sending its forces to Korea." Reinforcing Chiang's December comments to Rankin, Yeh told Dulles that a sound strategy was to hold Formosa first rather than to disperse forces to other theaters (Ibid., pp. 125–126).

200. Ibid., pp. 119–120. "State Department representatives remonstrated that UN allies and most Asian nations would oppose the insertion of Nationalist troops into the conflict, and that using them would wipe out any chance of an armistice" (Accinelli, p. 107).

201. In December 1936, Mao's Communists were on the verge of extinction at the hands of the Nationalists. However, Chiang's commanders insisted that he confront Japanese forces, which had occupied Manchuria and were menacing China south of the Great Wall. Chiang called off the campaign against Mao, joining with him in a shaky united front against Japan. It may thus be said that Japanese aggression saved Mao and that North Korean aggression saved Chiang.

202. The chiefs continued, "For the foreseeable future, and until conditions in the Far East have become peaceful and stable, the United States should take such measures as may be necessary to deny Formosa to any Chinese regime aligned with or dominated by the USSR" (*FRUS, 1952–1954, Vol. XIV, China and Japan, Part 1*, p. 16).

203. Vice President Richard Nixon spoke to this point in a December 23, 1953, oral report he made to the National Security Council. Nixon had recently returned from a four-week trip to Asia, including four days on Formosa. As to Nationalist troops he commented, "I would say morale is tops, much better than I had any idea. They are being sustained by the hope of return to the mainland in a military action" (*FRUS, 1952–1954, Vol. XIV, China and Japan, Part 1*, p. 347).

204. *FRUS, 1952–1954, Vol. XIV, China and Japan, Part 1*, p. 39.

205. Accinelli notes, "The Paramount American interest in Taiwan lay in the strategic advantage derived from retaining access to the island as a potential wartime base for U.S. military operations, while foreclosing its military exploitation by the Soviet Union, particularly in the event of hostilities" (Accinelli, p. 8).

206. *FRUS, 1952–1954, Vol. XIV, China and Japan, Part 1*, p. 39.

207. Ibid., pp. 49–50.

208. Ibid., p. 50.

209. A pillar of the Republican foreign policy establishment and a special consultant to the State Department, John Foster Dulles was the lead negotiator for the United States. The Nationalists were chagrined at being excluded (Rankin, p. 110). According to New Zealand's foreign minister, Sir Thomas MacDonald, the San Francisco treaty generated formation of the ANZUS Treaty between Australia, New Zealand, and the United States. In his oral history at Princeton University, MacDonald said, "Well, out of the Japanese Treaty, of course, came the desire to form ANZUS. We didn't know how the Japanese were going to go. We felt that if their militaristic ideas came to

the surface again and were acted on, then obviously we had to have some reasonable guarantee that we had a friend or two around the Pacific, and ANZUS was the result" (MacDonald, p. 7). General Matthew Ridgway confirms this in his own oral history. "Mr. Dulles said that there had developed on the part of Australia and New Zealand an attitude of unwillingness to go along with the peace treaty which would not closely restrict the right of Japan to rearm unless Australia and New Zealand got an assurance that we would come to their aid if a rearmed Japan should attack them." Oral History, Matthew B. Ridgway, Princeton University Library, p. 25. http://arks.princeton.edu/ark:/88435/7d2790309 (accessed February 10, 2022).

210. Australia's ambassador to the United States, Sir Percy Spender, characterized Dulles's view that a generous and non-punitive treaty needed to be concluded with Japan. "Mr. Dulles view was, very definitely, that any treaty which sought to impose upon a defeated enemy conditions which were unduly restrictive and which, in the end, they would resent and throw aside, was dangerous, and therefore wisdom dictated that we should make a peace with them which would be a peace which would give them a sense of honor and . . . would not cause them to lose face." Oral History, Sir Percy Spender, Princeton University Library, p. 2. http://arks.princeton.edu/ark:/88435/6969z604f (accessed December 12, 2020).

211. Dewey writes, "After years of insults by our government and what he believes to be our abandonment of China after the war, the Generalissimo's feelings swept aside all argument. . . . The final exclusion of Free China from the Japanese treaty had again humiliated the government of China before the world; defeated Japan was to be allowed the power of the victor, to choose whether she would sign a peace treaty with her old enemy, the Nationalist government of China, which won the war, or with the Communist usurper, Mao Tse-tung" (Dewey, pp. 134–135). Rana Mitter observes that the PRC's exclusion was a casualty of the Korean War, which may have been a dispositive factor in preventing the normalization of relations between the United States and mainland China. "The 1951 Treaty of San Francisco, which was supposed to mark the final settlement of the war in Asia, excluded the People's Republic. But blame for this exclusion rests on both actors in the dispute. The United States refused to recognize Mao's regime, excluding an emergent power from a role in defining a regional settlement. And China, with Stalin's support, backed up North Korea in its attack on South Korea, making a swift settlement with the United States close to impossible" (Mitter, p. 223).

212. Oral History of Chiang Kai-shek and Madame Chiang Kai-shek, Princeton University Library, p. 4, http://arks.princeton.edu/ark:/88435/pc289q35m (accessed December 27, 2020), pp. 31–32.

213. It was not a given that the United States and Japan would ally in a security arrangement. Japan considered alternatives. Former Japanese foreign minister Katsuo Okazaki states in a 1964 oral history that the Japanese government under Prime Minister Shigeru Yoshida had considered a strategy of neutrality, but ultimately rejected it as impractical. "We prepared two different kinds of security systems. One was to write a security pact between the United States and Japan, as it is now. But Mr. Yoshida was very careful in those matters. He requested the Foreign Office to prepare some other kind of security system . . . that Japan adopt a complete neutral policy

with the understanding of the United States and Soviet Russia. . . . But, after all, it was not found feasible." Katsuo Okazaki Oral History, Princeton University Library, p. 4, http://arks.princeton.edu/ark:/88435/tb09jb93v (accessed December 27, 2020). Accinelli says of Yoshida, "His own preference, however, would have been to pursue diplomatic contacts with the Communist government rather than with Chiang's routed regime. . . . Yet he necessarily subordinated these views to the paramount objective of ending his country's prolonged occupation and aligning Japan with the predominant economic and military power of the United States" (Accinelli, p. 83).

214. Karl Rankin comments, "It was not easy to persuade President Chiang and the Legislative Yuan of the acceptability of a separate treaty. However, there were certain provisions of special interest to China and Japan which could not easily have been included in the multilateral agreement. This provided a face-saving device for China as well as possible practical advantages" (Rankin, p. 116).

215. Oral History of Chiang Kai-shek and Madame Chiang Kai-shek. Peace was also made easier by the Nationalists' postwar posture toward Japan. In Chiang's words, "Following Japan's unconditional surrender, the Chinese government with a view to re-establishing long-term friendly relations with Japan, immediately announced that it would adopt not a vengeful, but a magnanimous, policy of 'let bygones be bygones' toward Japan" (Ibid., p. 2). The Yoshida government in Japan received this very well. Foreign Minister Okazaki states, "We had very friendly feelings toward Nationalist China, especially we were grateful to Generalissimo Chiang Kai-shek when he declared at the end of the war that Chinese people should not revenge the Japanese people on what Japan did in the past" (Okazaki, p. 7).

Chapter 4

1953—A New Administration Arrives in Washington

As Dwight D. Eisenhower prepared to assume the presidency in 1953, he and his advisers considered revising Truman's mission for the Seventh Fleet. Under the proposed new orders, the fleet would continue to shield Formosa from the PRC but would cease to block Nationalist Chinese attacks against the mainland.

In a conversation on January 2, 1953, Secretary of State-designate John Foster Dulles previewed this shift for the Nationalists' Foreign Minister George Yeh. In a memorandum to Eisenhower about that conversation, Dulles wrote, "I told him that it was possible that the present instructions to the Seventh Fleet to defend the Chinese Communist mainland might be altered without altering their instructions to aid in the defense of Formosa."[1] Feeling unduly constrained by Truman's directive, Chiang welcomed the change. "I would say that the modification President Eisenhower introduced with regard to the functions or duties of the Seventh Fleet in the Taiwan Strait was definitely an improvement. The earlier arrangement whereby the Seventh Fleet would on one hand safeguard us from Communist attack and on the other hand guarantee the Chinese Communists against external attack was not a reasonable one."[2]

Immediately thereafter, Dulles and Eisenhower met in New York with British prime minister Winston Churchill.[3] A memo from the Executive Secretariat at the State Department reads, "Mr. Dulles said there was not a great deal of discussion about Formosa but that he had informed Mr. Churchill that the new administration would want to change the mission of the Seventh Fleet so as to take away the prohibition against any attack on the mainland as an adjunct to the Chinese Communists when they are attacking us."[4]

Concerned that the "unleashed" Nationalists would use the opportunity to launch attacks on the PRC, the British government was alarmed. London instructed its embassy to warn the State Department that abandoning Truman's policy of neutralizing the strait would have "great international political repercussions." The embassy made this representation on January 28.[5]

On January 30, 1953, US assistant secretary Allison informed the British that Eisenhower had decided to make the change anyway. "In no part of the world does the United States or any other of the free nations take action which in effect uses its armed forces to protect Communist territory," said Allison.[6]

Concurrently, acting secretary of state H. Freeman Matthews cabled Rankin in Taipei, requesting he seek an appointment with Chiang to convey the following message:

> President Eisenhower presently plans to announce in his State of the Union message February 2 that he is issuing instructions that the Seventh Fleet no longer is to be charged with shielding the mainland of China. The Seventh Fleet, however, will continue under present orders to prevent attack from the mainland on Formosa and the Pescadores. The President will also say that this order implies no aggressive intent on the part of the US. This action does not itself represent any change in the policies of the US Government concerning the extension of military and economic assistance to the Government of the Republic of China.

Rankin was instructed that Chiang must make no disclosure of the altered policy until Eisenhower publicly announced it. Moreover, he told Rankin to avoid giving implication that the United States was inviting Taipei to request increased American military or economic assistance.[7]

Rankin met Chiang on January 31, 1953, then reported to State that the generalissimo received the plan well. "He is gratified," said Rankin, "by President Eisenhower's intent to take this 'judicious' step of great 'moral significance.'"[8]

General Douglas MacArthur chimed in, also on January 31, with a public statement that claimed Truman's decision had freed up Chinese troops to move from coastal areas to Korea and emboldened the PRC to enter the war. "It laid the basis for altering the localized character of the Korean conflict and set the stage for further involvements just as appeasement and indecisiveness have always done. The modification of the Seventh Fleet order should be supported by all loyal Americans who respective of party. It certainly is time for this change."[9]

London was far less sanguine about the revision, looking at the Nationalist government as a relic that could not survive unless propped up by the United States. Neither Churchill nor Attlee had been Chiang's advocate. On February 2, Foreign Secretary Anthony Eden made known British qualms. "Her Majesty's Government regret this decision which they consider will have unfortunate political repercussions particularly in the United Nations. They do not think that it will carry with it compensating military advantages or will help in any way towards a solution of the Korean conflict."[10] However, Eisenhower could not be turned around.[11]

The president announced the new policy in an address to a Joint Session of Congress on February 2, 1953. Eisenhower declared:

> In June 1950, following the aggressive attack on the Republic of Korea, the United States Seventh Fleet was instructed both to prevent attack upon Formosa and to ensure that Formosa should not be used as a base of operations against the Chinese Communist mainland.
>
> This has meant, in effect, that the United States Navy was required to serve as a defensive arm of Communist China. Regardless of the situation in 1950, since the date of that order the Chinese Communists have invaded Korea to attack the United Nations forces there. They have consistently rejected the proposals of the United Nations Command for an armistice. They recently joined with Soviet Russia in rejecting the armistice proposal sponsored in the United Nations by the Government of India. This proposal had been accepted by the United States and 53 other nations.
>
> Consequently, there is no longer any logic or sense in a condition that required the United States Navy to assume defensive responsibilities on behalf of the Chinese Communists, thus permitting those Communists, with greater impunity, to kill our soldiers and those of our United Nations allies in Korea.
>
> I am, therefore, issuing instructions that the Seventh Fleet no longer be employed to shield Communist China. This order implies no aggressive intent on our part. But we certainly have no obligation to protect a nation fighting us in Korea.[12]

Walter Robertson, who served as assistant secretary of state for Far Eastern Affairs, noted that apart from purely military considerations in the strait, the revised orders were intended to pressure Beijing to conclude the Korean conflict.[13] Also as part of that strategy, Eisenhower passed the word to China through British and Indian channels that he would not tolerate a protracted stalemate and was open to using nuclear weapons if necessary.[14]

In the congressional debate that immediately followed Eisenhower's speech, Democrats did not take exception to this policy change. However, several complained that the way Eisenhower had framed the issue was misleading. They argued that while Truman had undeniably protected Formosa from the Communists, Eisenhower left a distorted impression that protecting the PRC from the Nationalists had been equally important. Because Chiang lacked the capacity for major raids, Truman's order shielded the PRC from nothing consequential. Thus, said the Democrats, Eisenhower's change was more symbolic than substantial.[15]

In general, the "unleashing" of Chiang was well received in the press and in Congress, although it provoked early Senate discussion about what he would do with his newfound authority.[16] Senator John Sparkman (D-AL) noted that Chiang had disclaimed the need for US ground forces to recover the mainland, but not American naval and air capacity. "I do not believe that he could ever make a successful large-scale raid without such coverage," declared Sparkman. "If he cannot make a crossing without such United States protection, does the President intend to commit United States naval and air forces for this purpose?" Senator Herbert Lehman (D-NY) agreed that Chiang could not invade without "widespread and comprehensive support from the United States" and demanded that the American people and US allies should be advised of the implications of the new policy.[17] The scope of US obligations to Chiang would soon command much more attention in Congress.

DEEPER COORDINATION IN DEFENSE PLANNING

In anticipation of Eisenhower's address, Chiang and Rankin met on January 31. The generalissimo argued, and Rankin agreed, that defense planning between the United States and Nationalist China needed enhanced coordination.

Chiang addressed the vulnerability of Nationalist-held islands, just offshore from China. These involved two tiny groupings, each named from the largest island in its group: Quemoy [Kinmen] and Matsu [Mazu].[18] Being so proximate to the coast, they were highly vulnerable to PRC attack. At the same time, they served to connect the ROC to the mainland in ways that Formosa itself, 100 miles to the east, could not. The Nationalists would raise this concern often, hoping to include them within the protection of the Seventh Fleet. However, the Americans worried that Chiang was trigger-happy to renew combat with the Communists and that bringing Quemoy and Matsu within the protection of the Seventh Fleet made war with China more likely. Accordingly, Rankin made no commitments on the islands but did receive Chiang's commitment to initiate a policy of consulting MAAG-Formosa before launching any significant attacks on Communist-held territory.

In his memoirs, Rankin noted that Chiang wishfully interpreted Eisenhower's directive as signaling support for their return to the mainland. "Our position in Formosa remained basically unchanged, owing to the tangible factors which continued to govern; but the Chinese, not unnaturally, interpreted our step as suggesting the possibility of American support for offensive action on their part," this misimpression could not be allowed to take root. In the memoirs, Rankin wrote: "To minimize the danger of any misunderstanding, I therefore took the occasion of my call on President Chiang to ask that no such action be initiated by his armed forces, particularly if aircraft or armor were involved, without consulting the senior American military officer on Taiwan, General Chase. He readily agreed. To this extent the Chinese government was 'unleashed'—unfortunate word—and a moment later, 'neutralized' once more."[19]

In March, the JCS undertook the first major step under the new administration to upgrade US-ROC defense cooperation. It involved a draft directive to the Commander-in-Chief Pacific, Admiral Arthur Radford. The draft proposed basing patrol and reconnaissance aircraft on Formosa, joint US-Nationalist planning for Formosa's defense, coordinated training exercises, and development of plans for potential offensive action by the Nationalists. It provided, "In the event of air or sea attack against US forces, they will take immediate and aggressive self-defense measures, but retaliatory action against targets on the Chinese mainland will be taken only with the approval of the JCS."[20]

On March 27, a joint JCS-State meeting to discuss the directive occurred at the Pentagon. Air Force Chief of Staff General Hoyt Vandenberg highlighted that it increased the potential for confrontation with the Soviet Union:

> As I understand it, we are getting ready unilaterally since this is purely a US undertaking to protect Formosa. If the Chinese Communists should mount an air attack on Formosa, we would counter it. This would undoubtedly involve attacks on the mainland. Given the Sino-Russian agreement, there would be every possibility that Russia would assist the Chinese Communists. In that case, we would really be getting into a war with the USSR and China all by ourselves. It seems to me that if that is the policy everybody involved should clearly recognize the implications.[21]

Warning that Chiang was highly motivated to provoke a war, Vandenberg continued, "We have to realize that Chiang Kai-shek is a strong headed sort of person. He is going to have planes with which he can, if he wants to, attack the Communist mainland. If he does, and there are Communist attacks in retaliation, I think we should fully understand the kind of flypaper that we are stuck on."

Army Chief of Staff General James Lawton Collins suggested the draft be modified. "I personally part company with the Directive when it calls for Radford to conduct joint offensive planning with the Chinese."[22]

The cause for Collins's concern was scheduled US upgrades to Chiang's forces, specifically, the scheduled delivery to him of F84 aircraft. Vandenberg observed, "The 84s are fighter bombers of considerable range, and with these they could undertake bombardment well into Chinese Communist territory." Collins added, "We have revised the mission of the Seventh Fleet so that now a barrier is removed against offensive action by the Chinese Nationalists and, whereas before the Nationalists had no offensive capability, we are now providing them with an offensive capability in the form of jet aircraft, and it will be difficult if not impossible for Radford to judge whether any Chinese Communist attack is provoked or unprovoked."[23]

JCS chairman General Omar Bradley remarked, "He could bomb the Chinese coast and that might well bring Communist retaliation. I am inclined to share Collins' worry about joint offensive planning."[24] The chiefs struck the reference.

On March 31, Deputy Secretary of State H. Freeman Matthews reported the chiefs' concerns to Dulles and recommended that the question of controlling Chiang be urgently addressed. "As you know, Chiang Kai-shek will be very unhappy if an armistice is achieved in Korea: he wants to broaden the conflict, not end it. He may well be tempted to undertake some adventures with his F-84s, either with or without a deliberate intention of involving the US in a broader war with Communist China. I think we should study possible ways to prevent this happening."[25]

Dulles fully agreed. "I share these worries. I understand we are attempting to get an agreement with Chiang Kai-shek that he will not use the new equipment we give him against the China mainland without our prior consent. I consider this of the utmost importance."[26]

In an April 8 meeting of the National Security Council, the secretary emphasized this point. According to the meeting's Memorandum of Discussion, "It was therefore necessary to secure very quickly a commitment from Chiang Kai-shek that he would not use these aircraft recklessly and in a fashion to embarrass United States policy. Until this commitment had been obtained, Secretary Dulles recommended that the United States stop delivery of any more aircraft to the Chinese Nationalist Government." The president concurred. Thus, the NSC Action Item read, "Pending such a commitment, further shipments to the Chinese Nationalist Government of jet planes from the United States should be stopped and the transfer to the Chinese Nationalist Government of jet planes already shipped should be delayed."[27]

As finally negotiated between the JCS and State, the directive to Radford included this language:

> In coordinating plans with Chi Govt for offensive use of ChiNat Forces, commitment must be secured that these forces will not engage in offensive opns considered by the United States to be inimical to best interests of the United States. In particular you shld make clear that United States is undertaking no commitment to counter Commie mil actions which are consequences of ChiNat offensive undertaken without prior concurrence of United States authorities.[28]

Rankin and Chase brought these issues forward at an April 13 Taipei meeting with Chiang and Yeh. The Americans stated that the United States sought a "formal understanding from the Chinese Government not to engage in offensive military operations which the US considers inimical to its best interests." Yeh replied with a general assurance but sought clarification. What sort of operations would be "inimical?" Chiang wondered about guerilla operations, which were undertaken by local commanders. What would need American approval and what would not? The question, for the moment, was rhetorical and not answered.[29]

Dulles contacted Rankin on April 17, telling him to advise the foreign minister that the United States would expect to be consulted about any actions involving the use of US-supplied weaponry in offensive operations. The secretary also proposed to leverage Taipei until he got the understanding the United States wanted. Thus, he added, "In seeking such commitment, you should if and when you consider it helpful inform Chinese Government that jet aircraft now scheduled early delivery Formosa cannot be delivered until commitment obtained."[30]

The agreement that the Americans insisted upon came on April 22. The Nationalist Chinese note read:

> As a result of discussions with Government of USA, Government of Republic of China agrees in principle that Government of USA will be consulted for any offensive military operations against mainland of China which would radically alter a pattern or tempo of operations hitherto undertaken. As to exact implication of words pattern or tempo of present operations, Chinese government has designated General Chow Chih-jou, Chief of General Staff to enter into further discussion with Major General William C. Chase, Chief of USMAAG in Taipei.

In turn, General Chow sent a note to General Chase reading, "I wish also to reassure you that with the exception of employment of MDAP jet aircraft for the defense of Taiwan and necessary reconnaissance patrol missions, prior consultation with US authorities will be made on all future offensive operations involving use of US MDAP jet aircraft."[31]

On April 28, the National Security Council authorized shipment of the F84s to proceed.

The concerns the Joint Chiefs and State expressed about Chiang's eagerness to attack the mainland were well placed. On May 27, Howard Jones, a US diplomat in Taipei, cabled State to summarize a conversation between Chiang and Rankin. He also transmitted a plan of action prepared by the Nationalist Chinese Foreign Ministry to topple the Communist government. The plan asserted that doing so was a "prerequisite to putting a permanent stop to expansion of Soviet imperialism in Asia." It claimed that Nationalist Chinese ground forces would bear the burden of an invasion, with the United States limited to logistical backing. It stated that the Nationalists would raise an army consisting of 60 divisions of regular forces and reserves.[32] Chiang told Rankin mobilization and training to implement the plan could be completed in two or three years if the United States provided sufficient economic help. But he emphasized that time was of the essence. If the Communists remained in power for at least three more years, they would be entrenched. Chiang cautioned, "We will then not be able to dislodge Chinese Commies without becoming involved in war with Soviet Russia."[33]

Chiang returned to these warnings and themes repeatedly in meetings with many high-level Americans who visited Taipei. [34]

EARLY OVERTURES FOR A MUTUAL DEFENSE TREATY

With Eisenhower now in office, Chiang felt encouraged that the time was ripe for deeper security cooperation with the United States. His three principal contacts were Dulles; Walter S. Robertson, the assistant secretary of state for Far Eastern Affairs; and Karl L. Rankin, initially Chargé d'Affaires in Taipei and then US ambassador. While none gave Chiang support for a campaign to return to the mainland, each was far more sympathetic to his regime than had been Acheson, Marshall, and their subordinates. In July 1953, another Nationalist supporter, Admiral Arthur Radford, assumed chairmanship of the JCS. Nevertheless, as friendly to Chiang as these appointments would appear, the administration approached him cautiously. Committed to ending the Korean War and wary about being drawn into another conflict in Asia, they avoided being trapped into Chiang's planning and strategies.[35]

Shortly after Eisenhower's inauguration, Chiang asked his ambassador, Wellington Koo, to explore how strengthened ties might include a mutual defense treaty. It was the first mention to the Americans of such a pact. In his oral history, Koo recounts:

> In March of 1953, when the new Republican Administration was barely two months in office, I received instructions from the Foreign Ministry to bring to the United States Government's attention certain proposals to increase military cooperation between the United States and the Republic of China. On this basis I sought Secretary of State Dulles' views on these proposals, which included the negotiation and conclusion of a Chinese American mutual defense treaty. Our conversation took place on March 19, 1953.[36]

Koo proposed starting with a Washington-Taipei bilateral pact, with the possibility of linking it to a general Asian security arrangement later. If Dulles reacted well, the Nationalists would prepare a draft. But Dulles was hesitant. He wanted to know what territories the Nationalists proposed to include within its framework. Was a treaty to be limited solely to Formosa and the

Pescadores or was it also to encompass Nationalist-held islands offshore from the Chinese coast? As Koo recounted, Dulles worried that "if these islands were included within the scope of the pact and were attacked by the Communists, or if the Chinese Nationalists launched attacks against the mainland from them and the Communists should retaliate, the United States would be obliged to come to help the Nationalists. It entailed a responsibility which the United States might not be ready to assume at present."[37]

On the other hand, Dulles felt excluding the islands would damage the Nationalists prestige and raise questions about their sovereignty. "He believed the Nationalist government would not want to give the impression that the islands along the coast, up which it now controlled, were not under its legitimate sovereignty."[38]

Mindful about being sucked into the unresolved civil war, Dulles observed that it was much easier to make a military security pact with a country that was at peace and enjoyed settled borders.[39]

Koo said he was sure a way could be found to resolve these questions. Inasmuch as the United States was already providing defense assistance to his government, he considered the primary benefit of the pact to be political and psychological, rather than military. As he put it:

> Diplomatically it would be a sign of moral support for the United States to the international position of the government of Free China. Psychologically it would produce a tonic effect on the Chinese people on the mainland as well as in free China and overseas, because such a pact would increase their hopes for the liberation of the mainland and assure them that when whatever the Communists might do in Asia, the United States would not let Taiwan disappear from the map of the free world.[40]

Assistant Secretary John M. Allison also attended the meeting and prepared a Memorandum of Conversation. He wrote, "The Ambassador referred to US security pacts with Australia, New Zealand, and the Philippines as well as with Japan, and expressed the opinion that these should be rounded out by the conclusion of a pact with the Government on Formosa."[41]

Allison's notes reflect Dulles's caution. "The Secretary said that the United States would not want to make a treaty which would result in a commitment for the United States to go to war on the mainland of Asia and that it would be extremely difficult, and might in fact be embarrassing, to the Chinese Government, to limit the effect of any treaty to just Formosa and the Pescadores."

Notwithstanding his skepticism and cautious attitude, Dulles promised to give the issue further study.[42]

Koo made no further formal overtures on the pact to the State Department for the remainder of 1953, although he concedes that periodically he kept the idea in play. "I may have hinted at the desirability of such a pact in various speeches or informally in conversations with State Department and congressional figures."[43] For the time being, Koo focused on strengthening other aspects of Formosa's military cooperation with the United States.

Meanwhile, Chiang was promoting a triumphant return to the mainland and spoke of it publicly and often. Professor Robert Accinelli commented, "The swift recovery by force of arms of the lost Nationalist domain on the continent was the unceasing refrain of the Generalissimo and his inner circle. Keeping this goal alive was necessary, they believed, to sustain the morale of the civilian and military refugees who had joined them in exile."[44]

Chiang claimed to be optimistic for success because the Communist military had suffered losses in Korea and would need to rebuild.[45] If the war there continued, as Chiang expected it might, he predicted the Communists would grow weaker and the balance of power would shift in his direction. However, by June, warring parties in Korea reached an armistice to stop the fighting. It had the effect of dampening Chiang's invasion plans.[46]

Under the circumstances, Chiang reprioritized his thinking and again focused on concluding a mutual defense treaty. Writing to Eisenhower on June 7, he declared:

> Relative to the general situation in the Far East, it is recognized that, after the truce, the threat to the security of the Asian countries may yet remain. To cope with possible recurrence of such aggression the aggregate and individual strength of the free peoples in Asia must be increased. . . . Now is the time for the American Government to consider giving emphatic assurance to the anti-Communist countries in Asia, more especially those that are under the direct menace of Soviet Russia and Communist China, namely, the Republic of Korea, the Republic of China, Thailand, and Indochina, that they will be given effective aid to increase their military strength for defense. And to ensure the peace of Asia, it appears necessary that the American government declares to hold itself now ready to conclude bilateral or multilateral mutual security pacts with the directly menaced states mentioned above.[47]

Shortly thereafter, Chiang held a meeting with Admiral Arthur Radford, by now elevated to chairman of the JCS. He told the admiral that given the potential for a Korean armistice, it was important for Eisenhower to affirm that the United States would remain in Asia and not abandon the region to Communism. Chiang added that such a declaration should be reinforced by continuing to station US forces in Korea or establishing some form of Pacific defense union. Radford assured him Eisenhower would stand fast in Asia and was likely to conclude a series of bilateral or small multilateral defense pacts rather than to seek a comprehensive security agreement.[48]

On June 24, the generalissimo again wrote to Eisenhower, this time to endorse South Korean president Syngman Rhee's request for a mutual security treaty between the United States and the Republic of Korea. Rhee had been very nervous about the armistice and wanted the war to continue. If the fighting would cease, he at least wanted US security guarantees.[49] "This request of the Government of the Republic of Korea," said Chiang, "should receive your immediate and most favorable consideration so that the signature of such a pact may precede the signature of any truce arrangements."[50]

The Eisenhower administration recoiled from Rhee's attempt to prolong the war and to any inference that Chiang might support it. In a June 24 cable to Rankin, Dulles instructed the ambassador to let Chiang know "that Rhee's attempt to force US troops to fight indefinitely in Korea at Rhee's behest will not succeed." The United States was willing to cut Rhee loose if he attempted to remove Korean forces from the United Nations command.[51] "Plans are being formulated so that, if Rhee persists, responsibility for Korea will be left wholly to ROK forces. . . . We believe this will be disastrous for Korea but see no alternative to Rhee's absolute refusal to accept armistice and his threat to withdraw his forces from UNC[52] on a few hours' notice." Dulles added a final sentence, sure to get Chiang's attention, "Effect of military disaster to ROK in Korea and possible US withdrawal from Korea would doubtless require reconsideration of US-Formosa policy with result not now predictable."[53]

In his memoirs, Ambassador Rankin described how the misunderstanding developed. "Someone in Washington apparently had been persuaded that President Chiang was encouraging the Korean President in his alleged intransigence. An unfortunate message had been drafted in Washington, seemingly without adequate coordination, because of our overriding desire for a truce, and transmitted to the Chinese."[54]

Chiang reacted badly to the implications of Dulles's message, because he believed it mischaracterized his position and constituted a threat to his regime.[55] Rankin met with Chiang on July 1 to try to set things straight and reduce the tension. The ambassador cabled a meeting summary to State, "I said that the subject was an extremely sensitive one in Washington; I suggested that President Chiang consider the Secretary's message in this light and the possible consequent reconsideration of US-Formosa policy not as a threat but as a simple statement of fact. Obviously, many angles of US policy toward the Far East would have to be reconsidered in the event of a disaster in Korea."

Rankin also advised him of where the Nationalists stood in Washington. The assessment differed from what Chiang might have expected when Eisenhower replaced Truman. "It should not be assumed that the coming into power of a Republican administration was necessarily a net gain for Free China. In some respects, it was in others, it might not be. The Chinese government had undoubtedly benefited in various ways particularly since

1950 from the fact that support for Free China had been a domestic political issue in the United States. But the Republicans who had favored all-out aid under a Democratic administration might tend to be more conservative and restrained now that their party was in power."[56]

The ambassador's visit failed to calm the situation. For months thereafter, Chiang remained uneasy. When Walter Robertson, assistant secretary of state for Far Eastern Affairs, called at Taipei at the end of December 1953, Chiang brought up Dulles's telegram, indicated he still felt injured by it, and claimed his attitude toward Rhee had been misunderstood. He complained that he had sent a private message to Rhee, urging cooperation. The discord continued to fester until mid-January 1954 when the secretary wrote to Chiang to heal the rift. He had misunderstood the generalissimo's true actions, Dulles said, "I had not known of this and greatly appreciate what you did. We highly value your friendship, and I am personally grateful for the cooperation you have shown in meeting our common problems."[57]

To gain Rhee's agreement, and to forestall outright abandoning him, the United States agreed to his request for a mutual defense treaty. But there was a price. As Eisenhower explained in a June 30 reply to Chiang, Rhee would have to get on board with the armistice. "We have indicated to President Rhee our willingness under appropriate conditions to enter into a mutual security arrangement with the Government of the Republic of Korea. I am sure that you will agree, however, that for such an arrangement to be effective it must of necessity be based on mutual understanding cooperation and shared responsibility in achieving the common objective. Without these, a mutual security pact would be unworkable and meaningless."[58] The Korean War armistice was signed at Panmunjom on July 27, 1953, followed by the US-ROK treaty, which was signed on October 1, 1953.

Watching the Korean treaty come to fruition, Chiang became more anxious that he had not a pact of his own.[59] He redoubled his efforts. He and Foreign Minister George Yeh raised the topic with Vice President Nixon during Nixon's trip to Formosa in early November. The vice president and Mrs. Nixon were Chiang's house guests. Nixon and the generalissimo had 8 hours of private discussions, with only their interpreters present.[60]

In a November 18 communication to State, Rankin outlined why the Nationalists considered the matter so important. They reasoned that an accord would cement relations with the United States, which had been troubled and turbulent before Korea and could again unravel. "Official opinion here would expect no important practical changes in US support for Free China as a result of concluding security pact," wrote Rankin. "However, such a pact would be regarded as having considerable political significance and would allay fears of possible shift in United States policy toward recognition and United Nations admission of Peiping regime. In other words, United States policy toward free China would be widely considered to have assumed medium to long-term instead of short-term character. Grievance that security pact given to ex-enemy Japan and withheld from ally China also would be removed."[61]

Foreign Minister Yeh followed up on Nixon's visit with a letter to the vice president, transmitted through Rankin. Yeh's main arguments were that a pact would put relations "on a more permanent basis" and that it would dispel nagging apprehension on Formosa and among overseas Chinese that, under pressure from allies, "the United States would abandon Free China and recognize the Chinese Communists."

Yeh noted that much progress had been made in bilateral relations since the time of the 1949 Acheson White Paper, which he characterized as "intended to justify the abandonment of China." Much like the Communists, although for different reasons, the KMT felt betrayed and were outraged by the publication of the "White Paper." The Nationalists felt it distorted history and unfairly cast them in a bad light. As Yeh put it, "the Truman-Acheson China policy has now been repudiated." Even so, Yeh observed, the relationship between Washington and Taipei lacked a "concrete character" and a sense of permanence.[62]

At the same time, Eisenhower had finalized the agreement with South Korea. In its aftermath, Yeh observed, "the feeling has been gaining ground that if the United States could afford to conclude a pact with Korea, she could equally well, if not better, afford to conclude one with Free China along similar lines."[63]

Yeh concluded with a wry comment about the reception that a pact would receive in the Republican-controlled Congress, where anti-Communist sentiment was vivid and pro-Chiang legislators were outspoken. "Knowing as little of your internal politics as I do, I am in no position to say whether or not a pact with Free China would have the support of your legislators, but I am inclined to believe that those among your legislators who have consistently favored giving support to my government will not oppose it."[64]

On December 18, Yeh handed Rankin a draft mutual security pact, based on the text used in the ANZUS, Philippines, and Korean treaties. It provided that either party would regard an attack on Pacific "territories which are now or may hereafter be under its control" as an attack also on itself.[65]

The full text in the Nationalist draft read:

The Parties to this Treaty,

Reaffirming their faith in the purpose and principles of the Charter of the United Nations and their desire to live in peace with all peoples and governments of the free world, and more particularly to strengthen the peace and security in the Pacific area;

Recalling with mutual pride the historic relationship which brought their two peoples together in a common struggle against imperialistic aggression during the last war;

Recognizing that international Communism is a source of threat to world peace, human freedom and national independence, and that solidarity and mutual assistance among the countries of the Pacific area are urgently needed to meet such a threat and thereby to contribute to the cause of peace and freedom; and

Desiring to strengthen their present efforts for collective defense for the preservation of peace and security pending the development of a more comprehensive system of regional security in the Pacific area, therefore agree as follows

Article 1: The parties to this treaty undertake to settle by peaceful means in accordance with the principles of the Charter of the United Nations any international dispute in which they may be involved.

Article 2: In order more effectively to achieve the objective of this treaty the parties separately and jointly by self-help and mutual aid will maintain and develop their individual and collective capacity to resist armed attack.

Article 3: The parties through their foreign ministers or their deputies will consult together from time to time regarding the implementation of the treaty and whenever in the opinion of either of them the territorial integrity, political independence, or security of either of the parties is threatened by external armed attack in the Pacific.

Article 4: Each party regards an attack in the Pacific area on either of the parties in territories which are now or may hereafter be under its control as an attack on both parties and would act to meet the common danger in accordance with its constitutional processes.

Article 5: For purposes of article 4, an armed attack on either of the parties is deemed to include an armed attack on the metropolitan territory of either of the parties, or on the island territories under its jurisdiction in the Pacific or on its armed forces, public vessels, or aircraft in the Pacific.

Article 6: This treaty does not affect and shall not be interpreted as affecting in any way the rights and obligations of the parties under the Charter of the United Nations or the responsibility of the United Nations for the maintenance of international peace and security.

Article 7: This treaty shall be ratified by the parties in accordance with their respective constitutional processes and shall come into force as from the day of exchange of instruments of ratification which shall be affected at _____

Article 8: This treaty shall remain in force indefinitely. Either party may terminate it on one year after notice has been given to the other party

The language of Article 5 covered the Nationalist-occupied islands of Quemoy and Matsu, each close to the mainland. This presented the United States with a problem. The Americans thought the provision unwise because it escalated the chances of war with Communist China. At the same time, America considered it dangerous to leave the impression that it would never respond if there was an assault on the islands. And there was a further issue, as Rankin set out in his memoirs. A pact devoted solely to the defense of Formosa and the Pescadores "would suggest the abandonment of Free China of all hope that the mainland would ever be freed from the Communists and might also be taken to imply that the door was being left open to American recognition of the Peiping regime as master of the huge China mainland." He added that leaving things in that posture "would have unfortunate political repercussions throughout East Asia."[66]

NOTES

1. *FRUS, 1952–1954, Vol. XIV, China and Japan, Part 1*, p. 125.

2. Chiang and Madame Chiang, p. 6.

3. Ousted from 10 Downing Street in the British elections of 1945, Churchill returned after the elections of 1951.

4. *FRUS China and Japan*, p. 126.

5. Ibid., p. 129.

6. Ibid., p. 133.

7. Ibid., p. 132.

8. Rankin noted, "In subsequent conversation with Foreign Minister, I learned President Chiang's reference to 'moral significance' meant mission of Seventh Fleet was now what it should have been since 1950, which would have had considerable influence on development of the Korean War in Generalissimo's opinion" (Ibid., pp. 135–136). Accinelli reports that "even before the inauguration, Chiang signaled his expectation that the incoming administration would jettison the misguided practices of its predecessor in shaping overall Asian policy and relations with his government" (Accinelli, p. 111).

9. Senator William F. Knowland inserted MacArthur's statement into the *Congressional Record*. MacArthur also said, "Actually it was this protection which permitted the transfer of the very Communist armies assigned to the coastal defenses of central China for the attack upon our forces in Korea. Indeed, the concept of such sanctuary immunity unquestionably predominantly influenced Red China to enter the Korean conflict after the North Korean armies had been destroyed" (*Congressional Record*, February 13, 1953, p. 1060).

10. Ibid., p. 136. In its Statement of Policy 166/1, issued November 6, 1953, the National Security Council soberly assessed the divergence of views in the non-Communist world toward how best to interface with Beijing and focused on the basis for British attitudes.

"It is all too evident that the Free World will not act as a unit toward Communist China and the divisions of the Free World over attitudes toward Communist China tend to engender emotional heat of an intensity similar to that engendered by the China issue in domestic US opinion. India under Nehru's leadership continues to believe that the best way to approach the problem is to attempt to wean Mao's regime away from Russia by extensive promotion of non-Communist contacts with Communist China. Partly because of their desire to keep in step with India, partly from their fears about Hong Kong, and partly because of the important place which the idea of the China market occupies in British thought and politics, the UK leans toward the thesis that the Chinese Communists should be accorded conciliatory treatment."

(Ibid., pp. 305–306) NSC 146/2, also issued on November 6, noted, "Western European nations have been sensitive to any US policy which involved the possibility of extended hostilities in the Far East or a diversion of US resources to Asia. There has been a widespread belief in Western Europe, the Middle East, South Asia, and Southeast Asia that Chiang Kai-shek and his government are vestiges of the past which few mainland Chinese would be willing to support if they attempted to return to the mainland" (Ibid., pp. 324–325).

11. Professor Shu Guang Zhang writes that the objective of "unleashing" Chiang was to pressure the Chinese Communists to conclude the war in Korea. Shu Guang Zhang, *Deterrence and Strategic Culture: Chinese-American Confrontations, 1949–1958* (Ithaca, NY: Cornell University Press, 1992), p. 200.

12. Dwight D. Eisenhower, Annual Message to the Congress on the State of the Union, Online by Gerhard Peters and John T. Woolley, The American Presidency Project, https://www.presidency.ucsb.edu/node/231684.

13. Robertson, p. 35.

14. Walter Judd recalls that Eisenhower, frustrated by what he deemed to be Chinese stalling at armistice negotiations, sent an ultimatum through the British and the Indians to Beijing, threatening the possible use of nuclear weapons to end the war. As Judd recounts it, the president said he would have "no inhibitions as to territory and weapons" (Judd, p. 120). Jung Chang and Jon Halliday write, "Mao gambled that America would not expand the war to China. Chinese cities. and industrial bases, could be protected from US bombing by the Russian air force. And as for atomic bombs, his gut feeling was that America would be deterred by international public opinion, particularly as Truman had already dropped two—both on an Asian country. Mao took precautions for himself, though. During the Korean War, he mostly holed up in a top-secret military estate outside, Peking in the Jade Spring Hills, well equipped with air raid shelters" (Chang and Halliday, p. 362).

15. In Senate Floor debate on February 4, 1953, Senator Hubert Humphrey argued,

"It is my honest opinion that the statement pertaining to the use of the 7th Fleet is but part of the truth. It is in fact a rewriting of the history of our time. . . . This falsification of history has no place in a democracy, and I submit that the full intent and purport of this section of the State of the Union message is merely to state . . . that the United States Navy was required to serve as the defensive arm of Communist China. Mr. President that is part of the fact. The rest of the fact is that the Seventh Fleet served to protect our own installations, our own troops, and serve to protect the security of the forces upon Formosa."

Oklahoma Democrat Mike Monroney added, "It seems to me, as the distinguished senator has said, that it is stretching logic a little to assume that our Navy was protecting some 2 million communist troops from action by 300,000 or 3 at the time untrained and unequipped troops of Chiang Kai-shek" (*Congressional Record*, February 4, 1953, pp. 872–873). On February 6, Alabama Democrat John Sparkman declared, "I do not see how anyone can properly argue that it was actually in factually a protection to the mainland of China, when no one was capable of assaulting the mainland of China." And Illinois Democrat Paul Douglas called Eisenhower's comments about the Fleet protecting mainland China "ungracious" and "in error." Arkansas Democrat J. William Fulbright asked Sparkman, "If the removal of protection from Red China is of no great consequence, as I understand the Senator to say, then does the President's statement constitute any real change in existing policy at all." "No," Sparkman answered. *Congressional Record*, February 6, 1953, pp. 915–920.

16. Accinelli, p. 115.

17. *Congressional Record*, February 6, 1953, pp. 915–920.

18. On April 24, 1954, Rankin cabled State with his own views about the offshore islands, which he thought the Communists would move against before attacking Formosa. "As matters stand today, the Communists can take all of those islands if they wish, unless we are prepared to help defend certain of them, which are of particular importance, with US naval and air forces. Are we prepared to do this, or shall we simply dare the Communists to attack them and risk their loss in the near future, with consequent damage to the defenses of Formosa and serious loss of face by both Free China and the United States?" (Ibid., p. 193).

19. Rankin, p. 155. Of the term "unleash," Walter Robertson adds, "I always took umbrage at that word, because you're speaking of the President of a country as if he was a little dog let around on a leash. But Eisenhower never used that term. Secretary Dulles never used that term. That one was made up in the press" (Robertson, p. 33).

20. *FRUS 1952–1954, Vol. XIV, China and Japan, Part 1*, pp. 162–163.

21. Ibid., p. 165.

22. Ibid., p. 166.

23. Ibid., p. 168.

24. Ibid., p. 167.

25. Ibid., p. 170.

26. Ibid.

27. Ibid., p. 181.

28. Ibid., p. 174.

29. Ibid., pp. 190–191.

30. Ibid., pp. 191–192.

31. Ibid., p. 193.

32. At 15,000 soldiers per division, that size force would be approximately 750,000.

33. *FRUS 1952–1954, Vol. XIV, China and Japan, Part 1*, pp. 197–198.

34. For example, in October and November 1953, two US senators, fourteen representatives, and five admirals visited Formosa. All had meetings with senior officials and most met with Chiang personally (Ibid., p. 334).

35. "Although it appeared at first glance that Eisenhower and Dulles had joined the camp of Chiang's avid rooters, this was far from the case. The two men . . . believed that Europe, not Asia, was the premier battleground of the Cold War. . . . Privately, they were far from dewy-eyed admirers of the leadership of Chiang. . . . While publicly championing Chiang's government, the two leaders never endorse its plans for mainland reconquest" (Accinelli, p. 113).

36. Koo, p. H-238.

37. Ibid., p. H-239.

38. Ibid.

39. Ibid.

40. Ibid., p. H-241.

41. *FRUS, 1952–1954, Vol. XIV, China and Japan, Part 1*, p. 158.

42. Ibid.

43. Ibid.

44. Accinelli, p. 99.

45. Garver, p. 76.

46. Ibid., p. 77.

47. *FRUS, 1952–1954, Vol. XIV, China and Japan, Part 1*, pp. 203–204. Koo notes, "All these questions were closely interrelated. Any increase in military cooperation with the United States was a step in the direction of its formalization in a bilateral defense treaty; any bilateral treaty . . . was conceived of, on both the Chinese and American sides, as a link in the general defense system in Asia against Communism. It was a matter of circumstance as to what aspect could most fruitfully be urged at any particular time" (Koo, p. H-242).

48. *FRUS, 1952–1954, Vol, XIV, China and Japan*, Part 1, p. 206.

49. Walter Robertson recounts, "You were having these public demonstrations in Korea against the Armistice. Syngman Rhee was saying that any cease fire that left the Communists entrenched in North Korea was just sounding the death knell for the Republic of Korea—that it would only be a question of time when they would seek the appropriate opportunity to overrun all of Korea again, and he would rather lose now, trying to make an effort to save it, than to sign an Armistice agreement which would leave the Communists entrenched in Korea" (Robertson, p. 20).

50. *FRUS, 1952–1954, Vol, XIV, China and Japan*, Part 1, p. 213.

51. Robertson states that Rhee had been promised a mutual defense treaty and economic assistance, but the price was that he not resist the armistice or engage in unilateral military action. "If he went ahead without our support, the Communists would annihilate 2/3 of the forces and we would be faced with the problem of how we get our own forces out. . . . And so we had to let him know that under no circumstances we would support him in a unilateral movement of forces and that he would have to keep his forces under the United Nations Command" (Robertson, pp. 23–24).

52. ROK is the abbreviation for Republic of Korea (South Korea). UNC is the abbreviation for United Nations Command, which was comprised mostly of US and ROK troops.

53. *FRUS, 1952–1954, Vol. XIV, China and Japan, Part 1*, p. 214.

54. Rankin, p. 166.

55. Ibid.
56. Ibid., p. 222.
57. Ibid., pp. 349–350.
58. Ibid., p. 217.
59. Chiang was especially concerned that the issue of PRC membership in the United Nations, which the United States had deferred during the war, would come to the forefront. But public opinion in the United States, embittered by China's role in Korea, was set against the idea, as was the administration. "A July 1953 opinion poll showed that 60% of those surveyed disapproved seating the Chinese Communists in the Security Council, even if they agreed to peace terms in Korea" (Accinelli, p. 129).
60. Rankin, p. 188.
61. *FRUS 1952–1954, Vol. XIV, China and Japan, Part 1*, p. 333. In his memoirs, Rankin wrote,

"Developments since the Korean Armistice had further confirmed me in the opinion that only by a formal treaty of mutual defense could we expect to maintain among our Chinese friends the morale essential to a long-term program of cooperation. United States support for Free China in the event of military attack or similar threat to its existence was implicit in our actions since mid-1950. Our legal position, however, was unilateral. The aid and support we were giving could be terminated at any time, however unlikely such a reversal of policy might appear. I was convinced only by a formal bilateral agreement which need not go beyond what the United States would actually do in any case, could optimum results be expected from our large-scale aid to the Republic of China." (Rankin, p. 186)

62. Ambassador Karl Rankin observed, "The 'White Paper' atmosphere was still very much in evidence when I arrived in Taipei. The Chinese Government considers that the United States let them down badly in publishing that document. . . . They hold that the 'White Paper' does not tell the whole story, and that additional documents which they possess would, if published, have a devastating impact upon the 'White Paper's' thesis" (Rankin, p. 128).
63. On February 3, 1953, Chargé Rankin cabled the State Department about Nationalist concerns in being left out of the security structure America was building in the Far East, including worries that the United States would back away from recognizing them as the legal government of China. "The Chinese Nationalists are keenly aware of the fact that while the United States has signed a security pact with the ex-enemy Japan, no formal and continuing commitment has been made to Nationalist China, either as to the defense of Formosa or as to their legal position with reference to the island." He added, "The Nationalists do not exclude the possibility that the US may at some future date favor turning Formosa over to a 'trustee' or even to a China mainland regime which had promised to behave. US commitments on these points would help consolidate the structure of mutual confidence between the US and Nationalist China which has been laboriously re-erected since 1950" (Rankin, p. 152). At the time of Mao's victory in 1949, Dulles himself had considered the alternative of "trusteeship" for Formosa but, due to Republican politics and the Korean War, had since abandoned the idea (Immerman, p. 119).

64. Ibid., pp. 344–345. Richard H. Immerman recounts, "For more than a year prior to the outbreak of the crisis, Chiang had been drawing on his many sympathizers in the US press, Congress, and the State Department to lobby the Eisenhower Administration to agree to a mutual defense pact" (Immerman, p. 125).

65. Ibid., p. 343.

66. Rankin, pp. 195–196. Early in 1955, Dulles reconsidered his views. He worried that excluding the islands from express mention in the Mutual Defense Treaty left the PRC with the impression that the United States would not defend them (Immerman, p. 127). The United States succeeded in narrowing this provision in the treaty language. Article V reads, "Each Party recognizes that an armed attack in the West Pacific Area directed against the territories of either of the Parties would be dangerous to its own peace and safety and declares that it would act to meet the common danger in accordance with its constitutional processes." For purposes of the Republic of China, Article VI defines "territories" as Taiwan and the Pescadores, as well as "such other territories as may be determined by mutual consent." In his oral history, Chiang characterized this outcome. "It is true that the offshore islands are not specifically mentioned in the Sino-American Mutual Defense Treaty of 1954, but Article Six of that treaty provides for the defense of other territories under the control of the Republic of China, to be determined by both parties as essential to the defense of Taiwan and the Pescadores." Madame Chiang added, "we thought that was sufficient to guarantee" (Chiang and Madame Chiang, pp. 9–10).

Figure 1 In Cairo, Egypt, November 1943, (L–R) Generalissimo Chiang Kai-shek, President Franklin D. Roosevelt, Prime Minister Winston Churchill, and Madame Chiang. The Cairo Declaration stated that "all the territories Japan has stolen from the Chinese, such as Manchuria, Formosa, and the Pescadores, shall be restored to the Republic of China." *Source*: CPA Media Pte LTD/Alamy Stock Photo.

Figure 2 President Harry S. Truman Taking the Oath of Office Following the Death of President Franklin D. Roosevelt, April 12, 1945. *Source*: US Senate Historical Office.

Figure 3 President Truman and the Secretary of State He First Appointed, James F. Byrnes (1945–1947). *Source*: Senate Historical Office.

Figure 4 President Truman and Some of His Closest Advisers, (L–R) Dean Acheson, Averell Harriman, and George Marshall. *Source*: Harry S. Truman Library.

Figure 5   US Ambassador to China Patrick Hurley in Chungking with Chairman Mao Zedong before Failed Negotiations to Produce a Coalition Government, August 1945. *Source*: Everett Collection Historical/Alamy Stock Photo.

Figure 6   Chiang Kai-shek and Mao Zedong in Chungking, 1945. Their profound mistrust of one another undermined efforts to create a coalition government. *Source*: FHLC 20217/Alamy Stock Photo.

Figure 7   Chairman Tom Connally (D-TX) of the Senate Foreign Relations Committee from 1941 to 1947 and from 1949 to His Retirement in 1953. Pictured in 1949 with Secretary of State George Marshall (1947–1949). *Source*: US Senate Historical Office.

Figure 8   Senate Foreign Relations Chairman Tom Connelly with Secretary of State Dean Acheson (1949–1953) and US Ambassador-at-Large Philip Jessup. *Source*: US Senate Historical Office.

Figure 9 Chairman Walter George (D-GA) of the Senate Foreign Relations Committee in the 84th Congress (1955–1957). George was a senator for 30 years. In 1955, he shepherded the Formosa Resolution and the Mutual Defense Treaty through the Senate. *Source*: US Senate Historical Office.

Figure 10 Madame Chiang Kai-shek with Senators Everett Dirksen (R-IL), John Sparkman (D-AL), Hubert Humphrey (D-MN), and Margaret Chase Smith (R-ME). Madame Chiang lobbied strenuously in both the Executive Branch and with friends in Congress for more assistance to the Nationalist Chinese. *Source*: US Senate Historical Office.

Figure 11   Senator Herbert Lehman (D-NY) Strongly Believed That Powers Granted under the Formosa Resolution Should Be Limited to the Defense of Formosa and the Pescadores and Exclude the Islands of Quemoy and Matsu Adjacent to the Chinese coast. *Source*: Steve Cox, SuperStock/Alamy Stock Photo.

Figure 12   Senator Estes Kefauver (D-TN), a Leading Opponent of Both the Formosa Resolution and the Mutual Defense Treaty. The following year, in 1956, he ran for vice president on the Democratic ticket. *Source*: US Senate Historical Office.

Figure 13 **Senator William F. Knowland (R-CA), Majority Leader from July 1953 to 1955 and Minority Leader from 1955 to 1959.** He was Nationalist China's leading advocate in the Senate. *Source*: US Senate Historical Office.

Figure 14 **Dominating the Debate on Both the Formosa Resolution and the Mutual Defense Treaty, Senator Wayne Morse (D-OR) Criticized the Idea of Preemptive War.** *Source*: US Senate Historical Office.

Figure 15 Deeply Mistrustful of Chiang Kai-shek, Senator Russell Long (D-LA) Feared He Would Trap the United States into a War to Recover the Mainland. *Source*: US Senate Historical Office.

Figure 16 Senator H. Alexander Smith (R-NJ), Republicans' Top Asia Hand on the Senate Foreign Relations Committee and Staunch Ally of the Nationalist Cause. *Source*: US Senate Historical Office.

Figure 17 Republican Whip and a Member of the Armed Services Committee, Senator Leverett Saltonstall (R-MA) Was an Eisenhower Stalwart. *Source*: US Senate Historical Office.

Figure 18 Senator William Langer (R-ND) was the Sole Republican to Oppose the Formosa Resolution and the Mutual Defense Treaty. *Source*: US Senate Historical Office.

Figure 19 Former Representative Walter Judd (R-MN), Testifying in Congress. A former medical missionary in China, Dr. Judd was Generalissimo Chiang Kai-shek's most outspoken supporter in the House of Representatives.

Figure 20 President Dwight D. Eisenhower Signs the Formosa Resolution. Observing (L–R) are Senator Walter George, Secretary of State John Foster Dulles, Senator William Knowland, Senator Alexander Wiley, and House Minority Leader Joseph Martin.

Chapter 5

Rising Tensions in the Strait

Although fighting stopped in Korea, Asia was not at peace. Conflicts with Communists proliferated on other fronts, with Formosa once again at risk. The Nationalists anticipated that as Mao redirected his attention from Korea, trouble loomed for them. As Wellington Koo has written, "As the Korean Armistice had recently been signed, it was only logical to expect that the government on Taiwan would be subject to increased pressures from Communists on the Mainland."[1] Elsewhere, a catastrophe loomed for France in Indochina, where Paris sought to restore a colonial empire disrupted by Japanese wartime occupation. In May 1954, Communist forces under Ho Chi Minh and Vo Nguyen Giap forced a surrender of the French garrison at Dien Bien Phu. With that defeat, Paris's dreams of a return to Indochina collapsed.

Alarmed at the prospect of further Communist advances across multiple venues, the United States and its allies organized Southeast Asia Treaty Organization.[2] Negotiations took several months and concluded in September 1954. SEATO was conceived to neutralize Communist threats to South Vietnam and the remainder of non-Communist Southeast Asia.[3] As Walter Robertson explains, "The only effective way of preventing further Communist encroachments and aggression in Asia was to put them on notice that there was a military force, a concerted action of nations involved, that would prevent their doing so. That was the purpose of starting SEATO."[4]

Headquartered in Bangkok, SEATO joined Asian and Pacific regional partners Australia and New Zealand, Pakistan, Thailand, and the Philippines, with the United States, the United Kingdom, and France. However, Nationalist China was excluded.[5]

Barriers existed to involving Chiang in a multilateral security system. In a Statement of Policy published in November 1953 (NSC 146/2), the National Security Council saw three impediments: some Pacific countries did not recognize Chiang's government; some that did, like Australia and New Zealand, questioned its effectiveness; and some were reluctant to ally with Chiang given his ultimate objective to overthrow the Communist government. Given these attitudes, the inclusion of Nationalist China in a multilateral pact was problematic.[6]

There was another important distinction between America's other security arrangements in the region and one with Chiang. The other pacts were purely defensive in purpose, but an arrangement with Nationalist China seemed to have a different dimension—a potential shield to protect an ally who had aggressive designs on an adversary.

Might Chiang, intent on reconquest of the mainland, provoke aggression that would involve the United States?[7] Given his often-expressed ambitions, the prospect worried the Americans.[8] Having worked for peace in Korea, the administration was wary of being drawn into another land war in Asia, especially one that could widen to engage the Soviet Union.[9]

Although the United States did not consider Chiang's ambitions achievable, it worried that a mutual defense treaty might offer a backstop that would induce him to try. On the other hand, the United States also feared destroying Nationalist morale if it disabused Chiang of the prospect.[10] As Laura Tyson Li comments, "The notion of a 'return to the mainland' by military force was recognized as pure fantasy by the Americans, but diplomats were careful not to speak of this to the Chiangs. Unrealistic as the idea was, it served the crucial purpose of buoying morale among Chiang's followers."[11]

If hope disintegrated, there was the prospect that Chiang might seek to preserve himself by making peace with his adversaries. The practical result could be a "one-country, two systems" solution, which the PRC later used when Hong Kong reunified with China and which they hoped would lure Taiwan back to the motherland. Historian John Garver wrote that the threat was credible, notwithstanding years of tension between the two sides. "If US policy threatened continued Nationalist rule over Taiwan, the possibility of a deal between the Nationalists and the Communists was very real," Garver surmised.

The alternatives of Formosan independence or a two-China policy had no appeal for Chiang. Garver wrote, "Nationalist leaders were Chinese patriots committed to the establishment of China as a leading world power. They had no interest in becoming instruments of the permanent alienation of Taiwan from the Chinese nation, a role that would condemn them to being recorded by future Chinese historians as traitors to the Han race."[12]

Chiang's insistence on a "one-China" policy did not square with American interests, which involved keeping Formosa in friendly hands, avoiding war with China, and seeking an accommodation with the PRC that would split it from the Soviets.[13]

American policymakers were confined, however, by the knowledge that both Beijing and Taipei were committed to a one-China policy, to include Formosa. When Dr. Henry Kissinger visited China in 1971, as a precursor to President Richard Nixon's trip the following year, Chinese premier Zhou Enlai made clear the PRC's view that there could not be two Chinas or one China, one Taiwan. The artful language of the Shanghai Communiqué, issued at the end of Nixon's visit, thus states, "the United States acknowledges that all Chinese on either side of the Taiwan Strait maintain there is but one China and that Taiwan is part of China."

THE PRC IS AGITATED

For their part, Communists closely followed US encirclement efforts around the periphery of China and were alarmed. None was of greater concern, however, than the proposed treaty with Chiang. Monitoring travel to Formosa by US military leaders and statements by senior US officials, the Chinese were agitated that a US-ROC pact might materialize.[14] They believed it was a serious affront to China's territorial integrity.[15] Thomas Stolper observes, "The prospect of a Mutual Defense Treaty between Washington and Taipei was at the heart of Peking's concern for its sovereignty and territorial integrity. A binding American commitment to defend Taiwan would, by itself, be enough to eliminate the possibility of repossessing the island for an indefinite period."[16]

Aware that a treaty might develop, the PRC began a public campaign of official statements and press commentary against it.[17] The Communists were also concerned that the United States might organize a multilateral Northeast Asia alliance and include Chiang in it.[18] Professor Shu Guang Zhang cites commentary in the *People's Daily* [*Renmin Ribao*] of August 8, 1954, complaining that the United States "seeks to link up these two military blocks [in the Southeast and Northeast Asia] to form a hostile encirclement of China and to tie the Asian countries together with the Syngman Rhee clique and the Chiang Kai-shek gangsters as tools for US aggression against China."[19]

The Chinese were determined to preempt the alliance from materializing. Mao worried that a treaty would divide China much as Korea and Vietnam had been divided.[20] Thus, he wrote to Zhou on July 23, 1954, "in order to break up the collaboration between the United States and Chiang Kai-shek, and keep them from joining together militarily and politically, we must announce to our country and to the world the slogan of liberating Taiwan."[21] Military action would soon reinforce such sloganeering. As Gordon H. Chang and He Di noted about Mao, "over the years, he had accumulated much experience in using controlled military action for discrete political purposes."[22]

PRESSING THE NATIONALIST CASE HARDER

The United States had been lukewarm to initial Nationalist overtures about the treaty. Six weeks after the Nationalists had given Rankin the draft treaty, there had been no American response. Early in 1954, Koo received instructions to press the issue with the State Department. The urgency became increasingly acute because the Foreign Ministry decided that even if a multilateral pact materialized, it was unlikely to include the ROC. Thus, a bilateral treaty was the best available option. In a February 23 cable to Koo, Foreign Minister Yeh wrote, "Our policy, in the actual circumstances, is to lay emphasis on the conclusion of a Sino-American security pact and we will exert ourselves to the full in order to bring it about at an early date."[23]

To persuade the State Department, Yeh instructed Koo to lobby congressional Republicans. "Please also confidentially approach members of the Senate and House of Representatives, who are both friendly to us and influential with the United States Government, to push this matter." Yeh suggested a series of talking points for use with Republicans. These arguments included:

> Although the people at large in Asia believe the United States is not likely to abandon its anti-communist stand, they are deeply apprehensive that the United States, in the end, would accord recognition to the Communists and recognize two Chinas. Although this kind of view originated mainly from members of the Democratic Party in the United States, the general drift of public opinion in various places in East Asia is to make similar prognostications.
>
> Since taking over the reins of government, the Republican Party has not been able to free itself of the policy mold cast by the former Democratic Party. It has continued the containment policy in the Far East, although this kind of policy has already been proven ineffective and non-productive. If the present American administration were really to try to benefit from this failure of the Far Eastern policy of the Democratic Party and repair the situation in order to make gains, then the conclusion of a security treaty with us would constitute a real benefit.[24]

Further driving Taipei's angst was a forthcoming Geneva Conference to resolve outstanding questions over Indochina and Korea. It was set to convene at the end of April. The United States and the People's Republic of China would be among the governments attending, but Nationalist China would not be present. Koo received from his Foreign Ministry (otherwise referred to in his papers as the Waichiaopu) a summary of a March 2 conversation between Yeh and Rankin. According to the summary, "the Minister expressed the hope that the United States government would reach a decision on the matter before long. If a pact could be signed, or at least announced, before the Geneva conference, it would, he felt, achieve the additional effect of forestalling certain fears and speculations."[25]

The periodic Nationalist inquiries at State were politely deflected. Dulles was traveling or busy working on other matters. As Geneva grew nearer, State did exactly the opposite of what the Nationalists wanted. It put discussion of the treaty on the back burner.[26]

Taipei became increasingly apprehensive. The Foreign Ministry had assigned the negotiations a code name—TANG-AN. It cabled Koo on March 15 to check on progress, but there was none. Koo writes, "The Minister, who was feeling anxious about the matter, wanted to know if Dulles had returned to Washington or given any indication of his views before his departure from the capital, or if there had otherwise been any developments regarding TANG-AN. But there had not been any new developments. The State Department was preoccupied with the situation in Indochina and the preparations for the Geneva Conference on Indochina and Korea."[27]

On April 7, Koo raised the issue in person with Assistant Secretary of State Walter Robertson, who responded that, due to work on Geneva, Dulles had not had time to consider it. Robertson also mentioned that Dulles would need to discuss the idea with key senators, which would be impossible before Geneva, and thereafter to review the issue with the NSC.[28]

On April 16, Yeh wrote to Koo to express disappointment at the delays on the bilateral pact as well as at his government's exclusion from multilateral negotiations, which finally had gained momentum. Taipei felt like the odd man out. This was particularly acute since the Philippines was part of the multilateral arrangements. These negotiations would culminate in the September 2, 1954, signing in Manila of the SEATO Treaty. "I am afraid that our position has not been given full consideration by the State Department," Yeh lamented.[29]

The Nationalist government had pushed so persistently for a treaty that it is easy to assume it saw nothing but benefits from it. But that is not so. Koo wrote to Yeh on May 13 to outline drawbacks as well. The ambassador explained that concluding an agreement would be a psychological plus with the public, but that it would not materially enhance his government's access to military or economic assistance. And there was a major negative. A treaty would restrain the Nationalists' freedom of action to attack and retake the mainland. Koo felt that the advantages and disadvantages of a treaty were about equal. Koo wanted Taipei to consider these points. However, he pledged to continue pressing the question with Dulles if securing the treaty remained a high priority for Taipei.[30]

In his oral history, Koo recounted the reasoning that had prompted his communication to Yeh. "The fact was that I had thought all along this proposed pact had advantages and disadvantages, with the basic disadvantage being the restraint the treaty would put on our freedom of action to carry out our goal of regaining the mainland. . . . I wanted to caution the government that despite immediate psychological advantages to flow from a security pact with the United States, it would put a restraint by treaty on our freedom to attack and ultimately retake the mainland."

But Yeh did not agree. Responding on May 15, he indicated that the primary reason for the treaty was to put the bilateral defense relationship on a legal basis, and that the treaty was more useful psychologically than militarily. Yeh said the issue of restraints had been addressed in the Nationalists' original draft. "If we could obtain agreement on our draft," Yeh argued, "any efforts on our part to retake the mainland would not fall within the scope of the treaty and therefore the treaty would not in any way entail any restriction."[31] The Foreign Minister again urged Koo to push the draft with Dulles.[32]

Koo had convinced himself that Chiang's truculent and frequent pledges to return to the mainland would be fulfilled soon. Why else would the Nationalists have invested so much in training and modernizing their military? "All along, I hoped and believed that the repeatedly announced policy of retaking the mainland was to be carried out soon. . . . There were some 600,000 troops in Formosa in all branches, such as artillery, armored corps, Navy, etc. and a minimum of 85% of the budget was being spent annually on the armed forces."

However, to his surprise, the ambassador learned that Chiang would not assault the mainland without American help. "I really did not see clearly at the time that the government would not attack the mainland until the outbreak of such a general war ensured it of American assistance in that undertaking."

On May 19, Koo and Dulles met at the State Department. Koo writes, "I found the secretary very deliberate in his reply to my question about the proposed bilateral security pact. He seemed to be very cautious in choosing the right words and in framing his sentences while gazing out of the window pensively."

The secretary indicated that the Nationalists and Communists remained in a state of civil war. To avoid being mired in a continuing conflict, the United States had refrained from making an agreement with South Korea until after the armistice. The pact obligated Washington to assist only if there were an attack on territories then governed by the South Korean government or later brought under its control by lawful means. If South Korea instigated an attack on North Korea, the United States would not be required to help, nor would it assist in defending South Korea in case of North Korean retaliation. This understanding was set out in the negotiating record as well as in a letter addressed to President Rhee. Koo reports, "Was it meant, I asked, that only in the case of North Korea resuming hostilities on her initiative against South Korea will the pact apply in the view of the United States? Mr. Dulles answered in the affirmative."[33]

The secretary said that the United States sympathized with the Nationalist's aim to recover China, but America did not wish to engage in hostilities on the mainland. He would not agree to put the United States in that position.

At the same time, he was reluctant to insist on language that seemed to stifle the Nationalists' ambitions and damage the morale of their military. Dulles struggled with how to reconcile these contradictions.[34]

Koo responded that Taipei's draft was defensive in nature and did not necessarily require American involvement if the Nationalists initiated an attack. But Dulles remained uncomfortable with the draft and unsure how America could assist Chiang without being drawn into an unwanted war. Koo reports, "He said the general situation in the Far East was full of uncertainties and he hoped the developments would be such that Nationalist China could try to recover the mainland and succeed in its attempt. Perhaps the United States could then help."

TROUBLE IN THE TACHENS

Meanwhile, there had been clashes between Communist and Nationalist forces concerning the Tachen [Dachen] Islands, some 30 miles off the mainland coast of Chekiang [Zhejiang] Province. They were then Nationalist controlled, but some 200 miles distant from Formosa. Uncertain whether the United States would help Chiang defend offshore holdings, Mao began with a probe. In mid-January 1955, the PRC attacked Yijiangshan, a small island from the Tachens group, taking care to avoid conflict with US forces in the area.[35] The Nationalists brought their concerns to the administration. At the State Department, Koo discussed them with the China desk officer, Walter McConaughy, who was alarmed about the Communist strategy. Koo replied that the Tachens as well as the offshore islands adjacent to the mainland were vital to Nationalist China's security and that the ROC must continue to occupy them.

All these islands were vulnerable to a concerted Communist attack unless the United States stood with the Nationalists to defend them. In his memoirs, Koo noted that when Eisenhower changed the Seventh Fleet's orders, "We asked the American side to take advantage of the opportunity to publicly announce its solicitude for these outlying or offshore islands, so as not to let them fall into the enemy hands, and to include them within the area patrolled by the Seventh Fleet as a caution and warning to the enemy." However, the Americans did not comply. From Taipei's perspective, Washington's diffidence was damaging. "As a result, the enemy, knowing for certain that the United States was not disposed to join in the protection of the offshore islands had begun to plot action against them."[36]

Yeh sought unsuccessfully to correct this situation by seeking an American declaration that stated the defense of the offshore islands was as important as a defense of Formosa and the Pescadores, and that the Seventh Fleet would have the mission of preventing a Communist takeover of the islands, mainly Quemoy and Matsu.[37] Again, the United States did not comply.

GIVING ASSURANCES

As treaty discussions hobbled along, Taipei realized that the defense of the offshore islands presented a significant complication. Koo wrote, "The outbreak of serious clashes with Communist forces in the Taiwan Strait and Taipei's desire to reintroduce our requests of the previous July involving American commitment to the numerous offshore islands under the control of our government made it clear that the question of scope of application of the proposed treaty would, as Mr. Dulles himself had implied in the recent conversation, be a prominent issue in the negotiations for a bilateral treaty."

A related barrier was how to restrain Chiang so that America would not be forced into a war, said Koo. "The United States could not afford and had no intention to bind itself to automatic defense of a country which could at any time of its own choosing attack an enemy and invite retaliation."[38]

To ease negotiations, the Nationalists offered concessions. When retired US general James Van Fleet met with Chiang on May 27, the generalissimo indicated Taipei would consult with the United States before launching any large-scale military action and would not undertake any unilateral action. Moreover, while the Nationalists wanted the offshore islands to be protected, Taipei was willing to stipulate they would not be used for attacks against the mainland, unless otherwise agreed to with the United States.[39]

Nevertheless, the needle remained stuck. Koo visited Dulles on July 1, shortly before returning to Taipei for consultations. The secretary did not bring up the treaty. Believing that Dulles would have spoken about it if there was something to discuss, Koo let matters rest.

On July 3, Koo hosted a luncheon for US ambassador Karl Rankin, who was in Washington on home leave. Rankin brought with him minutes of a conversation he had on June 17 with Yeh at the Foreign Ministry. The dominant topic was the treaty.

In that conversation, Yeh asserted that the principal reason for the pact was political and psychological, rather than military. It would establish a stable legal framework for the bilateral relationship and communicate an unshakeable US commitment to Free China. But the minister also sought to assuage US fears about being drawn unwittingly into a Nationalist-instigated war. Thus, the minutes stated:

> Mr. Dulles might have had in mind a retaliatory attack on Taiwan by the Com-
> munist brought about by an attack on the mainland by the forces of the Chinese

Government. If such should be the case, his attention was to be drawn to the promises already made by President Chiang that the Chinese Government would not launch any major military operation against the mainland without prior consultation with the United States Government. Therefore, any possibility that the proposed pact might be brought into play in the event of a retaliation by the Communists was guarded by this commitment of the Chinese Government.[40]

On July 15, Koo and Rankin met at Twin Oaks, the Chinese ambassador's residence. Rankin noted that Dulles remained very cautious. The secretary seemed to believe Chiang, like Syngman Rhee, was a headstrong and intemperate anti-Communist. Rankin thought that did not square with reality and told Koo he would try to temper the secretary's views. Rankin believed that the Nationalist army was well trained but poorly equipped and was in no position to retake the mainland. And Chiang was a more measured leader than Rhee and would not attack unilaterally without a reasonable prospect for success.

Koo replied that he concurred with Rankin's assessment of the military situation. He noted in his memoirs, "I said the ambassador was quite right in emphasizing the capabilities of the Chinese Nationalist army. Even when it was fully equipped, it could not undertake a large-scale operation against the mainland without adequate air and naval support from the United States, especially in view of the growing strength of the Chinese Communist Air Force and Navy."[41]

Rankin confirmed for Koo that the United States had no intention of supporting an invasion of mainland China but would continue to provide arms to Formosa for defensive purposes. Soon thereafter, Koo left Washington for Taipei.

Meanwhile, friction in the region escalated. On July 23, Chinese Communist aircraft downed a British civilian airliner en route from Singapore to Hong Kong. In Congress, there were angry speeches. On July 26, in the vicinity of Hainan Island, US planes shot down two Chinese aircraft. And in Congress, there were more angry speeches. As Koo noted, "United States Congressional reaction to the second incident off Hainan was even stronger than that to the first, with Senate leaders appealing for national unity in the face of this 'hour of peril.'"[42]

Even though the immediate tensions subsided, the perilous situation seemed to provoke a reassessment in Washington of the benefits of having a treaty. As Koo framed it, "As I was in Taipei at the time, I had no ready firsthand access to what was being thought or said in Washington circles about the matter, for example, if and how it affected State Department thinking about the Sino-American defense pact, the timeliness of its conclusion, and the scope of its application. It was thus really a matter of speculation. But that the whole affair made those on both sides of the Pacific Ocean more sharply and painfully aware of this dangerous situation in Formosa and the adjacent area and its implications is attested to by the events which followed in the course of that year."[43]

CONCERNS AMONG ALLIES

The territorial reach of the Mutual Defense Treaty was not just a point of contention in Washington. US allies also had major qualms. While they understood, and indeed supported, defending Formosa and the Pescadores, they could not fathom why America needed to back Chiang on the offshore islands.[44] In particular, Britain was outspoken. It worried that bringing the defense perimeter so close to the Chinese coast could trigger a conflict prejudicial to London's interests in the region or needlessly involve its American ally in a major war.[45]

Chiang's treaty proposal was on the agenda at a July 31 meeting of the JCS. Chairman Bradley and Chief of Naval Operations William Fechteler agreed that, from a purely military perspective, Quemoy and Matsu were not essential to Formosa's defense.[46] If the Communists intended to launch an assault, defenders on the islands would quickly be overwhelmed and not offer an effective barrier to an amphibious attack. The chiefs did not support broadening the mission of the Seventh Fleet to protect the islands, although they acknowledged the political value to the Nationalists of holding them if possible.[47]

Chiang was fully committed to holding Quemoy and Matsu. He believed they connected Nationalist China to the mainland and stated he would defend them without American support if necessary.[48] Garver comments, "From Chiang Kai-shek's perspective, the offshores where 'springboards' for offensive operations against the mainland, including, ultimately, its recovery. Both symbolically and materially, Nationalist retention of at least several of the offshores was vital for the return."[49] When pressing the United States for a mutual defense treaty, Chiang urged that an American commitment to defend the islands be part of it.

Both as to the defense of the offshores and recovery of the mainland, Chiang's priorities and Eisenhower's were different. Chiang was aware of that and counted it in a list of sore points and resentments he held against the United States, which also included Roosevelt's deal-making at Yalta and Truman's pressure to shoehorn him into a coalition government.[50] While the administration would have preferred to see Chiang govern mainland China, if possible, Eisenhower and Dulles were not anxious to risk a major war to make it happen.[51]

Ambassador Rankin cabled State to describe how Chiang spoke to foreign guests about conquering the mainland:

> If he considers his listeners to be particularly sympathetic to his point of view, or if they are successful in drawing him out, Chiang will expand on his central theme: a return to the China mainland of his armed forces and his government as the only practicable means of liberating China from Communist control. . . . He estimates that a successful landing in South China would require 600,000 men, which would be well within the manpower resources of Formosa. Within three to six months after establishing a substantial beachhead, exploiting it as an opportunity might warrant and defeating all attempts to dislodge his forces, he confidently expects to gain the active support of the local population concerned and to see the beginning of a large-scale defection from the Communist forces to his.[52]

The United States would not support Chiang's ambitions. Vice President Nixon summarized the situation in a December 23, 1953, oral report to the National Security Council. "There is a considerable minority which believes that it is essential that the United States and other nations plan now for a program which would militarily overthrow the Chinese Communist government." But, Nixon continued, "The United States has rejected it." Thus, he asked, "What do we do about Formosa? This is difficult. We must tell them they cannot go back to the mainland."[53]

The United States needed Chiang safe and stable on Formosa to protect American interests there. And that safety depended on American support.[54] However, Chiang wanted more than just security on Formosa. Washington always kept in mind that Chiang's hunger to go on the offensive could embroil the United States in a war it did not want and might not easily contain. Much as during World War II, Chiang's interests and America's diverged.

AN ASSESSMENT OF US POSTURE TOWARD CHINA

On November 6, 1953, a year after Eisenhower's election, the National Security Council issued NSC 166/1, a Statement of Policy about China. It was not only accurate for its time, but prescient for the present day. "The emergence of a strong, disciplined, and revolutionary Communist regime on mainland China has radically altered the power structure in the Far East," it began. It noted that "the Chinese Communists have established strong, centralized political control over mainland China and have so far succeeded in coping with their economic problems." PRC military capabilities were considerable, the NSC observed, "sufficient to make invasion of China very costly. Mao would not be content just to consolidate his position on the mainland," the NSC said. "The Nationalist and Communist imperatives of the Peiping regime impel the Chinese Communists toward eventual recapture of historically Chinese territories which the US and the West now hold or protect." Nor was it likely that the United States could improve relations through appeasement. "Even if particular Far Eastern issues were resolved to the satisfaction of Peiping, the Chinese Communists, as Communists, would continue to maintain a basic hostility to the West in general and the US in particular."[55]

The NSC concluded that "it would be in the interest of the United States to secure a reorientation of the Chinese Communist regime or its ultimate replacement by a regime which would not be hostile to the United States."

However, the NSC identified as unacceptable several strategies that might be used to realize this objective. They included "the overthrow or replacement of the Chinese Communist regime by the use of US armed force; support with US forces of an attempt by the Chinese Government on Formosa forcibly to overthrow the Chinese regime; or concessions to Communist China designed to overcome the regime's basic hostility to the West." One such concession, stated to be out of bounds, was "the recovery of Formosa and other historically Chinese territory."[56]

The NSC painted a cataclysmic picture of the costs of US engagement in a war against China. It assessed,

"It is not possible to precisely forecast the end result of full exercise of US military capabilities against Communist China because of the variables which would be introduced by USSR counteraction. It is highly probable that an all-out US military effort against Communist China undertaken with the design of overthrowing the Peiping regime would result in Russian military intervention and quite possibly in global war. Such an undertaking would in any case bear high costs for the US, probably including full US mobilization, would commit to the China theater a high proportion of US forces, might absorb a considerable proportion of the US atomic stockpile and of US atomic carriers, and would probably result in the splitting of a US-led coalition.[57]

The NSC judged that, notwithstanding its reasonably well-developed and sizable military, Nationalist China was unlikely to be successful in its own defense, stating, "Without US naval and air protection, Formosa could probably not defend itself against Communist attack." Nevertheless, the NSC characterized Chiang's government as a "considerable asset" to the American position in East Asia for both symbolic and material reasons. It declared, "The existence of the Chinese government on Formosa offers an at least symbolic alternative to Communist control of the mainland and helps to frustrate the Communist objective of gaining international acceptance as the sole representative of the Chinese people. Taiwan also offers material competition to Peiping as a center for the loyalties of the overseas Chinese. The military forces of the Nationalists constitute the only readily available strategic reserve in the Far East and as such assist in discouraging the Chinese Communists from further military adventure."[58]

In the second Statement of Policy also issued on November 6 (NSC 146/2), the NSC outlined several approaches with respect to Nationalist China. They involved the US engagement in the defense of Formosa, backstopping the Nationalists in defending the offshore islands, and covertly assisting the Nationalists in their periodic pinprick raids on Communist territory.[59] Among the steps mentioned were:

- Effectively incorporate Formosa and the Pescadores within US Far East defense positions by taking all necessary measures to prevent hostile forces from gaining control thereof, even at grave risk of general war, and by making it clear the United States will so react to any attack.
- Without committing US forces, unless Formosa or the Pescadores are attacked, encourage and assist the Chinese National Government to defend the Nationalist-held offshore islands against Communist attack, and to raid Chinese Communist territory and commerce.
- Encourage and covertly assist the Chinese National Government to develop and extend logistical support of anti-communist guerrillas on the mainland of China for purposes of resistance and intelligence.

However, the NSC stopped short of making open-ended commitments to bankroll Chiang's government or to support a military operation to return him to the mainland. Instead, it advocated that the administration "continue efforts to show our continuing friendship for the Chinese National Government and the Chinese people while avoiding any implication of US obligation to underwrite the Government or to guarantee its return to power on the mainland."[60]

TAKING UNDER ADVISEMENT

In the early weeks of 1954, State took Chiang's proposal for a mutual defense treaty under advisement. Yeh continued to ask the US embassy in Taipei about the administration's reaction. Nationalist anxiety was rising because of a conference being arranged in Geneva to address issues emanating from the wars in Korea and Indochina. The conference was scheduled to start in late April. The PRC would be at the conference table, which the Nationalists feared might lead to Beijing's admission to the United Nations or even American recognition of the Communist government. Concluding the mutual security pact would provide Taipei timely reassurance of US support, Yeh stressed.[61]

Chiang's supporters in Congress echoed his concerns. As historian David Allan Mayers has noted, "Congressional pressures directed at Dulles before the Geneva Conference were aimed at discouraging any intention he may have entertained about meeting Chou En-lai or improving Sino-American relations."[62]

On February 25, Assistant Secretary of State Robertson sent a memorandum to Dulles recommending agreement in principle to the Nationalist proposal, with a caveat that safeguards be added to prevent "involuntary extension of current United States commitments as to the defense of Formosa and the Pescadores." Robertson contended that a pact would improve Nationalist morale, elevate the ROC to similar status with other US allies in the region, calm anxiety about the Geneva Conference, openly reaffirm US support for the Nationalist government, and be consistent with US policies in Asia. He requested permission to draft such a revised text, asked that the NSC decide as to the advisability of a treaty with Chiang, and recommended that negotiations with Taipei, if they were to occur, commence before the Geneva conference.[63]

The secretary informally addressed Robertson's memo two days later, in an internal meeting memorialized by Walter McConaughy of the Office of Chinese Affairs. Dulles acknowledged that Robertson had made strong arguments but was uncomfortable with the timing and would not be pressured or rushed. "He anticipated that any announcement before the Geneva Conference as to a security pact with Formosa would not be palatable to the governments or the public of Great Britain and France. It might be construed as provocative and calculated to prejudice the chances for any agreement at Geneva." McConaughy added, "He thought that the study of the issue would have to be very carefully prepared. He said that complex and important issues were involved, and he was not ready to make a decision now."[64]

Facing this reluctance, Robertson persisted. On March 31, 1954, he wrote a further memo to Dulles in which he argued, "commencing negotiations with the Chinese before the Geneva Conference would strengthen our negotiating posture at the conference by making clear at the outset our completely firm position on the Formosa issue." He again recommended that the secretary approve the negotiation of a treaty and that State secure NSC approval so that negotiations could commence before the conference.

But Dulles was not on board.[65] On April 8, he sent a message to the embassy in Taipei. It read, "Department has decided not to take any action before Geneva conference with respect to proposed bilateral mutual security treaty with Chinese Government. Available time for necessary careful consideration of matter with key congressional leaders is insufficient. Decision was without prejudice to later consideration of question." The Nationalists were informed.

Meanwhile, conditions in the Taiwan Strait grew more complicated due to midsummer rumors that the United States would consider entering a mutual defense pact with Chiang.[66]

Concerned about the implications these developments would pose for Chinese territorial integrity, and the prospect of further containment of China, Beijing was determined to be heard and to deter the United States if possible.[67] Zhou Enlai escalated threats that China intended to "liberate" Formosa and that the United States must not interfere.[68] Eisenhower pushed back. Asked at an August 17 press conference about Zhou's boast, the president noted that a Communist invasion "would have to run over the Seventh Fleet."[69]

THE SHELLING BEGINS

On September 3, 1954, Dulles arrived in Manila to sign the SEATO Treaty, which the PRC also opposed. Irritated by US efforts to contain them through alliances, including the rumored one with the ROC, and ongoing Nationalist harassment from coastal islands, the Communists struck back. Historians Gordon H. Chang and He Di report that the memoirs of General Ye Fei, the Communist commander in Fujian, reveal he received orders to shell Quemoy as a response to "Nationalist military provocations in the area and the rumored negotiation of a mutual defense treaty between Washington and Taibei [Taipei]."[70]

There were additional reasons for the shelling. With the Korean armistice in hand, Mao sought an opening to finish the civil war.[71] An active conflict in the strait would spotlight the risks of including the Nationalists in SEATO.[72] And it would foster divisions between America and its European allies over US policy in the region.

Finally, there was a domestic political value in using conflict with a foreign enemy to spike enthusiasm for the Communist revolution. Professor Chen Jian notes that on July 27, the CCP Central Committee had sent Zhou a wire reading, "The introduction of the task is not just for the purpose of undermining the American-Jiang plot to sign a military treaty; rather, and more important, by highlighting the task we mean to raise the political consciousness and political alertness of the people of the whole country; we mean to stir up our people's revolutionary enthusiasm, thus promoting our nation's socialist reconstruction."[73]

On September 3, PRC artillery began shelling the Nationalist island of Quemoy, adjacent to the mainland coast.[74] In 5 hours, some 6,000 shells landed.[75] Two American soldiers died in the bombardment. In the aftermath of the Korea stalemate and the setback in Vietnam, Washington was highly sensitive to any PRC moves in the strait and attributed to China's highly aggressive intent.[76] On the way home from Manila, Dulles stopped in Taipei to discuss the worsening strait crisis with Chiang.

In addition to the civilian population, a garrison of Nationalist troops was stationed on Quemoy.[77] Additional Nationalist forces were present on Matsu,[78] further to the north. Quemoy was 6 miles from the mainland, across from the port of Amoy [Xiamen]. Matsu was 10 miles offshore from Foochow [Fujian]. The islands were tiny, Quemoy compromising 60 square miles and Matsu only 12 square miles.

In his memoirs, Eisenhower noted that the shelling initiated a lengthy crisis that was one of the most difficult of his presidency. It was, he said, "a sequence of events which was to extend through nine months, threaten a split between the United States and nearly all its allies, and seemingly carry the country to the edge of war."[79]

The president's biographer William I. Hitchcock elaborated on the dilemma the administration confronted. "Eisenhower could signal indifference to the shelling, effectively abandoning the small offshore islands to the Red Chinese. But that would undermine Chiang, damage America's prestige in Asia, and cause a firestorm of protest by the Asia-First Republicans at home. Or Eisenhower could declare America's unalterable support for the tiny islands and reply to Chinese attacks with a war on China."[80]

For the Nationalists, the islands had psychological and military importance. Chiang had been exploiting them to disrupt shipping along the Chinese coast and considered using them as a staging area in a campaign to recover the mainland. Eisenhower wrote:

> Chiang's forces held the offshore islands for several reasons. The most important was Chiang's conviction that if he lost Quemoy and Matsu, his main forces would lose their will to fight. . . . To Chiang and his people, Quemoy and Matsu would one day be steppingstones for the reinvasion of their homeland. Meanwhile, the possession of these islands enabled Chiang to preserve for his forces a jumping off place for guerrilla raids on the mainland (these had been discontinued, however, in the summer of 1953), to sustain the morale of anti-Communist Asiatics in other areas of the southwest Pacific, and to compel the Communists to tie down troops to guard against the threat which island-based forces posed.[81]

American intelligence analysts surmised that the Communists were not likely to invade the islands, much less initiate an attack on Taiwan, because of uncertainty over the US response. According to Professor Robert Accinelli, it was a diversion. "The bombing of Quemoy, besides serving a political purpose by drawing international attention to the PRC's vehement opposition to the status quo in the Taiwan area, and to the rumored negotiation of a mutual security pact between Washington and Taipei, appears to have been a diversionary move in the planned campaign against the northernmost Nationalists islands,"[82] meaning the vulnerable Tachens group further north. Indeed, a successful campaign to seize the Tachens would take place four months later.

MILITARY AND DIPLOMATIC OPTIONS

The JCS, comprised of Chairman Arthur Radford, Army Chief of Staff Matthew Ridgway, Chief of Naval Operations Robert Carney, and Air Force Chief of Staff Nathan Twining, met with the president on Sunday, September 12 in Colorado. Six days earlier, the chiefs had voted 3–1 to recommend that the United States must assist Chiang in defending Quemoy and Matsu and that such assistance should include bombing the mainland. General Ridgway dissented from this strategy.[83]

With the exception of Ridgway, the chiefs attempted to convince Eisenhower.[84] But the president was more cautious, believing such operations could not easily be confined.[85] "We're not talking now about a brush-fire war," he told them. "We're talking about going to the threshold of World War III." Should there be a general war, the president added, "the logical enemy will be Russia, not China, and we'll have to strike there." Uncertain as well about whether a major conflict would enjoy public support or backing from traditional US allies, Eisenhower rejected the recommendation.[86]

In the face of Eisenhower's opposition, Dulles floated a diplomatic solution. He suggested working with allies to seek a cease-fire resolution in the United Nations Security Council.[87] Believing that the United States would realize domestic and international political benefits from making the overture, Eisenhower concurred.[88]

In a September 29 meeting in London, Dulles raised the idea with British foreign secretary Anthony Eden and New Zealand high commissioner Sir Frederick Dodge. They agreed upon a plan to have New Zealand submit the cease-fire issue to the Security Council. It was ultimately to be codenamed Operation Oracle.[89] Success was improbable. It depended on avoiding a Soviet veto and securing cooperation from both Chiang and the Communists. It was soon clear America had further groundwork to do with its Nationalist ally, which would never be comfortable with or trusting of UN intervention in the crisis.[90] Four months would pass until the time seemed ripe to advance Oracle in the United Nations.

Meanwhile, the shelling continued, which China intended as a warning to rethink making a mutual defense treaty with Chiang. The barrage was a reminder that tightening relations with the ROC meant intervening in an ongoing civil war.[91]

THE UNITED STATES COMES AROUND

Beijing's belligerence proved counterproductive, with the crisis lending greater urgency for both the United States and ROC to conclude a pact.[92] As Communist efforts to derail the treaty escalated, negotiations accelerated.[93]

However, PRC tactics served to reinforce Dulles's conviction that a treaty should not expressly cover any of the offshore islands under Nationalist occupation. In this fashion, the United States would not commit to defending positions of marginal military value, unless it judged that assaults on those holdings to imperil Formosa itself.[94] Retaining flexibility, the secretary left unspecified whether the United States would defend them.

In late November, the United States and the ROC reached an understanding. The treaty would expressly cover only Formosa and the nearby Pescadores Islands, with no specific requirement to protect Quemoy and Matsu.[95] However, out of concern that outright refusal to defend the offshores would undermine Nationalist morale, the treaty would also not preclude that.[96] Instead, it could also cover other territories that "may be determined by mutual agreement." These could be defended if a move against them was deemed by both treaty partners as a precursor to an attack on Formosa itself.[97] That left President Eisenhower in control of when, if at all, American forces would be deployed and their degree of engagement. As Newton observes, "the vagueness was intended to create uncertainty in China without committing the United States to wage a major war over a minor outpost."[98] It was a crucial principle, which laid the foundation for the policy of "strategic ambiguity" that has governed US relations with Taiwan since 1979, when President Jimmy Carter recognized the People's Republic of China and withdrew from the Mutual Defense Treaty with the ROC.

By insisting military action could not be undertaken without mutual agreement of the United States and the Republic of China, Dulles cabined-in Chiang's more adventurous instincts. With an exception for emergencies to act in self-defense, he accepted an American veto before forces could be committed.[99] The generalissimo acceded to these terms because he understood that he could not move against the PRC without substantial US support.[100] Eisenhower required that the Nationalists agree to an exchange of notes that to this effect.[101] Chiang asked that the notes remain secret, but Eisenhower insisted on making them public.[102]

Historians Gordon H. Chang and He Di write that Mao did not understand the reasons for the side letters or their importance. "Isolated in the international community, with relatively limited information, and with Leninist assumptions about the relationship of imperialism and semi-colonies, Mao could not know that there were serious strains in the US-Nationalist relationship or that Washington, uneasy about the Nationalist activities, wanted to limit Chiang Kai-shek's attacks on mainland forces. He mistakenly assumed that Chiang was little more than a puppet of the United States."[103]

As treaty negotiations were wrapping up, tensions with Beijing continued to rise. On November 22, a Chinese military tribunal imposed long sentences on 13 American airmen who had been captured during the Korean War, provoking further anger and threats of retribution in Congress.[104]

Dulles and the ROC's foreign minister George Yeh signed the Mutual Defense Treaty in Washington on December 2, 1954.[105] The exchange of notes was done on December 10 and made part of the treaty papers the administration sent to the Senate. After the Senate consented to the treaty, the parties would exchange instruments of ratification. Complaining that the treaty was, in effect, "a deed of transfer designed to make the US occupation of Taiwan permanent and legitimate," Beijing denounced the pact, declaring it null and void, and warned of "grave consequences."[106]

As China scholar Guangqiu Xu notes, "Beijing was enraged once more. To show its determination to maintain sovereignty within its territories, Beijing was resolute about using its military power again. At the beginning of 1955, military actions continued unabated against the offshore islands."[107]

The fundamentally defensive character of the US-ROC treaty was, in a way, like the 1950 pact between the PRC and the USSR. Article 1 of that treaty obliged each party to come to the aid of the other if attacked. It was not a blank check for either party to act as an aggressor and expect backup from its allies.[108]

On January 11, 1955, Eisenhower submitted the treaty to the Senate, which immediately referred it to the Committee on Foreign Relations. Hearings would begin before the end of the month.

THE TACHENS UNDER ATTACK

Meanwhile, the Communists launched aerial bombardment of the Tachens. Chiang's garrison was exposed, making it difficult to establish a well-contained defense perimeter and complicating America's objective to avoid an elevated risk of war with China.

Unwilling at first to cede any Nationalist-held territory, Chiang's instinct was to stand fast on the Tachens. Through his ambassador, Wellington Koo, he sought assurance of US logistical and moral support.[109]

At a January 12, 1955, meeting with Assistant Secretary of State Walter Robertson, Koo stressed that the American response would influence the generalissimo's decision on whether to stand fast or evacuate.[110] Koo stated that while there could be some argument over the military utility of the Tachens to Formosa's defense, the psychological importance of retaining them was indisputable and their loss would gravely damage Nationalist prestige.[111] Koo asked for an official statement to condemn the Communists' assault on the Tachens and to hold out the possibility of American intervention. He further asked that the Seventh Fleet be deployed closer to the islands and that logistical support be markedly increased.[112]

On January 18, 1955, after a series of aerial strikes, the Communists initiated an amphibious action on the lightly defended island of Yijiangshan in the Tachens group.[113] After 2 hours, the island fell. The Communists touted their victory as a step toward finishing the civil war. PRC radio proclaimed that "the victory shows that the Chinese people are unshakable in their determined will to fight for the liberation of Taiwan. Our people will use all their strength to fulfill that task."[114]

Negotiating the Mutual Defense Treaty had not deterred the attack because the accord only explicitly covered Formosa and the Pescadores, and ambiguity led Mao to believe that other Nationalist territories, such as the Tachens, would be unprotected.[115] The consequence was Mao's miscalculation about US intentions, mirrored by an American miscalculation that action in the Tachens was the initial stage of something bigger in the strait. As Gordon H. Chang and He Di remark, "By misinterpreting each other's intentions and signals, both sides, in taking what each consider to be prudent and justifiable actions, contributed to an increasingly dangerous situation."[116]

On January 19, the day after the fall of Yijiangshan, Dulles held a meeting at the State Department meeting with Foreign Minister George Yeh, who assured the secretary that the Nationalists were prepared to defend the remainder of the Tachens. He complained that the Seventh Fleet had kept further away from the islands than normal, giving the impression they would be abandoned.

Yeh asked that American officials refrain from suggesting that the Tachens were indefensible and unimportant. In fact, Yeh noted that the Tachens had served an important strategic purpose. They were reasonably proximate to Shanghai and had been used to harass shipping in the Shanghai region and southward along the coastline of Zhejiang Province. As well, they functioned as Nationalist listening posts. Thus, as Chen Jian writes, "seizing these islands would greatly enhance the PRC's coastal security in the Shanghai-Zhejiang region."[117]

Yeh warned that conflict in the Tachens could escalate into an attack on Formosa itself. As a strategy to stabilize the situation, Yeh urged that the islands be brought within the Seventh Fleet's patrol area.[118]

Dulles resisted, commenting that protecting the Tachens would necessitate deploying two carriers, half the American carrier fleet in Asia.[119] That kind of a commitment could not be justified, the secretary said. Dulles suggested that the Nationalists consider evacuation to avoid further attrition of their resources.[120]

Following his meeting with Yeh, Dulles lunched with Eisenhower at the White House. The secretary advised the president that Chiang should quit the Tachens and that the United States should provide logistical support for the evacuation. In exchange, the United States could abandon ambiguity and announce an intention to stand fast on Quemoy.[121] Dulles described it as "more defensible than the Tachens" and that it "served a more valuable military purpose than the Tachens." Eisenhower concurred with this strategy.[122]

After conversing with Eisenhower, Dulles returned to the State Department for a further meeting with Yeh. The secretary stated the United States would assist in the evacuation of the Tachens, would announce it was prepared to join the ROC in defending Quemoy, and would work in the UN Security Council for a cease-fire resolution. According to the Memorandum of Conversation, "the Secretary said he believed the announcement as to the protection of Quemoy would largely offset the adverse morale factor involved in a withdrawal from the Tachens. The action could be represented as a regrouping designed to concentrate the Chinese Government forces in more tenable positions. It could be held out as a trimming-down operation. It could be emphasized that China and the US will stand shoulder to shoulder in a consolidated position." The mention of China in this instance refers to Nationalist China and not the PRC.

Assistant Secretary Robertson told Yeh these protective actions would not await Senate approval of the treaty and could involve preemptive steps in response to a Communist buildup. It would not be necessary to await an actual attack.

Dulles and Yeh then discussed the resolution the administration would seek to authorize the use of military force. It would be explicit as to the defense of Formosa and the Pescadores and be flexible enough to embrace other contingencies. However, the secretary said that consultations on Capitol Hill would have to begin immediately, and he could not be certain whether a Congress controlled by the opposite party would go along. Most important to the effort was Senate Foreign Relations Committee chairman Walter George (D-GA), who Dulles routinely and assiduously cultivated.[123] The secretary cautioned that George was "extremely reluctant to take any action which might lead to war with Communist China."[124] Yeh responded that he would seek the views of his government on the evacuation and the remainder of the plan.[125]

On January 20, Dulles held a meeting at the State Department with House and Senate leaders from both parties, and the chairmen and ranking minority members of the Senate Foreign Relations Committee, Senate Armed Services Committee, House Foreign Affairs Committee, and House Armed Services

Committee. Admiral Arthur Radford, chairman of the JCS, also attended. The crisis over the offshore islands was the principal focus.

The secretary stated that Chiang's position in the Tachens was unsustainable. The island group was too far from Formosa to be defended against raids from the Chinese mainland except by carrier-based forces. Too much of the US naval strength in the region would be deployed for that purpose. The administration would not make a commitment of that magnitude.

Dulles argued that the Communist objective was not to nibble away at Nationalist offshore positions but to trap Chiang into making untenable defenses and then to go after Formosa once Nationalist forces had been decimated. Thus, the United States proposed an orderly Nationalist withdrawal from the Tachens and reinforcement of places like Quemoy that could be more readily defended from Formosan airfields.[126]

Senator Alexander Wiley (R-WI), the ranking minority member on the Senate Foreign Relations Committee, wondered whether the United States expected the PRC to interfere. Radford predicted that Communist seaborne harassment was unlikely and asserted that the United States could defend against airborne attacks without the need for hot pursuit back to mainland bases.[127]

House Minority Leader Joe Martin (R-MA) inquired whether the Nationalists had agreed to abandon the Tachens. Not yet, Dulles responded, but they were aware they could no longer supply the islands on their own. Failure to withdraw from the Tachens and regroup would trigger cascading defeats for the Nationalists in all their offshore positions. As that occurred, it would jeopardize up to a third of trained Nationalist troops. Under such conditions, Chiang's remaining forces might refuse to fight, and American troops would be needed to deny Formosa to the Communists.

Dulles told his guests that the Communists turned up the pressure on the Tachens to intimidate the United States from completing the Mutual Defense Treaty, which had been negotiated but was still pending in the Senate and could not be ratified without its consent. If the Senate would quickly approve the treaty so it could be ratified, that would demonstrate a refusal to be deterred and, he suggested, the Communists might step back.

The administration also promised to pursue diplomacy. He previewed the idea that the United States would seek a cease-fire resolution at the United Nations. Bringing it forward would strengthen international pressure against the Communists. It would also assure America's European allies that Washington was seeking to avoid war.[128] However, the secretary also said that a Soviet veto was probable, which would kill the prospects for a cease-fire resolution. Finally, Dulles previewed for the legislators an alternative strategy, involving a congressional resolution to authorize Eisenhower to use military force. No one in the meeting protested.

NOTES

1. Koo, p. F-371.

2. Foster Rhea Dulles comments on the direct correlation between the creation of SEATO and the results in Geneva, which acknowledged Communist control over North Vietnam and the potential of extension of such control over the remainder of Vietnam. "The effect of the Geneva settlement on American policy was a prompt renewal of the drive for a collective defense treaty to prevent further direct or indirect communist aggression in Southeast Asia. With North Vietnam lost to the other side, this appeared to the Eisenhower administration as more necessary than ever" (Foster Rhea Dulles, p. 146).

3. Professor Robert Divine states that "SEATO and the new American commitment to South Vietnam marked the administration's attempt to salvage whatever it could from what the National Security Council termed the 'disaster' in Indochina." However, he observes "the absence of such influential Asian nations as India, Indonesia, and Burma made SEATO suspect from the outset, as did the failure to include any automatic provisions for collective action against aggression." Robert A. Divine, *Eisenhower and the Cold War* (Oxford: Oxford University Press, 1981), p. 54.

4. Robertson, p. 72.

5. Dulles' biographer, Stephen Kinzer, notes that SEATO lacked key characteristics of the NATO alliance and never proved to be a robust anti-Communist mechanism. "Despite his efforts, SEATO never became a major political or military force. Its member states . . . committed themselves only to 'consult' in case of emergency, not to come to each other's defense in time of war or establish a joint military command." Kinzer adds that the pressure tactics the secretary of state and his brother, CIA director Allen Dulles, used to coax other countries to join were ineffective, if not counterproductive. "SEATO may have done more harm than good. Foster, often with quiet help from Allen, used all the pressure he could muster to pull regional leaders in. The most popular among them were neutralists who wanted fewer, not more, military alliances in the world" (Kinzer, p. 198).

6. Ibid., p. 315. "Because Chiang's regime was unacceptable to most Asian governments—the price of recognizing it against Peking's wishes was steep—the United States could not assure Taiwan's protection through a multilateral security pact and consequently had to enter into a bilateral treaty" (Mayers, p. 140).

7. Garver writes, "US policy required careful management of the contradiction between maintaining Nationalist morale and checking Nationalist actions that might entangle the United States in a war with China. To fulfill its assigned role in containing Communist China, Nationalist China had to be strong and confident. Yet the stronger and more confident the Nationalists became, the more they were able to draw the United States into confrontations with Communist China" (Ibid., p. 88).

8. In an August 20, 1953, dispatch to State, Ambassador Rankin set out four considerations he believed should guide US policy on this delicate question. He noted that a return to the mainland was the central aim of the Nationalist Government, that such a return was contingent upon American support, that the United States could not make advance commitments of support, but that it should not exclude the possibility

of giving it "under some future circumstances when it would appear to be in the American national interest" (Rankin, p. 176). Vice President Richard Nixon visited Taiwan from November 8 to 12, 1953. At the conclusion of his trip, he reported to Dulles, "I was extremely careful in my public and private statements in Formosa to avoid expressing any approval of military action to return to the mainland" (*FRUS 1952–1954, Vol. XIV, China and Japan, Part 1*, p. 331).

9. In 1979, the Senate debated the Taiwan Relations Act, legislation made necessary when President Jimmy Carter decided to recognize the PRC as the legitimate government of China. The United States had deep economic and cultural relations with Taiwan, which it wished to continue on an informal basis, and wished to support Taiwan's security even though Carter had withdrawn from the 1955 Mutual Defense Treaty that is a major subject of this book. Senator John Glenn (D-OH), a member of the Senate Foreign Relations Committee, sought to restrain his colleagues' enthusiasm for embracing Taiwan's defense. He admonished against "blank check" security guarantees in which Taiwan would feel emboldened to seek independence from China. The Senate heeded Glenn's warning and rejected an amendment that would have escalated the US commitment beyond the level the committee recommended.

10. "Not all Nationalist leaders were equally committed to the doctrine of returning to the mainland. Among the Nationalist elite, no one dared to openly challenge Chiang Kai-shek's belief that return to the mainland was the supreme mission for which all could be sacrificed. But there were some Nationalist leaders who understood that the reality of Communist China's immense power made such an outcome unlikely at least short of a major US-PRC war" (Ibid., p. 74).

11. Li, p. 235. NSC 162/2, the Eisenhower administration's initial policy statement on China, acknowledged that the CCP was in firm control of the country and was unlikely to be dislodged without a major war involving the use of atomic weapons and substantial numbers of US troops (Immerman, p. 119). In his interview with the Dulles Oral History Project at Princeton University, Walter Robertson was asked whether the United States ever led Chiang to believe support would be forthcoming for a return to the mainland. "Q: Did we ever hint that circumstances might arise in which we would provide the necessary support? A: No. Q: Was our position made completely and explicitly clear to Chiang? A: Absolutely. There wasn't anybody in the world that understood it any clearer than he did" (Robertson, pp. 36–37).

12. John W. Garver, *The Sino-American Alliance: Nationalist China and American Cold War Strategy in Asia* (Armonk, NY: M.E. Sharpe, Inc., 1997), p. 84.

13. Ibid., p. 113.

14. Shu Guang Zhang, p. 192.

15. Thomas E. Stolper, *China, Taiwan, and the Offshore Islands* (London: Routledge, 2018), p. 55. "The Chinese leaders believed that the United States would neither easily swallow its military 'defeat' in Korea or accept a diplomatic set back in Indochina. The next act of American imperialism, the Central committee concluded, might be to expand the military conflict onto the mainland from the Taiwan Strait" (Shu Guang Zhang, p. 190).

16. Stolper, p. 21.

17. Ibid., p. 35.

18. Ibid., p. 37.

19. Shu Guang Zhang, p. 191. Writing in *Foreign Affairs* in 1957, Secretary Dulles addressed the scope and purpose of US collective security policy. He stated,

> "the forces of NATO, now including the Federal Republic of Germany, stand guard over the treaty-defined North Atlantic region, which includes the vital area of Western Europe. In the West Pacific and Far East, the SEATO and ANZUS pacts and four bilateral treaties established the principle that the threat to one is the concern of all. In the Middle East, the Baghdad Pact and the Eisenhower Doctrine assure collective response to Communist aggression at points to special danger or weakness. This near worldwide system of regional collective security has served all the participants well. It has deterred aggression and given much needed assurance to people who are especially exposed to attack. We must, in candor, admit that all of the participants do not look upon these arrangements alike. Some consider them broad political alliances, binding the parties, at least morally, to support each other, generally. But the vast net result has been to further the application of the principle of collective security within the society of nations."

John Foster Dulles, "Challenge and Response in United States Policy," *Foreign Affairs*, October 1957.

20. Gordon H. Chang and He Di, note that, "politically, acquisition of Taiwan was central to the unification of Chinese territory, and China could not accept any treaty arrangement between the United States and the Nationalists that formerly separated Taiwan from the mainland or established an independent status for Taiwan" (Chang and Di, p. 1508).

21. Ibid., p. 193. Of Mao, Zhang writes, "in his judgment., proclaiming the liberation of Taiwan would demonstrate to Washington that any military alliance with Chiang could lead to war with China, which, Mao believed, the United States could not afford, and for which the United States was not yet ready" (Ibid., p. 194).

22. Chang and Di, p. 1509.

23. Koo, p. H-243.

24. Ibid., p. H-244.

25. Ibid., p. H-248.

26. State also had in mind the views of the British and French, who were cool to the idea of a US-ROC pact, believing it would escalate tensions in the region, even though the Geneva Conference was aimed at reducing tensions (Shu Guang Zhang, p. 204).

27. Koo, p. H-249. State told Koo that the review process was complicated and that the Nationalists were not being ignored. "When we asked whether 'under consideration' meant there were still difficulties, the representative replied that the State Department must first consult the Defense Department and then bring the matter before the National Security Council for a decision, that 'under consideration' was a fact and did not mean that the State Department felt there were difficulties concerning it" (Ibid.).

28. Ibid., pp. H-250–251.

29. Ibid., p. H-252.

30. Ibid., pp. H-256–257.

31. Ibid.

32. Yeh wrote to Koo about the impossibility of establishing an East Asian multilateral security alliance due to divisions among US allies in the region. In particular, South Korea would not ally with Japan. Therefore, a workable security structure would have to involve a series of bilateral pacts. These already existed between the United States and Japan, South Korea, and the Philippines. A similar arrangement must be concluded with the Republic of China, Yeh insisted.

33. Ibid., pp. H-261–262.

34. Ibid.

35. Shu Guang Zhang, p. 218.

36. Koo., pp. H-265–266.

37. Ibid., p. H-266.

38. Ibid., pp. H-266–267.

39. Ibid., pp. H-268–269. Van Fleet was recently retired from active duty. He had commanded the US Eighth Army and US Forces in Korea. He highly esteemed Chiang and the Nationalist army. In a January 29, 1954, television interview on the *Longines Chronoscope*, Van Fleet was asked, "Do you think that this army we are supporting in Formosa now under Chiang Kai-shek is a drain on the American taxpayer or do you think it serves some valuable purpose?" Van Fleet responded, "They're worth their weight in American boys. It costs very little. We get 21 divisions for a very small price, for the price of one American division." He was further asked, "Do you think there will ever be a purpose for those people there or just to divert a Communist army away from other areas?" He responded, "They have a tremendous pressure on the mainland of China right now, and the day may come when we would like to have a ready army to take advantage of some opportunity." Longines-Wittnauer with James Van Fleet, National Archives and Records Administration—ARC Identifier 95881/ Local Identifier LW-LW-286.

40. Koo, pp. H-274–275.

41. Ibid., p. H-281.

42. Ibid., p. H-286.

43. Ibid., p. H-287

44. On November 2, 1954, Eisenhower told the NSC about the importance of keeping in step with US allies on the matter of war over the offshore islands. The allies wouldn't support it, the president claimed (Garver, p. 124).

45. Quemoy was so close to the port of Amoy (Xiamen), in China's Fukien (Fujian) Province that it could easily be seen from the coast.

46. Bradley observed that neither of the islands had a port suitable for launching an amphibious attack. *FRUS 1952–1954, Vol. XIV, China and Japan, Part 1*, p. 240.

47. Ibid., pp. 240–241.

48. "The abandonment of the offshores would not, in itself, critically affect the defense of Taiwan. The PLA would gain open access from Xiamen (Amoy) and Fuzhou (Foochow), the two major ports it would use for a large-scale assault on Taiwan, and Taiwan would lose forward radar facilities useful for early warning. Against these losses were the major gains derived from drawing the defense perimeter down the middle of the Taiwan Strait, where US air and naval superiority could be brought fully into play" (Garver, p. 125).

49. Ibid., p. 127.

50. Ibid. These efforts included conditioning a requested loan of $500 million on Chiang's forming a coalition government, as well as an arms embargo against the Nationalists. As Walter Robertson describes it, "When General Marshall came and spent another 13 months not being able to get an agreement for a coalition the loan was never made. During that period of the Marshall mission, we cut off ammunition to Chinese troops which had been trained and equipped with American equipment by General Wedemeyer, at the same time that the Russians were supplying the Chinese Communists with Japanese arms and equipment" (Robertson, p. 8). Professor William Stueck has a different interpretation of the embargo, making it seem less consequential. "In August, under pressure from the Communists and wanting to discourage the Nationalists from seeking a military victory, which they were unlikely to achieve, Marshall actually suspended US licenses for the export to China of combat equipment related to the civil war. The Nationalists, however, already possessed adequate stocks of such materiel." Under some pressure from Congress, military assistance resumed in early 1947 (Stueck, pp. 101–103).

51. Twentieth-century history illustrated problems with allowing weak countries to provoke conflicts their stronger allies could not avoid. One vivid example of the "tail wagging the dog" was Germany's decision in July 1914 to give Austria unconditional support in the latter's conflict with Serbia. The immediate cause of tension was the June 25, 1914, assassination by pro-Serbian terrorists of Austrian archduke Franz Ferdinand; however, problems between Vienna and Belgrade had been brewing for some time. Austria decided to give Serbia an ultimatum, believing it would be rejected. The response would be a pretext for Austrian military action. To buttress its position, especially in light of an alliance between Serbia and Tsarist Russia, Austria sought and received assurances of support from its German ally. Berlin did not condition its backing, so it is said to have given Vienna a "blank check." Doing so triggered rapid mobilizations by allies to both disputing parties, and a full-scale war that none of the combatants intended.

52. In his oral history, Walter Robertson noted that the Nationalists believed conditions on the mainland were ripe to overthrow the Communist government. "Now, the Chinese on Taiwan—they'd get awfully good intelligence reports from the mainland. They knew of the unrest, and the hunger, and the uprising, and the liquidation. And they felt very sincerely that an attack there, properly supported, would win back China. They were forever pressing us for our consent to do it" (Robertson, p. 37).

53. The distrustful and dismissive tone of administration communications about Chiang troubled Rankin, the principal US envoy in Taipei. On April 10, he sent a note to Walter McConaughy, director of the State Department's Office of Chinese Affairs. He inquired, "Is our approach to be characterized by the evident dislike and distrust of the Chinese National regime? . . . Are we to proceed on the assumption that this government is not to be trusted, either as regards its operations in general or as a repository for confidences touching upon matters of mutual interest?" In the alternative, he asked, "should we treat Free China as we do our more favored friends among the free nations? . . . While not ignoring their faults, should we work with the Chinese on the basis of their relative cooperativeness, reliability, and effectiveness in

building strength to oppose Communism?" (*FRUS 1952–1954, Vol. XIV, China and Japan, Part 1*, pp. 348–349).

54. At a January 26, 1954, NSC meeting, Eisenhower had an exchange with Admiral Arthur Radford, who had succeeded General Bradley as chairman of the JCS. Radford observed that if Truman had not interposed the Seventh Fleet in 1950, the Communists would have emerged victorious. The meeting summary states, "Admiral Radford believed they could have gotten ashore on Formosa and ultimately have secured the whole island. This was true four years ago and it would be still be true today if American forces were not interposed, since the Chinese Communists had such a great logistical advantage over the Chinese Nationalists in the shape of men and junks to transport them" (Ibid., p. 356).

55. Ibid., pp. 279–280.

56. Ibid., pp. 280–281.

57. Ibid., p. 303. The NSC statement acknowledged the diversity of strong views on China among countries friendly to the United States.

"Because of the variety of these views, no US policy toward Communist China will meet support from all of the Free World. Because of the intensity of emotional and national feelings on the subject of Communist China any US policy toward Communist China will encounter strenuous and vocal objections from at least some of the countries of the Free World. Because of both the variety and emotional intensity of these views, US attempts to impose on other countries adoption of its own program toward Communist China, whatever that program may be, will have dangerously divisive effects on the Free World coalition. . . . The United States can avoid the most dangerously divisive potentials of the Chinese Communist issue by refraining from excessive pressure on its friends to follow American policies with respect to Communist China." (Ibid., p. 306)

58. Ibid., p. 300. Thus, the United States conceived of Nationalist China as a beacon of anti-Communism. Providing a meaningful contrast to Beijing not only for Chinese under direct ROC governance but to inspire Chinese everywhere, even within the PRC. Walter Robertson covered this in his oral history, saying, "We consider that the Republic of China is the only alternative to Communism for millions of Chinese—many of those on the mainland who have never accepted the Communist regime, the 12 million on Formosa, the some 10 or 12 million scattered throughout Asia. And so we thought that it was important to have this alternative to Communism for Chinese everywhere, and we made a mutual defense treaty where we would protect the Republic of China against aggressive attack" (Robertson, p. 76).

59. "Ever since the Chinese intervention in Korea, the JCS had kept open the option of an offensive role for nationalist troops" (Accinelli, p. 101).

60. *FRUS 1952–1954, Vol. XIV, China and Japan, Part 1*, pp. 308–309. In Statement of Policy NSC 146/2, the NSC noted, "Geographically, Formosa and the Pescadores are a portion of our offshore defense positions. Their retention in friendly hands is essential to the conduct of air and naval operations in the defense of these positions. Mere neutralization of these islands would not meet US military strategic needs."

61. Ibid., p. 367.

62. Mayers states that a reason for the anxiety was an inference drawn from comments the secretary made in the aftermath of the Korean armistice. "As recently as November 1953, Dulles had caused a stir in Taiwan and among Chiang's congressional supporters because of some apparently loose remarks. He seemed to imply that the American line toward China was softening and that if Peking should renounce aggression and quit taking orders from the Soviet Union, perhaps China would be eligible for American recognition and UN admission" (Mayers, p. 128).

63. *FRUS 1952–1954, Vol. XIV, China and Japan, Part 1*, pp. 367–368.

64. Ibid., p. 369. Richard Immerman observes, "Dulles kept putting him off. He worried about the potential loss of flexibility and recognized that the European allies would look askance at the United States assuming an additional military obligation in Asia, especially if that obligation was to protect Nationalist China. More important, he suspected that once guaranteed of US protection, the Generalissimo would feel no compunction about provoking a PRC attack on Taiwan" (Immerman, p. 125).

65. Ibid., pp. 400–401.

66. Mayers, pp. 136–137.

67. Stolper, pp. 38–39. Stolper observes,

"In the winter of 1954–55, Peking's immediate goal was to deter the United States from making a formal defense treaty with Taipei, but the leaders of the PRC seemed to have taken a long view of the problem of Taiwan and may have thought that the United States isolated in this matter might eventually be brought to withdraw a commitment made in the hope that others would someday join in upholding it. This would have been entirely in keeping with the Maoist strategy of isolating the most diehard elements of an enemy coalition in the belief that a favorable turn in the situation could be won later on." (Stolper, pp. 54–55)

68. Since mid-July 1954, Zhou had been under instructions from Mao to turn up the heat on liberating Formosa. In a July 23 telegram, Mao told Zhou, "After the end of the Korean War, we failed to highlight the task to the people in the whole country in a timely manner, we failed to take necessary measures and make effective efforts in military affairs, on the diplomatic front, and also in our propaganda to serve this task. If we do not highlight this task now, and if we do not work for it, we are committing a serious political mistake" (Quoted in Chen, p. 168).

69. Guangqiu Xu, *Congress and the US-China Relationship: 1949–1979* (Akron, OH: University of Akron Press, 2007), p. 115. Shu Guang Zhang recounts, "It is clear that even though Washington officials did not believe the Communist Chinese shelling would lead to an attack on Taiwan, they were certain that a Chinese seizure of Jinmen or Mazu would immediately damage US prestige in the region and threaten US security interests in the long run. It was generally agreed that the United States would have to react to this challenge" (Shu Guang Zhang, p. 207).

70. Gordon H. Chang and He Di, "The Absence of War in the US-China Confrontation Over Quemoy and Matsu in 1954–1955: Contingency? Luck? Deterrence?" *The American Historical Review*, Vol. 98, No. 5 (1993), p. 1507.

71. "To Communist China, Taiwan represented a strategic threat as well as a highly embarrassing piece of unfinished business. Mao Zedong desperately desired the destruction of Chiang's outpost, and in July 1954 he asked the Chinese military to

draw plans for an invasion to 'liberate' Taiwan from foreign control. As a preliminary move, China had to seize a group of tiny islands right off its coastline that Chiang's Nationalists had held since 1949 that could hamper China's military operations" (Hitchcock, p. 205). The issue of territorial integrity was a paramount concern for China. The Taiwan question has to be seen in the context of Chinese history, especially during the Century of Humiliation beginning in 1839 with the Opium War. As noted by Thomas E. Stolper, "Peking's great concern for China's sovereignty and territorial integrity was well founded in experience. Manchuria, Mongolia, Sinkiang [Xinjiang], Tibet, and Taiwan had all been detached from China at one time or another and to one degree or another during Mao's lifetime. The United States was only the latest in a long line of foreign powers which, viewed from Peking, threatened grave damage to China's sovereignty and territorial integrity" (Stolper, p. 15).

72. Immerman, p. 122.

73. Quoted in Chen, p. 169.

74. Movement of Seventh Fleet ships in the vicinity of the offshores had failed to deter the bombardment (Garver, p. 123). Two American military advisers were killed in the bombardment. Led by Admiral Arthur Radford, a majority of the JCS unsuccessfully recommended to Eisenhower that the United States retaliate by bombing China (Kinzer, p. 199). In Manila, the United States, the UK, France, Australia, New Zealand, Pakistan, the Philippines, and Thailand signed the SEATO Treaty.

75. Immerman, p. 123.

76. Chang and Di, p. 1505.

77. There were actually two islands, close together, Quemoy and Little Quemoy. References in this book and other texts are to the larger island.

78. There were 19 islands in the Matsu chain. Reference to Matsu concerns the main one of these islands.

79. Dwight D. Eisenhower, *Mandate for Change: 1953–1956* (New York, NY: Doubleday & Company, 1963), pp. 459–460.

80. William I. Hitchcock, *The Age of Eisenhower: America and the World in the 1950s* (New York, NY: Simon & Schuster, 2018), p. 205.

81. Eisenhower, p. 461. Wellington Koo reports that Nationalist general Sun Li-jen, a senior officer who was politically estranged from Chiang, saw marginal value using the offshore islands as a launching point to assault the mainland.

"General Sun went on to say . . . that holding these islands and defending them at great cost on the ground of their value as a springboard for an attack on the mainland was a mistaken idea, since to succeed in attacking the mainland and establishing a beachhead, surprise was an important factor. In the case of these islands, there could be no surprise, and the Communists had taken all necessary measures against any such eventuality on their side opposite these islands. Any successful attempt to establish a beachhead on the mainland would have to be made elsewhere on the coast." (Koo, p. H-362)

82. Accinelli, p. 159.

83. Divine, p. 56.

84. Eisenhower, p. 463. Senator Mike Mansfield (D-MT) recalls that Eisenhower's longtime confidant, Undersecretary of State Walter Bedell Smith, concurred with Ridgway. Mansfield reports that Smith was the sole dissenter on the State Department

senior staff and that Dulles himself was committed to the idea of bombing mainland China in retaliation for the attacks on Quemoy and Matsu. Michael J. Mansfield Oral History, Princeton University Library, pp. 5–6. http://arks/princeton.edu/ark:/88435/ f7623j85w (accessed February 8, 2022).

85. Professor Foster Rhea Dulles says of Eisenhower, "He did not believe an attack on China could be limited or controlled as had been the case in the Korean War. In the existing circumstances he was unwilling to intervene to protect the offshore islands let alone encourage the Nationalists to invade the mainland" (Foster Rhea Dulles, p. 151).

86. Eisenhower, p. 464, Newton, p. 176. Mansfield states, "It was the President's decision which kept it from coming to pass" (Mansfield, p. 7). Accinelli states that Eisenhower considered "the likelihood of a wider conflict with China, the primacy of the global contest with the Soviet Union, the lack of sufficient military resources to keep pace with an unchecked proliferation of strategic commitments, constitutional restraints, and the need for public and allied support" (Accinelli, p. 162).

87. Professor Shu Guang Zhang notes that the UN gambit would serve to rally international opinion behind the United States and to enhance US relations with its allies. If the Chinese Communists resisted, they would be seen as the aggressor and the issue of admitting the PRC to the United Nations could be further deferred. Finally, it could provoke tensions in relations between China and the USSR, if the Soviets were forced to back up Chinese recalcitrance (Shu Guang Zhang, pp. 210–211). Accinelli notes that Dulles believed the United States would be in a stronger position to intervene militarily for having tried and exhausted a diplomatic remedy (Accinelli, p. 163).

88. Mansfield, p. 7. As Hitchcock describes it, Eisenhower and Dulles were playing for time (Hitchcock, p. 206).

89. The British interest was to halt the hostilities in the strait, keep the Americans from committing to defend the offshore islands, secure Chiang's agreement to withdraw from the islands, and keep Formosa from being used as a base to attack the mainland (Accinelli, p. 171).

90. Ibid., p. 196.

91. Stolper, p. 39. Shu Guang Zhang, p. 216.

92. "The unstable situation in the Strait, coupled with the need to win Chiang over to the UN initiative, had convinced Dulles, who had tilting toward a defense pact since late summer, that the moment was now opportune to grant the Generalissimo the alliance he had long craved" (Accinelli, pp. 167–168).

93. Professors Gordon H. Chang and He Di remark, "To bolster its commitment to the nationalists, the Eisenhower administration completed negotiation of a mutual defense treaty and received a blank check from Congress in early 1955, the so-called Formosa Resolution, for the use of American forces to defend Taiwan island and the nearby Pescadores" (Chang and Di, p. 1502).

94. Stolper, pp. 50–51. William Hitchcock recounts that the purpose of crafting the treaty in this way was "to gain credit for supporting Taiwan while avoiding the burden of an explicit commitment to defend the disputed islands" (Hitchcock, pp. 206–207).

95. In a February 4, 1955, meeting with Yeh and Koo, Under Secretary Herbert Hoover, Jr. (the former president's son) advised his guests that due to an understanding that the administration had entered with Congress, the United States could not make any public announcement that it would support defense of the offshore islands (Stolper, p. 70).

96. Garver, p. 125.

97. The administration considered that such ambiguity might deter Beijing while currying favor from US allies who could be expected to stand aside from a conflict limited to the islands but would support a defense of Formosa. Ibid.

98. Jim Newton, *Eisenhower: The White House Years* (New York, NY: Doubleday, 2011), p. 176.

99. In his memoirs, Rankin writes, "On June 28, Foreign Minister Yeh informed me that if a mutual defense treaty could be concluded President Chiang would agree to seek the prior agreement of the United States before undertaking any important military action. This was reported to Washington" (Rankin, p. 197). At the end of July, Rankin prepared a report for State in which he declared, "The Chinese government on Formosa does not expect an American commitment, either direct or implied, to sponsor its return to the mainland. Rather, it seeks a confirmation of United States intent to assist in the defense of Formosa on a longer-term basis, if only by implication, than has so far been admitted. No less important to the Chinese would be the political support implicit in the bilateral pact, irrespective of its exact provisions, which would place them on a par with Japan and Korea in this respect" (Ibid., p. 199).

100. "Privately, he thought this was 'intolerable' and a humiliation, but the treaty was 'a light of hope in the darkness'" (Taylor, p. 475).

101. Robert Divine observes that the treaty was a way to placate members of his own party who were calling for more resolute action on Chiang's behalf. But he adds, "At the same time, by insisting on restraining Chiang Kai-shek, the President protected himself against danger of automatic involvement in one of the Generalissimo's military adventures. Once again Eisenhower had displayed skilled manipulation of an extremely ambiguous diplomatic and domestic political situation" (Divine, p. 57. Taylor, p. 47n5).

102. Accinelli, p. 176.

103. Chang and Di, p. 1508.

104. Senator Knowland proposed to Eisenhower that the United States retaliate by imposing a naval blockade along the Chinese coast and Senator McCarthy suggested Chiang's forces attack the mainland. However, Eisenhower refrained from a belligerent response (Taylor, p. 475). The United Nations General Assembly instructed Secretary General Dag Hammarskjold to work for the airmen's release. Bilateral US-China talks in Geneva, which began in 1955, led to their release.

105. Accinelli observes that the Nationalists had negotiated well. "They had benefited from Dulles' eagerness to soften their resistance to the UN initiative and to expedite the negotiations so as to move ahead with Oracle in concert with the British" (Accinelli, pp. 176–177).

106. Stolper, pp. 52–53.

107. Xu, p. 116.

108. The language of Article 1 of the Treaty of Friendship, Alliance, and Mutual Assistance reads, "The two Contracting Parties undertake to carry out jointly all necessary measures within their power to prevent a repetition of aggression and breach of the peace by Japan or any other State which might directly or indirectly join with Japan in acts of aggression. Should either of the Contracting Parties be attacked by Japan or by States allied with Japan and thus find itself in a state of war, the other Contracting Party shall immediately extend military and other assistance with all the means at its disposal." The same framework underpinned the 1940 Tripartite Pact, signed by Germany, Italy, and Japan. None of the signatories could be brought into a war if one of its partners was an aggressor. Article 3 of that pact stated, "Germany, Italy and Japan agree to co-operate in their efforts on aforesaid lines. They further undertake to assist one another with all political, economic and military means when one of the three contracting powers is attacked by a power at present not involved in the European war or in the Chinese-Japanese conflict." Thus, when Japan attacked the United States, Germany was not legally bound to declare war on the United States, although it chose to do so.

109. Rankin did not believe the United States would help Chiang to continue occupying the Tachens, so that their defense would be solely the ROC's responsibility (Rankin, p. 169).

110. Ibid., p. 14.

111. Ibid.

112. Ibid., pp. 16–17.

113. Planning for the assault began in early 1954 after Mao rejected the advice of his military advisers to attack Quemoy in the aftermath of the Korean armistice. Mao wanted to move on the Tachens first (Chen, p. 167). Gordon H. Chang and He Di argue that American ambiguity about defense of Nationalist-controlled islands was counterproductive in the Tachens because Mao concluded the United States would not defend them. "If Washington, instead of avoiding explicit commitments to the defense of the offshore islands, had consistently demonstrated its determination to defend the islands, Mao would not have been likely to approve the assault on the Dachens" (Chang and Di, p. 1512).

114. *Foreign Relations of the United States: China 1955–1957, Volume II* (Washington, DC: US Government Printing Office, 1986), p. 82.

115. Chang and Di, p. 1515.

116. Ibid., pp. 1514–1515.

117. Chen, p. 167.

118. Ibid., p. 29. Chen Jian notes that the Tachens were reasonably proximate to Shanghai.

119. At a January 20 State Department briefing for congressional leaders, Dulles explained that the Tachens were so close to the mainland and so distant from Formosa that Communist pilots could conduct bombing runs and return to base before the Nationalists could intercept them. Under those conditions, the only useful platform for Nationalist pilots would be carriers (Ibid., p. 56).

120. Ibid., pp. 39–40.

121. Dulles believed the Communists would assault the Tachens and other offshore islands, as a path to the larger objective of overrunning Formosa. To deter them,

ambiguity must be abandoned, and American policy must be more vividly expressed (Accinelli, p. 187).

122. Chen, p. 42. See also Qu, p. 116. Professor Robert Accinelli believes that, in hardening their response, the Americans misread Communist intentions. "Evidence was lacking at this time at the Chinese were even massing their forces for an assault on Quemoy and Matsu, let alone preparing to invade Taiwan" (Accinelli, p. 190).

123. According to Senator Mike Mansfield's 1966 oral history at Princeton University, Dulles actively cultivated Senator George. "Especially with Senator George, with whom he breakfasted at least once a week—most of the time, I believe, in Senator George's apartment, but much of the time, also, in the Secretary of State's office" (Mansfield, p. 2). George's biographer also recounts that "every Thursday, George and Dulles met in George's apartment in the Mayflower for breakfast, and Miss Lucy cooked eggs, bacon, and grits for them. At the meetings, Dulles briefed George on the latest foreign policy developments and suggested a strategy on how to meet them. The two men had formed a warm relationship in Dulles' short term in the Senate, and this deep respect flourished into a confident and comfortable informal working relationship." Jamie Cockfield, *A Giant from Georgia: The Life of US Senator Walter F. George, 1878–1957*, (Macon, Georgia: Mercer University Press, 2019), p. 398.

124. Thomas Stolper explains that "Peking did not act against the Tachens for tactical reasons alone, although if Peking had only the capture of the Tachens in mind, it could scarcely have chosen a better time to put heavy pressure on them than when the Senate was considering the MDT. The American administration was in no position to play games over those islands, for the Senate would have hesitated to consent to the MDT at a time when there was a possibility of war over territory of no importance to the United States" (Stolper, p. 57).

125. Ibid., pp. 49–50.

126. Dulles told Senator Wiley that one-third of Chiang's 300,000 troops were based on the offshore islands, principally on Quemoy (Ibid., pp. 56–58).

127. Ibid.

128. Ibid., p. 66.

Chapter 6

Eisenhower Goes to Congress

It was likely the United States would have to take unilateral steps to ensure Formosa's defense. Therefore, Eisenhower decided to seek a congressional resolution to authorize the use of US armed forces. Dulles anticipated the response from congressional Democrats that the president already had inherent constitutional authority as commander-in-chief without additional authorization. But the administration was determined to engage Congress anyway.

Eisenhower believed that a president could act unilaterally in case of an emergency or if Congress was not available. However, he thought that if Congress were in session, it must be consulted.[1] As well, mere ratification of the treaty by itself would not substitute for a congressional resolution. An authorization to use force was necessary to implement treaty obligations. The duration of the authorization could be for a designated amount of time or tied to a specific outcome, such as a UN cease-fire order.[2]

Prolonged ambiguity was not useful, Dulles thought. The administration hoped that the resolution and the treaty would send a plain message that the United States had reached the end of its patience and would not retreat. If the Communists were convinced of it, the crisis in the strait might stabilize.

On the afternoon of January 20, 1955, Dulles briefed the National Security Council on the prospect of further Communist attacks in the area and on the desperation of Chiang's position in the Tachens. Without American miliary intervention, which the United States had ruled out, the islands were indefensible, he said. But it must also be understood that abandoning them would damage Nationalist morale and send a negative message to US allies in the region. Dulles insisted that Washington must be clear.[3] America would help Chiang evacuate the Tachens and resist incursions against Quemoy and Matsu, if such appeared preparatory to an attack against Formosa itself.[4]

The secretary said that most of the congressional leadership understood the need for a resolution, with the key exception of House Majority Leader John McCormack, who argued that the president already had sufficient powers to intervene in the offshore islands.[5] Dulles expected that Congress would act quickly and favorably on a resolution once the president requested it.

Robert Cutler, Eisenhower's national security adviser, noted that existing US policy was silent on Quemoy and Matsu. He asked Dulles whether changing this policy to commit to their defense was likely to involve the United States in a war with China and wondered whether the secretary had explored that risk with Congress.[6]

The president disputed Cutler's premise. The current policy was one of "dangerous drift," and tempted aggression, Eisenhower said. Prospects for war would diminish if the United States spoke bluntly.[7]

Secretary of the Treasury George Humphrey was cautious. The Nationalist presence on Quemoy, so close to the Chinese mainland, tempted conflict. Humphrey was not against drawing a defense line to establish what the United States would and would not defend. However, he firmly opposed including Quemoy inside it.

Secretary of Defense Charles E. Wilson strongly agreed with Humphrey. The offshore islands were a constant provocation to the PRC and of no meaningful importance to the Nationalists who had no hope of using them to regain control of the mainland. For America, they were a peril. Better to abandon them, remove the irritant, and reaffirm the defense of Formosa. If the Communists chose to attack Formosa itself, they should know it would mean war with the United States.

Dulles argued that action against Quemoy presaged an assault on Formosa. The United States could not stand aside while all Chiang's offshore islands were abandoned, because that would damage Nationalist morale and undermine American prestige. Unless the Communists disclaimed interest in taking Formosa, Quemoy and Matsu must be held.[8]

Eisenhower asked Radford if Formosa could be defended if Chiang no longer controlled the offshores? Loss of the islands would weaken the Nationalists, Radford replied, because the Communists would be able to use the mainland ports of Amoy and Foochow as staging areas for an invasion.[9]

Vice President Nixon outlined the political environment in Congress for Eisenhower's resolution. Some Democrats would assert that the president's request was unnecessary. Chiang's supporters might criticize the administration for advising that the Tachens be abandoned. Other members would raise the prospect of war with China. Eisenhower understood these nuances but said the word that Americans most feared was "Munich."[10] He insisted that American policy must appear firm.

Nixon counseled against the president appearing personally before Congress to seek the resolution and urged that the president communicate by written message. Already disposed to dampen war anxiety, he concurred.

Eisenhower pressed on. He believed that war in Korea happened because it was unclear whether Western powers would resist an invasion. In this case, if the Executive and Legislative Branches locked arms, no one could doubt the US resolve. In his memoirs, he recounted, "I believed the Korean War had resulted, partially at least, from the mistaken Communist notion that under no circumstances would the United States move to the assistance of the Korean Republic. I resolved at this time no uncertainty about our commitment to defend Formosa should invite a major Communist attack."[11]

The previous day, Dulles sent Eisenhower a draft of the message to Congress. It referred to the strategic importance of Quemoy and Matsu. "Under present conditions, two groups of islands now held by the Republic of China would constitute useful stepping-stones in the hands of the Communists if they are determined to pursue their design to conquer Formosa."

Expanding US commitments was to be temporary, the draft continued. "Let me make my position crystal clear: I do not now suggest that the United States should permanently enlarge its defensive obligations beyond Formosa and the Pescadores." As well, the AUMF was to have an end point. "It might well expire on June 30, 1956, or whenever earlier I am able to report to the Congress, but the peace and security of the area are reasonably assured by international conditions created by the United Nations or otherwise."

The draft stressed that what Eisenhower sought was "authority for a limited use for a limited time of the Armed Forces of the United States in order to create a position of strength and security in a vital area that is openly challenged." It assured Congress, "let me emphasize that what I seek is no declaration of war nor what, in my opinion, will lead to war."[12] The White House took the draft under advisement. It would ultimately reject the idea of giving explicit assurances about Quemoy and Matsu.

On the evening of January 20, Dulles received Sir Roger Elkins, the British ambassador who wished to communicate his government's opposition to defending Quemoy and Matsu. The British thought anything that went beyond protecting Formosa and the Pescadores would complicate prospects for a cease-fire resolution in the United Nations.[13] Elkins stressed that the British worried about representations Dulles had made to Foreign Secretary Anthony Eden that the United States might use atomic weapons against Communist positions.[14]

The secretary replied that the long-term interest of the United States did not extend beyond Formosa and the Pescadores but emphasized the importance of Nationalist morale. If Chiang's troops felt marginalized and would not fight, the burden of holding Formosa would rest on the Americans. To avoid that problem, Quemoy could not be sacrificed.

At 9:00 a.m. on Friday, January 21, the National Security Council again convened. Dulles reported on his conversation with Elkins. He declared that a way to assuage London was to strip reference to Quemoy and Matsu from Eisenhower's statement, but to assure the Nationalists privately of American support.

The president reported on a conversation he had the previous day with House Speaker Sam Rayburn. The speaker had asserted that Eisenhower had sufficient power without congressional action and that seeking authorization looked like an admission to the contrary. Rayburn also worried about a filibuster in the Senate. Better to act first and seek congressional approval after the fact, Rayburn advised. He promised the president that Congress would respond promptly.[15]

Attorney General Herbert Brownell asked Eisenhower whether Rayburn's advice would cause him to reconsider. But the president told Brownell he would proceed with the request and communicate via written message.[16] Eisenhower's biographer, Stephen Ambrose, called the plan unprecedented. "The resolution Eisenhower wanted was something new in American history. Never before had Congress given the President a blank check to act as he saw fit in a foreign crisis."[17]

Eisenhower later wrote, "I stuck to my proposed message, the purpose of which was to inform the Chinese Communists of the United States' intensions, to dispel doubts in foreign capitals that the United States was acting on constitutional grounds, and to bolster Chinese Nationalist morale."[18]

For the remainder of the meeting, the NSC revised Dulles's draft and the text of the proposed resolution. The meeting's Memorandum of Discussion recited that the NSC "agreed that the President should request from Congress authority to use US armed forces, if necessary, for the purpose of securing Formosa and the Pescadores against armed attack, this authority to include the securing and protection of such related positions now in friendly hands, and the taking of such other measures as the President might judge to be appropriate for the security and defense of Formosa and the Pescadores." The memorandum also detailed that to secure this mission, the United States would "assist the Chinese Nationalists to defend the Quemoy Islands and the Matsu Islands from Chinese Communist attacks so long as such attacks are presumptively made by the Chinese Communists as a prelude to attack upon Formosa and the Pescadores."[19]

On the morning of Friday, January 21, Dulles and Assistant Secretary Robertson met at the State Department with Foreign Minister Yeh and Ambassador Koo. Dulles summarized Eisenhower's plans to seek a resolution and read the portions of the draft message. To the disappointment of his visitors, he clarified that it would not expressly mention Quemoy and Matsu.[20] However, Dulles assured them that the United States would assist in defending the islands as well as giving air and naval support to the evacuation of the Tachens. For that purpose, carriers from the Seventh Fleet were already being repositioned from the Philippines to Okinawa. If Communist forces attempted to interdict the evacuation, such as by bombing troop transports, the Americans would shoot down the planes.

Mindful of Chiang's political concerns over the Tachens evacuation, Yeh was pleased with the overall plan. Koo wondered how Congress would react to the resolution. The House would endorse quickly, Dulles assured him. The Senate, with its more liberal debate rules, might take a bit longer, but approval could be expected within a week.

Dulles mentioned the separate but related matter of the Mutual Defense Treaty and said that Chairman Walter George of the Senate Foreign Relations Committee had assured him of its prompt disposition. The resolution would not supplant action on the treaty.

Yeh noted that Taipei was very cool with the idea of a cease-fire resolution in the UN. Dulles responded that even if the proposal materialized, success was improbable. The Chinese Communists would argue that the controversy was China's internal affair and would not acknowledge the UN had any jurisdiction in the matter.[21]

On Saturday, January 22, 1955, Yeh and Koo saw Dulles again, returning to present Chiang's views on the Tachens, the offshore islands, the congressional resolution, the Mutual Defense Treaty, and the UN resolution. Chiang grudgingly agreed to withdraw from the Tachens, provided he had Washington's promise of naval and air support. Wanting to deflect press speculation that the Mutual Defense Treaty would be sidetracked once Congress agreed to the resolution, Chiang wanted the Senate to expedite the treaty's consideration. He was highly dubious about proceeding with the New Zealand resolution, arguing that it could foment discussion of divorcing Formosa from the mainland. Beijing and Taipei did not agree on much, but "two Chinas" was something they both ardently opposed.[22] Yeh added that the Tachens should be neutralized after the Nationalists left. Preventing them from being used as a Communist base would mitigate military problems that could arise from the evacuation. He did not present a plan for doing so, Finally, Yeh asked to review the wording of the cease-fire resolution before it was offered.[23]

On the evening of January 22, Chiang held a consultation with Ambassador Rankin to complain about the situation in the Tachens and the proposed cease-fire resolution. Chiang emphasized that the Nationalists opposed abandoning the Tachens. Withdrawal would generate grave problems for troop and civilian morale. However, he could not sustain his presence there without American support. Lacking an alternative, he agreed under US pressure to evacuate.

Even worse from his perspective was the cease-fire resolution. For Chiang, it evoked bitter memories of the 1946 Marshall mission, when similar American-promoted strategies had complicated the Nationalists' military position. Rankin said Chiang was convinced a cease-fire after the Tachens withdrawal "would compound bad effects and raise questions in every mind whether Free China would ever fight again. All efforts in recent years to build fighting spirit would be undermined."

Worried that US support was not durable, the Nationalists were forever sensitive to any sign of abandonment. And that is how they saw cease-fire proceedings at the UN. As Rankin later noted, "The effect of ceasefire proposal would be even more serious if it should precede exchange of ratification of mutual defense pact."[24]

In an oral history, given nine years later, Chiang framed the withdrawal as his own government's idea:

> The decision was primarily a military one. At the time we had to reinforce, to strengthen, the defense of Quemoy and Matsu, because we considered these two groups of offshore islands as absolutely essential to the successful defense of Taiwan. Now, by comparison, Tachen was less important in that context, so it was decided to move our forces on Tachen and take them to Quemoy and Matsu. That was the decision we reached, and your government—the United States government—was also in favor of our decision.[25]

In connection with the Tachens withdrawal, which the United States had in fact urged upon him, Chiang felt confident Washington would help him defend the offshore islands. Chiang's oral history interviewer asked him, "Was there any understanding with Secretary Dulles at that time, or later, that giving up the Tachens would be the last such evacuation that the President would countenance, and that this did not apply to Quemoy and Matsu? Did Secretary Dulles understand this? And did he give any reaction do it?" Chiang responded, "At the time, Mr. Dulles verbally promised us that, after our evacuation of the Tachen islands, the United States of America would jointly defend Quemoy and Matsu."[26]

Approximately 14,000 military personnel and 16,000 civilians were evacuated from the Tachens to Formosa. The following month, there was a further evacuation, this time of 6,000 persons from the Nanchi Island group, substantially to the south of the Tachens.

A RESOLUTION IS SUBMITTED TO CONGRESS

Eisenhower was convinced that Congress would authorize the use of military force if it believed it was necessary to defend Formosa.[27] The White House transmitted the message to Capitol Hill on January 24, 1955. "The most important objective of our nation's foreign policy is to safeguard the security of the United States by establishing and preserving a just and honorable peace," the president began. "In the western Pacific a situation is developing in the Formosa Straits that seriously imperils the peace and our security."

Eisenhower insisted that Formosa must be denied to the Communists. This had been a bedrock principle of American policy since the outbreak of the Korean War and Truman's interposition of the Seventh Fleet in the strait. Failure to execute the policy would breach the island chain that constituted a crucial line of defense for the United States and allied nations. Eisenhower continued, "In unfriendly hands Formosa and the Pescadores would seriously dislocate the existing, even if unstable, balance of morale, economic, and military forces upon which the peace of the Pacific depends." He recounted PRC attacks on the Tachens and on Quemoy, noting that these were but a prelude to a move against Formosa itself.

The president stated he hoped the United Nations would be able to bring an end to hostilities but that would take time. Meanwhile, it might be necessary for the US military to intervene.

The United States had been disturbed by the buildup of airfields and military forces on the mainland, as well as by the shelling of Quemoy, the president said. He warned, "We must be alert to any concentration or employment of Chinese Communist forces obviously undertaken to facilitate attack upon Formosa and be prepared to take appropriate military action."

What would America defend and under what circumstances would it do so? The Mutual Defense Treaty, then pending in the Foreign Relations Committee, mentioned only Formosa and the Pescadores. However, to mount a successful defense, it was necessary to take into account related circumstances, which might involve threats to Quemoy and Matsu. "I do not suggest that the United States enlarge its defensive obligations beyond Formosa and the Pescadores, as provided by the treaty now awaiting ratification. But unhappily, the danger of armed attack against that area compels us to take into account closely related localities and actions which, under current conditions, might determine the failure or success of an attack."

Eisenhower acknowledged that, as president, he already enjoyed wide authority to deploy the US military and said he would not hesitate to use it in emergency conditions. However, he pressed for a congressional resolution, arguing it demonstrated an indivisible foreign policy. "It will reduce the possibility that the Chinese Communists, misjudging our firm purpose and our national unity, might be disposed to challenge the position of the United States, and precipitate a major crisis which even they would neither anticipate nor desire."

To prevent accidental war, Eisenhower said, it must be clear the United States was prepared to act. Because a resolution would remove any doubt, it might de-escalate the conflict. "I hope, however, that the effect of an appropriate Congressional resolution will be to calm the situation rather than to create further conflict," the president stated.

The authority he sought was to be temporary and should be terminated once he could report to Congress that peace and security has been assured, by the action of the United Nations or otherwise.[28]

Finally, Eisenhower observed that the resolution was not a substitute for the treaty and urged that the Senate promptly give its advice and consent.

"Our purpose is peace," the president concluded.[29]

Identical versions of the Formosa Resolutions were introduced later that day, as H.J. Res. 159 in the House and S.J. Res. 28 in the Senate. Proceedings in the House would begin the next day, Tuesday, January 25, following a unanimous favorable vote in the House Committee on Foreign Affairs.[30]

THE FORMOSA RESOLUTION ON THE HOUSE FLOOR

As approved in House Foreign Affairs Committee, H.J. Res. 159 read:

> Joint resolution authorizing the President to employ the Armed Forces of the United States for protecting the security of Formosa, the Pescadores, and related positions and territories of that area:
>
> Whereas, the primary purpose of the United States, in its relations with all other nations, is to develop and sustain a just and enduring peace for all; and
>
> Whereas, certain territories in the West Pacific under the jurisdiction of the Republic of China are now under armed attack, and threats and declarations have been and are being made by the Chinese Communists that such armed attack is in aid of and in preparation for armed attack on Formosa and the Pescadores;
>
> Whereas, such armed attack if continued would gravely endanger the peace and security of the West Pacific area and particularly of Formosa and the Pescadores; and
>
> Whereas, the secure possession by friendly governments of the Western Pacific island chain, of which Formosa is a part, is essential to the vital interests of the United States and all friendly nations in or bordering upon the Pacific Ocean; and
>
> Whereas, the President of the United States on January 6, 1955, submitted to the Senate for its advice and consent a Mutual Defense Treaty between the

United States of America and the Republic of China, which recognizes that an armed attack in the West Pacific area directed against territories, therein described, in the region of Formosa and the Pescadores, would be dangerous to the peace and safety of the parties to the treaty: Therefore, be it.

Resolved, That the President of the United States be and he hereby is authorized to employ the armed forces of the United States as he deems necessary for the specific purpose of securing and protecting Formosa and the Pescadores against armed attack, this authority to include the securing and protection of such related possessions and territories of that area now in friendly hands, and the taking of such other measures as he judges to be required or appropriate in assuring the defense of Formosa and the Pescadores.

This resolution shall expire when the President shall determine that the peace and security of the area is reasonably assured by international conditions created by action of the United Nations or otherwise and shall so report to the Congress.

After reporting H.J. Res. 159, the committee went before the House Rules Committee, seeking a House Resolution (otherwise known as a "Rule") that would govern consideration during Floor proceedings. Chaired by Howard Smith (D-VA), the Rules Committee reported H.J. Res. 104, a highly restrictive resolution known as a closed rule. It provided there would be 2 hours of general debate on the Formosa Resolution, but no amendments. On the Floor, Smith explained the procedure:

> All that is before this Congress is that you are going to support the President's policy, or you are not going to do it. We did not think it ought to be cluttered up with proposed amendments that might reach far beyond the purposes of this resolution, in which it is the desire of all parties to make simple and clear to the whole world just what this country proposes to do and where we stand from now on out. That is what this resolution proposes to do. For that reason, the committee thought it wise that there should be no amendments offered to it and that we either voted up or down.[31]

House Majority Leader John McCormack (D-MA) spoke next. He supported Eisenhower's plea for the resolution as an expression of national unity. Long a member of the House Democratic leadership and a tough partisan, McCormack emphasized the need to demonstrate bipartisan solidarity, especially to the Soviets and Chinese. "It will convey to them with firmness and strength that a Republican Administration with a Democratic Congress does not mean a divided nation." Passing the resolution involved risks, he acknowledged, but they were risks worth assuming for the deterrent effect that he hoped it would have.[32]

McCormack's counterpart, Republican leader Joseph Martin, stressed that the policy behind the Formosa Resolution was not new. It was consistent with Truman's order of June 27, 1950, to the Seventh Fleet and Eisenhower's address to Congress of February 2, 1953."By this resolution, we take a further important step and make clear to the Communists what the character of our reaction would be. This resolution authorizes the President to employ armed force against the attacking forces, allowing them no safer havens or steppingstones, and without waiting until their convoys are approaching Formosan beaches."[33]

Remaining debate on the rule closely tracked and reinforced the leadership's arguments. The sole murmur of dissent came from Representative Edith Green (D-OR), who announced support for the resolution but lamented that the United Nations was not being used as a mechanism to resolve the crisis. "Placing Formosa under the jurisdiction of the United Nations for a period of several years would be far preferable to a course of action which bolsters the repudiated regime of Chiang Kai-shek, and which could very likely lead to war," Green said.

After an hour's debate, the rule passed by voice vote. Thereafter, House Foreign Affairs chairman James Richards (D-SC) successfully moved that the House resolve itself into the Committee of the Whole for the purpose of considering H.J. Res. 159 under its terms.

The previous autumn, Richards had traveled through Asia. He encountered doubt about American commitments in the face of ongoing Communist pressure. "One of the strongest impressions I brought back was the uncertainty among the peoples of those countries that we would fight to stop further aggression," Richards reported. He argued that passage of the Formosa Resolution would do much to assuage those doubts.

Representative Overton Brooks (D-LA) wanted to know if the resolution put any restrictions on Eisenhower's use of a nuclear weapon? "There is nothing in this resolution that restricts it or authorizes it," answered Richards. That was what Brooks wanted to hear. "At least there is no restriction to it; he is able to use it if he needs it."[34]

Minnesota's Walter Judd was the most outspoken member of the House of Representatives on China issues. A former medical missionary, Dr. Judd served a total of 10 years in China. Arriving in Congress in 1943, he was a leader in the successful effort that year to repeal the Chinese exclusion laws. A staunch supporter of Chiang Kai-shek and a forceful anti-Communist, Judd was an outspoken advocate for the China Lobby. In Floor debate on the Formosa Resolution, he defined the matters at issue in stark terms. "It is the security of the island chain from the Aleutians to Australia. It is the freedom of the remaining 800 million free people in Asia. It is the security of the United States," he exclaimed.

Judd believed that, in constructing its Cold War policies, America had given too little attention to the centrality of China. He thought the Communists were more realistic. "The war in China was the one we did not want to bother with, but they were determined to win." Judd analogized the geography of Asia to a giant hand. China was the palm, and its neighbors were the fingers. Control of the palm meant control of the fingers, altogether involving a large land mass and an immense population. Given these stakes, non-Communists must awaken and resist. "This resolution is not just to save one island and some outposts, but to help keep free over one-third of the human beings in the world and keep the world balance of power from being turned overwhelmingly against us."[35]

Representative Donald L. Jackson (R-CA) spoke of an anti-Communist world under siege following aggression in Korea, Indochina, and the Formosa Strait. The resolution was a policy watershed. "Our allies in the Philippines, Japan, Formosa, Australia, and New Zealand will know that we intend no further retreat in the Orient."

Concerned that Congress was giving Eisenhower an unprecedented degree of authority, Congressman Arthur Winstead (D-MS) announced his reluctant support. "The President's message asks the Congress to concur, in advance, in any move which he directs which might later require the outright declaration of war. This is something new in the history of the United States. Nevertheless, I will support the resolution, for I am convinced that the defense of Formosa is absolutely necessary if Communist aggression is to be stopped."[36]

Representative Paul J. Kilday (D-TX) worried about the precedent the resolution might establish for restricting the future exercise of presidential power over the armed forces. He worried about the implication that the president could not deploy the military without Congress's express permission. And he did not want Congress to micromanage American troop deployments, by either failing to authorize force or imposing limitations on its use. Finally, he wanted to ensure that military commanders would not have control over nuclear weapons. Congress had written into law that only the president would have such authority. Nothing in the Formosa Resolution should be construed as modifying that power, Kilday urged. "I do not want Members of this House or of the other body, or anyone else hereafter to raise the question should the President act without having submitted previously a request to the Congress for specific authority in that instance. I want to preserve his constitutional powers as written and preserve them inviolate."[37]

Speaker Sam Rayburn worried that passing the resolution would carry the negative inference that the president had no authority other than that which Congress specifically bestowed. "This should not be taken as a precedent that the President of the United States . . . should feel it is his duty to come before the Congress and ask for a resolution such as this." Rayburn went on, "If the President had done what is proposed here without consulting with the Congress, he would have had no criticism from me."[38]

Judd concurred with Kilday about presidential power but stressed that the resolution was helpful to project national unity. "The only qualm I had in consideration of this resolution was that it might be construed as setting a precedent limiting the power that I think he has under the Constitution. That is, I do not think it is necessary for the President to come to Congress for this authority, but I think it is better for him to do so because it makes our national position stronger before those who threaten war before the world."

Representative Sid Yates (D-IL) had several questions for Chairman Richards as the general debate wound down. Did the chairman construe the resolution as a declaration of war, either actual or contingent, against the Chinese Communists? "I do not consider it as a declaration of war," Richards replied. "I feel personally that if events transpired that made the president feel a declaration of war was necessary that he would have to come to Congress to get it." Did the resolution's elastic language that read "and the taking of such other measures as he judges to be required or appropriate" authorize Eisenhower to attack the mainland? "I do not so construe it," answered the chairman. "It would authorize the president to take physical possession of the islands in friendly hands, which we would say would be islands in the hands of the Nationalist Chinese. It would not authorize him to take possession of anything on the ground on the mainland, but would authorize him, I think, to attack the mainland if he deemed it necessary in support of the defenses of Formosa." Finally, Yates asked if the resolution required the United States to "go it alone" if the United Nations did not effect a cease-fire. "I construe the resolution not as requiring the government of the United States to go to alone if action is not taken by the United Nations but permitting it to go it alone," Richards said. "I would like to state that it is my understanding— and I believe that it is the understanding of the executive department of the government—that we are going to handle this situation whether the United Nations does get into it or not."[39]

Yates thought the resolution was premature and should await action in the Senate on the Mutual Defense Treaty. However, based on the president's request for moral support and the recommendation of the House Foreign Affairs Committee, he would vote aye.

Time for debate having expired, and no amendments being in order, the House voted on passage of the joint resolution. The tally was 410–3, with 11 members not voting. Only Representatives Graham Barden (D-NC) and Timothy Patrick Sheehan (D-IL), as well as Graham Siler (R-KY) voted no.

The rules, precedents, and mechanisms of the House serve to make it a legislative juggernaut when its leadership wants prompt action. That was the case with the Formosa Resolution. Within a day of the moment the House received it, the resolution received action at both the Foreign Affairs and Rules Committees and was considered on the Floor under a procedure allowing for very limited debate and no amendments at all. Issues that might have provoked or been evidence of dissent were essentially buried in the House but would surface in vigorous and active debate in the Senate.

On January 25, the day the House acted, Eisenhower met with Senate Minority Leader Knowland. The president told him:

> You know, Senator, sometimes we are captains of history. Formosa is a part of a great island barrier we have erected in the Pacific against Communist advance. We are not going to let it be broken. . . . We just can't permit the Nationalists to sit in Formosa and wait until they are attacked, and we just can't try to fight another war with handcuffs on as we did in Korea. If we see the Chinese Communists building up in their forces for an invasion of Formosa, we are going to have to go in and break it up.[40]

The same day, US intelligence agencies issued a National Intelligence Estimate concerning the probable situation in the strait if Congress approved Eisenhower's request. The NIE predicted that the Communists would continue to assert that Formosa was China's domestic matter, denounce US interference, and brag about Nationalist evacuation of the Tachens.[41] The estimate did not expect the Communists to attack American forces assisting the evacuation, although it did not rule that out. If fighting with the United States occurred, the estimate projected, the Chinese would seek to activate their mutual defense pact with the Soviets. The estimate assumed the Soviets would intervene, to maintain the Sino-Soviet alliance and to prevent destruction of the Chinese Communist regime. Congressional approval of the Formosa Resolution would not deter the Communists from probing actions to test US policy, it said.[42]

Chinese Communist reaction to Eisenhower's message was soon forthcoming. A *New York Times* dispatch from Tokyo reported, "Breaking a three-day silence on the President's move, the Peiping government radio last night called the President's message to Congress a 'barefaced war cry.' It accused the United States of 'plotting to extend its aggression beyond Taiwan [Formosa] and the Penghu [Pescadores] islands.' The Communist radio heard here called General Eisenhower's action a serious step in preparation for a new war."[43]

The Senate: Floor Debate before Hearings on the Formosa Resolution

On January 24, before committee proceedings on S.J. Res. 28 commenced, Senator Mike Mansfield (D-MT) took the Senate Floor. By then, he had spent a dozen years in Congress and was widely regarded among his colleagues and others as one of its experts on Asia.[44]

Mansfield expressed concern that the administration appeared to be rushing the Formosa Resolution through the Senate, putting it in the queue ahead of the Mutual Defense Treaty. He questioned the urgency. "If there was an impending crisis, why did not the President come in person to present the facts to the Congress? Why was the Senate not advised sooner?" The Senate should not act hastily, Mansfield implored. "The situation in the vicinity of Formosa is not one which lends itself to improvisation. We have slipped into a difficult position there. It will grow more difficult unless this government acts with a high degree of responsibility."[45]

So that his colleagues might better understand the US interest and legal position in Formosa, Mansfield reviewed the history of the island's sovereignty. Japan had taken it from China after an 1895 war. Although Japanese claims were internationally recognized, including by the United States, China believed that it had ceded sovereignty under duress and sought to regain it.

Formosa was an important strategic asset for Japan during World War II, said Mansfield, providing a launching pad for many air and naval attacks against American forces. During the war, the United States sought to wrest it away from the Japanese and, looking ahead, to prevent it from ever again being used by a hostile power. "Our vital interest in Formosa was obvious," he observed. "It was to deny the island, insofar as it was in our power to do so, to any group or nation which would use it for aggressive purposes in the western Pacific."[46]

Thus, the United States agreed in November 1943 to the Cairo Declaration, which Prime Minister Winston Churchill and Generalissimo Chiang Kai-shek cosigned with Roosevelt. "Under the terms of the agreement," said the senator, "the return of Formosa and the Pescadores to the Republic of China was pledged." Mansfield accurately characterized the declaration as a promise and not a treaty, and stated that it did not, by itself, adjust sovereignty over Formosa. "It did not under international law transfer the title of the islands to China. They remained technically under the sovereignty of Japan at least until the end of World War II."[47]

When the war ended, and it was possible for the Nationalist Chinese government to occupy the island, Mansfield said, the US strategic interest appeared to have been satisfied, pending a final peace treaty with Japan. But Mao's triumph in China and the onset of the Korean War changed things.

We had no interest in acquiring Formosa for ourselves, but only in preventing it from falling into the hands of the Communist aggressors. We supplied the Chinese Nationalist Government on Formosa with military and economic aid, while the Seventh Fleet was ordered to patrol the Strait. . . . We had to proceed in these circumstances to negotiate a peace treaty with Japan. By the terms of the treaty, Japan renounced all claims to Formosa. We and the other nations involved insisted on that renunciation as a safeguard against renewal of aggression from that source. The treaty, however, left indeterminate the legal status of the island, pending a clarification of the situation in the Far East.[48]

Stated otherwise, Japan had given up sovereignty without transferring ownership. Chiang was occupying Formosa without a formal territorial settlement. Notwithstanding Beijing's claims that sovereignty was indisputably Chinese, Mansfield argued that "we have as much a right to declare what the future of these islands shall be as do our allies. In our hands collectively lies the final authority to determine what shall be the final disposition of the Pescadores and Formosa."[49]

Under these conditions, Mansfield argued, the United States had a basis to intervene in the strait to assure its own security and regional stability. "Armed Forces of the United States are in that region for one purpose. They are there, or should be there, only to prevent Formosa and the Pescadores from falling into the hands of forces of Communist aggression which might ultimately be aimed at this country."

The senator believed the administration should vigorously pursue negotiations in the United Nations, thinking that a stable cease-fire might lead to a political solution. He considered that an overall settlement could involve four benchmarks: acknowledgment that the United States had no territorial claims in the region, restating that Japan had relinquished all territorial claims to Formosa, affirming that the island would not again become a springboard for aggression in the western Pacific, and resolution of sovereignty in accordance with the wishes of inhabitants of the islands.[50]

While Mansfield appreciated the president coming to Congress, he argued that Eisenhower already had ample constitutional authority and the resolution was unnecessary. "The President is to be congratulated and thanked for taking us into his trust in this case," Mansfield said, but noted, "There is a separation of authority as between the Executive and the Legislative Branches of our government, and under the Constitution there are certain elements of responsibility which are his."[51]

THE SENATE: HEARINGS ON THE
FORMOSA RESOLUTION COMMENCE

At 3:15 p.m. on January 24, 1955, in the US Capitol Building, the Senate Foreign Relations Committee met jointly with the Senate Armed Services Committee to commence closed-door testimony on the resolution.[52] In all, 26 senators were present, 14 from Foreign Relations and 12 from Armed Services. Georgia's senators headed the two committees: Walter George for

Foreign Relations and Richard Russell for Armed Services. Together George and Russell had 55 cumulative years of Senate service.

George chaired the proceedings. As he explained in his introductory statement, the combined hearing was necessary because the resolution implicated both foreign policy, which was in his committee's jurisdiction, and military execution, which involved Armed Services.

Dulles was the first witness. When PRC commenced shelling, he stated, the United States did not immediately react. However, the administration reassessed after the assault on the Tachens and repeated belligerent statements about liberating Formosa.[53]

Such rhetoric gave context to Beijing's strategy, which was not simply to oust Chiang from the islands. Instead, the Communists signaled they would press ahead to an outright assault on Formosa itself. "I think that we are forced to assume that is their probable intention," the secretary said.[54]

In the face of such escalation, America's reaction must be very firm. It would send a crucial message, not just to the Communists but also to treaty partners in South Korea, Japan, and the Philippines. Indecisiveness would confuse and disappoint US allies and destroy the morale of the Nationalist military.[55] If that happened, negative consequences would cascade. "You could have a very rapid disintegration in the position of the free countries all along that offshore island chain, and I believe that its tenability by US forces or by forces friendly to the United States would at that point become extremely precarious."[56]

Leaving the Tachens was in the Nationalists' best interest, the secretary testified. The islands were too distant from Formosa, overextending Chiang's defenses.[57] However, Quemoy and Matsu presented a different situation. They were directly opposite Formosa, far closer to it than the Tachens, and more directly related to its security. An attack on Formosa was likely to be launched from the mainland ports of Amoy and Foochow. Nationalist forces just offshore were well placed to interdict such assaults. "These two island positions block the exit to those harbors and constitute a very considerable obstacle to the possible invasion of Formosa by an amphibious operation," he stated.[58]

However, such strongholds still required people willing to defend them. If the Nationalists lost faith in US commitments, morale would collapse and defenses would not stand. Dulles testified that the prospect of unraveling was real and near. "Unless something is done at this stage, the entire situation will disintegrate to a point which is beyond the possibility of recovery."[59] A collapse would imperil control of Formosa, threaten US interests, and increase the prospects of war with China and the Soviet Union.[60]

Forfeiting Formosa would have major implications for the entire US posture in the western Pacific, he underscored. American strategy was based on controlling a chain of locations, beginning in the north with the Aleutian Islands of Alaska, continuing southwest to the Japanese main islands and Korea, and onward to Okinawa. Then came Formosa, followed by the Philippines, Australia, and New Zealand. All these lands, except Formosa, either belonged directly to the United States or were subject to treaties to which it was a party. "That whole position is regarded as vital to the United States," Dulles stated.[61]

Loss of Formosa would break the chain. Thus, the United States had two mutually consistent imperatives: to guarantee Chiang's defense and to reinforce its own security interests. "We don't operate there just out of an act of kindness to the Chinese Nationalists. We are there because that whole position from the Aleutians down to New Zealand is vital to us, and it is certainly the view of the Joint Chiefs of Staff that any breach in that line would be a grave disaster for the United States."[62]

Reinforcing this point, Senator William F. Knowland (R-CA) asked Dulles whether failure to hold the line would jeopardize US forces stationed in forward positions in Korea, Japan, Okinawa, and the Philippines. Dulles acknowledged that and said it was the reason for Truman's 1950 order placing the Seventh Fleet into the Taiwan Strait.[63]

Dulles knew that some senators preferred to resolve tensions through the United Nations.[64] No country had been more instrumental in its founding than America, and it was under a United Nations Security Council Resolution that the North Korean invasion was challenged. Dulles assured them the UN option would be explored, but cautioned he was skeptical of success. He anticipated that either the Soviets or the Chinese Communists would refuse to cooperate. The PRC had repeatedly avowed that the Formosa problem was a domestic matter for China alone to resolve, without external influence. The secretary quoted Zhou Enlai, who declared, "Taiwan is an inalienable part of Chinese territory. The liberation of Taiwan is a matter of China's sovereignty and internal affairs. No outside interference is allowed."[65]

Zhou had argued that the United Nations Charter prohibited it from intervening in a country's domestic jurisdiction and declared that China would not acquiesce in any UN directives. Dulles remarked, "I do not have a great deal of hope that they will be able to come up with a satisfactory solution of the matter because the Chinese Communists have repeatedly made clear that they will not accept any decision by the United Nations in this matter."[66]

Senator Russell referred to the president's message, which said, "We must be alert to any concentration or employment of Chinese Communist forces obviously undertaken to facilitate attack upon Formosa and be prepared to take appropriate military action."[67]

Did this statement connote anticipatory attacks against force concentrations massing in Chinese ports? And under what conditions, if any, would it involve the use of American troops? Dulles responded that Eisenhower would consider preemptive bombing, if necessary, but added, "There is no reason in sight for using ground forces in the area." However, he cautioned, "That assumes, of course, the continuing loyalty of the Chinese Nationalist forces. If they should become hopelessly discouraged, then we would be faced with the problem of sending our own ground forces to Formosa to at least stiffen them up."[68]

Was holding Quemoy essential to the defense of Formosa, Russell inquired? Strategically important, but not essential, Dulles answered. The larger question was morale. Picking off the islands would not necessarily make Taiwan militarily vulnerable, but it could sap the Nationalists' will to fight. In his testimony, Dulles returned repeatedly to this overarching concern about morale.[69]

Little more than five years had passed since Mao proclaimed the People's Republic of China. But for the Korean War, it is likely the Nationalist government in Taiwan would not have survived. The PRC made international declarations of its intention to unite Taiwan with the mainland. People in Taiwan were facing siege conditions and living under a martial law government. The offshore islands were under ongoing assault, and the Tachens had been vacated. Under those conditions, it was reasonable to question whether Nationalist forces would stand fast and what expedient steps the United States take to ensure they did. "There is not in contemplation any firm or perpetual obligation with respect to these islands," Dulles stated. "Our reactions there will be what seems to be dictated by circumstances and events, of which the morale factor is at the present time a very important one."[70]

Senator Alben Barkley (D-KY) doubted that it was possible to avoid the use of American troops. "Notwithstanding all these destructive weapons, we still have to follow up with an army, and I doubt very much if this Chinese operation will be much different as it flows along . . . but I think we are indulging in wishful thinking when we say that it will not be necessary to use ground troops."[71]

If Quemoy were attacked, asked Senator Ralph Flanders (R-VT), was the United States obligated to respond? Not legally or even implicitly so, answered Dulles. "We are not making any promises to the Chinese Nationalists or anybody else as to what we are going to do," he emphasized. "The decision rests with us."

Senator H. Alexander Smith (R-NJ) spoke of setting red lines, which meant declaring in advance circumstances that would trigger a US response. Smith believed the United States should make explicit that Quemoy and Matsu would be protected, but Dulles disagreed. He argued that if boundaries were demarcated, anything not expressly included would implicitly not be defended. That would generate a situation like the Acheson statement of

January 12, 1950, which laid out specific US defense interests in the Pacific without mentioning Korea. "We found that it was almost impossible to draw a line in terms of concrete named specific places and to say, 'this is it' and nothing else is it," Dulles replied, adding, "If you say, 'nothing else is it,' then all you do is to let the enemy run around the lines you have indicated."[72]

Was there a meaningful prospect for a Security Council cease-fire resolution, asked Senator Harry Flood Byrd (D-VA)? Dulles was doubtful. If the UN could not be productive, would the United States act on its own? Dulles answered affirmatively. "We will not feel dependent upon getting affirmative approval of the United Nations," he told the senator.[73]

Senator John Sparkman (D-AL) returned to the question of whether the resolution was even necessary?[74] In his message, Eisenhower stated he would act based on his inherent powers, if it was necessary to do so before Congress had an opportunity to legislate.[75] If the president could proceed without permission, why should Congress act at all? There were two major reasons, Dulles replied, one legal and the other political. Passing the resolution would clarify that the president was not relying solely on implied powers.[76] "Even if there was no doubt whatever about the legal position, even it was perfectly clear the President did have this authority, I believe it would be indispensable that the Congress should indicate its concurrence." Moreover, other nations would know that Americans of both parties were unified behind the policy. "Unless the American people, unless the Congress, are in back of this thing, and unless the whole world knows they are back of it, I do not think this operation would be successful."[77]

Ending any such speculation was important to avoid miscalculation and keep the peace, the secretary stressed. "What we are trying to do there is not to get into a war, but to keep out of a war, and at the same time to preserve the vital interests of the United States."[78]

In an exchange with Senator George Aiken (R-VT), Dulles elaborated on the need for a more resolute policy. The United States had been patient in response to a series of Communist provocations, he said. America pursued an armistice in Korea, rather than a widened war against China. The United States had not entered the war in Indochina, instead joining negotiations to curb the conflict. But the Communists continued to push. In the strait, they had become more belligerent. "Now this thing comes along so that you have got three successive episodes over a period of approximately five years which show a pattern of aggression. I don't know how many times Axis powers have to be aggressive before we took account of the fact that they were basically aggressive in their mood."[79]

The Communists would interpret anything other than American firmness as an invitation to press the advantage. "I do not think it will be stopped by anything less than a very clear declaration, an action on the part of our government that makes it clear to them if they are going to pursue that course, it is going to mean general war." Dulles claimed that being steadfast, rather than escalatory, was the best way to avoid war. Otherwise, he said, "There will be one of these miscalculations which I have often said is the greatest breeder of war there is."[80]

Dubious that a conflict could be confined to the strait, Senator Hubert Humphrey (D-MN) worried about an open-ended war with China. He recalled that, during the Korean conflict, General MacArthur had advised expanding the war across the Chinese border and toppling the Communist government. Would Eisenhower be tempted to follow suit? Dulles was emphatic that Eisenhower would not. The president had inherited the Korean conflict, with China as an enemy. Rather than extend the war, which he could have done, Eisenhower pursued an armistice. "I would say that the same considerations that influenced the President at that time, in that way, would influence him in a parallel situation."[81]

Senator John Stennis (D-MS) questioned whether help might materialize from US treaty allies if hostilities broke out. Dulles assessed those other nations would contribute little more than token forces to such a conflict, and that, apart from the Nationalist Chinese, the effort would be principally American.[82]

Next up was Barkley, who inquired whether the authority in the proposed resolution was so broad that it would cover a major war if hostilities with China erupted. Dulles answered that the resolution would be sufficient for the degree of conflict the administration anticipated, but Eisenhower would return to Congress in the event a major war developed. "There is no question whatever in my mind that any large-scale operation could not be conducted without recognition of the fact by the Congress and without the readiness of the Congress to appropriate the necessary funds, and exercise the necessary controls," he noted. While such steps could be taken without a formal declaration, said Dulles, Eisenhower had in mind a contained situation and was not seeking open-ended authority. The administration would come back to the Hill if things grew more severe.[83]

Finally, Barkley asked whether the administration had any plans to use American armed forces to restore Chiang's control of the mainland. Dulles assured the senator, "Absolutely nothing."[84]

Highly suspicious of Chiang's motives, Senator Homer Capehart (R-IN) framed a scenario in which the Nationalists would instigate provocations against the PRC, the Communists would retaliate, and Eisenhower would be forced to respond. "I don't want to place him in a position where he is calling the turn and where he is doing things under this resolution that forces our President to act, which in turn starts a war on the mainland between the United States and China or the United States and Russia." The senator pressed the witness, "If we are going to have a war with China or Russia, I don't want to see it precipitated by Chiang Kai-shek, and you assure me that that cannot happen and will not happen."[85] "Yes sir," Dulles emphasized.

Senator Knowland was both the Senate minority leader and Taiwan's foremost ally in the Senate.[86] He insisted that the offshore islands must be defended because of the military importance of nearby mainland ports. "Both of them furnish facilities for the concentration of large numbers of amphibious craft of the nature that would be used in any operation of this kind, it would be open to that purpose were it not for the fact that the Republic of China controls for the time being at least the blocking islands of those two harbors," the senator observed.[87] Dulles would not commit to defend the islands, but he concurred with Knowland's analysis. The issue was whether a Communist move against the islands was the precursor to an attack on Taiwan itself. If so, Eisenhower was likely to step in.

Senator Wayne Morse (D-OR) turned to the question of preventive war. He noted that the United States had never been the aggressor in a conflict. He was troubled by the predated authorization of force and the possibility of preemptive action against China. If America was labeled the aggressor, its moral standing would be damaged. Dulles responded that the concept of first aggressor must take account of reality, such as the need to take out military resources before they were deployed. "I think that the definition of what is aggression must necessarily adapt itself to modern conditions of warfare," Dulles said. "While it would be extremely nice to wait and do nothing until after we were sure that the other fellow was an aggressor, the fact is that if we adopt that policy, we will probably never live to hear the opinion of the court which will commend us."[88]

Shortly thereafter, Dulles completed his appearance before the committee. After nearly 4 hours, the hearing adjourned, to commence the following morning with the appearance of the JCS.

SENATE HEARINGS CONTINUE: JANUARY 25, 1955

On January 25, the combined committees reconvened in the Old Supreme Court Chamber to hear testimony from Admiral Arthur W. Radford, chairman of the JCS. Accompanying him were the service chiefs from the Army, Navy, Air Force, and Marine Corps. Radford affirmed that the chiefs unanimously supported Eisenhower's efforts to stabilize the Formosa area, adding, "I feel very strongly, as Secretary Dulles did yesterday, that . . . if we take no action at this time, we will lose our position in the western Pacific, we will lose it completely, and in the not-too-distant future. The only hope of avoiding a much larger struggle is to take firm action in this limited area at this time."

Failure to act would convey the impression of American weakness, on which Beijing would capitalize, he said. "They will have the definite feeling that whenever they threaten us, we will back down, and we will see them starting into Southeast Asia, and undoubtedly we will lose Japan, which is the great prize in the western Pacific for the Communists."[89]

Senator Russell asked Radford whether the offshore islands were crucial to the defense of Formosa and if the United States had any commitment, even implicit, to defend them. Radford answered that, from a military perspective, the islands were not essential and that the United States had no such understanding. Russell was generally satisfied. "I am somewhat concerned about this idea of adopting Quemoy and Matsu as part of the defenses of Formosa. I think there would be much more of a danger of being drawn into a war of a generation's length if we had our defense line there rather than the island of Formosa."[90]

Although the islands were not militarily essential, Radford cautioned, they remained consequential. They blocked two harbors that would be used to conduct an amphibious attack, so Formosa's defense would be easier if friendly forces occupied them. "For that reason," Radford stressed, "I would favor assisting the Chinese Nationalists to hold them."[91]

The United States had invested heavily in political stability and military strength of Chiang's government, Radford continued. He stated that, since 1950, America had spent more than $800 million to support the Chinese Nationalist army.[92] "They are part of our military strength in the Far East, and we do not want to lose them."[93]

Radford believed that the United States bore heavy responsibility for the Communist triumph on the mainland. He referred to American efforts to facilitate the creation of a coalition government by leveraging Chiang. "One of the things that a country does when they allow themselves to be equipped by another country, they usually put themselves in a position where that country can shut off spare parts and ammunition, and the equipment itself is worthless." The United States had done that during the Chinese civil war. Radford recounted, "There was a time in order to get Chiang Kai-shek to take certain action, we placed certain restrictions on him, and we shut off his supplies. In that interval of time, the Communists went ahead, violated their agreements, moved their forces around, and they were able to win a military victory." He lamented, "I think we can blame ourselves largely for the success of the Communists in conquering China."[94]

Radford reprised the morale issue. The steadfastness of Chiang's troops could not be assumed. "We have great concern over holding the loyalty of the troops that are available to us on Formosa," he said. If the United States did not show it was determined to backstop those forces, Nationalist resistance might dissipate. He again referred to the history of the Chinese civil war, in which considerable numbers of Nationalist forces surrendered or defected when they saw no hope of winning. Were there a danger of something similar happening, "there is a possibility that we would have to take action to hold Formosa ourselves."[95]

Russell was troubled about the effect on public opinion in Asia if it appeared the United States started the conflict. Who would decide whether a preemptive strike could be made against the mainland, he asked?

The United States would carefully monitor any buildup of forces, Radford replied, and assess its size and likely purpose. It would be the president's decision to order a preemptive strike, and under the proposed resolution, it was a matter completely within his discretion.[96] Radford added that if the PRC attacked American positions, such as naval vessels, the commander of the Seventh Fleet would have the authority to respond in hot pursuit and attack the planes and the bases from which they came.[97]

Senator Leverett Saltonstall (R-MA) asked Radford about how military leaders such as Omar Bradley, George Marshall, and Douglas MacArthur regarded the relationship of Formosa to US national security.[98] Each of them considered it vital to deny Formosa to the Communists, Radford responded. He outlined their reasoning, "Formosa, in unfriendly hands, because of its size, could accommodate air forces that could force us to abandon our base at Okinawa. I mean, they would outflank us, and with jet aircraft the threat to the Philippines, Okinawa, would be very, very great."[99]

Did the United States have sufficient forces in the region to back up its tough rhetoric, asked Senator Margaret Chase Smith (R-ME)? "Under the contingencies that may arise and basing it upon the intelligence we have, we have enough power to carry on the operations which might occur," Radford assured her. Suppose the response from the PRC was more severe than the administration anticipated? The United States would reinforce with assets already in the region, including ground forces, the admiral indicated, and, if necessary, the president would come to Congress for additional support.[100] However, Radford stressed, with 350,000 Nationalist Chinese combat troops available, he did not foresee any necessity for American ground forces to augment them.[101]

Radford testified that it would be unwise to allow the expanding Chinese military threat to continue indefinitely, without US intervention.[102] In the short term, America could supply Nationalist positions on the islands to offset buildups on the mainland. However, there was a point of saturation to that strategy, Radford said. Eisenhower's objective was to stabilize the situation before a large-scale conflict became inevitable.[103]

In his message, Eisenhower stated: "We must be alert to any concentration or employment of Chinese Communist forces obviously undertaken to facilitate attack upon Formosa and be prepared to take appropriate military action."

This meant disabling the Chinese before they gathered decisive strength and before they launched an attack. Senator Henry M. Jackson (D-WA) wanted clarification. "It is my understanding that if in the next two years no action is taken and there is this big critical build-up . . . then we would seize the initiative and possibly move against them?" Radford affirmed, "that is what the President says in his message."[104]

Would preemptive action involve the use of nuclear weapons against the Chinese mainland, Senator Mansfield inquired? Radford responded that such use would be unlikely, but he did not rule it out. "I would not hesitate to recommend it if I thought we had to use them to defend ourselves, defend our forces."[105]

Humphrey was puzzled. No one had suggested that an attack on Formosa was imminent. But the administration had asked that the resolution be considered ahead of the Mutual Defense Treaty. What was the urgency? Humphrey did not understand the sequencing.

Radford responded that the timing of the resolution was related to the expected evacuation of the Tachens, which generated a sense of crisis in the region. Although Chiang had not yet ordered a withdrawal, and was reluctant to do so, it seemed imminent.[106] The administration worried that it would tempt the Communists to ratchet up pressure elsewhere. Eisenhower wanted to be able to respond.

Passing the resolution and having the Senate approve the Mutual Defense Treaty would alter the psychology and make it easier for Chiang to give ground, commented Radford. It would ease his awkward domestic politics and serve as a warning to Beijing against trying to capitalize on its success in the Tachens.[107]

Was there evidence that the PRC was preparing to escalate, Humphrey inquired? Radford noted a substantial movement of ground forces near the coastal ports of Amoy and Foochow. He claimed that the buildup of air forces could follow quickly, leading Humphrey to ask, "So your testimony is that there is a present and prevailing threat immediately against the Straits of Formosa beyond Quemoy Island, is that correct?" "Absolutely," said Radford.[108] The admiral elaborated on what would happen if the Communists were not preempted:

> The Communists have announced that they are going to take Formosa and the Pescadores, and we have our choice of waiting until they decide they are ready to do it, by which time we may have lost one-third of the ground troops of Chiang Kai-shek that we equipped in these outlying islands, and we would have just that many less men to defend the island of Formosa. We might even have questionable loyalty if they are beaten and defeated. We have a great stake in this area.[109]

All the chiefs shared Radford's assessment, including Army Chief of Staff, General Matthew Ridgway. Ridgway had a reputation as an independent thinker. At the time of the 1954 siege of Dien Bien Phu, he had strongly dissented from a Joint Chiefs recommendation that the United States intervene to support beleaguered French forces. In the Formosa Strait crisis, he opposed US intervention to protect Quemoy and Matsu. Nevertheless, when Senator Knowland asked him about the importance of Formosa to the US strategic position in the Pacific, Ridgway answered, "The retention of Formosa and the Pescadores in the hands of a friendly government is essential to the vital interest of the United States."[110]

In later testimony, Ridgway noted that if the conflict expanded to the Chinese mainland, it was likely to require the use of ground forces. "I do not believe that you can compel the capitulation of a people like the Chinese with their loosely organized society by air action alone. I think that is a fundamental fallacy, I have always thought so, and I have stated so publicly on many occasions."[111] In testimony, Ridgway estimated an effective US force could involve a very large troop commitment, "at a minimum on the order of several hundred thousand."[112]

The general worried that defending the offshore islands was likely to draw America into that ground war on the Chinese mainland, as expressed in an exchange with Senator Morse:

Senator Morse: "General Ridgway, does the possibility of defending the Matsu Islands and Quemoy increase the probability of the Army being called upon to use ground forces on the mainland of China?"
General Ridgway, "Very definitely in my judgment, yes, sir."
Senator Morse: "That gives you concern?"
General Ridgway: "That gives me concern That is the root of my concern."[113]

Senator Sam Ervin (D-NC) doubted whether it was realistic to imagine a conflict might be narrowly contained. Ervin said, "We would be very foolish to delude ourselves into thinking that it might not be necessary for us to commit almost everything we have, that is, every branch of our service, including infantry and Marines, would we not?" Radford agreed. "Senator," he said, "I have tried to make it plain that the actions contemplated under this resolution can vary almost from a small defensive action all the way up to World War III, and the question of the decision in that respect will not be ours, it will be the Communists."[114]

Senator Capehart again wondered about Chiang's ability to aggravate tensions by attacking the mainland, and then relying upon the United States for help when the PRC responded.[115] The admiral assured him that Chiang had pledged not to do that and would be unable to draw in the United States against its will. "Chiang has no way of involving us in a war on the mainland unless we want to be involved," Radford observed, "because he is absolutely dependent upon our equipment and assistance. . . . At the present time, we have a commitment from him that he will undertake no offensive action against mainland targets without our concurrence."[116]

Capehart concluded that if Chiang was prevented from attacking the mainland, and the PRC was stopped from attacking Taiwan, the United States had endorsed a two-China policy. "This resolution is a resolution to stabilize this whole business, turning Formosa over to the Nationalists, with our guarantee of defense, and protection, and turning the mainland over to the Chinese Communists, is it not?" "Well, you might put it that way," Radford conceded.[117]

Senator Morse resumed his argument about preemptive war. He asserted the resolution authorized the president to commit an act of aggression against the PRC before the Communists acted against the United States. "Do you know," he asked Radford, "of any incident in the history of the United States where our government has ever committed an act of aggression before an act of war was committed against us?" The witness mentioned several cases where the United States had sent troops to stabilize a situation. Morse thought they were not analogous circumstances.

Morse differentiated between the Nationalists' claims to Formosa from those they made elsewhere. Morse considered this distinction to be important under international law and in courting world opinion. He noted that the Tachens and the offshore islands were territories on which China had uninterrupted claims. The outstanding issue in that case was not whether the land was Chinese, but which version of the Chinese government should rule it. Involving the United States in the dispute was intervening in a civil war, Morse claimed. However, he said, Formosa was different. Chinese sovereignty was interrupted because China had ceded legal control to Japan.

Notwithstanding Chiang's occupation of the island, Formosa's legal status remained nebulous. The Cairo Declaration had not resolved it. If America protected Formosa, the senator argued, it was fulfilling an obligation it assumed in World War II. "There has been a long break in the chain of continuity of Chinese sovereign rights over Formosa," noted Morse. "Therefore, any legal claims that we might have to exercise a protectorate over Formosa differs from the legal claims we might have of exercising a protectorate over the Tachens."[118]

The senator had emerged as the resolution's principal critic. He pursued two major complaints. The first was overbreadth. By not expressly restricting US defense commitments to Taiwan and the Pescadores, he said, the resolution in effect enlarged the Mutual Defense Treaty then submitted to the Senate. The second involved opening the door to preventive war, which contradicted settled American policy and invited Chiang to take provocative action. "I do not share the point of view that you could be absolutely sure that they would not create such an incident," he declared.[119]

Senator George disputed that the resolution exceeded the scope of the treaty. George noted that while the treaty did not explicitly embrace the offshore islands, it provided for the defense of Formosa and the Pescadores as well as such other areas as might be agreed upon by the United States and the Republic of China. Given the elasticity of the language, George believed that the resolution and the treaty were consistent.[120]

Senator Russell led Radford through a series of questions about the Nationalists' military position. The admiral stated that the chiefs concluded that US assistance would be needed for Chiang to invade the mainland or even to defend Formosa. Later that day, Radford enlarged on this point.

> If it was going to be a landing made against a very strongly fortified position, we might elect to come in because it would be our operation, they couldn't do it without our help, to give them some trained US troops to assist in the initial landing. . . . They couldn't undertake any return to the mainland, not only without our immediate support, transportation, air cover, but continuing logistics support after they had gone in land. We would have to give them airplanes, supply them the fuel. We would probably bring it in US tankers to where they unloaded. It would be a major operation that we would have to support from the beginning.[121]

Shortly thereafter, the hearing ended.

THE RESOLUTION IS REPORTED

The combined committee agreed to reconvene on Wednesday, January 26, to act on the Senate version, S.J. Res. 28.[122] Just after 10:00 a.m, it opened its markup session. Humphrey proposed an amendment to strike the provision that said, "this authority to include the security and protection of such related positions and territories of that area now in friendly hands." This language implicitly authorized Eisenhower to defend the offshore islands. Had Humphrey's amendment been adopted, the resolution would provide for the defense of Formosa and the Pescadores but nothing else.

Humphrey endorsed Morse's view that the legal status of Formosa and the Pescadores was distinct from other Nationalist-occupied positions. The Tachens and the offshore islands were Chinese beyond question, subject to sovereignty disputes between rival Chinese governments.[123] But, like many of his Senate colleagues, Humphrey claimed that the status of Formosa was different. As such, he reasoned that defending Formosa was not meddling in the civil war.[124] "The resolution, as presented to us, involves an element of risk as it pertains to the offshore islands that I believe to be unwarranted. I further believe that it may very well involve us in that aspect of the Chinese civil war on those offshore islands, which is not the case with Formosa because Formosa as to its ultimate disposition and jurisdiction is still an unsettled question in the area of international law. Formosa was dealt with by the Treaty of Japan and the Declaration of Cairo. The offshore islands have never been specifically dealt with."[125]

Humphrey wanted the resolution amended to strike the words "such other positions." The remaining language was sufficient for the president's purposes. To go further would serve notice "to the world and to our enemies that we are not only going to defend Formosa and the Pescadores, but we are going to get up within three and four miles of the coastline."[126]

Humphrey cited JCS testimony that the islands were not militarily essential to the defense of Formosa.[127] There was no material benefit to amplify the risk of war with the mainland.[128]

Knowland opposed the Humphrey amendment, claiming that adopting it would invite the PRC to seize the islands. While the administration had not deemed them essential to Formosa's defense, it acknowledged they were strategically beneficial. "I think we all heard the testimony of the responsible military officials of this government, and the Secretary of State, and the message of the President of the United States to the effect that there are certain islands which have a controlling position over the harbors out of which a major invasion of Formosa and the Pescadores could take place and that if those harbors were made available to the invasion fleets, it would facilitate the action of the Chinese Communists against Formosa and the Pescadores."[129]

Saltonstall argued the amendment would imperil Formosa because it hampered the United States from responding to an attack launched from the offshore islands rather than the mainland. "What we want to do is to give our Air Force and our Navy the best possible opportunity to protect Formosa and give our security with the least possible bloodshed by our boys," he said. That meant giving American commanders maximum flexibility. "I think to allow these air attacks to allow the possibility of Navy helping . . . makes it essential to leave this resolution in its broader terms."[130] Senators Smith and Bourke Hickenlooper (R-IA) followed with statements about the need to deny the Communists staging areas.

Joining Knowland in opposition, Senator Russell focused on deterrence. "This is not a diplomatic maneuver, gentlemen. . . . We are putting them on notice by this action, according to the testimony here, that if they expand their airfields in the immediate area of these islands, whether they are in our hands or those of the Chinese Nationalists or the Chinese Reds, that we reserve the right to attack the mainland of China."

Barely 18 months after the armistice in Korea, the United States might again be engaged in combat in Asia. Russell very much hoped to avoid that, worried about being caught in a quagmire, and urged colleagues to be realistic about the magnitude of what was at stake. "This is an ultimatum, and if it is not respected by the Communist government of China, why we might as well reconcile ourselves to the fact that it means war. It does not mean any partial war, it means a war with the most populous nation on earth, and it may last for a long time."

Russell was willing to accept that risk and not to micromanage Eisenhower's handling of the situation. "If we are prepared to attack the mainland of China, I am no longer disposed to quibble about Quemoy and Matsu," he said.[131]

Senator Byrd was much less willing than Russell for America to bear that burden. "I believe that a land war with China would be a catastrophe of the greatest magnitude to this country. It would last for years and years, perhaps generations. No nation has ever conquered China in her history, and I do not think any nation will ever conquer China."[132]

Unlike many Senate colleagues who valued Nationalist China as an anti-Communist ally, Byrd did not. He believed Chiang would miss no opportunity to draw the United States into a war with the PRC to recover the mainland. "Chiang Kai-shek is obsessed with the idea that if he can land on the shores of China, that the populace of China would rally to his support. He is obsessed with that idea. There is nothing that he will not do if he can compel us by some action that he will take to force us to get into a war with China." Byrd emphasized that Chiang and the United States had divergent, if not contradictory, objectives. Referring to the generalissimo and Madame Chiang, he said, "I have not got confidence in either one of them. They have their own purposes to win in this matter and those purposes are contrary to ours. They want to get back in control of China itself, and I understand from the military men here that that is not our purpose."[133]

Byrd considered the resolution overbroad and unnecessarily provocative. He announced he would support Humphrey's amendment, which he thought would improve upon, but fail to cure, the resolution's fundamental defects. In addition, Byrd was troubled that it could be implemented immediately, without first looking to the United Nations to defuse tensions. Therefore, he announced he would oppose the resolution, even though he planned to vote for the Mutual Defense Treaty.

Senator Estes Kefauver (D-TN) reinforced Byrd's position. "Supporting Chiang on these islands would place us in a position where we have a somewhat unreliable ally who could make decisions over which we would have little or no control, which might bring about actions which would bring us into war," claimed Kefauver. Best to support Humphrey's narrowing amendment, he thought, because it would reduce the chance of war as well as the prospect of alienating international public opinion. Beyond question, the islands were Chinese territory. Kefauver observed that "any ordinary person, I think, would kind of have a natural inclination to feel, 'well, after all, these have always been Chinese territory, and you cannot blame the Chinese Communists for not wanting to have a hostile enemy there.'"[134]

Defending Formosa was different, Kefauver argued. "I think we can make a strong case before the nations of the world where they will join us if we limit our defense activity to the Pescadores and Formosa. We can make a strong case because we are there in a trusteeship arrangement which has been delegated to some extent to China. Other the nations joined us in winning the Pacific war and so we have some obligation."[135]

Chairman George denied that the resolution authorized a land war on the Chinese mainland. Its scope was much narrower, authorizing support, if necessary, for the Nationalists on Quemoy and Matsu, but not an invasion. "My interpretation of it is that he could not invade (China) under the authority which the Congress is giving in this resolution."

> Byrd differed. "Suppose it was essential, as he regarded it, to the defense of Formosa, what then?"
> George answered, "You're not authorizing the seizure and the protection of anything except territories in friendly hands."
> Byrd challenged him. "Is it your opinion, then, that these islands that are so close to China, if they could be bombarded by artillery fire, that we are prohibited from firing into China?"

George rebutted, "I'm not saying what the President is prohibited from doing under a much broader power then the resolution. But the Congress here is asked to pass the resolution and the resolution as it is drawn is limiting the authority to use the armed forces for the purposes that I have specified." Later, George added. "We are limiting the use of these armed forces to that territory only that is now in friendly hands, and that excludes, as far as our consent and approval, the invasion to the mainland of China."[136]

The Humphrey amendment would unnecessarily restrict the president, complained Senator Barkley. He observed, "We are surely not willing that he or our government sit there on Formosa or the Pescadores like a decoy duck and wait for them to take off from Quemoy or Matsu or anywhere else, and the effect of this amendment would result in that. . . . As much as I sympathize with our trepidation in adopting this resolution, I think we have got to give the President authority without tying his hands or clipping him in the exercise of his judgment."[137]

Taking a longer view, Barkley doubted that conditions in the Far East could be meaningfully stabilized by armistices that postponed true reckoning. "We have a ceasefire in Korea, which has not settled anything, and we have one in Indochina, which has not settled anything, and we can plaster Asia with ceasefire agreements, and they do not mean anything, but the final reckoning must someday come when all these questions must be settled, and it may be easier to settle them now rather than to wait."[138]

While Barkley would vote no on the amendment, he shared Senator Byrd's distaste for Chiang. "I have not either patience with him or faith in him and I have not for a long time," he noted.[139]

Debate ended. George put the question on the Humphrey amendment. Eight senators voted in the affirmative and twenty were negative, so the amendment failed.

Senator Kefauver proposed a substitute for the text of S.J. Res. 28. It contained a lengthy preamble setting out some of the historical frameworks for the standoff in the strait. It repeated Kefauver's assertion, made during the hearings, that the final legal status of Formosa remained undetermined, allowing the United States to engage in its defense without involvement in a civil war. The preamble called for United Nations intervention and asserted American responsibility to protect Formosa while UN action was pending.[140]

Kefauver explained, "This is, of course, an effort to separate our position in Formosa and the Pescadores from that in the offshore islands, recognizing that a civil war does exist between Chiang and the offshore islands and the mainland, setting up our obligation under the Japan Surrender Treaty, asking and stating our willingness to have the United Nations consideration of this."[141]

The Kefauver substitute was defeated. Again, eight senators voted in the affirmative and twenty in the negative.

Following that vote, the combined committee ordered S.J. Res. 28 reported. On final passage, 27 senators voted aye. Senators Wayne Morse and William Langer (R-ND) voted no.

THE FORMOSA RESOLUTION IS
REPORTED FROM COMMITTEE

On January 26, Chairman George submitted the Committee Report. It noted that the Chinese Communists firmly intended to defeat the Nationalists and unite Formosa and the Pescadores with the mainland and declared that the resolution was designed to "stabilize the area" by committing the United States to take preventive action.[142]

The report acknowledged that such a commitment involved risks. The Communists might nonetheless take provocative action, such as grouping their forces "in such a way as to present a clear and immediate security threat." The president might have to launch a preemptive attack. As the report stated, "This resolution would be indicative of congressional support for such action."[143]

A further danger would be that a conflict with China would be widened to engage the Soviet Union. China and the USSR were bound by a 1950 treaty, which stated: "In the event of one of the High Contracting Parties being attacked by Japan or states allied with it, and thus being involved in a state of war, the other High Contracting Party will immediately render military and other assistance with all the means at its disposal." Because the United States was allied with Japan, it was entirely possible the Sino-Soviet agreement could be interpreted to trigger Soviet intervention. In hearing testimony, the administration tended to discount this possibility, but did not rule it out.

The report stated that the senators as well as the administration hoped for some constructive action by the United Nations to defuse tensions. However, the committee noted that the PRC was unlikely to cooperate with UN cease-fire efforts, because it held that sovereignty over Taiwan was China's internal affair and that "outside interference" would be intolerable.[144]

At the administration's urging, the committee at markup rejected the Humphrey amendment to exclude the offshore islands from the resolution's coverage, the report noted. "Both Secretary Dulles and Admiral Radford testified at some length against the desirability of listing the individual islands covered by the resolution or spelling out in concrete terms the latitude and longitude of the areas to be defended. The joint committee agrees that, in this particular instance at least, it would seem unwise to define too precisely the geographic scope of the resolution. Such action might handicap our country by depriving it of flexibility that may be needed to meet unforeseen situations that might arise in the future."[145]

Finally, the report addressed the question of whether, considering the president's constitutional powers, the resolution was even necessary at all. It acknowledged differences of opinion among the senators but sidestepped them to say, "The resolution . . . does call for the two branches of the government to stand together in the face of a common danger. With such unity there can be no question that the necessary constitutional powers exist for such action as may be required to meet the kind of emergency contemplated by the resolution."[146]

On January 26, 1955, the committee filed its report. Before the Senate formally moved to consider the resolution, debate on the Floor began.

NOTES

1. Stolper, p. 59.
2. Ibid., p. 60.
3. Dr. Shu Guang Zhang quotes Dulles's comments from January 19, 1955, "Doubts as to our intentions were having a bad effect. It was in many quarters

assumed that we would defend the islands., and our failure to do so indicated that we were running away when actual danger appeared" (Shu Guang Zhang, p. 212).

4. Stolper, p. 71. Thomas Stolper notes that, for the PRC, protesting Nationalist occupation of the offshores was useful in gaining world sympathy, but it never took its attention off its ultimate objective of Taiwan. "Everyone agreed that the offshore islands were juridically part of the mainland. But Peking consistently defined the issue in terms of Taiwan and rejected all attempts to define the issue more narrowly" (Stolper, p. 84).

5. Another congressional leader who doubted the necessity of the resolution was Senator Mansfield. In his oral history, he recounts, "I think it's a bad precedent. I don't think that these resolutions are necessary. The President either has or hasn't the powers as Commander-in-chief and President, or if he hasn't, then he ought to come to Congress for additional powers. But he doesn't need the powers which these resolutions—all of them—have given him in any instance that I can recall" (Mansfield, p. 12).

6. Stolper, p. 74.

7. Hitchcock, p. 207.

8. In his oral history, Walter Robertson states, "The Chinese Communists made the decision pretty simple for us because they were giving statements, all the time, but they were determined to liberate Formosa. As far as they were concerned, they didn't give a hang about these two little islands off their coast. What they wanted was the big prize, Formosa" (Robertson, p. 43).

9. Stolper, p. 81. The Joint Chiefs' position was that the islands were not vital for the defense of Formosa, in the sense that Formosa could still be defended without them. Radford was emphasizing that abandoning the islands made such defense substantially more complicated. It should be added that most of the chiefs, including Radford, also thought that Chiang should hold on to the Tachens, with the notable dissent in that instance from Army Chief of Staff Ridgway (Immerman, p. 123).

10. Ibid., p. 82. Eisenhower's referred to the infamous Munich conference of 1938 between Germany, Britain, Italy, and France, which led to abandonment to Hitler of Czechoslovakia's Sudetenland region. The conference had come to be seen as disreputable and had given the word "appeasement" very bad connotations. The president's point was that the United States could not appease the Communists or postpone confronting the issues arising from the crisis.

11. Eisenhower, p. 467.

12. Ibid., pp. 83–85.

13. Ambassador Rankin described strategy in the United Nations, codenamed Operation Oracle. "The plan was for New Zealand to introduce a resolution, with the support of the United States and the United Kingdom, calling for a secession of hostilities in the Formosa Strait. It was hoped that the Chinese Government, as a member of the Security Council, would go along with whatever course of action we might propose, on the assumption that the Soviets would oppose such an action in any case. The Communists would thus be placed in the wrong once more before world opinion, and another procedural victory gained for our side" (Rankin, p. 210). Chiang was dubious of this strategy (Taylor, p. 475). Like Mao, Chiang considered

tensions in the strait and internal Chinese concern and not susceptible to international intervention or negotiation.

14. Stephen E. Ambrose, *Eisenhower the President, Vol. II* (New York: Simon & Schuster, 1984), p. 239. Stephen Kinzer notes that Dulles's relationship with Eden was frequently testy. "He considered Foreign Secretary Eden soft, weak, and unwilling to confront the Soviet menace. . . . According to one of Foster's close aides, he had absolutely no regard for Eden's position on world affairs and believed 'you could simply not count on the British.' Eden, who fruitlessly pleaded with Foster to soften his attitude toward China, returned his low esteem. He considered Foster a narrow-minded ideologue and deplored his vivid denunciations of Communism" (Kinzer, p. 201). Richard H. Immerman recounts that Eden believed the United States had already decided to defend the islands, notwithstanding public ambiguity. Such a policy did not sit well with the foreign secretary. "Eden particularly distrusted Dulles" (Immerman, p. 124). In a 1964 oral history, Sir Leslie Munro, New Zealand's ambassador to the United States, mentions that Eden considered it was the role of the British and the Soviets to restrain their allies and tone down the possibility of conflict. "Eden always took the line that the Russians would be the people who would restrain the Chinese and the British would be the people who would restrain the Americans." Oral History Sir Leslie Knox Munro, Princeton University Library, p. 23, http://arks .princeton.edu/ark:/884335/r/781wn314 (accessed December 20, 2020).

15. *FRUS, China 1955–1957, Vol. II*, p. 91. Eisenhower was seeking a more substantial grant of authority that had been given to any president, apart from a declaration of war. Stephen Ambrose notes, "The resolution Eisenhower wanted was something new in American history. Never before had Congress given the president a blank check to act as he saw fit in a foreign crisis. Fully aware of the unprecedented nature of his request, Eisenhower talked with all the congressional leaders before submitting it" (Ambrose, p. 232).

16. "Whether constitutionally required or not, and the Administration's position was divided on this question, the President adamantly insisted that Congress must authorize the commitment of US forces to defend the islands" (Immerman, p. 127).

17. Ambrose, p. 232.

18. Eisenhower, p. 467.

19. *FRUS, China 1955–1957, Vol. II*, pp. 95–96.

20. "The resolution granted Eisenhower a blank check to use US force in the Taiwan Strait, but it was so blank that Chiang claimed that he had been betrayed. The reservations expressed by the NSC and European allies had heightened Eisenhower's and Dulles' own concerns about the United States becoming a hostage to the Nationalists' resistance to yielding an iota of control over any of the offshore islands" (Immerman, p. 128).

21. *FRUS, China 1955–1957, Vol. II*, pp. 99–104.

22. Walter Robertson emphasizes that both the Communists and Nationalists also rejected the idea of two Chinas in the United Nations. "There was never any time when the Chinese Communists would have accepted membership to the United Nations as long as Nationalist China was seated there" (Robertson, pp. 86–87).

23. *FRUS, China 1955–1957, Vol. II*, pp. 107–111.

24. Ibid., pp. 112–113.

25. Chiang and Madame Chiang, p. 12.

26. Ibid., p. 14.

27. Garver, p. 129.

28. The Formosa Resolution survived a major repeal effort in the Senate in 1972 and was finally repealed on October 26, 1974.

29. *Congressional Record*, January 24, 1955, pp. 625–626. Professor Robert Accinelli focuses on what the message omitted. "It concealed the defensive commitment to Quemoy and Matsu and inflated the present danger of an assault on Taiwan" (Accinelli, p. 192).

30. The vote was 28–0. The committee issued a brief report, indicating it was not taking a position on what it called "the field of controversy as to the respective limitations of power in the executive and legislative branches." In other words, the committee did not opine on the power of the president to act without congressional authorization or whether Congress could restrict powers that the president would otherwise enjoy under the Constitution. *Congressional Record*, January 25, 1955, p. 661.

31. *Congressional Record*, January 25, 1955, pp. 659–660. During the debate on the Formosa Resolution itself, Representative Robert Chiperfield (R-IL), who had been chairman of the Committee on Foreign Affairs during the 83rd Congress (1953–1955), addressed two reasons for a closed rule, which bars amendments. These were to avoid amendments on the issue of presidential powers and proposals that would establish geographic limitations for the use of such powers. Chipperfield stated, "There is a difference of opinion as to whether or not it was desirable in this resolution to establish specific geographical limits but after considered judgment it was felt that to do so would give our potential aggressors notice that we would not resist them beyond those geographical limits. It was felt best by Admiral Radford and Secretary Dulles not to delineate in terms of latitude and longitude the areas that are to be defended. The committee concurred in these views that precise definitions tended to tie the hands of the United States to an undesirable extent" (Ibid., p. 665). Avoided in the House because the Formosa Resolution came up under a closed rule, these issues would be front and center during Senate proceedings.

32. McCormack mentioned the need for presidents to use such powers unilaterally, when emergencies arise and Congress lacks time to act. He cited the example of the outbreak of the Korean War. *Congressional Record*, January 25, 1955, p. 659.

33. Ibid., p. 660.

34. Ibid., p. 664.

35. Ibid., p. 666.

36. Ibid., p. 670.

37. Ibid., pp. 672–673.

38. Ibid., p. 672.

39. Ibid., p. 680.

40. Gayle B. Montgomery and James W. Johnson, *One Step from the White House: The Rise and Fall of Senator William F. Knowland* (Berkeley, CA: University of California Press, 1998), p. 184.

41. On January 28, British diplomat Humphrey Trevelyan met in Beijing with Premier Zhou Enlai. Trevelyan reported that Zhou was "tense and absolutely uncompromising." Zhou characterized Eisenhower's message to Congress as a war message. He insisted that the Communists would continue to link the question of the offshore islands to Formosa, that these territories were nonnegotiable, that Beijing would liberate them, and did not fear war threats (Ibid., p. 154).

42. Ibid., pp. 124–128.

43. "Peiping Says US Issued 'War Cry.'" *New York Times*, January 28, 1955, p. 1.

44. Before being elected to the House in 1942, Mansfield had taught classes on Asian history at the University of Montana. Mansfield served in the Senate for a total of 24 years, the last 16 of which he was majority leader. In 1977, President Jimmy Carter appointed him ambassador to Japan. Mansfield continued in that post under President Ronald Reagan, serving in Tokyo for more than 11 years.

45. *Congressional Record*, January 24, 1955, p. 621.

46. Ibid.

47. Ibid.

48. Ibid.

49. Ibid.

50. Ibid., p. 622.

51. Ibid., p. 623. Although dubious of the necessity for the resolution, Mansfield wound up supporting it in committee and on the Floor. His biographer, Don Oberdorfer, explains, "With a concern for separation of powers, Mansfield argued that such an authorization by Congress was unnecessary because the President already possessed all the authority he needed to undertake military action as commander in chief and that awarding this 'authority' might suggest that he lacked such a capability until Congress acted. The Senate brushed this objection aside in regard to the Formosa Resolution, which then passed by a large majority in 1955 amid the continuing conflict in the Taiwan Strait. Mansfield was among those voting for it 'because circumstances leave us no other choice.'" Don Oberdorfer, *Senator Mansfield* (Washington, DC: Smithsonian Books, 2003), p. 143.

52. The hearing occurred in what is presently known as the Old Senate Chamber, then called the Old Supreme Court Chamber. Located on the corridor between the Rotunda and the present Senate chamber, the room housed the Senate between 1810 and 1859, and then the Supreme Court between 1860 and 1935. For the Bicentennial in 1976, the room was restored to look as it did during the Senate period. At the time of the 1955 hearing, it was vacant space, used for special events.

53. Dulles Hearing Testimony, p. 72.

54. Testimony of Secretary of State John Foster Dulles, January 24, 1955, *Executive Sessions of the Senate Foreign Relations Committee (Historical Series), Vol. VII*, Eighty-fourth Congress, First Session, 1955, p. 68.

55. Dulles told the committee that abandoning the Tachens was bad for Nationalist morale, but the damage could be mitigated by a forthright US commitment to Formosa's defense (Ibid., p. 74–75).

56. Ibid., p. 69. The following day, JCS chairman Arthur Radford expanded on this point, particularly with reference to Japan. He told the committee, "The great problem in the Far East at the moment is can we hold our essential allies out there?

Japan is very important. If Japan ever turned, ever went to the Communist side and they obtained the industrial know how and capacity of Japan, they would have tremendous strength out there and they would use it. We would practically be forced out of the Orient if that happened" (Ibid., p. 154).

57. Dulles told the senators, "These positions cannot be held without, in effect, pinning down there . . . a very considerable portion of the mobile forces that we have in that part of the world" (Ibid., p. 85). The following day, JCS chairman Arthur Radford underscored this point, "If the Chinese Nationalists are willing to withdraw, if we are willing to cover, that means they and we will not suffer the loss of the trained divisions and all their equipment, and from a military point of view that is very desirable not to lose that fighting force and its equipment" (Ibid., p. 217).

58. Ibid., p. 70.

59. Ibid., p. 71.

60. Ibid., p. 73.

61. Ibid., p, 71.

62. Ibid., p. 80.

63. Ibid., p. 109.

64. At the time, the Nationalist government held the China seat in the UN General Assembly and on the Security Council. While there had been efforts to replace it with the PRC, the United States had been strongly opposed, and the ouster went nowhere. Beijing did not gain the China seat until October 25, 1971, when the General Assembly adopted Resolution 2758 recognizing the PRC as China's legitimate government. By then, President Richard Nixon's opening to China had occurred. On July 15, 1971, after his National Security Adviser Henry Kissinger returned from secret exploratory meetings in Beijing, Nixon announced he would go to China the following year. At the time of the UN vote, Kissinger was back in Beijing to prepare the presidential visit. This time, Kissinger's trip was highly publicized. Between 1955 and 1971, the PRC had gained many new supporters of its bid for UN membership, mainly from postcolonial states in Asia and Africa. It is unlikely that the United States could have kept the PRC out of the UN even if relations between Washington and Beijing remained frozen, but the thaw sent a message. America's permanent representative, George H. W. Bush, worked hard to maintain the status quo, but was unsuccessful.

65. Senate hearings, p. 72.

66. Ibid.

67. Ibid., p. 75.

68. Ibid., p. 76. The next day, Admiral Radford, speaking for the Joint Chiefs, reaffirmed this perspective, telling Senator Saltonstall, "I do not believe that we, at any time, have favored the use of US ground forces on the mainland of China." However, Radford did not flatly rule it out, noting, "We are unable to forecast exactly what situation would develop, and we will have to be prepared to meet it as it develops, and we might have to use US ground forces somewhere for some purpose, and the resolution authorizes the use of the armed forces of the United States, which would include the Army and the Marine Corps." (Ibid., p. 195).

69. Nationalist will to fight was a key focus for the administration, whose national security policy centered on keeping the island in friendly hands. Historian

John Garver comments, "Because mainstream Republican leaders valued Nationalist Taiwan as an asset in containing Communist China, they feared that the loss of Taiwan would dangerously weaken containment. By asserting that particular US actions would lead to the collapse of Nationalist morale, Chiang was thus able to threaten to deny Taiwan to Washington" (Garver, p. 86).

70. Ibid.

71. Senate hearings, p. 202.

72. Ibid., p. 85. Dulles subsequently had a similar exchange with Senator Clifford P. Case (R-NJ). The senator noted that military necessity might dictate engaging in certain locations and bypassing others. If the resolution drew red lines, Case asked, "will we not create a psychological hazard if we fail to defend every one of them?" Dulles replied, "That was the reason, Senator, why we decided to avoid what many had thought might be desirable . . . an actual drawing of a line or naming by their names the islands and so forth which we are expected to hold" (Ibid., p. 103).

73. Ibid., p. 80.

74. For example, Senator Mansfield told Dulles that he appreciated the president consulting with Congress but worried about an inference that the president lacked inherent powers to act. The senator was also concerned about Congress arrogating to itself powers that rightly belonged to the Executive (Ibid., p. 101).

75. Eisenhower wrote, "Authority for some of the actions which might be required would be inherent in the authority of the Commander-in-Chief. Until Congress can act I would not hesitate, so far as my Constitutional powers extend, to take whatever emergency action might be forced upon us in order to protect the rights and security of the United States." Dwight D. Eisenhower, "Special Message to Congress Regarding United States Policy for the Defense of Formosa," January 24, 1955. The American Presidency Project. www.presidency.ucsb.edu (accessed March 2, 2022).

76. As Justice Robert Jackson stated in his concurring opinion in what is popularly known as the Steel Seizure case, "When the President acts pursuant to an express or implied authorization of Congress, his authority is at its maximum, for it includes all that he possesses in his own right plus all that Congress can delegate. In these circumstances, and in these only, may he be said (for what it is worth) to personify federal sovereignty" (*Youngstown v. Sawyer*, 343 US 579, 660 (1952)).

77. Senate hearings, p. 87.

78. Ibid., p. 87.

79. Ibid., p. 111.

80. Ibid., p. 112. Before the hearing concluded that day, Dulles revisited the necessity of risking war with China to defend American interests. "If we are not willing to take any risk of war with China, then we will be driven out of this whole Asian area and will fall back to the United States. That is the choice we have got to face. We have got to be prepared to take a risk of war with China, if we are going to stay in the Far East. If we are not willing to take that risk, alright, let's make that decision and we get out and we make our defenses in California" (Ibid., p. 130).

81. Ibid., p. 97.

82. Ibid., p. 101. The situation might be analogous to that of the Korean War, in which the United States supplied more than three-fourths of the non-Korean troops fighting on the side of the United Nations. Admiral Radford was later asked about

the possibility of multilateral forces under UN auspices. He demurred, "We do not expect any sizable contributions in this effort, except from Nationalist Chinese forces, and I do not understand, although I don't know, that the United Nations action would include calling on anyone else for forces" (Ibid., p. 198).

83. Ibid., p. 106.

84. Ibid., p. 110. The next day, Senator Sparkman asked JCS chairman Arthur Radford about whether the Nationalists had the capacity to recover the mainland on their own, Radford responded, "I think that the only way we could ever prove or disprove the question of whether Chiang would be able to go to the mainland and recover it would be to try it and . . . we know that would require naval and air support, logistics support, possibly some US ground troops to assist in at least the initial landing, and it would be such a major effort that we do not feel it should be tried" (Ibid., p. 150).

85. Ibid., pp. 114–115.

86. Journalist Evan Thomas writes, "Knowland was known as 'the Senator from Formosa' because of his fealty to the so-called China Lobby, which provided favors to Senators who backed the regime of Generalissimo Chiang Kai-shek. . . . At a dinner at the Nationalist Chinese embassy in Washington, Knowland had stood and with a shout joined in the toast 'Back to the Mainland!'. . . . 'Knowland has no foreign policy,' Eisenhower wrote in his diary, 'except to develop high blood pressure whenever he mentions the words 'Red China.'" Evan Thomas, *Ike's Bluff: President Eisenhower's Secret Battle to Save the World* (Little, Brown and Company, 2012), p. 153.

87. Ibid., p. 109.

88. Ibid., p. 121.

89. Ibid., p. 147.

90. Ibid., p. 134.

91. Ibid., p. 135.

92. Ibid., p. 139.

93. Ibid.

94. Ibid., p. 139.

95. Ibid. Radford explained, "Formosa is a key in our island defense chain in the Pacific and the loyalty of the armed forces of the Republic of China is of great importance to our military position in the Far East" (Ibid.). He told Senator Smith, "Our policy, insofar as possible, is to develop indigenous forces, the ground forces of indigenous people, for the indefinite period of the Cold War, and not only in the Far East. . . . We plan to supplement and assist those local forces with air power, US air and naval power, and reserve to ourselves the mobile strength of the US ground forces to be used where we want to use them" (Ibid., pp. 144–145).

96. Ibid., pp. 136–137.

97. Ibid., p. 136.

98. On June 14, 1950, MacArthur prepared a Top-Secret memo on Formosa. He wrote, "Since the fall of 1948 when the military capability of the Chinese Communist to engulf all of the mainland of China became clearly evident, I have been concerned as to the future status of Formosa and I have been convinced that the strategic interests of the United States will be in serious jeopardy if Formosa is allowed to be dominated by a power hostile to the United States." He noted that "the front line of the Far East

Command as well as the western strategic frontier of the United States rests today on the littoral islands extending from the Aleutians through the Philippine Archipelago. Geographically and strategically Formosa is an integral part of this offshore position which in the event of hostilities can exercise a decisive degree of control of military operations along the periphery of Eastern Asia." And he famously analogized Formosa to an "unsinkable aircraft carrier" that would be of immense value to the Soviet Union is allowed to fall into Communist hands. *FRUS, 1950, Korea, Vol. VII*, pp. 161–182.

99. Ibid., p. 143.

100. Ibid., pp. 155–156.

101. Ibid., p. 161.

102. Nationally syndicated columnist Stewart Alsop wrote in a January 26 article that, in October 1954, Radford had proposed bombing the Chinese mainland to hold Quemoy. At the time, said Alsop, Eisenhower rejected the plan. Alsop said that Radford persisted, and finally persuaded Secretary of State Dulles that preemptive bombing should be an option. Convinced, Dulles persuaded the president. Alsop stated, "In the end, the President decided on a curious compromise—the Tachens would be evacuated, while war would be risked, if necessary, to defend Quemoy, the most important Nationalist Island, and probably Matsu." Stewart Alsop, "It Could Mean War," *Washington Post and Times Herald*, January 26, 1955.

103. Senate Hearings, p. 157.

104. Ibid., p. 170.

105. Radford's statement was consistent with administration policy. John Garver states, "many officials, including Eisenhower, felt that the strong taboo that had developed against the use of atomic weapons was undermining the credibility of US power" (Garver, p. 131).

106. The US Navy would support the evacuation. In the January 25 hearing, Knowland asked Radford and each of the chiefs whether they anticipated the use of American ground forces in the Tachens. Each answered in the negative and gave the same response to his question about deploying US ground forces on the offshore islands (Senate hearings, pp. 186–187).

107. Radford stated, "We are trying to avoid having our allies suffer a very disastrous defeat which would have a bad psychological reaction all through the Far East" (Ibid., p. 163).

108. Ibid., p. 166.

109. Ibid.

110. Ibid., p. 183.

111. Ibid., p. 234. In an exchange with Senator Morse, Ridgway acknowledged that the Chinese might protract a land war through extensive use of guerilla tactics. Ibid.

112. Ibid., p. 237.

113. Ibid., pp. 240–241.

114. Ibid., p. 203.

115. During negotiations on the Mutual Defense Treaty, Chiang agreed to a side letter that stated deployment of forces from either signatory would have to be by

mutual agreement. The side letter was signed on December 10, 1954, eight days after the treaty was signed. On January 6, 1955, President Eisenhower submitted both to the Senate, along with a December 22, 1954, report from Secretary of State Dulles.

116. Senate hearings, p. 205.

117. Ibid., pp. 205–206.

118. Ibid., pp. 217–218.

119. Ibid., pp. 222–223.

120. Ibid., p. 230.

121. Ibid., p. 232.

122. The record of proceedings was kept classified until 1978, when the Senate Committee on Foreign Relations authorized its publication.

123. John Garver notes, "One consideration shaping US policy toward the offshores was the absence of a legal basis for US involvement with the offshore islands. The legal basis for US relations with Taiwan and the Pescadores after 25 June 1950 was the undetermined status of those islands which rested, in turn, on the fact that those islands had been transferred from Chinese to Japanese sovereignty in 1895 and then promised again to China with the Cairo Declaration of 1943. The smaller offshore islands, however, had never been under Japanese sovereignty. They had never been anything other than part of China" (Garver, pp. 114–115).

124. It must be stressed that the PRC strongly disputed this interpretation; for that matter, so did Chiang. The Shanghai Communiqué of February 1972 recognizes that Chinese on both sides of the strait believe there is one China and that Taiwan is part of it.

125. Senate hearings, p. 250.

126. Ibid., p. 251.

127. In his oral history, General Ridgway explained why he believed Quemoy was militarily inconsequential to either side. "You didn't need Quemoy to launch a full-scale attack against Formosa. It would have been helpful, but it was not essential. And as far as we were concerned, the seizure of Quemoy as a staging area for launching an assault against Red China was unsound because there wasn't any strategic objective on the mainland of China within hundreds of miles of Quemoy" (Oral History Ridgway, p. 34).

128. Senate hearings, p. 251.

129. Ibid., p. 252.

130. Ibid., p. 253.

131. Ibid., pp. 256–257.

132. Ibid., p. 259.

133. Ibid. Historian John W. Garver describes the divergent objectives between the United States and the ROC.

"Throughout the US-ROC alliance, there was a fundamental conflict about the basic purpose of the alliance. US leaders were generally committed to the strategy of containment, according to which Communist China was to be surrounded by a political-military zone intended to thwart Beijing's efforts to extend Communism into areas adjacent to China, and which would keep the Sino-Soviet alliance under pressure until that alliance broke apart. But unless Beijing imposed a major war in the United States through aggression against neighboring countries, the United States would not seek to overthrow or destroy China's Communist regime. The objective was to modify the behavior of China's Communist government, to weaken and isolate that regime, and to draw it away from the USSR, not to destroy the regime itself. Nationalist leaders, on the other hand, sought nothing less than the destruction of China's Communist regime and the state founded by that regime, the People's Republic of China." (Garver, pp. 73–74)

134. Professor Richard H. Immerman writes, "Chiang claimed legal jurisdiction (dubious) and that their possession by Taiwan was essential for its defense (more dubious). He exacerbated the controversy over the status of the island groups by using them for intelligence operations, to harass PRC shipping, and even to conduct coastal raids. To Peking, moreover, the deployment of some 50,000 Nationalist troops to Quemoy alone (another 5000 were stationed on Matsu) suggested that Chiang intended the islands to serve as steppingstones for his return to the mainland" (Immerman, p. 121).

135. Senate hearings, pp. 268–269.

136. Ibid., pp. 262–263.

137. Ibid., p. 273.

138. Ibid.

139. Ibid.

140. This preamble clause stated, "Whereas, the Treaty of Peace between the Allied Powers and Japan, signed September 8, 1951, under which Japan renounced all right title and claim to Formosa and the Pescadores pending definitive settlement of their future status, and pending such settlement, has recognized the jurisdiction of the Republic of China over these islands."

141. Senate hearings, p. 277.

142. S. Rept. 84–13, p. 1.

143. Ibid., p. 8.

144. Soviet diplomat, S.F. Antonov, relates a 1959 conversation with Mao that summarizes the Chinese view that Formosa could not be divided from the mainland and that the question of sovereignty over Formosa was purely China's internal affair.

"Mao Tse-tung noted that Comrade N.S. Khrushchev in his conversations with Eisenhower had spoken very firmly and correctly about the Taiwan question. Taiwan, continued Mao Tse-tung, is an inalienable part of China. Contrary to a number of countries, which after World War II had been divided in accordance with international agreements (Germany, Korea, Vietnam) on the Taiwan question, there had not been and were not any sort of international acts in which the separation of Taiwan from China had been mentioned. To the contrary, even during the war, in the Cairo Declaration, it had been decided that after the completion of military operations, Taiwan would be freed from its Japanese occupiers and returned to China."

"A Conversation with Mao, 1959," Cold War International History Project, www.mtholyoke.edu (accessed July 24, 2022).

145. S. Rept. 84–13, p. 9.

146. Ibid.

Chapter 7

The Formosa Resolution

Floor Proceedings

Senate Floor debate commenced before the Formosa Resolution was formally pending. It began with a speech on January 26, 1955, by Senator Russell Long (D-LA). He was unimpressed, and in fact dismayed, by the rapid and overwhelming vote in the House of Representatives. Noting that the resolution passed only one day after introduction, and without the benefit of a single hearing, Long urged the Senate not to act with similar dispatch. "It is well that the entire public of the United States should go into this matter with its eyes open," said Long. Extended proceedings, including the chance to propose amendments, would shed light on important topics the House had bypassed. A central issue involved the defense of Quemoy and Matsu. Long regarded it as a commitment the United States must avoid. "As a former member of the Committee on Armed Services, and as one who sat on that committee when President Truman ordered the Seventh Fleet to defend the Strait between Formosa and the mainland, I have never interpreted that obligation as extending to the small islands within easy artillery range of the Chinese mainland held by the Communists."

A further issue was whether the United States would launch preemptive bombing of the Chinese mainland to interdict the massing of Communist forces. As reported by the committee, the resolution appeared to permit it. "The mere concentration of Communist Chinese troops at any point along more than 200 miles of shoreland could serve as justification for heavy bombardment of Red Chinese ports," Long observed. "This is far more than our nation has thus far committed itself to do," he warned. "Thus far, the American people have not been informed of the implications of this joint resolution."[1]

But even if the American people were unaware, US allies were deeply concerned. Nervous in general about getting embroiled in an Asian war, the allies drew the line at defending the offshore islands. Thus, in a showdown, the United States and the Nationalists might stand alone. The senator pointed out, "We should realize that to become involved in a war with Russia under such circumstances would mean that the many allies, numbering more than 400,000,000 persons committed to our side in the event of Communist aggression, would have no obligation to come to our aid."[2]

Long was extremely wary of the Nationalists and the China Lobby, who he was sure would try to trap America into war by whatever means possible. Such a conflict was the only path to return to the mainland. "I fully believe that Chiang Kai-shek and his friends have no more certain purpose than to have the United States fully involved in all-out war with Red China, even if this should mean war with Russia."[3]

Senator Morse contended that passing the resolution was superfluous, because the Constitution already provided the president with sufficient authority to defend US national security. He argued that the resolution added nothing to those powers. "The President of the United States . . . has the emergency power which he needs to take whatever defensive course of action is necessary to protect the vital interests of the American people."

Thus, Congress was doing something that was both risky and unnecessary, Morse charged. The resolution amounted to a political blank check for any steps Eisenhower might take in the crisis. "We are being asked in effect to underwrite by our approval not only all the words of the resolution, but all the meanings of the resolution to be found between the lines, which are not written physically into the resolution." Having consented in advance to such a broad grant of authority, the senator predicted, Congress would be ill positioned to criticize the president later.[4]

As in the hearings, Morse tore into the idea of preemptive war. "I am opposed to the resolution in its present form because to all intents and purposes, I consider it amounts to a quasi-legalization of a preventive war," the senator claimed. Appearing to authorize it would sacrifice one of the cardinal principles of US foreign policy, he said. "A study of the history of American foreign relations will disclose that the most persuasive foreign policy weapon we have ever had, and the most precious foreign policy ideal a free people has ever had, has been the ideal of the free government of the United States never to commit an act of war, never to commit an act of aggression, and never to go to war, until war is made upon us."[5]

Whether or not one approved of the Communist government, Morse argued, no one could dispute that it had sovereign rights over mainland China. America had always respected the sovereign rights of all countries with which it was not at war. But a preemptive strike to disable potentially threatening Chinese forces would contradict that principle.

Notwithstanding assurances from the administration, Morse believed the Soviet Union would come to China's defense. "We have no reason to believe that Red China will act alone; we have no reason to believe that Red Russia will pay no heed or will give no consideration to her treaty commitments to Red China."[6]

Like several of his colleagues, Morse worried that Nationalist China would engineer a situation that backed the United States into a corner and made war probable. He charged, "The Nationalist Chinese believe their only hope of survival in the long run is to get the United States involved an all-out war on the mainland of China, which would result, they hope, in the final subjugation of the Communist regime."[7]

Morse argued that, as a victor in war, the United States bore a responsibility to defend Formosa and should treat it as a protectorate until arrangements could be made that assured peace. At the time of the Cairo Declaration, the United States had assumed that an allied government, Nationalist China, would be sovereign in Formosa after the Japanese formally renounced their claim. Washington could acquiesce to this because both US security and regional peace would be protected. However, by 1952, when Japan formally relinquished its claims, China was under Communist control. Morse believed that changed circumstances were decisive. If Washington acknowledged Communist rights to Formosa, regional peace and American interests would be imperiled. Thus, the senator said, the United States must maintain control, at least temporarily, recognizing neither Communist nor Nationalist sovereignty over the island. This reasoning contradicted both the PRC and ROC, which claimed that sovereignty conclusively transferred when the China reassumed physical control of Formosa.[8] On both sides of the strait, Cairo and Potsdam represented solemn commitments.

Longer term, Morse favored substituting a United Nations trusteeship for US control. "It is important to get the United Nations to relieve us of the unilateral course of action in respect to Formosa, but until it does, we have a clear duty in the interest of world peace to protect Formosa. The world cannot overlook the fact that we owed territorial obligations to Formosa because we took it from the Japanese and controlled it after World War II. Its return to China had not been implemented when it became a threat through our vital interests and to the peace in the Pacific."

However, protecting the offshore islands, whether tied or not to the defense of Formosa, was almost certain to require bombing mainland China.[9] If that occurred, China was likely to enjoy support from the Soviet Union while it was probable that the United States would be isolated. "Under the Chinese-Soviet defense pact, Russia could enter the war without NATO countries being under obligation to join with us," the senator said.[10]

Unless the resolution was amended to exclude the offshore islands and address only the defense of Formosa and the Pescadores, Morse pledged to vote against it.[11]

After Morse finished, Senator Knowland offered a spirited rebuttal. Morse's comments on preventive war were unsupported by the hearing testimony and left a dangerous misimpression. If left to stand uncorrected, they might cause the Communists to conclude a US strike was imminent, he noted. That could lead China or Russia to take preemptive action of their own, jeopardizing the Seventh Fleet and regional US bases.

Soviet propaganda could exploit Morse's criticism to cast the United States as the aggressor, Knowland added. The senator cited a news release from the Communist Party newspaper *Pravda*. "The Soviet newspaper Pravda charged today President Eisenhower's message to Congress on Formosa was 'brazen intervention' in Red China's internal affairs and an attempt to prepare an invasion of the mainland. . . . Both Houses of Congress are rushing through the consideration of this message. In question is the preparation of direct aggression by the United States Armed Forces against the continental territory of China."[12]

Eisenhower's objective was not to provoke a war, but to stabilize a volatile situation and America giving firm security guarantees to Chiang's government.[13] "I repeat," exclaimed the senator, "this is a resolution of peace. It is a resolution of stability. . . . There is not one iota of desire or intent . . . that the resolution be passed for the purposes of either making possible preventive war or aggression against the Chinese Communist regime, or any other regime."[14]

Knowland criticized the amendments that would eliminate defense of Quemoy and Matsu. "It would give a green light to the Chinese Communists to proceed to take those islands. We would be saying to them, 'you can feel absolutely certain that, with impunity, you can send your invading forces, your paratroopers, troops from amphibious craft into that line of islands regardless of their relationship to the safety of Formosa.'"[15]

The senator warned his colleagues that attacks on the offshore islands must be seen as preliminary to the effort to replace the Nationalists on Formosa. He quoted recent remarks from Premier Zhou Enlai. The premier had said, "The Government of the People's Republic of China has repeatedly and in solemn terms declared to the world: The Chinese people are determined to liberate their own territory of Taiwan (Formosa). They are using war threats and brandishing atomic weapons in an attempt to force the Chinese people into tolerating the occupation of Taiwan by the United States, giving recognition to the United States-Chiang Kai-shek Mutual Security Treaty, and permitting the use of Taiwan by the United States as a military base for preparing a new war. The Chinese people absolutely cannot tolerate this."[16]

Knowland derided Morse's suggestion that Formosa be governed under a United Nations trusteeship. He claimed Asians would look upon that as an extension of colonialism. There was a functioning government on Formosa. He thought unworkable the idea to replace it with a United Nations entity, whose policies would be subject to Soviet influence. "Do Senators expect them to disarm 350,000 of their own troops and place their lives and future at the tender mercy of an organization which would be subject to a Soviet veto? I think not."

Senator Kefauver contended that Congress must narrow the resolution to de-escalate matters. "I think war may come out of the present situation, whether any resolution is passed or not. . . . The Senate should endeavor to get the resolution in such shape that it will result in the least possible chance of war and still maintain our honor."

Eisenhower, Knowland, and others had claimed that passing the resolution would express national unity. Such unity was in fact available, Kefauver said, provided the resolution did not cover Quemoy and Matsu. "If it is unity the minority leader is seeking, all that is necessary is to see to it that we are kept from getting involved with Chiang on these little coastal islands."

The United States did not put Chiang on the islands and was not obliged to help him defend them, especially to launch an attack on the mainland, stated Kefauver. "We are not going to use the Armed Forces of the United States for the purpose of trying to keep Chiang Kai-shek on those islands, so he can mount an invasion of the mainland of China."

Kefauver was another of the senators who was openly contemptuous of Chiang. "His motive is not the same as ours," Kefauver declared. "Our motive is peace. His motive is the re-invasion of the continent of Asia." Everyone knew that would not be possible without American help, and Kefauver was certain that help should not be forthcoming.[17]

He would offer a substitute amendment that would omit reference to the yet unratified Mutual Defense Treaty, avoid stating a presumption that an attack on the islands was a precursor to an attack on Formosa, assert a legal basis for US protection of Formosa, welcome United Nations intervention, recognize the president's power to act rather than purport to authorize it, and strike reference to positions and territories "now in friendly hands." "I believe the reference to those islands must be eliminated from the resolution," Kefauver insisted. "They must be eliminated because I do not understand how we can operate in those islands without getting into a shooting war."[18]

Senator Margaret Chase Smith (R-ME) noted that the resolution would foreclose the kind of criticism Truman got for conducting the Korean War without express congressional authorization. "President Eisenhower," she said, "will have Democrats as well as Republicans in the same position with him, he will have placed them in the position of having shared the decision with him."

The resolution presented major questions that she hoped would be addressed in the Senate debate. Was it a "reserve declaration of war?" Would it result in admission of Communist China to the United Nations and US recognition of the Beijing government? Would the United States pursue a policy of preventing Chiang from invading the Chinese mainland? Considering cuts in the US defense budget, did the United States have sufficient military strength to back up all its firm talk?

"I am going to vote for this resolution," Smith announced, "because I think we must take a firm stand; and because I think Congress and the President should stand united on this issue, I hope the resolution is passed by unanimous vote."[19]

THE FORMOSA RESOLUTION ON THE
SENATE FLOOR: JANUARY 27, 1955

Shortly after the Senate convened on Thursday, January 27, the Democratic Whip, Earle Clements (D-KY), secured recognition to bring the Formosa Resolution to the Floor. Inasmuch as the Senate and House texts were identical, Clements moved that the Senate proceed to consider H.J. Res. 159, which the House had passed on the previous day. The Senate agreed to the motion by voice vote. S.J. Res. 28 would be set aside and there would be no further action on it. Floor action would be taken on the House Joint Resolution.

Chairman Walter George of the Committee on Foreign Relations, who managed the resolution to passage, began the debate. He appealed to senators to act promptly. If they did, and if amendments were not added, the resolution would make a strong impact for peace. However, he cautioned, "if it is long delayed, the psychological value of the action taken by the Congress of the United States will be very greatly minimized, if indeed not partially destroyed."

Rebutting arguments that the president already had the power to act, and the resolution was superfluous, George declared that Eisenhower was right coming to Congress, even if only to secure moral support from representatives of the American people. "I hope that no Democrat will be heard to say that because the President of the United States came to Congress, he is thereby subject to criticism."

George implored his colleagues to rally behind Eisenhower. "I ask this one question now: If the Congress of the United States is willing to withhold moral support to the President of the United States under existing conditions which are not disputed, what is the alternative? Let every Member answer, on his conscience, the question of what is his alternative?"

The senator described the developing military and political situation in the strait. A Communist assault on one of the Tachen Islands had been successful. Immediately thereafter, Premier Zhou Enlai had again affirmed the PRC's objective of "liberating" Formosa. The senator argued that China had been clear about its purposes, and that the Senate debate over Quemoy and Matsu amounted to a meaningless distraction. "Chou Enlai is not worried about the offshore islands," the chairman observed. "That is an issue which the American Senate is supposed to consider, talk about, exploit, and worry about. Zhou is not concerned about it. Has he said anything about taking the Tachen islands? Has he said anything about taking any other small island along the coast of China? Not at all. He has said 'you assert sovereignty over Formosa and the Pescadores Islands, and we propose to liberate those islands.'"

George dismissed the commentary, prominent in remarks from Morse and Kefauver, about preventive war. Such arguments primarily served to disturb US allies and reinforce Communist propaganda, he said.[20]

Some senators had expressed concern about war being instigated by a trigger-happy US commander or by the Nationalists. George worried that the sentiment might result in restrictive amendments. Thus, he collaborated with White House on a statement making clear that the president alone would decide whether to commit American forces. The administration issued it after negotiating with George on the wording.[21]

Released on January 27 by Eisenhower's press secretary James Hagerty, the statement read, "The President made it clear that these United States forces were designed purely for defensive purposes and that any decision to use United States forces other than in immediate self-defense or in direct defense of Formosa and the Pescadores would be a decision which he would take and the responsibility for which he has not delegated."[22]

As described in the *New York Times*:

> The purpose of the White House statement, it was made clear, was to end talk on Capitol Hill that the resolution authorizing the defense of Formosa was in any sense authority to carry on a preventive war aimed at Red China or the Soviet Union. It was designed, also, to answer questions as to whether Generalissimo Chiang Kai-shek, president of the Nationalist Government on Formosa, had in any sense received a go ahead for offensive maneuvers that might incite retaliation from the Chinese Communists.[23]

George believed the release should calm anxieties about accidental war.[24] He interpreted it for his colleagues. "For one thing, it means that neither the President of the Republic of China nor any of the officers of that government will start the war if one is started. But it means infinitely more than that. It means that no Admiral here or no line officer off the coast of China in the Formosa Straits or elsewhere will start it. It means, in explicit terms, the decision will be made here that it will be made a personal decision of the President of the United States and that he has delegated no authority to anyone else to make that decision." With that established, George asked, "Do Senators want anything more?"[25]

George turned to the issue of the offshore islands. He opposed the line drawing that Kefauver, Humphrey, and Morse deemed essential. The moment certain territories were put outside defense perimeter, the senator argued, the Communists were invited to seize them. "A great many people want someone to draw a line," said George. "I do not." Because he believed a takeover of Quemoy and Matsu presaged an attack on Formosa, George did not favor ceding an inch of Nationalist-held ground. "If we are going to defend effectively the island of Formosa or the Pescadores, we have to start in time to stop the invasion of those islands."

George disputed concerns that the resolution gave the president license to conduct warfare in China. He argued that it authorized the defense and securing of positions and territories then in friendly hands, and nothing more. Therefore, he said, it was language of limitation. Eliminating that provision would actually broaden Eisenhower's authority. "The President himself is asking that we agree, insofar as we can agree, to give him support not to go onto the mainland, and not to take any lands which are held by any people other than those who are friends of ours. He is asking that he be given the right, in this area, to secure and protect those lands that are now in friendly hands. That is what the President has asked for. It is a limitation upon his authority and power."[26]

The senator's biographer, Jamie Cockfield, considered his January 27 remarks to be one of the greatest speeches in a long career. "George's resounding voice laid waste to the resolution's opponents in a verbal carpet bombing," he wrote.[27]

New Jersey's H. Alexander Smith, the leading Foreign Relations Committee Republican on Asian issues, argued that tensions over Formosa could not be considered in isolation from two additional conflicts in Asia. One was Korea, which for 18 months had been under an armistice. Smith worried that the truce would not be durable. A second was Indochina, also under a truce that might not hold. His colleagues must put the strait crisis in context. "Unless we face the problem as an all-Asian problem, we run the risk of having it said 'this is just a battle to keep Formosa for Chiang Kai-shek'. . . . That is part of the picture, but the overall consideration is the whole Asia problem." Smith insisted that it was essential to support the structure of deterrence the administration erected.

Part of that system was the collective security arrangement known as the Southeast Asia Treaty Organization. Smith explained that in NATO the governing concept was that an attack on one was an attack on all, but that SEATO operated on a different principle. "We realized that in the far-flung areas of the Far East we could not assume that the responsibility of stating that an attack on one would be an attack on all. . . . Therefore, we adopted what was known as the Monroe Doctrine principle . . . that aggression anywhere would be a matter of concern to our own security and the security of the country attacked."

In addition, there were security pacts with Japan, the Philippines, South Korea, Australia, and New Zealand. To these would soon be added the Mutual Defense Treaty with Nationalist China. Smith explained, "Because we have been profoundly interested in Formosa as an outpost of strategic value to our own security, and as a protection for our bases in that area, we felt we should bring the Nationalist Chinese government into the same area of collective self-defense treaties." Smith recognized concerns from his colleagues that Chiang would try to leverage the pact into support for an invasion of the mainland, but he reassured senators that the administration had worked through appropriate safeguards, submitting into the *Congressional Record* an exchange of letters between Secretary Dulles and Foreign Minister George Yeh that, except in emergency circumstances involving self-defense, forces would not be deployed except by mutual agreement.

The Formosa Resolution was also integral to this security structure, Smith observed. "It has finally been decided without fear of contradiction, by a succession of governments, Democratic and Republican, that Formosa and the Pescadores are essential parts of our defense chain in that area; and that if that area falls into hostile hands, it will constitute a real threat to the free world into our own specific positions and responsibilities."

The resolution did not expressly include or exclude Quemoy and Matsu, the senator noted. That was purposeful, to give the president the fullest possible discretion on whether to defend them. It was possible that defense could involve a preemptive strike. Smith strongly disagreed that connoted a preventive war. The aggressor, he felt, was the side that had massed forces. "We could not be charged with aggression if we were to take appropriate defensive measures before we were attacked. . . . I do not see how it can be said that we are not entitled to take effective measures before the boats arrive at their destination and the troops strike the first blow."[28]

While Smith touted the benefits of ambiguity, Alabama's John Sparkman dissented. He thought it would be wiser to be clear about US intentions. "I believe we would be much better off if we said either 'yay' or 'nay' as to the defense of these two particular groups of islands. . . . That would remove the vagueness and uncertainty and the whole world, including the Chinese Communists would know we meant what we said." Sparkman did not quarrel with defending the islands and would disagree to amendments that attempted to exclude them.

Senator Herbert Lehman (D-NY) was greatly troubled by the prospect of war over Quemoy and Matsu. He distinguished between Formosa, which he said had not belonged to China "for generations" and the islands, which had "always belonged to China." In the aftermath of the war, observed Lehman, the United States was Formosa's "protector." However, defending the offshore islands was entirely different. "I think it will place us in a weakened position if we draw a defense line in the Far East to include Matsu and Quemoy, or the other islands near the Chinese coast. . . . If we did that, we would be taking sides in a civil war, not in a war to defend Formosa."[29]

Lehman took strong exception to the language that gave the president a free hand in "securing and protection of such related positions and territories now in friendly hands and the taking of such other measures as he judges to be required or appropriate in assuring the defense of Formosa and the Pescadores." He considered it far too elastic and feared it could lead to war. "I hold a very strong conviction about this—that clause should come out."[30]

Knowland challenged Lehman about the legal status of Formosa. "The Chinese Nationalists do not look at it in that way. Under the Cairo Declaration it was said that the Island of Formosa would be returned to the Republic of China; and the Republic of China is on Formosa and is in possession of it."

Knowland noted that the Nationalists considered defense of the offshore islands to be inextricable from the defense of Formosa proper, because controlling the islands kept the Communists from using key ports as staging areas for an invasion. The senator did not consider it America's place to challenge that reasoning or to tell Chiang to abandon them. Such foreign dictation would undermine Nationalist morale and the confidence of America's allies in the region and send the wrong message to the Communist Chinese. "Zhou Enlai would interpret it to mean that because of his threats and his huffing and puffing, the Senate of the United States decided to put shackles on the hands of the Commander in Chief."[31]

Late in the day, Morse took the Floor to dissect the White House statement and to renew his charge that the resolution authorized a preventive war. He argued the statement served only to clarify who had the responsibility for making decisions but did not limit the scope of what could be done, Morse said. "The resolution opens wide the door for taking action over and beyond the immediate defense of Formosa and the Pescadores and the President admits as much in his release."

While the statement was intended to calm fears of accidental war, it was insufficient for the senator. The statement placed no constraints on what Eisenhower might do. Morse implored his colleagues not to grant authority blindly. "I do not propose by pre-authorization, by predating, or by commitment in advance, without having before me the specific facts involving an incident which might justify the President asking for the exercise of such power, to give blanket approval to the President of the United States to proceed to commit an act of war against another nation."

Under the Constitution, only Congress had the responsibility to declare war. Morse claimed that the resolution amounted to delegating that power to the president. He implored his colleagues not to do so. "I respectfully submit that we have no right under our oaths of office to delegate that great constitutional obligation of Congress to anyone, not even to the President of the United States."

Morse contested George's argument that the resolution served to limit Eisenhower's power. "The language 'and the taking of such other measures as he judges to be required or appropriate' is a blanket grant of preventive war power to the President of the United States, if he decides to use it." The provision was not restrictive, but permissive. Eisenhower could take any step he pleased and claim it was necessary for the defense of Formosa, including a preventive act of war.

Senator Humphrey would soon offer his amendment striking the implicit reference to the offshore islands and the "such other measures" verbiage. Morse planned to support it. "The Senator from Minnesota proposes to eliminate that language and we are met with the argument that by removing that broad sweeping language from the resolution we broaden it. That is a bit of argumentation that defies all my understanding of logic." The senator explained, "Obviously, with the language 'to take such other measures' left in the resolution, it is perfectly clear that the President would have the power, most certainly, to order a strike against any point on the mainland of China. . . . Therefore, the conclusion is inescapable that striking such broad language from the resolution as the Humphrey amendment does cannot possibly result in broadening the resolution."

Morse was sure that the United States should not be defending Quemoy and Matsu. He believed they were militarily insignificant, belonged to China, and tempted reckless action. The resolution must be amended to preclude it. Doing so would eliminate a major possibility for conflict, Morse stated. The senator again emphasized that the United States had a right to defend Formosa but not to launch preemptive strikes against Chinese territory, even if the United States did not recognize the Communist government.

Two options were attractive to Morse. One was the Humphrey amendment to limit the scope of the resolution to defense of Formosa and the Pescadores and strike reference to the offshore islands. A second was an amendment from Senator Kefauver to defer US action while the United Nations endeavored to find a solution. Pending proceedings in the UN, the United States would commit to defend only Formosa and the Pescadores. Morse concluded, "unless we follow some such course of action, we shall not be giving the heed we should give to the risks of peace but will be enhancing the probability of the calculated risks of war."[32]

THE FORMOSA RESOLUTION ON THE
SENATE FLOOR: JANUARY 28, 1955

On the concluding day of proceedings on the Formosa Resolution, Senator Lehman spotlighted a contradiction. "We are told that there is an urgent necessity for the passage of this resolution. Yet at the same time, the President told us he already has all the legal authority he needs to perform the acts he proposes to perform under the terms of the pending resolution." If so, asked Lehman, why should the Senate rush to judgment? He insisted senators needed more time to consider the resolution's implications.

Lehman considered the contours of Eisenhower's policy in the strait to be ill-defined. If limited to the defense of Formosa and the Pescadores, the senator was on board. But the resolution was broader, and Lehman was not comfortable. He would not sanction using US forces to defend Quemoy and Matsu or even to support the Tachens evacuation. If the president wished to proceed on his own authority to do those things, that was his sole responsibility, Lehman said. But the Senate should not bless them in advance. "I am not going to support a congressional sanction for these activities," he declared. "I repeat that I am glad to support a congressional sanction for the defense of Formosa and the Pescadores. That is the furthest that I want to go."

Lehman felt somewhat reassured by Eisenhower's statement that major decisions would not be delegated. "I have great confidence in the personal integrity and patriotism of President Eisenhower. I appreciate his recognition of the fears that some of us have expressed and his desire to quiet those fears." But as was the case for Senator Morse, Lehman thought the statement was still not adequate. "He has quieted them," Lehman said, "only in small measure."

From Lehman's perspective, three things were still missing. There had been no reassurance about excluding Quemoy and Matsu, no justification for why the president needed a "blank check," and no reference of any kind to resolving the crisis within the United Nations.

The chief cause for his alarm was the language that allowed the president to take any measure he deemed appropriate to secure and protect positions and territories presently in friendly hands. Lehman asked, "What is it, other than a blank check signed by the Congress, for such action as the President or his military advisers should decide to take—action that can or may easily involve us in a war." He was troubled by the vagueness. No one necessarily knew who or what would be involved.

Again, Lehman said, the president could undertake all such measures on his own responsibility, subject to justifying them later to Congress and to the American people. But Congress should not be asked to approve them in advance. Summarizing the issue, the senator declared, "If this portion of the resolution proposes to give the President powers which he does not now have, I want to know for what I am voting. If this portion of the resolution merely approves in advance actions which the President already has the power to take, I think it not only unnecessary but unwise."

The senator laid out how Congress should exercise its constitutional responsibilities and where it should refrain from acting. "Ours is the responsibility to authorize specific action, and to authorize and to appropriate funds for specific and general activities, and to judge, after the fact, whether the President acted in accordance with his powers and responsibilities. Surely our duty is not to sanction in advance unspecified acts which are within the implicit powers and responsibilities of the President."

Lehman turned to the role of the United Nations. The administration indicated it would pursue a cease-fire in the UN, but the resolution said nothing about it. Left in that form, it would "serve notice that we have lost faith in the United Nations." Lehman thought it was a grave omission. He would support the Kefauver substitute to make explicit provision for the UN process. "We must speak boldly in this resolution of the United Nations and of our active desire to have the UN order a ceasefire and of our desire that the President urge in the UN such an action."

Above all, Lehman insisted, Congress must not even imply that the United States would defend Quemoy and Matsu. Acknowledging they were Chinese territory, he argued, "there is no juridical, legal, or historical basis for separating, alienating, or neutralizing those doorstep islands." If America chose to become involved in their protection, Lehman said, it would alienate allies and likely must act alone. The issue of the offshore islands had arisen during a recent debate in the British Parliament, he pointed out. Labor Party leader and former prime minister Clement Attlee made "a sharp and vigorous attack against this resolution and against our China policy." In response, Prime Minister Anthony Eden replied that "the offshore islands have always been regarded, and are now regarded by us, as part of China," and said that the British government did not believe the American defense line included them or would be extended to do so. However, if that was the understanding in London, it did not seem to hold true in Washington. "There is a clear indication, both in the message and in the resolution, as I read them, that we will regard any attempt on the part of the Communists to capture the islands like Quemoy and Matsu . . . as preparation for an attack on Formosa," justifying a US response. If that happened, he predicted, the British and other US allies would bail.

Lehman cautioned about reaching premature deductions over the massing of Chinese forces in coastal areas. Chiang's rhetoric about a return to the mainland had been escalating. In his 1955 New Year's Day message, Chiang declared, "A full scale war may break out at any time." He also predicted, "1955 will witness the further deterioration of international relations."[33] With these threats in mind, it was possible that the Communists were strengthening defenses against an invasion rather than preparing to attack across the strait.

While the United States should look to de-escalate this tenuous situation, the resolution was likely to ramp up the tension, Lehman charged. "This situation calls for a ceasefire order to preserve the peace. It calls for the re-leashing of Chiang Kai-shek and the leashing of the Chinese Communists by order and action of the United Nations."

Lehman endorsed the Kefauver substitute. If it did not pass, he would support the Humphrey amendment or would propose an amendment of his own. If none of those amendments passed, he would oppose the resolution.[34]

When Lehman finished, George announced that debate on a New Zealand-sponsored cease-fire proposal was expected to commence in the United Nations on Monday, January 31. It was imperative, he said, that Congress should complete work on the Formosa Resolution without further delay and with a heavily affirmative vote. "It is therefore important that at the beginning of that debate there should be a position of strength, and not of vacillation, on the part of the United States."[35]

Senator Humphrey was recognized to speak on his amendment. It would strike the language that read "the securing and protection of such related positions and territories of that area now in friendly hands and the taking of such other measures as he judges to be required or appropriate in assuring the defense of Formosa and the Pescadores."

Humphrey argued that the mandate to secure and protect could involve something apart from the defense of Formosa. He said testimony before the combined committees showed that the offshore islands were not essential for that purpose. Instead, it could mean a commitment "to use the forces of the United States to secure the island of Quemoy and the island of Matsu as objectives in themselves." That generated significant risks, he claimed, involving "the taking of American forces that much closer to the area of the Chinese mainland, with the possibility of entrapment and the possibility of a military debacle in a restricted area, and the possibility of furtherance of war on the Chinese mainland."

The senator feared the United States would have to assume those risks without traditional allies, such as Britain. London distinguished between Formosa, which it felt was of undetermined jurisdiction, and the offshore islands, which it considered disputed territory but unquestionably Chinese. The British would not fight for the islands because doing so meant involvement in a civil war. So, America would be isolated.

Humphrey sought to explain Eisenhower's statement that the president alone would make decision on major American deployments. The senator noted that Chiang's main objective, persistently and vociferously expressed, was to retake the mainland. But was impossible without support from the United States, Humphrey noted, which is why the Nationalists would look for ways to make it happen. "For the past six or seven years we have been hearing the story of the ability and capacity of the Generalissimo on Formosa to retake the mainland. That story is a myth, pure and simple. . . . If the mainland is ever to be retaken, it will be retaken with American power, American manhood, American blood, American money, and American armament." And that reality was the reason for Eisenhower's statement, Humphrey said. "The President is assuring Congress, by his decisions, that no one is to lead us into that trap."

Humphrey announced that he would vote for narrowing amendments and for the Kefauver substitute. It was Congress' responsibility not just to go along with president but to be a full participant in the policy process. "To be told in this instance that we cannot in any way modify the resolution is to deny Congress anything but the right to be a complete rubber stamp. . . . In the Constitution itself we find the words 'advice and consent' and not merely 'consent.'"

Humphrey said he would limit the authorization to the defense of Formosa, something to which the entire Congress was committed, and nothing more. "The language in the resolution pertaining to 'such related positions and territories of that area now in friendly hands' possibly commits Congress to a position which goes far beyond the defense of Formosa and the Pescadores."

If altered by Humphrey's amendment, the resolution would simply have read: "That the President of the United States be and is hereby authorized to employ the Armed Forces of the United States as he deems necessary for the specific purpose of securing and protecting Formosa and the Pescadores against armed attack."

The senator said he also intended to amend the resolution's preamble (the "whereas" clauses that precede and justify the "resolved" clause). The amendment would welcome UN intervention to produce a cease-fire and, as part of such an agreement, include a "definitive settlement of the future status of Formosa and the Pescadores in accordance with the principles of the United Nations Charter."[36] This comment provoked a vigorous response from Senator Paul Douglas (D-IL), who argued that such a cease-fire would chain Chiang Kai-shek to Formosa, eliminate the chances he could attempt to retake the mainland, collapse the morale of Nationalist troops, and quickly lead to Beijing's admission into the United Nations.[37] Humphrey never wound up proposing the amendment.

Humphrey announced that he would vote for the resolution if the amendments failed.

"The truth is that if the resolution should be defeated by the Congress, Mr. Eisenhower would still be President of the United States, still be Commander in Chief of the Armed Forces, still be the chief spokesman of the American foreign policy, but denied the confidence of the representatives of the people; and to the Communist world that would be a great day. . . . As a member of this body and as a citizen, I have no effective choice, I frankly state, but to support the resolution."[38]

North Dakota Republican William Langer followed Humphrey to the Floor and called up the First Amendment. It provided that the president could not use military force on the mainland of China, or to intervene in the defense of the offshore islands, except for the specific purpose of helping to withdraw Nationalist troops and civilians from those islands.

Langer observed that Eisenhower had been elected in 1952 on a peace platform. In Korea, the United States had borne the overwhelming part of the international burden. Eisenhower's promise to go to Korea and seek a way out of the conflict proved immensely popular with American voters, Langer said. But, just two years later, the situation in the strait threatened to move in the opposite direction. The senator wished to prevent American troops from being drawn into a land war in China. While he noted he could not stop Eisenhower from committing such forces under the president' own constitutional authority, Langer insisted that Congress must not have expressly permitted it. "It may be said that the President already has authority to send our armed forces anywhere in the world in order to protect Formosa, but certainly the Senate, if the amendment of the Senator from North Dakota were agreed to, would not have given the president that authority."[39]

Knowland rebutted. While Congress could not legally constrain the president's constitutional power, by adopting the Langer amendment it could impose moral restrictions on its use. If made public law, it could severely hamstring how Eisenhower responded to military provocations. For example, what if American forces supporting the Tachens withdrawal were attacked? "I do not think there is a single Member in the chamber who would expect our forces to be present as sitting ducks, to be fired upon and not permitted to fire back, that we could only pursue them to . . . within 12 miles of the China coast and that there we were to stop. Would we not be declaring publicly that the attackers would have a sanctuary at that point?"[40]

George Aiken (R-VT), who considered the Formosa Resolution as a deterrent to war, concurred. The Langer amendment would encourage conflict because it would provide the Communists safe havens behind which they could operate with impunity.[41]

One of Chiang's steadfast supporters, Herman Welker (R-ID), spoke at length about Communist provocations in Korea, Southeast Asia, and in the strait. These were either directly attributable to Communist China or supported by it, he observed. He supported the resolution without amendment as a message that the United States would stand its ground. "It would appear that the immediate purpose of the Chinese communists is to probe. They are conducting a testing action to determine whether or not we mean business in defending Formosa. And to my way of thinking the pending resolution of bodies the correct response. We do mean business and I think it is important that we make our intentions clear, so that the Chinese Communists can in no way misconstrue our intentions. The resolution of the consideration does just that." Beyond sending a message to Beijing, it would also signal non-Communist nations in Asia, who might otherwise lack confidence in the United States.[42]

John Bricker (R-OH) had argued during the Korean conflict that President Truman needed to seek approval from Congress before committing US forces to that war. Thus, he felt vindicated by Eisenhower's request for the Formosa Resolution. "This is not a simple or concurrent resolution which merely expresses the sense of the Senate or of the Congress. We are not called on here to express a purely advisory opinion. A joint resolution unlike a simple or concurrent resolution has legal force and effect. The Congress is authorizing the President to take certain action—action which may make a declaration of war a mere formality." If any senator thought that the president could simply act on his own, without need for congressional sanction, Bricker added, they should vote against the resolution.

Beyond the constitutional issue, Bricker thought the resolution was also important because the issues in the strait crisis were not simply military, but also political. As well, it was important for US allies and adversaries, as well as the American people, to know that the president and Congress stood united on the policy.[43]

Senator Morse returned to the Floor for final remarks. He again challenged George's position that the resolution limited Eisenhower's power. In fact, the "as he deems necessary" provision could not be broader, Morse said. It amounted to predated congressional approval for preemptive strikes against mainland China if the president considered them necessary to defend Formosa and the Pescadores. "We cannot escape the conclusion that if that is done it will constitute an act of war on the part of the United States against Red China before Red China commits an act of war against the United States," he thundered.

Quemoy and Matsu were Chinese territories, Morse repeated. Sovereignty was not disputed, so control was an unresolved issue in the Chinese civil war. To engage in their defense was to intervene in that war. "With the United States still claiming it should defend Quemoy and Matsu, what do these Chinese see? They see an opponent in a civil war, the Nationalist Chinese occupying those islands which they say, from the standpoint of their sovereign rights, belong to China." Morse was sure that would be a "bad historic precedent."[44]

Not only a bad precedent, Morse continued, but also escalatory and provocative. The resolution would put the Communists on notice that they could be preemptively struck. As a result, they could misinterpret US ship movements as preparation for such an assault and launch preemptive attacks of their own. "The resolution thereby creates an intolerable uncertainty," the senator observed.

Morse summarized his objections. As he construed it, the resolution allowed for preventive action. Because of that, it enabled the Communists to label the United States as an aggressor nation and weakened America's moral standing in the world. It increased the temptation for Chiang to provoke the Communists into attacking him, which would draw the United States into a war with China. And the role of the United Nations was insufficiently emphasized, including the option of establishing a trusteeship over Formosa. He concluded, "Now is the time to dissent, before legislation is passed which authorizes this sweeping power. It is a sweeping power. It is a dangerous power. There is not a word of limitation in the resolution with respect to the power. It is a preventive war power. I believe it greatly increases the probabilities of war. It tends too much in the direction of our running calculated risks of war and ignores the calculated risks of peace. I hope that history will prove all my fears are unfounded."[45]

Senator George made closing arguments for the committee. The resolution did not limit or purport to limit the president's constitutional authority, he said. What was limited was what Congress had agreed to support, that being the authority "to include the security and protection of such related positions and territories now in friendly hands." George noted, "It undoubtedly is a limitation, because it could not apply to any territories or positions in unfriendly or hostile hands. It is not strictly a limitation. I was not speaking technically. . . . It is a restriction upon the authority which the President may have, insofar as we express our judgment on it." The president could have wider powers under the Constitution, George conceded. "As to whether it limits his power under the constitution is an altogether different question. It is one with which I am not concerned here, and I do not think the Senate should be concerned with it."

George scornfully addressed the Langer amendment, which had been pending for much of the afternoon. The offshore islands were under the control of a regime that the United States recognized as the legitimate government of China. But Langer proposed that the United States not lift a finger in their defense and that the Nationalists evacuate them. What then, George asked? "What are we going to do with them when we get off? I ask any sensible man or woman in America, what is meant by that? Should we turn them over to the Reds, or get off quickly and turn them over to Peiping, a government which we have never recognized and take them away from the government which we have recognized and to which we have obligations?" The senator added. "I am under no such obligation to Communist China."

Agreeing to the sort of restriction that Langer proposed would have two consequences, George said. The Communists would seize the islands and the will of Nationalist forces to maintain the defense of Formosa would collapse. The United States had just signed a mutual defense treaty with the Nationalists but, by abandoning the offshore islands and leaving Chiang to fend for himself, would promptly be undermining its efficacy. "Here we are with an obligation under international law to defend Formosa, and yet we are asked to take action which can only benefit the enemy of Formosa, and which can only result in destroying the will to fight of every single soldier on Formosa. Is that not a beautiful way to keep our international obligations?"

A vote on the Langer amendment was drawing near. Senator Mansfield observed that the United States was implicitly embarked on a two-China strategy. If the resolution and related policies had the effect of preventing war, he said, it would be because it prevented China from attacking Formosa and stopped the Nationalists from attacking mainland China. In that way, it would operate much like Truman's 1950 interposition of the Seventh Fleet in the strait. "China will be split as definitively as Germany and Korea have been," said Mansfield. He predicted that if there were two Chinas, the Communists would accede to China's seat at the United Nations and the Nationalists would be expelled.

Mansfield opposed the Langer amendment and supported the resolution. "An adverse vote at this time, a failure to uphold the President, can only be interpreted throughout the world as a faltering of our resolve, with disastrous consequences to peace and free nations."[46]

Although Senator Capehart had been concerned that Chiang was motivated to provoke a Sino-American war, he announced that administration representations had reassured him. He concluded that the purpose of the resolution was solely to defend Formosa, and nothing wider, and that Eisenhower would firmly control whether American troops would be involved. "If we get into a war, we shall do it on our own initiative. I am thoroughly convinced that our officials are not going to permit Chiang Kai-shek to get us into a war."[47]

In brief remarks, Langer summed up his case. The debate had focused on the massing of forces near the Chinese coast and preemptive action that the United States might take to neutralize it. To avoid those strikes, China could simply move the buildup further inland, perhaps 100, 500, or 1,000 miles away. He asked, "Are we going to have the President use our armed forces to go that far and to attack the forces of the government of China before those forces attack us?" Foreseeing the United States being sucked into a protracted struggle on the Chinese mainland, Langer stated, "If five, six, seven, or eight years from now we find that our troops are still on the mainland of China, and if at that time the American people ask various Senators 'did you vote to send our boys there' the only answer Senators will be able to give is yes, if they vote in favor of the passage of the pending joint resolution."[48]

On the Langer amendment, three senators voted in favor. They were Langer, Morse, and Lehman. Eighty-three senators opposed the amendment, and ten senators did not vote.

Senator Kefauver called up his substitute amendment, which struck out and replaced all language of H.J. Res. 159. Morse and Lehman were his cosponsors. The substitute consisted of seven clauses in the preamble, followed by a "resolved" clause, which read:

> Resolved, That it is the sense of Congress—in light of the above-described situation and so long as it continues, pending effective action by the United Nations to maintain peace and security in the Formosa Straits and the waters surrounding Formosa and the Pescadores—the President has the authority to employ the Armed Forces of the United States if and as he deems necessary for the specific purpose of defending and protecting Formosa and the Pescadores from armed attack. That authority would include the taking of such other measures consistent with international law and our obligations under the United Nations Charter as he judges necessary or appropriate militarily in the defense of Formosa and the Pescadores.

In his memoirs, Eisenhower summarized the substitute in one sentence: "Senator Kefauver proposed turning over the protection of Formosa and the Pescadores to the United Nations and giving authority to the President only until the United Nations should act."[49]

Kefauver described a series of principles on which he based the substitute. First, to separate the offshore islands from the defense of Formosa and the Pescadores. He construed the pending resolution to embrace Quemoy and Matsu as fully as if they had been expressly named, claiming that his countrymen did not want to go to war over them.

> I do not believe the American people want to go to war in the defense of the coastal islands or to try to pull Chiang Kai-shek's chestnuts out of the fire. . . . Our interest is, and I hope it always will be, to stabilize that part of the world and to have peace. But that is not Chiang Kai-shek's interest. Chiang Kai-shek's interest is to get air cover in that area so that he will be able to move his troops onto the mainland and engage in a re-invasion of communist China. . . . The people United States do not want to go to war over some unnamed little coastal island off the Chinese mainland, an island about which they have never heard and do not care anything about.

Kefauver's comments, along with many similar remarks from other senators, were evidence of a brutal reality. In the anti-Communist spirit of the age, the United States was stuck with an ally who served American interests but who many senators distrusted, especially among Democrats.

The second principle asserted that defending Formosa was based on US legal responsibilities attendant to the peace treaty with Japan. Under the treaty, Japan had relinquished all claim to Formosa but the treaty itself did not convey title to it. "Until there is a treaty fixing their future status, we have a responsibility to defend them from armed attack."

The third principle was that the United States would expressly invite United Nations intervention to resolve the strait crisis. The resolution, as the House passed it, was silent on this point. While Eisenhower was open to a cease-fire, Kefauver thought the United States pursue it more aggressively. "We would not only welcome United Nations intervention, but we would exert our influence as a member of the UN to the uttermost to secure it." The senator argued that leaving the Formosa Resolution ambiguous over Quemoy and Matsu was counterproductive to this purpose. "Our stand in regard to the offshore islands is delaying and frustrating the efforts of our friends and allies in the United Nations to obtain a ceasefire agreement."

The fourth principle was that, pending UN action, the United States would protect the peace and security of Formosa, which was itself essential to the peace and security of the United States.

Kefauver reiterated that a resolution limited to the defense of Formosa and the Pescadores would win unanimous support in the Senate. "For that policy there is a legal, moral, and military basis." But he added, "My concern is that in the joint resolution Congress appears to be expressing a different policy."[50]

Voting on the Kefauver substitute, 11 senators were affirmative, all Democrats. Seventy-five senators were negative. Ten were absent.

Senator Lehman called up his amendment. Originally proposed by Senator Humphrey, it would leave intact language directly pertinent to Formosa and the Pescadores:

> Resolved, That the President of the United States be, and he hereby is authorized to employ the Armed Forces of the United States as he deems necessary for the specific purpose of securing and protecting Formosa and the Pescadores against armed attack.

As well, Lehman proposed to strike committee-reported language affecting the offshore islands:

> This authority to include the securing and protection of such related positions and territories of that area now in friendly hands and the taking of such other measures as he judges to be required or appropriate in assuring the defense of Formosa and the Pescadores.

Lehman implored his colleagues to pass the amendment. "I cannot conceive of anything more dangerous than what that which is now proposed. We have confidence in the President of the United States who now occupies that high office. We do not know what is going to happen in the future. What we do here tonight will be a precedent."[51]

In defending Formosa, Lehman was sure, the United States was on firm legal ground. China had given up claim to it in 1895. For 50 years, Japan exercised jurisdiction. After the war and the peace treaty, the United States assumed responsibility. "Communist China cannot claim that Formosa belongs to her. No other country, even though it recognizes Communist China, can claim that Formosa is a possession of or a part of the mainland of China." But that was not true of Quemoy and Matsu. Unlike the case of defending Formosa, protecting the islands would involve America in the civil war and kill off chances for a UN negotiation.

Congress must not relinquish its obligation to decide when to declare war, Lehman insisted. "If we pass this resolution, it will be a declaration that Congress is willing to abdicate its responsibilities and to place them unlimited, undefined, unspecified, and unreservedly, in the hands of the President of the United States."[52]

On the Lehman amendment, 13 senators voted aye. All were Democrats, except Langer. Seventy-four senators voted no. Nine senators did not vote. Among the absentees were Lyndon B. Johnson of Texas and John F. Kennedy of Massachusetts. Under a practice widely used at the time, a senator who was absent was able to make his position known by "pairing" either with another absentee of the opposite persuasion or with a senator who was present but withheld his vote. Thus, on the Lehman amendment, the *Congressional Record* reflects an announcement from Democratic Whip Earle Clements. "The Senator from Texas [Mr. Johnson] is paired with the Senator from Massachusetts [Mr. Kennedy]. If present and voting, the Senator from Texas would vote nay and the Senator from Massachusetts would vote yea."[53] Eisenhower called the disposition of the Lehman amendment "the key congressional vote on the entire subject."[54]

The vote on final passage of H.J. Res. 159 followed moments later. Eighty-five senators voted in the affirmative, three in the negative, and eight were absent. The negative votes came from Langer, Lehman, and Morse. All absentees, including Johnson and Kennedy, were announced as being in favor of the resolution.[55]

The overwhelming approval on final passage may have masked a degree of unease that senators chose to set aside in the spirit of the moment. Guangqiu Xu speculates, "The absence of partisan controversy on the joint resolution did not suggest real bipartisan support for the defense of Taiwan because the Democratic majority might have been forced, under the pressure of the

Republicans and the events, to accept a policy of full military support for Taiwan."[56]

Political scientist Robert David Johnson notes that the Formosa Resolution was a watershed for US foreign policy because it established a precedent for Eisenhower and future presidents to seek generously worded authorizations from Congress for the use of military force. "Events in the Middle East (1957), Cuba (1962), and Vietnam (1964) would prompt presidents to request comparable advance congressional approval to make war, and these legislatures would find it much harder given the Formosa Resolution precedent to resist."[57] The same might be said of the Desert Storm (1991) and September 11 (2001) AUMFs.

Knowland's biographers, Gayle B. Montgomery and James W. Johnson, write that the senator considered passage of the Formosa Resolution a great victory, in which he took pride years after he left the Senate. "Reflecting on that resolution in 1967, Knowland would call it a necessary act to tell the Communist world that the United States was willing to draw the line. He believed that had the United States taken similar action it might have averted World Wars I and II as well as the Korean War."[58]

NOTES

1. *Congressional Record*, January 26, 1955, pp. 735–736.

2. Ibid., p. 736.

3. There was a good basis for the senator's thinking. The eminent historian Nancy Bernkopf Tucker recounts Chiang's deeply embedded conviction, dating to a time when he was embroiled in civil war but had not yet lost the mainland. It was the belief that he was America's essential partner in a life and death struggle against Communism. "Chiang was convinced . . . that World War Three would soon break out between the United States and the Soviet Union. During this confrontation, Chiang would reconquer China and thereby eliminate Communism's eastern redoubt while the United States destroyed it in the West" (Tucker, p. 70).

4. Ibid., p. 738.

5. Ibid. In response, Eisenhower made a public statement on January 27, after Dulles previewed it with Chairman George. The statement said, "The President made clear that these forces were designed purely for defensive purposes and that any decision to use US forces other than in immediate self-defense or indirect defense of Formosa and the Pescadores would be a decision which he would take and the responsibility for which he has not delegated." *Foreign Relations of the United States 1955–1957, Vol. II, The China Area*, p. 141.

6. Ibid., p. 740.

7. *Congressional Record*, January 26, 1955, p. 742.

8. On this point, Morse inserted into the *Congressional Record* a Walter Lippmann column from January 24, 1955. Lippmann was of America's most

renowned journalists. He wrote, "Our right to defend Formosa rests on the fact that it is territory ceded by Japan about which the ultimate disposition has not been settled by any treaty. Even though both Chinese Governments claim Formosa as Chinese, even though we promised in 1943 at Cairo to restore it to the Republic of China, Formosa is not now, is not yet, Chinese territory. Because of that, our presence in Formosa is not intervention in the Chinese civil war." Walter Lippmann, "Reappraisal in the Formosa Strait," *Washington Post and Times Herald*, January 24, 1955.

9. Morse placed in the *Congressional Record* a *Washington Post* article from Stewart Alsop, in which the columnist wrote, "The extraordinary gravity of the decision which President Eisenhower has now taken is not fully appreciated in Congress or the country. The decision is, essentially, to bomb the Chinese mainland if this is deemed necessary for the defense of the Nationalist-held islands of Quemoy and Matsu." Alsop described Eisenhower's policy. "The President decided on a curious compromise—the Tachens would be evacuated, while war would be risked if necessary to defend Quemoy, the most important Nationalist island, and probably Matsu" (Ibid., p. 743).

10. US allies in Europe worried that the United States would be embroiled in a war in China and distracted from their defense (Garver, p. 79).

11. *Congressional Record*, January 26, 1955, p. 746.

12. Ibid., p. 751.

13. Knowland argued that stability would be achieved by firmly guaranteeing the security of Formosa and evacuating the militarily indefensible Tachens. The senator claimed that Chiang could not defend the Tachens because he lacked the air power to do so. "The Chinese Communists have superiority in the air. They can interfere with the resupply and reequipment of the Nationalist Chinese. Unless the Nationalist Chinese were either supported directly by us, or we could give them cover support for redeployment, it would mean a Dunkirk in that area of the world and would result in the loss of a substantial number of Chinese Nationalist troops who could better be used for the support and defense of the island of Formosa" (Ibid., p. 752).

14. Ibid., p. 753.

15. Ibid., pp. 752–753.

16. Ibid., pp. 755–756.

17. Ibid., pp. 760–761.

18. Ibid., p. 763.

19. Ibid., p. 765.

20. *Congressional Record*, January 27, 1955, p. 819.

21. Cockfield, p. 410.

22. *Congressional Record*, January 27, 1955, p. 819.

23. W.H. Lawrence, "White House Moves to Dispel Talk it Seeks a Preventive War," *New York Times*, January 28, 1955, p. 1.

24. The chairman's sense of the situation seemed borne out in press reports. William S. White, writing in the *New York Times*, noted, "Efforts in the Senate to limit President Eisenhower's authority to take war action in defense of Formosa were declining tonight. Strong reassurances from the White House and the Senate Democratic foreign policy leader, Senator Walter F George of Georgia, were dispersing

the small Senate bloc seeking to restrict the President." William S. White, "Efforts to Curb Eisenhower on Formosa Fade in the Senate," *New York Times*, January 28, 1955, p. 1. Robert Divine recounts, "The opposition in the Senate quickly dissolved after press secretary James Hagerty released a statement in the President's name stipulating that American forces would be used 'purely for defensive purposes' on the basis of a presidential decision 'which he would take and the responsibility for which he has not delegated'" (Divine, p. 59).

25. Later in the debate that day, Senator Knowland explained that "the reason for the President's statement was the misconstruction which had been placed on the resolution and the hearings, as was indicated on the Floor of the Senate in the debate yesterday in remarks which went out over the world, that this was not an effort on the part of the government, the people, and the President of the United States to start a preventive war and an aggressive war" (Ibid., p. 828).

26. *Congressional Record*, January 27, 1955, pp. 819–821.

27. Cockfield, p. 411. Contemporary opinion writers were also highly laudatory. Columnist David Lawrence said, "Seldom in the history of the United States Senate has there been an address of statesmanship comparable to that delivered by Senator Walter George of Georgia, Democrat, chairman of the Foreign Relations Committee, as he upheld President Eisenhower's request for unrestricted authority to use the armed forces to defend Formosa and the American defense line in the Far East. . . . The Georgia Senator made clear in his speech that this is not the time to give the enemy a privileged sanctuary of retreat, as was the case in Korea." David Lawrence, "Today in Washington—Senator George's Speech Hailed as Thrilling Show of Spirit," *New York Herald Tribune*, January 28, 1955. Columnist Arthur Krock wrote, "The chairman of the Senate Committee on Foreign Relations whose affectionate and reverent sobriquet is 'the old man' went at once to the heart of the issue today when he opened the formal Senate debate on the Formosa Pescadores resolution. . . . As Senator George pointed out today there is no common sense, or military sense, or any sense at all in giving advance specifications to a hostile government of exactly where and on what manifestations the line of defense will be drawn against its aggression." Arthur Krock, "In the Nation—The 'Old Man' Lays It on The Line," *New York Times*, January 28, 1955. In a C-SPAN interview in 1986, Senate parliamentarian Emeritus Floyd M. Riddick spoke of George's oratorical skills, "I used to think that George was the greatest orator I'd ever heard in the Senate. He never used a note. . . . He never spoke over 30 to 40 minutes and sometimes he had the ability to just make chills run down your back. He was so forceful in his statements." www.c-span.org/video/?126322-1/senate-parliamentarian (accessed February 27, 2022).

28. *Congressional Record*, January 27, 1955, pp. 821–825.

29. Ibid., p. 827.

30. Ibid.

31. Ibid.

32. Ibid., pp. 840–848.

33. *Congressional Record*, January 28, 1955, p. 959.

34. Lehman's remarks at *Congressional Record*, January 28, 1955, pp. 925–929.

35. Ibid., p. 929.

36. Ibid., pp. 934–936.

37. Ibid., pp. 934–937.

38. Ibid., pp. 929–939.

39. Ibid., pp. 939–940.

40. Ibid., pp. 945–946.

41. Ibid., p. 947.

42. Ibid., pp. 951–952.

43. Ibid., pp. 953–954.

44. Ibid., p. 956.

45. Ibid., pp. 959–960, 972–973.

46. Ibid., pp. 974–975.

47. Ibid., p. 979.

48. Ibid., p. 980.

49. Eisenhower, *Mandate*, p. 468.

50. *Congressional Record*, January 28, 1955, pp. 982–984.

51. Lehman was prescient on that point. In August 1964, President Lyndon Johnson asked Congress for a resolution authorizing military force to respond to a military incident in the Gulf of Tonkin. Johnson cited the broad authority given to Eisenhower in the Formosa Resolution. Congress acquiesced, and the Gulf of Tonkin resolution wound up being the predicate for the Vietnam War.

52. *Congressional Record*, January 28, 1955, pp. 986–987.

53. Ibid., p. 987. In his memoirs, Eisenhower took note of this situation.

"When this special vote was taken, by coincidence Senator Kennedy and Senator Johnson were in the hospital. But they felt so strongly about it as to announce themselves as paired: Senator Kennedy stood with Lehman, Morse, Kefauver, and the rest of the thirteen who wanted to write off Quemoy and Matsu; Lyndon Johnson joined with the ranks of the seventy-four in the majority, following the leadership of Senator Walter George of Georgia, who during the debate had declared that turning over Quemoy and Matsu to the Communists would cause a "disintegration that would . . . be swift, quick, speedy, and final," one which would "cut the heart out" of Nationalist troops." (Eisenhower, pp. 467–469)

54. Eisenhower, p. 468.

55. *Congressional Record*, January 28, 1955, p. 994.

56. Xu, p. 123.

57. Johnson, p. 67. Rhea Foster Dulles adds, "Congress was in some measure abdicating its responsibility in the conduct of foreign affairs by giving the president a free hand that could lead to war. In the case of both the four motion and Tonkin Bay resolutions, opposition was effectively silenced by appeals to patriotic unity" (Foster Rhea Dulles, p. 155).

58. Montgomery and Johnson, p. 185.

Chapter 8

After the Resolution, a Treaty

SEEKING REASSURANCE AT THE
STATE DEPARTMENT

In the late afternoon of January 27, while the Senate was debating the Formosa Resolution, Foreign Minister George Yeh and Ambassador Wellington Koo met at the State Department with Assistant Secretary Walter Robertson. Still concerned about the effect on Nationalist public opinion of a withdrawal from the Tachens, Yeh pressed the Americans for an explicit statement that the United States would defend Quemoy and Matsu. Robertson balked, noting that the resolution, which had just overwhelmingly passed in the House, authorized the president to defend all places in the region necessary for the defense of Formosa. That would implicitly include the offshore islands, Robertson noted, as Congress was aware when it authorized force. Yeh was not fully satisfied, but Robertson stood firm.

Koo pivoted to the Mutual Defense Treaty. Ratification remained a high priority for the Nationalists, and his government feared the treaty would be set aside now that Congress was addressing the resolution. Robertson assured him that the administration stood firmly behind the treaty, that no major opposition was anticipated, and that the Senate would move forward shortly after action on the resolution was complete.[1]

The following day, the Nationalists returned to the State Department to see Dulles. The secretary reaffirmed that the United States would not make a formal statement about defending the offshore islands and urged that Taipei issue no pronouncements that implied an American commitment to do so. Dulles warned that if the Nationalists issued a statement of that kind, it would contradict his testimony to Congress, and the United States might be forced to deny it. The resolution permitted Eisenhower to act in "related areas." That

263

provided all the flexibility the president needed. Amendments in the Senate to narrow it would be defeated, Dulles predicted.[2]

Yeh reported this conversation to the generalissimo, who remained agitated about Eisenhower's refusal to announce publicly a commitment to help the Nationalists defend Quemoy and Matsu. Chiang believed such a statement, timed with an announcement from Taipei on regrouping of forces, would mitigate his pressing political problem over the Tachen withdrawal. He had anticipated that Washington and Taipei would simultaneously issue announcements about US assistance in the Tachens and a joint declaration to defend the offshore islands.[3] But, unexpectedly, the administration demurred. Chiang summoned US ambassador Karl Rankin to express his dismay at what he saw as a commitment undone. According to Rankin, "Chiang seemed more nervous this evening than I remembered seeing him before. He appeared to think US about to let him down on Kinmen [Quemoy] and Matsu, presumably at British behest, without realizing implications in terms of immediate military situation and psychological effects here and elsewhere."[4] Chiang feared announcing a Tachens withdrawal unless he could simultaneously say something explicit about defending the offshore islands.

Anxious to avoid a public break with Chiang, the State Department briefed Eisenhower on a plan to calm the situation. In a January 30 White House meeting, acting secretary of state Herbert Hoover, Jr., met with the president. Eisenhower affirmed that the United States must reserve the right to assess the military situation on the islands and determine on its own whether US intervention was appropriate. "Our purpose in defending these areas is to defend Formosa and the Pescadores if they are threatened," said the president. "It is not a permanent commitment to defend any of these offshore islands." Not every action against the islands might be of the magnitude to justify an American response. Eisenhower added, "We must be the judge of the military situation that draws us in whether in Quemoy or elsewhere."[5] Eisenhower agreed to send Chiang a private message, reassuring him that the administration would press for Senate consent to the Mutual Defense Treaty and would consult with Taipei about any developments that might affect the defense of Formosa and the Pescadores.[6]

On the evening of January 31, Hoover cabled Ambassador Rankin with instructions that its contents be communicated directly, immediately, and confidentially to Chiang, with an admonition to Taipei not to divulge it. Citing the recently passed Formosa Resolution, the cable stated:

> Under present circumstances it is the purpose of the President to assist in the defense of Quemoy and Matsu against armed attack if he judges such attack is of a character which shows that it is in fact in aid of and in preparation for an armed attack on Formosa and the Pescadores and dangerous to their defense.

An attack by the Communists at this time on Quemoy or Matsu which seriously threatened their loss would be deemed by the President to be of this character.

The cable stressed that the United States would make such a determination unilaterally and that there were no preexisting understandings to the contrary. If the Nationalists implied there were, the United States reserved the right to deny them.[7]

The same evening, Robertson and McConaughy joined Yeh and Koo for dinner at the Chinese embassy. The Nationalists emphasized that the political problems associated with withdrawal would not be mitigated by private American reassurances. Chiang remained aggrieved and harbored suspicion that Quemoy and Matsu might be traded out for a UN-negotiated cease-fire. Robertson denied the possibility of such linkage.

Trying to calm Chiang, Robertson noted the overwhelming bipartisan vote in Congress for the Formosa Resolution, arguing that the outcome was far more significant than any declaration the United States might make about the offshore islands. He also promised that Senate hearings on the treaty would begin in three days, on February 2, a schedule somewhat accelerated by Eisenhower's intervention.[8]

On February 3, Hoover cabled Rankin that the United States was prepared to issue immediately a statement that it would support the Tachens withdrawal and take steps in the region to protect Formosa and the Pescadores. Not explicitly mentioning the offshore islands, the proposed statement read, "The United States Government has further advised the Chinese Government that with the object of securing and protecting Formosa in consonance with the congressional resolution approved January 29, 1955, the United States Government will extend assistance to the Republic of China in defending such related positions and territories now in its hands as the United States deems to be essential to the defense of Formosa and the Pescadores."[9]

The Nationalists remained unsettled about the US refusal to announce a commitment on Quemoy and Matsu. Mindful of Chiang's angst, Yeh tried again on the afternoon of February 3. Meeting at State with Robertson, he mentioned that Taipei was considering a unilateral statement about the islands. Concerned about what it might say or even imply, Robertson warned against it.

In the meantime, the Nationalists' position in the Tachens was becoming more precarious. Taipei had withheld asking for US assistance until a satisfactory announcement could be made about the withdrawal and redeployment. And for the generalissimo, that always meant including mention of Quemoy and Matsu. Since the Americans had not given him what he sought, Chiang had left the Tachens situation in abeyance. Now, Robertson emphasized that time was of the essence. If the Communists launched an assault, withdrawal would become more complicated. Do not delay requesting help, he stressed.[10] But the Nationalists continued to stall, wanting an express commitment about Quemoy and Matsu.[11]

In a White House meeting on February 5, Hoover discussed the situation with Eisenhower. Sensitive to congressional concerns that Chiang might manufacture a war with the Communists, the president worried about him delaying the withdrawal until armed conflict was unavoidable. Perhaps Chiang should be told that under such circumstances the United States would not help, Eisenhower suggested. However, before the meeting ended, a cable from Taipei arrived. It stated that a redeployment from the Tachens would occur and that American assistance was requested.[12]

Within 3 hours, Hoover messaged Rankin indicating that the United States would help with the evacuation.[13] Washington and Taipei then commenced an exchange of messages concerning the announcement the Nationalist government would issue. The final text read,

> In order to meet the new challenge of international Communist aggression, the Government of the Republic of China has decided to redeploy the forces defending certain offshore islands and to strengthen the defense of other important islands such as Quemoy, Matsu, etc., with the forces now in the Tachen Area. Through such consolidation, the defense of Taiwan and the Pescadores and other offshore islands will be further strengthened. The Government of the Republic of China in the spirit of Sino-American cooperation in the joint defense of their respective territories in the western Pacific has consulted with the United States Government concerning the redeployment of the forces in the Tachen Area.[14]

THE CEASE-FIRE RESOLUTION AT THE
UNITED NATIONS AND IN CONGRESS

On the same day the Senate passed the Formosa Resolution, Humphrey for himself and seven Democratic cosponsors introduced S. Res. 55, a resolution expressing the sense of the Senate that the United Nations should act to bring about a cease-fire in the Formosa Strait. The resolution was referred to the Committee on Foreign Relations, which solicited the State Department's views.

While that process was underway, things were happening at the UN, where Operation Oracle was finally active.[15] On January 31, 1955, at the request of New Zealand, the Security Council passed a resolution asking the PRC to participate in UN-sponsored cease-fire discussions. The vote in the Security Council was nine affirmative, one negative, and one abstention. The Soviet Union was the lone dissenter in what came to be known as the New Zealand Initiative. It could not exercise its veto in the Security Council because Sir

Leslie Munro of New Zealand, who was then presiding, ruled that the invitation involved a procedural issue, which was not subject to the veto.[16]

While Beijing framed its response, Foreign Relations met on February 1 to consider Humphrey's legislation. Chairman George had in hand a response from Assistant Secretary of State Thruston B. Morton, received that morning. The department was in general agreement with the resolution, but recommended its scope be amended by deleting the words "and in the Formosa Straits." Morton wrote, "The Department believes that it is important if there is to be any possibility of success for the proposed United Nations action, for such action to be pinpointed and directed at the so-called offshore islands which are the area of immediate concern." He continued, "since hostilities are presently confined to the offshore islands, the Department believes that an expression of Senate opinion should be likewise confined."[17] George seemed agreeable to this recommendation.

Soon after the committee meeting began, Senator Alexander Smith (R-NJ) voiced concern that the price of peace might involve appeasing Beijing, such as an arrangement where the islands would be turned over to the PRC in exchange for a cease-fire. "I would be strongly against this," cautioned Smith, "against any such approach which, I think, would be definitely detrimental to everything we've been trying to do out there in that area."

Senator Capehart reinforced Smith's concern about what the Communists would demand in exchange for its cooperation. Would China not seek possession of the offshore islands, membership in the United Nations, and diplomatic recognition by the United States?[18]

Humphrey responded that those would likely be Beijing's demands but noted the United States could veto any cease-fire arrangement of that nature. Capehart suggested it would be better to set the resolution aside for the time being, since proceedings at the UN were already underway. Passing the resolution might complicate America's flexibility to reject uncomfortable terms for the cease-fire. But Humphrey pressed on, emphasizing it was important to demonstrate that the Senate supported efforts to seek peace through UN auspices.[19]

Knowland argued that the Humphrey resolution unnecessarily complicated the Formosa situation. Both Houses of Congress had overwhelmingly passed the Formosa Resolution. The psychological effect of doing so would be mitigated by an extended or nuanced debate on cease-fire terms, he said. Proceedings on S. Res. 55 might be extended and divisive, as senators debated the resolution and proposed amendments. "For us to kind of give a blanket endorsement of a ceasefire with no conditions," stated Knowland,

> would be interpreted as the Senate beginning to weaken on the resolution which Congress has just passed, unless the resolution is strengthened to make sure that

we are not changing our position on the admission of Communist China into the United Nations and . . . without requiring the free world to again give up some territory or some people to the Chinese Communist. Now if we're going to get into that kind of a hassle on the floor, with six days of debate on each of those points, which undoubtedly would be raised, then I think we are going to help dilute and destroy some of the effectiveness of the resolution we almost unanimously passed.[20]

Because the Senate had just endorsed a military response to the strait crisis, Humphrey retorted, it also needed to support a diplomatic solution. "The question before the Senate is whether or not we are as interested in pursuing the course of arriving at a ceasefire as we are in pursuing the course which may arrive at all guns wide open."[21] Knowland reiterated that a cease-fire was likely to come with unacceptable terms, to which the Senate should avoid appearing agreeable.

Senators Capehart and Hickenlooper stated they would oppose the resolution because of concerns that passing it would commit them to back whatever conditions accompanied the cease-fire. "It seems to me that if this resolution is passed, then those who vote for it are almost bound to vote for any proposal which the United Nations comes up with on a ceasefire, and I am not prepared to do that," stated Hickenlooper.[22]

Aiken felt it would be counterproductive to bring S. Res. 55 to the Floor. He agreed with Knowland that senators would offer amendments, such amendments opposing PRC membership in the United Nations, that would be hard to reject but were likely to complicate the negotiations. "One of those amendments would undoubtedly be an anti-Red China seat in the United Nations, and it will undoubtedly pass by an overwhelming vote. I am wondering if that would knock any chance there might be for an honorable ceasefire into a cocked hat."[23]

Mansfield was one of the resolution's cosponsors but seemed taken aback at the controversy it had generated. If S. Res. 55 could not pass quickly and unanimously, he felt, it was better not to bring it forward. Mansfield moved to postpone consideration of the resolution, awaiting further developments in the UN situation.[24]

By voice vote, Mansfield's motion carried. Senator Morse was the sole dissenter.[25] Humphrey announced his intent to revive the resolution when the committee next met but, by then, the question was moot.

Before the matter could be brought forward in the United Nations, Oracle provoked decisive objections from both the Nationalists and the Communists.[26] In a televised interview on January 28, 1955, T. F. Tsiang, Nationalist China's Permanent Representative to the United Nations, expressed grave reservations about the cease-fire idea. "I'm opposed to it," he said. "In principle, I do not think that United Nations will perform any service to the cause of peace by taking up a resolution on ceasefire." Then he added, one of the reasons why we are opposed to this ceasefire . . . is that it might make difficult our future plans to recover the mainland."[27]

By a vote of 9–1 (the Soviet Union opposing and the Chinese Nationalists abstaining), the UN Security Council invited the PRC to parlay about a cease-fire, but the proposal met immediate resistance from the Chinese Communists. UN secretary general Dag Hammarskjold advised American ambassador Henry Cabot Lodge, Jr., of a February 3 communication from Premier Zhou Enlai. Beijing would not come to the UN because the Nationalists held China's seat on the Security Council. Zhou claimed such negotiations "would put China and the Chiang Kai-shek clique on an equal basis, asking for interference in Chinese internal affairs." He continued, "This whole activity is to put Chinese internal affairs in the international arena and create two Chinas, a theme openly discussed in the USA, which would mean violation of the UN Charter." It would be better for China and the United States to negotiate directly, Zhou argued. "If tension is to be alleviated, persuasion should be directed at the USA. China would not refuse to negotiate with the USA on this question." However, he added, "If the USA would think of using war threats to intimidate China or cause acceptance of the idea of two Chinas or continued occupation of Taiwan, it is a fantasy."[28]

In the aftermath of this rejection, Robert Bowie, the director of Policy Planning at State, prepared a memorandum for Dulles. Titled "Formosa Policy," the memo argued that the United States should shed the divisive burden of the offshore islands. "The free nations of Europe and Asia distinguish sharply between Formosa and the offshore islands," Bowie wrote. "In general, they support or acquiesce in our defense of Formosa. But they consider the offshore islands do not involve our security interests. . . . They feel that they are important only in terms of a ChiNat intention to attack the mainland and that the ChiComs cannot be expected to acquiesce in ChiNat retention of such strongholds in their harbors." The correct policy, he contended, "should be directed to disengaging from the offshore islands in a way which will not damage our prestige or leave any doubts as to our will to defend Formosa and the Pescadores." America should make clear that the change was not motivated by fear of the Chinese Communists but instead was the best policy to coalesce support for the defense of Formosa. "A program of obtaining the free world's support for our policy toward Formosa in exchange for abandoning the offshore islands would seem to me clearly to serve the US security interest," he concluded.[29]

Notwithstanding the urging of America's European allies, it was not a bargain Eisenhower would make. Dulles told British ambassador Sir Roger Makins on February 9 that the offshore islands must be considered in the context of Formosa's defense, not in isolation. The secretary saw attacks on the islands as preparatory to liberating Formosa itself. As the Communists did not separate these objectives, the United States could not either.[30]

THE SENATE CONSENTS TO THE MUTUAL DEFENSE TREATY: FEBRUARY 9, 1955

On Wednesday, February 9, 1955, Chairman George moved that the Senate consider the Mutual Defense Treaty between the United States and the Republic of China. He submitted for the *Congressional Record* the text of the treaty and four supplementary documents: a joint statement that the parties issued when negotiations concluded; statements that Dulles and Yeh issued on December 2, 1954, when signing the treaty; and December 10 letters between Dulles and Yeh to confirm their mutual understanding about joint agreements on the use of force.[31] The understanding, which appears in identical language in both letters, may be found in this book at the end of appendix C.

Unleashed by Eisenhower's 1953 orders to the Seventh Fleet, Chiang was thus "re-leashed" by these letters that restricted him from unilateral force deployments. The letters also controlled Chiang's ability to transfer large number of forces from Formosa to reinforce positions in the Tachens or the offshore islands. This was intended to prevent him from unduly raising the stakes on the offshore islands or generating a situation that would require supplementary American forces to backstop Formosa.

George opened the debate by explaining the purpose of the treaty. "It states clearly and unequivocally that an armed attack in the West Pacific area, including an attack specifically on the islands of Formosa and the Pescadores, would be dangerous to the peace and security of the United States. . . . I know of no competent military authority who would deny that it would be dangerous to the security interests of the United States should Formosa fall into unfriendly hands."

The Mutual Defense Treaty with the ROC was the sixth such pact that the United States had concluded in the region, George pointed out. The exclusion of Nationalist China from prior agreements had led to speculation that the United States might be willing to trade out Taipei's interests for a settlement with Communists and a recognition of the Beijing government. Uncertainty on these matters, compounded by the absence of a pact, had been damaging to relations with the Nationalists and to the morale of Chiang's troops, the senator said. But ratifying a treaty would put those anxieties to rest. "It seems to me that the approval of this treaty now will dispel any clouds of doubt that may exist on this point."

During Foreign Relations Committee deliberations on the treaty, three major issues had arisen, which George outlined. The first addressed the question of sovereignty over Formosa. Several times in the debate on the Formosa Resolution, senators had distinguished between the offshore islands, which were clearly Chinese, and Formosa, which they claimed was not. They noted that Japan had relinquished sovereignty without transferring it. So, the question arose: by ratifying the Mutual Defense Treaty, would the United States be saying that the Nationalists were sovereign in Formosa? After consulting with Dulles, the senators determined to address the issue in the committee report. It said, "It is the understanding of the Senate that nothing in the present treaty shall be construed as affecting or modifying the legal status or the sovereignty of the territories referred to in Article VI." As to Nationalist China, those were designated as "Taiwan and the Pescadores." George summarized, "It is our understanding that the legal status of the territories referred to in Article VI, namely Formosa and the Pescadores—whatever their status may be—is not altered in any way by the conclusion of this treaty."

The second was whether treaty obligations, which specifically embraced Formosa and the Pescadores, could be interpreted to extend to the offshore islands. At issue was the relationship of Article VI, which designated the places covered, to Articles II and V, which referred to mutual defense commitments. Article VI contained a sentence that stated, "The provisions of Articles II and V will be applicable to such other territories as may be determined by mutual agreement." Worried that the provision was too elastic and would allow for Quemoy and Matsu to come within the treaty's scope, Morse recommended deleting the sentence.

When testifying before Foreign Relations, and in effect to quiet these concerns, Dulles stated that extending coverage beyond Formosa and the Pescadores would amount to amending the treaty and, if it desired to do so, the administration would submit the issue to the Senate for its consent.

George explained why the committee was satisfied to leave the provision alone. "The committee felt, however, since similar language appears in the Southeast Asia pact that it would be unfortunate to strike it from the treaty with the Republic of China." Again, the committee addressed the issue in report language, which mirrored Dulles's testimony. "It is the understanding of the Senate that the mutual agreement referred to in Article VI, under which the provisions of Articles II and V may be made applicable to other territories, shall be construed as requiring the advice and consent of the Senate of the United States."

A final issue concerned the potential the Nationalists could instigate hostilities that would trigger American military obligations. As George noted, "Some members were concerned that, because of unique conditions in Formosa, some emphasis should be given to the idea that an armed attack against either of the parties which would bring the treaty into operation should be identified as an attack from the outside—that is, an external attack." To clarify this question, the committee included another provision in its report. "It is the understanding of the Senate that the obligations of the parties under Article V apply only in the event of external armed attack, and that military operations by either party from the territories held by the Republic of China shall not be undertaken except by joint agreement."

Fewer than two weeks had elapsed since Congress agreed to the Formosa Resolution (which, when Eisenhower signed it, became Public Law 84-4, also referred to as Public Law 4). George addressed the question of why the treaty was necessary when the Formosa Resolution was already in effect. He pointed out an important difference. "Public Law 4 was, in effect, a unilateral declaration of intent on the part of the United States. The treaty before us is a mutual understanding between two nations." As well, he said, the reach of Public Law 4 was broader than the treaty. "The treaty applies only to Formosa and the Pescadores. Public Law 4, however, applies to related positions and territories whose defense the President judges to be required to assure the defense of Formosa and the Pescadores." A final difference was the duration. Authority under the Formosa Resolution was to expire whenever the president reported to Congress that peace and security was reasonably assured. However, the treaty was to continue indefinitely, subject to termination by either party on one year's notice.

"In summary," said George, "aside from the fact that the pending treaty is considerably narrower in geographical coverage than is the resolution, the essential difference is that by the treaty the United States undertakes an international obligation whereas by the public law our action was unilateral and voluntary."

The Committee on Foreign Relations recommended that the Senate give its advice and consent to the treaty. As the chairman noted, the history of the Far East since the war had not been happy. The treaty was part of an overall American effort to stabilize the place. "The United States, supported by nearly every free country in the western Pacific, has made its intentions known. It intends that no other areas of the western Pacific shall fall under Communist control by the use of armed force."[32]

Senator Alexander Smith spoke of his meetings in recent years with Chiang, and the consternation felt in Nationalist China about being outside the array of security pacts that covered the western Pacific. "I had the feeling that the people of Formosa could not quite understand why they, of all the critical targets under assault by international Communism in the Far East, had been singled out, so to speak, and excluded from the general pattern of treaties with which we were entering into." Smith believed the concern was understandable and the treaty was overdue. Given the strategic importance of

Formosa, it was important that a well-trained and strongly motivated cadre of Nationalist troops occupy it. Otherwise, to deny Formosa to the Communist, American troops would have to be stationed there. "It is most essential not only that Formosa be kept in friendly hands, but also that Nationalist strength on the island be maintained." Smith added that the treaty would go far in reinforcing the morale of Nationalist forces, especially considering the unease the withdrawal from the Tachens had caused.

Smith stressed that the treaty was purely defensive in character. "I should like to emphasize that the treaty is not an instrument designed to facilitate our participation in offensive military operations against the mainland." This was reinforced by the exchange of notes between Secretary Dulles and Foreign Minister Yeh, Smith said.

He concluded by affirming that the US commitment to Chiang was ironclad. Reading from the committee report, Smith stated, "The treaty will give further evidence of our intention not to abandon a wartime ally who fought valiantly in a long and exhausting struggle against a common foe."[33]

Claiming he was "disturbed and concerned" by these matters being dealt with in the committee report, Senator Spessard Holland (D-FL) posed a question to Chairman George and Senator Smith. "Do these three statements of understanding operate in the same manner as would the adoption of reservations on the same subject and now are tantamount to the adoption of reservations?"[34]

George responded affirmatively. "Under all the circumstances in this particular case, and in relation to this particular treaty, and bearing in mind that the treaty is between the United States and the Republic of China only— the two parties to it—I think those statements of understanding are tantamount to reservations." The chairman made clear that the statements had been negotiated with the State Department and reflected interbranch agreement. "Certainly, there is the explicit and express approval of the Secretary of State as to those points on which it was thought desirable or even necessary to make any statements; and, therefore, they have been included in the report for the obvious reason that they do become substantially reservations in the particular situation in which we find ourselves." He further asserted that everything in the committee report had Executive Branch concurrence. "Therefore, these statements are tantamount to reservations so far as this treaty, this particular contract between the two governments, is concerned."

George clarified the distinction between reservations and understandings with respect to international law. There were differing degrees of solemnity, he said. Reservations require the agreement of all parties to a treaty, while understandings bind only the party that asserts them. As to the statements in the committee report, George stated, "while technically they are not reservations, and are not technically inserted in the resolution of ratification, they, nevertheless, become a part of it." He declared that he could speak with complete assurance that the Executive Branch was bound by the representations in the committee report and would not vary from them. Thus, although they were not formally incorporated in the resolution, their recitation in the report was tantamount to the same thing and carried the same solemnity.[35]

Smith explained that reservations had not been written because there was no ambiguity to address. He noted that Dulles was instrumental in crafting the report language, which was itself consistent with the secretary's exchange of notes with Yeh. Therefore, Smith argued, "no reservation of any sort is needed. The language speaks for itself."[36]

Drilling deeper into the statement about sovereignty over Formosa, Holland asked, "Was it the intention of the committee that in dealing with the Republic of China now occupying that area we would be acting in no way to affect, impair, or enlarge the title, right of possession, right of ownership, right of occupancy, or whatever right exists, leaving that question exactly as it now is for other determination?" Smith responded that Holland was correct. "We desired to make it crystal clear that we were not going into that subject in any way and that whatever the status was before the treaty was signed, it would be exactly the same after the treaty was signed."[37]

Knowland argued that the reason the sovereignty issue was not addressed by a reservation was because doing so would require acquiescence by the Republic of China. He doubted the Nationalists would concede that sovereignty over Formosa was unresolved. By addressing it in the report, that awkwardness was avoided. The senator declared US ratification of the treaty would not affect the question of sovereignty.[38]

That said, Knowland made clear his personal view that Chiang was already sovereign on Formosa. He referred to President Truman's statement of January 5, 1950, referring to the Cairo and Potsdam Declarations. Truman noted, "In keeping with these Declarations, Formosa was surrendered to Generalissimo Chiang Kai-shek, and for the past four years the United States and other allied powers have accepted the exercise of Chinese authority over the islands." Knowland observed that, on the same day, Secretary Acheson remarked, "The Chinese have administered Formosa for four years. Neither the United States nor any other ally ever questioned that authority in that occupation. When Formosa was made a province of China, nobody raised any lawyer's doubts about that. That was regarded as in accordance with the commitments."

Knowland considered that a commitment to return Formosa to Chinese sovereignty had been made and honored.[39] He put Truman's and Acheson's statements in the *Record* to prove it. By his lights, Formosa was Chinese. "In this instance there is a government which is occupying a province of its own country, and yet some nations of the world are willing to deal with nine and a half million human beings in another vast area of the world in an international poker game."[40]

Holland spoke up again to seek assurance that the State Department would feel bound by the statements in the committee report requiring mutual agreement before military engagement and limiting the scope of treaty coverage. Smith replied, "I can say without hesitation that the same restrictions would apply to the Department of State that would apply to Congress and that with the legislative history, which is being developed in connection with the treaty, it would be very difficult to evade the implications or the statements here made of the understanding."[41]

Senator Alexander Wiley (R-WI) stressed that the recent passage of the Formosa Resolution did not absolve the Senate from acting on the treaty. The resolution was a temporary unilateral measure, meant to expire when the crisis had passed. But the treaty was a more permanent, bilateral arrangement that was intended to survive the resolution.

Launching lengthy remarks, Senator Morse declared that it was not lawful to conclude a treaty with Chiang. "I shall vote against the so-called treaty because, in my judgment, it is not a treaty. By it we pledge ourselves to defend a government whose claim to the territory it rules at present is at best very doubtful. In my judgment, it is not an instrument of agreement with its sovereign power. Therefore, the document does not even meet the definition of a treaty."

Morse did not think the ROC enjoyed legal sovereignty over Formosa. Reading from a legal text, he stated, "The right to negotiate treaties is one of the tests of sovereignty." But the committee report said that the question of sovereignty remained undetermined. If that were so, how could the United States conclude a treaty with a non-sovereign partner. In the alternative, how could the Senate consent to the treaty and claim it was not judging the issue of sovereignty? "The treaty, in my judgment, seeks to give the world the impression that the Nationalist Chinese have sovereign rights in Formosa. I do not believe we can escape that deduction."[42]

Appearing to acknowledge Nationalist claims even implicitly was very dangerous for the United States, Morse said. Its caretaker rights, arising out of World War II, would disappear, and America would concede that the island was Chinese. Once that happened, Formosa would be indistinguishable from Quemoy and Matsu. Further American engagement on Formosa would amount to intervention in the civil war.[43]

Morse did not concede that the Cairo Declaration gave Chiang a right to Formosa.[44] The Nationalist occupation began when it was ordered by General MacArthur to accept the Japanese surrender there on behalf of the allied powers. That made the Nationalist troops an army of occupation not a representative of the local population. Morse reasoned, "The Chinese

Nationalist government had no more legal right unilaterally to make Formosa and the Pescadores a part of China than we would have had to make Germany a part of the United States." Defending Formosa and, in effect, protecting Chiang could and should be done without the treaty, said Morse.

Reprising his argument that the United States had rights in Formosa emanating from the Japanese surrender, and that Chiang was merely occupying the island, Morse declared a reservation was necessary to affirm sovereignty was unaffected.

The senator stated that report language alone would not do. The report was merely legislative history, which tribunals would ignore in favor of treaty provisions that were unambiguous on their face. "The so called qualifying or conditioning or limiting language of the Committee on Foreign Relations is not worth the paper it is written on so far as its legal effect before a world court is concerned." If the United States truly wished to avoid implicit recognition of Chiang's sovereignty, only a Senate-adopted reservation would do, and then only if Chiang's government agreed. But the committee did not propose a reservation, Morse said, precisely because it was unlikely the Nationalists would accept it. Dealing with the sovereignty issue in the committee report was an ineffective effort to sidestep the issue.

Adhering to the letter of international law would especially matter to Asian countries, who recognized US rights to act in Formosa, but who were otherwise fearful of Western imperialism. "From the time when Asiatic folklore and tradition can be drilled into their minds, they are brought up on the intellectual food that the great enemy of Asia is Western domination." Stepping outside a clearly delineated legal framework would feed Communist propaganda that America had imperialistic designs, Morse said. He argued there was a vast difference between stopping the Communists from taking over of Formosa and defending the Nationalist regime.

Morse reviewed twentieth-century Chinese history to demonstrate that Chiang's own inadequacies had caused the Nationalists to be toppled from power. "When I listen to the sentimental, emotional descriptions of the Nationalist Chinese regime, I pinch myself to make certain that I am hearing correctly, because history shows clearly that the Generalissimo never controlled North China."

The region to which the senator referred was Communist dominated during World War II and thereafter. It would have been impossible for Chiang to have dislodged them without American help, Morse observed. And even then, his government would have been propped up by a foreign power and not by indigenous support. "The fact is that to have placed the Generalissimo in control in north China would have required thousands of American Marines, and the Generalissimo would have stayed in control just as long as American Marines were maintained there to keep him in control."

The senator continued, "It would have been necessary to keep him there with guns and Marines because northern Chinese would have had none of it. . . . That tiny little war blazed more fiercely and finally turned into a holocaust and the Generalissimo was driven off the mainland of China. There was no doubt about the fact that the Chinese people wanted no more of him, and he took refuge on the islands near the coast and on Formosa."

The senator had little faith in Chiang's army. He thought they were incapable of recovering the mainland on their own and would be unlikely to prevail even with American help. "I dissent from the point of view being expressed to the American people that this is an effective military force. I think it would collapse unless we were to fill its ranks with thousands of American Marines and other foot soldiers and bring in the Navy and American air pilots to fight the battle." Morse stated. "I do not wish to become involved in any agreement with a Nationalist Chinese leader with such a record of ineffectiveness as that of the Generalissimo."

US allies shared this disdain for Chiang, said Morse. It was one thing for them to backstop America in holding Formosa, based on its crucial geographic position. "That line of defense is not our line of defense alone; it is freedom's line of defense in the Pacific; and every free nation in the world has an interest in that line." But it was another to support the Nationalist government in its claims to the offshore islands. No ally would join with the United States to do that. "They have said plainly that they will not stand behind and support that line unless we make it a line which runs through and includes Formosa and the Pescadores but stays away from the mainland of China."

Morse argued that an unintended consequence of the Mutual Defense Treaty was that it would separate Washington from its allies. "We are dealing with an agreement which involves the protection of a Nationalist Chinese regime which many of our allies fear, which they do not trust, and which they believe will try to lead the free world into a war on the mainland of China." If the Senate consented to the treaty and the administration ratified it, the United States would stand alone in the region against a Sino-Soviet monolith, he predicted. That could not be in America's best interest. "I will not be a party to creating a division of opinion between us and our allies over the Nationalist Chinese."

Morse turned to Article VI, which provided treaty coverage could be extended by mutual agreement to other territories beyond Formosa and the Pescadores. He inserted into the *Congressional Record* a memorandum from Benjamin V. Cohen, former legal counsel at the Department of State, who wrote that the treaty, as submitted, could be modified by Eisenhower and Chiang without further Senate action. Morse concurred with Cohen's conclusion that such an action would markedly change the treaty and was an unwarranted and unprecedented delegation.[45]

Morse claimed that, because of the Cohen memorandum, the State Department represented that extending the area of coverage would require Senate action to amend the treaty. The committee report included the same stipulation. If that were true, Morse asked, why include the provision in the first place?

He answered his own question. "The major argument which has been advanced . . . is that it is in other treaties." But Morse claimed the situation in Formosa was not comparable. "It was in other treaties when there was no question about the sovereign rights of the party on the other side. It has been in other treaties with governments which were not involved in civil wars. It has been in other treaties with governments which did not raise the great concern that the Nationalist Chinese raise all over Asia, within the boundaries of the countries friendly to us. And that sentence is just so much surplusage in all those treaties as it is in this one too." Morse argued it should be stricken.

The senator concluded by offering four reasons to oppose the treaty: it increased the danger of war, complicated the determination of sovereignty rights, was a pact with an unrepresentative "government of military occupation," and not an agreement that would be recognized under international law as between two sovereign powers.[46]

With Senators Lehman and Langer as cosponsors, Morse submitted two reservations:

> The Senate advises and consents to the ratification of this treaty with the understanding that the last sentence of Article VI of the treaty shall have no force or effect.
>
>   The Senate advises and consents to the ratification of this treaty with the understanding that nothing in the treaty shall be construed as affecting or modifying the legal status or sovereignty of the territories to which it applies.

Before voting began, Senator Lehman took the Floor to deny that there was a need for the treaty at all, asking "What, precisely, does the treaty add to the position and posture we took in the Formosa Resolution? Why do we need to approve this treaty, binding our country not only for the present to meet the present situation, but binding us with the bands of constitutional strength far into the indefinite future to meet situations which we cannot possibly foresee today?"

Reciting the history of the Formosa Resolution, Lehman added, "It was my belief—and that belief was rather widely held—that the passage of the resolution certainly eliminated the necessity of a treaty with the Chiang Kai-shek regime."

Especially with the Formosa Resolution in place, Lehman felt, proceedings on the Mutual Defense Treaty were unduly rushed. The administration had submitted the treaty on January 6. Foreign Relations reported it on February 7, only two days prior, and after a hearing with only Secretary Dulles as a witness. The committee report had just become available. What was the hurry? Lehman noted that the Senate had given other pacts, such as the Treaty of Versailles and the North Atlantic Treaty, extended consideration. Thus, "why should we ratify the Formosa Treaty in such haste?"

Lehman theorized that the treaty was being moved urgently to stabilize Chiang's government. "We are being asked to approve the establishment of a permanent military tie with a regime that is undeniably weak and, according to my information, steadily growing weaker. It is whispered that this treaty is necessary to shore up that regime, to strengthen it to prevent it from toppling over. And it is indicated that haste is necessary for this purpose."[47]

Senator Dennis Chavez (D-NM) raised a question. If the treaty was truly for defensive purposes and not just a shield for an effort to recover the mainland, should not the Senate adopt a reservation to that effect? Lehman concurred, warning that "what I think many Members of the Senate do not understand is that the interests of the United States and the interests of Chiang Kai-shek may very readily be at complete variance, and in all probability will be." Lehman was not satisfied with the exchange of letters between Secretary Dulles and Foreign Minister Yeh. The Senate must also adopt a reservation on the requirement for mutual consent to launch military action so that the restraint was within the treaty document itself.

Lehman thought the treaty implicitly recognized Chinese sovereignty. Like Morse, he considered it highly inadvisable. "Will not Communist China now claim legal justification for aggression against Formosa and the Pescadores? Will the Communists not say: 'We are merely putting down an insurrection in a territory which even the United States recognizes as being part of China proper?'" To guard against this inference, report language masquerading as reservation would not do. Finally, Lehman concurred with Morse that a reservation was needed on Article VI, so that the scope of the treaty was expressly confined.[48]

The presiding officer outlined the standard process the Senate would follow in determining whether and under what circumstances it would give its consent. He announced that amendments to the treaty text were in order first, and that after disposition of the amendments was complete, the Senate would incorporate any that had been adopted into the resolution of ratification. If senators had reservations or understandings to propose, they would then be offered to that document. Thereafter the Senate would vote on the resolution of ratification, which was the mechanism by which the Senate would consent to the treaty, under such additional terms and conditions as the Senate had chosen to add.

Morse proposed an amendment to the treaty text, adding a new sentence at the end of Article VIII. It read:

This treaty does not affect or modify and shall not be interpreted as affecting or modifying the legal status or sovereignty of the territories to which it applies.

On the vote, 11 senators were in the affirmative, 10 Democrats plus Langer. Fifty-seven senators were in the negative. Twenty-eight senators did not vote, including Majority Leader Lyndon Johnson and Senator John F. Kennedy. Majority Whip Earle Clements announced that Johnson would have voted nay. Kennedy did not take a position.

Morse offered a second amendment, this one to strike the last sentence of Article VI. As submitted by the president, that sentence read:

The provisions of Article II and V will be applicable to such other territories as may be determined by mutual agreement.

Chairman George responded to this by noting Dulles's commitment during the hearings that the administration would not expand coverage without returning to the Senate for consent to a amend the treaty. Dulles's word had been sufficient for the committee, George said, so it had rejected the identical amendment by a vote of 11–2. He asked senators, "Have we no confidence in anybody? The Committee on Foreign Relations gave this question earnest consideration, and I think there was no reasonable doubt about it. Otherwise, more than two members of the committee would not have voted in favor of the resolution of ratification."

Knowland interjected that adopting the amendment would cause a delay because it would necessitate renegotiating with Chiang's government.

George concurred, and then added, "This is in our report. It is specifically in the report and is specifically in the testimony of the Secretary of State. It would be true if no one had said it because there can be no enlargement of a treaty unless the proposed enlargement is submitted to the Senate and is agreed to by the Senate. Why should the Senate make itself ridiculous? Why should it attach this sort of amendment to the treaty? To do so would be beyond my comprehension."

On the second Morse amendment, 10 senators voted aye, 9 Democrats and Langer. Sixty senators voted no. Twenty-six did not vote. Johnson was announced in the negative. Kennedy took no position.

No further amendments were presented to the treaty, so the resolution of ratification was placed before the Senate. It read:

Resolved (two-thirds of the Senators present concurring therein), that the Senate advise and consent to the ratification of Executive A, 84th Congress, 1st session, the Mutual Defense Treaty between the United States of America, and the Republic of China, signed at Washington on December 2nd, 1954.

Morse offered his reservations concerning sovereignty and Article VI. The Senate rejected each by voice votes.

No further reservations were proposed. The Senate then voted on consenting to the resolution of ratification. On that vote, 65 senators voted aye. Six opposed. They were Morse, Lehman, and Langer, who had also opposed the Formosa Resolution, joined by Democrats Kefauver, Chavez, and Albert Gore of Tennessee. Twenty-five senators did not vote. Johnson was announced as being affirmative. Kennedy took no position.

The Mutual Defense Treaty between the United States and the Republic of China entered into force on March 3, 1955.

Both the Formosa Resolution and the Mutual Defense Treaty received overwhelming votes in Congress. As historian Foster Rhea Dulles notes, an important reason for this was the trust many Americans placed in Eisenhower's judgment. "For the most part they went along with it on the easy assumption that in this aspect of his policy, as on so many other issues at home or abroad, Ike really knew best."[49] The week that the Senate consented to the Mutual Defense Treaty, the president's approval rating in the Gallup Poll stood at 73%.[50]

NOTES

1. *FRUS 1955–1957 Vol. II China*, p. 144.
2. Ibid., pp. 152–156.
3. *FRUS 1955–1957 Vol. II, China*, p. 167.
4. Ibid., pp. 166–167. Chiang believed that the British would oppose an open commitment to defend Quemoy and Matsu because such would undercut the New Zealand and British Oracle initiative in the United Nations for a cease-fire. In a follow-up meeting the next day in Taipei, Chiang told Rankin that anything that the Communists could interpret as weakness or indecision would enhance prospects of war, the responsibility for which would rest with the allies (Ibid., p. 168). In any case, Oracle ran aground when the Chinese Communists refused an invitation to come to the United Nations and simply reaffirmed their demand that the United States quit Formosa (Ibid., p. 202). Rankin noted in his memoirs the Communist posture was so unyielding that it deflected criticism away from Chiang. "Fortunately, however, the Soviet and Red Chinese reaction was so uncompromising that any criticism of the Republic of China, because of its unwillingness to participate in what it considered spurious ceasefire negotiations, was avoided" (Rankin, p. 213).
5. *FRUS, 1955–1957 Vol. II, China*, p. 175.
6. Ibid. Eisenhower expanded on this thinking in a February 1 letter to Supreme Allied Commander, Europe, Alfred Gruenther. The president wrote,

"If the solution we adopt should state flatly that we would defend the principal islands of the offshore group (Quemoy and the Matsus), we would now please the Chinese

Nationalists, but we would frighten Europe and of course even further infuriate the Chinese Communists. By announcing this as a policy, we would be compelled to maintain in the area, at great cost, forces that could assure the defense of islands that are almost within wading distance of the mainland. This defensive problem could be extremely difficult over the long term and I think that the world in general, including some of our friends, would believe us unreasonable and practically goading the Chinese Communists into a fight. We could get badly tied down by any such inflexible public attitude."

The president continued, "We must make a distinction (this is a difficult one) between an attack that has only as its objective the capture of an offshore island and one that is preliminarily a movement to an all-out attack on Formosa" (Ibid., pp. 191–192). The Communists did not interfere in the evacuation (Shu Guang Zhang, p. 219).

7. *FRUS, 1955–1957 Vol. II, China,* pp. 182–183.
8. Ibid., pp. 187–189.
9. Ibid., pp. 203–204.
10. Ibid., pp. 205–207.
11. Accinelli, pp. 196–197.
12. *FRUS, 1955–1957 Vol. II, China,* pp. 221–222.
13. Hoover's text read,

"I have the honor to refer to your Excellency's note dated February 5, 1955, stating that the Government of the Republic of China has decided to withdraw its armed forces from the Tachen Islands for purposes of redeployment and consolidation and to evacuate such civilians as desire to leave these islands, and requesting the United States Government to assist in and to provide protective cover for such withdrawal of its armed forces and evacuation of civilians. I have the honor to inform your Excellency that the United States Government agrees to extend protection to and assist in the redeployment of the armed forces of the Government of the Republic of China from the Tachen Islands and the evacuation of such civilians as desire to leave those islands. The United States Government has issued appropriate orders to its military forces in the area to implement this decision" (Ibid., pp. 224–225).

14. Ibid., pp. 230–231.
15. Before moving ahead, Britain had sought an open US commitment not to promise help in defense of Quemoy until the result in the Security Council was first known. The United States would not explicitly do so, but the British let matters proceed anyway. In a Memorandum for the Record, Assistant Secretary of State for European Affairs Livingston Merchant wrote, "I should add, as my own judgement that the British Government, in agreeing to move ahead on Oracle without acceptance by us of the commitment they sought in the terms they used, was relying on its understanding derived from the series of conversations that the purpose of the United States was to reduce the risk of war and to avoid involving itself in a situation in which it relinquished to the Chinese nationalists or shared with them the power of grave decision" (*FRUS, 1955–1957, Vol. 2 China,* p. 180).
16. Thomas J. Hamilton, "UN Invites Red China to Join Talks to Halt Fighting on Coastal Isles," *New York Times,* February 1, 1955, p. 1.
17. Senate Report, p. 773.

18. US recognition of the PRC was then a highly remote possibility. For instance, on November 9, 1953, a reporter asked Dulles whether the ban on recognizing Communist China was forever. The secretary responded,

"I do not think that this Administration has ever said that it would be forever opposed to a recognition of a Communist government in China. We have said that so long as the Communist government in China is a proclaimed aggressor in Korea and has not purged itself, so long as it is promoting aggression in Indochina, and so long as it is in general conducting itself in a way which is not becoming of a nation which presumably has the obligations that are expressed in the (United Nations) Charter, so long as these conditions exist, it seems to us quite out of order to consider the matter."

(*FRUS, 1952–1954, Vol. XIV, China and Japan, Part 1*, pp. 330–331) According to Karl Rankin, the Chinese Nationalists were convinced Washington would have recognized the People's Republic in 1950, but for Communist mistreatment of American diplomatic personnel and property in the aftermath of Mao's takeover (Rankin, p. 172).

19. *FRUS, 1955–1957, Vol. 2 China*, pp. 288–289.

20. Ibid., p. 292.

21. Ibid., p. 293.

22. Ibid., p. 298.

23. Ibid., p. 299.

24. Ibid., p. 302.

25. Morse argued,

"I think that unless you get this principle incorporated in an action by the Senate almost immediately, more harm will be done than good attained by trying to do it at a later date, because at the present time the United Nations has taken jurisdiction; It has jurisdiction. We are a party to its jurisdiction. The whole Asiatic situation should be settled by the United Nations and not by the United States. We are running the great danger in the eyes of many segments of the world of giving the impression that we are going to go along only if we like it, and that is not the way to try a case before a great international tribunal when you are subject to the jurisdiction of the tribunal." (Ibid., p. 303)

26. Ibid., p. 465, 469.

27. Interview with Ambassador T.F. Tsiang, *Longines Chronoscope*, January 28, 1955.

28. *FRUS, 1955–1957 Vol. II China*, pp. 231–232.

29. Ibid., pp. 239–240.

30. Ibid., pp. 244–245.

31. These materials appear in the *Congressional Record* of February 9, 1955, pp. 1379–1380.

32. *Congressional Record*, February 9, 1955, pp. 1380–1382.

33. Ibid., pp. 1382–1383.

34. Ibid., p. 1385.

35. Ibid., p. 1384.

36. Ibid.

37. Ibid., pp. 1384–1385.

38. Ibid., p. 1385.

39. On this point, the Communists and Nationalists would agree. Both considered Formosa (Taiwan) to be part of China. Their dispute was whether Beijing or Taipei was the legitimate government of the entire country. Thus, the Shanghai Communiqué, issued at the end of Nixon's February 1972 visit, contains an American declaration that "The United States acknowledges that all Chinese on either side of the Taiwan Strait maintain there is but one China and that Taiwan is part of China. The United States Government does not challenge that position."

40. *Congressional Record*, February 9, 1955, pp. 1387–1388.

41. Ibid., p. 1385.

42. Morse placed in the *Congressional Record*, an article that appeared in the February 9, 1955, *Washington Post and Times Herald* by Herbert Elliston, who wrote,

> "How can you sign a treaty with a government without recognizing that it has a habitation as well as a name? The treaty refers only to Formosa and the Pescadores. Surely then it implies an extension of free China sovereignty to Formosa. . . . Secretary Dulles by the way in answer to this point says that nowhere in the treaty is the word sovereignty used and that the text, moreover, does not carry that implication. On this reasoning . . . we have made a solemn pact with the government-in-the-sky a government with no legitimate site on the mainland or in Formosa. Here is a *reductio ad absurdum*. Clearly the Nationalist authorities on Formosa would never have signed and not the present instrument if they shared Mr. Dulles interpretation of it."

Herbert Elliston, "Questions on the Formosa Treaty," *Washington Post and Times Herald*, February 9, 1955.

43. Morse placed in the record of memorandum by Benjamin V. Cohen, former legal counsel at the State Department. As to the sovereignty issue, Cohen noted "the formal recognition of Formosa and the Pescadores as territories of the Republic of China would give substance to the claim of the Chinese Communists that an armed attack on these islands is not an international aggression on their part but civil war in which the right and purpose of other nations forcibly to intervene would be open to serious doubt and question." *Congressional Record*, February 9, 1955, p. 1396.

44. As to the Cairo Declaration, Benjamin V. Cohen stated,

> "It is true that the Cairo Declaration which was reaffirmed in the Potsdam Proclamation asserted the purpose of the representatives of the United States, the United Kingdom, and Nationalist China was to restore Formosa and the Pescadores to the Republic of China. But such purpose has not yet been carried out by any duly ratified peace treaty and much has happened in the meanwhile. The situation has been so altered on the mainland of China as to raise grave doubt whether that purpose can now be carried out, as it was assumed it could be, with regard to the principles of the Atlantic Charter and the Charter of the United Nations." (Ibid.)

45. Cohen wrote,

> "This provision would enable the President by agreement with the Republic of China to extend the scope of the principal articles of the treaty to any or all of the islands off

the shore of the mainland of China and even to the mainland of China itself, without the advice and consent of the Senate or approval of Congress. Any such extension of the treaty could radically change and transform the nature of the treaty and impose new and grave responsibilities on the United States. This provision is a dangerous and unprecedented delegation of the treaty- ratifying power of the Senate, without specification of any standards to govern the exercise of the delegated power." (Ibid., p. 1397)

46. Senator Morse's remarks are found at *Congressional Record*, February 9, 1955, pp. 1388–1398.

47. Lehman's theory might not be far-fetched. Chiang was greatly concerned about the political effects of the Tachens withdrawal, and the Eisenhower administration was worried about the collapse of Nationalist morale. Both these problems would be mitigated with ratification of the Mutual Defense Treaty.

48. Senator Lehman's comments are found at *Congressional Record*, February 9, 1955, pp. 1403–1411.

49. Foster Rhea Dulles, p. 156.

50. American Presidency Project: Approval Ratings for POTUS, Dwight D. Eisenhower, www.presidency.ucsb.edu (accessed July 9, 2022).

Chapter 9

Defend or Abandon Quemoy and Matsu

Late in the day on February 10, Foreign Minister Yeh visited the State Department to bid farewell to Dulles. About to return home, he sought parting advice, which Dulles dispensed frankly. It would be useful, Dulles said, for the Nationalists to level with their people and not pledge a near-term campaign to retake the mainland. Such an invasion could not be successful if Communist troops, which vastly outnumbered their Nationalist counterparts, remained loyal to the regime. Regaining the mainland was unrealistic unless the Communist government collapsed from internal dissension. Yeh responded that Chiang felt obliged to make such declarations to maintain his people's morale. Dulles replied that empty rhetoric and unfulfilled promises were likely to be even worse for morale. He commended to Yeh's attention the example of West German chancellor Konrad Adenauer, who proclaimed a policy of German reunification but refrained from offering a timetable. Impatient as Chiang might be, Yeh answered, the generalissimo was also a realist, capable of accepting unpalatable alternatives. Chiang's most immediate concerns, he said, were to avert: Communist Chinese admission to the UN, surrender of the offshore islands, recognition of the Communist government, and a UN trusteeship for Formosa.[1]

TENSIONS WITHIN THE ANGLO-AMERICAN ALLIANCE

With Senate agreement to the Mutual Defense Treaty in hand, Eisenhower penned a letter to Prime Minister Winston Churchill. "I realize that it has been difficult, at times, for you to back us up in the Formosa question and, for this reason, I want to give you a very brief account of our general attitude toward the various factors that have dictated the course of action we have taken," the president wrote.

The United States and Britain faced very divergent domestic opinion, the president noted. In America, many people vocally argued that more should be done to support Chiang Kai-shek, adding, "The number that would like to see us clear out of Formosa is negligible." However, Eisenhower observed, "I know that on your side of the water you have the exact opposite of this situation."

It was vital, the president declared, that the Communists do not have the capacity to breach the island barrier that Formosa represented.[2] Were they successful in doing so, the Philippines and Indonesia would be immediately exposed, and the entire region would soon fall under Communist domination. Thus, the United States had committed itself to hold Formosa, including helping Nationalist forces to become more capable of self-defense.

While Formosa must be a fortress, it should not be a jail, said Eisenhower. Chiang and his troops "are not content *now* to accept irrevocably and permanently the status of 'prisoners' on the island" (emphasis in the original). What sustained them was a conviction that they would one day return to the mainland. With that in mind, Chiang insisted on retaining Quemoy and Matsu, considering them stepping-stones for an invasion, not just a line of defense. Were the Communists to take over those islands, the situation would reverse. As Eisenhower noted, it "would mean the almost immediate conversion of that asset into a deadly danger."[3]

Nationalist morale must be sustained, the president wrote, and that meant reassuring Taipei that the offshore islands would be protected if related to defending Formosa and the Pescadores. Such was implicit in both the Formosa Resolution and the Mutual Defense Treaty.

Those documents vividly expressed American resolve, Eisenhower continued, diminishing the chance of miscalculation and an accidental war, including one that could involve the Soviet Union. "I devoutly hope that history's inflexible yardstick will show that we have done everything in our power, and everything that is right, to prevent the awful catastrophe of another major war."

Churchill replied several days later, in a letter that exposed significant differences between Washington and London. Britain would support American policy on the defense of Formosa, said the prime minister. "I feel strongly that it is a matter of honour for the United States not to allow Chiang Kai-shek and his adherents, with whom the United States have worked as allies for so many years, to be liquidated and massacred by Communist Chinese, who are alleged to have already executed in cold blood between two and three million of their opponents in their civil war." However, Churchill continued, Nationalist retention of the offshore islands was distinct from the main problem. He perceived no value in them as a defensive barrier. "I cannot see any decisive relationship between the offshore islands and the defense of Formosa." Instead, he considered their main function was to serve as "bridgeheads for a Nationalist invasion of Communist China."[4]As such, Nationalist occupation of the islands was risky, inviting provocations that could enmesh the United States. "They might all too easily become the occasion of an incident which would place the United States before the dilemma of either standing by while their allies were butchered or becoming embroiled in a war for no strategic or political purpose."[5]

Britain would not support such an invasion, Churchill stressed, nor even a conflict fought to prevent Communist seizure of the islands. "A war to keep the coastal islands for Chiang would not be defensible here."[6]

It was problematic for the United States to nurture, or even to inflate, Chiang's hopes for a return to the mainland, the prime minister observed.[7] While US policy was based on maintaining Nationalist morale, Churchill argued that "I do not think it would be right or wise for America to encourage him to keep alive the reconquest of the mainland in order to inspirit his faithful followers." "He deserves the protection of your shield but not the use of your sword," said Churchill.[8]

The British believed the Communist triumph of 1949 was irrevocable. "The hope of Chiang subduing Communist China surely died six years ago when Truman on Marshall's advice gave up the struggle on the mainland and helped Chiang into the shelter of Formosa."

Appropriate American policy would be to stand fast on Formosa, Churchill said, treat the offshore islands like the Tachens and facilitate Nationalist withdrawal from them, and announce that the United States would meet any Communist interference with appropriate conventional force.[9]

On February 16, a somewhat frustrated Eisenhower discussed Churchill's policy prescriptions with Dulles, who complained that the British did not sufficiently appreciate all the United States had done to put limits on Chiang. That included the treaty addendum restraining the use of force without American agreement, coaxing him into acquiescing to the Oracle project at the United Nations, and facilitating the Tachens evacuation.[10] Chiang had gone along with these measures reluctantly. The United States could not presently demand more from him, said the secretary.[11]

After consulting with Dulles, the president replied to Churchill. In a letter dated February 18, 1955, he defended American policy, making no accommodation to the British position. Mindful of Chiang's extreme reluctance to withdraw from the Tachens, Eisenhower contended that the United States could not force Chiang to desert Quemoy and Matsu, which were more dearly held. "This country does not have decisive power in respect of the offshore islands," he asserted. "We believe that Chiang would even choose to stand alone and die if we should attempt now to coerce him into the abandonment of those islands."

The president insisted that the strength and morale of the Nationalist army was of vital importance to the West, and that meant being sensitive to Chiang's interests and politics. Ramifications of the French defeat in Vietnam made sustaining Chiang especially important. "Only a few months back we had both Chiang and a strong well-equipped French Army to support the free world's position in Southeast Asia," Eisenhower declared. "The French are gone—making it clearer than ever that we cannot afford the loss of Chiang unless all of us are to get completely out of that corner of the globe."[12]

The president recounted the steps America had taken to prevent Chiang's ambition from thrusting it into war. However, he worried that the Communists would interpret further restraint as weakness. Rather than being assuaged, they would be emboldened. "There comes a point where constantly giving in only encourages further belligerency," Eisenhower noted.

Abandoning the offshore islands would not appease the Communists, he contended. "What they are really interested in is Formosa—and later on, Japan—and the coastal islands are marginal." He concluded that withdrawal from the islands could marginalize the Nationalist government or precipitate its collapse. "This retreat, and the coercion we would have to use to bring it about, would so undermine the morale and the loyalty of the non-Communist forces on Formosa that they could not be counted on."

Nor did Eisenhower believe the problem of eroded confidence would be limited to Chiang and his forces. "All of the non-Communist nations of the western Pacific, particularly Korea, Japan, the Philippines, and of course Formosa itself, are watching nervously to see what we do next. I fear that if we appear strong and coercive only toward our friends and should attempt to compel Chiang to make further retreats, the conclusion of these Asian peoples will be that they had better plan to make the best terms they can with the Communists."

The United States had sufficient expertise and record of prudence in dealing with East Asia that Britain should defer to it, Eisenhower urged. "I devoutly hope that there may be enough trust and confidence develop between our two peoples so that when judgments of this kind have to be made, each could, in the last analysis, trust the other in the areas where they have special knowledge and the greatest responsibility."[13]

Neither Eisenhower nor Churchill could persuade his opposite number.[14] On February 28, Dulles wired acting secretary Herbert Hoover, Jr., from Bangkok about a discussion with British foreign secretary Anthony Eden. According to Dulles, Eden "agreed Taiwan should not be lost to Communists, although remarked Churchill does not think island strategically important but will go along with us if we think so. If Chinese attacked Taiwan and we resist,

Eden believes public opinion in Commonwealth and free world generally will clearly understand and support US, whereas they will not if war results from defense of offshore islands."[15]

Later that day, Dulles outlined the continuing division for the president. Recounting his February 24 meeting with Eden, the secretary noted that the foreign minister was promoting a trade-off. "In general, Eden's line was that a further fall back by abandonment of Quemoy and Matsu would be justified by increased support of resultant position by Commonwealth and western European public opinion. He naturally attaches to this an importance which I feel fails to appraise adequately dangerous to non-Communist morale in Far East, notably in Taiwan, Korea, Japan, and the Philippines."[16]

Citing the problems with betraying Czechoslovakia at Munich, Dulles told Eden that the time not to yield had arrived. Eden grasped the analogy but believed the West could defuse tensions by accommodating Communist Chinese interests on the offshore islands. Disagreeing, Dulles deferred to Eisenhower. He wrote the president, "I said this was a grave decision where you would have to exercise final responsibility and that all the world could know you would do so with the sober sense of responsibility and dedication to peace with freedom."[17]

Not being able to gain closure with the British vexed Eisenhower and prompted him to write again to Churchill. The United States had asked London for a degree of deference on Far Eastern policy but had not received it. In a March 29 letter, the president noted with some dismay that, "Although we seem always to see eye to eye with you when we contemplate any European problems, our respective attitudes toward similar problems in the Orient are frequently so dissimilar as to be almost mutually antagonistic."

Eisenhower approached Churchill respectfully and took pains to avoid recriminations. "I beg of you *not* to think of this letter as a complaint, or as any effort to prove that we are right, and you are wrong" (emphasis in the original). Instead, the president's concern was to get both countries on the same page. "I am interested in one thing and one thing only—how can we and our two governments come closer together in our thinking?"

The core problem, as Eisenhower saw it, was a difference of opinion over "the probable extent of further Communist expansion in Asia." While such was of great concern to the United States, he said, "your own government seems to regard Communist aggression in Asia as of little significance to the free world future."

The president again reaffirmed the foundations of US policy. "As I once explained to you, we are not interested in Quemoy and Matsu, as such. But because of the conviction that the loss of Formosa would doom the Philippines and the remainder of the region, we are determined that it shall not fall into the hands of the Communists."

Never believing that Quemoy and Matsu were strategically important to the defense of Formosa, Eisenhower wrote that he would be glad if Chiang voluntarily withdrew from them. However, the president refused to force the issue. He would not "put so much pressure on him that he might give up the entire struggle in utter discouragement." Eisenhower believed that Formosa could not be held without Chiang's ground forces.

The president brought up an argument not expressed in his prior letters to the prime minister. The presence of Nationalist China as a counterweight to Chinese Communism was important to the Free World. There were Chinese émigré communities throughout Asia, Eisenhower noted, with some form of dual loyalty to their local government and to China. These could become a destabilizing element if loyalty to China meant loyalty to Beijing. "If the Chinese National Government should disappear, these émigré Chinese will certainly deem themselves subjects of the Chinese Communist Government and they will quickly add to the difficulties of their adopted countries."

Eisenhower asked, "Do not such possibilities concern you?"[18]

DULLES MEETS WITH CHIANG

On March 3, Dulles met with Chiang in Taipei for consultations and to ratify the Mutual Defense Treaty. The secretary opened with a presentation about why the United States had engaged the United Nations. Many nations would want the UN to play a peacemaking role, he said. Although Communist intransigence was likely to prevent success there, the United States had to exhaust that option. He emphasized that the United States had not tried to extend UN jurisdiction over Formosa, as some in the Nationalist government feared. "What we sought was simply a 'cease-fire resolution' which would stop the fighting, but not an attempt to deal with the substance of the respective claims," Dulles wrote.

The secretary turned to the offshore islands issue, which had been the topic of so much discussion with Foreign Minister Yeh and which still bothered Chiang. Dulles presented a portion of a statement he intended to make upon his departure from Taipei. Referencing the formal designation of the Formosa Resolution, it read:

> The decision as to the use of the armed forces of the United States and the scope of their use under Public Law 4 will be made by the President himself in light of the circumstances at the time and his appraisal of the intentions of the Chinese Communists.
>
> Since, however, the Matsu and Quemoy Islands, now in friendly hands, have a relationship to the defense of Taiwan such as the president may judge

their protection to be appropriate in assuring the defense of Taiwan and the Pescadores, our consultation covered also these coastal positions of the Republic of China.

It is the ardent hope of the United States that the Chinese Communists will not insist on war as an instrument of its policy.

As President Eisenhower said, "We would welcome action by the United Nations which might bring an end to the active hostilities in the area." The United Nations is exploring the possibility of a cease-fire, as are also other peace-loving nations.

I have, however, made clear that the United States will not enter into any negotiations dealing with the territories, or rights of the Republic of China except in cooperation with the Republic of China.

The secretary raised the subject of greatest sensitivity to Chiang: the return to the mainland.[19] Candidly, he told him that Free China should refrain from whipping up fervor when Nationalist success depended on conditions outside its control, such as fracturing within mainland China itself. Dulles emphasized:

> The main point I wish to make was that these opportunities which were quite likely to arise were not opportunities which could be created by the Republic of China alone or which could be dated. The opportunities would be created by forces apart from the Republic of China. Under those circumstances, it seemed rather foolish for the Republic of China to try to hold out dates when the forces of the Republic of China could successfully conquer the mainland. This was belittling and exposing the Republic of China to a measure of ridicule abroad.[20]

Chiang stressed that keeping hope alive for a return to the mainland was vital for public morale but affirmed he would not take aggressive action against the PRC without first consulting with Eisenhower.[21] He claimed that internal political considerations made it impossible for him to agree to a cease-fire resolution at the UN. Beyond that, he thought the cease-fire opened the door to two Chinas, which both he and the Communists strongly opposed.[22] As Ambassador Rankin later wrote, "Advocates of two Chinas have chosen to overlook the actual and prospective attitudes of the Chinese regimes in question. Both have repudiated the idea; neither has given any indication of willingness to accept it in any form, even tacitly."[23]

Chiang also worried about proposals, such as those from Britain to seat Communist China in the UN. He warned he could never accept it. "He hoped the US would understand that the Chinese Nationalist Government would never sit anywhere at the same table with the Chinese Communists, much less in the UN," Dulles reported. The secretary replied that the United States had no intention of supporting Beijing's admission.[24]

RESORT TO TACTICAL NUCLEAR WEAPONS

Back in Washington on March 6, Dulles conferred with Eisenhower to review the Chiang meeting. The secretary was pessimistic, saying that the situation in the strait was more difficult than he had previously judged. Steps thus far taken, such as passage of the Formosa Resolution and ratification of the Mutual Defense Treaty, had not caused the crisis to abate.[25] As Gordon H. Chang and He Di observe, "Mao was partly responsible for Dulles perception, since Mao wanted to keep the pressure on the United States, which he did through propaganda; and Washington officials could not clearly distinguish between what was propaganda and what was an expression of genuine intent."[26]

The president and the secretary considered the need to use tactical atomic weapons in the event of hostilities. Dulles recounted the conversation. "He said that with the number of planes we had in the Asian area, it would be quite impractical to accomplish the necessary results in the way of putting out airfields and gun emplacements without using atomic missiles." The secretary added, "This did not, of course, mean weapons of mass destruction."[27]

Thus, Eisenhower had agreed use of the weapons might be a military necessity and that introducing the idea might get Beijing's attention. To prepare the US public, he told Dulles to float the idea in a public statement.[28] However, the president was skeptical that the literal and political fallout could be confined. The tactical nuclear weapons to which Dulles referred had yields of 15 kilotons, nearly as large as the bombs used against Japan in 1945, and the airfields were situated in coastal areas near civilian populations. Major casualties would be essentially unavoidable.[29]

On March 10, Dulles briefed the National Security Council about his trip. He emphasized the issue of Nationalist morale, which he described as precarious. If the Communists were able to induce defections, as had happened during the civil war, the Nationalist army might collapse. It was "not inconceivable that with skillful bribery some of the Chinese Nationalist generals could be bought by the Communists," Dulles said.[30] "This had happened many times before in the history of China, and indeed one of the reasons for becoming a general in China was to get oneself bought."

The secretary reported that he advised Chiang to tone down the rhetoric about an early return to the mainland but had done so gingerly. In Gleason's memorandum, Dulles told the NSC that "employment of shock treatment methods would risk the loss of Formosa, and if that island were lost, the entire US position in Asia would be lost with it."[31]

At this March 10 meeting, the NSC considered the atomic weapons issue. According to the Memorandum of Discussion prepared by Everett Gleason of the NSC staff, Dulles argued the use of such weapons would be unavoidable and that the US public needed to be prepared for it. "Secretary Dulles called for urgent steps to create a better public climate for the use of atomic weapons if we found it necessary to intervene in the defense of the Formosa area. . . . Secretary Dulles thought that very shortly now the Administration would have to face up to the question of whether its military program was or was not in fact designed to permit the use of atomic weapons." If not properly conditioned, fear and anxiety could constrain their use. "We might wake up one day and discover that we were inhibited in the use of such weapons by a negative public opinion," Dulles said.[32]

On March 11, Dulles spoke at a cabinet meeting about impressions from his trip to the Far East. According to diary notes from Eisenhower's press secretary James Hagerty, Dulles said,

> I am concerned because the purposes of Red China are more virulent than I had realized before I left this country. I had talks with the Burmese Prime Minister and with Eden, who has been conducting conversations with the Communists of Peiping, and I must tell you this: The Chinese Reds have a fanatical determination to eradicate any impression of goodwill for the United States in their part of the world. I disagree with the British and I am sure that we are living in a fool's paradise if we have any idea that we can make an easy trade with the Communists for the offshore islands.

Following through on his meeting with Eisenhower, Dulles began to lay the groundwork for possible deployment of tactical nuclear weapons in the crisis. At a March 15 news conference, he said, "If we defend Quemoy and Matsu, we'll have to use atomic weapons. That alone will be effective against the mainland airfields."[33] In a presidential press conference the next day, Charles von Fremd of CBS News asked Eisenhower to clarify the administration's position. "Mr. President," von Fremd inquired, "yesterday at his news conference, Secretary of State Dulles indicated that in the event of general war in the Far East, we would probably make use of some tactical small atomic weapons. Would you care to comment on this and, possibly, explain it further?"

Eisenhower replied, "In any combat where these things can be used on strictly military targets and for strictly military purposes, I see no reason why they shouldn't be used just exactly as you would use a bullet or anything else." He expressed a caveat, "I believe the great question about these things comes when you begin to get into those areas where you cannot make sure that you are operating merely against military targets." However, Eisenhower added, "But with that one qualification, I would say, yes, of course they would be used."[34]

Behind a façade of nonchalance, the Chinese noted these warnings with concern. As historian Shu Guang Zhang comments, "To the Chinese leaders, US nuclear weapons may not have been an 'empty threat.' They were evidently not sure how willing Moscow would be to retaliate for a US nuclear strike against China, nor were they certain how willing the Chinese people would be to face the risk of massive destruction."[35]

Eisenhower's and Dulles' comments sparked a war scare in the United States, made worse by Chief of Naval Operations Admiral Robert Carney's public speculation near the end of March that the United States would conduct a preemptive nuclear strike to head off an expected attack on Matsu.[36] The lead headline in the March 26, 1955, *New York Times* read, "US Expects Chinese Reds to Attack Isles in April; Weighs All-Out Defense." *Times* columnist Anthony Leviero reported, "A significant change in policy and defense planning is under consideration here in the belief Red China will begin its campaign to capture Matsu and Quemoy about the middle of April. The first intimations of an abrupt hardening of this country's position may come in the White House meetings that President Eisenhower has scheduled with congressional leaders on Wednesday and Thursday."

As Leviero noted, no decision had been made to commit US forces to military conflict. "There is as yet no sign that President Eisenhower has decided to intervene militarily to prevent the capture of the islands. But military advisers are urging him to do so, and on an all-out basis. He is being urged if this country is drawn into the conflict to destroy Red Chinas industrial potential and thus end its expansionist tendencies. On such a basis, the United States would be committed to the use of atomic weapons in war for the second time."[37]

Reaction from Democrats was harsh. Party leaders such as Adlai Stevenson, Lyndon Johnson, Averill Harriman, and Dean Acheson denounced recklessness and unwarranted risk taking.[38] And even Dulles's ally, Walter George, was alarmed.[39]

Within the administration, pessimism abounded that the crisis in the Formosa Strait could be peacefully contained. Eisenhower considered this general sense of gloom exaggerated. In a March 26 diary entry, the president wrote, "Lately there has been a very definite feeling among the members of the Cabinet, often openly expressed, that within a month we will actually be fighting in the Formosa Straits. . . . I believe hostilities are not so imminent as is indicated by the forebodings of a number of my associates. . . . I have so often been through these periods of strain that I have become accustomed to the fact that most of the calamities that we anticipate never really occur."[40]

The following day, Eisenhower and Dulles met with senior members of the House of Representatives. Formosa was the major topic. The Communists in Asia had enjoyed a string of successes that contributed to an arrogant attitude, Dulles observed. He cited the Chinese intervention in Korea, which pushed UN forces back from the Chinese border at the Yalu River, the French defeat in Indochina, and the evacuation of the Tachens. The response by anti-Communist countries had been ineffectual, he complained, whetting an appetite for further conquests.

Reporting on discussions with the British and Australians, Dulles complained that US allies had a narrow perspective on the offshore islands and failed to consider how abandonment would undermine Nationalist morale. Eisenhower added that the allies would fully support the United States as to Formosa and the Pescadores but were wary to start a war over Quemoy and Matsu.

The president told his guests that the United States was not committed to combat over the islands but would assess the situation in the event of a Communist attack. It would be his preference to assist the Nationalists with arms but not troops.[41]

On Capitol Hill, dissension on the administration's Formosa policy simmered. Democrats such as Senators Morse, Lehman, Humphrey, and Long, as well as majority leader Lyndon Johnson, continued to express misgivings about defending Quemoy and Matsu. From outside Congress, the party's titular leader, Adlai Stevenson, proclaimed that the administration's priorities were misplaced. "Should we be plunged into another great war, the maintenance of our alliances and the respect and goodwill of the uncommitted nations of Asia will be far more important to us than the possession of these offshore islands by General Chiang Kai-shek ever could be."[42]

EISENHOWER MAKES AN ASSESSMENT
AND LOOKS FOR A WAY OUT

On April 5, Eisenhower sent a lengthy letter to Dulles, summarizing the Formosa situation and the policy choices confronting the administration. "Inspired by the enlightened self-interest of the United States, this country has committed itself, by treaty with the Chinese Nationalist Government, to the defense of Formosa and the Pescadores," the president began. Although Quemoy and Matsu were not specifically mentioned in the treaty, the president noted, the Nationalists would have "some right to assume" that America would assist in their defense.

Doing so would impose substantial costs on the United States, he said, because most of the world saw the offshore islands as part of China. US participation in their active defense "would forfeit the good opinion of much of the Western world," Eisenhower thought. There was, as well, domestic opposition to such engagement, which the president worried could be quite substantial and corrosive. Such divisions would be greatly compounded especially if, to assure military success, the United States used atomic weapons. It was unclear if the United States could prevail without them.[43]

Yet, the United States could not simply walk away, he observed. "Most observers assert that it would dismay the ChiNats, *whose morale and military efficiency are essential to the defense of Formosa—and the security of Formosa is essential to the best interests of the United States and the Western world*" (emphasis in the original). America could not urge that the islands be forsaken without causing that morale to collapse.

Eisenhower judged that the drumbeat of domestic and international criticism about defending the islands, much less the use of nuclear weapons, was problematic and not sustainable. Robert Accinelli writes, "the administration's nuclear bravado in March, far from stimulating a favorable domestic environment for atomic retaliation, had done quite the opposite, as the war scared testified. The Secretary and the President similarly realized that the employment of nuclear weapons would shock much of world opinion, especially in non-Communist Asia, and rattle the Western allies."[44]

Mindful of the need to keep the country and its allies behind him, Eisenhower to consider proactive steps to escape the political morass.[45] It was better to take the initiative "rather than to remain inert awaiting the inevitable moment of decision between two unacceptable choices," said the president. For Eisenhower, this meant exploring a significant policy shift, to convince Chiang to deemphasize the importance of Quemoy and Matsu, treat them as outposts, and provision and garrison them accordingly.[46] If this were done, neither Chiang nor the Americans would be committed to the islands' all-out defense. "The worldwide political advantages of such an arrangement would be incalculable," Eisenhower wrote. In addition, benefits would accrue in US politics. "For ourselves" said the president, "one of the greatest advantages would be a practically solidified public opinion in the United States."

But to have a chance of success, and to avoid backlash, the idea for a reconfigured policy must look like it came from Chiang himself, not be one imposed by the United States. "Any alteration in military and political planning should obviously be developed under his leadership; above all, there must be no basis for public belief that the alterations came about through American intervention or coercion," Eisenhower cautioned.

Care must be taken to choose the American who would surface the plan with Chiang, he said. "The negotiator must be a man whom Chiang trusts and who is himself convinced of the soundness of this program."

The matter was urgent, the president told Dulles. "As you and I have fully agreed, there is no time for unnecessary delay."[47]

IMPLEMENTING THE PRESIDENT'S POLICY

To reflect and implement the president's vision, the State Department prepared a Draft Policy Statement. Dated April 8, 1955, it recited the American interest in preserving Free China. It began, "The security of Taiwan (including the Pescadores) is essential to the best interests of the United States and the Western World. In unfriendly hands, it would seriously threaten the security of the US and its allies in the Pacific."

However, the statement asserted that Nationalist retention of the offshore islands was not itself essential to US security interests. Thus, the administration did not agree that the islands be expressly covered by the Mutual Defense Treaty or the Formosa Resolution, and conditions would have to be assessed to determine whether US engagement was required. "It would be very difficult for the President to make an unconditional decision to defend the coastal positions," the statement read. For instance, an attack on the islands that the president did not consider a precursor to an attack on Formosa would not justify American intervention.

The statement listed three factors that favored US participation in the islands' defense.

- The islands served as natural barriers to harbors at Amoy and Fuchow that would be staging areas for an amphibious attack on Formosa.[48]
- More important, from a military perspective, was sustaining the will of Nationalist forces to fight. "The principal military reason for seeking to hold the two groups of islands is the estimated effect of their loss upon morale in Taiwan."
- Abandoning the islands could encourage more Communist aggression and weaken non-Communist resistance. "Loss of the Matsus and Quemoy—if attributed to our timidity—might create doubts in Japan and concern among our friends in Asia, particularly in Thailand, the Philippines, and Korea."

Countering these considerations, the statement set out five considerations.

- The proximity of the islands to the mainland made them inherently difficult to defend. "For the US to undertake their defense would commit our military prestige to a campaign under conditions favorable to the attacker," the statement noted.
- An effective defense was likely to require the use of atomic weapons.[49] Notwithstanding Dulles's assurances that the weapons would be targeted against military installations, the statement declared, "there would be a risk of large civilian casualties through after-effects, and indeed the inhabitants of Quemoy and even Taiwan might not be immune under certain atmospheric and wind conditions."
- A successful defense against an attack would not remove the incessant threat and would require tying down a major contingent of US and Nationalist forces to guard against periodic attacks. "A disproportionate

amount of our disposable, mobile reserves would be held down indefinitely in one sport, because our prestige would have become involved, even though involuntarily."

- The islands would not serve as a launching pad for a return to the mainland. If internal conditions on the mainland were such that a Nationalist return was possible, there would be better points to launch an attack. For largely symbolic reasons, Chiang had dangerously overcommitted his forces to island positions. "He is gambling his whole position in Taiwan and his future as a useful agent in helping to drive Communism from China."

- World opinion did not support going to war over the islands. "We have ample forewarning of the adverse character of world reaction that would follow any such action on our part, especially if we felt compelled to use atomic weapons," the statement said. It further observed, "If conflict in that region should spread to global proportions, we would be entering a life and death struggle under very great handicaps."

The statement added a further consideration. Much like the Japanese in the 1930s and 1940s, the Communists had latched on to the idea that Asia should manage its own affairs and be free of Western influence. Thus, it warned, "It is furthermore of the utmost importance that the issue should not take on the appearance of a struggle between races. A strong effort is being made by the Chinese Communists to create all-Asian sentiment against the white West. . . . It is important that if there is fighting around Taiwan, it should be primarily a fight between the Chinese Nationalists and the Chinese Communists, and not a fight between the 'white' Westerners and the 'yellow' Chinese."[50]

In light of these considerations, the statement concluded that neither America's prestige nor Chiang's should be tied to Quemoy and Matsu. Chiang was overcommitting himself to a circumstance whose risks far outweighed its symbolic value. "The lesson of Dien Bien Phu should not be forgotten," the statement warned. "Originally conceived to be an outpost of transitory value, it gradually became converted into a symbol, so that when it fell, all else fell with it." Without US support, the islands were "probably indefensible," it said, "and even with it, may not be defensible except by means which would defeat the larger common purpose."

Thus, it would be US policy to persuade Chiang to change course, and either disengage from the islands entirely or to treat them as outposts.[51]

On April 9, Robert Bowie, the State Department's director of Policy Planning, commented on the draft. In a Memorandum to Dulles, Bowie observed that, "To Chiang, the offshore islands are important not so much for the defense of Taiwan or for demonstrating Nationalist military prowess, but because they offer the most likely means for involving the US in hostilities with the Chinese Communists which could expand to create his opportunity for invasion." Bowie therefore reasoned that, "To treat the islands as expendable outposts would forfeit the prospect of such US military involvement. Consequently, Chiang can hardly be persuaded to do so unless he is completely convinced that the US has no intention of participating in their defense. And only a forthright public statement to the effect would be likely to convince him."

Bowie concluded that to avoid the appearance of US dictation, Chiang should have the choice of withdrawing from the islands or remaining there without US defense. But Bowie made clear which course was in America's interest. Chiang must withdraw. "Nationalist withdrawal would preclude the possibility that Chiang, even though agreeing to regard the islands as outposts, would continue to work to improve the prospects of subsequent US involvement," wrote Bowie. "Nationalist withdrawal would avoid the unsettling effects upon US opinion inherent, even with a prior US statement that it would not intervene, in standing by if the Communists should actually attack."[52]

THE ROBERTSON-RADFORD MISSION

The administration selected two emissaries to approach Chiang, Assistant Secretary of State Walter Robertson and Chairman of the JCS Admiral Arthur Radford.[53] The generalissimo knew them to be among his strongest advocates in Washington. On April 22, 1955, acting secretary Hoover transmitted a message to them that reflected the political delicacy of their assignment. "Your mission is to find in conversation mutual exploration some solution to the Formosa-Quemoy-Matsu problem that will be acceptable both to Chiang and to us," Hoover wrote. Avoiding the appearance of coercion was essential. "It is highly desirable that we avoid the position of urging upon him a solution which he cannot accept."

Robertson and Radford were in a very awkward spot. They would have to assert American unwillingness to defend Quemoy and Matsu per se and coax Chiang toward lessening his own commitments to the islands. These positions were contrary to firmly held Nationalist views. Hoover added, "The President is anxious that an area of understanding be reached that politically and psychologically avoids any indication of a lessening of our interest in the Generalissimo and at the same time achieves his recognition of the fact that the United States cannot be committed because of reasons important both to him and to this country to going to war in defense of the offshore islands."

At all costs, however, a rift with Chiang must be avoided. "Under no circumstances should there be allowed to develop an atmosphere which could preclude further conversations and negotiations, nor should there be any appearance of trying to force the Generalissimo to adopt a course which is unacceptable to him."[54]

Robertson and Radford arrived in Taipei on the morning of Sunday, April 24, and proceeded to the US embassy to confer with Ambassador Rankin. Later, Robertson cabled Dulles describing a "tense atmosphere of speculation" they encountered upon arrival. Preceding them were American news reports that their mission was to induce Chiang to leave Quemoy and Matsu, as well as reports from Hong Kong that the British government was pressing this strategy on the United States.[55]

Asked to speculate on Chiang's probable reaction to Eisenhower's proposal, Rankin said the generalissimo would be surprised that the United States was withdrawing support for defense of the offshore islands. Chiang would not concur that circumstances had changed to the degree that justified backing out. Although Rankin did not agree with the proposal, he accompanied Robertson and Radford to the meeting and promised to remain silent.

The meeting with Chiang took place on Monday evening, April 25, lasting for six and a half hours. Robertson began by reassuring the generalissimo of three key points: that the United States would not support any plan to neutralize Formosa, it would not recognize Communist China or support its admission to the United Nations, and it considered the Nationalist government as the legitimate government for the whole of China.[56]

Robertson said that rising tensions in the strait could lead to the outbreak of a war in which atomic weapons might be used. Should war occur, it was essential that President Eisenhower have the full backing of the American people and the greatest possible degree of support from world public opinion. To achieve that consensus, Robertson declared, the United States and the Chinese Nationalists must not strike the first blow. That meant no preemptive attack, even if the Communists continued to build airfields.[57] Robertson told Chiang that "President Eisenhower, with reluctance, has come to the decision that military disadvantages of unchecked buildup should be accepted at this time rather than we should be held responsible for initiating active hostilities which could readily spread to major war. President Eisenhower strongly feels that the moral and political advantages of avoiding the initiative in the fighting would more than offset the military disadvantages."

Robertson said Eisenhower believed strongly that US and world opinion would endorse protecting Formosa but not the offshore islands. And that was important. The war might widen into a global conflict. If the Soviet Union were drawn in, the United States would require the use of overseas bases, which might be denied if host countries did not support the war.

The vulnerability of Quemoy and Matsu made them weak defensive outposts and left the Nationalists exposed to the potential loss of troops, equipment, and face.[58] If it were possible to evacuate the islands, the United States would assist Chiang in substituting a more viable defensive position, said Robertson. That would include the use of naval power to command the sea lanes off the Chinese coast. In that way, the harbors of Amoy and Fuchow could not be used to stage an amphibious attack on Formosa and contraband and war-making materiel could be stopped. This interdiction would remain in place "until it was evident Red China had renounced its avowed purpose to take Formosa by force," Robertson indicated.[59]

The Americans had touched the political "third rail" of Nationalist China. Listening carefully, Chiang was polite but chagrined. He was also unpersuaded. He told Robertson that he would honor treaty obligations not to attack the mainland without American consent and he had agreed to evacuate the Tachens. But he would not abandon the offshore islands. To do so would cause his government to lose the respect of its own people, Chiang said.[60] He would defend Quemoy and Matsu even if he had to do so without US help. "He is fully aware of the danger of Chicom buildup but is prepared to take risk of receiving full onslaught of attack rather than give up two positions which would go against best Chinese tradition of patriotism," Robertson reported. Chiang said, "Soldiers must choose proper places to die. Chinese soldiers consider Quemoy-Matsu are proper places for them."

Chiang asked whether the United States had altered its position concerning assistance for the defense of the islands. He was referring to what he took to be American assurances to him from a cable on January 31, 1955, which stated that the United States would help defend the islands if an attack on them was construed as an attack on Formosa. The cable also said that the administration concluded that defense of the islands and defense of Formosa were in fact connected.

Expressly approved by Eisenhower, and delivered by Ambassador Rankin, the cable read, "Under present circumstances it is the purpose of the President to assist in the defense of Quemoy and Matsu against armed attack if he judges such attack is of a character which shows that it is in fact in aid of any in preparation for an armed attacked on Formosa and the Pescadores and dangerous to their defense. An attack by the Communists at this time on Quemoy or Matsu which seriously threatened their loss would be deemed by the President to be of this character."

Eisenhower's position had indeed changed, Radford responded, because the president concluded that a defense of the islands could not be made without resorting to atomic weapons. If used, that would have a highly adverse impact on public opinion worldwide, especially if they caused heavy civilian casualties. Foreign Minister Yeh asked whether defense was possible using only conventional arms. Radford answered that he could not guarantee a successful outcome if atomic weapons were not deployed.

Chiang wondered if the Americans had considered the effect withdrawing from the islands would have in non-Communist Asia. It would generate a grave psychological reaction, he predicted, as Asians would conclude the United States would not stand firm against the Communists.

The generalissimo and Madame Chiang temporarily withdrew from the meeting, but the conversation continued between Robertson and Yeh. The foreign minister recalled the negative effect on morale from the Tachens withdrawal, which was mitigated by the understanding, even if not publicly declared, that the United States would help defend Quemoy and Matsu. Robertson reported, "He indicated that further evacuation by military forces would result in loss of morale and deterioration of government position. He said he felt that to lose islands in battle would be less serious in effect upon morale than evacuation without fight."

Robertson urged the Nationalists to consider Eisenhower's offer, claiming that interdiction would be more effective against the Communists than trying to hold the islands. If Chiang accepted the plan, the two presidents could announce it jointly in a mutually agreed upon place.

Returning to the meeting, Chiang stated that he had been America's loyal ally, sensitive to its recommendations and political issues. He had withdrawn from the Tachens, hoping for an express US commitment to defend Quemoy and Matsu. When Eisenhower refused to make such a declaration, Chiang did not insist. "He had no desire to involve us in any armed conflict on behalf of the Government of China," reported Robertson.

Chiang said he did not believe the Communists would attack the islands independent of an assault on Formosa and did not think they would attack either without Soviet agreement. Therefore, he did not think war was imminent. Thus, he saw no reason to withdraw.

Evacuating Quemoy and Matsu would have a catastrophic psychological effect on his own government's prestige and America's, Chiang claimed. "Speaking among friends and in the greatest confidence, Gimo stated that if decision were made by Chinese Government to abandon Quemoy and Matsu none of Chinese people would support Government's decision. He would be unable to lead them."

Irritated as he was by the US proposal, Chiang claimed not to be surprised. He said that at the time of the Tachens withdrawal, he had forecast pressures would come to give up Quemoy and Matsu also. The British would be the instigators, as well as "some elements" in the United States. But Chiang said he did not expect such pressures to persuade Eisenhower.

Earlier in the evening, Radford had addressed military justifications for Eisenhower's decision. Robertson added a political dimension. As the administration made clear during Yeh's visits to the State Department, any US commitments concerning Quemoy and Matsu were unilateral decisions that could be withdrawn at any time the president thought conditions had changed. When Eisenhower sent his January 31 message, he considered "then prevailing circumstances," Robertson said. But political conditions had altered, to the point that Eisenhower could not ignore them. Robertson claimed that "tremendous opposition" had built up both in Congress and among the American people to a conflict over Quemoy and Matsu, especially if it required atomic weapons.[61] In light of these circumstances, "President Eisenhower could not now use US forces in defense of these islands without large loss of public support at home and abroad."

Chiang replied that he recognized Eisenhower's right to shift direction, but he would stay the course. Before the meeting broke for dinner, Robertson urged Chiang not to reject the proposal outright and to reserve further consideration. That got nowhere. As Robertson recounted, "Following dinner Gimo indicated quite firmly that he considered his answer to have been definitive and that he did not desire to resume discussions for the present."

The generalissimo departed. For a short while, the discussion continued with Foreign Minister Yeh, who conveyed Chiang's feeling of betrayal. "He stated that Gimo had not anticipated any proposal from US which would involve abandoning Quemoy and Matsu to Communists inasmuch as Gimo was so firmly convinced that he had been given positive assurances by President Eisenhower that US would participate in their defense under conditions such as now existed."[62]

Robertson and Radford met again with the generalissimo on April 26. Skeptical and upset, Chiang would not budge. As Robertson recounted, "Gimo indicated he understood fully details and implications of our proposal. He stated primary consideration was one of confidence and trust, secondly that any proposal must be within reasonable bounds of compliance to each party. He lacked faith in US ability to adhere in face of outside pressures to proposed interdiction of the seaborne traffic after having given up islands. The abandonment of his little remaining territory at this time would be completely unacceptable to his people and to overseas Chinese everywhere, shattering their confidence in him as well as the United States."

Chiang resurfaced past grievances in his relations with the United States, citing examples where American actions or advice had put him in untenable circumstances. He mentioned the secret Yalta agreements and pressures Marshall brought during the Chinese civil war. As Chiang described it, and Robertson chronicled, that because of a "series of agreements to meet expedient proposals by United States he found himself at point where further concessions would lead to ultimate calamity."

Robertson continued, "He did not question motives of United States in past or present situation but indicated very strongly and emotionally his conviction that further concessions impossible." Chiang asked that his apology for being unable to acquiesce be conveyed to President Eisenhower.

Both Chiang and Yeh asked that Eisenhower's change of heart not be announced, and that members of Congress not be told. Such disclosure would be a green light for the Communists to attack, they said.[63]

On April 29, Ambassador Rankin prepared a Memorandum for the Record, setting out his impressions from Chiang's meeting with the Americans. "His reactions were as I had predicted," Rankin wrote. Beyond his unwillingness to abandon the islands, Chiang considered the shipping interdiction proposal unrealistic, not because it was militarily unworkable, but because he had little faith in America's word. "He evidently had no confidence that the United States would actually participate in an effective shipping interdiction scheme in the face of strong and inevitable opposition by the British and others," said Rankin. "In his view the proposal meant giving up Kinmen and Matsu in return for another undertaking from which the United States would find reason for withdrawing."

Chiang's biographer, Jay Taylor, reveals that the generalissimo was privately appalled by the Robertson-Radford mission. Citing Chiang's diary, Taylor writes, "He thought the Americans were 'completely deceiving' and 'naïve and ignorant' to think he would believe them. He also believed the proposal was a British-originated plot to get him off the offshore islands."[64]

Much harm had been done to the bilateral relationship. Rankin continued, "This morning (April 29) Foreign Minister Yeh gave me his opinion that it would require a great deal of effort to repair the damage to Chinese confidence in the United States which had resulted from the above proposals."

The generalissimo did not find credible Robertson's argument that a change in US public opinion required Eisenhower to alter course. "It is evident that President Chiang and his close advisers are puzzled and disturbed. They cannot understand why following a course of action authorized by an almost unanimous vote of the American Congress as recently as January 28 should three months later threaten to 'split the United States wide open.'"

Chiang and his advisers attributed the change to incessant Commonwealth pressure to steer Eisenhower. "They are aware of no significant change in circumstances except for a certain amount of emotion generated in the American press and elsewhere supposedly as a result of influence brought to bear by fellow travelers, Europe-firsters and the inevitable British," said Rankin.

What did such fecklessness, as Chiang saw it, portend for the American posture in the region? "President Chiang evidently interprets all of this as indicating that the domestic position of the United States Government makes it incapable of pursuing a firm and consistent Far Eastern policy."

Chiang had been courteous to his guests, even though he flatly rejected the proposal. But behind the façade, he was profoundly distressed. Rankin observed, "Throughout the conversations President Chiang made a great effort to restrain himself, in deference to his visitors from Washington. He put his case frankly but with fewer outward signs of emotion than I have sometimes observed in talks with him when I was the only American present. However, in actual fact, I have the distinct impression never before to have seen him more deeply affected."[65]

There could be no meeting of the minds. Eisenhower viewed the offshore islands as an indefensible military burden that might be cast aside. Chiang saw them as fundamental to the legitimacy of his own regime and his claim to be sovereign over all of China. Thomas Stolper observes,

> On the face of it, the loss of a few small islands should not have been a catastrophe for Taipei. Peking's forces would still have to cross 100 miles of turbulent ocean to reach Taiwan. Taipei would still have a guarantee of defense from the most powerful nation in the world. The explanation for Chiang's refusal to quit Quemoy and Matsu lay in his fear of anything that would lead to drawing a clear line down the middle of the Taiwan Straits and hence to the formal separation of Taiwan from the rest of China. Such a separation would have meant abandoning hope for a Nationalist reconquest to the mainland, and that admission would have given the Nationalists only two choices: to create an independent Taiwan or to come to terms with Peking.[66]

Eisenhower had hoped for a different answer from Chiang but was not entirely surprised at the outcome. In his memoirs, the president wrote, "Despite my disappointment, I could not help reflecting that if I had been in his position, I might well have made the same decision."[67]

TENSIONS IN THE STRAIT DIMINISH

War appeared possible, but in April 1955, the PRC took a step to defuse the situation.[68] Attending a meeting of African and Asian leaders in West Java, Indonesia, otherwise known as the conference, Chinese foreign minister Zhou Enlai proposed negotiations between his country and the United States to resolve issues in the Taiwan Strait. On April 24, during his closing speech to delegates, Zhou said, "China and the United States should sit down and enter into negotiations to settle the question of relaxing and eliminating the tension in the Taiwan area; though, of course, this should in no way affect the Chinese people's just demand for the exercise of their sovereign rights and liberating Taiwan."[69]

The American reaction to Zhou's overture was generally positive. At a news conference on April 27, Eisenhower indicated openness to negotiating, at least about a cease-fire, adding the caveat that the United States would not negotiate about the interests of the Nationalist Chinese behind their backs. "Last Saturday it was stated we were not going to talk about the affairs of Nationalist China except with them present. I believe that Mr. Dulles made this point clear also at his own press conference, saying we would not discuss the affairs of the Chinese Nationalists behind their back; but that as a test of good intent, if the Chi-Com wanted to talk merely about cease-fire, we would be glad to meet with them and talk with them, but there would be no conferring about the affairs of the Chinese Nationalists."

Always sensitive to any possibility that they would be abandoned, the Nationalists were soon at the State Department for clarification. Ambassador Koo called on Dulles on May 5 to ask whether the United States had taken steps to arrange negotiations with the Chinese Communists. Washington had done nothing of the sort, Dulles assured Koo, referring him to the president's news conference of the day previous, in which Eisenhower noted that several countries had stepped forward to offer their services as intermediaries, but no arrangements had been made.[70] "As a matter of fact, as far as this country is concerned, we are sort of in a wait-and-see attitude," Eisenhower stated.

Anxious about what the United States might negotiate with the Communists, Koo wondered what could be discussed when one of the parties to hostilities, the ROC, was not and would not be at the table and the United States would not be bargaining on the ROC's behalf. He also noted speculation in Taipei that, as part of such discussions, the United States would recognize the Communist government.

Dulles attempted to reassure him on both grounds. The secretary clarified that Washington had no intention to recognize the PRC. In addition, he said, the United States hoped to secure assurances from the Communists that they would not attack Formosa and the Pescadores or the offshore islands. Dulles indicated he did not expect the Communists to agree.

The secretary stated that the United States took seriously the consultation provisions of Article IV of the Mutual Defense Treaty and affirmed that there would not be negotiations involving the ROC's essential interests without the Nationalists present. Referring to the 1945 Crimean Conference in which the Big Three had secretly bargained over China's sovereignty, Koo said he would report to Taipei that "there would be no second Yalta."[71]

POTENTIAL INTERMEDIARIES STEP UP

On May 27, Eisenhower received a message from Indian prime minister Jawaharlal Nehru, reporting on discussions between Zhou and India's foreign minister Krishna Menon, who had come to Beijing at Zhou's invitation. "While we were not speaking on behalf of any country or Government," Nehru wrote, "we have at the same time felt that we have contacts with and the friendship of the main parties concerned, namely United States and China, and some knowledge of their respective positions. This as well as recent developments in respect of the problem on both sides also encouraged the belief that ways of fruitful negotiations could be found."

Nehru was referring to a US decision to permit repatriation of Chinese persons who had been unable to return home after the founding of the People's Republic,[72] and a Chinese decision to release four US airmen of the so-called Fischer Group. Accusing the flyers of violating Chinese airspace during the Korean war, China had imprisoned them for two years.[73]

"The recent talks in Peking have led me to the belief that steps both to reduce tension and to pave the way for negotiation can be established, and the desire to bring about this exists," Nehru continued.[74]

On May 26, Zhou met with British ambassador Humphrey Trevelyan, with the hope that London would encourage the Americans to negotiate. According to a British memorandum of that conversation, "The Chinese Government considered that the main topic in the negotiations between the United States and the Chinese Government should be the easing and removal of tension in the Formosa area." Zhou differentiated between internal and international negotiations. He stressed that while Beijing would be willing to discuss peaceful unification with the Nationalists, Taipei could not have a seat at the table in any international meetings in which the PRC participated.[75]

By July 3, Dulles had met with intermediaries from India, Burma, and Indonesia, and listened to a myriad of proposals. However, no progress had been made in launching the negotiations and the American airmen were still confined. The secretary considered it was time to speak directly with the Chinese. In a memorandum to Under Secretary Hoover, Dulles wrote, "I am getting fed up with all the intermediaries."[76]

On July 11, Dulles sent a message to Beijing, via the British embassy.

Your and our consular representatives at Geneva have been having intermittent talks during the past year regarding the repatriation of civilians who desired to return to their respective countries. The results have been disappointing to us. It has been suggested that it would aid in settling this matter if these talks were conducted on a more authoritative level, and that this could facilitate further discussion and settlement of certain other practical matters now at issue between the two of us. If you think well of this, we will designate a representative of ambassadorial rank to meet on the above basis with your representative of comparable rank at Geneva on a mutually agreeable day.[77]

From Paris, Dulles cabled the State Department on July 16. He asked that congressional leaders be advised of his outreach to Zhou, and that the talks be understood as implementing Zhou's statement at Bandung and the US reply. Again referring to the Indians and Burmese, Dulles added, "We have come to the conclusion that operating through intermediaries is dangerous, particularly these intermediaries, and that direct contact is preferable." That notwithstanding, Dulles cautioned, no inference of diplomatic recognition could be made. The secretary indicated he would designate Ambassador U. Alexis Johnson to represent the United States in the negotiations.[78]

TALKS ARE PREPARED

On July 16, Dulles sent a message to Zhou via the British Foreign Office proposing that direct talks commence on August 1. Zhou agreed. An identical announcement was made in Washington and Beijing at 10:00 a.m., July 25, 1955. It read,

> As a result of communication between the United States and the People's Republic of China through the diplomatic channels of the United Kingdom, it has been agreed that talks held in the last year between consular representatives of both sides at Geneva should be resumed on ambassadorial level in order to aid in settling the matter of the repatriation of civilians who desire to return to their respective countries and to facilitate further discussions and settlement of certain other practical matters now at issue between both sides. The first meeting of ambassadorial representatives of both sides will take place on August 1, 1955, at Geneva.[79]

In a July 26 press conference, Dulles stated, "Both the Republic of China and the Chinese People's Republic claim that the area held by the other is part of China. But in connection with the Mutual Security Treaty which the United States made with the Republic of China, it was agreed that the Republic of China would not use force except as a matter of joint agreement, subject to action of an emergency character which was clearly an exercise of the inherent right of self-defense."

"We believe that the principle of non-recourse to force is valid not merely for the United States and its allies but that it is valid for all," Dulles went on. "We shall hope to find out in the forthcoming talks whether the Chinese

Communists accept the concept of a cease-fire in accordance with the United Nations principle of avoiding any use or threat of force which could disturb the peace of nations."

There was a chance the talks could be broadened beyond repatriation. "No doubt the Chinese Communists will have matters of their own to bring up. We shall listen to hear what they are, and if they directly involve the United States and Communist China, we will be disposed to discuss them with a view to arriving at a peaceful settlement."[80]

Ambassador Wellington Koo met with Robertson on July 28, wanting to know about the breadth of Johnson's mandate and ensuring it would not involve the rights and interests of the Republic of China.[81] Robertson assured him it would not.

What about a cease-fire? Could Johnson discuss that? Koo carried a message from Foreign Minister Yeh that expressed grave reservations about any such discussion. Yeh wrote, "Our two Governments have a formal understanding that no major military action will be undertaken in this area by either of us except by mutual agreement. The withdrawal from the Tachens has not brought about peace. Aggressive action in the Taiwan Strait has come and can only come from Peiping. Any offer from your representative to discuss ceasefire is likely to invite further demands from Peiping."

Yeh worried about the implications a cease-fire might have for reconquering China. Just as the Communists would not renounce force to gain control of Formosa, neither could the Nationalists do so without abandoning their quest to recover the mainland. "We shall abide by the understanding reached with you as our trusted ally," he said, "but may I emphasize again that any open cease-fire pledge on our part will destroy the very basis of our being and kill all hope of our brethren on the mainland for eventual liberation. I believe it is in our interest and yours to keep such hope alive. Our pledge to you must not be used or hinted at to trade for any Communist promise, which we know they will not honor. I shall much appreciate your assurance on this point."

Robertson refused to provide it. Although Koo asked several times, he would not exclude discussions that could secure a renunciation of force from the Communists. If that could be achieved, much tension would dissipate. The United States had a direct interest in exploring this issue, Robertson said, because the Mutual Defense Treaty bound it to defend Formosa if the PRC attacked.

Robertson told Koo that the United States supported the unification of Korea and of Germany but would not go to war to pursue it. Similarly, while the United States would defend Formosa, it would not support Nationalist efforts to unify China by force.

Johnson received his 18-point instructions from Dulles on July 29. They stated that the purpose of the talks in Geneva was to resolve repatriation issues, although the secretary added that "we are not, however, willing to promise political concessions to secure release of Americans held in China."

Dulles held out the possibility that "other practical matters now at issue between both sides" could be discussed. Prisoner of war exchanges and aviation safety protocols were examples. However, the talks could not embrace topics "which involve the rights of the Republic of China."

The United States should try to get an assurance that the Chinese People's Republic would renounce the use of force. "If the CPR representative contends that the use of force in the Formosa area is justifiable because this involves a domestic matter, that is, the unification of China, you may point out that the fact of a divided China is not basically different from the fact of a divided Korea, Germany, and Vietnam. It could be argued in each of these cases that unification is purely an internal matter. But in reality, resort to force would endanger international peace and security. The same applies to China."

Zhou Enlai addressed the National People's Congress on July 30, blaming the United States for tensions in the strait. The cause, he asserted, was "the United States' occupation of Chinese territory, Taiwan, and its interference with the liberation of China's coastal islands."

Referring to his Bandung Declaration, Zhou added, "During the Asian-African Conference, the Chinese government already proposed that China and the United States should sit down and enter into negotiations to discuss the question of easing and eliminating the tension in the Taiwan area." He continued, "There is no war between China and the United States," Zhou noted. "The peoples of China and the United States are friendly toward each other; the Chinese people want no war with the United States."

Although China would not renounce the possibility of force, Zhou affirmed that "conditions permitting, the Chinese people are ready to seek the liberation of Taiwan by peaceful means." Key to this happening was for the United States to step aside and cease supporting the Nationalists. "Provided that the United States does not interfere with China's internal affairs, the possibility of peaceful liberation of Taiwan will continue to increase. If possible, the Chinese government is willing to enter into negotiations with the responsible local authorities of Taiwan to map out concrete steps for Taiwan's peaceful liberation."

Unification was then, and would remain, a core issue for both the Communists and the Nationalists. On that much, they could agree. As Zhou Enlai stressed, "The Chinese people are firmly opposed to any ideas or plots of the so-called two Chinas."[82]

In his memoirs, Eisenhower describes the very broad range of advice he received for how to respond to the Formosa crisis. He recounts hearing from former British prime minister Clement Attlee that Chiang should be overthrown and from the sitting prime minister, Anthony Eden, that Chiang should be forced to relinquish Quemoy and Matsu. Senators Lehman, Morse, and Kennedy would have precluded America from defending those islands, while Admiral Arthur Radford would have intervened in the Tachens and bombed the mainland. Senator Knowland recommended blockading the Chinese coast. And some ideas were more far-reaching. Syngman Rhee suggested that the United States join him and Chiang in a war to liberate China from Communism.[83]

Eisenhower wrote, "The administration rejected all of these suggestions threading its way with watchfulness and determination through narrow and dangerous waters between appeasement and global war. For nine months the administration moved through treacherous crosscurrents with one channel leading to peace with honor and a hundred channels leading to war or dishonor."

"The hard way," he concluded, "is to have the courage to be patient."[84]

NOTES

1. *FRUS, 1955–1957 Vol. II China*, pp. 251–258. Before the outbreak of the Korean War, senior American strategists had considered the trusteeship idea. Assistant Secretary of State Dean Rusk and State Department special consultant John Foster Dulles were favorable to the idea, which would keep Formosa out of Communist hands even if Chiang's government collapsed (Tucker, p. 187). Once the war began, Truman interposed the Seventh Fleet in the strait, and Chiang had a new lease on life. "For the Nationalist Chinese, the struggle in Korea had come as if by magic at the last possible moment before disaster engulfed them" (*FRUS, 1955–1957 Vol. II China*, p. 198).

2. A March 16 National Intelligence Estimate assessed that, considering the Mutual Defense Treaty, the Chinese Communists could not seize Formosa and would not attempt to do so in 1955. However, if willing to absorb substantial casualties, the Communists could successfully attack Quemoy and Matsu, if the islands were defended by the Nationalists only. Continued bombardment and interdiction of supplies should be expected, said the NIE, in an effort to weaken the Nationalists' hold on the islands and to test US intentions. However, the Communists would be unlikely to seize the islands in 1955 if they concluded that doing so would provoke a conflict with the United States, including attacks on the Chinese mainland (Ibid., pp. 376–377).

3. Ibid. Stolper speculates that the PRC would not have moved solely against Quemoy and Matsu for the paradoxical reason that success might have destabilized Chiang and motivated the United States to assume control of Formosa with a puppet government (Stolper, p. 86).

4. American military planners did not share Churchill's assessment of the defensive importance of the islands. On February 24, chairman of the JCS, Arthur Radford, wrote, "Importance Matsu and Kinmen stems from psychological as well

as military considerations. They are part of Gimo's defense of Formosa. They are his outposts and warning stations, which block two key port areas, use of which Chicoms probably would want in any invasion attempt against Formosa. Their retention by ChiNats makes most difficult secret build up by Chicoms for invasion of Formosa and Pescadores." The Americans also placed far more emphasis than the British on the issue of morale. "Matsu and Kinmen offer Nationalist leadership their one hope for reestablishing themselves on the mainland. . . . Should we barter away their one hope so quickly, it could have serious repercussions psychologically among ChiNats and all through the Far East. Geographically and militarily, loss might be inconsequential, but diplomatic and psychological repercussions might be out of all proportion to its physical importance" (*FRUS, 1955–1957 Vol. II China*, p. 304).

5. *FRUS, 1955–1957, Vol. II China*, pp. 270–272.

6. Ibid.

7. Other Commonwealth countries shared this assessment of Chiang's prospects. In a 1964 oral history for Princeton University, former New Zealand foreign minister Sir Thomas MacDonald observed, "Well, that just didn't seem to be on. And until he had conditions right for getting to the mainland—and the conditions right meant he had a very large percentage of the population to be on his side. Well, nothing that we could learn—reading of articles, people who'd been in Communist China—nothing would indicate that position had been reached. And until he did reach that position that there was violent discontent all over the place and he had some hope of getting assistance from the local population—well, such an invasion just wasn't on." http://arks.princeton.edu/ark:/88435/6q182r41z (accessed February 7, 2022)

8. *FRUS, 1955–1957 Vol. II China*, pp. 270–272.

9. Ibid.

10. In a February 25 cable to the State Department from Bangkok, Dulles recited the constraints. "We made a treaty with the Republic of China which excluded from the treaty area all positions held by the Republic of China except Formosa and the Pescadores, which we committed ourselves to defend as against armed attack. We negotiated an agreement with the Republic of China whereby it agreed not to carry on offensive actions from any territory held by it except in agreement with the US and not to weaken the defense of Formosa by the diversion and expenditure elsewhere of elements of power contributed to it by the US" (Ibid., p. 310).

11. Ibid., pp. 276–277.

12. Stephen Ambrose notes the conflict between Eisenhower's and Churchill's views on the islands. "Eisenhower was saying that the loss of Quemoy and Matsu would lead to the loss of the entire western position in Asia. Churchill was not convinced. He said all that the Chicoms wanted was Quemoy and Matsu (and implied that he agreed with them that the islands rightly belonged to China)" (Ambrose, p. 236).

13. *FRUS, 1955–1957 Vol. II China*, pp. 293–295.

14. Walter Robertson recalls, "We had decided that we would not yield to the pressures of the British and others of our allies to force the Chinese off of these islands" (Robertson, p. 42).

15. Ibid., pp. 308–310. Eden accurately described opinion within the Common-wealth. In a March 14 Washington meeting with Dulles, Australian prime minister Robert Menzies noted that sentiment in the Australian House of Commons was that Quemoy and Matsu were unimportant to the defense of Formosa and should promptly be abandoned to the Communists. While Australia would support a war to defend freedom, it would not support going to war over the offshore islands. Dulles rebut-ted with an argument about destroying Nationalist morale and indicated the United States would not have sufficient troops to replace of Chiang's army on Formosa if that army lost the will to fight (Ibid., pp. 368–371). On March 16, British ambassador Sir Roger Makins dispatched a memorandum to the State Department reinforcing his country's position with military and political arguments. "We agree that the Chinese Communists will not accept the retention of Formosa by the Nationalists; but it is our belief that given the clear United States determination to defend Formosa (and the Pescadores) they will not in fact contest the issue by force." Makins continued,

"There may always be an explosion, but it seems to us that would be more likely to come at present from miscalculation than deliberate policy on the part of the Chinese. That is why in our view it is so important to exercise moderation in our statements and attitudes lest we frighten the Asians into China's arms. This is one of the reasons why we would like to see the coastal islands evacuated. Our judgment is based not only on the military case for evacuation but also on the fact that the American position would be easier to justify vis-a-vis world and Asian opinion were these islands not in question." (Ibid., pp. 374–375)

16. Ibid., p. 310.

17. Ibid., pp. 312–313.

18. Ibid., pp. 418–422.

19. An April 16, 1955, National Intelligence Estimate noted that, as to a return to the mainland, "actual expectations appear to have dimmed, notably among the higher civil and military echelons. . . . As long as three years ago officials in private conversations would admit that, contrary to public assurances, they actually harbored little hope of ever returning to the mainland except in the event of a general war" (Ibid., p. 482).

20. According to Chiang, Dulles supported the Nationalists' fervor to return to the mainland but de-emphasized the importance or use of military force in achieving that objective. If political conditions were not ripe, Dulles believed, force would be ineffective. As Chiang put it, "Mr. Dulles, throughout the discussions with us, expressed himself as being in sympathy with our national cause, and he was in favor of—would like to see us back on the mainland—to regain the mainland and all that. But he was trying to suggest that probably in trying to attain our goal, less importance be given, less emphasis be given, to the use of force than, say, to the use of political means" (Chiang and Madame Chiang, p. 27).

21. The April 16, 1955, NIE stated that "Chiang Kai-shek is the outstanding sym-bol of hope for return to the mainland and the chief creator and perpetuator of this hope. . . . His steadfastness and personifying return to the mainland has been respon-sible for sustaining this objective, however remote or infeasible it might be. . . . If

the Chinese Nationalists on Taiwan came to believe that there could be no return to the mainland, the effect upon morale and upon Chiang Kai-shek's personal prestige would be seriously adverse" (*FRUS, 1955–1957, Vol. II China*, p. 482).

22. In a March 13, 1955, letter to Assistant Secretary Robertson, US ambassador Rankin elaborated on Chiang's concern about two Chinas and actions that might be taken to lead to that outcome. "Probably much more serious to Free China's morale than the loss of additional small islands would be any formal steps toward the two Chinas project. From the Chinese point of view these might include the entry of the Peiping regime into the United Nations and or its recognition by the United States. Any cease-fire, except possibly of definitely limited duration, would have similar implications to them. Obviously, anything which would indicate definitive United States acquiescence in the Communist conquest of the Chinese mainland would represent irretrievable disaster in the Free Chinese eyes." Abandoning Quemoy and Matsu must be seen in the two-China context, said Rankin, because it would implicitly draw "a line down the Formosa Strait" (Ibid., p. 362).

23. Rankin, p. 234.

24. *FRUS, 1955–1957, Vol. II China*, pp. 320–328.

25. A March 10 memorandum of the National Security Council elaborates on Dulles's position. "At this particular moment, the United States could not sit idly by and watch the Chinese Nationalist forces on Quemoy and the Matsus sustain a terrific defeat or be wiped out without such repercussions that would be likely to lose Formosa itself as a result. Nor, on the other hand, could we force the Chinese Nationalists to agree to evacuate these offshore islands." (Ibid., p. 350). In a discussion with Dulles on the following day, Eisenhower concurred with this position. (Ibid., pp. 353–354).

26. Chang and Di, p. 1517.

27. Ibid., pp. 336–337. The following day, Dulles had a similar conversation with Senate Foreign Relations Committee chairman Walter George. He assured the senator that the atomic weapons that would be used were not weapons of mass destruction. "I said that the missiles we had in mind had practically no radioactive fall-out and were entirely local in effect" (*FRUS, 1955–1957, Vol. II China*, pp. 337–338). This relatively rosy assessment did not square with CIA estimates that a nuclear attack of the kind envisioned could kill 12–14 million civilians (Kinzer, p. 200). The Chinese also anticipated the Americans would use atomic weapons. Senior Chinese officers, including Su Yu, the PLA's deputy chief of staff, analyzed the possibility. According to M. Taylor Fravel, "most Chinese generals believed that nuclear weapons would be used in strategic bombing campaigns at the start of a war. When combined with the advent of jet propulsion, Su Yu described the future war in 1955 as starting with an 'atomic blitz' in which aircraft would be used to bomb industrial centers, cities, and military targets" (Fravel, p. 79).

28. Shu Guang Zhang, p. 213.

29. Evan Thomas, *Ike's Bluff: President Eisenhower's Secret Battle to Save the World* (New York: Little, Brown and Company, 2012), p. 139.

30. A March 16 memo from the Director of Central Intelligence Allen Dulles to his brother states, "There continues to be reason to believe that the problem of Chinese Nationalist vulnerability to subversion is more serious than is generally

recognized. . . . The Chinese Communists are clearly conducting a psychological warfare effort against the Chinese Nationalists, parallel with the military effort, as was the pattern in Communist operations during the civil war on the mainland. . . . Communist spokesmen have said both privately and publicly in recent months that they believe the island will fall through a combination of Communist military action and internal uprisings" (*FRUS, 1955–1957, Vol. II China*, pp. 380–381).

31. Ibid., pp. 344–350. The March 16 National Intelligence Estimate assessed that Nationalist withdrawal from the offshore islands, whether or not under US pressure, would have an adverse effect on morale and opinion on Taiwan, in South Korea, and in the Philippines, and could have a similar, though less pronounced effect in Southeast Asian countries. Elsewhere in the non-Communist world, the NIE said, the reaction would be relief (Ibid., p. 380).

32. Ibid., p. 347. A March 16 National Intelligence Estimate assessed the impact on world opinion from use of atomic weapons. It declared, "If the US used nuclear weapons against Communist China, the predominant world reaction would be one of shock. These reactions would be particularly adverse if these weapons were used to defend the offshore islands or destroy military concentrations prior to an all-out Communist Chinese attempt to take the offshore islands." Attitudes might be different if such weapons were used to stop an invasion of Taiwan (Ibid., p. 379).

33. Ambrose, p. 238. In a 1957 article for *Foreign Affairs*, Dulles further developed the case for tactical nuclear weapons. He wrote,

"the resourcefulness of those who serve our nation in the science and weapons engineering now shows that it is possible to alter the character of nuclear weapons. It seems now that their use need not involve vast destruction and widespread harm to humanity. Recent tests point to the possibility of possessing nuclear weapons the destructiveness and radiation effects of which can be confined substantially to predetermined targets. In the future. It may thus be feasible to place less reliance upon deterrence of vast retaliatory power. It may be possible to defend countries by nuclear weapons, so mobile, or so placed, as to make military invasion with conventional forces a hazardous attempt."

John Foster Dulles "Challenges and Response in United States Policy," *Foreign Affairs*, October 1957.

34. *The Public Papers of the President: Dwight D. Eisenhower: 1955* (Washington, DC: US GPO), p. 56. William Hitchcock notes that the threat was effective. "The nuclear-saber rattling had the desired effect. On April 23, the Chinese Foreign Minister, Zhou Enlai, announced that China wanted no war with the United States and stressed China's desire for friendship with the American people. The shelling of the islands fell off dramatically and the crisis was dispelled." At the same time, Hitchcock writes, the brinksmanship may have propelled China to build its own nuclear weapon, which it successfully tested in 1964 (Hitchcock, p. 209). However, Professor Chester Pach, Jr., questions the deterrent value of the threat, given Mao's views about the probability the United States would actually deploy such a weapon and China's ability to survive its use. "Mao Zedong often questioned the credibility of US threats and insisted that the Chinese could withstand any losses that came from a nuclear attack." Chester J. Pach, Jr. "Dwight D. Eisenhower Foreign Affairs," University

of Virginia Miller Center. Chen Jian offers a similar observation. "Mao would offer describe nuclear weapons as nothing but a 'paper tiger'" (Chen Jian, p. 190).

35. Shu Guang Zhang notes that, in the aftermath of the crisis, Mao was determined that China should have nuclear weapons capability. "Mao, having felt the threat of US nuclear attack, began to realize the real power of such weapons and, unable to secure any commitment from Moscow for a nuclear counterattack in the event of a US nuclear strike at China decided that China therefore needed to build its own nuclear weapons" (Shu Guang Zhang, pp. 221–222).

36. Divine, p. 63. "Furious with Carney and irate at the press for its sensation mindlessness, Eisenhower immediately moved to muzzle him and to correct the impression of an impending showdown. He apparently did not pause to consider how the nuclear warnings issued by him and other top officials might have contributed to the scare headlines he now deplored" (Accinelli, p. 217).

37. Anthony Leviero, "US Expects Chinese Reds to Attack Isles in April; Weights All-Out Defense," *New York Times*, March 26, 1955, p. 1.

38. Halperin, pp. 239–240. Ambrose, p. 239.

39. Accinelli, p. 218.

40. Ibid., p. 405.

41. Ibid., pp. 424–428.

42. Quoted in Foster Rhea Dulles, p. 159.

43. Eisenhower assessed that the islands would be difficult to defend because their location so close to the Chinese mainland would minimize the utility of US naval forces. Such proximity also increased vulnerability to an amphibious attack. "In view of the overwhelming land forces available to the Red Chinese and the strength of any bombardment that could be brought to bear on the islands, any successful defense would necessarily require counteraction against the mainland of China itself," the president wrote, adding that such action would likely mean use of atomic weapons. Even a successful defense would not remove the long-term threat, Eisenhower said, meaning that both the United States and the ROC, once committed, "would be led to immobilize more and more military strength for the single purpose of defending the offshore islands" (Ibid., pp. 446–447).

44. Accinelli, p. 221.

45. "Administration officials, though, were still trying to avoid the moment of decision between war and retreat in event that deterrence failed. To this end, Dulles recommended a withdrawal, combined with a naval blockade. He wanted to persuade Chang to evacuate the offshore islands, and then to blockade the 500 miles of Chinese coast along the Taiwan Strait, with elements of the Seventh Fleet and the Fifth Air Force already in the area" (Shi Guang Zhang, p. 215). Gordon H. Chang and He Di point out how escalatory the blockade would have been. "Neither Beijing nor Washington had wanted direct conflict, and Chiang's acceptance of the evacuation and blockade plan would have brought the situation precipitously close to an inadvertent war. As a provocative fait accompli, the blockade would have invited Communist retaliation, including clashes between US and Chinese forces" (Gordon H. Chang and He Di, pp. 1519–1520).

46. Walter Robertson recounts, "Now President Eisenhower is a military man and he, personally, from a purely strategic standpoint, did not give the islands the same strategic importance that the Chinese Nationalists did. We would have been delighted if the Chinese Nationalists had voluntarily evacuated these people and their forces there" (Robertson, p. 41).

47. *FRUS, 1955–1957, Vol. II China*, pp. 445–450.

48. The statement assessed that the same purpose could be served by naval vessels, thus drawing the conclusion that "the offshore islands are useful, but not essential, to the defense of Taiwan itself" (Ibid., p. 458).

49. This was especially true because of Eisenhower's "New Look" defense posture, which de-emphasized spending on the army and navy and invested more in aviation and nuclear weapons. According to Stephen Ambrose, "Because of the New Look, the United States did not have the strength to defend the islands by conventional arms" (Ambrose, p. 238).

50. A former medical missionary in China, Walter Judd had a similar perspective. In his oral history, he noted, "The whole Asian world, the whole two-thirds of the world, which is non-Caucasian, has always felt that the United States in a showdown will always stand with white people. We will always stand with the British and the French. This is why when we talk about our principles and so on, in Asia they don't pay much attention. They figure that we will never stand on principle if it's against our traditional allies, the whites, and especially the British and French" (Oral History, Judd, p. 129).

51. *FRUS, 1955–1957, Vol. II China*, pp. 455–463.

52. Ibid., pp. 473–475.

53. "Worried that the fall of the heavily defended offshore islands to China would be as damaging as the fall of Dien Bien Phu, Eisenhower had sent Walter Robertson, assistant Secretary of State for Far Eastern Affairs, and Admiral Arthur Radford, chairman of the Joint Chiefs of Staff to Taiwan in April 1955 to persuade Chiang to reduce his forces on the islands." Appu K Soman, "'Who's Daddy' in the Taiwan Strait: The Offshore Islands Crisis of 1958," *The Journal of American-East Asian Relations*, Vol. 3, No. 4 (Winter 1994), p. 375.

54. Ibid., pp. 501–502.

55. Ibid., p. 509.

56. Congress strongly opposed Communist China's admission to the United Nations. On July 15, 1954, the House unanimously passed a resolution to that effect. The Senate followed suit two weeks later with a similar provision in a foreign assistance appropriations bill (Rankin. p. 198). It was not the first time. For example, on July 21, 1953, the House passed a sense of the Congress resolution that the Communists were not entitled to China's seat in the UN. It passed 379–0. The Senate later concurred. To the degree there was controversy, it was over the idea, advanced by Knowland and other Nationalist supporters, that the United States should withdraw from the UN if the Chinese Communists were admitted. Democratic senators like Morse, Lehman, and Fulbright took exception to that approach. *Congressional Record*, July 2, 1954, pp. 9585–9588.

57. Five airfields were being built. Construction had begun in March 1955.

58. In his oral history, Robertson states, "He had 50,000 troops on Quemoy at that time, and President Eisenhower thought it was too heavy a concentration of his troops on these outposts. They ought to be defended all right, but they ought to be defended as outposts, so that if they were lost it wouldn't be a catastrophic thing" (Robertson, pp. 41–42).

59. "The purpose of the evacuation blockade proposal was to get the administration off the hook in the offshore islands, under conditions that would save face for Chiang and the United States and undergird the security of Taiwan. The removal of the Generalissimo's forces would eliminate the islands as a locus of conflict between the CCP and KMT, and as a potential *casus belli* for the United States. With the protection afforded by the Strait and the Seventh Fleet, the transplanted forces would be much safer on Taiwan. American prestige and military power would no longer remain handcuffed to the defense of militarily unessential territory that was constantly exposed to attack or intrusion from the nearby mainland." (Accinelli, p. 223)

60. Sir Walter Nash, New Zealand's ambassador to the United Nations, explained in an oral history that Quemoy and Matsu were especially important to Chiang because they were indisputably connected to mainland China. "The facts behind it were that Quemoy and Matsu were the only two places that Chiang Kai-shek had a foot in that was the mainland of China. Those were the only two places left because—not jumping off places necessarily, no—but this is the place of our own mainland that we hold." Nash, p. 9. http://arks.princeton.edu/ark:/88435/ks65hj48h (accessed February 6, 2022).

61. Historian Thomas E. Stolper notes that near-unanimous support in Congress for defending Formosa sharply eroded when the question involved defending the offshore islands. "The near unanimity of American opinion in favor of the defense of Taiwan disappeared when discussion turned to the offshore islands. Only the all-out backers of Chiang Kai-shek in the United States wanted a firm commitment to the offshores" (Stolper, pp. 10–11).

62. *FRUS, 1955–1957, Vol. II China*, pp. 510–517. A summary prepared by the Office of the Historian at the US State Department outlines the quid pro quo that Chiang thought the Americans had given following passage of the Formosa Resolution. "The US Government then announced its determination to defend Taiwan against Communist attack, although it did not specify the territory included within its defense perimeter. In exchange for a private promise to defend Jinmen and Mazu, however, Chiang Kai-shek agreed to withdraw his troops from Dachen, which was strategically ambiguous and difficult to defend." Office of the Historian, US Department of State, "The Taiwan Straits Crisis: 1954–55 and 1958."

63. Ibid., pp. 523–525.

64. Taylor, p. 481.

65. *FRUS, 1955–1957, Vol. II China*, pp. 528–531.

66. Stolper, p. 80.

67. Eisenhower, p. 482.

68. "A combination of factors—the limited initial objective, the concern about provoking the large-scale military conflict with the United States, and the fear of a US nuclear counterattack—eventually led the CCP leaders to look for a diplomatic solution to the tensions in the Taiwan Strait" (Shu Guang Zhang, p. 222).

69. Wilson Center Digital Archive, "Speech by Premier Zhou Enlai at the Closing Session of the Asian-African Conference," April 24, 1955. www.digitalarchive .wilsoncenter.org (accessed January 7, 2022).

70. Britain, India, Pakistan, Burma, and Indonesia had individually been involved in discussions with each side. The United States had not sought any of them to serve as an intermediary.

71. *FRUS, 1955–1957, Vol. II China*, pp. 545–549.

72. The plight of Chinese who came to the United States before 1949 as students and wished to repatriate but were denied permission to return home is set out in a front-page article by Harrison Salisbury in the June 3, 1955, *New York Times*. Salisbury writes, "A handful actually did return, but most were barred by detainer orders that the Immigration Service issued after the entry of Chinese Communist forces in the Korean War in 1950. This prevented most Chinese in the scientific, engineering, or technical fields from going back to China." Harrison Salisbury, "US is Criticized on China Students," *New York Times*, June 3, 1955, p. 1. See also Yelong Han, "An Untold Story: American Policy Toward Chinese Students in the United States 1949–1955," *The Journal of American-East Asian Relations,* Vol. 2, No. 1, Special Issue: The Impact of the Korean War (Spring 1993), pp. 77–99.

A related and highly celebrated case was that of Qian Xuesen, a leading rocket scientist, who served on the faculty of CalTech, but who came under suspicion for Communist sympathies and was detained in the United States for five years. After the United States deported him, Qian returned to China and became the father of China's jet propulsion and rocket programs, including the launch of the first Chinese satellite into space. "Qian Xuesen: The Man the US Deported – Who Then Helped China into Space," www.bbc.com, October 27, 2020 (accessed January 7, 2022). Eisenhower was personally involved in the decision to let Qian go. In a Memorandum of Conversation, dated June 10, 1955, Dulles wrote, "The President said he thought that the Chinese had come here with an implied understanding that they could go home. . . . He said he thought we should let all of the Chinese go back. I said there were two that Defense was dubious about because they had highly classified information. The President thought that this should not be an obstacle, that perhaps the information was not as valuable as we thought" (*FRUS, 1955–1957, Vol. II China*, pp. 588–589).

73. "Harold E. Fischer, Jr., An American Flyer Tortured in a Chinese Prison, Dies at 83," *New York Times*, May 8, 2009. His release and that of his compatriots had been the subject of inconclusive diplomacy by UN secretary general Dag Hammarskjold.

74. *FRUS 1955–1957 Vol. II China.*, pp. 574–575.

75. Ibid., pp. 580–583. Zhou also met with Indonesian prime minister Mohammed Ali, the essence of which the Indonesian ambassador conveyed to the State Department on June 13. Zhou told Ali that there were two issues to be settled by international negotiation. One was the activities of the Seventh Fleet and the other was the presence of the US military on Formosa. Such negotiations could be bilateral or involve other countries, but they could not include the Nationalists. The internal negotiation would be with the Nationalists only and concerned reunification with the mainland (Ibid., pp. 591–593).

76. *FRUS, 1955–1957, Vol. II China*, pp. 630–631. Referring to the Indians and the Burmese, Dulles wrote to Robertson on July 5, "As you know, I think there is a need to do something and I feel that some direct contacts are less dangerous than the kind of ineffectual intermediary activities of such persons as Menon and U Nu, who I think are not hardheaded enough to report accurately to us what the Chinese Communists really think or vice versa." (Ibid., p. 631). It was Zhou who had encouraged the used of intermediaries because ongoing Geneva talks with the United States on repatriation had been very unproductive (Ibid., p. 650).

77. Ibid., p. 643. Robertson was skeptical that the talks would produce much, or even that they could extend beyond repatriation issues without intruding upon the fundamental interests of the Nationalists (Ibid., pp. 648–649). GRC is an abbreviation standing for the Government of the Republic of China.

78. Ibid., pp. 658–659.

79. Ibid., p. 660.

80. Ibid., pp. 679–680.

81. Nervous about being sold out, the Nationalists regarded the US-PRC Geneva talks suspiciously. "The Chinese government on Taiwan regarded these Geneva sessions with grave misgivings. . . . But were these contacts with the Communists to continue in the manner that would lead to formal recognition of Peiping?" (Rankin, p. 247).

82. *FRUS, 1955–1957, Vol. II China*, pp. 688–689.

83. On July 28, 1954, Rhee spoke to a joint meeting of the US Congress. After outlining the resources available to win an anti-Communist crusade, he exclaimed, "The return of the Chinese mainland to the site of the free world would automatically produce a victorious end to the wars in Korea and Indochina and would swing the balance of power so strongly against the Soviet Union that it would not dare to risk war with the United States. Unless we win China back, an ultimate victory for the free world is unthinkable." "Text of Rhee's Address to Congress," *New York Times*, July 28, 1954, p. 2.

84. Eisenhower, *Mandate*, p. 483.

Chapter 10

A Crisis Renewed

A tense but nonetheless continuous peace existed in the region after the first Formosa Strait crisis abated.[1] On August 1, 1955, talks commenced in Geneva between the US ambassador to Czechoslovakia U. Alexis Johnson and the Chinese ambassador to Poland Wang Pingnan.[2]

Between the first talk and December 12, 1957, there were 73 such meetings.[3] Thereafter, Ambassador Johnson was reassigned. China was offered a replacement interlocutor of lower than ambassadorial rank but refused to meet with him. Thus, the discussions were suspended until September 1958, when they resumed, in Warsaw with US ambassador to Poland, Jacob Beam, representing the United States. Periodic meetings would continue there until 1970.[4] Although the sessions yielded little in the way of improvement in US-China relations, they were the sole avenue of Sino-American dialogue for many years.

After the 1955 crisis toned down, Chiang reinforced the Nationalist garrisons on the offshore islands, to the point that some 100,000 troops were stationed there, amounting to one-third of his total combat-ready forces.[5] American defense planners did not consider these forces, however substantial, to be strong enough to withstand a Communist assault on the islands without American help, but making vulnerable such a high proportion of his army put Chiang's survival at risk. Historian Appu Soman speculates that Chiang's reason for doing so was to raise the stakes for the survival of the Nationalist government and make it imperative for the United States to defend the islands.[6]

The Communists were to claim that the reinforcement and supply of these garrisons was a precipitating cause of a renewed strait crisis in 1958. Mao viewed with alarm America's downgrading of the Geneva talks, a May 1957 announcement that Washington would deploy tactical nuclear missiles to Formosa, and the further entrenchment of the US military on the island. Beijing believed the United States intended to occupy Formosa permanently, intruding on China's sovereignty and obstructing its unification.[7] According to Soman, "US policy appeared to the Chinese at be aimed at the creation of two Chinas at a minimum to threatening the very existence of the PRC."[8]

To prevent this, the Communists would have to upend the status quo. Thus, Mao sought a high-stakes fight that would trap the United States in an overextended commitment to Chiang. He saw obligations to the ROC as a noose for the United States that China could tighten at will.[9] He believed that a fresh crisis in the strait would drain American resources and drive a wedge between America and its key allies.[10]

A since-declassified 1966 study by the RAND Corporation for the Department of Defense provides a further explanation, rooted in China's desire to stand as a beacon to nonaligned countries. It noted an account from Wu Lengxi, a member of the Central Committee of the Chinese Communist Party.[11] Wu detailed comments that Mao himself made during a meeting of that body at the seaside resort of Beidaihe on August 23, 1958, in which the chairman said the commencement of the shelling would harmonize the PRC's interest in Formosa with anti-Western activity then occurring in the Middle East. Presumably, Arab and African countries, many of whom were antagonistic to the West, would find common ground with Beijing and support its posture against the United States.[12] Speaking before the Politburo Standing Committee, Mao declared, "Our demand is that the American armed forces withdraw from Taiwan and that Jiang's [Chiang's] troops withdraw from Jinmen and Mazu. If they do not do so, we will attack. Taiwan is too far away to be bombed, so we shell Jinmen and Mazu. This will surely produce a shock wave in the world. Not only will the Americans be shocked, but the Asians and the Europeans will be shocked too. The people in the Arab world will be delighted, and the vast masses in Asia and Africa will take our side."[13]

In picking this fight, Mao might assume higher risks because of changes in the military balance of power between the USSR and the United States. It appeared to have moved in the Soviets' favor in the years since 1955. The launch of the Sputnik in 1957 heralded advances in Soviet rocketry as did Moscow's announcement late that year that it had developed intercontinental missile capability. These developments generated lots of excitement in China and substantial anxiety in the United States. The RAND study argues they raised the stakes of confrontation with the Soviets and made America more cautious about foreign interventions.

China scholar Chen Jian states that Mao needed a foreign enemy when mobilizing the Chinese people for the mass campaign of industrialization and communal agriculture known as the Great Leap Forward. "Mao decided to bring China into this crisis primarily for the purpose of creating an extraordinary environment in which the full potential of the Great Leap Forward—a crucial episode in the development of Mao's grand enterprise of continuous revolution—would be thoroughly realized," Chen says. "The special way in which Mao used international tension to promote domestic mobilization reflected the Chairman's reading of a key factor shaping popular Chinese perceptions with the outside world, that is, the Chinese people's profound victim mentality." By confronting a foreign "aggressor" who he claimed was occupying and exploiting Chinese territory, Mao could exploit this nationalistic line of thinking. "Almost every time that China encountered an international crisis (no matter how the crisis began), the deep-rooted Chinese victim mentality would readily provide the Chinese leaders with a theme to encourage nationwide mobilization."[14]

On July 31, 1958, Soviet leader Nikita Khrushchev arrived in Beijing, for meetings that lasted until August 3. Professor Chen has reviewed both the Soviet and Chinese minutes of those sessions and concludes that Mao, allergic to being controlled by Moscow, never informed Khrushchev that he intended to shell Quemoy and Matsu.[15] When the shelling erupted on August 23, the Soviets worried it would provoke a major war. In early September, they sent Foreign Minister Andrei Gromyko to China to ascertain Mao's objectives. The Chinese advised Gromyko that the purposes of the bombardment were to spotlight the Formosa issue, to avert a two-China solution, and to stretch American resources, but that they did not intend an invasion of Taiwan or direct confrontation with the United States.[16] Reassured about the danger of war, Khrushchev soon sent two belligerent letters to Eisenhower warning of Soviet retaliation if the United States launched such an attack on mainland China.[17]

A CRISIS BEGINS

Given the mass rallies in China, a military buildup in Fujian Province, July air skirmishes over the strait, and Khrushchev's visit, Nationalist intelligence grew concerned that an assault would follow. Chiang sounded the alarm to American officials in a meeting on August 4. RAND states, "At this meeting, Chiang stated that the Khrushchev-Mao talks, which had just been concluded, were the most important event in the Far East in the past ten years and he predicted that the Chinese Communists might now take military action against Taiwan."[18]

Chiang pressed for an explicit American statement that the United States would defend the offshore islands.[19] Initially, the administration was reluctant to take that step. However, it was concerned that the deployment of so much of Chiang's army would lead to disaster if the islands were overrun.[20] Thus, it elected to warn the Chinese Communists that the United States believed an attack on the islands could careen into a wider war. For this purpose, the administration released August 23 correspondence from Dulles to House Foreign Affairs Committee chairman Thomas Morgan. It responded to a letter from Morgan inquiring about rising tensions in the region.[21] Dulles was candid. "We are, indeed, disturbed by the evidence of the Chinese Communist buildup, to which you refer. It suggests they might be tempted to try to seize forcibly Quemoy or Matsu islands. As you know these islands have been continuously in the hands of the Republic of China. Over the last four years the ties between these islands and Formosa have become closer and their interdependence has increased." Then, in a warning he meant for Beijing to receive, he continued, "I think it would be highly hazardous for anyone to assume that if the Chinese Communists were to attempt to change this situation by force and now to attack and seek to conquer these islands, that it could be a limited operation. It would, I fear, constitute a threat to the peace of the area. Therefore, I hope and believe that it will not happen."[22] This letter, which signaled that the United States might intervene but did not commit it to doing so, did not mollify Chiang, nor did it deter Beijing.

The Communists began shelling Quemoy on August 23, 1958, following troop buildups in mainland China and July air clashes over the strait. The first day's assault was especially intense.[23] The shelling continued at a somewhat reduced level for two months, accompanied by occasional strafing, and a two-week blockade by sea. In response, the Seventh Fleet patrolled the area and, beginning on September 6, assisted Nationalist convoys that resupplied Quemoy.[24]

Soon after the shelling began, the secretary wrote a memo to Under Secretary Christian Herter and Assistant Secretary Walter Robertson. In it, he revealed ambivalence about Chiang's use of the islands as a staging area to harass the PRC and to attempt to stir political upheaval on the mainland.

> I do not feel that we have a case which is altogether defensible. It is one thing to contend that the CHICOMS should keep their hands off the present territorial and political status of Taiwan, the Penghus, Quemoy, and Matsu and not attempt to change this by violence which might precipitate general war in the area. It is another thing to contend that they should be quiescent while this area is used by the CHINATS as an active base for attempting to foment civil strife and to carry out widespread propaganda through leaflets, etc. against the CHICOMS regime. We are, in effect, demanding that these islands be a privileged sanctuary from which the CHINATS can wage at least political and subversive warfare against the CHICOMS but against which the CHICOMS cannot retaliate.[25]

Dulles speculated that third-party intervention, such as through the United Nations, might prove useful at some stage to defuse tensions. He believed that holding out the possibility of diplomacy would be well received on Capitol Hill, which it was.

Unlike in the prior strait crisis, in which Eisenhower called upon legislators to join with him in a common cause, Congress on that same day adjourned for the remainder of the year. Nevertheless, the administration worked actively to keep key Members of Congress informed and to prevent opposition from germinating.[26] Moreover, the Formosa Resolution and the Mutual Defense Treaty were still in force, so the obligations to which Congress had so overwhelmingly consented were still active. There was no need for the president to seek fresh legislation. And use of authority already granted was fully within the president's discretion. This resolved legal questions, although political support in 1958 was to diminish greatly from what it had been in 1955.

In his memoirs, Eisenhower notes that there were substantial similarities in Chinese rhetoric and tactics between the 1958 crisis and the one that transpired three to four years earlier.[27] However, he considered the situation in 1958 to be more perilous because it was more probable to go nuclear.[28] Believing it might not be able to execute an effective intervention with conventional arms, the administration actively considered use of tactical nuclear weapons.[29]

"I did not doubt our total superiority," Eisenhower said in his memoirs, "but any large-scale conflict stimulated here was now less likely to remain limited to a conventional use of power. And, in the intervening years, the Soviets had added substantially to their arsenal of hydrogen bombs. In addition, the Chinese Communists had built an array of airfields in Fujian Province, near Quemoy, from which aerial attacks could be more easily launched against Quemoy and Matsu, and even Formosa."[30]

As in 1955, the Eisenhower administration thought that an assault on Quemoy and Matsu could be the first step to an attack on Formosa.[31] The administration assessed that, given the number of Communist forces and the nature of their military strategies, conventional weapons might not be adequate and use of tactical nuclear devices might be necessary.[32] Eisenhower knew that deploying such weapons could cause vivid domestic controversy and "a worldwide feeling of revulsion against the United States," but pondered that it might be mitigated if they were low yield, used solely against military targets, and minimized fallout and civilian impact. Bad as the political blowback would be, Eisenhower felt, losing a confrontation with the Communists would be worse for the United States.[33]

At the same time, it was unclear what kind of Communist attack was coming. US intelligence services did not believe there was likelihood that seizing

Quemoy would be followed immediately by an attack on Formosa.[34] But perhaps a broader assault would not be necessary. A failed defense of Quemoy, where Chiang had positioned substantial forces, might prove all that was necessary to collapse the morale of his army and undermine his legitimacy.[35]

Probing the contours of US policy toward Quemoy, on August 27, Chalmers Roberts of the *Washington Post* asked Eisenhower about Dulles's letter to Morgan. "Some people are reading Secretary Dulles' statement of last Saturday as indicating that this means we consider the islands more important than ever to the defense of Formosa itself. Would you comment on that?" Eisenhower responded.

> Well, they have this increased importance: what we call the Nationalist Chinese have now deployed about a third of their forces to certain of these islands west of the Pescadores, and that makes a closer interlocking between the defense systems of the islands with Formosa than was the case before that. Before that, I think, they were largely thought of as outposts, strongly held positions, but nevertheless outposts. Now, apparently, the philosophy is to hold the whole thing. It is part of the territory from which they hope to make their living, so there is a closer relationship than there was before.[36]

John Scali of the United Press International followed up by asking how seriously Eisenhower viewed the Communist attacks on Quemoy and whether there was the danger of direct American intervention to interdict them. The president referred to Dulles's letter to Morgan and let matters rest there.[37]

In any event, the spirit, if not the letter, of the Formosa Resolution appeared to require more direct linkage before the United States could intervene militarily. And such intervention was likely to generate widespread criticism, not only from Democrats and editorial writers, but also from US allies who had opposed Quemoy intervention in 1955 and whose views had not changed. Thus, the administration pursued a more limited strategy, one aimed at deterring the Communists from escalation that would force Eisenhower's hand.

At the same time, the president had privately concluded that the Communists must not be allowed to take Quemoy and must be discouraged from trying. "This modern possibility that 'for want of a nail, a shoe was lost,' had led to reaffirmation of the conclusion that Quemoy and Matsu were essential to America's security," Eisenhower wrote in *Waging Peace*.[38]

STRAINING THE "LEASH"

Fearing an amphibious landing on Quemoy, or the island's strangulation in a war of attrition, Chiang cabled the president on August 27 with three specific requests. The first was to make an explicit public commitment to defend Quemoy within the framework of the Formosa Resolution. Chiang asked for "a declaration in pursuance of the Congressional authorization of January 29. 1955, that the present Communist aggressive action against Kinmen constitutes a threat to the security of Taiwan and Penghu. Should the Communists continue their attack against the Kinmen complex or embark upon any aggressive plan against the Matsus, the United States Government would employ its military force to assist in the defense of these two island groups in order to ensure the security of Taiwan and Penghu." The second request was to provide for convoys to escort Nationalist vessels port to port between Formosa and Quemoy and Matsu, thus "make the entire Straits safe for shipping." Third, Chiang asked that the local commander, Vice Admiral Roland N. Smoot, be authorized to deploy necessary forces without the need for further authorization from Washington. "As Washington is far away from the front line," Chiang wrote, "and cannot keep up with the ever-changing war situation, the time-consuming telegraph in exchanges will cause delay which may lead to military disasters."

Chiang indicated that the Nationalists had exercised great self-restraint in the crisis to date because of commitments made at the time of the Mutual Defense Treaty to consult with the United States before undertaking military action. He wrote, "Normally, we would have retaliated in the exercise of our inherent right of self-defense by bombing at once the enemy's air and naval bases along the coast, or at least his gun positions around Kinmen. But I feel that in view of our joint defense agreement and our promise to hold consultations with the United States in such eventuality, we have exercised extreme self-restraint and have withheld our forces from taking proper retaliatory action."

Reminding Eisenhower of commitments made at the time of the Tachens withdrawal to consolidate Nationalist strength into more defensible positions, Chiang asserted that the offshore islands were inextricably connected to the security of the Republic of China. "The withdrawal from the Tachens was made known to our military forces and the civilian population including the Chinese overseas as a strategic move. The security of the Kinmen and Matsu Islands is therefore closely related to the destiny of the Republic of China. To fulfill our duty of self-defense and self-preservation, we must fight the fanatical aggressors blow for blow and guard every inch of our territory. For us, there is no alternative."[39]

The president did not accede to any of these requests.[40] However, "to allay the Generalissimo's concerns, as well as to make our position clear before the world," Eisenhower approved a document that edged closer to the declaration Chiang had been seeking. It took the form of a public statement from Dulles following his September 4 meeting with the president in Newport, Rhode Island.[41] The statement declared that Quemoy and Matsu had never been governed by the Communists; that the United States was bound by treaty to defend Formosa; and that the Formosa Resolution had authorized the president to secure and protect related positions, such as the islands. It observed that the Communists had been "harassing the regular supply of the military and civilian population of the Quemoys" and that such actions were part of announced PRC plans to seize the offshore islands and Formosa.

The secretary noted that, as of that time, the PRC had not launched an "all-out effort to conquer by force Taiwan (Formosa) and the offshore islands." Dulles continued, "Neither is it apparent that such efforts as are being made, or may be made, cannot be contained by the courageous, and purely defensive efforts of the forces of the Republic of China, with such substantial logistical support as the United States is providing." Under those circumstances, and referencing the Formosa Resolution, Dulles declared, "the President has not yet made any finding under the Resolution that the employment of the Armed Forces of the United States is required or appropriate in ensuring the defense of Formosa." But he warned, "The President would not, however, hesitate to make such a finding if he judged that these circumstances made this necessary to accomplish the purposes of the Joint Resolution. In this connection, we have recognized that the securing and protecting of Quemoy and Matsu have increasingly become related to the defense of Taiwan (Formosa). This is indeed also recognized by the Chinese Communists."[42]

Dulles called for a de-escalation of tensions. He said the United States did not require the Communists to renounce their territorial claims "however ill-founded we may deem them to be," but that Washington would insist, as it had in the years of talks in Geneva, on a "declaration of mutual and reciprocal renunciation of force," something the Communists had always rejected.[43]

After Dulles delivered these formal remarks, there was a second statement, attributed only to a "high official." According to the *New York Times*, the official said, "we would not probably wait until the situation was *in extremis* but we would judge in light of all the circumstances whether or not the situation was out of hand as far as the Nationalist Chinese alone were concerned."

The high official, not identified at the time as Dulles, was referenced in an adjacent *Times* article, titled "Red Bases Would be Bombed."[44] It reads, "A top administration official said today Chinese Communist airbases on the mainland would be bombed almost immediately if they were used to launch air attacks against Nationalist-held Quemoy. United States fighters and bombers would join, if needed, but only after President Eisenhower ordered such action as essential to defend Taiwan against Red Chinese invasion."[45]

The lead headline in the following day's *Times* read "US Decides to Use Force If Reds Invade Quemoy; Dulles Sees Eisenhower; Peiping is Warned."[46] Mao and the Chinese leadership took the admonition seriously, anticipating the possibility of a nuclear strike. They responded by declaring that Chinese territorial waters extended to 12 miles from the coast and warning the United States against escorting Nationalist convoys to Quemoy.[47]

Senator H. Alexander Smith spoke with Dulles soon after. Interviewed for the same *Times* story, Smith stated that the United States would "definitely" intervene to prevent a Communist takeover of the offshore islands. Later in the article, Senator Mansfield was quoted as saying Eisenhower should avoid psychological traps such as "face-saving" and "prestige." In the event of escalation, Mansfield urged, the president should consult with Congress. "I hope that if decision is in the offing, before it is made the President would call back to Washington the Democratic and Republican leaders of Congress with appropriate committee members to discuss the situation and in that way to give the rest of us indirect assurance that consideration is being given Congress as a whole."[48]

On September 6, Zhou Enlai issued a public statement that the bilateral talks, suspended for nine months, would soon resume. The United States responded positively.[49] As to Beijing's strategy in the beginning to deescalate, RAND concludes, "It would appear that by September 2, the Chinese Communists had come to the reluctant conclusion that the United States was neither going to force the Chinese Nationalists to abandon the offshore islands nor stand aside and allow the Chinese Communists to impose a successful blockade against GRC forces."[50]

On September 9, Dulles held a press conference in which he was asked directly, "has the United States made a decision to help Chiang Kai-shek defend Quemoy and Matsu?" The secretary reaffirmed his September 4 Newport statement, notwithstanding its ambiguity, and claimed its meaning was well understood. "There was no definitive decision because, as the statement pointed out, certain of the facts could not be known in advance of the event. But certainly, that statement was a significant statement. It has been so interpreted at least by the Chinese Communists and by the Soviet Union. Certainly, they see the significance in the statement."

Reporters pressed the case. Why shouldn't the United States be more definitive about whether it would defend Quemoy? Asserting that the Quemoy situation did not yet rise to the level of an attack on Formosa, Dulles responded,

> The terms of the resolution itself make perfectly clear that United States is to defend Taiwan and the Penghus. It also makes clear that it was the wish of the Congress that if the President found that related areas should be defended as part of that effort, then he should defend them. . . . You may recall that the treaty that we have covers only Taiwan and the Penghus. At the time of the ratification of that treaty we pointed out that if further area was to be brought under that treaty we would go back to Congress, the Senate, and ask for an amendment of the treaty. Therefore, it is quite clear, and I think we made it clear from the

beginning of this affair, that the offshore islands are not to be defended as such by the United States. If they are to be involved in what is in effect an attack upon areas which we are bound to defend, namely Taiwan and the Penghus, that we will meet that attack at that point. . . . This can only be done if there is an actual relationship between the two at the time in question.[51]

KHRUSHCHEV INTERVENES

Just as Eisenhower attempted to deter the Communists and limit their freedom of action, the Communists tried to do the same to Eisenhower. On September 7, Soviet premier Nikita S. Khrushchev sent the president a letter that he had previewed with the Chinese leadership several days earlier.[52] It began by blaming the United States for rising tensions. "As a result of the policy pursued by the United States with regard to China, and particularly the steps now taken by the American Government in the area of the Chinese island of Taiwan and the Taiwan Strait, a dangerous situation has emerged in the Far East. Mankind is again confronted with a direct threat of war." Khrushchev went on to justify the PRC's actions in the strait,[53] condemn the Chiang government, and advise the president that the USSR would take countermeasures if the United States took military action against mainland China:

> It would be a serious miscalculation for the United States to believe that one can make short work of China, just as some powers used to do in the past. Such a miscalculation would have grave consequences for the cause of world peace. Let us, therefore, make this quite clear since any misunderstanding and equivocal statements are the most dangerous things in such affairs. An attack on the People's Republic of China, which is a great friend, ally, and neighbor of our country, is an attack on the Soviet Union. Loyal to its duty, our country would do everything to defend, jointly with the People's Republic of China, the security of both countries and the interests of peace in the Far East and throughout the rest of the world.

Having pledged that the USSR would come to China's defense,[54] Khrushchev insisted he was not issuing ultimatums or making threats, just warning the United States about a circumstance that could spiral out of control. "Nothing could be more erroneous than to try to read in this message of mine an intention to put on color too thick, let alone any threats. All we want to do is call your attention to the situation in which no one would be able to get out of, neither you nor we, should a war break out in the Far East."[55]

Wanting to calm war fears, Eisenhower addressed the nation in a televised Oval Office address on the evening of September 11. He rejected responding to the current crisis by agreeing to surrender the offshore islands. "Shall we take the position that, submitting to threat, it is better to surrender pieces of free territory in the hope that this will satisfy the appetite of the aggressor and we shall have peace? Do we not still remember that the name of 'Munich' symbolizes a vain hope of appeasing dictators?"

The president told the country that the Communists would never be satisfied with grabbing Quemoy, and that permitting it would invite further territorial demands. "It is as certain as can be that the shooting which the Chinese Communist started August 23rd had, as its purpose, not just the taking of the island of Quemoy. It is part of what is indeed an ambitious plan of armed conquest." Where would it lead? Eisenhower went on, "This plan would liquidate all of the free world positions in the western Pacific area and bring them under captive governments which would be hostile to the United States and the free world. Thus, the Chinese and the Russian Communists would come to dominate at least the western half of the now friendly Pacific Ocean."

Eisenhower referred to Khrushchev's September 7 letter, but he rejected its demand that the United States abandon its allies in the region. Instead, the United States would stand by its cluster of treaty commitments as well as the Formosa Resolution. "Congress has made clear its recognition that the security of the western Pacific is vital to the security of the United States and that we should be firm."

To avert Chinese or Soviet miscalculation, the president affirmed that he would use the authority embedded in the Formosa Resolution if confronted with a Communist assault and claimed an attack on Quemoy would never be confined to the island itself. "There will be no retreat in the face of armed aggression, which is part and parcel of a continuing program of using armed force to conquer new regions. I do not believe that the United States can be lured or frightened into appeasement. I believe that in taking the position of opposing aggression by force, I am taking the only position which is consistent with the vital interests of the United States, and, indeed with the peace of the world."

Offering hope for an exit from the crisis, Eisenhower noted that the Geneva negotiations, suspended since the previous July, might soon resume, but added that, as before, the United States would take no position in the talks that would prejudice the interests of Nationalist China. If those meetings did not restart, or did not prove fruitful, he held out the prospect of negotiations under UN auspices. "If bilateral talks between ambassadors do not fully succeed, there is still the hope that the United Nations could exert a peaceful influence on the situation."

The president concluded, "The present situation, though serious, is by no means desperate or hopeless. There is not going to be any appeasement. I believe that there is not going to be any war."[56]

Partisan Discord and Public Opposition

Eisenhower's biographer, Stephen Ambrose, recounts that the broad unity on display during debates on the Formosa Resolution and the Mutual Defense Treaty was missing. Coming as the crisis did two months before the 1958 midterm election, partisan blame-casting was to be expected. Public opinion was similarly negative, driven by fears of nuclear war.[57]

As columnist James Reston wrote in the *New York Times* the morning after the president's speech, "General Eisenhower called for 'unity' in the crisis. But otherwise, he ignored the protests in Allies countries and among the opposition Democrats that the policy risked war over islands that were more important to Free China than to the free world or the principle of non-aggression."[58]

The RAND Corporation study notes that "Congressional criticism, particularly from Democratic Senators, increased in volume. It was reported in the press that congressional mail was heavy and strongly opposed to Administration policy. . . . Much of the criticism came from members of the Senate Foreign Relations committee and from other congressional leaders. The increasing Democratic attack on Administration policy caused fear that the Communists would interpret the debate as an indication that the United States would not act."[59] A highlight of this dissension came in the form of a letter from Senator Theodore Francis Green (D-RI), who in 1957 replaced Walter George as chairman of the Senate Foreign Relations Committee.[60] On September 29, Green wrote Eisenhower, expressing concern that conflict in the strait "may result in military involvement at the wrong time, in wrong place, and on issues not a vital concern to our security." The letter concluded with Green's assessment that the United States would be fighting without the support of America's allies or of the American people.[61] Green urged that the president call the Congress into special session if there was a danger of war with Communist China. And Senator Mike Mansfield warned that the United States would have to bear the burden of such a fight without help from America's traditional allies.[62]

WHERE ARE THE ALLIES?

Much as in 1954–1955, those allies were unnerved about fighting a war over Quemoy.[63] And, in turn, their attitude irritated Eisenhower and Dulles. The two met on the afternoon of September 11, hours prior to the president's broadcast, to lament the lack of support. In a memorandum of conversation Dulles approved, he said, "We discussed the regrettable failure of many of our allies to stand by us publicly in the present situation or indeed in any situation in which they do not see that their immediate interests are directly affected. I suggested that we should be thinking of steps to encourage a greater sense of solidarity with our allies less the several security systems of which we are a member begin to fall apart."[64]

On September 12, Eisenhower responded to Khrushchev's letter, noting that the renewed shelling began only three weeks after the premier had visited China and stating that Beijing's objective was not Quemoy but the overthrow of the Chinese Nationalist government. He told Khrushchev that the issue was whether the Communists would renounce the use of force in resolving their territorial claims. Referencing the Geneva meetings, Eisenhower stated, "In the past, the United States representative at these talks has tried by every reasonable means to persuade the Chinese Communist representative to reach agreement on mutual renunciation of force in the Taiwan area but the latter insistently refused to reach such agreement." The president urged Khrushchev to press the Communists to return to negotiations and desist from the use of force.[65]

Former president Harry S. Truman weighed in on September 14 with a nationally syndicated column supporting the US decision to stand firm regarding Quemoy. "I do not think there will be a war in the Pacific unless Red China launches it, and the Soviet Union abets it. It is just that plain," Truman began. "The probing tactics of the Chinese Communists over Quemoy and Matsu are part of a reckless campaign to determine whether they can get full support from the Kremlin and whether we will stand up to their use of force to take over Quemoy, Matsu and Formosa."

Truman was far more generous in his comment about Chiang than he was while in the White House. He reminded readers, "Lest we forget, Chiang Kai-shek was our ally during the Second World War. Stalin and Russia agreed to back his leadership of the Chinese people after long negotiations in Moscow. . . . The Russians later betrayed Chiang Kai-shek and began to work with Mao Tse-tung."

Notwithstanding the troubled management that led to his defeat in the civil war, Chiang merited America's loyalty, Truman continued. "Whatever we may think of Chiang Kai-shek's handling of his situation, or our own judgment of it at the time, he was our friend and ally during grave times, and he is still considered by millions as a symbol of a once free China."[66]

KHRUSHCHEV TRIES AGAIN

On September 19, Khrushchev replied to Eisenhower with a lengthy, even more vituperative letter, claiming that the president had missed the essence of the premier's earlier communication. "The essence of that message," Khrushchev said, "was to show the danger which threatens humanity if the

USA does not renounce its aggressive policy, which is constantly creating hotbeds with serious conflicts, first in one and then in another region of the world and has led to the creation in the present time of an especially tense situation in the Far East."

Khrushchev accused the United States of propping up the Nationalist government for its own military purposes: "Who can deny that without the support from the side of the USA there would long since not have existed either the Chiang Kai-shek clique or the so-called Taiwan problem. . . . It is clear to anyone that the US has unlawfully seized these islands because the preservation of the Chiang Kai-shek clique on Taiwan gives it the possibility of retaining in this area its armed forces and to threaten the CPR with war."

Charging America with supporting a two-China policy, Khrushchev claimed the Chinese people would repudiate any effort to dismember their state. Chiang, he added, was "merely a hated shadow of the past" that had no legitimacy in China. For that reason, it was not legitimate for the United States to have made a mutual defense treaty with the Nationalists. "This kind of treaty is invented and fabricated exclusively for concealment of aggression," he alleged.

Referencing the possibility that the United States would resort to nuclear weapons, Khrushchev threatened retaliation in kind. "Those who nurture plans for an atomic attack on the CPR should not forget that not only the USA, but the other side as well possesses atomic and hydrogen weapons and also the appropriate means for their delivery, and if such an attack is made on the CPR, the aggressor will immediately receive a proper repulse with these very means." Responsibility for war, he stated, would lie with Eisenhower personally.

Khrushchev repeated that an attack on China would be treated as an attack on the Soviet Union, and that the 1950 Treaty of Friendship and Alliance would be invoked. "We will fulfill completely the obligations we have assumed."

He appealed to the United States to defuse the tensions by withdrawing recognition from the Nationalist government and conferring it on Beijing. "If one does not conduct a line toward the preparation of war and indeed is guided by the ideas of peaceful cooperation, then it is most important to recognize the Government of the CPR."[67]

After consultation between Eisenhower and Secretary Herter, the United States decided to reject Khrushchev's letter. On September 20, the White House issued a statement to that effect. It read, "President Eisenhower received this morning from the United States Embassy in Moscow text of a lengthy communication from Chairman Khrushchev regarding the Far Eastern situation. This communication is replete with false accusations; it is couched in language that is abusive and intemperate; it indulges in personalities; it contains inadmissible threats. All of this renders the communication unacceptable under established international practice. Accordingly, it has been rejected and the United States Chargé d'Affaires in Moscow has been instructed to return the communication to the Soviet Government."[68]

BOMBING THE MAINLAND?

As the crisis lingered into later September, Chiang stepped up pressure on the American government to support him in bombing sites on the mainland. Doubtless, the PRC would retaliate, opening the door to a war to recover the mainland, A front-page *New York Times* story of September 24, 1958, carried the headline, "Chiang Reported Urging Attack Against Mainland." It described a 3-hour meeting held the previous day between Chiang and Admiral Harry D. Felt, the commander of US forces in the Pacific.

The *Times* reported:

> A high Nationalist source indicated that the present thinking of the Nationalist government, which President Chiang is believed to have expounded thoroughly to Admiral Felt for relay to Washington, runs along lines of immediate aerial bombardment of Communist coastal batteries and eventual landing of Nationalist forces on the mainland. Nationalist leaders see nothing unrealistic— as Asian neutralists and even many Americans do—in Generalissimo Chiang's hope of reconquering the Communist-held mainland within a reasonable length of time, this source declared.

The reason for Chiang's optimism was Nationalist perception of major discontent on mainland with Mao's Great Leap Forward, a plan of rapid industrialization that created massive disruption of Chinese agriculture and widespread famine. The *Times* continued, "Nationalist intelligence from the mainland has indicated that increasing unhappiness with tightening Communist oppression would swing millions of Chinese behind Nationalist forces once a landing was made, the Nationalist source said."

The *Times* indicated that the Nationalists seemed convinced that their long deferral of an assault on the mainland was ending. "Whether this thesis is accepted or not, the important political fact seems to be that the Nationalists are convinced of it and are in no mood for concessions to the Communists in Warsaw, in the United Nations, or elsewhere."[69]

But they would have to wait much longer. An adjacent story in the *Times* carried the headline "Washington Bars China Coast Raids." It said that American officials had ruled out any effort in the foreseeable future to bomb Chinese artillery based on the mainland and said that the United States would redouble efforts to seek a diplomatic solution, either in the ambassadorial-level Warsaw talks or at the United Nations.

Under the direction of Secretary Dulles, US officials bluntly told Chiang that Washington would exercise veto power under the Mutual Defense Treaty against a unilateral Nationalist attack on the mainland and would not acquiesce in American participation in such an attack. The story stated,

> Privately the Administration is understood to be taking a much more severe line with President Chiang Kai-shek than it is taking in public. He is said to have been left in no doubt that any new military attack on the mainland that would raise the possibility of involving the United States in direct military action against the Communists must be taken only with the United States approval.

The reason for the tough response was fear that aggressive Nationalist tactics would trigger treaty obligations to Chiang. The article continued, "Washington is taking this line because any Nationalist aerial attack on the Communist gun emplacements might lead to Communist pursuit of the Nationalist bombers back to Taiwan and probably to Communist attacks on Taiwan itself. Such attacks would presumably oblige the United States under its treaty with the Nationalist Chinese to enter the war."

The Dulles-Yeh side letters to the Mutual Defense Treaty were written to control the possibility of inadvertent war. Without them, the United States likely would not have entered the treaty in the first place and, if it had, securing Senate consent would have been much more difficult. Now they were the safeguard against cascading and retaliatory actions leading to war. Thus, the story adds, "Accordingly, Washington is insisting on a veto of any Nationalist action that might provoke a counter-attack on Taiwan."[70]

Public opinion in the United States supported a policy of defending Formosa but not being corralled into a conflict in Asia over the offshore islands, and Eisenhower and Dulles took notice of it.[71] According to historian George Eliades, mail to the State Department ran 80% against US intervention in the crisis, and public polls showed a similar percentage favoring peace negotiation through the United Nations before resorting to war.[72] Editorials in leading newspapers captured this sentiment. On September 25 the *New York Times* wrote,

> we are determined to defend Taiwan and the nearby Penghu islands against any armed attack in keeping with our mutual defense treaty with the Chiang Kai-shek regime and in the interest of the free world. On this there is overwhelming bipartisan agreement at home and considerable moral support from our chief allies. . . . These considerations do not apply to the offshore islands of Quemoy and Matsu. We have no treaty commitment to defend these islands which are purposely not included in the treaty area, and the president is authorized under

the Senate resolution to defend them only if an attack on them is obviously part of an attack on Taiwan. We have neither strong bipartisan support at home though or moral support from our chief allies to defend these islands, and if we tried to do so we would stand alone against a hostile world opinion.[73]

With American assistance, Seventh Fleet escorts of Nationalist convoys were able to keep Quemoy supplied and the crisis began to abate. As September turned to October, the Communists began to reduce tensions, offering on October 6 a temporary cease-fire. After de-escalatory talks between Dulles and Chiang later in the month, the PRC announced it would shell the islands only on odd-numbered days. This allowed for the safe resupply of Quemoy on alternate days without US escorts. Thus, the second strait crisis ended.

A VISIT FROM DULLES

Eisenhower had faced the dilemma that the offshore islands could not be successfully defended without resorting to nuclear weapons, and nuclear weapons could not be used without alienating the American people and US allies. To defuse the situation, he sent his secretary of state on a mission to see Chiang.

Dulles arrived in Taipei in mid-October with instructions from the president to increase the quantity and quality of military assistance to the ROC, especially amphibious lift capacity.[74] In exchange, he was to persuade the generalissimo to reduce the size of the troop deployment on Quemoy and to renounce the use of force to recover the mainland. Dulles was successful. On October 23, 1958, the United States and ROC issued a Joint Communiqué. In part, it read:

> The two Governments reaffirmed their dedication to the principles of the Charter of the United Nations. They recalled that the treaty under which they are acting is defensive in character. The Government of the Republic of China considers but the restoration of freedom to its people on the mainland is its sacred mission. It believes that the foundation of this mission resides in the minds and the hearts of the Chinese people and that the principal means of successfully achieving its mission is the implementation of Dr. Sun Yat-sen's three people's principles (nationalism, democracy, and social well-being) and not the use of force.[75]

Dulles and Eisenhower were well satisfied with this breakthrough. On the afternoon of October 23, 1955, the secretary sent a message through the Department of State. It was directed to Eisenhower on an "eyes only" basis. Dulles wrote, "Most importantly, in the communique we are issuing, the Chinese Nationalists declared their dependence upon political ideals rather than upon force to liberate the peoples of the China mainland. We had great difficulty in getting them to accept or at least publicly announced this important shift in emphasis. It will, I think, have important applications over the future."[76]

For nearly a decade on Formosa, the Nationalists held fast on a claimed right to retake the mainland by force, even though they knew they could not do so without substantial logistical assistance from the United States. And, as reflected in congressional debates and elsewhere, many Americans feared that Chiang sought to maneuver the United States into a conflict. Now, the Nationalists had renounced force as the means to solve cross-strait disputes, something the Communists had not done and, indeed, have not done to this day.

On October 24, 1958, Eisenhower reacted to the Joint Communiqué in a cable to Chiang. He said:

> I wholly endorse the communiqué. It sets forth our solidarity in the face of Chinese Communist armed attacks. Also, I consider it important that your Government should have declared that its success in restoring freedom to the mainland Chinese depends principally upon the minds and hearts of the Chinese people and not the use by your Government of force. This free world principle, not accepted by the Communists, sets us apart from them and morally above them. Your enunciation of that principle will, I am confident, be welcomed throughout the free world.[77]

Eisenhower held a news conference on Wednesday, November 5, after the Republican drubbing in the 1958 midterm elections. Late in the proceedings, he took a question from Robert Pierpoint of CBS News, who stated, "Mr. President, some people profess to see in our foreign policy, a weakening of our close ties. With Nationalist China, any move toward recognition of two Chinas existing side by side. I would like to hear your viewpoint on that." The president responded,

> Well, I have cautioned often that problems, and sometimes they are factors, the principal factors, gradually change. For example, in the latest communique signed by, or at least issued by, the Generalissimo and Foster Dulles, there was a statement that Nationalist China was intending to use political—or I believe the word "peaceful" is there—at least political means in their attempt to win back the mainland instead of military affairs. Well now, you see, there is something always changing in this problem. As far as I am concerned, some our position has not changed as long as Red China continues to do some of the things which we cannot possibly stomach.[78]

Ties with Nationalists would not weaken during Eisenhower's time or for more than a decade thereafter, until President Richard Nixon opened the door to China as a way to hedge relations with the Soviet Union and find a pathway to peace in Vietnam.

NOTES

1. During this period, there had been minor, periodic exchanges of artillery fire, most of it nonlethal. Morton H. Halperin, *The 1958 Taiwan Strait Crisis: A Documented History* (Santa Monica, CA: Rand Corporation, 1966), p. 1.

2. The talks were pretty much the only point of contact between the United States and the PRC until 1971, when Dr. Henry Kissinger made his breakthrough trip to China in anticipation of President Richard Nixon's trip the following year. In September 1955, Johnson and Wang were able to announce an agreement on the repatriation of nationals. Apart from that, there was little to no tangible progress at these meetings.

3. The meetings were suspended after Johnson informed the Chinese that he was being transferred and would be replaced by Mr. Edwin W. Martin, a representative of lower rank. The Chinese refused to accept this arrangement, insisting that the United States be represented at the ambassadorial level (Halperin, p. 17). On July 28, 1958, the United States proposed that the talks resume, with the US ambassador to Poland, Jacob Beam, representing the United States. Zhou Enlai accepted this proposal on September 6 and the talks resumed on September 23, this time in Warsaw. Harry S. Truman, "Truman Asks Firm Stand to Curb Peiping Thrusts," *New York Times*, September 14, 1958, p. 1.

4. Office of the Historian, US Department of State, "US-China Ambassadorial Talks 1955–1970," www.history.state.gov (accessed July 9, 2022).

5. As Eisenhower later wrote, "It seemed likely that his heavy deployment to these forward positions was designed to convince us that he was as committed to the defense of the offshore islands as he was through that of Formosa." Fears resurfaced that were expressed in Congress and elsewhere during the first strait crisis that Chiang might be trying to enmesh the United States into a war to recover the mainland. Eisenhower wrote, "To restrain him from his cherished ambition of aggressive action against the mainland was not always easy." Dwight D. Eisenhower, *Waging Peace: 1956–1961* (New York: Doubleday & Company, 1961), pp. 294–296. At a September 9, 1958, press conference, Dulles was asked whether the Nationalist buildup on Quemoy violated the terms of his agreement with Foreign Minister Yeh that there would be no significant depletion of the defensive strength available on Formosa. Dulles responded in the negative and said that while the United States did not support the buildup, it also did not oppose it. "State Department Transcript of Remarks Made by Dulles at his News Conference," *New York Times*, September 10, 1958, p. 8.

6. "It is even more likely that he intended to trap the United States into defending the islands, on the plea that their fall to China now would be catastrophic for the ROC. Indeed, as we shall see, Dulles used this argument to persuade Eisenhower to commit the United States to the defense of Quemoy and Matsu. The Nationalist reinforcement of these islands thus proved to be an important factor in determining whether or not the United States would intervene in this crisis" (Soman, p. 376).

7. Shu Guang Zhang, p. 228. "The provocative Nationalist activities, Dulles' uncompromising stance on China, the reinforcement of the offshore islands far beyond the requirements for its defense, and the arrival of the Matador missiles, presented China with a security threat its leaders could no longer ignore" (Soman, pp. 377–378).

8. Ibid., p. 378.

9. Chen Jian, p. 187.

10. Shu Guang Zhang, pp. 228–229. Chen Jian, p. 186.

11. "Although the Chinese Communists were later to claim that the cause of the crisis was the buildup of Chinese Nationalist troops on Quemoy, there is nothing to suggest that this was in fact a very likely or very important part of the Chinese Communist motivation. . . . Very little military activity of consequence appears to have been carried out from the offshore islands" (*New York Times*, September 10, 1958, p. 8).

12. "On the evening of the 23rd, I attended the Politburo's Standing Committee meeting chaired by Chairman Mao. At the meeting I learned the reason [for the bombardment]. In mid-July, American troops invaded Lebanon and British troops invaded Jordan in order to put down the Iraqi people's armed rebellion. Thereafter, the Central Committee decided to conduct certain military operations in the Taiwan Straits to support the Arabs' anti-imperialist struggle as well as to crack down on the Nationalist army's frequent and reckless harassment along the Fujian coast across from Jinmen and Mazu. . . . Mass rallies and parades were organized all over the country to support the Iraqi and Arab peoples and to protest against the American and British imperialists' invasions of the Middle East."

Wu added, "Chairman Mao talked first at the meeting of August 23. He said that the day's bombardment was perfectly scheduled." What Mao meant was that three days earlier, the UN General Assembly passed a resolution requesting American and British troops to withdraw from both Lebanon and Jordan. Mao thought that made American occupation of Taiwan look even more unjust. Wu reports, "Our demand was that American armed forces should withdraw from Taiwan, and Jiang's army should withdraw from Jinmen and Mazu. If they did not, we would attack. Taiwan was too far away to be bombed, so we shelled Jinmen and Mazu." "Memoir by Wu Lengxi, 'Inside Story of the Decision Making during the Shelling of Jinmen,'" August 23, 1958, History and Public Policy Program Digital Archive, Zhuanji wenxue (Biographical Literature, Beijing), no. 1, 1994: 5–11. https://digitalarchive.wilsoncenter.org/document/117009. As of mid-July, the Chinese government had been whipping up public sentiment about US intervention in Lebanon and tying it to the Taiwan question. This campaign included newspaper coverage in editorials and a July 17 "Get Out of the Middle East" rally in Beijing. At the rally, Peng Chen, a Politburo member, expressly conflated the two in an "anti-imperialist" message, declaring "We firmly believe that the people with justice on their side will triumph in the end with the east wind prevailing over the west wind" (Halperin, p. 21).

13. Quoted in Chen Jian, p. 182.

14. Chen Jian, p. 203. Gordon H. Chang and He Di remark that Mao used the 1955 crisis for much the same reason. "In terms of domestic propaganda, the campaign for

Taiwan would help rekindle the enthusiasm of the Chinese people for the New Chin after the conclusion of the Korean and Vietnam conflicts" (Chang and Di, p. 1509).

15. Ibid., p. 179.

16. Shu Guang Zhang, p. 255.

17. Chen Jian, p. 77.

18. Halperin, p. 34.

19. The RAND analysts consider that this was part of Chiang's ongoing strategy to draw the United States into a military confrontation against the Communists, perhaps leading to a conflict that could assist his return to the mainland. "For the Nationalists this could only be viewed as an opportunity to involve the United States in a major military action against the Chinese Communists, which was clearly their only hope for a return to the mainland" (Ibid., p. 98).

20. Soman, p. 379.

21. It responded to a letter that Morgan sent Dulles about signs of impending trouble in the region.

22. RAND comments, "In the letter to Morgan, Dulles had come very far toward satisfying the GRC request that he make a public statement that the United States would defend the offshore islands" (Halperin, p. 95).

23. It is estimated that, on August 23, the Communists fired 40,000 shells at Quemoy (Halperin, p. viii). Eisenhower writes that the first word that Communists might renew the shelling or take other action against Quemoy came through US intelligence reports on August 6, 1958. Soviet premier Nikita Khrushchev had just completed a visit to China. Eisenhower was unable to draw a definitive connection between the timing of Khrushchev's visit and the instigation of hostilities in the strait. Eisenhower, *Waging Peace*, pp. 292–293.

24. Ibid., p. 297. Soman, p. 382.

25. Quoted in Halperin, p. 102. The RAND report observes, "He was to continue to hold throughout the crisis, and to be the only one in Washington to express the belief that the Chinese Communists had been 'provoked' into their military move by some actions of the Chinese Nationalists and that if these actions could be eliminated a *modus vivendi* might be established" (Ibid., p. 103).

26. As his cultivation of Senator George would demonstrate, Dulles was very attentive to congressional relations. RAND describes how this was handled during the 1958 crisis. "About 30 key congressmen were to be sent a biweekly detailed confidential letter describing the situation very candidly. The letters were sent home since Congress was not in session, despite the fact that the congressman did not have facilities normally required for the receipt of confidential material. People at State, including Dulles, were always available to see congressman when they were in town" (Halperin, p. 104). At his September 9, 1958, press conference, Dulles emphasized that Congress was being kept well informed. "Let me say that efforts have been made, very considerable efforts have been made, to make contact with congressional leaders. It's not easy to do that at the present time when they are scattered throughout the country. But through telephone, where possible through private talks, and through written communications, there have been contacts made with the congressional leaders" (Dulles press conference, September 9, 1958).

27. For instance, both in 1954/1955 and in 1958, the Communists insisted that resolution of the Taiwan issue was an internal Chinese matter, not susceptible to foreign interference. In both instances, China accused the United States of occupying Taiwan, acting imperialistically, and intervening in China's internal affairs. Both times, China initiated armed hostilities against Quemoy and, even when tensions subsided, Beijing refused to abjure the use of force.

28. "At one point in 1958, the fighting over Kinmen became so intense that the American military deployed atomic bombs to an air base in southern Taiwan, where they reportedly stayed until 1974, just in case the Chinese Communists ever tried to invade and nothing else could stop their human wave tactics." Ian Easton, *The Chinese Invasion Threat* (Manchester, UK: Eastbridge Books, 2019), p. xxvii.

29. Soman, pp. 383–384.

30. Eisenhower, *Waging Peace*, p. 293.

31. Dr. Shu Guang Zhang states that the administration believed the Chinese Communists would probe US willingness to engage. If the United States reacted passively to attacks on the offshore islands, the Communists would press on to Taiwan (Shu Guang Zhang, p. 244).

32. "We recognized, however, that to be successful we might face the necessity of using small yield atomic weapons against hostile airfields, for from vastly dispersed locations, enemy bombers could concentrate their lethality on the target area of Formosa, the Pescadores, and the offshore islands. The immense geographical advantage, extremely difficult if not impossible to eliminate with conventional weapons, would have to be offset by our sheer power" (Eisenhower, *Waging Peace*, p. 295). See also Appendix O in *Waging Peace*, in which Eisenhower and Dulles state, "If the Communists, acting on the supposition that we will not actively intervene, seek to take Quemoy by assault and become increasingly committed, and if we then do intervene, there might be a period between the beginning of assault and irrevocable commitment when prompt and substantial US intervention with conventional weapons might lead the Chicoms to withhold or reverse their assault effort. Otherwise, our intervention would probably not be effective if it were limited to the use of conventional weapons" (Eisenhower, p. 692).

33. Ibid. The president and Dulles outlined their perspective on a collapse of American power in a September 4 memo, following their meeting at the Naval Air Station in Newport, Rhode Island. Paragraph 7 of that memo reads,

"If the foregoing occurred, it would seriously jeopardize the anti-Communist barrier consisting of the insular and peninsula positions in western Pacific, for example, Japan, Republic of Korea, Republic of China, Republic of the Philippines, Thailand, and Vietnam. Other governments in Southeast Asia such as those of Indonesia, Malaysia, Cambodia, Laos, and Burma, would probably come fully under Communist influence. U S positions in the area—perhaps even Okinawa, would probably become untenable, or unusable, and Japan, with its great industrial potential, would probably fall within the Sino-Soviet orbit. These events would not happen all at once but would probably occur over a period of a few years. The consequence in the Far East would be even more far reaching and catastrophic than those which followed when the United States allowed the Chinese mainland to be taken over by the Chinese Communists, aided and abetted by the Soviet Union." (Ibid., p. 692)

34. A Special National Intelligence Estimate, dated August 26, 1958, stated, "In view of US commitments to defend Taiwan and our estimate that neither communist China nor the USSR is willing to risk a major war at present, we believe that Communist China will not attempt to seize Taiwan or the Penghus during the next six months at least" (*FRUS, 1958–1960, Vol. XIX China*, p. 81).

35. The RAND report surmises, "The Chinese Communists probably had a general belief that the rapid deterioration of morale in Taiwan which would occur because of the fall of Quemoy in the loss of a large part of the Chinese Nationalist military capability, would open the way for subversive moves. It might lead, for example, to a fall from power of Chiang Kai-shek and the seizure of power by other Chinese Nationalist leaders who were willing to make a deal with the Chinese Communist regime" (Halperin, p. 175).

36. Public Papers of the President, 1958 Eisenhower, p. 641.

37. Ibid., p. 644.

38. Eisenhower, *Waging Peace*, pp. 294–295.

39. *FRUS 1958–1960 Vol. XIX China*, pp. 83–86. See also Eisenhower, *Waging Peace*, p. 298.

40. To avoid the likelihood of being hit by artillery fire, the United States escorted convoys up to 3 miles of Quemoy, but not closer. In September, the Communists declared a 12-mile limit, which would cover the offshore islands, but the United States refused to recognize it.

41. Eisenhower, *Waging Peace*, p. 299.

42. It was also noted by the Soviet Communists. In his memoirs, former foreign minister Andrei Gromyko characterized Dulles's comments as "armed blackmail, intended to frighten the Chinese people" (Gromyko, p. 251).

43. "Authorized Statement by the Secretary of State Following his Review with the President of the Situation in the Formosa Straits Area," Public Papers of the President, Dwight D. Eisenhower 1958 (Washington, DC: US Government Printing Office, 1959), pp. 687–698. Eisenhower writes that the statement was also meant to reassure Chiang who had written him a private and anguished letter that communications between Formosa and Quemoy were about to be cut and that Quemoy would be starved into submission. Eisenhower, *Waging Peace*, p. 298.

44. In a September 9, 1958, news conference, Dulles acknowledged that he was the "high official."

45. "Red Bases Would be Bombed," *New York Times*, September 6, 1958, p. 3.

46. *New York Times*, September 5, 1958, p. 1.

47. Shu Guang Zhang, p. 251.

48. E. W. Kenworthy, "Senator Affirms US Will to Fight," *New York Times*, September 6, 1958, p. 3.

49. Soman, p. 387.

50. Halperin, pp. 224–225. Asked at his September 9 press conference what the United States hoped to get from the talks, Dulles responded, "We hope that out of the talks will come at a minimum a *modus vivendi* which will assure that the issues there will not be resolved by recourse to force. If the issues themselves could be resolved, that would be a very good result, but that perhaps is too much to hope. I do not think it

is too much to hope that there can be a *modus vivendi* or a cease fire agreement reached which would assure that the issues would not be resolved by violent, aggressive action which would risk world war" (Dulles, September 9, 1958, press conference).

51. Dulles September 9, 1958. Press conference.

52. Chen Jian writes, "For the first time since the outbreak of the Taiwan Strait crisis. Zhou explained to the Soviets Beijing's aims in conducting the shelling. Zhou emphasized that by shelling Jinmen, Beijing, meant to have the Americans 'get stuck' in Taiwan, 'just as they've gotten stuck in the Middle East and the Near East.'" The shelling also had the purpose of focusing and rallying domestic opinion against a foreign enemy, he added. Zhou assured the Soviets the shelling would not be followed by an invasion of the offshore islands (Chen Jian, p. 188).

53. "China has every legitimate right to take all the necessary measures against the traitor Chiang Kai-shek. It is taking these measures on its own land and is not dispatching troops to the territories of other countries. These actions of the People's Republic of China are nothing but a lawful measure of self-defense stipulated in the UN Charter," Khrushchev wrote. "Message form Khrushchev to Eisenhower on Crisis in the Taiwan Strait Area," *New York Times*, September 9, 1958, p. 12.

54. Khrushchev advised Liu Xiao, China's ambassador to the USSR, that the Soviets had enhanced the position of their air forces in the Far East to deter a US-KMT attack on China. Through the ambassador, Mao responded that China had the situation in hand and did not anticipate a general war with the United States (Shu Guang Zhang, p. 255).

55. "Message from Khrushchev to Eisenhower on Crisis in the Taiwan Strait Area," *New York Times*, September 9, 1958, p. 12. The RAND report surmises that "the Chinese Communist may have hoped that the pressure from Khrushchev's letter plus domestic and international opposition to American engagement would cause the Administration to defuse the crisis by pressing Chiang to evacuate" (Halperin, p. 227).

56. Dwight D. Eisenhower, "Radio and Television Report to the American People Regarding the Situation in the Formosan Straits, September 11, 1958," *Public Papers of the Presidents of the United States: Dwight D. Eisenhower 1958* (Washington, DC: US Government Printing Office, 1959), pp. 694–700.

57. Soman cites a Gallup survey, in which 52% of respondents favored supporting the Nationalists if that led to full-scale war and use of nuclear weapons and only 28% supported such use, with 82% seeking a preemptive solution at the United Nations (Soman, p. 389).

58. James Reston, "President Says Nation Must Fight If Necessary to Bar Quemoy Fall; Sees No War; Urges Negotiations," *New York Times*, September 12, 1955, p. 1.

59. Appu Soman cites that of 640 letters received at the White House prior to September 9, 1958, 470 sought to keep the United States out of war, 39 supported Eisenhower, and 89 wanted to take the issue to the United Nations (Soman, p. 389).

60. Green was in line to chair Foreign Relations after the Democrats regained the Senate majority in the 1954 elections. Concerned about working with Green, Dulles and Eisenhower prevailed upon Senator Walter George to take the job. George had

seniority over Green on the committee but was chairing the Finance Committee. One senator could not chair two full committees at the same time. In 1955, George relinquished chairmanship of Finance to take Foreign Relations. In 1956, George did not seek reelection to the Senate. Upon George's retirement, Green became the most senior Democrat on Foreign Relations. Democrats retained the Senate majority and Green thus ascended to chairman.

61. Halperin, pp. 291–293.

62. Russell Baker, "Democrats Critical of Quemoy Policy," *New York Times*, September 12, 1958, p. 1.

63. Ambrose, p. 484. The Rand Corporation report details some of this allied opposition. For example, the Philippines sought to engage the UN to solve the crisis. Japan was not committed to support the United States. The Macmillan government in Britain said that its support for military action in the strait had been neither offered nor requested. The opposition Labor Party, the British press, and public opinion in the UK were opposed to war over Quemoy. Australia's prime minister declared that the ANZUS Pact was inapplicable to the situation and said his country had no obligation to defend the offshore islands. New Zealand's prime minister recommended that Formosa be converted into an independent and neutral nation. Germany remained disengaged (Halperin, p. 390). Mao understood this dissension as a liability for the United States and vainly hoped that it and American domestic opinion would cause Eisenhower to disengage from defense of the offshore islands (Shu Guang Zhang, p. 252).

64. Foreign Relations of the United States 1958–1960, Vol. XIX China, "Joint Communiqué" (Washington, DC: US Government Printing Office, 1996), p. 162.

65. Dwight D. Eisenhower, "Letter to Nikita S. Khrushchev, Chairman, Council of Ministers, USSR, on the Formosa Situation," *Public Papers of the Presidents of the United States: Dwight D. Eisenhower 1958* (Washington, DC: US Government Printing Office, 1959), pp. 701–703.

66. Harry S. Truman, "Truman Asks Firm Stand to Curb Peiping Thrusts," *New York Times*, September 14, 1958, p. 1.

67. *FRUS, 1958–1960, Vol. XIX China*, pp. 231–238.

68. Ibid., p. 248.

69. Robert Trumbull, "Chiang Reported Urging Attack Against Mainland," *New York Times*, September 24, 1958, p. 1.

70. "Washington Bars China Coast Raids," *New York Times*, September 24, 1958, p. 1.

71. "He told Dulles that the opinion poll data 'shook' him. He was prepared to abandon the offshore islands but could not say so publicly. The heavy cost of the Formosa operation weighed on his mind. . . . The pressure of domestic and international opinion finally forced a change in Dulles' thinking. Even while talking tough, he had foreseen that a lasting solution to the problem would involve removal of the Nationalist threat to China from the offshore islands" (Soman, p. 391).

72. George C. Eliades, "Once More into the Breach: Eisenhower, Dulles, and Public Opinion During the Offshore Islands Crisis of 1958," *The Journal of American-East Asian Relations*, Vol. 2 (Winter 1993), p. 357.

73. "Taiwan and the Offshore Islands," *New York Times*, September 25, 1958.

74. Shu Guang Zhang, p. 264.

75. *FRUS, 1958–1960, Vol. XIX China*, "Joint Communiqué" (Washington, DC: US Government Printing Office, 1996), pp. 442–444.

76. Ibid., "Telegram from Secretary of State Dulles to the Department of State," p. 444.

77. Ibid., "Telegram from the Department of State to the Embassy in the Republic of China," p. 446. It should be noted that 54 of the 73 meetings that Ambassador Johnson had with Ambassador Wang, the United States asked the PRC for a renunciation of force but was always rebuffed. *FRUS, 1958–1960, Vol. XIX China*, p. 203.

78. *Public Papers of the President of the United States: Dwight D. Eisenhower 1958* (Washington, DC: USGPO), p. 835.

Conclusion

The Communists launched a heavy day of shelling against Quemoy on June 17, 1960, to protest the visit of President Eisenhower to Taiwan. Eisenhower arrived for a two-day visit hours after the shelling ceased, the only time an American president has ever set foot on the island.[1] The total 86,000 shells in fewer than 4 hours exceeded the one-day record by more than 27,000 rounds.

Accompanying this barrage was a statement from the Chinese army. It announced:

> In support of the just struggle of the people of the Asian countries against Eisenhower's gangster trip, in support of the just struggle of our patriotic compatriots in Taiwan, Penghu, Quemoy, and Matsu against Eisenhower's gangster trip, and to show the great Chinese people's contempt and scorn for Eisenhower, we have decided that, in accordance with the rule of shelling on odd days on June 17, the eve of Eisenhower's arrival in Taiwan, and on June 19, the day of his departure from Taiwan, a demonstration of arms against the United States and shelling to "welcome and see off" Eisenhower will be conducted at the Quemoy front.

The army helpfully added, "For your safety, advance notice is hereby given."[2]

In Taipei, Eisenhower received what the *New York Times* called a "tumultuous reception."[3] Greeted by some 300,000 people, and hosted by generalissimo and Madame Chiang, the president pledged at a mass rally that the United States would stand fast with Nationalist China.

> You may be assured that our continuing the search for peaceful solutions to outstanding international problems does not reflect the slightest lessening of our determination to stand with you, and with all our free neighbors of the Pacific, against aggression. The United States does not of course recognize the claim of

the war-like and tyrannical Communist regime in Peiping. In the United Nations we support the Republic of China, a founding member, as the only rightful representative of China in that organization. The American people deeply admire your courage and striving so well to keep the cause of liberty alive here in Taiwan in the face of the menacing power of Communist imperialism. Your accomplishments provide inspiration to us all.[4]

Eisenhower's 1960 trip was the first time since the 1943 conference in Cairo that Chiang had met with a US president and was a true high point in US relations with Nationalist China. Within a few years, the United States became mired in the Vietnam War and arguments festered in Congress and elsewhere that US policies in Asia were misaligned. For example, in March 1966, the Senate Foreign Relations Committee held seven days of hearings on "US Policy with Respect to Mainland China."[5] In October 1967, private citizen Richard Nixon authored his influential article in *Foreign Affairs*, titled "Asia After Vietnam," in which he famously argued, "taking the long view, we simply cannot afford to leave China forever outside the family of nations, there to nurture its fantasies, cherish its hates, and threaten its neighbors. There is no place on this small planet for a billion of its potentially most able people to live in angry isolation."[6] Other voices emphasizing these themes were also heard, such as Senator Mansfield, Senator Jacob Javits (R-NY), and Senator Edward Kennedy (D-MA).

Slowly but inexorably, major US allies began to join the British in shifting recognition from Taipei to Beijing. France was the first, in 1964.[7] Italy did so in 1970. West Germany, Japan, Australia, and New Zealand followed in 1972, all in the aftermath of President Nixon's opening to China early that year. The Philippines and Thailand acted in 1975.

The United States kept faith with Chiang Kai-shek during the generalissimo's lifetime, even though Nixon had set the process of normalization in motion and the United States and PRC had opened transitional government-to-government liaison offices in each other's capital in 1973. Chiang passed away on April 5, 1975, at the age of 87. His son, Chiang Ching-kuo became president after a three-year interim period. He died in 1988, a year after lifting martial law in Taiwan.[8]

UNIFICATION OR SEPARATISM

Lee Teng-hui, who had been Chiang Ching-kuo's vice president, followed him into office. Lee was a force for democracy and set in motion a process that led to direct elections for both the Legislative Yuan and the presidency. Beijing believed Lee was also a force for separatism,[9] so when he ran in 1996 to become the first democratically elected president, China sought to intimidate Taiwan's voters with a series of missile launches, which began in July 1995 and ended in March 1996. This belligerence became known as the Third Taiwan Strait Crisis. In response, US president Bill Clinton ordered US naval vessels to traverse the strait several times in 1995 and two aircraft carrier strike groups to locate near Taiwan in March 1996, at the time of the voting.[10] In that era, the Chinese military was in no position to contest American power, and it unhappily backed down. Lee won the election on March 23, 1996, and the crisis abated.[11]

China drew a firm conclusion about America and China's future. As Peking University scholar Wang Jisi summarizes, "In Beijing's view, the crisis left little doubt that Washington would be a major stumbling block to unification."[12]

Humiliated by its inability to deter the US military or to influence the Taiwan election, China launched a massive modernization of its armed forces, which has significantly altered the balance of power in the strait. Twenty-five years after the Third Strait Crisis, China has the world's largest navy and other powerful means of force projection. As Stanford's Oriana Skylar Mastro has written, "in some areas, Chinese military capabilities already surpass America's—in shipbuilding, land based conventional ballistic and cruise missiles, and integrated air defense systems. China possesses the third largest nuclear arsenal in the world, one that is undergoing major modernization."[13]

In the present day, peaceful uniting of Taiwan with mainland China appears exceedingly elusive. This has been especially true since the 2016 election of Tsai Ing-wen [Cai Yingwen] of the Democratic Progressive Party to Taiwan's presidency and her reelection in 2020. Accusing the DPP of instigating separatism, Beijing has responded belligerently, with repeated military activity in the vicinity of Taiwan, cutbacks in economic relations and people-to-people contact, campaigns intended to bar Taiwan from international forums, and inducing Taiwan's remaining diplomatic partners to abandon it.[14]

At the same time, China's relations with the United States have badly fractured.[15] While Taiwan is by no means the sole reason, it is the single most combustible irritant. Escalating tensions involve not just impediments to unification but China's conviction that the United States is encouraging separatism to undermine Communist rule and to weaken and contain China. The Chinese have not lately arrived at this conclusion. In 1989, unrest and violence in Tiananmen Square sparked apprehensions, well founded or not, about US involvement. And misgivings have persisted through other circumstances. Peking University scholar Wang Jisi remarks, "closer ties, however, also fed Chinese suspicions that the Americans intended to sow the seeds of dissent in China and eventually topple the CCP. . . . Ever since, any time the CCP has encountered political turmoil at home, it has believed the United States to be a hidden hand."[16] Whether this is paranoia or realism, it obviously provides little basis for trust in Sino-American relations. Tension over Taiwan very much fits this paradigm.

In August 2022, the State Council of the People's Republic of China issued a White Paper titled "The Taiwan Question and China's Reunification in the New Era." In its preamble, the paper states,

> Resolving the Taiwan question and realizing China's complete reunification is a shared aspiration of all the sons and daughters of the Chinese nation. It is indispensable for the realization of China's rejuvenation. It is also a historic mission of the Communist Party of China (CPC). The CPC, the Chinese government, and the Chinese people have striven for decades to achieve this goal.[17]

The Communist government has never wavered in pursuit of this objective, which it expressed in the Anti-Secession Law of March 14, 2005. This statute is reprinted in this book at appendix D and expresses the one-China principle; the policy of One Country, Two Systems; and the prospect of coercion if Taiwan refuses to unify with the mainland.

Public reaction sharply diverges, depending on whether the respondent lives on the mainland or on Taiwan. According to state media, the Chinese people stand firmly behind this policy. In addition, Professor Mastro cites survey data indicating that 70% of mainlanders strongly support the use of force to compel Taiwan to unify with the mainland.[18]

Meanwhile, the people of Taiwan look at unification with the mainland in quite the opposite way and staunchly reject the One Country, Two Systems model. This sentiment was vivid even before China's 2020 imposition of a national security law in Hong Kong. In an opinion survey that Taiwan's Mainland Affairs Council conducted in 2019, 79% of respondents rejected "One Country, Two Systems" form of governance, 84% opposed unification by force, and 88% wanted unification to be decided by popular vote in Taiwan.[19] After the crackdown in Hong Kong, such opinions can only have firmed up.

At the 2022 Aspen Security Forum, Chinese ambassador to the United States Qin Gang noted that 'One Country, Two Systems' was originally designed for Taiwan but was first put into practice in Hong Kong in 1998 after the PRC assumed control from the British. For the arrangement to work, he explained, there must be allegiance to a single country, even if political and economic arrangements vary under that flag. "'One Country' is the precondition for 'Two Systems.' If there's no 'One Country' where are 'Two Systems?'"

Qin alleged that, in Hong Kong, there were activists who wanted to separate from China. "What has happened in Hong Kong over the past three years is that some people did not want 'one country' and did not want Hong Kong to be part of China. They over-emphasized the differences and over-stressed 'two systems.'" Beijing imposed the national security law to end the confusion, he said. "What the central government is doing is to set the record straight, correct those wrongdoings, and put Hong Kong back to order."

The ambassador claimed that it would be premature to conclude the "One Country, Two Systems" formula was unworkable. "We have confidence to make 'One Country, Two Systems' successful. And it's a good example for the reunification of China."[20]

Speaking with US journalists on August 17, 2022, Qin reiterated, "'One Country, Two Systems' is still the most inclusive solution to resolve the Taiwan question. . . . Different political systems are not an obstacle to reunification, and they are not a pretext to separate Taiwan from China." He continued, "We believe it has fully considered Taiwan's realities and it's conducive to Taiwan's long-term stability and prosperity."[21]

EDGING AWAY FROM THE ONE-CHINA POLICY

As tensions in the strait rise, so does the prospect of Sino-American confrontation. Both the Trump and Biden administrations have moved closer to breaching the one-China policy, while professing adherence to it.[22] Each step has blurred the four-decade old barrier to official relations with Taiwan, and each has evoked Beijing's vigorous objections. Even though there are no formal diplomatic contacts between the United States and Taiwan, relations between them are stronger now than when they were uneasy allies.

In mid-August 2022, the United States Trade Representative announced the opening of negotiations for a bilateral trade agreement between the United States and Taiwan, a move the PRC opposes as a violation of the one-China policy.[23] To adhere to the policy, or at least to its letter, negotiations will be conducted between the American Institute in Taiwan and the Taipei Economic and Cultural Representative Office in the United States.[24] The announcement came in the immediate aftermath of the launch of another Biden initiative in the region, the Indo-Pacific Economic Framework, from which Taiwan was omitted. As reported in the *Financial Times*, "the US announced the 'US Taiwan Initiative on Twenty-first Century Trade' just days after it unveiled the regional Indo-Pacific Economic Framework that excluded Taiwan, partly because some southeast Asian nations involved were concerned about antagonizing China, which claims sovereignty over the country."[25] PRC reaction was strong. Through its spokesperson Shu Jueting, the Chinese Ministry of Commerce asserted, "China always opposes any form of official exchanges between any country and the Taiwan region of China."[26]

The trade initiative echoes the creation of SEATO in the 1950s, when Chiang was excluded from a regional security arrangement because of qualms from some of the participants, only to have him conclude a bilateral defense pact with the United States.

CONGRESS STEPS BACK AND LEANS FORWARD

In the present day, Taiwan enjoys immense support in Congress. This is manifested by legislation such as the Taiwan Travel Act,[27] which elevates US government contacts with Taiwan, and the Taiwan Allies International Protection and Enhancement Initiative Act.[28] Other Taiwan measures, even more consequential to degrading the one-China policy, frequently circulate in Congress and have broad support. They would enhance arms sales and military cooperation, formalize trade relations, and alter the nature of the unofficial relationship that now exists. The PRC vocally opposes all this legislation.[29] However, few in Congress seem to pay much attention to its objections.

The incautious and pugnacious atmosphere on Capitol Hill differs markedly from that which existed when the Taiwan Relations Act was passed in 1979. Enacted within four months of normalized relations between the United States and the People's Republic of China, the legislation was intended to regularize and stabilize economic and cultural relations with Taiwan. But, mindful of building a relationship with the PRC, Congress took care not to contradict the basis for normalization, which included avowal of the one-China policy and that Taiwan was part of China.[30]

The act stated that normalized diplomatic relations rested on the expectation that the future of Taiwan would be settled peacefully.[31] It committed the United States to the sale of defensive arms to Taiwan and to the capacity to resist coercion against Taiwan[32] and that the United States shall maintain the capacity to help Taiwan resist coercion.[33] It legislatively preempted a potential legal dispute by providing that Twin Oaks, a 21-acre DC estate owned by the Chinese government since the 1930s, would remain the property of Nationalist China rather than allowing the PRC to succeed in ownership.[34] Moreover, it created the American Institute in Taiwan to conduct unofficial relations with the people on Taiwan.[35] Amendments offered at the time to upgrade the relationship to something official were rejected.[36]

So was an amendment by Senator Charles Percy (R-IL) that would have stated it was US policy "to consider any effort to resolve the Taiwan issue by other than peaceful means a threat to the peace and security of the Western Pacific and to the security interests of the United States." In opposing this amendment, Senator John Glenn (D-OH) of the Senate Foreign Relations Committee spoke in a manner reminiscent of debates on the Formosa

Resolution and the Mutual Defense Treaty. Glenn worried that the Percy language was so stringent the United States could not avoid a fight that Taiwan itself had provoked. The amendment created "a serious risk of being pulled into a conflict not of our own choosing," Glenn charged. "We would be hard pressed, if this amendment is approved, to go against that request from Taiwan." He continued. "Why do we want to lead Taiwan into thinking we will make a commitment to them we are not likely to honor in the crunch? Why do we want to mislead our friends around the world into thinking we would make that kind of commitment? Why do we want to mislead the people in the People's Republic of China into thinking that we would have a knee jerk reaction to events beyond our control?"[37]

Elevating the US defense commitment into something akin to the Mutual Defense Treaty, without the controls of the Dulles-Yeh side letters, the amendment was defeated.[38] Senator Joe Biden (D-DE) was outspoken in opposing it and other amendments that had been proposed. He argued that normalization had allowed the United States to turn a corner in relations with Asia from which it must not regress. "Passage of amendments to this bill, which would, in effect, create a second China. It would lay the basis for another 30 years of fiction, of illusion, of instability," Biden declared.[39]

Taiwan's present strength in Congress and the Executive reflects its demonstrable commitment to democracy and its posture as a spunky underdog. It is also a consequence and a key driver of an overall deterioration in US-China relations that summons old and troubling memories. Hallmarks of the downward spiral are confrontational Chinese diplomacy, truculent military posturing, embracing a destabilizing post-Soviet authoritarian, human rights problems, and bilateral economic tensions. These are countered by strengthened US alliances around China's perimeter, an increasing tendency to construe China as hostile, and diminished American regard for what China insists are its core interests and redlines. On both sides, trust is collapsing. Major economic and psychological decoupling is underway. It affects not only supply chains and other business interests, but academic, cultural, and tourist exchanges as well. A robust and diverse structure of relationships between China and the United States, constructed over many decades, is being dismantled brick by brick.

In this toxic atmosphere of suspicion, no problem is thornier or more dangerous than Taiwan. Professor Yan Xuetong of Tsinghua University warns, "Although China has not given up the principle of peaceful unification to date, it may abandon it if Taiwan announces *de jure* independence. The more other countries support Taiwan secessionist policies, the more the PLA will carry out military exercises to deter Taiwan."[40] In the 1950s, miscalculations were very problematic. Mao's assumptions about America's intentions—its relationship with Chiang, and US misunderstandings about the Communists, led to two crises in the strait and the potential for nuclear deployment. Things have changed, but maybe not that much.

PROBLEMS COMPOUND

It will be recalled that the one-China policy involves US recognition of the PRC as the sole legal government of China and acknowledgment, even if not acceptance, of Beijing's claim that Taiwan is part of China. Thus far, this has been the policy of 10 presidents, starting with Nixon. Notwithstanding some tense moments, it has kept the peace in the strait.

However, the Chinese increasingly question whether adherence is real. American claims of fealty, which would tend to calm Chinese anxiety, are belied by actions that heighten suspicion. The terms and trend of US legislation; stiff rhetoric in Congress; visits to Taiwan by American lawmakers, most notably House Speaker Nancy Pelosi;[41] heightened Executive Branch interface; and multiple impromptu Biden assertions about a defense commitment to Taiwan have incensed Beijing and fed nationalist sentiment that America seeks to contain and weaken the country.[42]

Thus, China contends that while the United States observes the letter of the one-China policy, it stretches the spirit. The 2022 State Council White Paper provides:

"External interference is a prominent obstacle to China's reunification. Still lost in delusions of hegemony and trapped in a Cold War mindset, some forces in the US insist on perceiving and portraying China as a major strategic adversary and a serious long-term threat. They do their utmost to undermine and pressurize China, exploiting Taiwan as a convenient tool. The US authorities have stated that they remain committed to the one-China policy and that they do not support 'Taiwan independence.' But their actions contradict their words. They are clouding the one-China principle in uncertainty and compromising its integrity."[43]

Wang Jisi claims that China interprets circumventions of the one-China policy as consistent with long-standing efforts to undermine the leadership of the Communist Party and cripple the country. The assumption appears to be that the United States has never accepted the permanence of Communist rule in China. Wang writes, "The conventional wisdom in Beijing holds that the United States is the greatest external challenge to China's national security, sovereignty, and internal stability. Most Chinese observers now believe that the United States is driven by fear and envy to contain China in every possible way." He continues, "Although American policy elites are clearly aware of how that view has taken hold in Beijing, many of them miss the fact that from Beijing's perspective, it is the United States and not China that has fostered this newly adversarial environment, especially by carrying out what the CCP views as a decades-long campaign of meddling in China's internal affairs with the goal of weakening the party's grip on power."[44] These apprehensions are well developed in China, with roots back to the Maoist period.

Beijing's suspicion of malevolent Western motives, understandable when the United States actively isolated the PRC, denying it recognition and blocking it from membership in the UN, has continued notwithstanding years of active and favorable Western engagement. Princeton University professor Aaron Friedberg notes that engagement tended to exacerbate these misgivings rather than calming them, because the Chinese interpreted it as a way for the West to coopt, change, and dominate the PRC rather than truly accept it on its own terms:

> From the start, the CCP leadership saw engagement as a trap set for them by the West, a of a clever strategy for transforming Chinese society, eroding the foundations of the Party's authority, and causing its eventual collapse in their own removal from power. . . . As they saw it, their country was the last bastion of socialism, in an American-dominated international system that embodied, reinforced, and sought to promulgate liberal democratic values. Accepting Washington's seemingly warm welcome to join in that system would expose Beijing to mounting pressures to abandon its principles and adopt the West values at its as its own.[45]

It is not peculiar that the Chinese Communist Party would come to such conclusions. In promoting engagement with domestic audiences, Western leaders have advertised these very objectives. For example, on March 9, 2000, President Bill Clinton proposed granting the PRC Permanent Normal Trade Relations status, which ended the need for annual waivers of US law that would have otherwise imposed onerous tariff burdens on China. In his remarks that day, the president said, "China is a one-party state that does not tolerate opposition. It does deny citizens fundamental rights of free speech and religious expression. It does defend its interests in the world and some-times in ways that are dramatically at odds from our own. But the question is not whether we approve or disapprove of China's practices. The question is what's the smartest thing to do to improve those practices?" Clinton con-cluded, "If you believe in a future of greater openness and freedom for the people of China, you ought to be for this agreement."[46]

While the PRC has not evolved in ways the West had hoped,[47] Taiwan has transformed into a prosperous, multiparty democracy, very different from the martial law regime that existed there when the Shanghai Communiqué was announced. Given dramatic changes in how the United States relates to the PRC and to Taiwan, key US opinion leaders contend, as Dulles concluded in 1954, that strategic ambiguity tempts misunderstanding and should be forsworn in favor of a declared commitment to defend Taiwan.[48] If this course is followed, the Mutual Defense Treaty, which ended more than 40 years ago, will de facto be revived, raising the issue of safeguards that shielded the United States from being unwittingly drawn into war. It may be one thing to defend Taiwan if Beijing grows impatient and attacks it, and another if Taiwan declares independence and an attack follows. The Dulles-Yeh letters were a precaution to keep the tail from wagging the dog.

Speaking in Washington, DC, at the Heritage Foundation on March 23, 2022, former secretary of state Mike Pompeo decried both the policy of ambiguity and the idea that Taiwan is part of China. "When the bad guys in the world don't exactly know how the West will respond, there is risk they will miscalculate. . . . One of the central features of making sure that Taiwan has the capacity to defend itself is the world recognizing what we all know to be true: it is not part of China, that if it became part of China this wouldn't be reunification, this would be an aggressive action to destroy the sovereignty of an independent country."[49]

Meeting with President Tsai Ing-wen in Taipei in July 2022, former US secretary of defense Mark Esper contended that strategic ambiguity should be abandoned and that the one-China policy had "outlived its usefulness."[50] Speaking at the Aspen Security Forum, just after his return from Taiwan, Esper observed that the premise behind the policy, as expressed in the Shanghai Communiqué, no longer stands. The communiqué recited that Chinese on both sides of the strait agreed there was one China, and Taiwan was part of it, but disagreed as to who was the legitimate government. No one would have more strenuously agreed with that statement than Chiang Kai-shek. However, Esper explained that people on Taiwan now "identify as Taiwanese, not Chinese, and they long ago renounced any ambition to return to the mainland and claim it."[51]

The Taiwan Strait is the Berlin of the twenty-first century, a place of persistent and combustible tension. If strategic competition between the United States and China ever intensifies to the level of military conflict, with the potential for nuclear deployment, the most likely issue will be Taiwan.

NOTES

1. The stop in Taiwan was part of a journey that also took Eisenhower to the Philippines, South Korea, and Okinawa. Japan was originally on the itinerary as well but the trip was cancelled by the Japanese government after violent Communist-inspired demonstrations protesting a new Japanese-American Security Treaty, which Japan approved soon thereafter.

2. "Text of Peking's Warning to Quemoy," *New York Times*, June 18, 1960, p. 2.

3. Jacques Nevard, "Eisenhower is Hailed in Taiwan; Reds Shell Quemoy 'In Contempt'; Tokyo Leftists Keep Up Protests," *New York Times*, June 18, 1960, p. 1.

4. *The Public Papers of the Presidents of the United States, Dwight D. Eisenhower 1960*–61 (Washington, DC: US GPO), p. 505.

5. United States. Congress. Senate. Committee on Foreign Relations. (1966). *U.S. Policy with Respect to Mainland China: hearings before the United States Senate Committee on Foreign Relations, Eighty-Ninth Congress, second session, on Mar. 8, 10, 16, 18, 21, 28, 30, 1966* (Washington, DC: US GPO).

6. Richard Nixon, "Asia After Vietnam," *Foreign Affairs*, Vol. 46, No. 1 (October 1967), p. 121.

7. Garrett Martin, "Playing the China Card," *Journal of Cold War Studies*, Vol. 10, No. 1 (Winter 2008), pp. 52–80.

8. Eric Pace, "Chiang Ching-kuo Dies at 77, Ending a Dynasty on Taiwan," *New York Times*, January 14, 1988, p. 1.

9. Beijing's rhetoric against Lee became hostile in 2014. As CNN explains, "The reason for all the vitriol was Lee's announcement in July that henceforth bilateral ties between Taipei and Beijing should be on a 'special state-to-state' basis." "Why Beijing Fears Taiwan's Lee Teng-hui," www.cnn.com (accessed August 9, 2022). Lee also spoke at commencement ceremonies at his alma mater, Cornell University, on June 9–10, 1995. The Clinton administration at first refused to grant Lee a visa, but under pressure from Congress, relented. The Chinese leadership was dismayed.

10. "China's huge exercises around Taiwan were a rehearsal, not a signal, says Oriana Skylar Mastro," *The Economist*, August 10, 2022 (accessed August 11, 2022)

11. It must be noted that during the First and Second Taiwan Strait crisis, the military imbalance was even greater. The Soviet Union agreed in 1955 to assist China in the development of a nuclear weapon. See "Chinese Nuclear History," digitalarchive.wilsoncenter.org (accessed September 1, 2022). In 1960, the Soviets reversed course and withdrew all technical assistance. China had to develop the bomb indigenously from that point forward. It did not successfully test a nuclear device until 1964. Therefore, in 1958, if the United States was going to be deterred, it would be because of the potential for Soviet intervention or the international and domestic opposition to the use of nuclear weapons.

12. Wang Jisi, "The Plot Against China? How Beijing Sees the New Washington Consensus," *Foreign Affairs*, July/August 2021.

13. Mastro, *Economist*. China is substantially expanding its nuclear arsenal, both in terms of silos and mobile land platforms, and submarines. Tong Zhao, of the Carnegie Endowment for International Peace, writes about the rationale. "During the Cold War, the Soviet Union felt that keeping up with the United States' nuclear arsenal was necessary for it to achieve real political equality with Washington. Today, similar reasoning seems to be behind China's nuclear buildup—a belief that the United States won't drop its hostility against China unless its hand is forced by robust Chinese strategic power." Tong Zhao, "What's Driving China's Nuclear Buildup," Carnegie Endowment for International Peace, August 5, 2022, www.carnegieendownment.org (accessed August 9, 2022).

14. Stanford Professor Oriana Skylar Mastro comments, "Chinese President Xi Jinping has made clear his ambition to resolve the Taiwan issue, grown markedly more aggressive on issues of sovereignty, and ordered the Chinese military to increase its activity near the island. He has also fanned the flames of Chinese nationalism and allowed discussion of a forceful takeover of Taiwan to creep into the mainstream of the Chinese Communist Party. The palpable shift in Beijing's thinking has been made possible by a decades-long military modernization effort, accelerated by Xi, aimed at allowing China to force Taiwan back into the fold." Oriana Skylar Mastro, "The Taiwan Temptation: Why Beijing Might Resort to Force," *Foreign Affairs*, July/August 2021.

15. It has become a largely zero-sum competition. Writing in *Foreign Affairs*, Cornell University's Jessica Chen Weiss speaks of a "global struggle" and observes, "The United States seeks to perpetuate its preeminence and an international system that privileges its interests and values. China sees US leadership as weakened by hypocrisy and neglect, providing an opening to force others to accept its influence and legitimacy. On both sides there is a growing fatalism that a crisis is unavoidable and perhaps even necessary." Jessica Chen Weiss, "The China Trap: US Foreign Policy and the Perilous Logic of Zero-sum Competition," *Foreign. Affairs*, September/October 2022.

16. Wang Jisi, "The Plot Against China? How Beijing Sees the New Washington Consensus," *Foreign Affairs*, July/August 2021. Aaron L. Friedberg, *Getting China Wrong*, (Cambridge, UK: Polity Press, 2022), p. 94.

17. As we have seen, China has expressed these sentiments since the founding of the People's Republic. There has never been a moment when these views have been relaxed. For example, 50 years ago, in the Shanghai Communiqué, the Chinese side stated, "the Government of the People's Republic of China is the sole legal government of China; Taiwan is a province of China which has long been returned to the motherland; the liberation of Taiwan is China's internal affair in which no other country has the right to interfere; and all US forces and military installations must be withdrawn from Taiwan. The Chinese Government firmly opposes any activities which aim at the creation of 'one China, one Taiwan,' 'one China, two governments,' 'two Chinas,' an 'independent Taiwan' or advocate that 'the status of Taiwan remains to be determined.'"

18. Wang Jisi, *Foreign Affairs*. The Chinese military has been psychologically conditioned to undertake this mission. Ian Easton comments, "Invading Taiwan is at the heart of the armed wing of the CCP, which is known as the People's Liberation Army (PLA). The war plan for fighting a 'Taiwan Liberation' campaign is tattooed onto the PLA's corporate memory. It is something that has been indoctrinated and encoded into the minds of all top-level officers. This offensive operation shapes their lives and institutions. It defines them and gives their military service purpose and meaning" (Easton, p. 2).

19. "Taiwan Public Rejects One Country, Two Systems," March 21, 2019, www .mac.gov.tw (accessed August 10, 2022).

20. Aspen Security Forum, "Fireside Chat with Ambassador Qin Gang," July 20, 2022.

21. Embassy of the People's Republic of China in the United States of America, "Transcript of Ambassador Qin Gang's Interview with US Mainstream Media 2022/08/17 18:50."

22. In Trump's case, problems began when he was president-elect and accepted a congratulatory call from Tsai Ing-wen. After some hedging about his views on the one-China policy, Trump affirmed fealty to it. However, as his administration proceeded, and especially after launching a trade war with the PRC and the advent of the Covid-19 pandemic, Trump became far less cautious. In January 2021, Secretary of State Mike Pompeo lifted long-standing restrictions on official US government contacts with Taiwan. "The US-Taiwan relationship need not and should not be hackled by self-imposed restrictions of our permanent bureaucracy." BBC News. "Pompeo: US to Lift Restrictions on Contacts with Taiwan." www.bbc.com (accessed August 19, 2022). This announcement followed the July 2020 visit to Taiwan by Secretary of Health and Human Services Alex Azar and the August 2020 visit by Under Secretary of State Keith Krach.

23. "In Beijing, Ministry of Commerce spokeswoman Shu Jueting said mainland China firmly opposed the US-Taiwan trade initiative." "The Chinese side has always opposed any form of official exchanges between any country and the Taiwan region of China, including the negotiation and signing of any agreement of a sovereign or official nature," Shu said. Robert Delaney and Lawrence Chung, "US-Taiwan trade: Washington announces start of talks for bilateral agreement with an eye on Beijing," *South China Morning Post*, August 18, 2022, www.scmp.com (accessed August 18, 2022).

24. "United States and Taiwan Commence Formal Negotiations on US-Taiwan Initiative on 21st Century Trade," www.ustr.gov (accessed August 18, 2022).

25. Felicia Schwartz "US and Taiwan to hold trade talks amid China tensions," *Financial Times*, August 18, 2022, www.ft.com (accessed August 22, 2022).

26. "US Announces Trade Talks with Taiwan and China Immediately Shows its Wrath," August 18, 2022, www.cbsnews.com (accessed Augustb19, 2022).

27. PL 115–135. The legislation promotes intergovernmental contacts at all levels between the United States and Taiwan, chipping away at decades-long US policy to avoid such contacts. See Gerrit van der Wees, "The Taiwan Travel Act in Context," *The Diplomat*, March 19, 2018, www.thediplomat.com (accessed August 11, 2022).

28. PL 116–135. The legislation promotes Taiwan's diplomatic and economic relationships. See Mercy Kuo, "Trump and the TAIPEI Act," *The Diplomat*, April 21, 2022. www.thediplomat.com (accessed August 11, 2022).

29. Arms sales to Taiwan evoke a harsh reaction from China and usually involve a suspension of dialogue or cooperation with the United States. In his August 17, 2022, meeting with US journalists, Chinese ambassador Qin Gang claimed that the quality and quantity of weapons supplied to Taiwan violates the US-China Joint Communiqué of August 17, 1982. He stated, "We haven't seen the United States honor its commitments. . . . The quantities are more, and the qualities are more sophisticated. This is written in black and white in the international document. The United States government has reneged on this commitment." Embassy of the People's Republic of

China, "Transcript of Ambassador Qin Gang's Interview with the US Mainstream Media 2022/08/17 18:50."

30. The US-PRC Normalization Communiqué, announced December 15, 1979, read:

1. The United States of America and the People's Republic of China have agreed to recognize each other and to establish diplomatic relations as of January 1, 1979.

2. The United States of America recognizes the Government of the People's Republic of China as the sole legal Government of China. Within this context, the people of the United States will maintain cultural, commercial, and other unofficial relations with the people of Taiwan.

3. The United States of America and the People's Republic of China reaffirm the principles agreed on by the two sides in the Shanghai Communiqué and emphasize once again that:

4. Both wish to reduce the danger of international military conflict.

5. Neither should seek hegemony in the Asia-Pacific region or in any other region of the world and each is opposed to efforts by any other country or group of countries to establish such hegemony.

6. Neither is prepared to negotiate on behalf of any third party or to enter into agreements or understandings with the other directed at other states.

7. The Government of the United States of America acknowledges the Chinese position that there is but one China and Taiwan is part of China.

8. Both believe that normalization of Sino-American relations is not only in the interest of the Chinese and American peoples but also contributes to the cause of peace in Asia and the world.

The United States of America and the People's Republic of China will exchange Ambassadors and establish Embassies on March 1, 1979.

31. The Taiwan Relations Act provides:

(b) It is the policy of the United States—

(3) to make clear that the United States decision to establish diplomatic relations with the People's Republic of China rests upon the expectation that the future of Taiwan will be determined by peaceful means;

(4) to consider any effort to determine the future of Taiwan by other than peaceful means, including by boycotts or embargoes, a threat to the peace and security of the Western Pacific area and of grave concern to the United States;

32. The Taiwan Relations Act provides:

SEC. 3. (a) In furtherance of the policy set forth in section 2 of this Act, the United States will make available to Taiwan such defense articles and defense services in such quantity as may be necessary to enable Taiwan to maintain a sufficient self-defense capability.

(b) The President and the Congress shall determine the nature and quantity of such defense articles and services based solely upon their judgment of the needs of Taiwan, in accordance with procedures established by law. Such determination of Taiwan's defense needs shall include review by United States military authorities in connection with recommendations to the President and the Congress.

(c) The President is directed to inform the Congress promptly of any threat to the security or the social or economic system of the people on Taiwan and any danger to the interests of the United States arising therefrom. The President and the Congress shall determine, in accordance with constitutional processes, appropriate action by the United States in response to any such danger.

33. The Taiwan Relations Act states that it is US policy "6) to maintain the capacity of the United States to resist any resort to force or other forms of coercion that would jeopardize the security, or the social or economic system, of the people on Taiwan."

34. The Taiwan Relations Act provides: "For all purposes under the laws of the United States, including actions in any court in the United States, recognition of the People's Republic of China shall not affect the ownership of or other rights or interests in properties, tangible and intangible, and other things of value, owned or held on or prior to December 31, 1978, or thereafter acquired or earned by the governing authorities on Taiwan."

35. The Taiwan Relations Act declares that unofficial relations between the United States and Taiwan shall be conducted through the mechanism of the American Institute in Taiwan.

"SEC. 6. (a) Programs, transactions, and other relations conducted or carried out by the President or any agency of the United States Government with respect to Taiwan shall, in the manner and to the extent directed by the President, be conducted and carried out by or through—

(1) The American Institute in Taiwan, a nonprofit corporation incorporated under the laws of the District of Columbia, or (2) such comparable successor nongovernmental entity as the President may designate."

36. For example, an amendment by Senator Gordon Humphrey (R-NH) to elevate the America Institute on Taiwan into a formal liaison office lost 38–57. An amendment by Senator Robert Dole (R-KS) to subject the AIT director to Senate confirmation lost 38–54. Those votes occurred on March 7, 1979. In the House, an amendment by Rep. Ken Cramer (R-CO) to mandate the United States to act if Taiwan were attacked was defeated 149–221, and amendment by Rep. Robert Lagomarsino (R-CA) to specify conditions under which recognition of the PRC would be withdrawn was defeated 169–197. An amendment by Rep. Dan Quayle to elevate representation to a liaison office 172–181. All these House votes occurred on March 12, 1979.

37. *Congressional Record*, March 8, 1979, p. 4323.

38. The amendment by Senator Charles Percy (R-IL) stating that a non-peaceful resolution of the Taiwan question would threaten US security interests lost 42–50 on March 9, 1979.

39. *Congressional Record*, March 8, 1979, p. 4325.

40. Yan Xuetong, "Becoming Strong: The New Chinese Foreign Policy," *Foreign Affairs*, July/August 2021, pp. 13–14.

41. China objects every time a congressional delegation stops in Taiwan, but never more vigorously than when House Speaker Nancy Pelosi visited in August 2022, and it does not accept the rationale that Congress is an independent branch and beyond presidential control. In his sit-down with American journalists after that visit, Chinese

ambassador Qin Gang explained the basis for the protest. "Over the past decades, China has opposed congressional visits to Taiwan because we believe that they are in violation of the one-China principle and the three joint communiqués. They violate the commitment of the United States of not developing official relations with Taiwan. Congress is part of the government of the US. It's not an independent, uncontrollable branch. It's obliged to abide by the foreign policy of the United States." Embassy of the People's Republic of China, "Transcript of Ambassador Qin Gang's Interview with the US Mainstream Media 2022/08/17 18:50."

42. Wang Jisi points out,

"the CCP believes that all these perceived attempts to foment dissent and destabilize China are part of an integrated American strategy to westernize (xihua) and split up (fenhua) China and prevent the country from becoming a great power. The central government and Chinese official media acknowledge no distinctions among the US government executive branch, the US Congress, American media, and American-based nongovernmental organizations. The CCP views all American institutions and individuals that criticize or take action against Beijing as players in a well-planned, well-organized campaign of subversion, and the party brands any Chinese citizen or group that has in one way or another being backed by the United States or American organizations as a "stooge" or "political tool" of Washington."

Wang Jisi, "The Plot Against China? How Beijing Sees the New Washington Consensus," *Foreign Affairs*, July/August 2021.

43. "The Taiwan Question and China's Reunification in the New Era, August 2022." The paper details a range of complaints that it says proves the United States is hollowing out its one-China commitment.

"They are contriving "official" exchanges with Taiwan, increasing arms sales, and colluding in military provocation. To help Taiwan expand its "international space," they are inducing other countries to interfere in Taiwan affairs, and concocting Taiwan-related bills that infringe upon the sovereignty of China. They are creating confusion around what is black and white, right and wrong. On the one hand, they incite separatist forces to create tension and turmoil in cross-straits relations. On the other hand, they accuse the mainland of coercion, pressurizing Taiwan, and unilaterally changing the status quo, in order to embolden these forces and create obstacles to China's peaceful reunification."

44. Wang Jisi, "The Plot Against China? How Beijing Sees the New Washington Consensus," *Foreign Affairs*, July/August 2021.

45. Aaron L. Friedberg, *Getting China Wrong* (Cambridge, UK: Polity Press, 2022), p. 94.

46. "Full Text of Clinton's Speech on China Trade Bill," *New York Times*, March 9, 2000.

47. "Neither carrots nor sticks have swayed China as predicted. Diplomatic and commercial engagement have not brought political and economic openness. Neither U.S. military power nor regional balancing has stopped Beijing from seeking to displace core components of the U.S.-led system. And the liberal international order has failed to lure or bind China as powerfully as expected." Kurt M. Campbell and Ely Ratner, "The China Reckoning," *Foreign Affairs*, March/April 2018.

48. See, for example, Richard Haass and David Sacks, "American Support for Taiwan Must be Unambiguous," *Foreign Affairs*, September 2, 2020.

49. The 2022 B.C. Lee Lecture Featuring the Honorable Mike Pompeo, www .heritage.org (accessed July 30, 2022).

50. Lawrence Chung, "Former US Defence Chief Says One-China Policy Has Outlived Its Usefulness," *South China Morning Post*, July 19, 2022, www.scmp.com (accessed July 30, 2022).

51. Aspen Security Forum, "Fireside Chat on the Future of Taiwan with Mark Esper," July 22, 2022.

Appendix A

Text of President Eisenhower's Message to Congress on The Formosa Resolution

January 24, 1955

To the Congress of the United States:

The most important objective of our nation's foreign policy is to safeguard the security of the United States by establishing and preserving a just and honorable peace. In the Western Pacific, a situation is developing in the Formosa Straits, that seriously imperils the peace and our security.

Since the end of Japanese hostilities in 1945, Formosa and the Pescadores have been in the friendly hands of our loyal ally, the Republic of China. We have recognized that it was important that these islands should remain in friendly hands. In unfriendly hands, Formosa and the Pescadores would seriously dislocate the existing, even if unstable, balance of moral, economic and military forces upon which the peace of the Pacific depends. It would create a breach in the island chain of the Western Pacific that constitutes, for the United States and other free nations, the geographical backbone of their security structure in that Ocean. In addition, this breach would interrupt North-South communications between other important elements of that barrier and damage the economic life of countries friendly to us.

The United States and the friendly Government of the Republic of China, and indeed all the free nations, have a common interest that Formosa and the Pescadores should not fall into the control of aggressive Communist forces.

Influenced by such considerations, our government was prompt, when the Communists committed armed aggression in Korea in June 1950, to direct our Seventh Fleet to defend Formosa from possible invasion from the Communist mainland.

These considerations are still valid. The Seventh Fleet continues under Presidential directive to carry out that defensive mission. We also provide military and economic support to the Chinese Nationalist Government, and we cooperate in every proper and feasible way with that Government in order to promote its security and stability. All of these military and related activities will be continued.

In addition, there was signed last December a Mutual Defense Treaty between this Government and the Republic of China covering Formosa and the neighboring Pescadores. It is a treaty of purely defensive character. That Treaty is now before the Senate of the United States.

Meanwhile Communist China has pursued a series of provocative political and military actions, establishing a pattern of aggressive purpose. That purpose, they proclaim, is the conquest of Formosa.

In September 1954 the Chinese Communists opened up heavy artillery fire upon Quemoy Island, one of the natural approaches to Formosa, which had for several years been under the uncontested control of the Republic of China. Then came air attacks of mounting intensity against other free China islands, notably those in the vicinity of the Tachen group to the north of Formosa. One small island (Ichiang) was seized last week by air and amphibious operations after a gallant few fought bravely for days against overwhelming odds. There have been recent heavy air attacks and artillery fire against the main Tachen Islands themselves.

The Chinese Communists themselves assert that these attacks are a prelude to the conquest of Formosa. For example, after the fall of Ichiang, the Peiping Radio said that it showed a "determined will to fight for the liberation of Taiwan (Formosa). Our people will use all their strength to fulfill that task."

Clearly, this existing and developing situation poses a serious danger to the security of our country and of the entire Pacific area and indeed to the peace of the world. We believe that the situation is one for appropriate action of the United Nations under its charter, for the purpose of ending the present hostilities in that area. We would welcome assumption of such jurisdiction by that body.

Meanwhile, the situation has become sufficiently critical to impel me, without awaiting action by the United Nations, to ask the Congress to participate now, by specific resolution, in measures designed to improve the prospects for peace. These measures would contemplate the use of the armed forces of the United States if necessary to assure the security of Formosa and the Pescadores.

The actions that the United States must be ready to undertake are of various kinds. For example, we must be ready to assist the Republic of China to redeploy and consolidate its forces if it should so desire. Some of these forces are scattered throughout the smaller offshore islands as a result of historical rather than military reasons directly related to defending Formosa. Because of the air situation in the area, withdrawals for the purpose of redeployment of Chinese Nationalist forces would be impractical without assistance of the armed forces of the United States.

Moreover, we must be alert to any concentration or employment of Chinese Communist forces obviously undertaken to facilitate attack upon Formosa and be prepared to take appropriate military action.

I do not suggest that the United States enlarge its defensive obligations beyond Formosa and the Pescadores as provided by the Treaty now awaiting ratification. But unhappily, the danger of armed attack directed against that area compels us to take into account closely related localities and actions which, under current conditions, might determine the failure or the success of such an attack. The authority that may be accorded by the Congress would be used only in situations which are recognizable as parts of, or definite preliminaries to, an attack against the main positions of Formosa and the Pescadores.

Authority for some of the actions which might be required would be inherent in the authority of the Commander-in-Chief. Until Congress can act, I would not hesitate, so far as my Constitutional powers extend, to take whatever emergency action might be forced upon us in order to protect the rights and security of the United States.

However, a suitable Congressional resolution would clearly and publicly establish the authority of the President as Commander-in-Chief to employ the armed forces of this nation promptly and effectively for the purposes indicated if in his judgment it became necessary. It would make clear the unified and serious intentions of our Government, our Congress and our people. Thus, it will reduce the possibility that the Chinese Communists, misjudging our firm purpose and national unity, might be disposed to challenge the position of the United States, and precipitate a major crisis which even they would neither anticipate nor desire.

In the interest of peace, therefore, the United States must remove any doubt regarding our readiness to fight, if necessary, to preserve the vital stake of the free world in a free Formosa, and to engage in whatever operations may be required to carry out that purpose.

To make this plain requires not only Presidential action but also Congressional action. In a situation such as now confronts us, and under modern conditions of warfare, it would not be prudent to await the emergency before coming to the Congress. Then it might be too late. Already the warning signals are flying.

I believe that the threatening aspects of the present situation, if resolutely faced, may be temporary in character. Consequently, I recommend that the Resolution expire as soon as the President is able to report to the Congress that the peace and security of the area are reasonably assured by international conditions, resulting from United Nations action or otherwise.

Again, I say that we would welcome action by the United Nations which might, in fact, bring an end to the active hostilities in the area. This critical situation has been created by the choice of the Chinese Communists, not by us. Their offensive military intent has been flaunted to the whole world by words and by deeds. Just as they created the situation, so they can end it if they so choose.

What we are now seeking is primarily to clarify present policy and to unite in its application. We are not establishing a new policy. Consequently, my recommendations do not call for an increase in the armed forces of the United States or any acceleration in military procurement or levels of defense production. If any unforeseen emergency arises requiring any change, I will communicate with the Congress. I hope, however, that the effect of an appropriate Congressional Resolution will be to calm the situation rather than to create further conflict.

One final point. The action I request is, of course, no substitute for the Treaty with the Republic of China which we have signed and which I have transmitted to the Senate. Indeed, present circumstances make it more than ever important that this basic agreement should be promptly brought into force, as a solemn evidence of our determination to stand fast in the agreed Treaty area and to thwart all attacks directed against it. If delay should make us appear indecisive in this basic respect, the pressures and dangers would surely mount.

Our purpose is peace. That cause will be served if, with your help, we demonstrate our unity and our determination. In all that we do we shall remain faithful to our obligations as a member of the United Nations to be ready to settle our international disputes by peaceful means in such a manner that international peace and security, and justice, are not endangered.

For the reasons outlined in this message, I respectfully request that the Congress take appropriate action to carry out the recommendations contained herein.

DWIGHT D. EISENHOWER

Dwight D. Eisenhower, Special Message to the Congress Regarding United States Policy for the Defense of Formosa. Online by Gerhard Peters and John T. Woolley, The American Presidency Project, https://www.presidency.ucsb.edu/node/233556.

Appendix B

Text of the Formosa Resolution

Joint Resolution by the Congress

Washington, January 29, 1955

Whereas, the primary purpose of the United States, in its relations with all other nations, is to develop and sustain a just and enduring peace for all; and

Whereas, certain territories in the West Pacific under the jurisdiction of the Republic of China are now under armed attack, and threats and declarations have been and are being made by the Chinese Communists that such armed attack is in aid of and in preparation for armed attack on Formosa and the Pescadores.

Whereas, such armed attack if continued would gravely endanger the peace and security of the West Pacific area and particularly of Formosa and the Pescadores; and

Whereas, the secure possession by friendly governments of the Western Pacific Island chain, of which Formosa is a part, is essential to the vital interests of the United States and all friendly nations in or bordering upon the Pacific Ocean; and

Whereas, the President of the United States on January 6, 1955, submitted to the Senate for its advice and consent to ratification of a Mutual Defense Treaty between the United States of America and the Republic of China, which recognizes that an armed attack in the West Pacific area directed against territories, therein described, in the region of Formosa and the Pescadores, would be dangerous to the peace and safety of the parties to the treaty: Therefore be it

Resolved by the Senate and House of Representatives of the United States of America in Congress assembled, That the President of the United States be and he hereby is authorized to employ the Armed Forces of the United States as he deems necessary for the specific purpose of securing and protecting Formosa and the Pescadores against armed attack, this authority to include the securing and protection of such related positions and territories of that area now in friendly hands and the taking of such other measures as he judges to be required or appropriate in assuring the Defense of Formosa and the Pescadores.

This resolution shall expire when the President shall determine that the peace and security of the area is reasonably assured by international conditions created by action of the United Nations or otherwise and shall so report to the Congress.

Appendix C

Text of the US Mutual Defense Treaty with the Republic of China and Related Letters of Understanding

The Parties to this Treaty,

Reaffirming their faith in the purposes and principles of the Charter of the United Nations and their desire to live in peace with all peoples and all Governments, and desiring to strengthen the fabric of peace in the West Pacific Area,

Recalling with mutual pride the relationship which brought their two peoples together in a common bond of sympathy and mutual ideals to fight side by side against imperialist aggression during the last war,

Desiring to declare publicly and formally their sense of unity and their common determination to defend themselves against external armed attack, so that no potential aggressor could be under the illusion that either of them stands alone in the West Pacific Area, and

Desiring further to strengthen their present efforts for collective defense for the preservation of peace and security pending the development of a more comprehensive system of regional security in the West Pacific Area,

Have agreed as follows:

ARTICLE I

The Parties undertake, as set forth in the Charter of the United Nations to settle any international dispute in which they may be involved by peaceful means in such a manner that international peace, security and justice are not endangered and to refrain in their international relations from the threat or use of force in any manner inconsistent with the purposes of the United Nations.

ARTICLE II

In order more effectively to achieve the objective of this Treaty, the Parties separately and jointly by self-help and mutual aid will maintain and develop their individual and collective capacity to resist armed attack and communist subversive activities directed from without against their territorial integrity and political stability.

ARTICLE III

The Parties undertake to strengthen their free institutions and to cooperate with each other in the development of economic progress and social well-being and to further their individual and collective efforts toward these ends.

ARTICLE IV

The Parties, through their Foreign Ministers or their deputies, will consult together from time to time regarding the implementation of this Treaty.

ARTICLE V

Each Party recognizes that an armed attack in the West Pacific Area directed against the territories of either of the Parties would be dangerous to its own peace and safety and declares that it would act to meet the common danger in accordance with its constitutional processes.

Any such armed attack and all measures taken as a result thereof shall be immediately reported to the Security Council of the United Nations. Such measures shall be terminated when the Security Council has taken the measures necessary to restore and maintain international peace and security.

ARTICLE VI

For the purposes of Article II and V, the terms "territorial" and "territories" shall mean in respect of the Republic of China, Taiwan and the Pescadores, and in respect of the United States of America, the island territories in the West Pacific under its jurisdiction. The provisions of Article II and V will be applicable to such other territories as may be determined by mutual agreement.

ARTICLE VII

The Government of the Republic of China grants, and the Government of the United States of America accepts, the right to dispose such United States land, air and sea forces in and about Taiwan and the Pescadores as may be required for their defense, as determined by mutual agreement.

ARTICLE VIII

This Treaty does not affect and shall not be interpreted as affecting in any way the rights and obligations of the Parties under the Charter of the United Nations or the responsibility of the United Nations for the maintenance of international peace and security.

ARTICLE IX

This Treaty shall be ratified by the United States of America and the Republic of China in accordance with their respective constitutional processes and will come into force when instruments of ratification thereof have been exchanged by them at Taipei.

ARTICLE X

This Treaty shall remain in force indefinitely. Either Party may terminate it one year after notice has been given to the other Party.

IN WITNESS WHEREOF the undersigned Plenipotentiaries have signed this Treaty.

DONE in duplicate, in the English and Chinese languages, at Washington on this second day of December of the Year One Thousand Nine Hundred and Fifty-four, corresponding to the second day of the twelfth month of the Forty-third year of the Republic of China.

Exchange of Notes Between Secretary of State John
Foster Dulles and Chinese Foreign Minister George Yeh

The Secretary of State to the Chinese Minister of Foreign Affairs

DEPARTMENT OF STATE

WASHINGTON

December 10, 1954

Excellency:

I have the honor to refer to recent conversations between representatives of our two Governments and to confirm the understandings reached as a result of those conversations, as follows:

The Republic of China effectively controls both the territory described in Article Six of the Treaty of Mutual Defense between the Republic of China and the United States of America signed on December 2, 1954, at Washington and other territory. It possesses with respect to all territory now and hereafter under its control the inherent right of self-defense. In view of the obligations of the two Parties under the said Treaty and of the fact that the use of force from either of these areas by either of the Parties affects the other, it is agreed that such use of force will be a matter of joint agreement, subject to action of an emergency character which is clearly an exercise of the inherent right of self-defense. Military elements which are a product of joint effort and contribution by the two Parties will not be removed from the territories described in Article 6 to a degree which would substantially diminish the defensibility of such territories without mutual agreement.

Accept, Excellency, the assurances of my highest consideration.

John Foster Dulles

Secretary of State of the United States of America

His Excellency George K. C. Yeh

Minister for Foreign Affairs of the Republic of China

[English Text of Note II]

December 10, 1954

Excellency:

I have the honor to acknowledge the receipt of Your Excellency's Note of today's date, which reads as follows: [See note I]

I have the honor to confirm, on behalf of my government, the understanding set forth in Your Excellency's Note under reply.

I avail myself of this opportunity to convey to Your Excellency the assurances of my highest consideration.

George K. C. Yeh

Minister for Foreign Affairs of the Republic of China

His Excellency John Foster Dulles

Secretary of State of the United States of America

Appendix D

The Anti-Secession Law of 2005

Anti-Secession Law (Adopted at the Third Session of the Tenth National People's Congress on March 14, 2005)

Article 1 This Law is formulated, in accordance with the Constitution, for the purpose of opposing and checking Taiwan's secession from China by secessionists in the name of "Taiwan independence," promoting peaceful national reunification, maintaining peace and stability in the Taiwan Straits, preserving China's sovereignty and territorial integrity, and safeguarding the fundamental interests of the Chinese nation.

Article 2 There is only one China in the world. Both the mainland and Taiwan belong to one China. China's sovereignty and territorial integrity brook no division. Safeguarding China's sovereignty and territorial integrity is the common obligation of all Chinese people, the Taiwan compatriots included.

Taiwan is part of China. The state shall never allow the "Taiwan independence" secessionist forces to make Taiwan secede from China under any name or by any means.

Article 3 The Taiwan question is one that is left over from China's civil war of the late 1940s.

Solving the Taiwan question and achieving national reunification is China's internal affair, which subjects to no interference by any outside forces.

Article 4 Accomplishing the great task of reunifying the motherland is the sacred duty of all Chinese people, the Taiwan compatriots included.

Article 5 Upholding the principle of one China is the basis of peaceful reunification of the country.

To reunify the country through peaceful means best serves the fundamental interests of the compatriots on both sides of the Taiwan Straits. The state shall do its utmost with maximum sincerity to achieve a peaceful reunification.

After the country is reunified peacefully, Taiwan may practice systems different from those on the mainland and enjoy a high degree of autonomy.

Article 6 The state shall take the following measures to maintain peace and stability in the Taiwan Straits and promote cross-Straits relations:

(1) to encourage and facilitate personnel exchanges across the Straits for greater mutual understanding and mutual trust;
(2) to encourage and facilitate economic exchanges and cooperation, realize direct links of trade, mail and air and shipping services, and bring about closer economic ties between the two sides of the Straits to their mutual benefit;
(3) to encourage and facilitate cross-Straits exchanges in education, science, technology, culture, health and sports, and work together to carry forward the proud Chinese cultural traditions;
(4) to encourage and facilitate cross-Straits cooperation in combating crimes; and
(5) to encourage and facilitate other activities that are conducive to peace and stability in the Taiwan Straits and stronger cross-Straits relations.

The state protects the rights and interests of the Taiwan compatriots in accordance with law.

Article 7 The state stands for the achievement of peaceful reunification through consultations and negotiations on an equal footing between the two sides of the Taiwan Straits. These consultations and negotiations may be conducted in steps and phases and with flexible and varied modalities.

The two sides of the Taiwan Straits may consult and negotiate on the following matters:

(1) officially ending the state of hostility between the two sides;
(2) mapping out the development of cross-Straits relations;
(3) steps and arrangements for peaceful national reunification;
(4) the political status of the Taiwan authorities;
(5) the Taiwan region's room of international operation that is compatible with its status; and
(6) other matters concerning the achievement of peaceful national reunification.

Article 8 In the event that the "Taiwan independence" secessionist forces should act under any name or by any means to cause the fact of Taiwan's secession from China, or that major incidents entailing Taiwan's secession from China should occur, or that possibilities for a peaceful reunification should be completely exhausted, the state shall employ non-peaceful means and other necessary measures to protect China's sovereignty and territorial integrity.

The State Council and the Central Military Commission shall decide on and execute the non-peaceful means and other necessary measures as provided for in the preceding paragraph and shall promptly report to the Standing Committee of the National People's Congress.

Article 9 In the event of employing and executing non-peaceful means and other necessary measures as provided for in this Law, the state shall exert its utmost to protect the lives, property and other legitimate rights and interests of Taiwan civilians and foreign nationals in Taiwan, and to minimize losses. At the same time, the state shall protect the rights and interests of the Taiwan compatriots in other parts of China in accordance with law.

Article 10 This Law shall come into force on the day of its promulgation.

Appendix E

Maps of China and Taiwan

MAPS: CHINA

A map of modern China. Manchuria is the large area in the northeast. It is nearly 400,000 square miles in size and is large than any country in Europe. Taiwan (Formosa) lies approximately 100 miles off the southeastern Chinese coast. The offshore islands of Kinmen and Mazu (Quemoy and Matsu) are just off the coast, near Fujian. The Tachen Islands, which China seized in early 1955, are not far to the east of Hangzhou.

https://www.cia.gov/the-world-factbook/countries/china/map

MAPS: TAIWAN

https://www.cia.gov/the-world-factbook/countries/taiwan/map

The island of Taiwan (Formosa), since 1949 the home of the Chinese Nationalist government. Martial law was in effect from 1949 to 1988. Today it is a prosperous democracy, over which China asserts sovereignty claims, and which has not declared its independence.

Bibliography

Abramson, Rudy. *Spanning the Century: The Life of W. Averell Harriman*. New York: William Morrow and Company, Inc., 1992.

Accinelli, Robert. *Crisis and Commitment: United States Policy Toward Taiwan 1950–1955*. Chapel Hill, NC: University of North Carolina Press, 1996.

Ambrose, Stephen E. *Eisenhower the President, Vol. II*. New York: Simon & Schuster, 1984.

Atkinson, Brooks. "Long Schism Seen." *New York Times*, October 31, 1944.

Atkinson, George W. "The Sino-Soviet Treaty of Friendship and Alliance." *International Affairs* (Royal Institute of International Affairs) Vol. 23, No. 3 (July 19, 1944), pp. 357–366.

Baker, Russell. "Democrats Critical of Quemoy Policy." *New York Times*, September 12, 1958.

Barboza, David. "John Leighton Stuart, China Expert, is Buried There at Last." *New York Times*, November 19, 2008.

Bernstein, Richard. *China 1945: Mao's Revolution and America's Fateful Choice*. New York: Alfred A. Knopf, 2014.

Bianco, Lucien. *Origins of the Chinese Revolution, 1915–1949*. Palo Alto, CA: Stanford University Press, 1971.

Billingham, Anthony. "The Man and the Woman Whom China Obeys." *New York Times Magazine*, November 7, 1937.

Carter, Carolle J. *Mission to Yenan: American Liaison with the Chinese Communists, 1944–1947*. Lexington, KT: University of Kentucky Press, 2021.

Chang, Gordon H. and He Di. "The Absence of War in the US-China Confrontation Over Quemoy and Matsu in 1954–1955: Contingency? Luck? Deterrence?" *The American Historical Review*, Vol. 98, No. 5 (1993), pp. 1500–1524.

Chang, Iris. *The Rape of Nanking*. New York: Penguin Books, 1998.

Chang, June and Jon Halliday. *Mao: The Unknown Story*. New York: Alfred A. Knopf, 2005.

Chen, Jian. *China & the Cold War*. Chapel Hill, NC: University of North Carolina Press, 2001.

Chiang, Kai-shek. *China's Destiny*. New York: Roy Publishers, 1947.

Chiang, Kai-shek. *Soviet Russia in China: A Summing Up at Seventy*. New York: Farrar, Strauss, and Cudahy, 1957.

Chiang, Kai-shek and Madame Chiang Kai-shek. *Oral History*. Princeton University Library. Public Policy Papers, 1964. http://arks.princeton.edu/ark:/88435/pc289q35m.

Churchill, Winston S. *The Second World War, Vol. IV: The Hinge of Fate*. London: Cassel, 1951.

Cockfield, Jamie. *A Giant from Georgia: The Life of US Senator Walter F. George, 1878–1957*. Macon, Georgia: Mercer University Press, 2019.

Davies, Jr. John Paton. *China Hand*. Philadelphia, PA: University of Pennsylvania Press, 2012.

Davies, Jr. John Paton. *Dragon by the Tail: American, British, Japanese, and Russian Encounters with China and One Another*. New York: W.W. Norton & Company, Inc., 1972.

Delaney, Robert and Lawrence Chung. "US-Taiwan Trade: Washington Announces Start of Talks for Bilateral Agreement with an Eye on Beijing." *South China Morning Post,* August 18, 2022. www.scmp.com.

Dewey, Thomas E. *Journey to the Pacific*. Garden City, NY: Doubleday, 1952.

Dikotter, Frank. *The Tragedy of Liberation: A History of the Chinese Revolution 1945–1957*. New York: Bloomsbury Press, 2013.

Divine, Robert. *Eisenhower and the Cold War*. Oxford: Oxford University Press, 1981.

Dulles, Foster Rhea. *American Policy Toward Communist China, The Historical Record: 1949–1969*. New York: Thomas Y. Crowell Company, 1972.

Dulles, John Foster. "Challenge and Response in United States Policy." *Foreign Affairs*, October 1957.

Durdin, F. Tillman. "Red Envoys Ordered Out." *New York Times*. March 1, 1947.

Durdin, F. Tillman. "Worth Twenty Divisions." *New York Times*. September 14, 1941.

Easton, Ian. *The Chinese Invasion Threat*. Manchester: Eastbridge Books, 2019.

Eliades, George C. "Once More into the Breach: Eisenhower, Dulles, and Public Opinion During the Offshore Islands Crisis of 1958." *The Journal of American-East Asian Relations*, Vol. 2 (Winter 1993). pp. 347–367.

Elliston, Herbert. "Questions on the Formosa Treaty." *Washington Post and Times Herald*. February 9, 1955.

Eisenhower, Dwight D. *Mandate for Change: 1953–1956*. New York: Doubleday & Company, 1963.

Eisenhower, Dwight D. *Waging Peace: 1956–1961*. New York: Doubleday & Company, 1965.

Elkins, W. F. "Fascism in China: The Blue Shirts Society 1932–37." *Science and Society*, Vol. 33, No. 4 (Fall-Winter 1969), pp. 426–433.

Esherick, Joseph W. *The World War II Dispatches of John Stewart Service*. New York: Random House, 1974, p. 249.

Fairbank, John King. *The Great Chinese Revolution: 1800–1985*. New York: Harper & Row, 1986.

Fairbank, John King. *The United States and China*. Cambridge: Harvard University Press, 1971.

Feis, Herbert. *The China Tangle*. Princeton, NJ: Princeton University Press, 1953.

Fenby, Jonathan. *Chiang Kai-shek: China's Generalissimo and the Nation He Lost*. New York: Carroll & Graf Publishers, 2004.

"Foreign Relations: Until the Dust Settles." *Time,* March 7, 1949.

Fravel, M. Taylor. *Active Defense*. Princeton, NJ: Princeton University Press, 2019.

Friedberg, Aaron L. *Getting China Wrong*. Cambridge: Polity Press, 2022.

Garver, John W. "Chiang Kai-shek's Quest for Soviet Entry into the Sino-Japanese War." *Political Science Quarterly*, Vol. 102, No. 2 (Summer, 1987), pp. 295–316.

Garver, John W. *The Sino-American Alliance: Nationalist China and American Cold War Strategy in Asia*. Armonk, NY: M.E. Sharpe, Inc., 1997.

Gromyko, Andrei. *Memoirs*. New York: Doubleday, 1989.

Guo, Xixiao. "Paradise or Hell Hole? US Marines in Post-World War II Chinam." *The Journal of American-East Asian Relations*, Vol. 7, No. 3/4 (Fall-Winter 1998), pp. 157–185.

Halperin, Morton H. *The 1958 Taiwan Strait Crisis: A Documented History*. Santa Monica, CA: Rand Corporation, 1966.

Hamilton, Thomas J. "UN Invites Red China to Join Talks to Halt Fighting on Coastal Isles." *New York Times*, February 1, 1955.

Han, Yelong. "An Untold Story: American Policy Toward Chinese Students in the United States 1949–1955." *The Journal of American-East Asian Relations*, Vol. 2, No. 1, Special Issue: The Impact of the Korean War (Spring 1993).

Hasegawa, Tsuyoshi. *Racing the Enemy: Truman, Stalin, and the Surrender of Japan*. Cambridge: Belknap Press, 2006.

Heiferman, Ronald Ian. *The Cairo Conference of 1943*. Jefferson, NC: McFarland & Company, Inc., 2011.

Hitchcock, William I. *The Age of Eisenhower: America and the World in the 1950s*. New York: Simon & Schuster, 2018.

Huang, Grace. "Madame Chiang's Visit to America." In Joseph W. Esherick and Matthew T. Combs, Eds., *1943: China at the Crossroads*. Ithaca, NY: Cornell University 2018.

Huang, Hua and Li Xicabing (Translator). "My Contacts with John Leighton Stuart After Nanjing's Liberation." *Chinese Historians*, 5:1, 47–56, DOI: 10.1080/1043643x, 1992,11876866.

Hull, Cordell. *The Memoirs of Cordell Hull*. New York: Macmillan Company, 1948.

Hutchings, Graham. *China 1949: Year of Revolution*. London: Bloomsbury Academic, 2021.

Immerman, Richard E. *John Foster Dulles: Piety, Pragmatism, and Power in US Foreign Policy*. Wilmington, DE: Scholarly Resources, Inc., 1999.

Johnson, Robert David. *Congress and the Cold War*. Cambridge: Cambridge University Press, 2006.

Judd, Walter H. *Oral History, Eisenhower Administration Project Number 117.* Columbia University, 1979.

Karon, Tony. "Madame Chiang Kai-shek, 1898–2003." *Time*, October 24, 2003.

Kinzer, Stephen. *The Brothers: John Foster Dulles, Allen Dulles, and Their Secret World War.* New York: Henry Holt and Company, 2013.

Koo, Wellington. *The Wellington Koo Memoir.* New York Times Oral History Program, Chinese Oral History Project of the East Asian Institute of Columbia University.

Kristof, Nicholas D. "The Horror of 2–28: Taiwan Rips Open the Past." *New York Times*, April 3, 1992.

Krock, Arthur. "In the Nation – The 'Old Man' Lays It on The Line." *New York Times*, January 28, 1955.

Kuo, Helen. "China's Leaders Speak." *New York Times*, April 18, 1943.

Kurtz-Phelan, Daniel. *The China Mission: George Marshall's Unfinished War.* New York: W.W. Norton & Company, 2018.

Lawrence, W. H. "White House Moves to Dispel Talk it Seeks a Preventive War." *New York Times*, January 28, 1955.

Leviero, Anthony. "US Expects Chinese Reds to Attack Isles in April; Weights All-Out Defense." *New York Times*, March 26, 1955.

Levine, Steven I. "On the Brink of Disaster: China and the United States in 1945." In Harry Harding and Yuan Ming, Eds., *Sino-American Relations 1945–1955: A Joint Assessment of a Critical Decade.* Wilmington, DE: Scholarly Resources, 1989.

Li, Laura Tyson. *Madame Chiang Kai-shek: China's Eternal First Lady.* New York: Atlantic Monthly Press, 2006.

Liebman, Henry R. "Mme. Chiang Flying to US to Get Help." *New York Times*, November 29, 1948.

Lippmann, Walter. "Reappraisal in the Formosa Strait." *Washington Post and Times Herald*, January 24, 1955.

Lynch, Michael. *The Chinese Civil War 1945–49.* Oxford: Osprey Publishing, Ltd., 2010.

MacDonald, Sir Thomas. *Oral History.* Princeton University Library. Public Policy Papers, 1964.

"Madame." *Time*, March 1, 1943.

"Man and Wife of the Year." *Time*, January 3, 1938.

"Man of Feeling." *Time*, February 7, 1949.

Mansfield, Michael J. *Oral History.* Princeton University Library. Public Policy Papers. http://arks/princeton.edu/ark:/88435/f7623j85w.

Mao, Zedong. "Farewell, Leighton Stuart!" *Selected Works of Mao Zedong.* www.marxists.org.

Mastro, Oriana Skylar. "The Taiwan Temptation: Why Beijing Might Resort to Force." *Foreign Affairs*, July/August 2021.

Mayers, David Allan. *Cracking the Monolith: US Policy Against the Sino-Soviet Alliance, 1949–1955.* Baton Rouge, LA: Louisiana State University Press, 1986.

MacDonald, Sir Thomas. *Oral History.* Princeton University Library. http://arks.princeton.edu/ark:88435/6q182r41z.

Mehta, Gaganvihari Lallubhai. *Oral History*. Princeton University Library. Public Policy Papers, 1966. http://arks.princeton.edu./ark:88435/02871214j.

Messer, Robert L. "Roosevelt, Truman, and China: An Overview." In Harry Harding and Yuan Ming, Eds., *Sino-American Relations 1945–1955: A Joint Assessment of a Critical Decade*. Wilmington, DE: Scholarly Resources, 1989.

Miller, Merle. *Plain Speaking: An Oral Biography of Harry S. Truman*. New York: Berkley Publishing Corporation, 1973.

Mitter, Rana. *China's Good War*. Cambridge, MA: The Belknap Press of Harvard University Press, 2020.

Montgomery, Gayle B. and James W. Johnson. *One Step from the White House: The Rise and Fall of Senator William F. Knowland*. Berkeley, CA: University of California Press, 1998.

Munro, Leslie Knox. *Oral History*. Princeton University Library. Public Policy Papers, 1964. http://arks.princeton.edu/ark:/884335/r/781wn314.

Nash, Sir Walter. *Oral History*. Princeton University Library. Public Policy Papers, 1964. http://arks.princeton.edu/ark:/88435/ks65hj48h.

Nevard, Jacques. "Eisenhower is Hailed in Taiwan; Reds Shell Quemoy 'In Contempt'; Tokyo Leftists Keep Up Protests." *New York Times*, June 18, 1960.

Newton, Jim. *Eisenhower: The White House Years*. New York: Doubleday, 2011.

Nixon, Richard. *RN: The Memoirs of Richard Nixon*. New York: Grosset & Dunlap, 1978.

Oberdorfer, Don. *Senator Mansfield*. Washington, DC: Smithsonian Books, 2003.

Okazaki, Katsuo. *Oral History*. Princeton University Library. Public Policy Papers, 1964. http://arks.princeton.edu/ark:/88435/tb09jb93v.

Oshinsky, David M. *A Conspiracy So Immense: The World of Joe McCarthy*. New York: Oxford University Press, 2005.

Pach, Jr., Chester J. *Dwight D. Eisenhower Foreign Affairs*. University of Virginia, Miller Center.

Pakula, Hannah. *The Last Empress: Madame Chiang Kai-shek and the Birth of Modern China*. New York: Simon & Shuster, 2009.

Pantsov, Alexander V. and Steven I. Levine. *Mao: The Real Story*. New York: Simon & Schuster, 2012.

Pepper, Suzanne. *Civil War in China: The Political Struggle 1945–1949*. Lanham, MD: Rowman & Littlefield Publishers, 1999.

Peraino, Kevin. *A Force So Swift: Mao, Truman, and the Birth of Modern China 1949*. New York: Crown Publishing Group, 2017.

Plokhy, S. M. *Yalta: The Price of Peace*. New York: Penguin Group, 2010.

Preston, Diana. *Eight Days at Yalta: How Churchill, Roosevelt, and Stalin Shaped the Post-War World*. London: Picador, 2019.

Rankin, Karl. *China Assignment*. Seattle, WA: University of Washington Press, 1964.

Reardon-Anderson, James. *Yenan and the Great Powers*. New York: Columbia University Press, 1980.

Reston, James. "President Says Nation Must Fight If Necessary to Bar Quemoy Fall; Sees No War; Urges Negotiations." *New York Times*, September 12, 1955.

Ridgway, Matthew B. *Oral History*. Princeton University Library. Public Policy Papers, 1964. http://arks.princeton.edu/ark:/88435/7d2790309.

Robertson, Walter S. *Oral History*. Princeton University Library. Public Policy Papers, 1965. http://arks.princeton.edu/ark:/88435/3n204436h.

Salisbury, Harrison E. "US is Criticized on China Students." *New York Times*, June 3, 1955.

Schram, Stuart. *Political Leaders of the Twentieth Century: Mao Tse-Tung*. Westport, CT: Praeger Publishers, 1966.

Schwartz, Felicia. "US and Taiwan to Hold Trade Talks Amid China Tensions." *Financial Times*, August 18, 2022. www.ft.com

Sheridan, Michael. *The Gate to China: A New History of the People's Republic and Hong Kong*. New York: Oxford University Press: 2021.

Sherwood, Robert E. *Roosevelt and Hopkins: An Intimate History*. New York: Harper & Brothers, 1948.

Smith, H. Alexander. *Oral History*. Princeton University Library. Public Policy Papers, 1964.

Spender, Sir Percy. *Oral History*. Princeton University Library. Public Policy Papers http://arks.princeton.edu/ark:/88435/6969z604f.

Soman, Appu K. "'Who's Daddy' in the Taiwan Strait: The Offshore Islands Crisis of 1958." *The Journal of American-East Asian Relations*, Vol. 3, No. 4 (Winter 1994). pp. 378–398

Stephenson, Charles. *Stalin's War on Japan: The Red Army's Manchurian Strategic Offensive Operation, 1945*. Yorkshire: Pen & Sword Books, 2021.

Stimson, Henry L. *On Active Services in Peace and War*. New York: Harper Brothers, 1947.

Stolper, Thomas E. *China, Taiwan, and the Offshore Islands*. London: Routledge, 2018.

Stuart, John Leighton. *Fifty Years in China: The Memoirs of John Leighton Stuart Missionary and Ambassador*. New York: Random House, 1954.

Stueck, William. "The Marshall and Wedemeyer Missions: A Quadrilateral Perspective." In Harry Harding and Yuan Ming, Eds., *Sino-American Relations 1945–1955: A Joint Assessment of a Critical Decade*. Wilmington, DE: Scholarly Resources, 1989.

Tanner, Harold M. *Where Chiang Kai-shek Lost China*. Bloomington, IN: Indiana University Press, 2015.

Tao, Wenzhao. "Hurley's Mission to China and the Formation of US Policy to Support Chiang Kai-shek Against the Chinese Communist Party." In Harry Harding and Yuan Ming, Eds., *Sino-American Relations 1945–1955: A Joint Assessment of a Critical Decade*. Wilmington, DE: Scholarly Resources, 1989.

Taylor, Jay. *The Generalissimo: Chiang Kai-shek and the Struggle for Modern China*. Cambridge, MA: The Belknap Press of Harvard University Press, 2009.

"Text of Peking's Warning to Quemoy." *New York Times*, June 18, 1960.

The China White Paper (originally issued as *United States Relations with China: With Special Reference to the Period 1944–1949*) Department of State Publication 3573, Far Eastern Series 30). Stanford, CA: Stanford University Press, 1967.

The Public Papers of the President: Dwight D. Eisenhower: 1955. Washington, DC: US GPO.

The Public Papers of the Presidents of the United States, Dwight D. Eisenhower 1960–61. Washington, DC: US GPO.

The United States and Communist China in 1949 and 1950: The Question of Rapprochement and Recognition: A Staff Study. Committee on Foreign Relations United States Senate, Washington, DC: US GPO, 1973.

Thomas, Evan. *Ike's Bluff: President Eisenhower's Secret Battle to Save the World*. Little, Brown and Company, 2012.

Tong, Hollington K. *Chiang Kai-shek's Teacher and Ambassador; An Inside View of the Republic of China from 1911–1958*. Bloomington, IN: AuthorHouse, 2005.

Trumbull, Robert. "Chiang Reported Urging Attack Against Mainland." *New York Times*, September 24, 1958.

Truman, Harry S. "Truman Asks Firm Stand to Curb Peiping Thrusts." *New York Times*, September 14, 1958.

Tsou, Tang. *America's Failure in China*. Chicago, IL: University of Chicago Press, 1962.

Tuchman, Barbara W. "If Mao Had Come to Washington: An Essay in Alternatives." *Foreign Affairs*, October 1972.

Tuchman, Barbara W. *Stilwell and the American Experience in China: 1911–1945*. New York: The Macmillan Company, 1970.

Tucker, Nancy Bernkopf. *Patterns in the Dust: Chinese-American Relations and the Recognition Controversy: 1949–1950*. New York: Columbia University Press, 1983.

United States. US Department of State. *Foreign Relations of the United States 1943: The Conferences at Cairo and Tehran*. Washington, DC: US GPO, 1961.

United States. US Department of State. *Foreign Relations of the United States, The Far East: China 1947, Vol. VII*. Washington, DC: US GPO, 1972.

United States. US Department of State. *Foreign Relations of the United States, The Far East: China 1948 Volume VIII*. Washington, DC: US GPO, 1973.

United States. US Department of State. *Foreign Relations of the United States. The Far East: China 1949, Vol. IX*. Washington, DC: US GPO, 1974.

United States. US Department of State. *Foreign Relations of the United States, 1952–1954, Vol. XIV, China and Japan, Part 1*. Washington, DC: US GPO, 1985.

United States. US Department of State. *Foreign Relations of the United States, 1955–1957, China Vols. I and II*. Washington, DC: US GPO, 1986.

United States. US Department of State. *Foreign Relations of the United States, 1969–1976, Vol. XVII, China 1969–1972*. Washington, DC: US GPO, 2006.

United States. US Department of State. *Foreign Relations of the United States 1958–1960, Vol. XIX China*. Washington, DC: US GPO, 1996.

Wang, Jisi. "The Plot Against China: How Beijing Sees the New Washington Consensus." *Foreign Affairs*, July/August 2021.

"Washington Bars China Coast Raids." *New York Times*, September 24, 1958.

Weiss, Jessica Chen. "The China Trap: US Foreign Policy and the Perilous Logic of Zero-Sum Competition." *Foreign. Affairs*, September/October 2022.

White, Theodore F. and Annalee Jacoby. *Thunder Out of China.* New York: William Morrow & Company, 1946.

Xu, Guangqiu. *Congress and the US-China Relationship: 1949–1979.* Akron, OH: University of Akron Press, 2007.

Yan, Xuetong. "Becoming Strong: The New Chinese Foreign Policy." *Foreign Affairs*, July/August 2021.

Zhang, Baijia. "Chinese Policies Toward the United States, 1937–1945." In Harry Harding and Yuan Ming, Eds., *Sino-American Relations 1945–1955: A Joint Assessment of a Critical Decade.* Wilmington, DE: Scholarly Resources, 1989.

Zhang, Shu Guang. *Deterrence and Strategic Culture.* Ithaca, NY: Cornell University Press, 1992.

Index

Note: Page numbers followed by "n" denote endnotes.

About the Author

Martin B. Gold is a recognized authority and author on matters of congressional rules and parliamentary strategies, and he frequently advises senators and their staffs on these matters. He has served for a decade on the adjunct faculty at George Washington University. In 2022, he received the College of Professional Studies Faculty Excellence Award.

Mr. Gold is the author of eight previous books, all focusing on Congress exclusively or involving Congress as a key actor. This includes four editions of *Senate Procedure and Practice*; *Forbidden Citizens: Chinese Exclusion and the US Congress*; *A Legislative History*; *A Legislative History of the Taiwan Relations Act: Bridging the Strait*; and *The Twenty-Second Amendment and the Limits of Presidential Tenure: A Tradition Restored*. It also includes *The Grand Institution: A Profile of the United States Senate*, which was translated in China and published in Beijing.

Before a wide range of domestic business, professional, and academic audiences, Mr. Gold speaks about Congress as well as political and public policy developments.

He has been a guest lecturer at Tsinghua University, the Beijing Foreign Studies University, the Beijing International Studies University, Moscow State University, the Moscow State Institute of International Relations, the State Parliament of Ukraine, and the Federation Council of the Federal Assembly of the Russian Federation.

Mr. Gold is a member of the Council on Foreign Relations, the National Committee on US-China Relations, the Asia Society, and the Cosmos Club of Washington, DC.

He lives in the nation's capital with his wife, Celeste, who loves Congress as much as he does.

www.ingramcontent.com/pod-product-compliance
Lightning Source LLC
Chambersburg PA
CBHW032308280326
41932CB00009B/737